DIMENSIONS OF HUMAN BEHAVIOR

FOURTH EDITION

Note From the Author: The Educational Policy and Accreditation Standards of the Council on Social Work Education, adopted in 2008 and revised on March 27, 2010, lays out 10 core social work competencies that should guide curriculum design in social work education programs. Competencies are practice behaviors that integrate knowledge, values, and skills. The 7th competency "Apply knowledge of human behavior and the social environment" is the explicit focus of this book and its companion volume *Dimensions of Human Behavior: The Changing Life Course.* That has been the focus of the books for all previous editions. In this 4th edition of the *Dimensions of Human Behavior* books, however, we have been more intentional about integrating all 10 core competencies while keeping the central focus on knowledge about human behavior and the social environment.

We have added material to assist the reader to engage in personal reflection related to social work's purpose and approach. Critical thinking questions have been added to each chapter to assist the reader in ongoing critical examination of personal biases, conceptual frameworks, and empirical research. The content on diversity and social and economic justice continues to be expanded in this 4th edition, with greater attention to issues of global social justice. New material on the changing social contexts of social work practice is introduced, most notably in terms of recent brain research, social policy initiatives, new technological developments, and global societal trends.

The 10 core competencies and the related practice behaviors are presented below followed by a grid that indicates which of the core competencies are addressed in some fashion in each chapter. You might find it helpful to review these core competencies from to time to time as you are learning more and more about what it means to be a social worker.

COUNCIL ON SOCIAL WORK EDUCATION
EDUCATIONAL POLICY AND ACCREDITATION STANDARDS

Educational Policy 2.1 – Core Competencies

2.1.1—Identify as a professional social worker and conduct oneself accordingly. Social workers

- advocate for client access to the services of social work;

- practice personal reflection and self-correction to assure continual professional development;

- attend to professional roles and boundaries;

- demonstrate professional demeanor in behavior, appearance, and communication;

- engage in career-long learning; and

- use supervision and consultation.

2.1.2—Apply social work ethical principles to guide professional practice. Social workers

- recognize and manage personal values in a way that allows professional values to guide practice;

- make ethical decisions by applying standards of the National Association of Social Workers Code of Ethics and, as applicable, of the International Federation of Social Workers/International Association of Schools of Social Work Ethics in Social Work, Statement of Principles;

- tolerate ambiguity in resolving ethical conflicts; and

- apply strategies of ethical reasoning to arrive at principled decisions.

2.1.3—Apply critical thinking to inform and communicate professional judgments. Social workers

- distinguish, appraise, and integrate multiple sources of knowledge, including research-based knowledge, and practice wisdom;
- analyze models of assessment, prevention, intervention, and evaluation; and
- demonstrate effective oral and written communication in working with individuals, families, groups, organizations, communities, and colleagues.

2.1.4—Engage diversity and difference in practice. Social workers

- recognize the extent to which a culture's structures and values may oppress, marginalize, alienate, or create or enhance privilege and power;
- gain sufficient self-awareness to eliminate the influence of personal biases and values in working with diverse groups;
- recognize and communicate their understanding of the importance of difference in shaping life experiences; and
- view themselves as learners and engage those with whom they work as informants.

2.1.5—Advance human rights and social and economic justice. Social workers

- understand the forms and mechanisms of oppression and discrimination;
- advocate for human rights and social and economic justice; and
- engage in practices that advance social and economic justice.

2.1.6—Engage in research-informed practice and practice-informed research. Social workers

- use practice experience to inform scientific inquiry and
- use research evidence to inform practice.

2.1.7—Apply knowledge of human behavior and the social environment. Social workers

- utilize conceptual frameworks to guide the processes of assessment, intervention, and evaluation; and
- critique and apply knowledge to understand person and environment.

2.1.8—Engage in policy practice to advance social and economic well-being and to deliver effective social work services. Social workers

- analyze, formulate, and advocate for policies that advance social well-being; and
- collaborate with colleagues and clients for effective policy action.

2.1.9—Respond to contexts that shape practice. Social workers

- continuously discover, appraise, and attend to changing locales, populations, scientific and technological developments, and emerging societal trends to provide relevant services, and
- provide leadership in promoting sustainable changes in service delivery and practice to improve the quality of social services.

2.1.10(a)-(d)—Engage, assess, intervene, and evaluate with individuals, families, groups, organizations, and communities. Social workers

- substantively and effectively prepare for action with individuals, families, groups, organizations, and communities;
- use empathy and other interpersonal skills;
- develop a mutually agreed-on focus of work and desired outcomes;
- collect, organize, and interpret client data;
- assess client strengths and limitations;
- develop mutually agreed-on intervention goals and objectives;
- select appropriate intervention strategies;
- initiate actions to achieve organizational goals;
- implement prevention interventions that enhance client capacities;
- help clients resolve problems;
- negotiate, mediate, and advocate for clients;
- facilitate transitions and endings; and
- critically analyze, monitor, and evaluate interventions.

Chapter	Professional Identity	Ethical Practice	Critical Thinking	Engage Diversity	Human Rights & Justice	Research-Informed Practice	Human Behavior	Policy Practice	Practice Context	Engage, Assess, Intervene,& Evaluate
1	√	√	√	√	√	√	√		√	√
2	√	√	√	√	√	√	√	√	√	√
3	√		√	√	√	√	√	√	√	√
4	√	√	√	√		√	√		√	√
5	√	√	√	√	√	√	√		√	√
6	√	√	√	√	√	√	√		√	√
7	√	√	√	√	√	√	√	√	√	√
8	√	√	√	√	√	√	√		√	√
9	√		√	√	√	√	√	√	√	
10	√		√	√	√	√	√		√	√
11	√	√	√	√	√	√	√			√
12	√	√	√	√	√		√	√	√	
13	√	√	√		√		√	√	√	
14	√		√		√		√	√	√	
Total Chapters	14	10	14	12	13	11	14	7	13	10

Dimensions of Human Behavior: Person and Environment and Social Work Core Competencies

DIMENSIONS OF HUMAN BEHAVIOR

PERSON AND ENVIRONMENT

FOURTH EDITION

ELIZABETH D. HUTCHISON
Virginia Commonwealth University

AND CONTRIBUTORS

Los Angeles | London | New Delhi
Singapore | Washington DC

For information:

SAGE Publications, Inc.
2455 Teller Road
Thousand Oaks, California 91320
E-mail: order@sagepub.com

SAGE Publications Ltd.
1 Oliver's Yard
55 City Road
London EC1Y 1SP
United Kingdom

SAGE Publications India Pvt. Ltd.
B 1/I 1 Mohan Cooperative Industrial Area
Mathura Road, New Delhi 110 044
India

SAGE Publications Asia-Pacific Pte. Ltd.
33 Pekin Street #02-01
Far East Square
Singapore 048763

Printed in the United States of America.

Library of Congress Cataloging-in-Publication Data

Dimensions of human behavior. Person and environment / [authored by] Elizabeth D. Hutchison and contributing authors.—4th ed.
   p. cm.
 Includes bibliographical references and index.
 ISBN 978-1-4129-8879-7 (pbk.)

   1. Social psychology. 2. Human behavior. 3. Social structure. 4. Social service. I. Hutchison, Elizabeth D. II. Title: Person and environment.

HM1033.D56 2011
302--dc22   2010018631

This book is printed on acid-free paper.

    11 12 13 14 10 9 8 7 6 5 4 3 2

Acquisitions Editor:	Kassie Graves
Editorial Assistant:	Veronica Novak
Production Editor:	Karen Wiley
Copy Editor:	Teresa Herlinger
Typesetter:	C&M Digitals (P) Ltd.
Proofreader:	Jennifer Gritt
Indexer:	Molly Hall
Cover Designer:	Edgar Abarca
Marketing Manager:	Stephanie Adams

Brief Contents

Detailed Contents

Case Studies

Preface

In the preface to the first edition of this book, I noted that I have always been intrigued with human behavior. I didn't know any social workers when I was growing up—or even that there was a social work profession—but I felt an immediate connection to social work and social workers during my junior year in college when I enrolled in an elective entitled Introduction to Social Work and Social Welfare. What attracted me most was the approach social workers take to understanding human behavior. I was a sociology major, minoring in psychology, and it seemed that each of these disciplines—as well as disciplines such as economics, political science, and ethics—added pieces to the puzzle of human behavior; that is, they each provided new ways to think about the complexities of human behavior. Unfortunately, it wasn't until several years later when I was a hospital social worker that I began to wish I had been a bit more attentive to my course work in biology, because that discipline holds other pieces of the puzzle of human behavior. But when I sat in that Introduction to Social Work and Social Welfare course, it seemed that the pieces of the puzzle were coming together. I was inspired by the optimism about creating a more humane world, and I was impressed with an approach to human behavior that clearly cut across disciplinary lines.

Just out of college, amid the tumultuous societal changes of the late 1960s, I became an MSW student. I began to recognize the challenge of developing the holistic understanding of human behavior that has been the enduring signature of social work. I also was introduced to the tensions in social work education, contrasting breadth of knowledge versus depth of knowledge. I found that I was unprepared for the intensity of the struggle to apply what I was learning about general patterns of human behavior to the complex, unique situations that I encountered in the field. I was surprised to find that being a social worker meant learning to understand my own behavior, as well as the behavior of others.

Since completing my MSW, I have provided services in a variety of social work settings, including hospitals, nursing homes, state mental health and mental retardation institutions, community mental health centers, a school-based program, public child welfare programs, and a city jail. Sometimes the target of change was an individual, and other times the focus was on bringing about changes in dyadic or family relationships, communities, organizations, or social institutions. I have also performed a variety of social work roles, including case manager, therapist, teacher, advocate, group facilitator, consultant, collaborator, program planner, administrator, and researcher. I love the diversity of social work settings and the multiple roles of practice. My varied experiences strengthened my commitment to the pursuit of social justice, enhanced my fascination with human behavior, and reinforced my belief in the need to understand human behavior holistically.

For almost 30 years, I taught courses in Human Behavior in the Social Environment to undergraduate students, MSW students, and doctoral students. The students and I struggled with the same challenges that I encountered as a social work student in the late 1960s: the daunting task of developing a holistic understanding of human behavior, the issue of breadth versus depth of knowledge, and discovering how to use general knowledge about human behavior in unique practice situations. Increasingly, over time, my students and I also recognized a need to learn more about human and social diversity, and to build a knowledge base that provided tools for promoting social justice. My experiences as student, practitioner, and teacher of human behavior led me to write this book.

MULTIDIMENSIONAL UNDERSTANDING OF HUMAN BEHAVIOR

Social work has historically used the idea of person-in-environment to develop a multidimensional understanding of human behavior. The idea that human behavior is multidimensional has become popular with most social and behavioral science disciplines. Recently, we have recognized the need to add the aspect of time to the person–environment construct, to capture the dynamic, changing nature of person-in-environment.

The purpose of this book is to help you to breathe life into the abstract idea of person-in-environment. As I did in the first three editions, I identify relevant dimensions of both person and environment, and my colleagues and I present up-to-date reports on theory and research about each of these dimensions. All the while, we encourage you to link the micro world of personal experience with the macro world of social trends—to recognize the unity of person and environment. We help you make this connection by showing how several of the same theories have been used to understand dimensions of both person and environment. A companion volume to this book, *The Changing Life Course,* builds on the multiple dimensions of person and environment analyzed in this book and demonstrates how they work together with the dimension of time to produce patterns in unique life course journeys.

BREADTH VERSUS DEPTH

The most difficult challenge I have faced as a student and teacher of human behavior is to develop a broad, multidimensional approach to human behavior without an unacceptable sacrifice of depth. It is indeed a formidable task to build a knowledge base both wide and deep. After years of struggle, I have reluctantly concluded that although both breadth and depth are necessary, it is better for social work to err on the side of breadth. Let me tell you why.

Social workers are doers; we use what we know to tell us what to do. If we have a narrow band of knowledge, no matter how impressive it is in its depth, we will "understand" the practice situations we encounter from this perspective. This will lead us to use the same solutions for all situations, rather than to tailor solutions to the unique situations we encounter. The emerging risk and resilience literature suggests that human behavior is influenced by the many risk factors and protective factors inherent in the multiple dimensions of contemporary social arrangements. What we need is a multidimensional knowledge base that allows us to scan widely for, and think critically about, risk factors and protective factors and to craft multipronged intervention programs to reduce risks and strengthen protective factors.

To reflect recent developments in the social and behavioral sciences, this book introduces dimensions of human behavior that are not covered in similar texts. Chapters on the biological and spiritual dimensions of person, the physical environment, social institutions, and social movements provide important insights into human behavior not usually covered in social work texts. In addition, we provide up-to-date information on the typically identified dimensions of human behavior.

GENERAL KNOWLEDGE AND UNIQUE SITUATIONS

The purpose of the social and behavioral sciences is to help us understand *general patterns* in person–environment transactions. The purpose of social work assessment is to understand *unique configurations* of person and environment dimensions. Those who practice social work must interweave what they know about unique situations with general knowledge. To assist you in this process, as we did in the first three editions, we begin each chapter with one or more case studies, which we then interweave with contemporary theory and research. Most of the stories are composite cases and do not correspond to actual people known to the authors. In this fourth edition, we continue to expand upon our efforts in the last three editions to call more attention to the successes and failures of theory and research to accommodate human diversity related to gender, class, race and ethnicity, culture, sexual orientation, and disability. More important, we have extended our attention to diversity by being very intentional in our effort to provide a global context for understanding person–environment transactions. The attention to the global world has once again expanded in this edition. Finally, greater attention has been paid to the impact of new technologies on all dimensions of the person and environment.

ABOUT THIS BOOK

The task of developing a solid knowledge base for doing social work can seem overwhelming. For me, it is an exciting journey, because I am learning about my own behavior as well as the behavior of others. What I learn enriches my personal life as well as my professional life. My colleagues and I wanted to write a book that gives you a state-of-the-art knowledge base, but we also wanted you to find pleasure in your learning. We have tried to write as we teach, with enthusiasm for the content and a desire to connect with your process of learning. We continue to use some special features that we hope will aid your learning process. As in the first three editions, key terms are presented in bold type in the chapters and defined in the Glossary. As in the second and third editions, we present orienting questions at the beginning of each chapter to help the reader to begin to think about why the content of the chapter is important for social workers. Key ideas are summarized at the beginning of each chapter to give readers an overview of what is to come. Critical thinking questions are presented throughout all chapters. Active learning exercises are presented at the end of each chapter.

The bulk of this fourth edition will be familiar to instructors who used earlier editions of *Dimensions of Human Behavior: Person and Environment*. Many of the changes that are included came at the suggestions of instructors and students who have been using the third edition. All chapters have been updated to reflect recent census data, developing trends, and cutting-edge research.

NEW IN THIS EDITION

The more substantial revisions for this edition include the following:

- Even more content has been added on globalization.

- More content has been added on the neoliberal philosophy.

- Attention has been given to the impact of the severe global economic recession that began in late 2007.

- Even more content has been added on human diversity.

- More attention is given to postmodern culture and postmodern approaches to understanding human behavior.

- More content has been added on the impact of the new mass media technologies on person and environment.

- Some new exhibits have been added and others updated.

- Several new case studies have been added to reflect contemporary issues.

- The Families chapter has been rewritten, with more emphasis on diversity of family structures, as well as economic and cultural diversity in family life.

- Web resources have been updated. Visit www.sagepub.com/hutchisonpe4e for more information.

ONE LAST WORD

I imagine that you, like me, are intrigued with human behavior. That is probably a part of what attracted you to social work. I hope that reading this book reinforces your fascination with human behavior. I also hope that when you finish this book, and in the years to come, you will have new ideas about the possibilities for social work action.

Learning about human behavior is a lifelong process. You can help me in my learning process by letting me know what you liked or didn't like about the book.

—*Elizabeth D. Hutchison*
ehutch@vcu.edu

Acknowledgments

A project like this book is never completed without the support and assistance of many people. A fourth edition stands on the back of the first three editions, and by now I have accumulated a very large number of people to whom I am grateful.

Steve Rutter, former publisher and president of Pine Forge Press, shepherded every step of the first edition, and provided ideas for many of the best features of the second edition, which are carried forward in the third, and now, this fourth edition. Along with Paul O'Connell, Becky Smith, and Maria Zuniga, he helped to refine the outline for the second edition, and that outline continues to be used in this book.

The contributing authors and I are grateful for the assistance Dr. Maria E. Zuniga offered during the drafting of the second edition. She contributed the Meza family case study in Chapter 9 and provided many valuable suggestions for how to improve the coverage of cultural diversity in each chapter. Her suggestions improved the second edition immensely and have stayed with us as lasting lessons about human behavior in a multicultural society.

I am grateful once again to work with a fine group of contributing authors. They were gracious about timelines and incorporating feedback from reviewers. Most important, they were committed to providing a state-of-the-art knowledge base for understanding the multiple dimensions of human behavior across the life course.

We were lucky to be working again with the folks at Sage. It has been wonderful to again have the disciplined and creative editorial assistance of Kassie Graves. In December 2009, I was lucky enough to have an invigorating day of meetings with Kassie, and a host of other folks at Sage who manage the various stages of turning ideas into books and getting them into the hands of students and faculty. Associate Editor Leah Mori brought creative energy to some of the visual aspects of the book, and did so in such a competent and pleasant way. Veronica Novak has been a steady assistant for the last three editions, managing the flow of work and responding to my many questions and requests. Teresa Herlinger was an exquisite copy editor who added some good humor to a task that could become tedious. And, finally, Karen Wiley was once again a capable production editor.

I am grateful to my former faculty colleagues at Virginia Commonwealth University (VCU) who set a high standard for scientific inquiry and teaching excellence. They also provided love and encouragement through both good and hard times. My conversations about the human behavior curriculum with colleagues Rosemary Farmer, Stephen Gilson, Marcia Harrigan, Holly Matto, Mary Secret, and Joe Walsh over many years have stimulated much thinking and resulted in many ideas found in this book.

My students over almost 30 years also deserve a special note of gratitude. They taught me all the time, and many things that I have learned in interaction with them show up in the pages of this book. They also provided a great deal of joy to my life journey. Those moments when I learn of former students doing informed, creative, and humane social work are special moments, indeed. I have also enjoyed receiving e-mail messages from students from other universities who are using the books, and I have found their insights to be very helpful.

My deepest gratitude goes to my husband, Hutch. Since the first edition of this book was published, we have weathered several challenging years and experienced many celebratory moments. He is constantly patient and supportive and often technically useful. But, more important, he makes sure that I don't forget that life can be great fun.

Finally, I am enormously grateful to a host of reviewers who thoughtfully evaluated the third edition and provided very useful feedback about how to improve upon it. Their ideas were very helpful in framing our work on this fourth edition.

Jiunn-Jye Sheu
University of Florida

Kathy M. Elpers
University of Southern Indiana

Ted Watkins
Texas State University

Soma Sen
San Jose State University

Alfred T. Kisubi
University of Wisconsin Oshkosh

Louis Laster
University of Texas at Arlington

Gloria Duran Aguilar
Florida A&M University

Cheri Carter
Temple University

Larry G. Morton II
Eastern Michigan University

To all my former students, who challenged me to think critically and expand my understanding of diversity, and who made the social work classroom a very exciting place to be.

PART

A Multidimensional Approach for
Multifaceted Social Work

- Caroline O'Malley is knocking at the door of a family reported to her agency for child abuse.

- Sylvia Gomez and other members of her team at the rehabilitation hospital are meeting with the family of an 18-year-old male who is recovering from head injuries sustained in a motorcycle accident.

- Mark Bernstein is on the way to the county jail to assess the suicide risk of an inmate.

- Helen Moore is preparing a report for a legislative committee.

- Juanita Alvarez is talking with a homeless man about taking his psychotropic medications.

- Stan Weslowski is meeting with a couple who would like to adopt a child.

- Andrea Thomas is analyzing the results of a needs assessment recently conducted at the service center for older adults where she works.

- Anthony Pacino is wrapping up a meeting of a cancer support group.

- Sam Belick is writing a social history for tomorrow's team meeting at the high school where he works.

- Sarah Sahair has just begun a meeting of a recreational group of 9- and 10-year-old girls.

- Jane Kerr is facilitating the monthly meeting of an interagency coalition of service providers for substance-abusing women and their children.

- Ann Noles is planning a fund-raising project for the local Boys' and Girls' Club.

- Meg Hart is wrapping up her fourth counseling session with a lesbian couple.

- Chien Liu is meeting with a community group concerned about youth gang behavior in their neighborhood.

- Mary Wells is talking with one of her clients at the rape crisis center.

- Nagwa Nadi is evaluating treatment for posttraumatic stress disorder at a Veteran's Administration hospital
- Devyani Hakakian is beginning her workday at an international advocacy organization devoted to women's rights.

What do these people have in common? You have probably guessed that they all are social workers. They work in a variety of settings, and they are involved in a variety of activities, but they all are doing social work. Social work is, indeed, a multifaceted profession. And because it is multifaceted, social workers need a multidimensional understanding of human behavior. This book provides such an understanding. The purpose of the two chapters in Part I is to introduce you to a multidimensional way of thinking about human behavior and to set the stage for subsequent discussion. In Chapter 1, you are introduced to the multiple dimensions of person, environment, and time that serve as the framework for the book, and you are introduced to social work's emphasis on diversity, inequality, and social justice. You also are given some tools to think critically about the multiple theories and varieties of research that make up our general knowledge about these dimensions of human behavior. In Chapter 2, you encounter eight theoretical perspectives that contribute to multidimensional understanding. You learn about their central ideas and their scientific merits. Most important, you consider the usefulness of these eight theoretical perspectives for social work.

CHAPTER

Setting the Stage

A Multidimensional Approach

Elizabeth D. Hutchison

OPENING QUESTIONS

• What is it about people, environments, and time that social workers need to understand?

• Why is it important for social workers to understand the roles that diversity and inequality play in human behavior?

KEY IDEAS

As you read this chapter, take note of these central ideas:

1. This book provides a multidimensional way of thinking about human behavior in terms of changing configurations of persons and environments.

2. Although person, environment, and time are inseparable, we can focus on them separately by thinking about the relevant dimensions of each.

3. Relevant personal dimensions include the biological, the psychological, and the spiritual.

4. Nine dimensions of environment that have relevance for social work are the physical environment, culture, social institutions and social structure, dyads, families, small groups, formal organizations, communities, and social movements. These dimensions have been studied separately, but they are neither mutually exclusive nor hierarchically ordered.

5. Social work puts special emphasis on diversity, inequality, and the pursuit of global social justice.

6. Knowledge about the case, knowledge about the self, values and ethics, and scientific knowledge are four important ingredients for moving from knowing to doing.

7. This book draws on two interrelated logical and systematic ways of building scientific knowledge: theory and empirical research.

Case Study

Manisha's Quest for Dignity and Purpose

Manisha is a 57-year-old Bhutanese woman who resettled in the United States in early 2009. She is eager to tell her story, which she does with the help of an interpreter. Manisha describes her childhood as wonderful. She was the youngest of seven children born to a farming family in a rural village of Bhutan. Although there was little support for education, especially for girls, Manisha's parents valued education, and she was one of five girls in her village school, where she was able to finish the second grade. As was tradition, she married young, at age 17, and became a homemaker for her husband, who was a contractor, and the four sons they later had. Manisha and her husband had a large plot of farmland and built a good life. They were able to develop some wealth and were sending their children to school. She says that they were managing well and living in peace.

In 1988, the political climate began to change and the good times ended. Manisha says she doesn't really understand how the problem started because in Bhutan, women were excluded from decision making and were given little information. As she talks, she begins to reflect that she has learned some things about what happened, but she still doesn't understand it. What she does recall is that the Bhutanese government began to discriminate against the Nepali ethnic group to which she belongs. News accounts indicate that the Druk Buddhist majority wanted to unite Bhutan under the Druk culture, religion, and language. The Nepalis had a separate culture and language and were mostly Hindu, while the Druks were Buddhist. Manisha says she does not know much about this, but she does recall that suddenly Nepalis were denied citizenship, were not allowed to speak their language, and could no longer get access to jobs. Within a family, different family members could be classified in different ways based on ethnicity.

Manisha recalls a woman who committed suicide as the discrimination grew worse. She also remembers that the Nepali people began to raise their voices and question what was happening. When this occurred, the Bhutanese government sent soldiers to intimidate the villagers and undermine the Nepali resistance. It is evident that Manisha is controlling her emotions as she tells about cases of rape of Nepali women at the hands of the Bhutanese soldiers and recalls that the soldiers expected Nepali girls and women to be made available to them for sexual activity. She reports that government forces targeted Nepali families who had property and wealth, arresting them in the middle of the night and torturing and killing some. Families were forcefully evicted from their property. She recalls families who had to flee at night, sometimes leaving food on their tables.

One day when Manisha was at the market, the soldiers arrested her husband and took him to jail; she didn't know where he was for 2 days. He was in jail for 18 months. She remembers that she and her sons would hide out, carefully watch for soldiers, and sneak back home to cook. She was afraid to be at home. Finally, one day she was forced to report to the government office and there she was told to leave and go to Nepal. She says that until then, she was just a simple housewife who was tending her gardens and cooking for her family. She told the government representative that she couldn't leave because her husband was in jail and she needed to care for her children. She tried to survive, living with other families, and she managed to live that way for a year.

Finally, Manisha heard that her husband would be released from jail on condition that he leave the country. By this time, neighbors had started to flee, and only four households were left in her village. She sent her youngest son with friends and neighbors who were fleeing. A few days later, her husband was released. He said he was too afraid to stay in their home, and they too had to flee. Manisha did not want to leave, and as she tells her story, she still talks longingly of the property they had to leave behind. But the next morning, she and her husband and their other three sons fled the country. It was a 3-day walk to the Indian border, where Manisha and her family lived on the banks of a river with other Nepalis who had fled. Her sons ranged in age from 6 to 19 at this time. Manisha recalls that many people died by the river and that there was "fever all around."

After 3 months, Manisha and her family moved to a refugee camp in Nepal, the largest of seven Nepali refugee camps. They spent 17 years in this camp before coming to the United States. The 18 months of imprisonment affected her husband such that he was not able to tolerate the close quarters of refugee camp living; he lived and worked in the adjacent Nepali community and came to visit his family. The four boys were able to attend school in the camp.

(Continued)

(Continued)

The camp was managed by the United Nations High Commissioner for Refugees (UNHCR) whose representatives started to build a forum for women. Manisha says that many of the women were, like her, from rural areas where they had been self-reliant, eating what they grew and taking care of their families. Now they were dependent on other people. The facilities at the camps were closely built and crowded. There was always a need for cash; the refugees were given food, but money was needed for other things, like clothes and personal hygiene items. Oxfam, an international aid organization, started a knitting program, and the women were able to sell their knitted items, which provided much-needed cash. Manisha recalls that many of the women were emotionally disturbed and needed support. Some committed suicide. She began to provide moral support to other women and to disabled children, and she worked as the camp's Deputy Secretary for 3 years.

Manisha's family wanted desperately to get back to Bhutan, but they began to realize that that would not happen. They also learned that Nepal would not give citizenship to the refugees even though they had a shared culture. So, Manisha and her family decided to resettle in the United States where they had been assured by UNHCR workers that they would have a better life. The family resettled in three stages. First, Manisha and her husband came to the United States along with their youngest son and his wife. The older sons and their families resettled in two different waves of migration. They all live in close proximity. Some of Manisha's sons and daughters-in-law are working and some are not, but most are employed only part time. Some work in hotel housekeeping, and one daughter-in-law works in a hospital. Manisha and her husband have not been able to find work, and she suggests that the language barrier is greater for them than for their sons and their families. She says they are all struggling financially and worry because they need to repay the costs of transportation from Nepal to the United States. But mostly, Manisha wants to find a job because she wants to make a contribution and have self-respect. In the camp in Nepal, she had been working and was on the go. Now, she says she lives behind closed doors. She and her husband are taking English as a second language (ESL) classes, but she feels strongly that she needs to be out at work so that she has a chance to practice English. She has given some thought to the type of work she could do, such as folding laundry or working in a school cafeteria. She thinks she could do those jobs, even with her limited English proficiency. She and her husband continue to practice their Hindu faith at home, but they are not able to attend the nearest Hindu Center, which is 15–20 miles from their apartment, as often as they would like. The social worker at the Refugee Resettlement Program is concerned about Manisha and other women who are isolated and unhappy.

—*Beverly B. Koerin and Elizabeth D. Hutchison*

SOCIAL WORK'S PURPOSE AND APPROACH: INDIVIDUAL AND COMMUNITY WELL-BEING

As eventful as it has been, Manisha's story is still unfolding. As a social worker, you will become a part of many unfolding life stories, and you will want to have useful ways to think about those stories and effective ways to be helpful to people like Manisha and her community of Bhutanese refugees. The purpose of this book and its companion volume, *The Changing Life Course*, is to provide ways for you to think about the nature and complexities of the people and situations that are at the center of social work practice. To begin to do that, we must first clarify the purpose of social work and the approach it takes to individual and collective human behavior. This is laid out in the 2008 Educational Policy and Accreditation Standards of the Council on Social Work Education:

The purpose of the social work profession is to promote human and community well-being. Guided by a person and environment construct, a global perspective, respect for human diversity, and knowledge based on scientific inquiry, social work's purpose is actualized through its quest for social and economic justice, the prevention of conditions that limit human rights, the elimination of poverty, and the enhancement of the quality of life for all persons. (p. 1)

This book elaborates and updates the person and environment construct that has guided social work intervention since the earliest days of the profession. The element of time is added to the person and environment construct to call attention to the dynamic nature of both people and environments. The book identifies multiple dimensions of both person and environment and draws on ongoing scientific inquiry, both conceptual and empirical, to examine the dynamic understanding of each dimension. Special attention is paid to globalization, diversity, human rights, and social and economic justice in examination of each dimension. In this chapter, the multidimensional approach to person and environment is presented, followed by discussion of diversity, inequality, and the pursuit of social justice from a global perspective. After a brief discussion of the process by which professionals like social workers move from knowing to doing, the chapter ends with a discussion of how scientific knowledge from theory and research informs social work's multidimensional understanding of human behavior.

A MULTIDIMENSIONAL APPROACH

If we focus on the _person_ in Manisha's story, it appears that she was born with a healthy biological constitution, which allowed her to work on the family farms and nurture four sons. She describes no difficulty in managing the strenuous 3-day walk to the Indian border as she fled Bhutan. She survived while many people died by the river and later, in the refugee camp, she survived and found new purpose when many others died of damaged bodies or broken spirits. We might wonder whether these hardships have taken their toll on her biological systems in ways that will show up later as health problems. We can wonder the same about the harsh conditions of her husband's 18-month imprisonment. Manisha appears to have emotional resilience, but she is struggling to maintain belief in her ability to find dignity and purpose in her new life in the United States. Her Hindu faith continues to be a source of comfort for her as she strives to maintain hope for the future.

If we focus on the _environment_, we see many influences on Manisha's story. Consider first the physical environment. Manisha lived in relative comfort, first on her father's and then her husband's farm, for almost 40 years, where she was able to spend much of her day outside helping to turn farmland into food for her family. She still grieves the loss of land and the freedom she had to roam it. From there, she endured a long hike and a few months of survival in a poorly sheltered camp by the river. Her next stop was a crowded refugee camp where she faced a level of dependence she had not previously known. After 17 years, she and her family left the camp to establish a new life in the United States where she lives with her husband in a small apartment that leaves her feeling isolated.

Culture is an aspect of environment that exerts a powerful influence in Manisha's story. Culture influenced the fact that she received limited, if any, education and that she be married at what may appear to us to be an early age. Her culture also held that women lack power and influence and are not involved in affairs outside the home, and yet Manisha assumed a powerful role in holding her family together after her husband was imprisoned. She also developed a very public role in the refugee camp and grieves the loss of that role in which she felt she was making a contribution to the public good. Although there were many challenges in the camp, she was living among people who shared her culture, language, and religion. She is struggling to adapt to a new, fast-moving culture where language is a constant barrier and her religious beliefs are in the minority. But culture is an important part of Manisha's story in another way. Culture clash and cultural imperialism led the Bhutanese government to discriminate against and then banish the Nepali ethnic group. Unfortunately, such cultural conflict is a source of great international upheaval.

Manisha's story has been powerfully influenced by the geopolitical unrest that began just as she was entering middle adulthood. Her relationships with social institutions have changed over time, and she has had to learn new rules based on her changing place in the social structure. Prior to 1988, she enjoyed high status in her village and the respect that comes with it. She lived in peace. She still does not understand why the Bhutanese government suddenly began to discriminate against her ethnic group, and she grieves the loss of property, status, and homeland that came out of this unrest. She is grateful to the United Nations for their support of the Bhutanese refugees and to the United States for welcoming some to resettle here. Unfortunately, she and her family have resettled in the United States in the midst of the worst global economic recession since the Great Depression of the 1930s. They are all struggling to find work that will allow them to have some of the self-reliance they experienced in Bhutan.

Another dimension of the environment, family, is paramount to Manisha. She is lucky to have her husband living with her again and all of her children nearby. None of her siblings was resettled in the same city, however, and they are spread across several countries at this time; some are still in the Nepali camp awaiting resettlement. She is not even sure what has happened to much of her large extended family. Manisha's children and grandchildren are central to her life, and they give her hope for the future. Manisha and her husband are devoted to each other, but must adjust to living together again after living in separate quarters for many years. In some ways, Manisha led a much more independent life in the refugee camp than back in Bhutan, and she came to value that independence. She and her husband are still negotiating this change from traditional gender roles. Her husband has enormous sadness about all that the family lost after the situation changed for them in Bhutan, including the loss of social status and self-reliance.

Small groups, organizations, and communities have been important forces in Manisha's life, but she has had little direct contact with social movements. In the refugee camp, she participated in some focus groups that the UNHCR conducted with the women in the camps. She is enjoying the relationships she is developing with her ESL class; she draws courage from the companionship and the collegial sense of "we are all in the same boat" that she gets from the weekly classes.

Several organizations have been helpful to her and her family since they fled Bhutan. First, she is grateful for the UNHCR for all of the resources that they put into running the Nepali refugee camps. Second, she has high praise for Oxfam International, which started the knitting program in the camps. In the United States, she is grateful for the assistance of the refugee resettlement program that sponsored her family, and is especially appreciative of the ESL program they run and the moral support provided by the social worker. She would like to have more contact with the Hindu Center, but the distance does not make that easy.

Manisha moved from a farming village, where she was surrounded by open land, extended family, and long-term friends, to a poorly sheltered camp by the river, where fear and confusion were the driving force of relationships and loss of loved ones was a much too common occurrence. Next, she moved to a crowded refugee camp, where disease and despair were common, but where she also found her voice and played an important role in helping other women and their children. She enjoyed her leadership position as Deputy Secretary of the camp and liked the active life she created in this role. Now, she has moved to a city in the United States where many people are willing to help, but everything seems strange, and the language barrier is a serious impediment. She feels isolated and lonely in her small apartment.

Manisha is aware that some members of her Nepali ethnic group developed a resistance movement when the Bhutanese government began to discriminate against them. She is also aware that some refugees in the Nepali refugee camps have resisted the idea of resettlement to the United States and other countries because they think that resettlement will dilute the pressure on Bhutan to repatriate the Nepalis. As much as Manisha would love to be repatriated, she and her family decided that resettlement in the United States was their best chance for a good future.

Time is also an important part of Manisha's story and there are many trace effects of earlier times in her current story. She thinks of her 40 years in Bhutan as a time that moved by too fast, but left her with many happy memories that she now cherishes. The 17 years in the refugee camp seemed to move very slowly at first, but Manisha was able to develop a rhythm to her life that kept time moving. These were also years when Manisha and her husband lived in separate quarters, and their relationship still suffers from such a long period of partial separation. Experiences with past environments have left them with a preference for rural environments and a discomfort with too much privacy, which they experience as isolation. Discrimination, imprisonment, escape, crowded camp, and resettlement have been powerful life events for Manisha and her family and continue to affect their current life. Most notably, Manisha's husband is uncomfortable in situations involving confinement, food shortage, or harsh authority figures, which appears to be related to the 18 months in prison, an experience he does not talk about, not even with Manisha. Both Manisha and her husband still grieve the loss of their farm and long to see it again. They also long for a time of life that was much simpler, living with their children on their farm with family and friends all around. The language barrier is the most persistent reminder that this is not home, but it takes on special meaning because it reminds them of the time when the Bhutanese government prohibited the use of the Nepali language in schools. Manisha sees that her children and grandchildren are living in the present rather than the past, and she is trying to do that as well.

Manisha's story is a good illustration of the dynamic nature of the person and environment over time, and it illustrates why the person and environment must be put within the context of time. What made Manisha decide to take an active role in providing support and comfort to other women in the refugee camp? Was it something within her, something about her physical and social environment, or something about her life course phase? Or a combination of all three? What will her life be like in 10 years? How about the lives of her husband, her children, and her grandchildren? What factors will influence their futures? How will they look back on this time in their lives? It is impossible to focus on person, environment, and time independently; they are inseparable.

As suggested above, social work has historically recognized human behavior as an interaction of person with environment. The earliest social work practice book, *Social Diagnosis,* written by Mary Richmond in 1917, identified the social situation and the personality of the client as the dual foci of social work assessment. The settlement house movement put heavy emphasis on the environmental elements of person–environment interactions, but environment was deemphasized, and intrapsychic factors were emphasized when social work began to rely on psychodynamic theory in the 1920s. In the late 1960s, however, social work scholars began to focus on the environment again when general systems theory and other related formulations were incorporated into the way social work scholars think about human behavior (R. Anderson & Carter, 1974; Bloom, 1984; Germain, 1973; Hartman, 1970; G. Hearn, 1958, 1969; C. Meyer, 1976; Pincus & Minahan, 1973; Siporin, 1975).

In recent times, ecological theory, which addresses the relationships between organisms and their environments, has become the dominant theoretical approach across a number of behavioral science disciplines (Gardiner & Kosmitzki, 2008). These approaches have renewed social workers' interest in the social sciences and helped them to understand the processes and activities involved in the relationships between person and environment. The multidimensional approach of this book is rooted in the systems perspective.

Today, a vast multidisciplinary literature, of both theory and research, is available to help us in our social work efforts. The good news is that the multifaceted nature of this literature provides a broad knowledge base for the varied settings and roles involved in social work practice. The bad news is that this literature is highly fragmented, "scattered across more than thirty fields" (Kirk & Reid, 2002, p. 207). What we need is a structure for organizing our thinking about this multifaceted, multidisciplinary, fragmented literature.

The multidimensional approach provided in this book should help. This approach is built on the three major elements of human behavior: person, environment, and time. Although in this book and the companion volume, *The Changing Life Course,* we focus on each of these elements separately, keep in mind that no single element can be entirely understood without attention to the other elements. Person, environment, and time are not simple concepts, and they can best be thought of as **multidimensional**, that is, as having several identifiable dimensions. We can get a clearer picture of these three elements if we think about the important dimensions of each—what it is that we should study about person, about environment, and about time. Exhibit 1.1 is a graphic overview of the dimensions of person, environment, and time discussed in this book. Exhibit 1.2 defines and gives examples for each dimension.

Keep in mind that **dimension** refers to a feature that can be focused on separately but that cannot be understood without also considering other features. The dimensions identified in this book are usually studied as detached or semidetached realities, with one dimension characterized as causing or leading to another. However, I do not see dimensions as detached realities, and I am not presenting a causal model. I want instead to show how these dimensions work together, how they are embedded with each other, and how many possibilities are opened for social work practice when we think about human behavior this way. I am suggesting that humans engage in **multidetermined behavior,** that is, behavior that develops as a result of many causes. I do think, however, that focusing on specific dimensions one at a time can help to clarify general, abstract statements about person and environment—that is, it can put some flesh on the bones of this idea.

Personal Dimensions

Any story could be told from the perspective of any person in the story. The story at the beginning of this chapter is told from Manisha's perspective, but it could have been told from the perspectives of a variety of other persons such as the Bhutanese king, Manisha's husband, one of her children, one of her grandchildren, a UNHCR staff member, one of the women supported by Manisha in the camp, the social worker at the refugee resettlement agency, or Manisha's ESL teacher. You will want to recognize the multiple perspectives held by different persons involved in the stories of which you become a part in your social work activities.

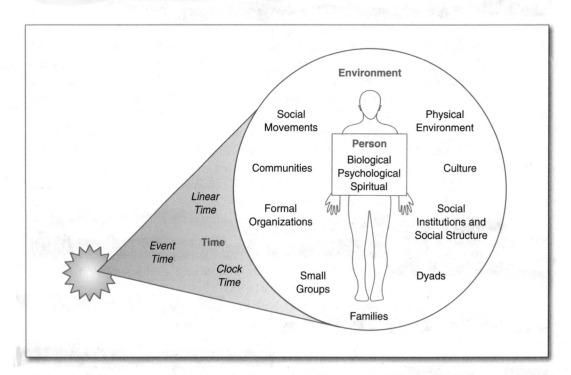

▲ **Exhibit 1.1**   Person, Environment, and Time Dimensions

Dimension	Definition	Examples
Personal Dimensions		
The Biological Person	The body's biochemical, cell, organ, and physiological systems	Nervous system, endocrine system, immune system, cardiovascular system, musculoskeletal system, reproductive system
The Psychological Person	The mind and the mental processes	Cognitions (conscious thinking processes), emotion (feelings), self (identity)
The Spiritual Person	The aspect of the person that searches for meaning and purpose in life	Themes of morality; ethics; justice; interconnectedness; creativity; mystical states; prayer, meditation, and contemplation; relationships with a higher power
Environmental Dimensions		
The Physical Environment	The natural and human-built material aspects of the environment	Water, sun, trees, buildings, landscapes
Culture	A set of common understandings, evident in both behavior and material artifacts	Beliefs, customs, traditions, values
Social Structure and Social Institutions	Social Structure: A set of interrelated social institutions developed by humans to impose constraints on human interaction for the purpose of the survival and well-being of the collectivity	Social Structure: Social class
	Social Institutions: Patterned ways of organizing social relations in a particular sector of social life	Social Institutions: Government, economy, education, health care, social welfare, religion, mass media, and family
Dyads	Two persons bound together in some way	Parent and child, romantic couple, social worker and client
Families	A social group of two or more persons, characterized by ongoing interdependence with long-term commitments that stem from blood, law, or affection	Nuclear family, extended family, chosen family

▲ **Exhibit 1.2** *(Continued)*

Dimension	Definition	Examples
Small Groups	Collections of people who interact with each other, perceive themselves as belonging to a group, are interdependent, join together to accomplish a goal, fulfill a need through joint association, or are influenced by a set of rules and norms	Friendship group, self-help group, therapy group, committee, task group, interdisciplinary team
Formal Organizations	Collectivities of people, with a high degree of formality of structure, working together to meet a goal or goals	Civic and social service organizations, business organizations, professional associations
Communities	People bound either by geography or by network links (webs of communication), sharing common ties, and interacting with one another	Territorial communities such as neighborhoods; relational communities such as the social work community, the disability community, a faith community, a soccer league
Social Movements	Large-scale collective actions to make change, or resist change, in specific social institutions	Civil rights movement, poor people's movements, disability movement, gay rights movement
Time Dimensions		
Clock Time	Time in terms of clocks and calendars	Hours, days, workdays, weekends
Event Time	Time in terms of signals from the body and from nature	Hunger signals time to eat; natural signs signal time to plant and harvest
Linear Time	Time in terms of a straight line	Past, present, future

▲ **Exhibit 1.2**   Definitions and Examples of Dimensions of Person, Environment, and Time

You also will want tools for thinking about the various dimensions of the persons involved in these stories. For many years, social work scholars described the approach of social work as *psychosocial,* giving primacy to psychological dimensions of the person. Personality, ego states, emotion, and cognition are the important features of the person in this approach. Currently, however, social workers, like contemporary scholars in other disciplines (e.g., Bandura, 2001; E. Garland & Howard, 2009; C. MacDonald & Mikes-Liu, 2009; Sadock & Sadock, 2007; P. White, 2005), take a **biopsychosocial approach.** In this approach, human behavior is considered to be the result of interactions of integrated biological, psychological, and social systems. Psychology is seen as inseparable from biology; emotions and cognitions affect the health of the body and are affected by it (Adelman, 2006). Increasingly, neurobiologists write about the "social brain," recognizing that the human brain is wired for social life but also that the social environment has an impact on brain structure and processes (Cacioppo et al., 2007; Frith & Frith, 2010).

In recent years, social work scholars and those in the social and behavioral sciences and medicine have argued for greater attention to the spiritual dimension of persons as well (Carley, 2005; Faull & Hills, 2006; M. Richards, 2005; Watts, Dutton, & Gulliford, 2006). Developments in neuroscience have generated new explorations of the unity of the biological, psychological, and spiritual dimensions of the person. For example, recent research has focused on the ways that emotions and thoughts, as well as spiritual states, influence the immune system (Kimura et al., 2005; Woods, Antoni, Ironson, & Kling, 1999) and health practices (C. Park, Edmondson, Hale-Smith, & Blank, 2009). One research team has explored the impact of spirituality and religiosity on mental health and found that thankfulness protects against major depression (Kendler et al., 2003). In this book, we give substantial coverage to all three of these personal dimensions: biological, psychological, and spiritual.

Environmental Dimensions

Social workers have always thought about the environment as multidimensional. As early as 1901, Mary Richmond presented a model of case coordination that took into account not only personal dimensions but also family, neighborhood, civic organizations, private charitable organizations, and public relief organizations (see Exhibit 1.3). Like contemporary social workers, Richmond saw the environment as multidimensional, including in her model many of the same dimensions of environment covered in this book and presented in Exhibit 1.1.

Several models for classifying dimensions of the environment have been proposed since Mary Richmond's time. Among social work scholars, Ralph Anderson and Irl Carter made a historic contribution to systemic thinking about human behavior with the first edition of their *Human Behavior in the Social Environment: A Social Systems Approach* (1974), one of the earliest textbooks on human behavior authored by social workers. Their classification of environmental dimensions has had a significant impact on the way social workers think about the environment. Anderson and Carter divided the environment into five dimensions: culture and society, communities, organizations, groups, and families. Social workers (see, e.g., Ashford, LeCroy, & Lortie, 2010) have also been influenced by Uri Bronfenbrenner's (1989, 1999) ecological perspective, which identifies four interdependent, nested categories or levels of systems:

1. *Microsystems* are those that involve direct, face-to-face contact between members.

2. *Mesosystems* are networks of microsystems of a given person.

3. *Exosystems* are the linkages between microsystems and larger institutions that affect the system, such as the family system and the parent's workplace or the family system and the child's school.

4. *Macrosystems* are the broader influences of culture, subculture, and social structure.

Some recent models have added the physical environment (natural and designed environments) as a separate dimension. Failure to include the physical environment has most notably hampered social work's ability to respond to persons with physical disabilities. Recent research on the connection between the physical environment and healing has special relevance for social workers in many settings.

To have an up-to-date understanding of the multidimensional environment, social workers need knowledge about the eight dimensions of environment described in Exhibit 1.2 and presented as chapters in this book: the physical environment, culture, social institutions and social structure, families, small groups, formal organizations, communities, and social movements. We also need knowledge about dyadic relationships—those between two people, the most basic social relationships. Dyadic relationships receive attention throughout the book and are emphasized in Chapter 5, which focuses on the psychosocial person. Simultaneous consideration of multiple environmental dimensions provides new possibilities for action, perhaps even new or revised approaches to social work practice.

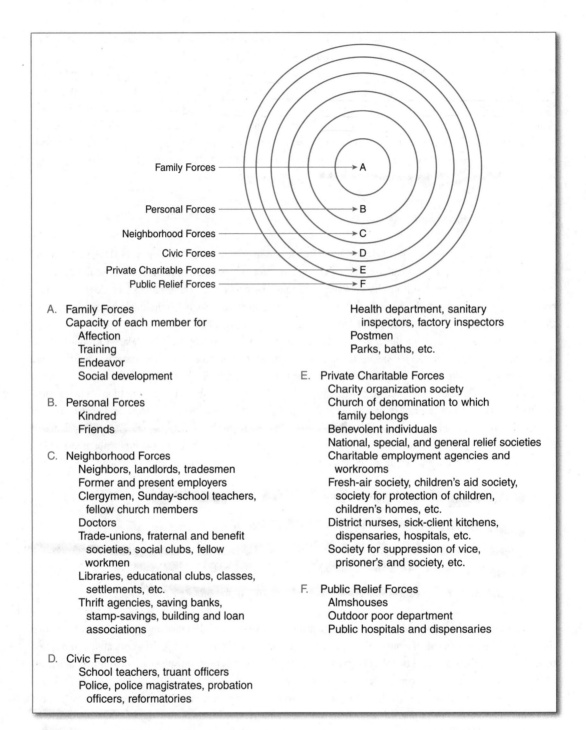

Family Forces ────────────────► A

Personal Forces ──────────────► B

Neighborhood Forces ──────────► C

Civic Forces ─────────────────► D

Private Charitable Forces ─────► E

Public Relief Forces ──────────► F

A. Family Forces
    Capacity of each member for
        Affection
        Training
        Endeavor
        Social development

B. Personal Forces
        Kindred
        Friends

C. Neighborhood Forces
        Neighbors, landlords, tradesmen
        Former and present employers
        Clergymen, Sunday-school teachers,
          fellow church members
        Doctors
        Trade-unions, fraternal and benefit
          societies, social clubs, fellow
          workmen
        Libraries, educational clubs, classes,
          settlements, etc.
        Thrift agencies, saving banks,
          stamp-savings, building and loan
          associations

D. Civic Forces
        School teachers, truant officers
        Police, police magistrates, probation
          officers, reformatories

        Health department, sanitary
          inspectors, factory inspectors
        Postmen
        Parks, baths, etc.

E. Private Charitable Forces
        Charity organization society
        Church of denomination to which
          family belongs
        Benevolent individuals
        National, special, and general relief societies
        Charitable employment agencies and
          workrooms
        Fresh-air society, children's aid society,
          society for protection of children,
          children's homes, etc.
        District nurses, sick-client kitchens,
          dispensaries, hospitals, etc.
        Society for suppression of vice,
          prisoner's and society, etc.

F. Public Relief Forces
        Almshouses
        Outdoor poor department
        Public hospitals and dispensaries

▲ **Exhibit 1.3**   Mary Richmond's 1901 Model of Case Coordination

▲ **Photo 1.1**   Three dimensions of human behavior are captured in this photo—person, environment, and time.

These dimensions are neither mutually exclusive nor hierarchically ordered. For example, a family is sometimes referred to as a social institution, families can also be considered small groups or dyads, and family theorists write about family culture. Remember, dimensions are useful ways of thinking about person–environment configurations, but you should not think of them as detached realities.

Time Dimensions

When I was a doctoral student in a social work practice course, Professor Max Siporin began his discussion about social work assessment with the comment, "The date is the most important information on a written social work assessment." This was Siporin's way of acknowledging the importance of time in human behavior, of recognizing that person–environment transactions are ever changing, dynamic, and flowing.

We are aware of the time dimension in the ongoing process of migration in Manisha's story. And, you may be interested, as I am, in the process of acculturation in which she and her family are now engaged. As will be discussed in Chapter 8, **acculturation** is a process of changing one's culture by incorporating elements of another culture. When the Bhutanese government tried to impose a different culture, religion, and language on the Nepali ethnic group, they, not surprisingly, resisted. In the refugee camps, their culture, religion, and language were practiced without conflict. Now that Manisha's family has resettled in the United States, they must find a way to live in a multicultural society that is nevertheless dominated by Anglo culture, Christianity, and the English language. Think about the complexity of the developmental tasks involved in adapting to that culture change.

Acculturation happens over time, in a nonlinear process, with new situations and opportunities to learn, negotiate, and accommodate. Manisha recognizes that her development of English proficiency skills depends to a large degree on opportunities to be in situations where she must use those skills and observe other people using the English language. She is interested in learning about her new culture's roles while still keeping her culture of origin. No doubt she will become bicultural over time, given her adaptability in developing new gender roles in the refugee camp. Most likely, the different members of her family will acculturate at different paces, with her grandchildren leading the way (Bush, Bohon, & Kim, 2010). Twenty years ago, research indicated that men adapted to cultural change faster than women, but more recent research indicates that immigrant women often have a faster pace of acculturation than their spouses (Falicov, 2003).

When I think of time, I tend to think of clocks, calendars, and appointments. And I often seem to be racing against time, allowing the clock to tell me when an event should begin and end. This is the way most people in affluent countries with market economies think of time. This approach to time has been called *clock time* (Lauer, 1981; R. Levine, 2006). However, this approach to time is a relatively new invention, and many people in the contemporary world have a very different approach to time (Rosen, 2004). In nonindustrialized countries, and in subcultures within industrialized countries, people operate on *event time,* allowing scheduling to be determined by events. Robert Levine provides numerous examples of event time. Signals from the body, rather than the hour on the clock, dictate when to eat. Activities are guided by seasonal changes: When the rainy season comes, it is time for planting. Appointments are flex-

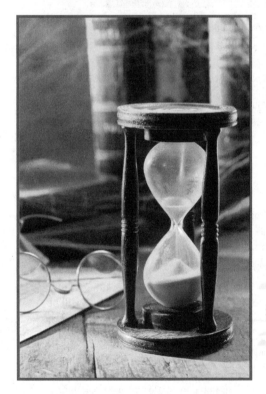

ible: "I will see you tomorrow morning when the cows go out to graze." The length of an event may be explained by saying, for example, "The storm lasted as long as a rice-cooking." Monks in Burma have developed their own alarm clocks, knowing it is time to get up when there is enough light to see the veins in their hands (Thompson, 1967, cited in Levine, 2006). In agricultural societies, the most successful farmers are the ones who can be responsive to natural events rather than to scheduled events. Manisha's life was organized around cues from the natural world rather than the clock when she lived in Bhutan, just as my grandfather's was on his farm in rural Tennessee.

Anthropologists report that some event time cultures, such as that of the Hopi of the U.S. Southwest, and some Arab cultures have no language to distinguish past, present, and future time. However, clock time cultures often use the concept of **time orientation** to describe the extent to which individuals and collectivities are invested in three temporal zones—past, present, and future time— known as **linear time.** Research indicates that cultures differ in their time orientation. Traditional cultures are more invested in the past, and advanced industrial cultures are more invested in the future (Hofstede, 1998). In reality, some situations call for us to be totally immersed in the present, others call for historical understanding of the past and its impact on the present, and still others call for attention to future consequences and possibilities. Recently, Western behavioral scientists have begun to incorporate Eastern mindfulness practices of being more fully present in the current moment (present orientation) to help people buffer the persistent stresses of clock

▲ **Photo 1.2** Time is one of the three dimensions outlined in this text for studying human behavior. It recognizes that people and environments are ever changing, dynamic, and flowing.

time and goal monitoring (future orientation) (see, e.g., Boyatzis & McKee, 2005). People in fast-paced, clock time societies often berate those who are less attentive to the clock while at the same time bemoaning the hold the clock has on them. Research also indicates that there are age-related differences in time orientation, with older adults tending to be more past oriented than younger age groups (Shmotkin, 1991). There are also individual variations in time orientation. For example, researchers have found that trauma survivors who experienced the most severe loss are more likely than other trauma survivors to be highly oriented to the past (Holman & Silver, 1998; E. Martz, 2004). This is something to keep in mind when we interact with refugees, military men and women who have served in war zones, and other groups who have an increased likelihood of having a history of trauma. It is also important for social workers to be aware of the meaning of time for the individuals and communities they serve.

Sometimes the pace of change is more rapid than at other times—for example, the pace of change accelerated in 1988 for Manisha and her family and again when they resettled in the United States. There is also a temporal scope, or duration, to social and personal change. In linear time, the scope of some events is brief, such as a birthday party, an automobile accident, termination from a job, winning the lottery, or a tornado. Werner, Altman, and Oxley (1985) refer to these brief events as *incidents*; in this book and the companion volume, they are called **life events.** Although life events are brief in scope, they may produce shifts and have serious and long-lasting effects. It is important to note the role of perception when discussing both the pace of change and the duration of an event (Rappaport, Enrich, & Wilson, 1985). It is easy to imagine that the 3 months that Manisha and her family spent in the camp by the river seemed longer than 3 months in a more peaceful time on their farm in Bhutan.

Other events are long and complex transactions of people and environments. Werner et al. (1985) refer to these longer events as *stages*; it is this dimension of time that has been incorporated into life stage theories of human behavior. As will be explained in Chapter 2, however, life stage theories have been criticized for their overstatement of the universality of the sequence of stages and of the timing of human behavior. In contrast, a **life course perspective** assumes that each person's life has a unique, long-term pattern of stability and change but that shared social and historical contexts produce some commonalities. In some ways, Manisha's life journey is unique, but in other ways, her journey is similar to that of other members of the Nepali ethnic group from Bhutan. The life course perspective is the topic of Chapter 1 in the companion volume.

Critical Thinking Questions 1.1

How would our understanding of Manisha's story change if we had no knowledge of her prior life experiences in Bhutan and the Nepali refugee camp—if we only assessed her situation based on her current functioning? What personal and environmental dimensions would we note in her current functioning?

DIVERSITY, INEQUALITY, AND THE PURSUIT OF SOCIAL JUSTICE: A GLOBAL PERSPECTIVE

The Council on Social Work Education requires that social work educational programs provide a global perspective to their students. What exactly does that mean, and why is it valued? We are increasingly aware that we are part of an interconnected world, and Manisha's story is one reminder of this. But just how connected are we? In her book *Beyond Borders: Thinking About Global Issues,* Paula Rothenberg (2006) writes, "A not so funny, but perhaps sadly true, joke going around claims that people in the United States learn geography by going to war" (p. xv). Certainly, we have learned something about the maps of Afghanistan and Iraq, but what do we know about the map of Bhutan? A global perspective involves much more than geography, however. Here are some aspects of what it means to take a global perspective:

- To be aware that my view of the world is not universally shared, and others may have a view of the world that is profoundly different from mine

- To have a growing awareness of the diversity of ideas and cultural practices found in human societies around the world

- To be curious about conditions in other parts of the world and how they relate to conditions in our own society

- To understand where I fit in global social institutions and social structure

- To have a growing awareness of how people in other societies view my society

- To have a growing understanding of how the world works, with special attention to systems and mechanisms of inequality and oppression around the world

We have always been connected to other peoples of the world, but those connections are being intensified by **globalization,** a process by which the world's people are becoming more interconnected economically, politically, environmentally, and culturally. It is a process of increased connectedness and interdependence that affects people around the world (Eitzen & Zinn, 2006). This increasing connectedness is, of course, aided by rapid advancements in communication technology. There is much debate about whether globalization is a good thing or a bad thing, a conversation that will be picked up in Chapter 9 as we consider the globalization of social institutions. What is important to note here is that globalization is increasing our experiences with social diversity and raising new questions about inequality, human rights, and social justice.

Diversity

Diversity has always been a part of the social reality in the United States. Even before the Europeans came, the Indigenous people were divided into about 200 distinct societies with about 200 different languages (Parrillo, 2009). Since the inception of the nation of the United States of America, we have been a nation of immigrants. We value our nation's immigrant heritage and take pride in the ideals of equality of opportunity for all who come. However, there have always been tensions about how we as a nation will handle diversity. Will we be a *melting pot* where all are melted into one indistinguishable model of citizenship, or will we be a *pluralist society* in which groups have separate identities, cultures, and ways of organizing but work together in mutual respect? Pioneer social worker Jane Addams was a prominent voice for pluralism during the early 20th century, and that stance is consistent with social work's concern for human rights.

However, it is accurate to say that some of the diversity in our national social life is new. Clearly, there is increasing racial, ethnic, and religious diversity in the United States, and the mix in the population stream has become much more complex in recent years (Parrillo, 2009). The United States was 87% White in 1925, 80% White in 1950, and 72% White in 2000; by 2050, it is projected that we will be about 50% White (Prewitt, 2000). Why is this happening at this time? A major driving force is the demographic reality that native-born people are no longer reproducing at replacement level in the wealthy postindustrial nations, which, if it continues, ultimately will lead to a declining population skewed toward advanced age. One solution used by some countries, including the United States, is to change immigration policy to allow new streams of immigration. The current rate of foreign-born persons in the United States is lower than it has been throughout most of the past 150 years, but foreign-born persons are less likely to be White than when immigration policy, prior to 1965, strictly limited entry to persons of color. With the recent influx of immigrants from around the globe, the United States has become one of many ethnically and racially diverse nations in the world today. In many wealthy postindustrial countries, including the United States, there is much anti-immigrant sentiment, even though the economies of these countries are dependent on such migration. Waves of immigration have historically been accompanied by anti-immigrant sentiment. There appear to be many reasons for anti-immigrant sentiment, including fear that new immigrants will dilute the "purity" of the native culture, racial and religious bias, and fear of economic competition. Like other diverse societies, we must find ways to embrace the diversity and seize the opportunity to demonstrate the human capacity for intergroup harmony.

On the other hand, some of the diversity in our social life is not new but simply newly recognized. In the contemporary era, we have been developing a heightened consciousness of human differences—gender differences, racial and ethnic differences, cultural differences, religious differences, differences in sexual orientation, differences in abilities and disabilities, differences in family forms, and so on. We are experiencing a new tension in navigating the line between cultural sensitivity and stereotypical thinking about individuals and groups. It is the intent of this book to capture the diversity of human experience in a manner that is respectful of all groups, conveys the positive value of human diversity, and recognizes differences *within* groups as well as *among* groups.

As you seek to honor differences, keep in mind the distinction between heterogeneity and diversity (Calasanti, 1996). **Heterogeneity** refers to individual-level variations—differences among individuals. For example, as the social worker whom Manisha consults, you will want to recognize the ways in which she is different from you and from other clients you serve, including other clients of Bhutanese heritage. An understanding of heterogeneity allows us to recognize the uniqueness of each person and situation. **Diversity,** on the other hand, refers to patterns of group differences. Diversity recognizes social groups, groups of people who share a range of physical, cultural, or social characteristics within a category of social identity. As a social worker, besides recognizing individual differences, you will also want to be aware of the diversity in your community, such as the distribution of various ethnic groups, including those of Bhutanese heritage. Knowledge of diversity helps us to provide culturally sensitive services.

I want to interject a word here about terminology and human diversity. As the contributing authors and I attempted to uncover what is known about human diversity, we struggled with terminology to define identity groups. We searched for consistent language to describe different groups, and we were dedicated to using language that identity groups would use to describe themselves. However, we ran into challenges endemic to our time related to the language of diversity. It is not the case that all members of a given identity group at any given time embrace the same terminology for their group. As I write this paragraph, I am listening to news reports about the political uproar over Senator Harry Reid's use of the word *Negro* to refer to then-presidential candidate Barack Obama. Yesterday, I heard a news report about the U.S. Census Bureau using Negro as racial category in the 2010 census. Staff at the Census Bureau argue that this is the term preferred by older African Americans. However, the young African American reporter said the word is not in his vocabulary. Similar examples could be found for other ethnic groups. As we reviewed literature from different historical moments, we recognized the shifting nature of terminology. In addition, even within a given historical era, we found that different researchers used different terms and had different decision rules about who composes the membership of identity groups. Add to this the changing way that the U.S. Census Bureau establishes official categories of people, and in the end, we did not settle on fixed terminology to consistently describe identity groups. Rather, we use the language of individual researchers when reporting their work, because we want to avoid distorting their work. We hope you will not find this too distracting. We also hope that you will recognize that the ever-changing language of diversity has both constructive potential to find creative ways to affirm diversity and destructive potential to dichotomize diversity into *the norm* and *the other.*

Inequality

Attending to diversity involves recognition of the power relations between social groups and the patterns of opportunities and constraints for social groups. If we are interested in the Bhutanese community in our city, for example, we will want to note, among other things, the neighborhoods where they live, the quality of the housing stock in those neighborhoods, the comparative educational attainment in the community, the occupational profile of the community, and the comparative income levels. When we attend to diversity, we not only note the differences between groups, but also how socially constructed hierarchies of power are superimposed on these differences.

Recent U.S. scholarship in the social sciences has emphasized the ways in which three types of categorizations—gender, race, and class—are used to develop hierarchical social structures that influence social identities and life chances (Rothenberg, 2007; Sernau, 2006). This literature suggests that these social categorizations create **privilege**, or unearned advantage, for some groups and disadvantage for other groups. In a much-cited article, Peggy McIntosh (2007) has pointed out the mundane daily advantages of White privilege that are not available to members of groups of color, such as, "can be sure that my children will be given curricular materials that testify to the existence of their race" and "Whether I use checks, credit cards, or cash, I can count on my skin color not to work against the appearance of financial reliability." We could also generate lists of advantages of male privilege, adult privilege, upper-middle-class privilege, heterosexual privilege, ability privilege, Christian privilege, and so on. McIntosh argues that members of privileged groups benefit from their privilege but have not been taught to think of themselves as privileged. They take for granted that their advantages are "normal and universal" (Bell, 1997, p. 12). For survival, members of nonprivileged groups must learn a lot about the lives of groups with privilege, but groups with privileged status are not similarly compelled to learn about the lives of members of nonprivileged groups.

Michael Schwalbe (2006) argues that those of us who live in the United States also carry "American privilege," which comes from our dominant position in the world. (I would prefer to call this "U.S. privilege," since people living in Canada, Ecuador, and Brazil also live in America.) According to Schwalbe, among other things, American privilege means that we don't have to bother to learn about other countries or about the impact of our foreign policy on people living in those countries. Perhaps that is what Rothenberg (2006) was thinking of when she noted ignorance of world geography among people who live in the United States. American privilege also means that we have access to cheap goods that are produced by poorly paid workers in impoverished countries. As you will see in Chapter 9, the income and wealth gap between nations is mind-boggling. Sernau (2006) reports that the combined income of the 25 richest people in the United States is almost as great as the combined income of 2 billion of the world's poorest people. The average per capita income in Bhutan is $1,440 in U.S. dollars, compared to $46,040 in the United States (UNICEF, n.d.). It is becoming increasingly difficult to deny the costs of exercising American privilege by remaining ignorant about the rest of the world and the impact our actions have on other nations.

As the contributing authors and I strive to provide a global context, we encounter current controversies about appropriate language to describe different sectors of the world. Following World War II, a distinction was made between First World, Second World, and Third World nations, with First World referring to the Western capitalist nations, Second World referring to the countries belonging to the socialist bloc led by the Soviet Union, and Third World referring to a set of countries that were primarily former colonies of the First World. More recently, many scholars have used this same language to define global sectors in a slightly different way. *First World* has been used to describe the nations that were the first to industrialize, urbanize, and modernize. *Second World* has been used to describe nations that have industrialized but have not yet become central to the world economy. *Third World* has been used to refer to nonindustrialized nations that have few resources and are considered expendable in the global economy. However, this approach has begun to lose favor in the past few years (Leeder, 2004). Immanuel Wallerstein (1974, 1979) uses different language but makes a similar distinction; he refers to wealthy *core* countries, newly industrialized *semiperiphery* countries, and the poorest *periphery* countries. Other writers divide the world into *developed* and *developing* countries, referring to the level of industrialization, urbanization, and modernization. Still others divide the world into the *Global North* and the *Global South*, calling attention to a history in which the Global North colonized and exploited the resources of the Global South. Finally, some writers talk about the *West* versus the *East*, where the distinctions are largely cultural. We recognize that such categories carry great symbolic meaning and can mask systems of power and exploitation. As with diversity, we attempted to find a respectful language that could be used consistently throughout the book. Again, we found that different researchers have used different language and different characteristics to describe categories of nations, and when reporting on their findings, we have used their own language to avoid misrepresenting their findings.

It is important to note that privilege and disadvantage are multidimensional, not one-dimensional. One can be privileged in one dimension and disadvantaged in another; for example, I have White privilege but not gender privilege. As social workers, we need to be attuned to our own *social locations*—where we fit in a system of social identities, such as race, ethnicity, gender, social class, sexual orientation, religion, ability/disability, and age. We must recognize how our own particular social locations shape how we see the world, what we notice, and how we interpret what we "see."

This is not easy for us, because in the United States, as a rule, we avoid the topic of class and don't like to admit that it shapes our lives (Sernau, 2006). It is important for social workers to acknowledge social inequalities, however, because our interactions are constantly affected by inequalities. In addition, there is clear evidence that social inequalities are on the rise in the United States. In the last couple of decades, the United States gained the distinction as the most unequal society in the postindustrial world, and the gap continues to widen in the midst of the deep economic recession that officially began in December 2007 (Sernau, 2006).

The Pursuit of Social Justice

There is another important reason that social workers must acknowledge social inequalities. The National Association of Social Workers (NASW) Code of Ethics identifies social justice as one of six core values of social work and mandates that "Social Workers challenge social injustice" (NASW, 1999). To challenge injustice, we must first recognize it and understand the ways that it is embedded in a number of societal institutions. That will be the subject of Chapter 9 in this book.

Suzanne Pharr (1988) has provided some useful conceptual tools that can help us recognize injustice when we see it. She identifies a set of mechanisms of oppression, whereby the everyday arrangements of social life systematically block opportunities for some groups and inhibit their power to exercise self-determination. Exhibit 1.4 provides an overview of these mechanisms of oppression. As you review the list, you may recognize some that are familiar to you, such as stereotyping and perhaps blaming the victim. There may be others that you have not previously given much thought to. You may also recognize, as I do each time I look at the list, that while some of these mechanisms of oppression are sometimes used quite intentionally, others are not so intentional but occur as we do business as usual. For example, when you walk into your classroom, do you give much thought to the person who cleans that room, what wage this person is paid, whether this is the only job this person holds, and what opportunities and barriers this person has experienced in life? Most likely, the classroom is cleaned in the evening after it has been vacated by teachers and students, and the person who cleans it, like many people who provide services that make our lives more pleasant, is invisible to you. Giving serious thought to common mechanisms of oppression can help us to recognize social injustice and think about ways tochallenge it.

In recent years, social workers have expanded the conversation about social justice to include *global* social justice. As they have done so, they have more and more drawn on the concept of *human rights* to organize thinking about social justice, but ideas about human rights are in the early stage of development (see Mapp, 2008; Reichert, 2006; Wronka, 2008). In the aftermath of World War II, the newly formed United Nations (1948) created a Universal Declaration of Human Rights (UDHR), which spelled out the rights to which all humans were entitled, regardless of their place in the world, and this document has become a point of reference for subsequent

Economic Power and Control	Limiting of resources, mobility, education, and employment options to all but a few
Myth of Scarcity	Myth used to pit people against one another, suggests that resources are limited and blames people (e.g., poor people, immigrants) for using too many of them
Defined Norm	A standard of what is good and right, against which all are judged
The Other	Those who fall outside "the norm" but are defined in relation to it, seen as abnormal, inferior, marginalized
Invisibility	Keeping "the other's" existence, everyday life, and achievements unknown
Distortion	Selective presentation or rewriting of history so that only negative aspects of "the other" are included
Stereotyping	Generalizing the actions of a few to an entire group, denying individual characteristics and behaviors
Violence and the Threat of Violence	Laying claim to resources, then using might to ensure superior position
Lack of Prior Claim	Excluding anyone who was not originally included and labeling as disruptive those who fight for inclusion
Blaming the Victim	Condemning "the others" for their situation, diverting attention from the roles that dominants play in the situation
Internalized Oppression	Internalizing negative judgments of being "the other," leading to self-hatred, depression, despair, and self-abuse
Horizontal Hostility	Extending internalized oppression to one's entire group as well as to other subordinate groups, expressing hostility to other oppressed persons and groups rather than to members of dominant groups
Isolation	Physically isolating people as individuals or as a "minority" group
Assimilation	Pressuring members of "minority" groups to drop their culture and differences and become a mirror of the dominant culture
Tokenism	Rewarding some of the most assimilated "others" with position and resources
Emphasis on Individual Solutions	Emphasizing individual responsibility for problems and individual solutions rather than collective responsibility and collective solutions

▲ **Exhibit 1.4**   Common Mechanisms of Oppression

SOURCE: Adapted from Pharr (1988).

definitions of human rights. Joseph Wronka (2008) argues that human rights are the bedrock of social justice. He identifies five core notions of human rights as suggested by the UDHR:

- *Human dignity:* equality and freedom

- *Nondiscrimination:* based on race, color, sex, language, religion, political opinion, national or social origin, property, birth, or other status

- *Civil and political rights:* freedom of thought, religion, expression, access to information, privacy, and fair and public hearing

- *Economic, social, and cultural rights:* to meaningful and gainful employment, rest and leisure, health care, food, housing, education, participation in cultural life, special care for motherhood and children

- *Solidarity rights:* to a just social and international order, self-determination, peace

Mapp (2008) suggests that three main barriers prevent full access to human rights: poverty, discrimination, and lack of access to education. Manisha has experienced all three of these barriers at some point in her life.

Critical Thinking Questions 1.2

What impact is globalization having on your own life? Do you see it as having a positive or negative impact on your life? What about for Manisha? Do you think globalization is having a positive or negative impact on her life?

KNOWING AND DOING

Social workers, like other professional practitioners, must find a way to move from knowing to doing, from "knowing about" and "knowing that" into "knowing how to" (for fuller discussion of this issue, see Hutchison, Charlesworth, Matto, Harrigan, & Viggiani, 2007). We *know* for the purpose of *doing.* Like architects, engineers, physicians, and teachers, social workers are faced with complex problems and case situations that are unique and uncertain. You no doubt will find that social work education, social work practice, and even this book will stretch your capacity to tolerate ambiguity and uncertainty. That is important because, as Carol Meyer (1993) has suggested, "There are no easy or simple [social work] cases, only simplistic perceptions" (p. 63). There is evidence that social workers have a tendency to terminate the learning process too early, to quest for answers, as opposed to appreciating the complexity of the process that may lead to multiple possible solutions (Gambrill, 2006). There are four important ingredients of "knowing how" to do social work: knowledge about the case, knowledge about the self, values and ethics, and scientific knowledge. These four ingredients are intertwined in the process of doing social work. The focus of this book is on scientific knowledge, but all four ingredients are essential in social work practice. Before moving to a discussion of scientific knowledge, I want to say a word about the other three ingredients.

Knowledge About the Case

I am using *case* to mean the situation at hand, a situation that has become problematic for some person or collectivity, resulting in a social work intervention. Our first task as social workers is to develop as good an understanding of the situation as possible: Who is involved in the situation and how are they involved? What is the nature of the relationships of the people involved? What are the societal, cultural, and community contexts of the situation? What are the contextual constraints as well as the contextual resources for bringing change to the situation? What elements of the case are maintaining the problematic situation? How have people tried to cope with the situation? What preference do the involved people have about the types of intervention to use? What is the culture, and what are the social resources of the social agency to whose attention the situation is brought? You might begin to think about how you would answer some of these questions in relation to Manisha's situation.

It is important to note that knowledge about the case is influenced by the quality of the relationship between the social worker and client(s). There is good evidence that people are likely to reveal more aspects of their situation if they are approached with commitment, an open mind, warmth, empathic attunement, authentic responsiveness, and mutuality (Hepworth, Rooney, Rooney, Strom-Gottfried, & Larsen, 2010). For example, as Manisha becomes comfortable in the interview, feeling validated by both the interviewer and the interpreter, she begins to engage in deeper reflection about what happened in Bhutan. At the end of the interview, she expresses much gratitude for the opportunity to tell her story, noting that this is the first chance she has had to put the story together and that telling the story has led her to think about some events in new ways. This can be an important part of her grieving process. The integrity of knowledge about the case is related to the quality of the relationship, and the capacity for relationship is related to knowledge about the self.

But knowledge about the case requires more than simply gathering information. We must select and order the information at hand and decide if further information is needed. This involves making a series of decisions about what is relevant and what is not. It also involves searching for recurring themes as well as contradictions in the information. For example, it is important for the refugee resettlement social worker to note a strong theme of the desire for purpose and self-respect in Manisha's story. Equally important is the information that Manisha shares about the knitting project sponsored by Oxfam. This may provide a clue for further program development to meet the needs of the community of Bhutanese refugees. It is also important to note Manisha's lingering confusion about why her peaceful world in Bhutan got turned upside down. This suggests that Manisha and other Bhutanese refugees might benefit from narrative exercises that help them to make sense of these experiences.

To assist you in moving between knowledge about the case and scientific knowledge, each chapter in this book begins, as this one does, with one or more case studies. Each of these unique stories suggests what scientific knowledge is needed. For example, to work effectively with Manisha, you will want to understand some things about Bhutan, the Nepali ethnic group, Hinduism, grief reactions, the acculturation process, challenges facing immigrant families, and cross-cultural communication. Throughout the chapters, the stories are woven together with relevant scientific knowledge. Keep in mind that scientific knowledge is necessary, but you will not be an effective practitioner unless you take the time to learn about the unique situation of each person or collectivity you serve. It is the unique situation that guides what scientific knowledge is needed.

Knowledge About the Self

In his book *The Spiritual Life of Children,* Robert Coles (1990) wrote about the struggles of a 10-year-old Hopi girl to have her Anglo teacher understand Hopi spirituality. Coles suggested to the girl that perhaps she could try to explain her tribal nation's spiritual beliefs to the teacher. The girl answered, "But they don't listen to hear *us*; they listen to hear themselves" (p. 25, emphasis original). This young girl has captured, in a profound way, a major challenge to our everyday personal and professional communications: the tendency to approach the world with preconceived notions that we seek to validate by attending to some information while ignoring other information. The capacity to understand oneself is needed in order to guard against this very human tendency.

Three types of self-knowledge are essential for social workers: understanding of one's own thinking processes, understanding of one's own emotions, and understanding of one's own social location. We must be able to think about our thinking, a process called *metacognition.* We also must be able to recognize what emotions get aroused in us when we hear stories like Manisha's and when we contemplate the challenges of the situation, and we must find a way to use those emotions in ways that are helpful and avoid using them in ways that are harmful. Although writing about physicians, Gunnar Biorck (1977) said it well when he commented that practitioners make "a tremendous number of judgments each day, based on inadequate, often ambiguous data, and under pressure of time, and carrying out this task with the outward appearance of calmness, dedication and interpersonal warmth" (p. 146).

In terms of social location, as suggested earlier, social workers must identify and reflect on where they fit in a system of social identities, such as race, ethnicity, gender, social class, sexual orientation, religion, ability/disability, and age.

The literature on culturally sensitive social work practice proposes that a strong personal identity in relation to important societal categories, and an understanding of the impact of those identities on other people, is essential for successful social work intervention across cultural lines (see Lum, 2007). This type of self-knowledge requires reflecting on where one fits in systems of privilege.

Values and Ethics

The process of developing knowledge about the case is a dialogue between the social worker and client system, and social workers have a well-defined value base to guide the dialogue. Six core values of the profession have been set out in a preamble to the Code of Ethics established by the National Association for Social Workers (NASW) in 1996 and revised in 1999. These values are service, social justice, dignity and worth of the person, importance of human relationships, integrity, and competence. The value of social justice was discussed earlier in the chapter. As demonstrated in Exhibit 1.5, the Code of Ethics articulates an ethical principle for each of the core values. Value 6, competence, requires that we recognize what science there is to inform our work. It requires understanding the limitations of the available science for considering the situation at hand, but also that we use the strongest available evidence to make practice decisions. This is where scientific knowledge comes into the picture.

1. Value: Service

   Ethical Principle: Social workers' primary goal is to help people in need and to address social problems.

2. Value: Social Justice

   Ethical Principle: Social workers challenge social injustice.

3. Value: Dignity and Worth of the Person

   Ethical Principle: Social workers respect the inherent dignity and worth of the person.

4. Value: Importance of Human Relationships

   Ethical Principle: Social workers recognize the central importance of human relationships.

5. Value: Integrity

   Ethical Principle: Social workers behave in a trustworthy manner.

6. Value: Competence

   Ethical Principle: Social workers practice within their areas of competence and develop and enhance their professional expertise.

▲ **Exhibit 1.5**   Core Values and Ethical Principles in NASW Code of Ethics

SOURCE: Copyright 1999. National Association of Social Workers, Inc., NASW Code of Ethics

Critical Thinking Questions 1.3

What emotional reactions did you have to reading Manisha's story? What did you find yourself thinking about her story? Where do you see Manisha fitting in systems of privilege? Where do you see yourself fitting? How might any of this impact your ability to be helpful to Manisha?

SCIENTIFIC KNOWLEDGE: THEORY AND RESEARCH

Ethical social workers are always searching for/recalling what is known about the situations they encounter, turning to the social and behavioral sciences for this information. Scientific knowledge serves as a screen against which the knowledge about the case is considered. It suggests **hypotheses,** or tentative statements, to be explored and tested, not facts to be applied, in transactions with a person or group. Because of the breadth and complexity of social work practice, usable knowledge must be culled from diverse sources and a number of scientific disciplines. **Science,** also known as scientific inquiry, is a set of logical, systematic, documented methods for answering questions about the world. Scientific knowledge is the knowledge produced by scientific inquiry. Two interrelated approaches to knowledge building, theory and empirical research, fit the scientific criteria of being logical, systematic, and documented for the public. Together, they create the base of knowledge that social workers need to understand commonalities among their clients and practice situations. In your course work on social work research, you will be learning much more about these concepts, so I only provide a brief description here to help you understand how this book draws on theory and research.

Theory

Social workers use theory to help organize and make sense of the situations they encounter. A **theory** is a logically interrelated set of concepts and propositions, organized into a deductive system, which explains relationships among aspects of our world. As Elaine Leeder (2004) so aptly put it, "To have a theory is to have a way of explaining the world—an understanding that the world is not just a random series of events and experiences" (p. 9). Theory is a somewhat imposing word, seemingly abstract and associated with serious scholars, but it has everyday utility to social workers:

> Scratch any social worker and you will find a theoretician. Her own theoretical perspectives about people and practice may be informed by theories in print (or formal theories) but are put together in her own way with many modifications and additions growing out of her own professional and personal experience. (W. Reid & Smith, 1989, p. 45)

Thus, theory gives us a framework for interpreting person and environment and planning interventions. Theories focus our attention on particular aspects of the person–environment–time configuration.

Other terms that you will often encounter in discussions of theories are model, paradigm, and perspective. *Model* usually is used to refer to a visual representation of the relationships between concepts, *paradigm* most often means a way of seeing the world, and *perspective* is an emphasis or a view. Paradigms and perspectives are broader and more general than theory.

If you are to make good use of theory, you should know something about how it is constructed. **Concepts** are the building blocks of theory. They are symbols, or mental images, that summarize observations, feelings, or ideas. Concepts allow us to communicate about the phenomena of interest. Some relevant concepts in Manisha's story are culture, Hinduism, Buddhism, cultural conflict, refugee, acculturation, loss, grief, dignity, and self-reliance.

Theoretical concepts are put together to form **propositions,** or assertions. For example, loss and grief theory proposes that the loss of a person, object, or ideal leads to a grief reaction. This proposition, which asserts a particular relationship between the concepts of loss and grief, may help the refugee resettlement social worker understand some of the sadness, and sometimes despair, that she sees in her work with Bhutanese refugee families. They have lived with an accumulation of losses—loss of land, loss of livelihood, loss of roles, loss of status, loss of extended family members, loss of familiar language and rituals, and many more.

Theories are a form of **deductive reasoning,** meaning that they lay out general, abstract propositions that we can use to generate specific hypotheses to test in unique situations. In this example, loss and grief theory can lead us to hypothesize that Bhutanese refugees are grieving the many losses they have suffered.

Social and behavioral science theories are based on **assumptions,** or beliefs held to be true without testing or proof, about the nature of human social life. These theoretical assumptions have raised a number of controversies, three of which are worth introducing at this point (Burrell & Morgan, 1979; P. Y. Martin & O'Connor, 1989; Monte & Sollod, 2003):

1. Do the dimensions of human behavior have an **objective reality** that exists outside a person's consciousness, or is all reality based on personal perception **(subjective reality)**?

2. Is human behavior determined by forces beyond the control of the person **(determinism)**, or are people free and proactive agents in the creation of their behavior **(voluntarism)**?

3. Are the patterned interactions among people characterized by harmony, unity, and social cohesion or by conflict, domination, coercion, and exploitation?

The nature of these controversies will become more apparent to you in Chapter 2. The contributing authors and I take a middle ground on all of them: We assume that reality has both objective and subjective aspects, that human behavior is partially constrained and partially free, and that social life is marked by both cohesion and conflict.

Empirical Research

Traditionally, science is equated with empirical research, which is widely held as the most rigorous and systematic way to understand human behavior. Research is typically viewed, in simple terms, as a problem-solving process, or a method of seeking answers to questions. If something is empirical, we experience it through our senses, as opposed to something that we experience purely in our minds. The process of **empirical research** includes a careful, purposeful, and systematic observation of events with the intent to note and record them in terms of their attributes, to

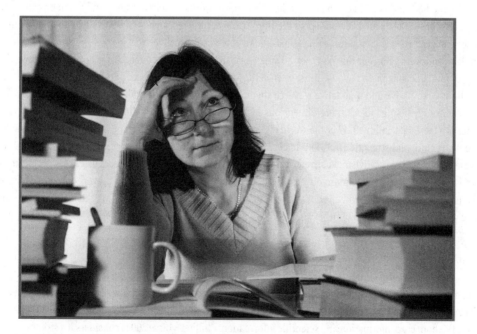

▲ **Photo 1.3** Theories and research about human behavior are boundless and constantly growing. Active readers must question what they read.

look for patterns in those events, and to make our methods and observations public. Like theory, empirical research is a key tool for social workers: "The practitioner who just conforms to ongoing practices without keeping abreast of the latest research in his or her field is not doing all possible to see that his or her clients get the best possible service" (Rubin & Babbie, 1993, p. xxv).

Just as there are controversies about theoretical assumptions, there are also controversies about what constitutes appropriate research methods for understanding human behavior. Modern science is based on several assumptions, which are generally recognized as a **positivist perspective:** The world has an order that can be discovered, findings of one study should be applicable to other groups, complex phenomena can be studied by reducing them to some component part, findings are tentative and subject to question, and scientific methods are value-free. **Quantitative methods of research** are the preferred ones from the positivist perspective. These methods use quantifiable measures of concepts, standardize the collection of data, attend only to preselected variables, and use statistical measures to look for patterns and associations (Schutt, 2009).

Over the years, the positivist perspective and its claim that positivism = science have been challenged. Critics argue that quantitative methods cannot possibly capture the subjective experience of individuals or the complex nature of social life. Although most of these critics do not reject positivism as *a way* of doing science, they recommend other ways of understanding the world and suggest that these alternative methods should also be considered part of science. Various names have been given to the alternative methods. We will be referring to them as the **interpretist perspective,** because they share the assumption that reality is based on people's definitions of it and research should focus on learning the meanings that people give to their situations. This is also referred to as a *constructivist perspective*.

Interpretists see a need to replace quantitative methods with **qualitative methods of research,** which are more flexible, experiential, and are designed to capture how participants view social life rather than to ask participants to respond to categories preset by the researcher (Schutt, 2009). Participant observation, intensive interviewing, and focus groups are examples of qualitative methods of research. Interpretists assume that people's behavior cannot be observed objectively, that reality is created as the researcher and research participants interact. Researchers using qualitative methods are more likely to present their findings in words than in numbers and to attempt to capture the settings of behavior. They are likely to report the transactions of the researcher and participant as well as the values of the researcher, because they assume that value-free research is impossible.

In this controversy, it is our position that no single research method can adequately capture the whole, the complexity, of human behavior. In fact, "we must often settle for likely, approximate, or partial truths" (Kirk & Reid, 2002, p. 16). Both quantitative and qualitative research methods have a place in a multidimensional approach, and used together they may help us to see more dimensions of situations. Alvin Saperstein (1996) has stated our view well: "Science is a fabric: its ability to cover the world depends upon the existence of many different fibers acting together to give it structure and strength" (p. 163). This view has much in common with postpositivism, which developed in response to criticism of positivism. **Postpositivism** is a philosophical position that recognizes the complexity of reality and the limitations of human observers. It proposes that scientists can never develop more than a partial understanding of human behavior (Schutt, 2009). Nevertheless, science remains the most rigorous and systematic way to understand human behavior.

Critical Use of Theory and Research

You may already know that social and behavioral science theory and research have been growing at a fast pace in modern times, and you will often feel, as McAvoy (1999) aptly put it, that you are "drowning in a swamp of information" (p. 19), both case information and scientific information. Phillip Dybicz (2004) considers it a strength of the profession that social workers have been more willing than other social and behavioral scientists and professionals to wade into the swamp. Ironically, as you are drowning in a swamp of information, you will also be discovering that the available scientific information is incomplete. You will also encounter contradictory ideas that must be held simulta-neously and, where possible, coordinated to develop an integrated picture of the situation at hand. That is, as you might guess, not a simple project. It involves weighing available evidence and analyzing its relevance to the situation at hand. That requires critical thinking. **Critical thinking** is a thoughtful and reflective judgment about alternative views and contradictory information. It involves thinking about your own thinking and the influences on that think-ing, as well as a willingness to change your mind. It also involves careful analysis of assumptions and evidence. Critical thinkers also ask, "What is left out of this conceptualization or research?" Throughout the book, we will call out criti-cal thinking questions to support your efforts to think critically.

As you read this book and other sources of scientific knowledge, you will want to begin to think critically about the theory and research that they present. You will want to give careful thought to the credibility of the claims made. Let's look first at theory. It is important to remember that although theorists may try to put checks on their biases, they write from their own cultural frame of reference and from a particular location in the social structure of their society. So, when taking a critical look at a theory, it is important to remember that theories are generally created by people of privileged backgrounds who operate in seats of power. The bulk of theories still used today were authored by White, middle- to upper-class Western European men, and men in the United States with academic appointments. Therefore, as we work in a highly diversified world, we need to be attentive to the possibilities of biases related to race, gender, culture, religion, sexual orientation, abilities/disabilities, and social class—as well as professional or occupational ori-entation. One particular concern is that such biases can lead us to think of disadvantaged members of society or of members of minority groups as pathological or deficient.

Social and behavioral science scholars disagree about the criteria for evaluating theory and research. However, I recommend the criteria presented in Exhibit 1.6 because they are consistent with the multidimensional approach of this book and with the value base of the social work profession. (The five criteria for evaluating theory presented in Exhibit 1.6 are also used in Chapter 2 to evaluate eight theoretical perspectives relevant to social work.) There is agreement in the social and behavioral sciences that theory should be evaluated for coherence and conceptual clar-ity as well as for testability and evidence of empirical support. The criterion of comprehensiveness is specifically related to the multidimensional approach of this book. We do not expect all theories to be multidimensional in nature, but critical analysis of a theory should help us identify deterministic and unidimensional thinking where they exist. The criterion of consistency with emphasis on diversity and power arrangements examines the utility of the theory for a profession that places high value on social justice, and the criterion of usefulness for practice is essential for a profession.

Just as theory may be biased toward the experiences of members of dominant groups, so too may research be biased. The result may be "misleading and, in some cases, [may lead to] outright false conclusions regarding a minor-ity" (Monette, Sullivan, & DeJong, 2008, p. 8). Bias can occur at all stages of the research process.

• Funding sources and other vested interests have a strong influence on which problems are selected for research attention. For example, several critics have suggested that governmental agencies were slow to fund research on acquired immune deficiency syndrome (AIDS) because it was associated in the early years with gay males (Shilts, 1987).

• Bias can occur in the definition of variables for study. For example, using "offenses cleared by arrests" as the definition of crime, rather than using a definition such as "self-reported crime involvement," leads to an overestima-tion of crime among minority groups of color, because those are the people who are most often arrested for their crimes (Hagan, 1994).

• Bias can occur in choosing the sample to be studied. Because there are fewer of them, members of minority groups may not be included in sufficient numbers to demonstrate the variability within a particular minority group. Or a biased sample of minorities may be used (e.g., it is not uncommon to make Black/White comparisons on a sam-ple that includes middle-class Whites and low-income Blacks).

Criteria for Evaluating Theory

Coherence and conceptual clarity. Are the concepts clearly defined and consistently used? Is the theory free of logical inconsistencies? Is it stated in the simplest possible way, without oversimplifying?

Testability and evidence of empirical support. Can the concepts and propositions be expressed in language that makes them observable and accessible to corroboration or refutation by persons other than the theoretician? Is there evidence of empirical support for the theory?

Comprehensiveness. Does the theory include multiple dimensions of persons, environments, and time? What is included and what is excluded? What dimension(s) is (are) emphasized? Does the theory account for things that other theories have overlooked or been unable to account for?

Consistency with social work's emphasis on diversity and power arrangements. Can the theory help us understand diversity? How inclusive is it? Does it avoid pathologizing members of minority groups? Does it assist in understanding power arrangements and systems of oppression?

Usefulness for social work practice. Does the theory assist in the understanding of person-and-environment transactions over time? Can principles of action be derived from the theory? At what levels of practice can the theory be used? Can the theory be used in practice in a way that is consistent with the NASW Code of Ethics?

Criteria for Evaluating Research

Corroboration. Are the research findings corroborated by other researchers? Are a variety of research methods used in corroborating research? Do the findings fit logically with accepted theory and other research findings?

Multidimensionality. Does the research include multiple dimensions of persons, environments, and time? If not, do the researchers acknowledge the omissions, connect the research to larger programs of research that include omitted dimensions, or recommend further research to include omitted dimensions?

Definition of terms. Are major variables defined and measured in such a way as to avoid bias against members of minority groups?

Limitation of sample. Does the researcher make sufficient effort to include diversity in the sample? Are minority groups represented in sufficient number to show the variability within them? When demographic groups are compared, are they equivalent on important variables? Does the researcher specify the limitations of the sample for generalizing to specific groups?

Influence of setting. Does the researcher specify attributes of the setting of the research, acknowledge the possible contribution of the setting to research outcomes, and present the findings of similar research across a range of settings?

Influence of the researcher. Does the researcher specify his or her attributes and role in the observed person-environment configurations? Does the researcher specify his or her possible contributions to research outcomes?

Social distance. Does the researcher attempt to minimize errors that could occur because of literacy, language, and cultural differences between the researcher and respondents?

Specification of inferences. Does the researcher specify how inferences are made, based on the data?

Suitability of measures. Does the researcher use measures that seem suited to, and sensitive to, the situation being researched?

▲ **Exhibit 1.6**   Criteria for Evaluating Theory and Research

- Bias can occur in data collection. The validity and reliability of most standardized measuring instruments have been evaluated by using them with White, non-Hispanic respondents, and their cultural relevance with ethnic minorities is questionable. Language and literacy difficulties may arise with both written survey instruments and interviews. Several potential sources of errors when majority researchers gather data from members of minority groups are mistrust and fear, the motivation to provide what is perceived to be wanted, shame and embarrassment, joking or making sport of the researcher, answering based on ideal rather than real, and inadequacy of questions— e.g., asking about a monthly income with families that will have to do a complex computation of incomes of different family members: "income from selling fruit and Popsicles on weekends, income from helping another family make cheese once every two to three weeks, extra money brought in by giving haircuts and permanents to neighborhood women, or occasional childcare and sewing" (Goodson-Lawes, 1994, p. 24).

As with theory evaluation, there is no universally agreed-upon set of criteria for evaluating research. We recommend the nine criteria presented in Exhibit 1.6 for considering the credibility of a research report. These criteria can be applied to either quantitative or qualitative research. Many research reports would be strengthened if their authors were to attend to these criteria.

A WORD OF CAUTION

This book covers two of the three elements of human behavior: person and environment. The third element, time, is covered in a companion volume titled *Dimensions of Human Behavior: The Changing Life Course.*

In this book, Part I includes two stage-setting chapters that introduce the framework for the book and provide a foundation for thinking critically about the discussions of theory and research presented in Parts II and III. Part II comprises four chapters that analyze the multiple dimensions of persons—one chapter each on the biological person, the psychological person (or the self), the psychosocial person (or the self in relationship), and the spiritual person. The eight chapters of Part III discuss the environmental dimensions: the physical environment, culture, social institutions and social structure, families, small groups, formal organizations, communities, and social movements.

Presenting personal and environmental dimensions separately is a risky approach. I do not wish to reinforce any tendency to think about human behavior in a way that camouflages the inseparability of person and environment. I have taken this approach, however, for two reasons. First, the personal and environmental dimensions, for the most part, have been studied separately, often by different disciplines, and usually as detached or semidetached entities. Second, I want to introduce some dimensions of persons and environments not typically covered in social work textbooks and provide updated knowledge about all the dimensions. However, it is important to remember that no single dimension of human behavior can be understood without attention to other dimensions. Thus, frequent references to other dimensions throughout Parts II and III should help develop an understanding of the unity of persons, environments, and time.

IMPLICATIONS FOR SOCIAL WORK PRACTICE

The multidimensional approach outlined in this chapter suggests several principles for social work assessment and intervention, for both prevention and remediation services:

- In the assessment process, collect information about all the critical dimensions of the changing configuration of person and environment.

- In the assessment process, attempt to see the situation from a variety of perspectives. Use multiple data sources, including the person(s), significant others, and direct observations.

- Allow people to tell their own stories, and pay attention to how they describe the pattern and flow of their person–environment configurations.

- Use the multidimensional database of information about critical dimensions of the situation to develop a dynamic picture of the person-environment configuration.

- Link intervention strategies to the dimensions of the assessment.

- In general, expect more effective outcomes from interventions that are multidimensional, because the situation itself is multidimensional.

- Pay particular attention to the impact of diversity and inequality on the unique stories and situations that you encounter.

- Allow the unique stories of people and situations to direct the choice of theory and research to be used.

- Use scientific knowledge to suggest tentative hypotheses to be explored in the unique situation.

KEY TERMS

acculturation	heterogeneity	privilege
assumptions	hypotheses	propositions
biopsychosocial approach	interpretist perspective	qualitative methods of
concepts	life course perspective	research
critical thinking	life events	quantitative methods
deductive reasoning	linear time	of research
determinism	multidetermined behavior	science
dimension	multidimensional	subjective reality
diversity	objective reality	theory
empirical research	positivist perspective	time orientation
globalization	postpositivism	voluntarism

ACTIVE LEARNING

1. We have used multiple dimensions of person, environment, and time to think about Manisha's story. If you were the social worker at the refugee resettlement agency that sponsored her family's resettlement, you would bring your own unfolding person–environment–time story to that encounter. With the graphic in Exhibit 1.1 as your guide, write your own multidimensional story. What personal dimensions are important? What environmental dimensions? What time dimensions? What might happen when these two stories encounter each other?

2. Select a social issue that interests you, such as child abuse or youth gangs. List five things that you "know" about this issue. Think about how you know what you know. How would you go about confirming or disproving your current state of knowledge on this topic?

WEB RESOURCES

Each chapter of this textbook contains a list of Internet resources and Web sites that may be useful to readers in their search for further information. Each site listing includes the address and a brief description of the contents of the site. Readers should be aware that the information contained in Web sites may not be truthful or reliable and should be confirmed before the site is used as a reference. Readers should also be aware that Internet addresses, or URLs, are constantly changing; therefore, the addresses listed may no longer be active or accurate. Many of the Internet sites listed in each chapter contain links to other sites containing more information on the topic. Readers may use these links for further investigation.

Information on topics not included in the Web Resources sections of each chapter can be found by using one of the many Internet search engines provided free of charge on the Internet. These search engines enable you to search using keywords or phrases, or you can use the search engines' topical listings. You should use several search engines when researching a topic, as each will retrieve different Internet sites. Below, we list the search engines first.

Google
www.google.com

bing
www.bing.com

cuil
www.cuil.com

Ask
www.ask.com

YAHOO!
www.yahoo.com

Excite
www.excite.com

Lycos
www.lycos.com

There are several Internet sites that are maintained by and for social workers, some at university schools of social work and some by professional associations:

Council on Social Work
Education (CSWE)
www.cswe.org

CSWE is the accrediting body for academic social work programs; site contains information about accreditation, projects, publications, and links to a number of social work–related Web sites.

Information for Practice
www.nyu.edu/socialwork/ip/

Site developed and maintained by Professor Gary Holden of New York University's School of Social Work contains links to many federal and state Internet sites as well as journals, assessment and measurement tools, and sites maintained by professional associations.

International Federation of Social Workers
www.ifsw.org

Site contains information about international conferences, policy papers on selected issues, and links to human rights groups and other social work organizations.

National Association of Social
Workers (NASW)
www.naswdc.org

Site contains professional development material, press room, advocacy information, and resources.

Social Work Access Network (SWAN)
www.sc.edu/swan/

Site presented by the University of South Carolina College of Social Work contains social work topics, list of schools of social work, upcoming conferences, and online chats.

Social Work and Social Services Web
Sitestp://gwbweb.wustl.edu/Resources/Pages/socialservic
esresourcesintro.aspx

Site presented by the George Warren Brown School of Social Work, Washington University, St. Louis, Missouri, contains links to resources for a wide variety of social issues and social service organizations.

CHAPTER

2

Theoretical Perspectives on Human Behavior

Elizabeth D. Hutchison and Leanne Wood Charlesworth

OPENING QUESTIONS

- What theories are needed to understand the multiple dimensions of person, environment, and time involved in human behavior?

- What criteria should social workers use to evaluate theories of human behavior?

KEY IDEAS

As you read this chapter, take note of these central ideas:

1. The systems perspective sees human behavior as the outcome of reciprocal interactions of persons operating within linked social systems.

2. The conflict perspective draws attention to conflict, inequality, dominance, and oppression in social life.

3. The rational choice perspective sees human behavior as based on self-interest and rational choices about effective ways to accomplish goals.

4. The social constructionist perspective focuses on how people learn, through their interactions with each other, to understand the world and their place in it.

5. The psychodynamic perspective is concerned with how internal processes such as needs, drives, and emotions motivate human behavior.

6. The developmental perspective focuses on how human behavior unfolds across the life course.

7. The social behavioral perspective suggests that human behavior is learned as individuals interact with their environments.

8. The humanistic perspective emphasizes the individual's inherent value, freedom of action, and search for meaning.

Case Study

Intergenerational Stresses in the McKinley Family

The hospice social worker meets three generations of McKinleys when she visits their home in an upper midwestern city. She is there because the family has requested hospice services for Ruth McKinley, the 79-year-old mother of Stanley McKinley. Ruth has a recurrence of breast cancer that has metastasized to her lungs; she is no longer receiving aggressive treatment and her condition is deteriorating. Upon entering the house, the social worker meets 50-year-old Stanley, his 51-year-old wife, Marcia, and their 25-year-old daughter, Bethany, who takes the social worker to a bedroom to meet her grandmother. She gives Ruth a gentle pat and introduces the social worker. Ruth smiles at Bethany and greets the social worker. Bethany leaves the room to give some privacy to the social worker and her grandmother.

(Continued)

(Continued)

The social worker spends about 20 minutes with Ruth and finds her weak but interested in talking. Ruth says she knows that she is receiving hospice care because she is dying. She says she has lived a good life and is not afraid of dying. She goes on to say, however, that there are some things on her mind as she thinks about her life. She is thinking a lot about her estranged daughter who lives several states away, and she does not want to die with this "hardness between us." She also is thinking a lot about Stanley, who is unemployed, and hoping that he can find a spark in his life again. Bethany is very much on her mind, as well. She says she worries that Bethany is sacrificing too much of her young life to the needs of the family. As Ruth grows tired, the social worker ends the conversation, saying that she would like to visit with Ruth again next week so that they can talk some more about Ruth's life and the things that are on her mind.

Back in the living room, the social worker talks with Stanley, Marcia, and Bethany. She learns that Ruth moved into Stanley and Marcia's home 5 years ago after she had a stroke that left her with left-sided paralysis. At that time, Stanley and Marcia took out a second mortgage on their house to finance some remodeling to make the home more accessible for Ruth, providing her with a bedroom and bathroom downstairs. They also put in a much-needed new furnace at the same time. Bethany speaks up to say that her grandmother is the kindest person she knows and that they were all happy to rearrange their home life to make Ruth comfortable. Marcia notes that it seemed the natural thing to do, because Ruth had taken care of Bethany while Marcia worked during Bethany's early years. After Ruth came to live with them, Stanley continued to work at a print shop, and Marcia changed to the evening shift in her job as a police dispatcher. Bethany arranged her work and part-time community college studies so that she could be available to her grandmother between the time her mother left for work and her father returned from his workday. She took charge of preparing dinner for her dad and grandmother and giving Ruth a daily bath.

This arrangement worked well for 4 years. Bethany speaks fondly of the good times she and her grandmother had together as Bethany provided direct care to her grandmother, and her grandmother showered her with stories of the past and took a lively interest in her life, often giving her advice about her romantic life. Marcia breaks in to say that life has been tough for the past year, however, and her voice cracks as she says this. She recounts that they learned of the recurrence of Ruth's breast cancer 11 months ago and of the metastasis 5 months ago. For a few months, Stanley, Marcia, and Bethany juggled their schedules to get Ruth to doctor visits, chemotherapy treatments, and bone scans, until Ruth and the oncologist decided that it was time to discontinue aggressive treatment.

Then, 7 months ago, Stanley lost his job at the printing company where he had worked since getting out of the army, and he has been unsuccessful in finding new work. They were still managing financially with the help of unemployment checks until Marcia took a tumble down the stairs and injured her back and hip 4 months ago. She had surgery, which was followed by complications, and has been out of work on disability. She is expecting to go back to work next week. Bethany says she has wanted to work more to bring more money into the home, but she has also been needed at home more to fill in for Marcia. She lost one job because of too many absences and has pieced together two part-time jobs that give her a little more flexibility. She worries, however, about having no health insurance because she needs ongoing treatment for asthma. Marcia says that Stanley has been a wonderful caregiver to her and his mom, but she knows that the caregiving has interfered with his job search and is wearing him down.

Stanley enters the conversation to report that they have been unable to make mortgage payments for the past 3 months, and the bank has notified him that they are at risk of facing foreclosure. He becomes despondent as he tells this. He says they have been in the house for 15 years and had always paid the mortgage on time. The second mortgage for the remodeling is adding to the current financial pinch.

He says he is in a quandary about what to do. Marcia is going back to work soon, but she is still not strong enough to provide much physical care to Ruth. In addition, he is not at all optimistic that he will find a job in the near future. His former boss has now closed the printing shop because she lost some of her large clients. Stanley wonders if he should retrain for another occupation, but knows that this is not a good time for him to try to do that, with his mother's deteriorating condition. Bethany suggests that she should take some time off from school and find a job working nights so that she can give her dad time to look for jobs during the day. She has graduated from community college and been accepted into a bachelor's degree program in nursing. She says she is feeling too sad about her grandmother and too worried about the family's future to do well in school anyway. Besides that, she would like to be able to spend more time with her grandmother before she dies. At this point, Marcia breaks down and cries, sobbing that she just wants to give up: "We work so hard but nothing goes our way. I don't know where we will go if we lose the house."

As the family talks about their problems and possible solutions, the social worker recalls that she has heard something about a community program that provides counseling to people who are in jeopardy of home foreclosure. She wonders if that could help the McKinley family.

MULTIPLE PERSPECTIVES FOR A MULTIDIMENSIONAL APPROACH

The unfolding story of the multigenerational McKinley family may be familiar to you in some ways, but it is also unique in the way these particular persons and environments are interacting over time. As a social worker, you need to understand these details about the situation of the family. However, if you are to be helpful in improving the situation, you also need some scientific knowledge that will assist you in thinking about its unique elements. As suggested in Chapter 1, the range of knowledge offered by a multitheoretical approach is necessary when taking a multidimensional approach to human behavior. The purpose of this chapter is to introduce you to eight theoretical perspectives that are particularly useful for thinking about changing situations of persons and environments: systems perspective, conflict perspective, rational choice perspective, social constructionist perspective, psychodynamic perspective, developmental perspective, social behavioral perspective, and humanistic perspective. In Chapter 1, we defined *theory* as a logically interrelated set of concepts and propositions, organized into a deductive system, which explains relationships among aspects of our world. We suggested that a *perspective*, in contrast to a theory, is broader and more general—an emphasis or view. Each of the perspectives discussed in this chapter is composed of a number of diverse theories. Each of these perspectives is European American in heritage, but in recent years, each has been influenced by thinking in other regions of the world.

We have selected these eight theoretical perspectives because they have stood the test of time, have a wide range of applications across dimensions of human behavior, and are used in empirical research. Each has been reconceptualized and extended over time. In this volume, margin notes are used in Chapters 3 through 14 to help you recognize ideas from specific perspectives. Our purpose in this chapter is to introduce the "big ideas" of the eight perspectives, and not to present a detailed discussion of the various theories within the perspectives. We do call attention, however, to some of the most recent extensions of the perspectives. We want to lay the groundwork for your understanding of the variations of the perspectives discussed in subsequent chapters. If you are interested in a more in-depth look at these theoretical perspectives, you might want to consult an excellent book titled *Contemporary Human Behavior Theory: A Critical Perspective for Social Work* (Robbins, Chatterjee, & Canda, 2006a).

Besides presenting an overview of the big ideas, we analyze the scientific merit of the perspectives and their usefulness for social work practice. The five criteria for critical understanding of theory identified in Chapter 1 provide the framework for our discussion of the perspectives: coherence and conceptual clarity, testability and empirical support, comprehensiveness, consistency with social work's emphasis on diversity and power arrangements, and usefulness for social work practice. Four of the perspectives introduced in this chapter are based in sociology, four are based in psychology, and several have additional interdisciplinary roots. This diversity reflects the history of the social work profession: Social work scholars began with a preference for sociological knowledge, moved over time to a preference for psychological knowledge, and have recently come to seek knowledge of both environmental and personal factors. This recent trend is consistent with the multidimensional approach of this book.

As noted in Chapter 1, diversity and inequality are major themes of this book. In earlier versions of the eight perspectives, few theorists acknowledged the importance of looking at diverse persons in diverse environments. Each of the perspectives has continued to evolve, however, and the perspectives are being reconstructed to better accommodate diversity and address inequality. Some theory critics suggest that this shift to greater emphasis on diversity and inequality represents a paradigm, or worldview, shift (e.g., Schriver, 2004). Other theory critics, on the other hand, argue that the eight perspectives discussed here have undergone continual change, but not such revolutionary change as to be labeled a paradigm shift (e.g., Ritzer & Goodman, 2004). These critics suggest that the perspectives have stood the test of time because they have, over time, become much more self-conscious about diversity and inequality. Whether or not the attention to diversity and inequality constitutes a paradigm shift, we agree that it has been a major and positive trend in behavioral science theorizing.

Another major trend in behavioral science theory is that although much of recent theorizing fits within existing categories of theoretical perspectives, theoretical synthesizing is blurring the boundaries between perspectives (Ritzer & Goodman, 2004). Theorists are being influenced by each other, as well as by societal changes, and have begun to borrow ideas from each other and to build new theory by combining aspects of existing theory. As you read about each of the perspectives, think about not only how it can be applied in social work practice, but also how well it represents all the complexities of human behavior in its current form.

SYSTEMS PERSPECTIVE

When you read the case study at the beginning of this chapter, you probably thought of it as a story about a family system—a story about Ruth, Stanley, Marcia, and Bethany McKinley—rather than "Ruth McKinley's story," even though the hospice case file reads "Ruth McKinley." You may have noted how Ruth's, Stanley's, Marcia's, and Bethany's lives are interrelated, how they influence one another's behavior, and what impact each of them has on the overall well-being of the family. You may be thinking about the reciprocal roles of caregiver and care recipient and how the family members keep adjusting their caregiving roles to accommodate changing care needs. You also may note that this family, like other families, has a boundary indicating who is in and who is out, and you may be wondering if the boundary around this family allows sufficient input from friends, extended family, neighbors, religious organizations, and so on. You may also have noted the influence of larger systems on this family, particularly the insecurities in the labor market and the gaps in the health care system. Medicare coverage for hospice care is an important resource for the family as they cope with the end-of-life care needs of Ruth. You can see, in Exhibit 2.1, how these observations about the McKinley family fit with the big ideas of the systems perspective.

The systems perspective sees human behavior as the outcome of reciprocal interactions of persons operating within linked social systems. Its roots are very interdisciplinary. During the 1940s and 1950s, a variety of disciplines—including mathematics, physics, engineering, biology, psychology, cultural anthropology, economics, and sociology—began looking at phenomena as the outcome of interactions within and among systems. Mathematicians and engineers used the new ideas about system feedback mechanisms—the processes by which information about past behaviors in a system are fed back into the system in a circular manner—to develop military technology for World War II; scientists at Bell Laboratories used the same ideas to develop transistors and other communication technology (Becvar & Becvar, 1996). Later, George Engel (1977) used the same ideas to develop a biopsychosocial model of disease.

Social workers were attracted to the systems perspective in the 1960s, as they shifted from a psychiatric model to one that was more inclusive of environment. Social work has drawn most heavily from the work of sociologists Talcott Parsons and Robert Merton, psychologists Kurt Lewin and Urie Bronfenbrenner, and biologist Ludwig von Bertalanffy. The social workers who first adopted the systems perspective were heavily influenced by *functionalist sociology*, which was the dominant sociological theory during the 1940s and 1950s. In functionalism, social systems are thought to be orderly and remain in a relatively stable state, also known as *homeostasis* or *equilibrium*. Each part of the system serves an essential function in maintaining the system, and the functions of the various parts are coordinated to produce a well-functioning whole. System processes and structures such as rules and roles serve to maintain system stability. Although this systems approach did not deny the possibility of system change, it was more concerned with the mechanisms of system maintenance and stability.

In the systems perspective, the structure of roles has been an important mechanism for maintaining system balance. Role refers to the usual behaviors of persons occupying a particular social position. Consider the roles played by each person in the McKinley family and the stresses the family has faced as a result of role transitions over the past year. Stanley has lost his role as family provider and has needed to increase his caregiving role. He has struggled to find time and energy for the job search. Marcia took on the role of care recipient rather than caregiver. Bethany faced new challenges in juggling worker, student, and caregiver roles. She seems to be indicating that she is experiencing some role overload.

There was substantial growth in interest in the use of the systems perspective in social work during the 1970s, but by the end of the decade, social workers became dissatisfied with the perspective on two counts. First, the perspective was seen as too abstract and, second, the emphasis on stability seemed too conservative for a profession devoted to social change. Throughout the 1980s, some social work scholars tried to correct for these shortcomings with the continual development of ecological and dynamic systems approaches (e.g., Germain & Gitterman, 1980). Social workers (e.g., Bolland & Atherton, 1999; Hudson, 2000; K. Warren, Franklin, & Streeter, 1998) took renewed interest in the systems perspective in the 1990s as they began to make use of chaos theory and the related complexity theory. Chaos theory emerged in mathematics in the 1960s, took hold in a number of natural science disciplines in the 1970s, and revitalized the systems perspective in the social sciences, but interest in chaos theory has waned somewhat in the first decade of the 21st century.

Whereas traditional systems theories emphasize system processes that produce stability, **chaos theory** and the closely related complexity theory emphasize systems processes that produce change, even sudden, rapid, radical change. This difference in understanding about change and stability in social systems is explained by propositions

---

- Systems are made up of interrelated members (parts) that constitute a linked whole.
- Each part of the system impacts all other parts and the system as a whole.
- All systems are subsystems of other larger systems.
- Systems maintain boundaries that give them their identities.
- The dynamic interactions within, between, and among systems produce both stability and change, sometimes even rapid, dramatic change.

▲ **Exhibit 2.1**   Big Ideas of the Systems Perspective

▲ **Photo 2.1** The pieces of this globe come together to form a unified whole—each part interacts and influences the other parts—but the pieces are interdependent, as suggested by the systems perspective.

central to chaos theory. Traditional systems theories proposed that system stability results from *negative feedback loops* that work like a thermostat to feed back information that the system is deviating from a steady state and needs to take corrective action. Chaos theory recognizes negative feedback loops as important processes in systems and acknowledges their role in promoting system stability. In addition, it proposes that complex systems produce *positive feedback loops* that feed back information about deviation, or should we say innovation, into the steady state in such a way that the deviation reverberates throughout the system and produces change, sometimes even rapid change. The change-producing feedback may come from within the system or from other systems in the environment.

Like earlier systems theories, chaos theory emphasizes that all systems are made up of subsystems, and all systems also serve as subsystems in other systems. Subsystems are always adjusting to each other and their environments, and the resultant changes are continuously being fed back. This results in a constant state of flux, and sometimes small changes in systems can reverberate in such a way as to produce very sudden and dramatic changes. Recently, chaos theory has been recommended as a useful approach for clinical social workers and clinical psychologists as they assist clients in trying new solutions to long-standing problems (M. Lee, 2008) and to recreate themselves in times of transition (Bussolari & Goodell, 2009).

One issue about which the various versions of the systems perspective disagree is the permeability, or openness, of systems' boundaries to the environment. Functionalist sociology seemed to assume that interactions take place within a *closed system* that is isolated from exchanges with other systems. The idea of systems as closed was challenged by dynamic systems theories, most recently chaos theory, which assumes a more *open system* as the healthy system. As Exhibit 2.2 illustrates, an open system is more likely than a closed system to receive resources from external systems.

Recently, *deep ecology* has emerged with an emphasis on the notion of the total interconnectedness of all elements of the natural and physical world (Besthorn & Canda, 2002; Ungar, 2002). Sociologist John Clammer (2009) suggests that deep ecology, with its addition of connections to the natural and physical worlds, can help to bridge Western and Eastern social science. The emerging *globalization theories* also emphasize the openness of systems, calling our attention to, among other things, how Stanley McKinley's job opportunities are connected to the increasingly globalized economy (Z. Bauman, 1998; U. Beck, 1999; Giddens, 2000).

On the other hand, recent theorizing in sociology has argued the case of the closed system. Niklas Luhmann's (1987) general systems theory, which has lately gained popularity in sociology, suggests that in highly complex societies, systems tend to become fragmented and closed to each other. They develop different languages and cultures and, consequently, cannot receive (hear and understand) feedback from each other. Luhmann calls such systems *autopoietic*. The events of September 11, 2001, and many other recent happenings, remind us that even in a context of rapid international communication and a global economy, cultures may remain very isolated from the feedback of other cultures. The seemingly impermeable cultural boundaries between the United States and Middle Eastern nations speak to this. Luhmann's theory of closed systems has not been used in the U.S. social work literature, but it has been a popular approach among European social workers (see Wirth, 2009).

This is how the criteria for evaluating theory apply to the systems perspective:

• *Coherence and conceptual clarity.* Although it has been popular over time, the systems perspective is often criticized as vague and somewhat ambiguous. Functional sociology has been particularly vulnerable to criticisms that its concepts are poorly, or inconsistently, defined. Although chaos theory and complexity theory have greater consistency in use of terms than earlier approaches did, concepts in these theo-

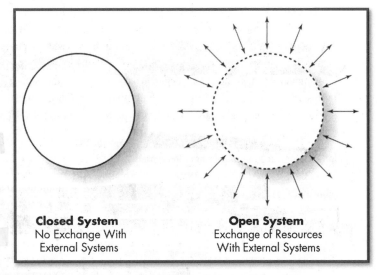

Closed System
No Exchange With
External Systems

Open System
Exchange of Resources
With External Systems

▲ **Exhibit 2.2**   Closed and Open Systems

ries remain highly abstract and often confusing in their generality. In reality, chaos theory and complexity theory emerged in applied mathematics, and concepts from them are still being developed in the social sciences. There are recent attempts by social workers to extrapolate concepts from these theories (e.g., Bolland & Atherton, 1999; Hudson, 2000; K. Warren et al., 1998), but scholars have not yet stated or explained the concepts of these theories in the simplest and clearest way possible. A recent article by Mo Yee Lee (2008) makes great progress in this area.

• *Testability and evidence of empirical support.* Poorly defined and highly abstract concepts are difficult to translate into measurable variables for research. Nevertheless, a long tradition of research supporting a systems perspective can be found in anthropology and sociology (see J. White & Klein, 2008d, for a discussion of the use of the systems perspective to study family systems). The systems perspective has been greatly strengthened in recent years with developments in brain research, epidemiology, and a rapidly expanding empirical literature on ecological risk and resilience (Corcoran & Walsh, 2006; M. Fraser, 2004; Hutchison, Matto, Harrigan, Charlesworth, & Viggiani, 2007). Research methods, such as lengthy time series analyses, have been developed in the natural and social sciences for studying concepts of chaos and complexity, but these methods are still rarely used in social work.

• *Comprehensiveness.* Clearly, the systems perspective is devoted to the ideal of comprehensiveness, or holism. It can, and has, incorporated the various dimensions of human systems as well as various dimensions of environmental systems, nonhuman as well as human. Systems theorists recognize—even if they do not always make clear—the social, cultural, economic, and political environments of human behavior. They acknowledge the role of external influences and demands in creating and maintaining patterns of interaction within the system. Early theorizing in the systems perspective did not deal with the time dimension—the focus was always on the present. But recent formulations have attempted to add a time dimension to accommodate both past and future influences on human behavior (see Bronfenbrenner, 1989; Ford & Lerner, 1992; Hannerz, 1992; Wachs, 1992). Certainly, chaos theory and complexity theory give implicit, if not always explicit, attention to time with their emphasis on dynamic change. Globalization theory calls attention to the impact of speedy communications on world systems (Giddens, 2000; Virilio, 2000).

• *Diversity and power.* Although diversity is not addressed in most systems theorizing, recent versions of the systems perspective, with their attention to complexity and continuous dynamic change, open many possibilities for diversity. Furthermore, while most systems theorists do not address the role of power in systems transactions, some can accommodate the idea of power differentials better than others. Traditional systems theories that were influenced by functionalist sociology assumed that social systems are held together by social consensus and shared values. The emphasis on system equilibrium and on the necessity of traditional roles to hold systems together can rightly be criticized as socially conservative and oppressive to those who lack power within the system. Contemporary systems theory has begun to recognize power and oppression; conflict is seen as necessary for change in chaos theory, and some versions of globalization theory call attention to how powerful nations exploit the cultures, economies, and political arrangements of less powerful nations (McMichael, 2008).

- *Usefulness for social work practice.* The systems perspective is more useful for understanding human behavior than for directing social work interventions, but several social work practice textbooks were based on the systems perspective in the 1970s and 1980s (see Germain & Gitterman, 1980; C. Meyer, 1983; Pincus & Minahan, 1973; Siporin, 1975). The primary value of the systems perspective is that it can be used at any level of practice. It also has merit because it surpasses other perspectives in suggesting that we should widen the scope of assessment and intervention and expect better outcomes from multidimensional interventions (Hutchison, Matto, et al., 2007). Chaos theory can even be used by social workers to input information into a client system to facilitate rapid change, thereby enhancing possibilities for brief treatment, and group process can be used as reverberating feedback to produce change (K. Warren et al., 1998). In fact, social workers who work from a family systems perspective (e.g., Carter & McGoldrick, 2005a) have for some time used methods such as family genograms, and other forms of feedback about the family, as information that can produce change as it reverberates through the family system. Mo Yee Lee (2008) provides a number of examples of how clinical social workers can use chaos and turbulence to help clients open to new ways of looking at and resolving problems.

CONFLICT PERSPECTIVE

As she thinks about the McKinley family, the hospice social worker is struck by Stanley and Marcia's growing sense of powerlessness to manage the trajectories of their lives. A major theme in their story, like the stories of so many other families during the current recession, is lack of power in both the labor market and the housing market. Worries about access to health care are another part of the story, and one is reminded of recent political debates about health care funding. It remains to be seen what impact the federal health insurance law passed in March 2010 will have on families like the McKinleys. While the systems perspective helps us think about how interdependent the family members are, you may be thinking that they have some competing interests in relation to scarce resources of time and money. For example, Bethany's educational goals are in competition with the caregiving needs of Ruth and Marcia. The hospice social worker knows that communications can become tense in families facing similar situations of scarce resources, as members assert their self-interests, and she wants to know more about how the McKinley family negotiates competing interests. She is also curious about the history of gender roles in this family and how those have been affected by Stanley's unemployment. Compare these observations with the central ideas of the conflict perspective, presented in Exhibit 2.3.

The **conflict perspective** has become popular over and over again throughout history, with roots that can be traced back to German philosopher George Hegel (1770–1831) and Italian philosopher Niccolo Machiavelli (1469–1527), and perhaps even further, drawing attention to conflict, dominance, and oppression in social life (R. Collins, 1994; Ritzer, 2008b). The conflict perspective typically looks for sources of conflict and causes of human behavior in the economic and political arenas, and more recently in the cultural arena. In sociology, the conflict perspective has two traditions: a utopian tradition that foresees a society in which there is no longer a basis for social conflict, and a second tradition that sees conflict as inevitable in social life.

The roots of contemporary conflict theory are usually traced to the works of Karl Marx and his collaborator Friedrich Engels, as well as the works of Max Weber. Marx (1887/1967) and Engels (1884/1970) focused on economic

- Groups and individuals try to advance their own interests over the interests of others as they compete for scarce resources.
- Power is unequally divided, and some social groups dominate others.
- Social order is based on the manipulation and control of nondominant groups by dominant groups.
- Lack of open conflict is a sign of exploitation.
- Members of nondominant groups become alienated from society.
- Social change is driven by conflict, with periods of change interrupting long periods of stability.

▲ **Exhibit 2.3** Big Ideas of the Conflict Perspective

structures, suggesting that the capitalist economic system is divided into capitalists and workers. Capitalists decide what is to be done and how to do it, and they own the products produced by the workers as well as the means of production. Capitalists pay workers as little as they can get away with, and they, not the workers, reap the benefits of exploiting natural resources. According to Marx, this system produces *false consciousness:* Neither capitalists nor workers are aware that the system is based on exploitation; workers think they are getting a fair day's pay, and capitalists think workers are fairly rewarded. Marx proposed, however, that workers are capable of recognizing the exploitation and achieving *class consciousness,* but capitalists are incapable of recognizing the exploitation in the system.

Weber (1904–1905/1958) rejected this singular emphasis on economics in favor of a multidimensional perspective on social class that included prestige and power derived from sources other than economics. Contemporary conflict theory tends to favor Weber's multidimensional perspective, calling attention to a confluence of social, economic, and political structures in the creation of inequality (Allan, 2007; Appelrouth & Edles, 2007; Ritzer, 2008b). Jürgen Habermas (1984, 1981/1987) and other **critical theorists** argue that as capitalism underwent change, people were more likely to be controlled by culture than by their work position. Our lives became dominated by the culture industry, which is controlled by mass media. Critical theorists suggest that the culture industry plays a major role in turning workers into consumers, calling attention to the role of the advertising industry in exploiting consumers. They suggest that in the contemporary world, workers work very hard, sometimes at second and third jobs, in order to consume. They describe the exploitation of consumers as a pleasant kind of control: People spend more and more time working to be able to shop, and shopping becomes the major form of recreation. Working and shopping leave little time for reflective or revolutionary thinking. Of course, this approach to conflict theory continues to recognize the supremely important role of the economic system, which is a very important part of the McKinley family situation at the current time.

Immanuel Wallerstein (1974, 1979) is a neo-Marxist who has focused on international inequality. He proposed that the capitalist world system is divided into three geographic areas with greatly different levels of power: A *core* of nations dominates the capitalist worldwide economy and exploits the natural resources and labor in other nations. The *periphery* includes nations that provide cheap raw materials and labor that are exploited to the advantage of the core. The *semiperiphery* includes nations that are newly industrializing; they benefit from the periphery but are exploited by the core.

Power relationships are the focus of the conflict perspective. Some theorists in the conflict tradition limit their focus to the large-scale structure of power relationships, but many theorists, especially critical theorists, also look at the reactions and adaptations of individual members of nondominant groups. These theorists note that oppression of nondominant groups leads to their *alienation,* or a sense of indifference or hostility.

Lewis Coser (1956) proposed a **pluralistic theory of social conflict,** which recognizes that more than one social conflict is going on at all times, and that individuals hold cross-cutting and overlapping memberships in status groups. Social conflict exists between economic groups, racial groups, ethnic groups, religious groups, age groups, gender groups, and so forth. Thus, it seeks to understand life experience by looking at simultaneous memberships—for example, a White, Italian American, Protestant, heterosexual, male semiskilled worker, or a Black, African American, Catholic, lesbian, female professional worker. Feminist theorists have developed a pluralistic approach called *intersectionality theory,* which recognizes vectors of oppression and privilege, including not only gender, but also class, race, global location, sexual orientation, and age (see P. H. Collins, 1990).

Although early social workers in the settlement house tradition recognized social conflict and structured inequality, and focused on eliminating oppression of immigrants, women, and children, most critics agree that social workers have not drawn consistently on the conflict perspective over time (Robbins et al., 2006a). Concepts of power and social conflict were revived in the social work literature in the 1960s (Germain, 1994). In the past decade or so, with renewed commitment to social justice in its professional code of ethics and in its curriculum guidelines, social work has drawn more heavily on the conflict perspective to understand dynamics of *privilege,* or unearned advantage, as well as discrimination and oppression. Social workers have used the conflict perspective as a base to develop practice-oriented **empowerment theories,** which focus on processes that individuals and collectivities can use to recognize patterns of inequality and injustice and take action to increase their own power (e.g., Gutierrez, 1990, 1994; J. Lee, 2001; S. Rose, 1992, 1994; Solomon, 1976, 1987). Both in their renewed interest in domination and oppression and in their development of practice-oriented empowerment theories, social workers have been influenced by **feminist theories,** which focus on male domination of the major social institutions and present a vision of a just world based

▲ **Photo 2.2** This homeless woman on a street in prosperous Beverly Hills, California, is one of many examples of unequal power in the global economy, a focus of the conflict perspective.

on gender equity. Feminist theories emphasize that people are socialized to see themselves through the eyes of powerful actors. Like Marx, most feminist theorists are not content to ask, "Why is it this way?" but also ask, "How can we change and improve the social world?" Scanzoni and colleagues (Scanzoni & Szinovacz, 1980) have been interested in whether and, if so, how gender power arrangements change as women become the more stable economic provider in families, a situation that has now occurred in the McKinley family as well as many other families around the world.

Here is how the conflict perspective rates on the five criteria for evaluating social work theory:

• *Coherence and conceptual clarity.* Most concepts of the conflict perspective are straightforward—conflict, power, domination, inequality—at least at the abstract level. Like all theoretical concepts, however, they become less straightforward when we begin to define them for the purpose of measurement. Across the various versions of the conflict perspective, concepts are not consistently used. One major source of variation is whether power and privilege are to be thought of as objective material circumstances, subjectively experienced situations, or both. In general, theories in the conflict tradition are expressed in language that is relatively accessible and clear. This is especially true of many of the practice-oriented empowerment theories developed by social workers. On the other hand, most recent conflict theorizing in the critical theory tradition is stated at a high level of abstraction.

- *Testability and evidence of empirical support.* Conflict theory has developed, in the main, through attempts to codify persistent themes in history (R. Collins, 1990). The preferred research method is empirical historical research that looks at large-scale patterns of history (see Mann, 1986; McCarthy & Zald, 1977; McMichael, 2008; Skocpol, 1979; Wallerstein, 1974, 1979). As with other methods of research, critics have attacked some interpretations of historical data from the conflict perspective, but the historical analyses of Michael Mann, Theda Skocpol, and Immanuel Wallerstein are some of the most influential works in contemporary sociology. In addition to historical analysis, conflict theorists have used experimental methods to study reactions to coercive power (see Willer, 1987; Zimbardo, 2007) and naturalistic inquiry to study social ranking through interaction rituals (R. Collins, 1981). Contemporary conflict theorists are also drawing on network analysis, which plots the relationships among people within groups, and are finding support for their propositions about power and domination. Family researchers have used conflict theory, specifically the concept of power, to study family violence (J. White & Klein, 2008a).

- *Comprehensiveness.* Traditionally, the conflict perspective focused on large-scale social institutions and social structures, such as economic and political institutions. In the contemporary era, Randall Collins (1990) is a conflict theorist who has made great efforts to integrate conflict processes at the societal level with those at the community, small group, and family levels. Collins suggests that we should recognize conflict as a central process in social life at all levels. Family theorists propose a conflict theory of families (J. White & Klein, 2008d). Traditional conflict theories propose that oppression of nondominant groups leads to a sense of alienation, and recent empowerment theories give considerable attention to individual perceptions of power. The conflict perspective does not explicitly address biology, but it has been used to examine racial and social class health disparities. Most conflict theories do consider dimensions of time. They are particularly noteworthy for recommending that the behavior of members of minority groups should be put in historical context, and indeed, as discussed above, empirical historical research is the research method that many conflict theorists prefer.

- *Diversity and power.* The conflict perspective is about inequality, power arrangements, and systems of oppression. It helps us look at group-based patterns of inequality. In that way, it also assists us in understanding diversity. The pluralist theory of social conflict and feminist intersectionality theory, both of which recognize that individuals have overlapping memberships in a variety of status groups, are particularly useful for considering human diversity. A major strength of the conflict perspective is that it discourages pathologizing members of minority groups by encouraging recognition of the historical, cultural, economic, and political context of their behavior. Empowerment theories guide practice interventions that build on the strengths of members of minority groups.

- *Usefulness for social work.* Concepts from the conflict perspective have great value for understanding power dimensions in community, group, and family relationships, as well as the power differential between social worker and client. Clearly, the conflict perspective is crucial to social work because (a) it shines a spotlight on how domination and oppression might be affecting human behavior; (b) it illuminates processes by which people become estranged and discouraged; and (c) it encourages social workers to consider the meaning of their power relationships with clients, particularly nonvoluntary clients (Cingolani, 1984). The conflict perspective is essential to the social justice mission of social work. In recent years, social workers have been in the forefront of developing practice-oriented empowerment theories, and the conflict perspective has become as useful for recommending particular practice strategies as for assisting in the assessment process. Empowerment theories provide guidelines for working at all system levels (e.g., individual, family, small group, community, and organization), but they put particular emphasis on group work because of the opportunities presented in small groups for solidarity and mutual support. With the addition of empowerment theories, the conflict perspective can not only help us to understand how the McKinley family came to feel powerless, but also help us think about how we can assist individual family members, as well as the family as a whole, to feel empowered to improve their situation. Social movement theories (see Chapter 14), which are based in the conflict perspective, have implications for the mobilization of oppressed groups, but the conflict perspective in general provides little in the way of specific policy direction.

RATIONAL CHOICE PERSPECTIVE

Another way to think about the McKinley family is to focus on the resources that each member brings to the ongoing life of the family, and each member's sense of fairness in the exchange of those resources. You might note that Ruth has diminishing resources to offer to the family, but the rest of the family seems to derive satisfaction from caring for her. Marcia indicates that it is only fair that they care for her now because of the care Ruth provided to Bethany when she was a young child (not to mention the care she provided to Stanley in his formative years). Stanley's ability to provide economic resources to the family has diminished, and we might wonder how this has affected his sense of providing his "fair share" of resources to the family. Marcia has gotten satisfaction over the years from her caregiving role in the family, and her ability to bring this resource to the family has been compromised. On the other hand, the economic resources she brings into the family have become more important since Stanley became unemployed. Bethany provides economic resources as well as caregiving resources, and there is no evidence that she considers her contributions to the family to be unfair. She is weighing the long-term rewards of education against the short-term costs of adding a rigorous educational program to an already overtaxed life. Exhibit 2.4 reveals a fit between these observations about the McKinley family and the central ideas of the rational choice perspective.

The **rational choice perspective** sees human behavior as based on self-interest and rational choices about effective ways to accomplish goals. Human interaction is seen as an exchange of resources, and people make judgments about the fairness of the exchange. The perspective is interdisciplinary, with strong roots in utilitarian philosophy, economics, and social behaviorism. Social workers are most familiar with the rational choice perspective as it is manifested in social exchange theory in sociology, rational choice models of organizations, public choice theory in political science, and the emerging social network theory. The rational choice perspective comes out of a very old tradition in social thought (J. White & Klein, 2008c), but the roots of contemporary sociological theories of rational choice are generally traced to Claude Lévi-Strauss, George Homans, and Peter Blau. Other major theorists include John Thibaut and Harold Kelley, James March and Herbert Simon, Michael Hechter, James Coleman, James Buchanan, Richard Emerson, and Karen Cook.

Social exchange theory starts with the premise that social behavior is based on the desire to maximize benefits and minimize costs. A basic belief is that social relationships occur in a social marketplace in which people give in order to get. Persons with greater resources in a social exchange hold what is often unacknowledged power over other actors in the exchange. In the early development of social exchange theory, Homans (1958) insisted that behavior could be understood only at the psychological level, denying the relevance of the cultural and social environments. Homans was particularly forceful in attacking the view that individual behavior is influenced by role expectations that emanate from sociocultural systems. More recent formulations of social exchange theory have moved from this

---

- People are rational and goal-directed.
- Human interaction involves trade of social resources, such as love, approval, information, money, and physical labor.
- Social exchange is based on self-interest, with actors trying to maximize rewards and minimize costs.
- Values, norms, and expectations, as well as alternatives, influence the assessment of rewards and costs.
- Reciprocity of exchange is essential to social life.
- Power comes from unequal resources in an exchange.

▲ **Exhibit 2.4**   Big Ideas of the Rational Choice Perspective

position toward a greater emphasis on the social, economic, political, and historical contexts of social exchanges (see Levi, Cook, O'Brien, & Faye, 1990; Markovsky, 2005). These formulations would emphasize how relationships in the McKinley family are influenced by the structure of the labor market and political decisions about governmental support systems, including health care. Beginning with the work of Peter Blau (1964), social exchange theorists and researchers have taken a strong interest in how power is negotiated at all levels, from interactions between two people to *Realpolitik*, or balance of power, among nations. Particularly noteworthy in this regard are Emerson's (1972a, 1972b) power-dependency theory and Cook's (1987) exchange network theory.

Rational choice theory is currently popular in sociology, health promotion, and family studies. In sociology, James Coleman (1990) used rational choice theory to explore possible incentives to encourage actors to behave in ways that are more beneficial to others. For example, he has proposed lifting the legal immunity of members of corporate boards to encourage them to act in a more prosocial manner. In the health promotion literature, a number of rational models have been proposed to understand risky health behaviors and to extrapolate prevention strategies from them. Two of those models are the *health belief model* (HBM) (M. Becker, 1974; M. Becker & Joseph, 1988) and the *theory of reasoned action* (Ajzen & Fishbein, 1977; Hornik, 1991). In family studies, social exchange theory has been used to understand mate selection, divorce, and caregiver burden (Dainton & Zelley, 2006).

Some feminists have criticized exchange theory on the grounds that its emphasis on rational calculation of personal advantage is a male attitude and does not represent the female perspective (Ritzer, 2008b). This criticism might be shared by ethnic groups who have traditionally been more collectivist, and less individualist, than White Anglo-Saxon Protestant Americans. In fact, Homans (1958) developed his American version of exchange theory partially in reaction to Lévi-Strauss's French collectivist version, which argued that social exchange is driven by collective, cultural, and symbolic forces and is not based simply on self-interest (Ekeh, 1974). Karen Cook and her colleagues (Cook, O'Brien, & Kollock, 1990) have undertaken a synthesis of social exchange and symbolic interaction theories (see the discussion of the social constructionist perspective in this chapter), recognizing the possibility that different people hold different definitions of fairness and positive outcomes in social exchange. We can imagine, for example, that some young adults in Bethany McKinley's position would consider it unfair to be involved in provider and caregiving roles in their family of origin.

Thibaut and Kelley's concepts of comparison level and comparison level alternatives are also useful in understanding different definitions of rewards and costs (Kelley & Thibaut, 1978; Thibaut & Kelley, 1959). *Comparison level*, a standard for evaluating the rewards and costs of a given relationship, is based on what the evaluator expects from the relationship. It has been used to understand why some people stay in abusive relationships. *Comparison level alternative* is the lowest level of outcomes a person will accept in light of alternative opportunities. This concept has been used to understand how people make decisions about seeking divorce. Some rational choice theorists have used the concept of *opportunity costs* to refer to the cost of forgoing the next-most attractive alternative when choosing a particular action. Researchers across a wide range of disciplines are using statistical methods to calculate the opportunity costs of particular courses of action, such as conserving natural habitats (Naidoo & Adamowicz, 2006) or prescribing antidepressant medications instead of cognitive behavioral therapy (Hollinghurst, Kessler, Peters, & Gunnell, 2005).

Theorists in the rational choice tradition are also advancing **social network theory**, which actually has intellectual roots in the systems perspective. Still in the early stages of development, social network theory already provides useful tools for person and environment assessments and holds great promise for the future. Social networks are typically presented visually as sociograms, which illustrate the relations among network members (see Hartman, 1995; C. Meyer, 1993). Members of the network—individuals, groups, or organizations—are represented as points, and lines are drawn between pairs of points to demonstrate a relationship between them. Arrows are often used to show the flow of exchanges in a relationship. These graphic displays illuminate such issues as network size, density of relationships, strength of relationships, reciprocity of relationships, and access to power and influence. Sociograms are usually called **ecomaps** in the social work literature. An ecomap of the McKinley family is presented in Exhibit 2.5.

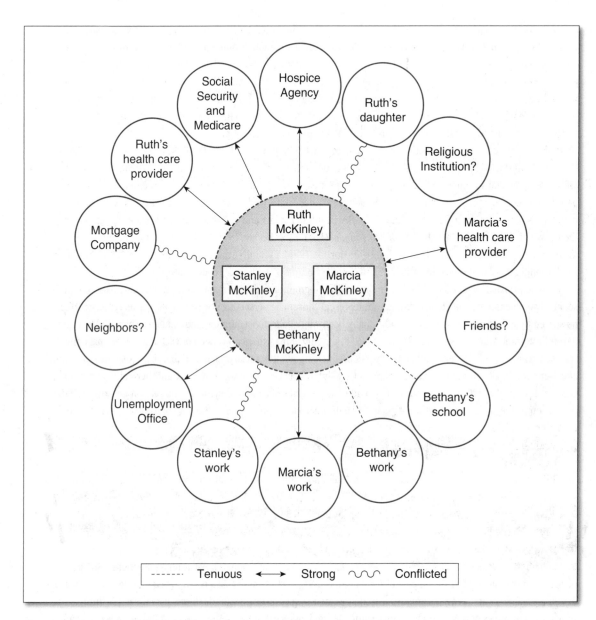

▲ **Exhibit 2.5** Ecomap of the McKinley Family

Here is an analysis of how well the rational choice perspective meets the criteria for judging social work theory:

• *Coherence and conceptual clarity.* As the rational choice perspective has developed, two conceptual puzzles have emerged, one at the individual level and one at the collective level. At the individual level, there is a question about the individual's capacity to process information and make rational decisions. At the collective level, the question is how is collective action possible if each actor maximizes rewards and minimizes costs. To their credit, recent theorists have embraced these puzzles. New developments in the rational choice perspective emphasize the limits to rational choice in social life (see Cook et al., 1990; Emerson, 1972a, 1972b; Levi et al., 1990; March & Simon, 1958). James Coleman (1990) is particularly noted for his attempts to employ rational choice theory to activate collective action for the purpose of social justice. There is still much internal inconsistency among most rational choice theories, however, about the nature and extent of rationality, with some theorists more willing than others to recognize the limits of human rationality.

- *Testability and empirical support.* The rational choice perspective has stimulated empirical research at several levels of analysis, with mixed results. Cognitive psychologists Daniel Kahneman and Amos Tversky (1982, 1984) dealt a blow to the rational choice perspective in the 1980s. They reported research findings that individual choices and decisions are often inconsistent with assumed rationality and that, indeed, situations are often too complicated for individuals to ascertain what is the most rational choice. On the other hand, more than modest support for the perspective has been found in research on dyads and families (see G. Becker, 1981; Nomaguchi & Milkie, 2005; Sprecher, 2005). A number of scholars have pointed out the difficulty of measuring rewards, costs, and fairness, because they are subjectively evaluated—what is rewarding to one person may not be rewarding to another. In response, researchers have developed the Marital Comparison Level Index (Sabatelli, 1984) and Parental Comparison Level Index (Waldron-Hennessey & Sabatelli, 1997). Researchers in a number of disciplines are attempting to find precise ways of measuring opportunity costs of alternative policies.

- *Comprehensiveness.* Although all strains of the rational choice perspective are interested in human interactions, the different strains focus on different dimensions of those configurations. Homans as well as Thibaut and Kelley were primarily interested in dyads. Ivan Nye (1982) has used the rational choice perspective to understand family life. Peter Blau (1964) came to be interested in larger structures. Coleman (1990) is interested in how individual actions get aggregated into collective action at the organizational and societal level. Network theory focuses on social interactions at the community, organizational, and institutional levels. In general, the rational choice perspective is weak in exploration of personal dimensions. It has also ignored the time dimension, except to respect the history of rewards and costs in past exchanges.

- *Diversity and power.* Although they were designed to look at patterns, not diversity, early rational choice theories provided some tools for understanding diversity in behaviors that come out of particular social exchanges. All theories in this perspective recognize power as deriving from unequal resources in the exchange process. Some versions of rational choice theory emphasize the ways in which patterns of exchange lead to social inequalities and social injustices. Although the rational choice perspective does not explicitly pathologize members of minority groups, those versions that fail to put social exchanges in historical, political, and economic contexts may unintentionally contribute to the pathologizing of these groups.

- *Usefulness for social work practice.* Some versions of rational choice theory serve as little more than a defense of the rationality of the marketplace of social exchange, suggesting a noninterventionist approach. In other words, if all social exchanges are based on rational choices, then who are we to interfere with this process? This stance, of course, is inconsistent with the purposes of social work. However, some theorists in this tradition, most notably James Coleman, have begun to propose solutions for creating social solidarity while recognizing the self-interestedness that is characteristic of Western, industrialized societies. These attempts have led Randall Collins (1994) to suggest that, out of all current social theories, contemporary rational choice theories have the greatest chance of informing social policy. On the other hand, Deborah Stone (2002) has skillfully demonstrated that the rational choice model is not a sufficient fit, and maybe not even a good fit, with the messy, nonlinear policy-making process. Family therapists use social exchange theory to guide prevention and intervention in marital and parent–child relationships, assisting family members to increase rewarding interactions and decrease unrewarding exchanges (J. White & Klein, 2008c). Social workers make use of social network theory at the micro level, to assess and enhance the social support networks of individual clients and families (K. Johnson, Whitbeck, & Hoyt, 2005; Pinto, 2006; Tracy & Johnson, 2007). Social work administrators and planners use social network theory to understand and enhance the exchange of resources in networks of social service providers (see Streeter & Gillespie, 1992).

SOCIAL CONSTRUCTIONIST PERSPECTIVE

As the hospice social worker drives back to the office, the McKinley family is on her mind. She thinks about Ruth and her end-of-life reflections about her life and social relationships. She hopes that she can be a good listener and a partner with Ruth as she makes meaning of her life. She recalls other clients who have made some changes in their life stories as they had a chance to reflect on them with her. She is curious about the story of the estrangement between Ruth and her daughter and wants to hear more about that from Ruth. She wonders if Ruth has been able to talk with Stanley and Bethany about her concerns for them and what meaning they might make of those concerns. The social worker also thinks about the story she heard from Stanley, Marcia, and Bethany. She thinks of Marcia's words, "nothing goes our way," and wonders whether this understanding of the world is shared by Stanley and Bethany—and, if so, how she might help them construct a different ending to the story they are telling themselves. The social worker also reflects on the way gender roles are defined in the family and would like to know more about how these roles have been negotiated over time in the family. You can see how her reflections are consistent with the social constructionist perspective by exploring Exhibit 2.6.

To understand human behavior, the **social constructionist perspective** focuses on how people learn, through their interactions with each other, to classify the world and their place in it. People are seen as social beings who interact with each other and the physical world based on *shared meanings,* or shared understandings about the world. In this view, people develop their understandings of the world and themselves from social interaction, and these understandings shape their subsequent social interactions.

The intellectual roots of the social constructionist perspective are usually traced to the German philosopher Edmund Husserl, as well as to the philosophical pragmatism of John Dewey and early theorists in the symbolic interaction tradition, including Charles Horton Cooley, W. I. Thomas, and George Herbert Mead. More recent theorists include Herbert Blumer, Erving Goffman, Alfred Schutz, Harold Garfinkel, Peter Berger, and Thomas Luckmann. Randall Collins (1994) suggests that social constructionist theorizing is the type of sociology that American sociologists do best.

To the social constructionist, there is no singular objective reality, no true reality that exists "out there" in the world. There are, instead, the shared subjective realities that are created as people interact. Constructionists emphasize the existence of multiple social and cultural realities. Both persons and environments are dynamic processes, not static structures. The sociopolitical environment and history of any situation play an important role in understanding human behavior. The social constructionist would, for example, call attention to how Stanley's understanding of himself as a worker is being influenced by the current economic recession.

The importance of subjective rather than objective reality has been summed up by the words of W. I. Thomas (Thomas & Thomas, 1928): "If men [sic] define situations as real, they are real in their consequences" (p. 128).

- Human consciousness, and the sense of self, is shaped by continual social interaction.
- Social reality is created when people, in social interaction, develop a common understanding of their world.
- People perform for their social audiences, but they are also free, active, and creative.
- Social interaction is grounded in language customs, as well as cultural and historical contexts.
- People can modify meanings in the process of interaction.
- Society consists of social processes, not social structures.

▲ **Exhibit 2.6**   Big Ideas of the Social Constructionist Perspective

Actually, social constructionists disagree about whether there is, in fact, some objective reality out there. Radical social constructionists believe there is not. They believe that there is no reality beyond our personal experiences. Most *postmodern theorists* fall in this category, arguing that there are no universals, including no universal truth, reality, or morality (Danto, 2008; Lyotard, 1984). The postmodernists accept that the world is "messy" and see no need to impose order on it. More moderate social constructionists believe that there are "real objects" in the world, but those objects are never known objectively; rather, they are only known through the subjective interpretations of individuals and collectivities (C. Williams, 2006).

Social constructionists also disagree about how constraining the environment is. Some see individual actors in social interactions as essentially free, active, and creative (Gergen, 1985). Others suggest that individual actors are always performing for their social audiences, based on their understanding of community standards for human behavior (Berger & Luckmann, 1966; Goffman, 1959). The dominant position is probably the one represented by Schutz's (1932/1967) *phenomenological sociology.* While arguing that people shape social reality, Schutz also suggests that individuals and groups are constrained by the preexisting social and cultural arrangements created by their predecessors.

The social constructionist perspective sees human understanding, or human consciousness, as both the product and the driving force of social interaction. Some social constructionists focus on individual consciousness, particularly on the human capacity to interpret social interactions and to have an inner conversation with oneself about them (Cooley, 1902/1964; Ellis, 1989; G. Mead, 1934). They see the self as developing from the interpretation of social interaction. Cooley introduces the concept of the *looking-glass self,* which can be explained as "I am what I think you think I am." The looking-glass self has three components: (1) I imagine how I appear to others, (2) I imagine their judgment of me, and (3) I develop some feeling about myself that is a result of imagining their judgments of me. George Herbert Mead (1959) suggests that one has a self only when one is in community and that the self develops based on our interpretation of the *generalized other,* which is the attitude of the entire community. Cynthia Franklin (1995) asserts that these cognitively oriented versions of social constructionism are best known as constructivism.

Other social constructionists put greater emphasis on the nature of social interactions, calling attention to gestures and language that are used as symbols in social interaction (Charon, 1998). These symbols take on particular meaning in particular situations. These social constructionists also see social problems as social constructions, created through claims making, labeling, and other social processes (Best, 1989).

The McKinley family is coping with a great deal of change in the external world as well as within their family system. The social constructionist perspective would encourage us to be interested in how they are describing and explaining these changes. For example, how do they understand their struggles in the labor market and the housing market? How much do they attribute their struggles to personal failings, to being victims of a globalized world economy that is creating more privilege for some and more disadvantage for others, or perhaps to corporate greed that caused a meltdown in the housing and financial markets? How do their attributions affect their sense of self-worth? The social constructionist perspective would also be interested in how the McKinley family understands the meaning of family and how they have developed this understanding in their ongoing interactions with each other and the world.

This is how the social constructionist perspective measures against the criteria for judging theories:

- *Coherence and conceptual clarity.* Social constructionism, both the original phenomenological and symbolic interactional concepts as well as the contemporary postmodern conceptualizations, is often criticized as vague and unclear. Over the past few decades, a great diversity of theorizing has been done within this broad theoretical perspective, and there is much fragmentation of ideas. Sociologists in the conflict and rational choice traditions have begun to incorporate social constructionist ideas, particularly those related to meaning making, which has further blurred the boundaries of this perspective. One challenge to the consistency of the social constructionist perspective is that it denies the one-absolute-truth, objective approach to reality while arguing that it is absolutely true that reality is subjective. It criticizes grand theorizing while presenting a grand theory of human behavior.

- *Testability and evidence of empirical support.* Because of the vagueness of its concepts, the social constructionist perspective has been criticized for being difficult to operationalize for empirical research. Social constructionists have responded in two different ways to this criticism. Some argue that it is naïve to think that any theory can be evaluated based on empirical evidence (Cole, 1992). However, many social constructionist proponents have challenged the criticism and offered alternative criteria for evaluating theory (see Witkin & Gottschalk, 1988). They also propose an alternative research methodology, constructivist research (Lincoln & Guba, 1985), which is sensitive to the context of the research, seeks the views of key parties, and takes into account the interactions involved in the research process (Schutt, 2009; C. Williams, 2006). Research in the postmodern tradition is interested in stories, not facts (Danto, 2008). Social constructionism has stimulated a trend in the behavioral sciences to use a mix of quantitative and qualitative research methodologies to accommodate both objective and subjective reality.

- *Comprehensiveness.* Social constructionism pays little attention to the role of biology in human behavior, with the exception of a few constructivist biologists (Maturana, 1988; J. Stewart, 2001; Varela, 1989). In some versions of social constructionism, cognitive processes are central (Mahoney, 1991), and the social construction of emotions is considered in others (Ellis, 1989). With the emphasis on meaning making, social constructionism is open to the role of religion and spirituality in human behavior. With its emphasis on social interaction, the social constructionist perspective is strong in attention to the social environment. It has been criticized, however, for failing to pay attention to the macro world of social institutions and social structure. Time, and the role of history, is respected in the social constructionist perspective, with many authors drawing attention to the historical era in which behavior is constructed. Reality, to the social constructionist, is a moving target (C. Williams, 2006).

- *Diversity and power.* With its emphasis on multiple social realities, the social constructionist perspective is strong in its ability to accommodate diversity. It has been criticized, however, for failure to provide the theoretical tools necessary for the analysis of power relationships (Coser, 1975; Ritzer, 2008b; C. Williams, 2006). Some critics have suggested that many contemporary postmodern versions of social constructionism, by ignoring power while focusing on multiple voices and multiple meanings in the construction of reality, reduce oppression to mere difference (C. Williams, 2006). These critics suggest that this reduction of oppression to difference masks the fact that some actors have greater power than others to privilege their own constructions of reality and to disadvantage the constructions of other actors. This criticism cannot be leveled at all versions of social constructionism, however. Social work scholars have been attracted to those versions of the social constructionist perspective that have incorporated pieces of the conflict tradition (E. Freeman & Couchonnal, 2006; Laird, 1994; Saleebey, 1994), particularly the early work of Michel Foucault (1969) on the relationship between power and knowledge. They propose that in contemporary society, minority or "local" knowledges are denied credibility in majority-dominated social arenas and suggest that social work practitioners can bring credibility to minority viewpoints by allowing oppressed individuals and groups to tell their own stories.

- *Usefulness for social work practice.* Social constructionism gives new meaning to the old social work adage, "Begin where the client is." In the social constructionist perspective, the social work relationship begins with developing an understanding of how the client views the situation and what the client would like to have happen. The current strong interest in solution-focused and narrative and storytelling therapies is based on the social constructionist perspective. Solution-focused approaches attempt to help clients construct solutions rather than solve problems. They are based on the assumption that clients want to change and are capable of envisioning the change they would like to see. Narrative therapy starts with the assumption that we all tell ourselves stories about our lives, developing dominant story lines and forgetting material that does not fit into them. A goal of therapy is to help clients see more realities in their story lines, with other possible interpretations of events (J. Walsh, 2010). The social worker should engage the client in thinking about the social, cultural, and historical environments in which his or her version of reality was constructed, which, for members of oppressed groups, may lead to empowerment through *restorying*, or revision of the story line (Greene & Cohen, 2005; Laird, 1994; Saleebey, 1994). Joseph Walsh suggests that narrative therapy can be particularly helpful to hospice patients who are reflecting on their life stories. That is, indeed, the approach of the hospice social worker who is working with Ruth McKinley and her family. At the level of groups and organizations, the social constructionist perspective recommends getting discordant groups to engage in sincere discussion of their disparate constructions of reality and to negotiate lines of action acceptable to all (C. Fox & Miller, 1995).

Critical Thinking Questions 2.1

The systems, conflict, rational choice, and social constructionist perspectives all pay attention to the environment that is external to individuals. It could be argued that the hospice social worker should only be focusing on Ruth McKinley's personal needs and reactions. How would you argue in favor of that approach? How would you argue against it?

PSYCHODYNAMIC PERSPECTIVE

Both Stanley and Marcia McKinley's despondence and loss of hope are apparent in their first meeting with the hospice social worker—and easy to understand. Think about the losses they have faced in the past year: loss of job (Stanley), loss of income (Stanley and Marcia), loss of valued roles (provider for Stanley and caregiver for Marcia), and loss of health (Marcia). They also face the impending loss of Ruth, the last surviving parent for them, and the possible loss of their home. This rapid accumulation of loss would challenge, even overwhelm, the adaptive capacities of most any human. Bethany is thinking of dropping out of school, a decision that will involve loss of a dream, at least temporarily. In the midst of all that loss, we also note the deep attachment that all four family members—Ruth, Stanley, Marcia, and Bethany—have for each other. This suggests that early nurturing environments supported the development of secure attachments. As we explore the McKinley family's situation from the psychodynamic perspective (see Exhibit 2.7), these and other ideas emerge.

The **psychodynamic perspective** is concerned with how internal processes such as needs, drives, and emotions motivate human behavior. The perspective has evolved over the years, moving from the classical psychodynamic emphasis on innate drives and unconscious processes toward greater emphasis on the adaptive capacities of individuals and their interactions with the environment. The origins of all psychodynamic theories are in the work of

---

- Emotions have a central place in human behavior.
- Unconscious, as well as conscious, mental activity serves as the motivating force in human behavior.
- Early childhood experiences are central in the patterning of an individual's emotions and, therefore, central to problems of living throughout life.
- Individuals may become overwhelmed by internal or external demands.
- Individuals frequently use ego defense mechanisms to avoid becoming overwhelmed by internal or external demands.

▲ **Exhibit 2.7**   Big Ideas of the Psychodynamic Perspective

Sigmund Freud; other prominent theorists in the evolving psychodynamic perspective include Carl Jung, Anna Freud, Melanie Klein, Margaret Mahler, Karen Horney, Heinz Hartmann, Robert W. White, Donald Winnicott, Otto Kernberg, Heinz Kohut, and Erik Erikson. More recent formulations of the perspective include ego psychology, object relations, self psychology, and relational-cultural theories. We will elaborate on these more recent developments later.

To trace the evolution of the psychodynamic perspective, it is essential to begin with its Freudian roots. Sigmund Freud looked at the human personality from a number of interrelated points of view; the most notable are his drive or instinct theory, topographical theory, structural theory, and psychosexual stage theory, summarized below. Freud revised each of these approaches to human personality over time, and different followers of Freud have attended to different aspects of his theoretical works, further revising each of them over time.

- *Drive or instinct theory.* This theory proposes that human behavior is motivated by two basic instincts: *thanatos,* or the drive for aggression or destruction, and *eros,* or the drive for life (through sexual gratification). Recent revisions of drive theory have suggested that human behavior is also motivated by drives for mastery (see D. Goldstein, 1996) and for connectedness (Borden, 2009).

- *Topographical theory of the mind.* Topographical theory proposes three states of mind: conscious mental activities of which we are fully aware; preconscious thoughts and feelings that can be easily brought to mind; and unconscious thoughts, feelings, and desires of which we are not aware but which have a powerful influence on our behavior. Although all psychodynamic theorists believe in the unconscious, the different versions of the theory put different emphases on the importance of the unconscious in human behavior.

- *Structural model of the mind.* This model proposes that personality is structured around three parts: the *id,* which is unconscious and strives for satisfaction of basic instincts; the *superego,* which is made up of conscience and ideals and is the censor of the id; and the *ego,* which is the rational part of personality that mediates between the id and the superego. Freud and his early followers were most interested in the id and the pathologies that emanate from it, but later followers have focused primarily on ego strengths and the drive for adaptation. Both ego psychology and self psychology are part of this later tradition.

- *Psychosexual stage theory.* This theory proposes a five-stage model of child development, based on sexual instincts: the oral phase (birth to about 18 months), when the search for pleasure is centered in the mouth; the anal phase (from about 18 months to 3 years), when the search for pleasure is centered in the anus; the phallic phase (ages 3–6), when the search for pleasure is centered in the genitals; the latency phase (ages 6–8), when erotic urges are repressed; and the genital phase (adolescence onward), when the search for pleasure is centered in the genitals and sexual intimacy. Freud asserted that there was no further personality development in adulthood. Recent revisions of psychodynamic theory, starting with the work of Erik Erikson (1963), have challenged that idea. Although they still give primacy to the childhood years, they suggest that personality continues to develop over the life course. Recent theories put less emphasis on sexual instincts in stage development.

Let's turn now to some revisions of Freudian theory. *Ego psychology* gives primary attention to the rational part of the mind and the human capacity for adaptation. It recognizes conscious as well as unconscious attempts to cope, and the importance of both past and present experiences. Defense mechanisms, unconscious processes that keep intolerable threats from conscious awareness, play an important role in ego psychology (see E. Goldstein, 2001). *Object relations theory* studies how people develop attitudes toward others in the context of early nurturing relationships, and how those attitudes affect the view of the self as well as social relationships. In this tradition, John Bowlby's attachment theory has become the basis for a psychobiological theory of attachment (Barnekow & Kraemer, 2005; Kraemer, 1992). *Self psychology* focuses on the individual need to organize the personality into a cohesive sense of self and to build relationships that support it (see E. Goldstein, 2001). *Relational-cultural theory,* also known as relational feminist theory, proposes that the basic human drive is for relationships with others. The self is understood to develop and mature through emotional connectedness in mutually empathic relationships, rather than through a process of separation and independence as proposed by traditional object relations theory. Human connectedness is emphasized, human diversity acknowledged, and human difference normalized rather than pathologized (Borden, 2009; Freedberg, 2007). You will read more about the psychodynamic perspective in Chapter 4.

Here are the criteria for evaluating theories as applied to the psychodynamic perspective:

- *Coherence and conceptual clarity.* Criticisms that the psychodynamic perspective lacks logical consistency are directed primarily at Freud's original concepts and propositions, which were not entirely consistent because they evolved over time. Ego psychology and object relations theorists strengthened the logical consistency of the psychodynamic perspective by expanding and clarifying definitions of major concepts. Theories in the psychodynamic perspective are also criticized for the vague and abstract nature of their concepts.

- *Testability and evidence of empirical support.* Later psychodynamic theorists translated Freud's ideas into more measurable terms. Consequently, much empirical work has been based on the psychodynamic perspective. Contradictions in the research findings may be due in large part to the use of different definitions and measures. Some concepts, such as mastery or competence, have strong empirical support, but this support has been generated primarily by other schools of thought, such as developmental psychology and Albert Bandura's social behaviorism. Recent long-term longitudinal studies support the importance of childhood experiences, but also indicate that personality continues to develop throughout life (see E. Werner & Smith, 2001). There is growing evidence of the supremely important role that attachment plays in shaping development over the life course (see Trees, 2006).

- *Comprehensiveness.* Early psychodynamic theories were primarily concerned with internal psychological processes. Strong attention is paid to emotions, and in recent formulations, cognitions are also acknowledged. Although Freud assumed that biology determines behavior, he developed his theory several decades before neurological science began to uncover the biological base of emotions. Recently, however, psychodynamic theorists have begun to incorporate new developments in neurological sciences about early brain development into their formulations (see, e.g., Applegate & Shapiro, 2005). With the exception of Carl Jung, early psychodynamic theorists were not interested in the spiritual aspects of human behavior, typically viewing them as irrational defenses against anxiety. Recently, psychodynamically oriented social workers have attempted to integrate spirituality into their practice (see Northcut, 2000). As for environments, most psychodynamic theory conceptualizes them as sources of conflicts with which the individual must struggle. Relational-cultural theory, with its emphasis on supporting the growth of relationships and community, takes exception to that view. Overall, however, environments beyond the family or other close interpersonal relationships are ignored. This has led to criticisms of "mother blaming" and "family blaming" in traditional psychodynamic theories. Social, economic, political, and historical environments of human behavior are probably implied in ego psychology, but they are not explicated. As for time, the focus is on how people change across childhood. There has traditionally been little attempt to account for change after childhood or to recognize the contributions of historical time to human behavior, but the relational-cultural theory looks at relationships across the life course.

- *Diversity and power.* Traditional psychodynamic theories search for universal laws of behavior and their applicability to unique individuals. Thus, diversity of experience at the group level has been quite neglected in this tradition until recently. Moreover, in the main, "universal" laws have been developed through analysis of heterosexual men of White, Anglo-Saxon, middle-class culture. Feminists, as well as members of racial and ethnic minority groups, have criticized the psychodynamic bias toward thinking of people as autonomous individuals (Freedberg, 2007). These critics suggest that viewing this standard as "normal" makes the connectedness found among many women and members of racial and ethnic minority groups seem pathological. Recently, proponents of the psychodynamic perspective have tried to correct for these biases and develop a better understanding of human diversity (E. Goldstein, 1995).

Psychodynamic theories are strong in their recognition of power dynamics in parent–child relationships and in exploration of the lifeworlds of children. They are weaker, overall, in looking at power issues in other relationships, however, including gender relationships. Early on, Freud recognized gender differences, even gender inequality, but attributed them to moral deficits within women. Erik Erikson's theory of psychosocial development has a somewhat greater emphasis on social forces. However, Erikson's work has been criticized for its lack of attention to the worlds of women, racial minorities, and sexual minorities. It did not take into account the persistently hostile environments in which minority group members interact or the extraordinary coping strategies needed to negotiate those environments. In the contemporary era, psychoanalytic feminists have reworked Freud's ideas to focus on patriarchy, asking the question, "Why do men work so hard to maintain patriarchy and why do women put so little energy into challenging patriarchy?" (Lengermann & Niebrugge-Brantley, 2007). They propose that the answer to this question is found in the gender-based early child-rearing environment. African American social workers have proposed that social workers can help to empower African American clients by integrating empowerment theory and an Afrocentric perspective with the ego-strengthening aspects of ego psychology (Manning, Cornelius, & Okundaye, 2004). Relational-cultural theory was developed out of concerns about the male bias in existing psychodynamic theories.

- *Usefulness for social work practice.* Most versions of the psychodynamic perspective have included clinical theory as well as human behavior theory. Differences of opinion about principles of practice reflect the theoretical evolution that has occurred. Practice principles common to all versions of the psychodynamic perspective include the centrality of the professional–client relationship, the curative value of expressing emotional conflicts and understanding past events, and the goals of self-awareness and self-control. In contrast to the classical psychodynamic approach, recent formulations include directive as well as nondirective intervention, short-term as well as long-term intervention, and environmental manipulations—such as locating counseling regarding possible mortgage foreclosure for the McKinley family—as well as intrapsychic manipulations such as emotional catharsis. Ego psychology has also been used to develop principles for prevention activities in addition to principles of remediation (D. Goldstein, 1996). In general, however, the psychodynamic perspective does not suggest practice principles at the level of communities, organizations, and social institutions. Thus, from this perspective, it would not help you to think about how to influence public policy related to housing, income security, or access to health care.

DEVELOPMENTAL PERSPECTIVE

Another way to think about the McKinley family is to view their situation in terms of the developmental tasks that they face. You might note that Ruth McKinley is in late adulthood and engaged in a review of her life journey, attempting to make peace with the life she has lived. You might also note that Stanley and Marcia assumed caregiving responsibilities for Ruth 5 years ago while also continuing to provide support to Bethany as she moved into young adulthood. At the current time, their struggles to stay employed and hold onto their house are situations that were once thought to be "off time," or atypical, for individuals in middle adulthood, but have become more common for the current cohort of midlife adults. Bethany assumed a caregiving role with Ruth as she emerged into adulthood, and that also may seem off time. We can think about where she stands with the developmental markers typically associated with young adulthood: education/work, intimate relationship, leaving home, and starting career. These observations are consistent with the central ideas of the developmental perspective, summarized in Exhibit 2.8.

The focus of the **developmental perspective** is on how human behavior unfolds across the life course, how people change and stay the same over time. Human development is seen to occur in clearly defined stages based on a complex interaction of biological, psychological, and social processes. Each new stage involves new tasks and brings changes in social roles and statuses. Currently, there are two streams of theorizing in the developmental perspective, one based in psychology and one based in sociology.

- Human development occurs in clearly defined, age-graded stages.
- Each stage of life is qualitatively different from all other stages.
- Each stage builds on earlier stages.
- Human development is a complex interaction of biological, psychological, and social factors.
- Moving from one stage to the next involves new tasks and changes in statuses and roles.

▲ **Exhibit 2.8**   Big Ideas of the Developmental Perspective

▲ **Photo 2.3** Families are composed of people in different life stages, occupying different statuses and playing different roles, as suggested by the developmental perspective.

Life span or *life cycle theory,* based in psychology, focuses on the inner life during age-related stages. The study of life span development is rooted in Freud's (1905/1953) theory of psychosexual stages of childhood development, but Erikson (1963) has been the most influential developmental theorist to date because his model of development includes adult, as well as child, stages of development. Other early life cycle theorists include Margaret Mahler, Harry Stack Sullivan, and Jean Piaget. More recent developmental theorists include Daniel Levinson, George Vaillant, Roger Gould, Lawrence Kohlberg, Robert Havighurst, Joan Borysenko, Barbara Newman, and Philip Newman.

Erikson (1963) proposed an *epigenetic model of human development,* in which the psychological unfolding of personality takes place in sequences. Healthy development depends on the mastery of life tasks at the appropriate time in the sequence. Although life span theorists tend to agree with this epigenetic principle, there is also growing agreement that the stages are experienced in a more flexible way than Erikson proposed, with cultural, economic, and personal circumstances leading to some differences in timing and sequencing (Sollod, Wilson, & Monte, 2009).

For example, Bethany McKinley is thinking of postponing school and career development to be a support to her extended family in a stressful period in the life of the family. Stanley McKinley is faced with a need to rethink his occupational career at the age of 50.

Erikson divided the life cycle into eight stages, each with a special psychosocial crisis:

Stage 1 (birth–1 year): basic trust versus mistrust

Stage 2 (ages 2–3): autonomy versus shame, doubt

Stage 3 (ages 3–5): initiative versus guilt

Stage 4 (ages 6–12): industry versus inferiority

Stage 5 (ages 12–18 or so): identity versus role confusion

Stage 6 (early–late 20s): intimacy versus isolation

Stage 7 (late 20s–50s): generativity versus stagnation

Stage 8 (late adulthood): integrity versus despair

Early life span theorists, including Erikson, saw their models of development as universal, applying equally well to all groups of people. This idea has been the target of much criticism, with suggestions that the traditional models are based on the experiences of Anglo, White, heterosexual, middle-class men and do not apply well to members of other groups. This criticism has led to a number of life cycle models for specific groups, such as women (Borysenko, 1996), gay and lesbian persons (e.g., Troiden, 1989), and African Americans (Cross, Parham, & Black, 1991). Life span theories have also been criticized for failing to deal with historical time and the cohort effects on human behavior that arise when groups of persons born in the same historical time share cultural influences and historical events at the same period in their lives.

These criticisms have helped to stimulate development of the life course perspective in sociology. This relatively new perspective conceptualizes the life course as a social, rather than psychological, phenomenon that is nonetheless unique for each individual, with some common life course markers, or transitions, related to shared social and historical contexts (George, 1993). Glen Elder Jr. (1998) and Tamara Hareven (2000) have been major forces in the development of the life course perspective. In its current state, there are six major themes in this perspective: interplay of human lives and historical time; biological, psychological, and social timing of human lives; linked or interdependent lives; human capacity for choice making; diversity in life course trajectories; and developmental risk and protection. As you may recall, the life course perspective is the conceptual framework for the companion volume to this book.

The life course perspective would suggest that the timing of young adult transition markers for Bethany McKinley has been influenced by historical trends toward increasing levels of education and delayed marriage. It would also call attention to the impact of the global economic recession that began in December 2007 on Stanley's occupational trajectory. This perspective would emphasize how the life course trajectories of Stanley, Marcia, Bethany, and Ruth are intertwined, and how what happens in one generation reverberates up and down the extended family line. For example, Stanley, Marcia, and Bethany reorganized their work and family lives to care for Ruth after her stroke. Give some thought to how their life journeys might have been different if Ruth had not required care at that time. Or imagine what decision Bethany might be making about school if Marcia was in stronger health. This notion that families are linked across generations by both opportunity and misfortune is a central idea of the life course perspective, but you may also recognize it as consistent with the system perspective's emphasis on interdependence. The evolving life course model respects the idea of role transition that is so central to the developmental perspective, but it also recognizes the multiplicity of interacting factors that contribute to diversity in the timing and experience of these transitions.

Here is how the criteria for evaluating theories apply to the developmental perspective:

- *Coherence and conceptual clarity.* Classical developmental theory's notion of life stages is internally consistent and conceptually clear. Theorists have been able to build on each other's work in a coherent manner. Still in its early stages, the life course perspective has developed some coherence and beginning clarity about the major concepts. When viewing these two developmental streams together, contradictions appear in terms of universality versus diversity in life span/life course development.

- *Testability and evidence of empirical support.* Many of Erikson's ideas have been employed and verified in empirical research, but until recently, much of developmental research has been based on White, heterosexual, middle-class males. Another concern is that by defining normal as average, developmental research fails to capture the lifeworlds of groups who deviate even moderately from the average, or even to capture the broad range of behavior considered normal. Thus, empirical support for the developmental perspective is based to some extent on statistical masking of diversity. The life course perspective has offered a glimpse of diversity, however, because it has been developed, in general, from the results of longitudinal research, which follows the same people over an extended period of time. The benefit of longitudinal research is that it clarifies whether differences between age groups are really based on developmental differences or whether they reflect cohort effects from living in particular cultures at particular historical times. There is a growing body of longitudinal research in the life course tradition (see Elder & Giele, 2009).

- *Comprehensiveness.* The developmental perspective, when both theoretical streams are taken together, gets relatively high marks for comprehensiveness. Both the life span and the life course streams recognize human behavior as an outcome of complex interactions of biological, psychological, and social factors, although most theorists in both streams pay little attention to the spiritual dimension. The traditional life span approach pays too little attention to the political, economic, and cultural environments of human behavior; the life course perspective pays too little attention to psychological factors. Both approaches attend to the dimension of time, in terms of linear time, but the life course perspective attends to time in a more comprehensive manner, by emphasizing the role of historical time in human behavior. Indeed, the developmental perspective is the only one of the eight perspectives discussed here that makes time a major focus.

- *Diversity and power.* The early life span models were looking for universal stages of human development and did not attend to issues of diversity. More recent life span models have paid more attention to diversity, and diversity of pathways through life is a major theme in the life course perspective. Likewise, the traditional life span approach did not take account of power relationships, with the possible exception of power dynamics in the parent–child relationship. Moreover, traditional life span models are based on the average White, middle-class, heterosexual, Anglo-Saxon male and ignore the worlds of members of nondominant groups. Newer models of life span development have attempted to correct for that failure. Daniel Levinson's (1996) study of women's lives is noteworthy in that regard; it includes a sample of women diversified by race and social class and acknowledges the impact of gender power differentials on women's development. The life course perspective recognizes patterns of advantage and disadvantage in life course trajectories, and life course researchers have done considerable work on the accumulation of advantage and disadvantage over the life course (see Ferraro & Shippee, 2009).

- *Usefulness for social work practice.* Erikson's theory has often been used for assessment purposes in social work practice, and in a positive sense, the theory can aid indirectly in the identification of potential personal and social developmental resources. Traditional life span theories should be applied, however, only with recognition of the ethnocentrism expressed in them. They have traditionally suggested, for example, that there is one right way to raise a child, one "appropriate" type of relationship with the family of origin, and one "healthy" way to develop intimate relationships in adulthood. Although it is harder to extrapolate practice principles from the more complex, still-emerging life course perspective, it seems more promising for understanding diverse persons in diverse environments. It suggests that individuals must always be assessed within familial, cultural, and historical contexts. Overall, the developmental perspective can be viewed as optimistic. Most people face difficult transitions, life crises, and developmental or other challenges at some point, and many people have been reassured to hear that their struggle is "typical." Because the developmental perspective sees individuals as having the possibility to rework their inner experiences, as well as their family relationships, clients may be assisted in finding new strategies for getting their lives back on course. For example, Stanley McKinley could explore untapped talents and interests that might be used to get his occupational career moving again.

SOCIAL BEHAVIORAL PERSPECTIVE

The hospice social worker observed Bethany McKinley's warm and gentle interaction with her grandmother, Ruth. Therefore, she wasn't surprised later to hear Bethany describe Ruth as kind. She imagined that Ruth modeled kind behavior as she cared for Bethany when she was a young child. She also observed that Stanley, Marcia, and Bethany seemed to reinforce kind behavior in each other. She noticed how Stanley and Bethany put their arms around Marcia when she began to cry. The social worker was also struck by statements by both Stanley and Marcia that seem to indicate that they have lost confidence in their ability to make things happen in their lives. She understood how recent events could have undermined their confidence, but she was curious whether she had simply caught them on a down day or if, indeed, they no longer have expectations of being able to improve their situation. Viewing the McKinley family from a social behavioral perspective (see Exhibit 2.9) can lead to such assessment and questions.

Theories in the **social behavioral perspective**, sometimes called the social learning perspective, suggest that human behavior is learned as individuals interact with their environments. But behaviorists disagree among themselves about the processes by which behavior is learned. Over time, three major versions of behavioral theory have been presented, proposing different mechanisms by which learning occurs:

1. **Classical conditioning theory**, also known as respondent conditioning, sees behavior as learned through association, when a naturally occurring stimulus (unconditioned stimulus) is paired with a neutral stimulus (conditioned stimulus). This approach is usually traced to a classic experiment by Russian physiologist Ivan Pavlov, who showed, first, that dogs naturally salivate (unconditioned response) to meat powder on the tongue (unconditioned stimulus). Then, a ringing bell (conditioned stimulus) was paired with the meat powder a number of times. Eventually, the dog salivated (conditioned response) to the ringing of the bell (conditioned stimulus). In other words, an initially neutral stimulus comes to produce a particular behavioral response after it is repeatedly paired with

---

- Human behavior is learned when individuals interact with the environment.
- All human behavior is learned by the same principles of learning: association of environmental stimuli, reinforcement, imitation, and personal expectations and meaning.
- All human problems can be formulated as undesirable behavior.
- All behavior can be defined and changed.

▲ **Exhibit 2.9**   Big Ideas of the Social Behavioral Perspective

another stimulus of significance. Classical conditioning plays a role in understanding many problems that social work clients experience. For example, a woman with an alcohol abuse problem may experience urges to drink when in a location where she often engaged in drinking alcohol before getting sober. Anxiety disorders are also often conditioned; for example, a humiliating experience with public speaking may lead to a deep-seated and long-lasting fear of it, which can result in anxiety attacks in situations where the person has to speak publicly. This approach looks for antecedents of behavior—stimuli that precede behavior—as the mechanism for learning.

2. **Operant conditioning theory,** sometimes known as instrumental conditioning, sees behavior as the result of reinforcement. It is built on the work of two American psychologists, John B. Watson and B. F. Skinner. In operant conditioning, behavior is learned as it is strengthened or weakened by the reinforcement (rewards and punishments) it receives or, in other words, by the

▲ **Photo 1.4** Classical conditioning is traced to an experiment Russian physiologist Ivan Pavlov performed with dogs.

consequences of the behavior. Behaviors are strengthened when they are followed by positive consequences and weakened when they are followed by negative consequences. A classic experiment demonstrated that if a pigeon is given a food pellet each time it touches a lever, over time the pigeon learns to touch the lever to receive a food pellet. This approach looks for consequences—what comes after the behavior—as the mechanism for learning behavior. We all use operant conditioning as we go about our daily lives. We use *positive reinforcers,* such as smiles or praise, to reward behaviors that we find pleasing, in the hopes of strengthening those behaviors. *Negative reinforcers* are also used regularly in social life to stop or avoid unpleasant behavior. For example, the adolescent girl cleans her room to avoid parental complaints. Avoiding the complaints reinforces the room-cleaning behavior.

3. **Cognitive social learning theory,** also known as cognitive behavioral theory or social cognitive theory, with Albert Bandura as its chief contemporary proponent, suggests that behavior is also learned by imitation, observation, beliefs, and expectations. In this view, the "learner" is not passively manipulated by elements of the environment but can use cognitive processes to learn behaviors. Observing and imitating models is a pervasive method for learning human behavior. Bandura (1977a, 1986) proposes that human behavior is also driven by beliefs and expectations. He suggests that **self-efficacy** (a sense of personal competence) and **efficacy expectation** (an expectation that one can personally accomplish a goal) play an important role in motivation and human behavior. Bandura (2001, 2002) has recently extended his theory of self-efficacy to propose three models of **agency** (the capacity to intentionally make things happen): *personal agency* of the individual actor, *proxy agency* in which people reach goals by influencing others to act on their behalf, and *collective agency* in which people act cooperatively to reach a goal.

Although the different streams of social behavioral theorizing disagree about the mechanisms by which behavioral learning occurs, there is agreement that differences in behavior occur when the same learning processes occur in different environments. In this perspective, all human problems of living can be defined in terms of undesirable behaviors, and all behaviors can be defined, measured, and changed.

This is how the social behavioral perspective rates on the criteria for evaluating theories:

- *Coherence and conceptual clarity.* Although there are disagreements about the mechanisms of learning among the various streams of the social behavioral perspective, within each stream, ideas are logically developed in a consistent manner. The social behavioral perspective gets high marks for conceptual clarity; concepts are very clearly defined in each of the streams.

- *Testability and evidence of empirical support.* Social behavioral concepts are easily measured for empirical investigation because theorizing has been based, in very large part, on laboratory research. This characteristic is also a drawback of the social behavioral perspective, however, because laboratory experiments by design eliminate much of the complexity of person–environment configurations. Furthermore, all versions have had their "share of confirmations and disconfirmations" (Monte & Sollod, 2003, p. 578). In general, however, it seems fair to say that all streams of the social behavioral perspective have attained a relatively high degree of empirical support.

- *Comprehensiveness.* Overall, the social behavioral perspective sacrifices multidimensional understanding to gain logical consistency and testability. Although it accepts biology's impact on learning, little attention is paid to biology, except for the recent work of Bandura (2001, 2002), which recognizes the role of biology in human behavior, noting that in most spheres, while biology sets constraints on behavior, it also permits a wide range of behaviors. It is also important to note that contemporary research on neurophysiology and the immune system indicate that classical conditioning plays a role in physiological functioning (Farmer, 2009; Pert, 1997). Cognition and emotion are not included in theories of classical and operant conditioning, but they do receive attention in social cognitive theory. Spiritual factors are considered unmeasurable and irrelevant in classical and operant conditioning theories. They would be relevant only to the extent that they reinforce behavior. For this reason, many theorists and social workers see social behaviorism as dehumanizing. Although environment plays a large role in the social behavioral perspective, the view of the environment is quite limited in classical and operant conditioning. Typically, the social behavioral perspective searches for the one environmental factor, or contingency, that has reinforced one specific behavior. The identified contingency is usually in the micro system (such as the family) or sometimes in the meso system (e.g., a school classroom), but these systems are not typically put in social, economic, political, or historical contexts. One exception is Bandura's social cognitive theory, which acknowledges broad systemic influences on the development of gender roles. Social work scholars applying behavioral principles have also made notable efforts to incorporate a broader view of the environments of human behavior (Mattaini, 1997). Time is important in this perspective only in terms of the juxtaposition of stimuli and reinforcement. The social behaviorist is careful to analyze antecedents and consequences of behavior.

- *Diversity and power.* The social behavioral perspective receives low marks in terms of both diversity and power issues. Very little attention has been paid to recognizing diversity in human behaviors, and it is assumed that the same mechanisms of learning work equally well for all groups. Likewise, the social behavioral perspective attends little to issues of power and oppression. Operant behavioral theory recommends rewards over punishment, but it does not account for the coercion and oppression inherent in power relationships at every system level. It is quite possible, therefore, for the professional behavior modifier to be in service to oppressive forces. On the other hand, behavioral methods can be used to serve social work values (Thyer & Wodarski, 2007). Bandura (1986) writes specifically about power as related to gender roles. He and other theorists note that persons in nondominant positions are particularly vulnerable to **learned helplessness** (see Mikulincer, 1994; Seligman, 1992) in which a person's prior experience with environmental forces has led to low self-efficacy and expectations of efficacy. You may find the concepts of self-efficacy and learned helplessness particularly useful in thinking about both Stanley and Marcia McKinley's situations. Both have experienced some setbacks that may be leading them to expect less of themselves.

- *Usefulness for social work practice.* A major strength of the social behavioral perspective is the ease with which principles of behavior modification can be extrapolated, and it is probably a rare person who has not used social behavioral principles of action at some point. Social workers and psychologists have used social behavioral methods primarily to modify undesirable behavior of individuals. For example, systematic desensitization techniques are used to diminish or eradicate anxiety symptoms. Parent training programs often teach parents how to make more effective use of reinforcements to strengthen positive behaviors and weaken negative behaviors in their children. Social workers often model how to enact new behaviors for their clients. Dialectical behavior therapy teaches adaptive coping related to emotion regulation, distress tolerance, cognitive distortions, and interpersonal communication (J. Walsh, 2010). However, behavioral methods have not been used effectively to produce social reform. Richard Stuart (1989) reminds us that behavior modification was once a "social movement" that appealed to young social reformers who were more interested in changing social conditions that produce atypical behaviors than in changing systems for managing atypical behavior. Skinner's *Walden Two* (1948) was the impetus for attempts by these young reformers to build nonpunitive communities, which represented significant modification of social conditions (see Kinkade, 1973; Wheeler, 1973). Indeed, Bandura's (2002) recent conceptualization of proxy agency and collective agency has implications for social reform.

HUMANISTIC PERSPECTIVE

Consistent with the social work code of ethics, the hospice social worker who is making contact with the McKinley family believes in the dignity and worth of all humans. Her experiences as a hospice social worker have reinforced her belief that each person is unique, and even though she has worked with over 100 hospice patients, she expects Ruth McKinley's story to be in some ways unlike any other story she has heard. She is eager to hear more about how Ruth sees her situation and whether there are any things she would like to change in the limited time she has left. The social worker takes note of strengths she sees in the McKinley family, their love and kindness toward each other and their courage in the face of an accumulation of stress. She wants to hear more about how Stanley, Marcia, and Bethany are thinking about their relationships with Ruth and whether there are any changes they would like to make in that relationship during Ruth's final days. Her thoughts and planned course of action reflect the humanistic perspective, summarized in Exhibit 2.10.

The humanistic perspective is often called the "third force" of psychology, because it was developed in reaction to the determinism found in early versions of both the psychodynamic (behavior as intrapsychically determined) and behavioral (behavior as externally determined) perspectives (Sollod et al., 2009). We are using the term **humanistic perspective** to include humanistic psychology and existential psychology, both of which emphasize the individual's

---

- Each person is unique and has value.
- Each person is responsible for the choices he or she makes within the limits of freedom.
- People always have the capacity to change themselves, even to make radical change.
- Human behavior can be understood only from the vantage point of the phenomenal self—from the internal frame of reference of the individual.
- Behaving in ways that are not consistent with the true self causes anxiety.
- Human behavior is driven by a desire for growth, personal meaning, and competence, and by a need to experience a bond with others.

▲ **Exhibit 2.10**   Big Ideas of the Humanistic Perspective

freedom of action and search for meaning. We also extend the term to include transpersonal theory, which focuses on the spiritual aspects of human experience; the existential sociology tradition, which presents as a dominant theme the idea that people are simultaneously free and constrained, both active and passive agents; and the growing movement of positive psychology.

Like social constructionism, the humanistic perspective is often traced to the German phenomenological philosopher Edmund Husserl (Krill, 1986). It is also influenced by a host of existential philosophers, beginning with Søren Kierkegaard and including Friedrich Nietzsche, Martin Heidegger, Jean-Paul Sartre, Albert Camus, Simone de Beauvoir, Martin Buber, and Paul Tillich. Other early contributors to existential psychology include Viktor Frankl, Rollo May, Carl Jung, R. D. Laing, Karen Horney, and Erich Fromm. Perhaps the most influential contributions to humanistic psychology were made by Carl Rogers (1951) and Abraham Maslow (1962). Maslow is considered one of the founders of *transpersonal psychology*, which he labeled as the "fourth force" of psychology, and Ken Wilber (2006) has developed an increasingly influential transpersonal theory, which is discussed in Chapter 6.

Existential psychology, which developed out of the chaos and despair in Europe during and after World War II, presented four primary themes (Krill, 1996):

1. Each person is unique and has value.

2. Suffering is a necessary part of human growth.

3. Personal growth results from staying in the immediate moment.

4. Personal growth takes a sense of commitment.

It is the emphasis on the necessity for suffering that sets existentialism apart from humanism.

Abraham Maslow (1962), a humanistic psychologist, was drawn to understand "peak experiences," or intense mystical moments of feeling connected to other people, nature, or a divine being. Maslow found peak experiences to occur often among self-actualizing people, or people who were expressing their innate potentials. Maslow developed a theory of a **hierarchy of needs**, which suggests that higher needs cannot emerge in full motivational force until lower needs have been at least partially satisfied. Physiological needs are at the bottom of the hierarchy, and the need for self-actualization is at the top:

1. *Physiological needs:* hunger, thirst, sex

2. *Safety needs:* avoidance of pain and anxiety; desire for security

3. *Belongingness and love needs:* affection, intimacy

4. *Esteem needs:* self-respect, adequacy, mastery

5. *Self-actualization:* to be fully what one can be; altruism, beauty, creativity, justice

Carl Rogers (1951), another major humanistic psychologist, was interested in the capacity of humans to change in therapeutic relationships. He began his professional career at the Rochester Child Guidance Center, where he worked with social workers who had been trained at the Philadelphia School of Social Work. He has acknowledged the influence of Otto Rank, Jessie Taft, and the social workers at the Rochester agency on his thinking about the importance of responding to client feelings (Hart, 1970). He came to believe that humans have vast internal resources for self-understanding and self-directed behavior. He emphasized, therefore, the dignity and worth of each individual, and presented the ideal interpersonal conditions under which people come to use their internal resources to become "more fully functioning." These have become known as the core conditions of the therapeutic process: empathy, warmth, and genuineness.

Maslow is said to have coined the term "positive psychology" when he used it as a chapter title in his 1954 book, *Motivation and Personality*. **Positive psychology** is a relatively recent branch of psychology that undertakes the scientific study of people's strengths and virtues and promotes optimal functioning of individuals and communities. Proponents of positive psychology argue that psychology has paid too much attention to human pathology and not enough to human strengths and virtues (see C. Snyder & Lopez, 2007). Martin Seligman (1991, 1998, 2002), one of the authors of the concept of "learned helplessness," has been at the forefront of positive psychology, contributing the important concept of "learned optimism." Positive psychologists argue that prevention of mental illness is best accomplished by promoting human strength and competence. They have identified a set of human strengths that promote well-being and buffer against mental illness, including optimism, courage, hope, perseverance, honesty, work ethic, and interpersonal skills (C. Snyder & Lopez, 2007). The positive psychology approach is drawing on both Western and Eastern worldviews. A large focus on hope is rooted in Western thinking (McKnight, Snyder, & Lopez, 2007); whereas emphasis on balance, compassion, and harmony comes more from Eastern thinking (Pedrotti, Snyder, & Lopez, 2007).

This is how the humanistic perspective rates on the criteria for evaluating theories:

- *Coherence and conceptual clarity.* Theories in the humanistic perspective are often criticized for being vague and highly abstract, with concepts such as "being" and "phenomenal self." The language of transpersonal theories is particularly abstract, with discussion of self-transcendence and higher states of consciousness. Indeed, theorists in the humanistic perspective, in general, have not been afraid to sacrifice coherence to gain what they see as a more complete understanding of human behavior. The positive psychology movement is working to bring greater consistency and coherence to humanistic concepts.

- *Testability and evidence of empirical support.* As might be expected, empirically minded scholars have not been attracted to the humanistic perspective, and consequently until recently there was little empirical literature to support the perspective. A notable exception is the clinical side of Rogers's theory. Rogers began a rigorous program of empirical investigation of the therapeutic process, and such research has provided strong empirical support for his conceptualization of the necessary conditions for the therapeutic relationship: warmth, empathy, and genuineness (Sollod et al., 2009). The positive psychology movement is focusing, with much success, on producing empirical support for the role of human strengths and virtues in human well-being.

- *Comprehensiveness.* The internal life of the individual is the focus of the humanistic perspective, and it is strong in consideration of both psychological and spiritual dimensions of the person. With its emphasis on search for meaning, the humanistic perspective is the only perspective presented in this chapter to explicitly recognize the role of spirituality in human behavior. (Other theories of spirituality are discussed in Chapter 6.) In addition, Maslow recognizes the importance of satisfaction of basic biological needs. As might be expected, most theorists in the humanistic tradition give limited attention to the environments of human behavior. Taking the lead from existential philosophers, R. D. Laing sees humans as interrelated with their worlds and frowns on the word *environment* because it implies a fragmented person. In discussions of human behavior, however, Laing (1967, 1969) emphasizes the insane situations in which human behavior is enacted. Erich Fromm (1941) was heavily influenced by Karl Marx and is much more inclusive of environment than other theorists in the humanistic perspective, emphasizing industrialization, Protestant reformation, capitalism, and technological revolution as alienating contexts against which humans search for meaning. Although existential sociologists emphasize the importance of feelings and emotions, they also focus on the problematic nature of social life under modernization (see Fontana, 1984). A dehumanizing world is implicit in the works of Maslow and Rogers, but neither theorist focuses explicitly on the environments of human behavior, nor do they acknowledge that some environments are more dehumanizing than others. The positive psychology movement has begun to examine positive environments that can promote human strengths and virtues, including school, work, and community environments (C. Snyder & Lopez, 2007).

- *Diversity and power.* The humanistic perspective, with its almost singular consideration of an internal frame of reference, devotes more attention to individual differences than to differences between groups. The works of Fromm and Horney are striking exceptions to this statement. Karen Horney identified culturally based gender differences at a time when psychology either ignored gender or took a "biology as destiny" approach. She also lost favor among other psychodynamic theorists by reworking Freud's conceptualization of the Oedipus conflict and of feminine psychology to produce a more gender-sensitive perspective (Horney, 1939, 1967). In general, far too little attention is given in the humanistic tradition to the processes by which institutional oppression influences the **phenomenal self**—the individual's subjectively felt and interpreted experience of "who I am." Like the social constructionist perspective, however, the humanistic perspective is sometimes quite strong in giving voice to experiences of members of nondominant groups. With the emphasis on the phenomenal self, members of nondominant groups are more likely to have preferential input into the telling of their own stories. The social worker's intention to hear and honor the stories of each member of the McKinley family may be a novel experience for each of them, and she may, indeed, hear very different stories from what she expects to hear. Erich Fromm and Michael Maccoby (1970) illustrate this emphasis in their identification of the different lifeworlds of members of groups of different socioeconomic statuses in a Mexican village. Most significantly, Rogers developed his respect for the personal self, and consequently his client-centered approach to therapy, when he realized that his perceptions of the lifeworlds of his low-income clients in the Child Guidance Clinic were very different from their own perceptions (Hart, 1970).

- *Usefulness for social work.* If the social constructionist perspective gives new meaning to the old social work adage, "Begin where the client is," it is social work's historical involvement in the development of the humanistic perspective that gave original meaning to the adage. It is limited in terms of providing specific interventions, but it is consistent with social work's value of the dignity and worth of the individual. The humanistic perspective suggests that social workers begin by developing an understanding of how the client views the situation and, with its emphasis on the individual drive for growth and competence, it recommends a "strengths" rather than "pathology" approach to practice (Saleebey, 2006). George Vaillant (2002), a research psychiatrist, suggests that this attention to strengths is what distinguishes social workers from other helping professionals. From this perspective, then, we might note the strong commitment to helping one another displayed by the McKinley family, which can be the basis for successful intervention. At the organizational level, the humanistic perspective has been used by organizational theorists, such as Douglas McGregor (1960), to prescribe administrative actions that focus on employee well-being as the best route to organizational efficiency and effectiveness. Positive psychology is beginning to propose guidelines for developing positive environments in schools, workplaces, and communities.

Critical Thinking Questions 2.2

When it comes to theory or perspective, some people are one-theory/perspective people and find that one theory/perspective does an adequate job of explaining the world. Other people can be described as cluster people: They can identify about three theories (or perspectives) that work well for them in most situations. Still other people can best be described as multi-theoretical—they think the world calls for a larger range of theories (perspectives) than the cluster folks. After reading this chapter, how would you characterize your current thinking about which of these groups you fall into? What factors do you think influence your theoretical preferences?

THE MERITS OF MULTIPLE PERSPECTIVES

You can see that each of these perspectives puts a different lens on the unfolding story of the McKinley family, and that each has been used to guide social work practice over time. But do these different ways of thinking make you more effective when you meet with clients like the McKinleys? We think so. It was suggested in Chapter 1 that each situation can be examined from several perspectives, and that using a variety of perspectives brings more dimensions of the situation into view. Eileen Gambrill (2006) has suggested that all of us, whether new or experienced social workers, have biases that predispose us to do too little thinking, rather than too much, about the practice situations we confront. We are, she asserts, particularly prone to ignore information that is contrary to our hypotheses about situations. Consequently, we tend to end our search for understanding prematurely. One step we can take to prevent this premature closure is to think about practice situations from multiple theoretical perspectives.

The fields of psychology and sociology offer a variety of patterned ways of thinking about changing person–environment configurations, ways that have been worked out over time to assist in understanding human behavior. They are tools that can help us make sense of the situations we encounter. We do not mean to suggest that all eight of the perspectives discussed in this chapter will be equally useful, or even useful at all, in all situations. But each of these perspectives will be useful in some situations that you encounter as a social worker, and therefore should be in your general knowledge base. As a competent professional, you must view the quest for adequate breadth and depth in your knowledge base as an ongoing, lifelong challenge and responsibility. We hope that over time you will begin to use these multiple perspectives in an integrated fashion so that you can see the many dimensions—the contradictions as well as the consistencies—in stories like the McKinley family's. We encourage you to be flexible and reflective in your thinking and your "doing" throughout your career. We remind you, again, to use general knowledge only to generate hypotheses to be tested in specific situations.

IMPLICATIONS FOR SOCIAL WORK PRACTICE

The eight perspectives on human behavior discussed in this chapter suggest a variety of principles for social work assessment and intervention:

- In assessment, consider any recent role transitions that may be affecting the client. Assist families and groups to renegotiate unsatisfactory role structures. Develop networks of support for persons experiencing challenging role transitions.

- In assessment, consider power arrangements and forces of oppression, and the alienation that emanates from them. Assist in the development of advocacy efforts to challenge patterns of dominance, when possible. Be aware of the power dynamics in your relationships with clients; when working with nonvoluntary clients, speak directly about the limits and uses of your power.

- In assessment, consider the patterns of exchange in the social support networks of individual clients, families, and organizations, using ecomaps for network mapping when useful. Assist individuals, families, and organizations to renegotiate unsatisfactory patterns of exchange, when possible. Consider how social policy can increase the rewards for prosocial behavior.

- Begin your work by understanding how clients view their situations. Engage clients in thinking about the environments in which these constructions of self and situations have developed. When working in situations characterized by differences in belief systems, assist members to engage in sincere discussions and to negotiate lines of action.

- Assist clients in expressing emotional conflicts and in understanding how these are related to past events, when appropriate. Help them develop self-awareness and self-control, where needed. Assist clients in locating and using needed environmental resources.

- In assessment, consider the familial, cultural, and historical contexts in the timing and experience of developmental transitions. Recognize human development as unique and lifelong.

- In assessment, consider the variety of processes by which behavior is learned. Be sensitive to the possibility of learned helplessness when clients lack motivation for change. Consider issues of social justice and fairness before engaging in behavior modification.

- Be aware of the potential for significant differences between your assessment of the situation and the client's own assessment; value self-determination. Focus on strengths rather than pathology.

KEY TERMS

agency	empowerment theories	psychodynamic perspective
boundary	feedback mechanism	rational choice perspective
chaos theory	feminist theories	role
classical conditioning theory	hierarchy of needs	self-efficacy
cognitive social learning theory	humanistic perspective	social behavioral perspective
conflict perspective	learned helplessness	social constructionist perspective
critical theorists	operant conditioning theory	social exchange theory
developmental perspective	phenomenal self	social network theory
ecomaps	pluralistic theory of social conflict	systems perspective
efficacy expectation	positive psychology	

ACTIVE LEARNING

1. Reread the case study of the intergenerational stresses in the McKinley family. Next, review the big ideas of the eight theoretical perspectives in Exhibits 2.1, 2.3, 2.4, 2.6, 2.7, 2.8, 2.9, and 2.10. Choose three specific big ideas from these exhibits that you think are most helpful in thinking about the McKinley family. For example, you might choose this big idea from the systems perspective: Each part of the system affects all other parts and the system as a whole. You might also choose this big idea from the humanistic perspective: Human behavior is driven by a desire for growth, personal meaning, and competence, and by a need to experience a bond with others. Likewise, you might choose another specific idea from any of the perspectives. The point is to choose the three big ideas that you find most useful. Now, in a small group, compare notes with three or four classmates about which big ideas were chosen. Try to determine why these particular choices, and not others, were made by each of your classmates.

2. Break into eight small groups, with each group assigned one of the theoretical perspectives described in the chapter. Each group's task is to briefly summarize the assigned theoretical perspective and then explain the group's interpretation of the perspective's usefulness when applied to the McKinley family or another case scenario.

3. Choose a story that interests you in a current edition of a daily newspaper. Read the story carefully and then think about which of the eight theoretical perspectives discussed in this chapter is most reflected in the story.

Conflict Theory(ies) of Deviance
www.umsl.edu/~keelr/200/conflict.html

Site presented by Robert O. Keel at the University of Missouri at St. Louis, contains information on the basic premises of conflict theory as well as specific information on radical conflict theory and pluralistic conflict theory.

Humanistic Psychology
www.ahpweb.org/aboutahp/whatis.html

Site maintained by the Association of Humanistic Psychology, contains the history of humanistic psychology, information on Carl Rogers, the humanistic view of human behavior, methods of inquiry, and humanistic psychotherapies.

Personality Theories
www.webspace.ship.edu/cgboer/perscontents.html

Site maintained by C. George Boeree at the Psychology Department of Shippensburg University, provides an electronic textbook on theories of personality, including the theories of Sigmund Freud, Erik Erikson, Carl Jung, B. F. Skinner, Albert Bandura, Abraham Maslow, Carl Rogers, and Jean Piaget.

Sociological Theories and Perspectives
www.sociosite.net/topics/theory.php

Site maintained at the University of Amsterdam, contains general information on sociological theory and specific information on a number of theories, including chaos theory, interaction theory, conflict theory, and rational choice theory.

William Alanson White Institute
www.wawhite.org

Site contains contemporary psychoanalysis journal articles, training programs, and professional meetings.

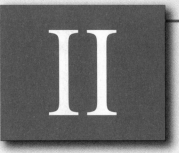

PART

II

The Multiple
Dimensions of Person

The multiple dimensions of person, environment, and time have unity; they are inseparable and embedded. That is the way I think about them and the way I am encouraging you to think about them. However, you will be better able to think about the unity of the three aspects of human behavior when you have developed a clearer understanding of the different dimensions encompassed by each one. A review of theory and research about the different dimensions will help you to sharpen your thinking about what is involved in the changing configurations of persons and environments.

The purpose of the four chapters in Part II is to provide you with an up-to-date understanding of theory and research about the dimensions of person. It begins with a chapter on the biological dimension and ends with one on the spiritual dimension. Because so much has been written about the psychological dimension, it is covered in two chapters: the first one about the basic elements of a person's psychology and the second one about the processes a person uses to maintain psychological balance in a changing environment.

With a state-of-the-art knowledge base about the multiple dimensions of persons, you will be prepared to consider the interactions between persons and environments, which is the subject of Part III. And then you will be able to think more comprehensively and more clearly about the ways configurations of persons and environments change across the life course. The discussion of the life course in the companion volume to this book, *The Changing Life Course*, attempts to put the dimensions of persons and environments back together and help you think about their embeddedness.

CHAPTER

The Biological Person

Stephen French Gilson

Acknowledgments: The author wishes to thank Elizabeth DePoy and Elizabeth Hutchison for their helpful comments, insights, and suggestions for this chapter.

OPENING QUESTIONS

- What do social workers need to know about the interior environment of human biology?

- How does knowledge of biology contribute to important roles that social workers play in individual and community health and illness?

KEY IDEAS

As you read this chapter, take note of these central ideas:

1. Although there are a variety of ways to think about our bodies, the approach proposed here locates understandings of the body within theories of environments—in this case, the interior environment. Environment is defined as a "set of conditions" (DePoy & Gilson, 2007), and thus interior environment theories are concerned with the description and explanation of embodied organic conditions, such as internal organ systems, genetics, interior psychological structures, processes, and so forth. Exterior environments are non-corporeal, or conditions that are not organic and not contained within the body (DePoy & Gilson, 2007). Although, for instructive purposes, we distinguish interior from exterior environments, we want to emphasize that the division is not clear and is often arbitrary, a key point to be considered and discussed in this chapter.

2. There is strong evidence of relationships among physical health, psychological health, and exterior environmental conditions. Biological functioning is the result of complex transactions among interior and exterior systems. No biological system operates in isolation from these other phenomena.

3. The nervous system is responsible for processing and integrating incoming information, and it influences and directs reactions to that information. It is divided into three major subsystems: the central nervous system, peripheral nervous system, and autonomic nervous system.

4. The endocrine system plays a crucial role in growth, metabolism, development, learning, and memory.

5. The immune system is made up of organs and cells that work together to defend the body against disease. Autoimmune diseases occur when the immune system mistakenly targets parts of the interior environment.

6. The cardiovascular system is made up of the heart and the blood circulatory system. The circulatory system supplies cells of the body with the food and oxygen they need for functioning.

7. The musculoskeletal system supports and protects the body and its organs and provides motion. The contraction and relaxation of muscles attached to the skeleton is the basis for voluntary movements.

8. The reproductive system is composed of both internal and external structures that are different for males and females.

Cheryl's Brain Injury

Cheryl grew up in rural Idaho in a large extended family of Anglo heritage and enlisted as a private in the army just after she finished her 3rd year in high school. After basic training, she was deployed to Iraq for active combat duty. Traveling en route to Baghdad, Cheryl's Humvee contacted an improvised explosive device (IED), causing Cheryl to sustain a closed head injury and multiple fractures. She was in a coma for 3 weeks.

Over a 6-month period, all of Cheryl's external bodily injuries, including the fractures, healed, and she was able to walk and talk with no apparent residual impairments. Cognitively and socially, however, Cheryl experienced change. Although able to read, she could not retain what she had just read a minute ago. She did not easily recall her previous knowledge of math and was not able to compute basic math such as addition and subtraction without the use of a calculator. She was slow in penmanship, taking at least 5 minutes to write her own name. Unlike her social behavior prior to the accident, Cheryl was often blunt in her comments, even to the point of becoming confrontational with friends without provocation.

Because of her observable recovery, everyone expected Cheryl to return to active duty, but 2 years after the accident, her family knows that she is not going to return to military service. Cheryl's ex-boyfriend, Sean, is about to get engaged to another woman, but Cheryl thinks that she is still dating Sean and that he will soon marry her. People who knew Cheryl before the accident cannot understand why her personality has changed so markedly, and they even say, "She's a completely different person!"

A Diabetes Diagnosis for Bess

Bess, a 52-year-old Franco-American woman who lives in rural Maine, was enjoying her empty nest just before the social worker met her. The youngest of her three children had married 6 months earlier, and although Bess was proud of what she had accomplished as a single mother, she was now ready to get on with her life. Her first order of business was to get her body back into shape, so she started on a high-carbohydrate, low-fat diet that she had read about in a magazine. Drinking the recommended eight glasses of water or more each day was easy, because it seemed that she was always thirsty. But Bess was losing more weight than she thought possible on a diet, and she was always cheating! Bess had thought that she would have to get more exercise to lose weight, but even walking to and from her car at the grocery store tired her out.

One morning, Bess did not show up at the country store where she worked. Because it was very unusual for her not to call and also not to answer her phone, a coworker went to her house. When there was no response to the knocking, the coworker and one of Bess's neighbors opened the door to Bess's house and walked in. They found Bess sitting on her couch, still in her nightclothes, which were drenched with perspiration. Bess was very confused, unable to answer simple questions with correct responses. Paramedics transported Bess to the local community hospital.

In the emergency room, after some blood work, a doctor diagnosed diabetes mellitus (diabetes). Because diabetes is common among middle-aged and older Franco Americans in this poor rural town, a social worker had already established an educational support group for persons with diabetes that Bess now attends.

Melissa's HIV Diagnosis

Melissa's "perfect life" has just fallen apart. As a young, Jewish, urban professional who grew up in a middle-class suburb in New York, Melissa had always dreamed of a big wedding at her parents' country club, and her dreams were about to come true. All the plans had been made, invitations sent out, bridesmaids' dresses bought and measured, and her wedding dress selected. All that remained was finalizing the menu and approving the flower arrangements. Because Melissa and her fiancé planned to have children soon after their marriage, she went to her physician for a physical exam 2 months before her wedding. As the doctor does with all of her patients, she asked if Melissa had ever been tested for HIV. Melissa said no, and gave her permission for an HIV test to be run with all the other routine blood work.

One week after her physical, the doctor's office called and asked Melissa to return for more blood work because of what was thought to be an inaccuracy in the report. Melissa went back to the office for more blood tests. Another week passed, but Melissa did not think again about the tests because she was immersed in wedding plans. Her physician called her at home at 8:00 one morning and asked her to come to her office after work that day. Because she was distracted by the wedding plans and a busy schedule at work, Melissa did not think anything of the doctor's request.

When she arrived at the doctor's office, she was immediately taken to the doctor's private office. The doctor came in, sat down, and told Melissa that two separate blood tests had confirmed that she was HIV positive. Melissa spent over 3 hours with her physician that evening, and soon thereafter she began to attend an HIV support group.

Melissa has never used illicit drugs, and she has only had two sexual partners. She and her fiancé had decided not to have unprotected intercourse until they were ready for children, and because they used condoms, he was not a prime suspect for passing along the infection. Melissa remembered that the man with whom she was involved prior to meeting her fiancé would not talk about his past. She has not seen this former lover for the past 3 years, ever since she moved away from New York.

Lifestyle Changes for Thomas

Thomas is a 30-year-old African American man who lives with his parents, both of whom are obese, as are his two older sisters. Thomas loves his mom's cooking, but some time ago realized that its high-fat and high-sodium content was contributing to his parents' obesity and high blood pressure.

In contrast, Thomas takes pride in watching his diet (when he isn't eating at home) and is pretty smug about being the only one in the family who is not obese. Being called "the thin man" is, to Thomas, a compliment. He also boasts about being in great physical shape, and exercises to the point of being dizzy.

(Continued)

(Continued)

After one of his dizziness episodes, a friend told him that he should get his blood pressure checked. Although Thomas knew of the high incidence of heart disease among African Americans, he never considered that he would have a problem. After all, he is young and in good physical shape. Out of curiosity, the next time Thomas stopped at his local drug store, he decided to use one of those self-monitoring machines to check his blood pressure. To his astonishment, the reading came back 200/105, which is quite high. Thomas now seeks a social worker's help to adopt some major lifestyle changes.

Case Study 3.5

Max's Post-Polio Syndrome

Max is from an Eastern European immigrant family that settled in a midwestern city in the United States. When he was 2 years old, he contracted polio that affected only his legs. He never had any breathing difficulties, nor was there any involvement in his arms. In fact, after 6 months in the hospital and another 6 months of therapy when he returned home, Max appeared to be "cured." Afterward, as he was growing up, there were no visible signs of previous illness. He clearly could keep up with his friends, except he could never run very long distances.

Forty-three years later, Max developed early symptoms of post-polio syndrome. He began to notice increasing weakness in his legs, unusual fatigue, and a lot of pain all over his body. A recent evaluation at a university clinic confirmed the diagnosis of post-polio syndrome, and the clinicians who saw him recommended that he consider getting the type of brace that is inserted in his shoes to support both ankles, as well as use forearm crutches for walking long distances. Max has earned his living all his life as a house painter. He needs help figuring out how to cope with these new developments and how to support his growing family.

Case Study 3.6

Juan and Belinda's Reproductive Health

Juan and Belinda, now both 17 years old, grew up in the same neighborhood of a southwestern city in the United States and attend the same church, St. Joseph's Catholic Church. They do not attend the same school, however. Belinda has received all of her education at the schools at St. Joseph's; Juan attended John F. Kennedy Elementary School and John Marshall Junior High, and he now attends Cesar Chavez High School. Since seventh grade, Juan has met Belinda after school and walked her home.

They both live in small, well-kept homes in a section of the community that is largely Spanish speaking with very strong influences from the wide variety of countries of origin represented by community residents: Mexico, Honduras, El Salvador, and Nicaragua, among others. The Catholic Church here is a dominant exterior environmental force in shaping community social, political, economic, and personal values and behaviors.

Both Juan's and Belinda's parents immigrated to the United States from Mexico, seeking to improve the opportunities for their future families. Juan's mother found a job as a housekeeper at a local hotel, where she now manages the housekeeping staff. His father began as a day laborer and construction worker, eventually moving up to become foreman of the largest construction company in the area. He anticipates beginning his own construction company within the next year. Belinda's mother is a skilled seamstress and was able to start her own tailoring business shortly after immigrating. Belinda's father, with a background in diesel mechanics, was able to find work at a large trucking company where he continues to work today.

Like many teenagers, Juan and Belinda face the difficulties of sorting out the complexities and the intricacies of their relationship. They feel very much in love, knowing in their hearts that they want to get married and raise a family. At 17, they are at the crossroads of intimacy, because they face conflicts about their sexuality with limited information and strong prohibitions against premarital sex. Following many of the teachings of their church and the urgings of their parents, Juan and Belinda have avoided much physical contact except for kissing and holding each other.

Like many communities in the United States, their community struggled with the question of just what information should be given to students about physical health and sexuality. Their community decided to limit the amount and type of information to the basics of female and male sexual anatomy and physiology. The result of this decision for Juan and Belinda was that they learned very little about sexual response and behavior, conception, pregnancy, childbirth, contraception, safe sex practices, or other areas that are critical in today's world. The decision by the school board was based on a belief that it was the family's responsibility to provide this information to their children. The school social worker at Cesar Chavez High School is aware of the moral conflicts that arise for youth in this community that in part result from limited sex education.

AN INTEGRATIVE APPROACH FOR UNDERSTANDING THE INTERSECTION OF INTERIOR BIOLOGICAL HEALTH AND ILLNESS AND EXTERIOR ENVIRONMENTAL FACTORS

As we think about the stories of Cheryl, Bess, Melissa, Thomas, Max, and Juan and Belinda, we can see that biology is an important dimension of their behavior. But despite growing agreement about the importance of biology in influencing human behavior and thus the need for social workers to be well informed in this arena, the profession is struggling to articulate exactly what social workers need to know about human biology, or what DePoy and Gilson (2008) refer to as a substantial part of the interior environment. Because social workers deal with people, and people comprise the corpus of human biology, social workers encounter biology and its reciprocal influence with exterior environmental conditions such as poverty, addictions, violence, and child abuse each time they interact with individuals. For instructive purposes, we distinguish interior from exterior environments on the basis of corporeality, or material that relates to the body (DePoy & Gilson, 2007). However, the division between the corporeal and non-corporeal is not clear. Consider for example a knee replacement. While it is not organic in composition, it is located beneath the skin and functions as integral to body stability and movement. But is it interior or exterior? What about eyeglasses, prostheses, or even clothes that preserve body temperature?

Returning to the cases of Cheryl, Bess, Melissa, Thomas, Max, and Juan and Belinda, their interior environments are the central reason they are seeking social work assistance. To be efficacious in meeting professional goals, social workers must have a working knowledge of the body's systems and the ways these systems interact with each other and with other interior and exterior environmental dimensions. Social workers also must be sufficiently informed about interior environment theory and knowledge in order to discuss details of biological functioning with clients when indicated (H. C. Johnson, 2001; Tangenberg & Kemp, 2002).

While the knowledge of biological structures and their function is foundational to understanding the interior environment, it is insufficient for social workers, in that social work decision making and activity require a complex mastery of knowledge about the interactions of interior and exterior environments. Moreover, understanding of how the interior environment contributes to human behavior (what people do and do not do and how they do what they do), appearance, and experience (DePoy & Gilson, 2004) is critical for informed social work practice as exemplified by each of the case studies above.

Approaching social work practice from well-accepted explanatory models such as biopsychosocial-spiritual and legitimacy (DePoy & Gilson, 2008) requires depth of knowledge not only of interior parts, but also of their complex, context-embedded interaction. Consistent with post-postmodern thinking, which colocates multiple fields of knowledge adjacent to and informing one another (DePoy & Gilson, 2008), social work's growing interest in human biology is essential for framing effective responses that consider the interstices of "mind–body interactions."

Systems frameworks describe and explain human phenomena as sets of interrelated parts. There are many variations and applications of systems approaches ranging from those that look at embodied or interior systems, to those that examine human systems composed of both humans and their exterior environments, and even extending to systems that do not contain embodied elements (DePoy & Gilson, 2008). At this point, there is a well-developed theory supported by rigorously conducted empirical evidence of the complex relationships among physical health, psychological health, and social experiences (DePoy & Gilson, 2008; Epel et al., 2006; Weitz, 2009). This is an exciting and rapidly changing knowledge base.

Systems perspective

In March of 2001, the National Institutes of Health sponsored a conference titled Vital Connections: The Science of Mind–Body Interactions (MacArthur Network on Mind–Body Interactions, 2001). This event was one of the most important in influencing new theory and knowledge linking interior and exterior systems and environments. Renowned scholars reported on several topics focusing on the interaction of exterior and interior environments that have been receiving and continue to receive intense research scrutiny—for example the neurobiology of human emotions, early care and brain development, the biology of social interactions, socioeconomic status (SES) and health, neuroendocrinology of stress, and the role of sleep in health and cognition. Scholarship at this conference revealed further evidence of the critical connections between environmental conditions and embodied phenomena, which were previously thought to be only tangentially related to one another. Throughout the 3-day conference, presenters theorized about the "integrative mechanisms" that link social and psychological dimensions to the brain and the rest of the body. Researchers were clear that we are just beginning to understand these mechanisms, and we need to be cautious not to exceed our data in any claims or beliefs about systems interactivity. Much of the current evidence emerged from animal studies and is now conducted with advanced computer modeling software. Its accuracy in explaining the human body remains probable but cautiously applied.

Although these attempts to understand mind–body connections have led to many important theories about health and illness, they may also be misinterpreted. Social workers therefore would be advised to heed the warning of a number of medical researchers and social critics against explaining behavior and emotion through a medicalized lens (see P. Conrad, 2007; Fischbach, quoted in McArthur Network on Mind–Body Interactions; Lane, 2007; Watters, 2010). Such a reductionist perspective may undermine our ability to consider the full range of exterior environmental influences on embodied phenomena. Moreover, medicalization serves to pathologize typical daily experience.

On the flipside of this caution, overattribution of physical experiences to psychological and social conditions fails to consider the interior environmental causes of illness. While we cannot forget that health and illness are influenced by exterior social, political, cultural, and economic environmental conditions (DePoy & Gilson, 2007; Saleebey, 2001), these are often invoked as one-way streets rather than being seen as part of a more complex interactive picture. While the efficiency of a single framework is seductive, such thinking may limit our ability to expansively identify the broad nature of problems and needs, and a range of appropriate interventions to resolve the problems (DePoy & Gilson, 2004, 2010).

The constructed perspective suggests that human phenomena are pluralistic in meaning. As an example, rather than being a singular, scientifically supported entity, through the lens of social construction, a physically disabling medical

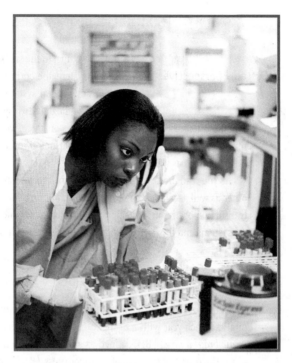

▲ **Photo** 3.1 A medical researcher examines data to test a hypothesis.

Social constructionist perspective

condition such as paralysis or low vision is defined in large part by its meaning from interior views as well as from political, social, cultural, and economic exterior environments (G. L. Albrecht, Seelman, & Bury, 2001; Barnett & Scotch, 2002; DePoy & Gilson, 2004; Gilson & DePoy, 2000, 2002). Thus, using social construction as explanatory, the experience of having atypical low vision can be interpreted as influenced by shared cultural understandings of the "expected roles" for persons with atypical vision, or by actions or inactions of political institutions to promote or impede this subpopulation's access to physical and social environments. We may automatically assume that an individual with atypical low vision is in need of professional intervention, when that person may in effect have his or her life well organized and function well in all chosen living and working environments. Thus, rather than being explained by the biological condition itself, limitation associated with an atypical biological condition may be a function of the exterior environment; the characteristics of the task; personal attitude; and available resources such as technology, assistance from family, friends or employees, accessible transportation, and welcoming, fully accessible communities (DePoy & Gilson, 2010).

As an example, although social workers do not make medical diagnoses for embodied conditions in the scope of our practice, the social work administrator who is developing or operating a shelter, a food kitchen, or an advocacy center may integrate medical and mental health services with employment, housing, financial, and companionship services (Gelberg & Linn, 1988; Nyamathi, Leake, Keenan, & Gelberg, 2000) within the larger considerations of the meaning of those services to the users and community context. Lowe (1997) has recommended a model of social work practice that promotes healthy communities as well as working with individuals, families, and groups to help them identify and advocate for their own health needs if they so choose. DePoy and Gilson (2004, 2010) have built on this model by proposing *legitimate communities*, defined as those that practice acceptance of ideas and appreciate and respond to the full range of human diversity.

A LOOK AT SIX INTERIOR ENVIRONMENT SYSTEMS

Systems perspective

Now we turn to the six biological systems that will be discussed in this chapter: the nervous system, the endocrine system, the immune system, the cardiovascular system, the musculoskeletal system, and the reproductive system. All the other biological systems (such as the digestive system, the respiratory system, and the urinary system) also warrant our attention, but with the limitations of space, we have chosen these six because they are commonly involved in many of the biologically based issues that social workers encounter, and thus can serve as a model for thinking about other systems as well.

As you read the descriptions of these six interior environment systems, keep in mind their connectedness with each other as well as with all environmental conditions. As we emphasize throughout, just as human behavior is a complex transaction of person and environment, biological functioning is the result of complex interactions among all biological systems and the environments in which they function. No one system operates in isolation from other systems.

Nervous System

In the first case study, you met Cheryl, who is like the more than 235,000 people in the United States who are hospitalized each year with a **brain injury (BI)**. In Cheryl's case, we are referring to what is commonly termed a *traumatic brain injury* (TBI), defined as an insult to the brain caused by an external physical force that may result in a diminished or altered state of consciousness (Brain Injury Association of America, 2001). Included here are what might be classified as mild brain injuries or concussions. Traumatic brain injuries include head injuries that result from falls, automobile accidents, infections and viruses, insufficient oxygen, and poisoning. Explosions caused by landmines and improvised explosive devices have been identified as one of the primary causes of TBI and interior environment problems in military personnel.

According to the Centers for Disease Control and Prevention (CDC, 2006a), approximately 1.4 million individuals sustain traumatic brain injury in the United States each year, accruing $60 billion yearly in hospital and injury-related costs (direct medical costs and indirect costs such as lost economic productivity). It is estimated that 2% of the population in the United States, or 5.3 million people, live with the atypical results of traumatic brain injuries. For children and young adults, TBI is the type of injury most often associated with deaths due to unintended injuries. The rates of TBI among African American children ages 0–4 are about 40% higher than those for White children. It is estimated that one in four adults with TBI is unable to return to work within one year after the injury.

Although the symptoms may be similar, *acquired brain injury* (ABI) is a different classification of brain injury. It does not result from traumatic injury to the head; is not hereditary, congenital, or degenerative; and it occurs after birth. Included in this category are oxygen deprivation (anoxia), aneurysms, infections to the brain, and stroke (Brain Injury Association of America, 2001).

Each type of BI may provoke specific atypical issues and behaviors for the individual. However, brain injury in general can affect cognitive, physical, and psychological skills. Atypical cognitive function may present as atypical language and communication, information processing, memory, and perception. Cheryl's atypical writing is an example, as well as a reflection of atypical fine motor skill. Atypical physical functioning often occurs, such as walking differently or not at all (problems with ambulation), and changes in balance and coordination, strength, and endurance. Atypical psychological changes may come from two different sources. They may be *primary*, or directly related to the BI; these include irritability and judgment errors. Or they may be *reactive* to the adjustments required to live with the atypical function caused by BI and its consequences, typically resulting in a diagnosis of depression and changes in self-esteem. Cheryl's difficulty in recognizing that Sean is not going to marry her and her misjudgments in other social situations are symptoms of the psychological consequences of her BI.

The **nervous system** provides the structure and processes for communicating sensory, perceptual, and autonomically generated information throughout the body. Three major subsystems compose the nervous system:

1. Central nervous system (CNS): the brain and the spinal cord

2. Peripheral nervous system (PNS): spinal and cranial nerves

3. Autonomic nervous system (ANS): nerves controlling cardiovascular, gastrointestinal, genitourinary, and respiratory systems

The brain sends signals to the spinal cord, which in turn relays the message to specific parts of the body by way of the PNS. Messages from the PNS to the brain travel back by way of a similar pathway (Carey, 1990; R. Carter, 2009). Note that Cheryl's brain injury affects only a part of her nervous system—in fact, only part of the CNS. Damage to other parts of the nervous system can have significant atypical effects, but here we focus on her brain injury because it is so closely linked with behavioral changes.

The human brain, which constitutes only about 2% of one's total body weight, may contain as many as 10 million neurons. Its three major internal regions are referred to as the forebrain, midbrain, and hindbrain. Viewed from the side (see Exhibit 3.1), the largest structure visible is the *cerebral cortex,* part of the forebrain. The cerebral cortex is the seat of higher mental functions, including thinking, planning, and problem solving. This area of the brain is more highly developed in humans than in any other animal. It is divided into two hemispheres—left and right—that are interconnected by nerve fibers. The hemispheres are thought to be specialized, one side for language and the other for processing of spatial information such as maps and pictures. Each hemisphere controls the opposite side of the body, so that damage to one side of the brain may cause numbness or paralysis of the arm and leg on the opposite side.

The cerebral cortex has four lobes, which are depicted in Exhibit 3.1. As Exhibit 3.2 explains, functions such as vision, hearing, and speech are distributed in specific regions, with some lobes being associated with more than one function. The frontal lobe is the largest, making up nearly one-third of the surface of the cerebral cortex. Lesions of any one of the lobes can have a dramatic impact on the functions of that lobe (Carpenter, 1991; R. Carter, 2009; Earle, 1987). Other forebrain structures process information from the sensory and perceptual organs and structures and send it to the cortex, or receive orders from cortical centers and relay them on down through central nervous system structures to central and peripheral structures throughout the body. Also in the forebrain are centers for memory and emotion, as well as control of essential functions such as hunger, thirst, and biological sex drive.

The midbrain is a small area, but it contains important centers for sleep and pain as well as relay centers for sensory information and control of movement.

In Exhibit 3.1, part of the hindbrain, including the cerebellum, can also be seen. The *cerebellum* controls complex motor programming, including

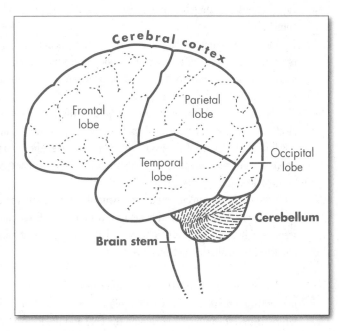

▲ **Exhibit 3.1**   Selected Areas of the Brain

Brain Region	Function
Frontal lobe	Motor behavior
	Expressive language
	Social functioning
	Concentration and ability to attend
	Reasoning and thinking
	Orientation to time, place, and person
Temporal lobe	Language
	Memory
	Emotions
Parietal lobe	Intellectual processing
	Integration of sensory information
Left parietal lobe	Verbal processing
Right parietal lobe	Visual/spatial processing
Occipital lobe	Vision

▲ **Exhibit 3.2**   Regions of the Cerebral Cortex

maintaining muscle tone and posture. Other hindbrain structures are essential to the regulation of basic physiological functions, including breathing, heart rate, and blood pressure. The brain stem connects the cerebral cortex to the spinal cord.

The basic working unit of all the nervous systems is the **neuron,** or nerve cell. The human body has a great diversity of neuronal types, but all consist of a cell body with a nucleus and a conduction fiber, an **axon.** Extending from the cell body are *dendrites,* which conduct impulses to the neurons from the axons of other nerve cells. Exhibit 3.3 shows how neurons are linked by axons and dendrites.

The connection between each axon and dendrite is actually a gap called a **synapse.** Synapses use chemical and electrical **neurotransmitters** to communicate. As the inset box in Exhibit 3.3 shows, nerve impulses travel from the cell body to the ends of the axons, where they trigger the release of neurotransmitters. The adjacent dendrite of another neuron has receptors distinctly shaped to fit particular types of neurotransmitters. When the neurotransmitter fits into a slot, the message is passed along.

Although neurotransmitters are the focus of much current research, scientists have not yet articulated all that positivist research reveals about what neurotransmitters do. Essentially, they may either excite or inhibit nervous system responses. But medical research has revealed very little about many of the neurotransmitters, and may not yet have identified them all. Here are a few:

• *Acetylcholine (ACh):* The first neurotransmitter identified (in 1914 by Henry Hallett Dale and confirmed as a neurotransmitter by Otto Loewi; they jointly received the Nobel Prize in Physiology or Medicine in 1936) is an excitatory neurotransmitter active in both the CNS and the PNS. Acetylcholine may be critical for intellectual activities such as memory.

- *Dopamine (DA):* This neurotransmitter, which is widely present in the CNS and PNS, is implicated in regulation of the endocrine system. Dopamine is thought to play a role in influencing emotional behavior, cognition, and motor activity.

- *Norepinephrine (NE):* Like dopamine, norepinephrine appears in many parts of the body. It may play a role in learning and memory and is also secreted by the adrenal gland in response to stress or events that produce arousal. Norepinephrine connects the brain stem with the cerebral cortex (Bentley & Walsh, 2006).

- *Serotonin:* Present in blood platelets, the lining of the digestive tract, and in a tract from the midbrain to all brain regions, this neurotransmitter is thought to be a factor in many body functions. Serotonin plays a role in sensory processes, muscular activity, thinking, states of consciousness, mood, depression diagnoses, and anxiety diagnoses (Bentley & Walsh, 2006).

- *Amino acids:* Some types of these molecules, which are found in proteins, are distributed throughout the brain and other body tissues. One amino acid, gamma aminobutyric acid (GABA), is thought to play a critical role in inhibiting the firing of impulses of some cells. Thus, GABA is believed to be instrumental in many functions of the CNS, such as locomotor activity, cardiovascular reactions, pituitary function, and anxiety diagnoses (Bentley & Walsh, 2006).

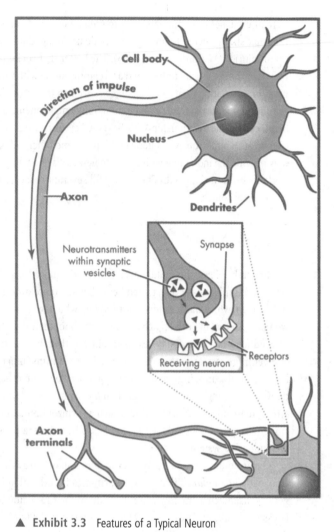

▲ **Exhibit 3.3** Features of a Typical Neuron

- *Peptides:* Amino acids that are joined together have only recently been studied as neurotransmitters. Opioids, many of which are peptides, play an important role in activities ranging from moderating pain to causing sleepiness. Endorphins help to minimize pain and enhance adaptive behavior (Carey, 1990; Sadock & Sadock, 2007).

Biologically, behavior is affected not only by the levels of a neurotransmitter but also the balance between two or more neurotransmitters. Psychotropic medications impact behaviors and symptoms associated with diagnoses of mental illness by affecting the levels of specific neurotransmitters and altering the balance among the neurotransmitters. Social workers approaching their work from a medical diagnostic perspective would be well advised to keep up on medical research about the effects of neurotransmitters on human behavior when working with individuals who are typically referred for medications evaluation and when following up with individuals who have been placed on medication treatment regimens (Bentley & Walsh, 2006).

For Cheryl, as for many people living with traumatic brain injury, her skills, abilities, and atypical changes may be affected by a variety of interior and exterior environment circumstances—including which parts of the brain were injured, her achievements prior to injury, her social and psychological supports, and the training and education that she is offered following her accident. Tremendous advances are being made in rehabilitation following brain injuries (W. Gordon et al., 2006). The better that social workers understand brain functions and brain plasticity, the more they can understand and communicate with medical personnel. We may be able to help with adjustment or adaptation to atypical changes as well as the recovery of functions. Cheryl could benefit from cognitive retraining, support in finding and maintaining employment, family counseling, and individual counseling that will help her end her relationship with Sean. A key to recovery for many individuals who have experienced similar trauma is an opportunity to interact with peers and other individuals with similar experiences. Such peer networks may provide the individual with access to new skills and a key link to exterior environment social support. A social worker who is working with Cheryl may fill several roles: case manager, advocate, counselor, resource coordinator, and referral source.

Endocrine System

Remember Bess, the middle-aged woman diagnosed with diabetes? If you had first met her in a nonhospital setting, you might have interpreted her behaviors quite differently. Because of the recent rural health initiative in Bess's town, which has a number of residents who have relocated from French Canada, it was not unusual to hear women speaking in both French and English about their diets and exercises, and initially you may have been quite pleased for Bess's success. If Bess had told you that she was tired, you might have suggested that she slow down and get more rest, or perhaps that she include vitamins in her diet. Sitting in the morning in her nightclothes on her couch and missing work might suggest alcohol or other drug use. Confusion, switching back and forth between speaking French and English in the same sentence, and inability to answer simple questions could signal stroke, dementia, or a mental illness such as schizophrenia. But only a thorough medical assessment of her interior environment revealed the cause of Bess's behaviors: a physical health condition traceable to a malfunction in the endocrine system.

The **endocrine system** plays a crucial role in our growth, metabolism, development, learning, and memory. It is made up of *glands* that secrete hormones into the blood system; those hormones bind to receptors in target organs, much as neurotransmitters do in the brain, and affect the metabolism or function of those organs (Besser & Thorner, 1994; Kapit, Macey, & Meisami, 2000; Mader, 2003; Rosenzweig, Breedlove, & Watson, 2004; Rosenzweig & Leiman, 1989). Distinguishing differences between hormones and neurotransmitters are often the distance of travel from the point of release to the target, as well as the route of travel. Hormones travel long distances through the bloodstream; neurotransmitters travel shorter distances from cell to cell, across the synaptic cleft.

Endocrine glands include the pineal, pituitary, thyroid, parathyroid, pancreas, and adrenal. Endocrine cells are also found in some organs that have primarily a non-endocrine function: the hypothalamus, liver, thymus, heart, kidney, stomach, duodenum, testes, and ovaries. Exhibit 3.4 lists some of the better-known glands and organs, the hormones they produce, and their effects on other body structures.

The most basic form of hormonal communication is from an endocrine cell through the blood system to a target cell. A more complex form of hormonal communication is directly from an endocrine gland to a target endocrine gland.

The endocrine system regulates the secretion of hormones through a **feedback control mechanism.** Output consists of hormones released from an endocrine gland; input consists of hormones taken into a target tissue or organ. The system is self-regulating. Similar to neurotransmitters, hormones have specific receptors, so that the hormone released from one gland has a specific target tissue or organ (Mader, 2003).

Systems perspective

Gland	Hormone	Effect
Hypothalamus	Releasing and release-inhibiting factors	■ Targets pituitary gland, which affects many hormonal activities
Pituitary	Adrenocorticotropic (ACTH) Growth (GH, somatotropic) Vasopressin Prolactin	■ Stimulates adrenal cortex ■ Stimulates cell division, protein synthesis, and bone growth ■ Stimulates water reabsorption by kidneys ■ Stimulates milk production in mammary glands
Testes	Androgens (testosterone)	■ Stimulates development of sex organs, skin, muscles, bones, and sperm ■ Stimulates development and maintenance of secondary male sex characteristics
Ovaries	Estrogen and progesterone	■ Stimulates development of sex organs, skin, muscles, bones, and uterine lining ■ Stimulates development and maintenance of secondary female sex characteristics
Adrenal	Epinephrine Adrenal Cortical Steroids	■ Stimulates fight-or-flight reactions in heart and other muscles ■ Raises blood glucose levels ■ Stimulates sex characteristics
Pancreas	Insulin Glucagon	■ Targets liver, muscles, adipose tissues ■ Lowers blood glucose levels ■ Promotes formation of glycogen, proteins, and fats
Thymus	Thymosins	■ Triggers development of T lymphocytes, which orchestrate immune system response
Pineal	Melatonin	■ Maintains circadian rhythms (daily cycles of activity)
Thyroid	Thyroxin	■ Plays role in growth and development ■ Stimulates metabolic rate of all organs

▲ **Exhibit 3.4** Selected Endocrine Glands and Their Effects

A good example of a feedback loop is presented in Exhibit 3.5. The hypothalamus secretes the gonadotropin-releasing hormone (GnRH), which binds to receptors in the anterior pituitary and stimulates the secretion of the luteinizing hormone (LH). LH binds to receptors in the ovaries to stimulate the production of estrogen. Estrogen has a negative effect on the secretion of LH and GnRH at both the pituitary and hypothalamus, thus completing the loop. Loops like these allow the body to finely control the secretion of hormones.

Another good way to understand the feedback control mechanism is to observe the results when it malfunctions. Consider what has happened to Bess, who has been diagnosed with the most common illness caused by hormonal imbalance: **diabetes mellitus.** Insulin deficiency or resistance to insulin's effects is the basis of diabetes. Insulin and

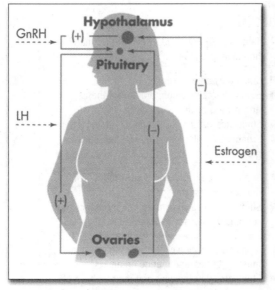

▲ **Exhibit 3.5**   An Example of a Feedback Loop

glucagon, which are released by the pancreas, regulate the metabolism of carbohydrates, the source of cell energy. They are essential for the maintenance of blood glucose levels (blood sugar). High blood glucose levels stimulate the release of insulin, which in turn helps to decrease blood sugar by promoting the uptake of glucose by tissues. Low blood sugar stimulates the release of glucagon, which in turn stimulates the liver to release glucose, raising blood sugar. In individuals with insulin deficiency, muscle cells are deprived of glucose. As an alternative, those muscle cells tap fat and protein reserves in muscle tissue as an energy source. The results include wasting of muscles; weakness; weight loss; and *metabolic acidosis,* a chemical imbalance in the blood. The increase in blood acidity suppresses higher nervous system functions, leading to coma. Suppression of the respiratory centers in the brain leads to death (Kapit et al., 2000).

Epidemiologists report a dramatic increase in the incidence of diabetes worldwide in recent years (Zimmet, Alberti, & Shaw, 2001). There are currently 23.6 million persons (7.8% of the population) in the United States who have diabetes. There are 17.9 million persons who have been diagnosed with diabetes, with an estimated 5.7 million having undiagnosed diabetes (National Institute of Diabetes and Digestive and Kidney Diseases [NIDDK], 2008). Nearly 800,000 new cases of diabetes are diagnosed each year, or 2,200 per day. The number of persons who have been diagnosed with diabetes has shown a steady increase over the past 15 years. It is estimated that $1 out of every $10 spent on health care in the United States is spent on diabetes and its consequences (American Diabetes Association, n.d.). Juvenile-onset diabetes (type 1) is found in children and young adults; risk factors may be autoimmune, genetic, or environmental. Non-Hispanic Whites are at greater risk of developing type 1 diabetes than other racial and ethnic groups. No known way to prevent type 1 diabetes exists. Maturity-onset diabetes (type 2), non-insulin-dependent diabetes mellitus, most commonly arises in individuals over the age of 40 who are also obese. Type 2 diabetes is associated with older age, obesity, family history of diabetes, history of gestational diabetes, impaired glucose metabolism, physical inactivity, and particular races/ethnicities. Latinos, Native Americans, Asian Americans, and non-Hispanic Blacks are twice as likely to have type 2 diabetes as non-Hispanic Whites. Gestational diabetes is a third type, a form of glucose intolerance diagnosed during pregnancy. This form of diabetes occurs more frequently among African Americans, Hispanic/Latino Americans, and Native Americans, than among other populations (NIDDK, 2008).

For Bess, as for many individuals with symptoms indicating the presence of a medical condition, a crucial role for the social worker is to facilitate access to and comprehension of information and knowledge about the symptoms and the diagnosed condition. Social workers can also aid in the translation of this information, so clients such as Bess, whose first language is French and who might not understand medical jargon, can grasp what is happening to them. The social worker may also help Bess begin to examine the lifestyle changes that may be suggested by this diagnosis. What might it mean in terms of diet, exercise, home and work responsibilities, and so forth? Bess may need assistance in working with her insurance company as she plans how her care will be financed. She may also need counseling as she works to adjust to life with this new medical diagnosis.

Rational choice perspective

Immune System

Melissa is far from alone in testing positive for HIV. The Centers for Disease Control and Prevention (CDC, 2009d) estimated that approximately 56,300 people were newly infected with HIV in 2006 (the most recent year that such diagnostic data was recorded). Nearly 1 out of every 250, or about 1 million Americans, is infected with the **human immunodeficiency virus (HIV),** the virus that causes **AIDS—acquired immunodeficiency syndrome.** In 2005, Glynn and Rhodes suggested that 24% to 27% of the people in the United States infected with HIV are not aware of their infection. It is estimated that the number of diagnoses of AIDS through 2007 in the United States and dependent areas was 1,051,875; the estimated number of people newly diagnosed with AIDS in 2007 in the United States and dependent areas was 35,962 (CDC, 2009a).

It has been estimated that 33.4 million (31.1 million–35.8 million) people are living with HIV worldwide, that 2.7 million (2.4 million–3.0 million) people were newly infected in 2008, and that 2 million (1.7–2.4 million) people died of AIDS-related illness in 2008 (Joint United Nations Programme on HIV/AIDS [UNAIDS], 2009). The good news is that according to the 2009 AIDS epidemic update by UNAIDS, new infections of HIV have been reduced 17% over the past 8 years. In addition, the number of AIDS-related deaths has declined 10% over the past 5 years.

Cumulatively, the estimated number of adults and adolescents diagnosed with AIDS in the United States and dependent areas is 1,009,200, with 810,676 cases in males; 198,544 cases in females; and 9,200 cases estimated in children under age 13. These represent point estimates, which result from adjustments of reported case counts (CDC, 2009a). Persons of all ages and racial and ethnic groups are affected. The cumulative estimates of the number of AIDS cases from the beginning of the epidemic through 2007 include 404,465 cases of AIDS among Whites (not Hispanic); 426,003 cases among Black African Americans (not Hispanic); 169,138 cases among Hispanics/Latinos; 7,511 cases among Asian/Pacific Islanders; 3,492 cases among American Indians/Alaska Natives; and 721 among Native Hawaiians/Other Pacific Islanders.

HIV/AIDS is a relatively new disease, and early in its history, it was assumed to be terminal. The introduction of highly active antiretroviral therapy (HAART) that became widespread in the United States in 1996 altered the perception of AIDS. It came to be seen as a chronic instead of terminal disease. The reality is that, although some are living longer with the disease, others are still dying young. In 2002, HIV/AIDS was the leading cause of death in the United States for Black (not Hispanic) females ages 25–44 (R. Anderson, 2002). The CDC in 2009 estimated that the number of deaths of persons with AIDS in the United States and dependent areas was 14,561; this included 14,105 adults and adolescents, and 5 children under age 13. The cumulative estimated number of deaths in the United States and dependent areas through 2007 was 583,298. This report further states that when considering only the 50 states and the District of Columbia, cumulative estimated number of deaths included 557,902 adults and adolescents, and 4,891 children under age 13 years (CDC, 2009a).

The Centers for Disease Control and Prevention (2009a) has also reported that the six common transmission categories for HIV are male-to-male sexual contact, injection drug use, male-to-male sexual contact *and* injection drug use, high-risk heterosexual (male–female) contact, mother-to-child (perinatal) transmission, and other (includes blood transfusions and unknown causes). According to the CDC (2005a), the fastest growing groups of persons reported with HIV have been men and women who acquire HIV through heterosexual contact, a group to which Melissa now belongs. Although HIV is more easily transmitted from men to women, it can be transmitted from women to men as well. Heterosexual transmission occurs mainly through vaginal intercourse.

Once a person is infected with HIV, the disease-fighting immune system gradually weakens. This weakened immune system lets other diseases begin to attack the body. Over the next few years, Melissa will learn a great deal about how her body protects itself or does not against disease and infection. The **immune system** is made up of organs and cells that work together to defend the body against disease (Kennedy, Kiecolt-Glaser, & Glaser, 1988;

Sarafino, 2008). When operating in an optimal manner, the immune system is able to distinguish our own cells and organs from foreign elements (Sarafino, 2008). When the body recognizes something as exterior or foreign, the immune system mobilizes body resources and attacks. Remember that we cautioned you about the arbitrary distinction between exterior and interior environments? Here is a good example: The foreign substance (which may be organic in composition and thus fit the definition of interior environment) that can trigger an immune response may be a tissue or organ transplant or, more commonly, an antigen. **Antigens** include bacteria, fungi, protozoa, and viruses.

Sometimes, however, the immune system is mistakenly directed at parts of the body it was designed to protect, resulting in **autoimmune diseases.** Examples include rheumatoid arthritis, rheumatic fever, and lupus erythematosus. With rheumatoid arthritis, the immune system is directed against tissues and bones at the joints. In rheumatic fever, the immune system targets the muscles of the heart. With lupus erythematosus, the immune system affects various parts of the interior environment, including the skin and kidneys (Sarafino, 2008).

Organs of the immune system are located throughout the body. They have primary involvement in the development of **lymphocytes,** or white blood cells (Sarafino, 2008). The main lymphatic organs include the following:

- Bone marrow: The largest organ in the body, it is the soft tissue in the core of bones. There are two types of bone marrow, red and yellow. Yellow bone marrow stores fat, which the body consumes only as a last resort in cases of extreme starvation. At birth, all bone marrow is red, but as the body ages, more and more red bone marrow is converted to yellow. In adults, red bone marrow is found in the sternum, ribs, vertebrae, skull, and long bones. The bone marrow produces both red (erythrocytes) and white (leukocytes and lymphocytes) blood cells.

- Lymph nodes: Small oval or round spongy masses distributed throughout the body (Sarafino, 2008). Lymph nodes are connected by a network of lymphatic vessels that contain a clear fluid called *lymph,* whose job is to bathe cells and remove bacteria and certain proteins. As the lymph passes through a lymph node, it is purified of infectious organisms. These vessels ultimately empty into the bloodstream.

- Spleen: An organ in the upper left quadrant of the abdomen. The spleen functions much like a very large lymph node, except that instead of lymph, blood passes through it. The spleen filters out antigens and removes ineffective or worn-out red blood cells from the body (Sarafino, 2008). An injured spleen can be removed, but the individual becomes more susceptible to certain infections (Mader, 2003).

- Thymus: Located along the trachea in the chest behind the sternum, the thymus secretes *thymosins,* hormones believed to trigger the development of T cells. *T cells,* white blood cells that mature in the thymus, have the task of slowing down, fighting, and attacking antigens (Mader, 2003).

The immune system's response to antigens occurs in both specific and nonspecific ways. **Nonspecific immunity** is more general. "Scavenger" cells, or phagocytes, circulate in the blood and lymph, being attracted by biochemical signals to congregate at the site of a wound and ingest antigens (Safyer & Spies-Karotkin, 1988; Sarafino, 2008). This process, known as *phagocytosis,* is quite effective but has two limitations: (1) Certain bacteria and most viruses can survive after they have been engulfed, and (2) because our bodies are under constant attack and our phagocytes are constantly busy, a major assault on the immune system can easily overwhelm the nonspecific response. Thus, specific immunity is essential (Safyer & Spies-Karotkin, 1988).

Specific immunity, or acquired immunity, involves the lymphocytes. They not only respond to an infection, but they also develop a *memory* of that infection and allow the body to make rapid defense against it in subsequent exposure. Certain lymphocytes produce **antibodies,** protein molecules designed to attach to the surface of specific invaders. The antibodies recruit other protein substances that puncture the membrane of invading microorganisms, causing the invaders to explode. The antibodies are assisted in this battle by T cells, which destroy foreign cells directly and orchestrate the immune response. Following the *primary response,* the antibodies remain in the circulatory system at significant levels until they are no longer needed. With reexposure to the same antigen, a *secondary immune response* occurs, characterized by a more rapid rise in antibody levels—over a period of hours rather than days. This rapid response is possible because, during initial exposure to the antigen, memory cells were created. *Memory T cells* store the information needed to produce specific antibodies. They also have very long lives (Safyer & Spies-Karotkin, 1988; Sprent & Surth, 2001).

The immune system becomes increasingly effective throughout childhood and declines in effectiveness in older adulthood. Infants are born with relatively little immune defense, but their immune system gradually becomes more efficient and complex. Thus, as the child develops, the incidence of serious illness declines. During adolescence and most of adulthood, the immune system, for most individuals, functions at a high level of effectiveness. As we age, although the numbers of lymphocytes and antibodies circulating in the lymph and blood do not decrease, their potency diminishes.

Developmental perspective

The functioning of the immune system can be hampered by a diet that is low in vitamins A, E, and C and high in fats and cholesterol, and by excess weight (Sarafino, 2008). There are also far more serious problems that can occur with the immune system, such as HIV, that are life threatening. HIV, like other viruses, infects "normal" cells and "hijacks" their genetic machinery. These infected cells in essence become factories that make copies of the HIV, which then go on to infect other cells. The hijacked cells are destroyed. A favorite target of HIV is the T cells that tell other cells when to start fighting off infections. HIV thus weakens the immune system and makes it increasingly difficult for the body to fight off other diseases and infections. Most of us host organisms such as fungi, viruses, and parasites that live inside us without causing disease. However, for people with HIV, because of the low T cell count, these same organisms can cause serious infection. When such a disease occurs or when the individual's number of T cells drops below a certain level, the person with HIV is considered to have AIDS (Cressey & Lallemant, 2007).

Melissa's life may undergo significant changes as symptoms of HIV infection begin to emerge. Melissa may be at increased risk for repeated serious yeast infections of the vagina, and she may also be at increased risk for cancer of the cervix and pelvic inflammatory disease. Both men and women are vulnerable to opportunistic diseases and infections such as Kaposi's sarcoma, cytomegalovirus (CMV), AIDS retinopathy, pneumocystis carinii pneumonia (PCP), mycobacterium tuberculosis, and Candida albicans (thrush); atypical functioning such as AIDS dementia, loss of memory, loss of judgment, and depression; and other symptoms such as gastrointestinal dysfunction/distress, joint pain, anemia, and low platelet counts. The social worker may help to educate Melissa about these increased risks. In order to protect her health and the health of others, Melissa will most likely be advised to take special precautions. She can be supported in staying well by getting early treatment, adopting a healthy lifestyle, and remaining hopeful and informed about new treatments (Patterson et al., 1996).

The social worker also may have a role to play in working with Melissa as she tells her family and fiancé about her diagnosis. Melissa and her fiancé may need advice about how to practice safe sex. The social worker should also be available to work with Melissa, her fiancé, and her family as they adjust to her diagnosis and the grief frequently associated with it. The social worker may explore reactions and responses of Melissa, her fiancé, and her parents to this health crisis.

Because of the tremendous costs for medications, particularly the new HAART, the social worker may link Melissa to sources of financial support. This aid will become increasingly critical if she gets sicker, her income declines, and her medical expenses increase. Given recent advances in medical diagnostics and therapeutics, recent estimates indicate that the lifetime costs of health care associated with HIV may be more than $385,200 per person who is diagnosed as an adult (Schackman et al., 2006). Treatment with HAART is not a cure, but it allows the individual with HIV to fight off other infections and live longer (Markowitz, 1997). However, side effects of some of the drugs are just as debilitating as the effects of AIDS.

In addition to providing Melissa with information about her immune system, HIV, AIDS, and other physical health issues, the social worker can advise Melissa of the protections guaranteed to her under the Americans with Disabilities Act of 1990. Melissa has joined an HIV support group, but the social worker may also offer to provide her with or refer her to counseling. The social worker may also have a role to play on behalf of all people with HIV/AIDS, working to address prevention and public health in part by providing HIV/AIDS education to business groups, schools, civic and volunteer associations, and neighborhood groups and by influencing policy to support public health HIV prevention initiatives.

Critical Thinking Questions 3.1

How important is it for Cheryl, Bess, and Melissa to be well informed about their medical conditions? How would you advise them about possible sources of information for their specific conditions? How should their social workers go about becoming better informed about their medical conditions?

Cardiovascular System

According to current estimates, 80 million people in the United States, or more than one in five, have one or more types of *cardiovascular disease* (CVD), the most common cause of death in this country (American Heart Association, 2009).

An estimated 73,600,000 people in the United States ages 6 and over have high blood pressure, over 17 million (17,600,000) have a history of coronary heart disease ("heart attack"), and 6.4 million have a history of having had a stroke. CVD claimed 831,272lives (34.3% of all deaths, or 1 of every 2.9 in 2006). Over 151,000 Americans killed by CVD in that year were under the age of 65. The final death rates from CVD per 100,000 population in the United States in 2006 were 306.6 for White males, 422.8 for Black males, 215.5 for White females, and 298.2 for Black females (American Heart Association, 2010). In 2005, strokes killed 143,579 people in the United States; in 2006, strokes killed 137,119 (American Heart Association, 2009). Stroke is the third leading cause of death (American Heart Association, 2006; U.S. Department of Health and Human Services, 2000). In the United States, stroke is the leading cause of serious, long-term disability (American Heart Association, 2009). The death rates per 100,000 population for stroke in 2006 were 41.7 for White males, 67.1 for Black males, 41.1 for White females, and 57.0 for Black females (American Heart Association, 2009). In 2003, the rates of stroke among Mexican Americans were 2.6% for males and 1.8% for females; among Hispanic persons or Latinos (male and female), the rate was 2.2%; it was 1.8% among Asians (male and female) and 3.1% among American Indians/Alaska Natives (males and females) (American Heart Association, 2006a). In the United States, the death rate from heart disease has been consistently higher in males than in females and higher among African Americans than among Whites (U.S. Department of Health and Human Services, 2000). The rate of nonfatal strokes for Blacks in the United States is 1.3 times that of non-Hispanic Whites, the rate of fatal stroke is 1.8 times greater, and the rate of death from heart disease is 1.5 times greater (American Heart Association, 2006).

Thomas's cardiovascular diagnosis is **high blood pressure (hypertension),** defined as a systolic blood pressure equal to or greater than (≥) 140 mm Hg and/or a diastolic blood pressure ≥90 mm Hg (his was 200/105). Blacks,

Puerto Ricans, Cubans, and Mexican Americans are all more likely to suffer from high blood pressure than are Whites, and the number of existing cases of high blood pressure is nearly 40% higher among Blacks than among Whites. An estimated 6.4 million Blacks have high blood pressure, with more frequent and severe effects than in other population subgroups (U.S. Department of Health and Human Services, 2000). The prevalence of hypertension among Blacks in the United States is among the highest rates in the world.

In 2006, it was estimated that one in three adults had high blood pressure, with 77.6% of those individuals having been aware of their condition. In 90%–95% of the cases of individuals with high blood pressure, the cause is unknown. The death rate from high blood pressure has steadily increased (by 19.5%) from 1996 to 2006, with the actual number of deaths having risen 48.1%. The death rates per 100,000 population from high blood pressure in 2006 were 15.6 for White males, 51.1 for Black males, 14.3 for White females, and 37.7 for Black females (American Heart Association, 2009). High blood pressure also tends to be more common in people with lower education and income levels (N. Adler, 2006).

The cost of cardiovascular disease and stroke in 2005 was estimated to exceed $394 billion, including $242 billion for health care expenses and $152 billion for lost productivity (CDC, 2005b). According to the American Heart Association (2006), the estimated combined direct and indirect cost associated with high blood pressure for 2006 is $63.5 billion.

To better understand cardiovascular disease, it is first important to gain insight into the functioning of the **cardiovascular system,** which is composed of the heart and the blood circulatory system (Kapit et al., 2000; Mader, 2003). The heart's walls are made up of specialized muscle. As the muscle shortens and squeezes the hollow cavities of the heart, blood is forced in the directions permitted by the opening or closing of valves. Blood vessels continually carry blood from the heart to the rest of the body's tissues and then return the blood to the heart. Exhibit 3.6 shows the direction of the blood's flow through the heart.

There are three types of blood vessels:

1. Arteries: These have thick walls containing elastic and muscular tissues. The elastic tissues allow the arteries to expand and accommodate the increase in blood volume that occurs after each heartbeat. Arterioles are small arteries that branch into smaller vessels called capillaries.

2. Capillaries: A critical part of this closed circulation system, they allow the exchange of nutrients and waste material with the body's cells. Oxygen and nutrients transfer out of a capillary into the tissue fluid surrounding cells and absorb carbon dioxide and other wastes from the cells.

3. Veins: These take blood from the capillaries and return it to the heart. Some of the major veins in the arms and legs have valves allowing the blood to flow only toward the heart when they are open and block any backward flow when they are closed (Kapit et al., 2000; Mader, 2003).

The heart has two sides (right and left), separated by the septum. Each side is divided into an upper and a lower chamber. The two upper, thin-walled chambers are called **atria.** The atria are smaller than the two lower, thick-walled chambers, called **ventricles.** Valves within the heart direct the flow of blood from chamber to chamber, and when closed, prevent its backward flow (Kapit et al., 2000; Mader, 2003).

As Exhibit 3.6 shows, the right side of the heart pumps blood to the lungs, and the left side pumps blood to the tissues of the body. Blood from body tissues that is low in oxygen and high in carbon dioxide (deoxygenated blood) enters the right atrium. The right atrium then sends blood through a valve to the right ventricle. The right ventricle then sends the blood through another valve and the pulmonary arteries into the lungs. In the lungs, the blood gives up carbon dioxide and takes up oxygen. Pulmonary veins then carry blood that is high in oxygen (oxygenated) from

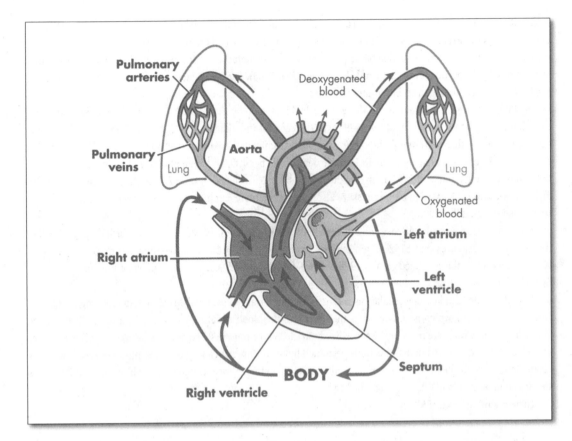

Pulmonary arteries

Deoxygenated blood

Pulmonary veins

Aorta

Lung

Lung

Oxygenated blood

Left atrium

Right atrium

Left ventricle

BODY

Septum

Right ventricle

▲ **Exhibit 3.6**   The Direction of Blood Flow Through the Heart

the lungs to the left atrium. From the left atrium, blood is sent through a valve to the left ventricle. The blood is then sent through a valve into the aorta for distribution around the body (Kapit et al., 2000; Mader, 2003).

Contraction and relaxation of the heart moves the blood from the ventricles to the lungs and to the body. The right and left sides of the heart contract together—first the two atria, then the two ventricles. The heart contracts ("beats") about 70 times per minute when the body is at rest. The contraction and relaxation cycle is called the cardiac cycle. The sound of the heartbeat, as heard through a stethoscope, is caused by the opening and closing of the heart valves.

Although the heart will beat independently of any nervous system stimulation, regulation of the heart is primarily the responsibility of the ANS. *Parasympathetic activities* of the nervous system, which tend to be thought of as normal or routine activities, slow the heart rate. *Sympathetic activities,* associated with stress, increase the heart rate. As blood is pumped from the aorta into the arteries, their elastic walls swell, followed by an immediate recoiling. The alternating expansion and recoiling of the arterial wall is the pulse. The normal pulse rate at rest for children ages 6–15 is 70-100 beats per minute; for adults age 18 and over, the normal pulse rate at rest is 60–100 beats per minute (Cleveland Clinic, 2005–2009).

Blood pressure is the measure of the pressure of the blood against the wall of a blood vessel. A *sphygmomanometer* is used to measure blood pressure. The cuff of the sphygmomanometer is placed around the upper arm over an artery. A pressure gauge is used to measure the *systolic blood pressure,* the highest arterial pressure, which results from ejection of blood from the aorta. *Diastolic blood pressure,* the lowest arterial pressure, occurs while the ventricles of the heart are relaxing. Medically desired and healthy blood pressure for a young adult is 120 mm of mercury systole over 80 mm of mercury diastole, or 120/80 (Kapit et al., 2000; Mader, 2003).

Blood pressure accounts for the movement of blood from the heart to the body by way of arteries and arterioles, but skeletal muscle contraction moves the blood through the venous system. As skeletal muscles contract, they push against the thin or weak walls of the veins, causing the blood to move past valves. Once past the valve, the blood cannot return, forcing it to move toward the heart.

High blood pressure has been called the silent killer, because many people like Thomas have it without noticeable symptoms. It is the leading cause of strokes and is a major risk factor for heart attacks and kidney failure.

Suddenly faced with startling information, such as a dramatic change in what was believed to be good health, Thomas might experience a range of responses, including but not limited to denial, questioning, self-reflection, self-critique, and even anger. The social worker can play many critical roles with Thomas. Perceptions of exterior conditions such as racial discrimination, daily hassles, and stressful life events place him at increased risk for having a stroke or dying as a result of his high blood pressure (Paradies, 2006). Social workers are uniquely positioned to see the links between external environment issues—such as vocational and educational opportunities, economics and income, housing, and criminal victimization—and interior environment health issues.

> Conflict perspective

On an individual level, possession of knowledge to access the benefits of medical examination and treatment would be warranted for Thomas. The social worker can participate in medical care by helping Thomas learn the essential elements of effective health practice, including knowledge of what it means to have high blood pressure, the causes, and strategies for decreasing the health risks. If medication is prescribed, the social worker can support the medication regimen and Thomas's decision about how to follow it.

The social worker also can process with Thomas a strategy for identifying and deciding on his preferred lifestyle changes to help lower his blood pressure. These may include examination of sources of stress and patterns of coping, diet, how much exercise he gets on a regular basis, and his social and economic external environmental conditions.

Because high blood pressure has been shown to run in families, the social worker can also work with Thomas's family to discuss lifestyle factors that might contribute to high blood pressure, such as exposure to stress, cigarette/tobacco use, a diet high in cholesterol, physical inactivity, and excess weight.

> Systems perspective

Because African Americans and some other minorities have been shown to be at increased risk for high blood pressure, the social worker may work with community organizations, community centers, and religious organizations to advance policy and public health practices to support education and prevention programs as well as a physician and health care provider referral program. These health issues have been shown to be related to exterior environment experiences of discrimination and prejudice, and thus the social worker should pay attention to the external environment issues that negatively affect groups and individuals.

Musculoskeletal System

Today, polio, a viral infection of the nerves that control muscles, has been nearly eradicated in industrialized countries. But in the middle of the 20th century, the disease was much more common, and it temporarily or permanently paralyzed both children and adults. The first outbreak of polio in the United States occurred in 1843 (University of Cincinnati, 2001–2010). According to the College of Medicine at the University of Cincinnati, in 1952 there were 21,000 cases of polio paralysis in the United States, with the last case of wild-virus acquired polio being diagnosed in 1979. By 1991, new cases of wild-virus acquired poliomyelitis syndrome had disappeared from the Western Hemisphere; by 1997, the Western Pacific was polio free; and by 2002, the European region was polio free (University of Cincinnati, 2001–2010). As of 2008, only four countries remain polio-endemic. This is down from more that 125 countries in 1998.

The four remaining countries are Afghanistan, India, Nigeria, and Pakistan (World Health Organization [WHO], 2008a). According to the World Health Organization (2006c), the total confirmed cases of polio diagnosed in 2006, as of July 27, was 597 for Africa, 0 for the Americas, 58 for the Eastern Mediterranean, 0 for Europe, 134 for Southeast Asia, and 1 for the Western Pacific. Of the 440,000 people living with polio in the United States, about 25 to 50% may be affected by **post-poliomyelitis syndrome (PPS),** progressive atrophy of muscles in those who once had polio (National Institute of Neurological Disorders and Stroke, 2006). Case Study 3.5, at the beginning of the chapter, involves Max, who has PPS.

PPS has many causes. Some of the symptoms may be the result of the natural aging of muscles and joints damaged by polio or by overuse of unaffected muscles. Unrelated medical conditions may lead to new symptoms in people who have had polio and a progression of earlier weaknesses. Unexplained atypical muscle atrophy and weakness may also develop. The overuse or repetitive use of weakened muscle fibers and tissues may lead to musculoskeletal pain, which in turn may lead to further atrophy, a need for increased rest, and possibly an increasing level of impairment (Gevirtz, 2006).

For Max, as for many people who have had polio, this onset of new symptoms is unexpected. It may signal increasing physical impairment, which may require new adjustments and adaptations. A social worker who is working with Max should first acquire a knowledge base and then identify his strengths, resources, and perceived needs for intervention.

At the center of PPS is dysfunction in the **musculoskeletal system,** which supports and protects the body and provides motion. The contraction and relaxation of muscles attached to the skeleton is the basis for all voluntary movements. Over 600 skeletal muscles in the body account for about 40% of our body weight (Mader, 2003). When a muscle contracts, it shortens; it can only pull, not push. Therefore, for us to be able to extend and to flex at a joint, muscles work in "antagonistic" pairs. As an example, when the hamstring group in the back of the leg contracts, the quadriceps in the front relax; this allows the leg to bend at the knee. When the quadriceps contract, the hamstring relaxes, allowing the leg to extend.

The contraction of a muscle occurs as a result of an electrical impulse passed to the muscle by a controlling nerve that releases acetylcholine. When a single stimulus is given to a muscle, it responds with a twitch, a contraction lasting only a fraction of a second. But when there are repeated stimulations close together, the muscle cannot fully relax between impulses. As a result, each contraction benefits from the previous contraction, giving a combined contraction that is greater than an individual twitch. When stimulation is sufficiently rapid, the twitches cease to be jerky and fuse into a smooth contraction/movement called *tetanus.* However, tetanus that continues eventually produces muscle fatigue due to depletion of energy reserves.

Skeletal muscles exhibit tone when some muscles are always contracted. Tone is critical if we are to maintain body posture. If all the muscle fibers in the neck, trunk, and legs were to relax, our bodies would collapse. Nerve fibers embedded in the muscles emit impulses that communicate to the CNS the state of particular muscles. This communication allows the CNS to coordinate the contraction of muscles (Kapit et al., 2000; Mader, 2003). In its entirety, the musculoskeletal system both supports the body and allows it to move. The skeleton, particularly the large heavy bones of the legs, supports the body against the pull of gravity and protects soft body parts. Most essential, the skull protects the brain, the rib cage protects the heart and lungs, and the vertebrae protect and support the spinal cord.

Bones serve as sites for the attachment of muscles. It may not seem so, but bone is a very active tissue, supplied with nerves and blood vessels. Throughout life, bone cells repair, remold, and rejuvenate in response to stresses, strains, and fractures (Kapit et al., 2000). A typical long bone, such as the arm and leg bones, has a cavity surrounded by a dense area. The dense area contains compact bone; the cavernous area contains blood vessels and nerves surrounded by spongy bone. Far from being weak, spongy bone is designed for strength. It is the site of red marrow, the specialized tissue that produces red and white blood cells. The cavity of a long bone also contains yellow marrow, which is a fat-storage tissue (Kapit et al., 2000; Mader, 2003).

Developmental perspective

Most bones begin as cartilage. In long bones, growth and calcification (hardening) begin in early childhood and continue through adolescence. Growth hormones and thyroid hormones stimulate bone growth during childhood.

Androgens, which are responsible for the adolescent growth spurt, stimulate bone growth during puberty. In late adolescence, androgens terminate bone growth.

Bones are joined together at joints. Long bones and their corresponding joints are what permit flexible body movement (Mader, 2003). Joints are classified according to the amount of movement they permit. Bones of the cranium, which are sutured together, are examples of immovable joints. Joints between the vertebrae are slightly movable. Freely movable joints, which connect two bones separated by a cavity, are called *synovial joints.* Synovial joints may be hinge joints (knee and elbow) or ball-and-socket joints (attachment of the femur to the hipbone). Exhibit 3.7 shows the structure of the knee joint. Synovial joints are prone to arthritis because the bones gradually lose their protective covering and grate against each other as they move (Mader, 2003).

The bones in a joint are held together by *ligaments,* while *tendons* connect muscle to bone.

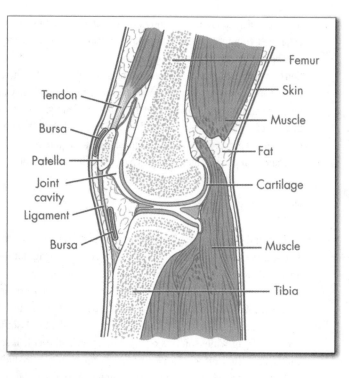

▲ **Exhibit 3.7**   Structure of the Knee Joint

The ends of the bones are capped by cartilage, which gives added strength and support to the joint. Friction between tendons and ligaments and between tendons and bones is eased by fluid-filled sacs called *bursae.* Inflammation of the bursae is called bursitis.

Although overuse is damaging to the musculoskeletal system, underuse is, too. Without a certain amount of use, muscles atrophy and bone density declines. Thus, the advice given to many individuals who were diagnosed with polio has been to "use it or lose it." Unfortunately, this advice may have inadvertently contributed to Max's post-polio symptoms.

Because of the commonly held perspective that individual independence is most desirable, it is not unusual for social workers and other health care professionals to discourage a person with a medical explanation for atypical function from using exterior environmental modifications and resources when they are not essential. These may include ramps, elevators, and electrically operated doors or assistive devices. **Assistive devices** are those products that are designated by the medical community to help a person to communicate, see, hear, or maneuver. Examples that have been used by individuals with atypical activity include manual wheelchairs, motorized wheelchairs, motorized scooters, and other aids that enhance mobility; hearing aids, telephone communication devices, assistive listening devices, visual and audible signal systems, and other aids that enhance an individual's ability to hear; and voice-synthesized computer modules, optical scanners, talking software, Braille printers, and other devices that enhance an individual's ability to communicate.

Those who believe that working to "overcome" challenges is a helpful approach in adjusting to or working with atypical function are well meaning. But hidden within this belief system is the impression that being labeled as "disabled" ascribes deficiency that makes an individual less than whole, less than competent, and less than capable. Having attended school before the Rehabilitation Act of 1973, the Individuals with Disabilities Education Act of 1975, and the Americans with Disabilities Act of 1990, Max's early years were spent in a world with little understanding or acceptance of his atypical gait. For Max, as for many people considered to be "disabled" on the basis of an atypical function, the pressure was and often is to "overcome" or to succeed in spite of a disability. Possibly, that interior and exterior environment pressure may have contributed to Max's current post-polio exacerbation.

The social worker has many options or none for working with Max. Max may choose to receive a thorough examination by a physician knowledgeable about polio and PPS and stop there. If Max seeks social services, the social worker will then be able to serve as a resource and referral agent. He or she may work with other rehabilitation professionals, such as physical therapists and occupational therapists, in identifying useful adaptations in Max's home and work environment that he could choose to use if he so desired. The social worker can provide counseling but may also refer Max to a PPS peer support group. Because Max might choose to acquire new technology, the social worker may also intervene with insurance companies reluctant to purchase expensive equipment.

Reproductive System

Juan and Belinda are at the age when an understanding of reproduction and sexuality is critical. In the United States, as in many countries around the globe, the typical age for the first experience of sexual intercourse is approximately 17, with 75% of high school seniors reporting having had sexual intercourse. Moreover, on average, there are almost 8 years for women and 10 years for men between first intercourse and first marriage (Alan Guttmacher Institute, 2006). According to the Centers for Disease Control and Prevention (2007), 47.8% of high school students reported having had sexual intercourse during their life, 45.9% for females and 49.8% for males. For high school students, 43.7% of White students reported that they had ever had sexual intercourse during their life; the percentage among Black students was 66.5%, and 52.0% among Hispanic students.

Contraception use has been increasing among sexually active teens in the United States. In 2006, an estimated 74% of sexually active females and 82% of sexually active males used contraception during their first experience with sexual intercourse (Alan Guttmacher Institute, 2006). This is an encouraging trend, but sexually active U.S. teens still lag behind sexually active teens in other wealthy countries in contraceptive use. This contributes to a higher incidence of teen pregnancy and sexually transmitted disease (STD) in the United States than in other wealthy countries (Alan Guttmacher Institute, 2002b). Annually, between 750,000 and 850,000 teenage females become pregnant in the United States, with between 75% and 95% of the teen pregnancies being unintended (Moss, 2004). The teen pregnancy rate in the United States declined 28% between 1990 and 2002. Among Black teenagers aged 15–19, the pregnancy rate fell by 40% during the same period; among White teenagers 15–19, the rate of decline was 34%; while among Hispanic teenagers 15–19 of any race, the pregnancy rate increased slightly from 1991–1992, but by 2002 was 19% lower than the 1990 rate (Alan Guttmacher Institute, 2006). The teen birth rate began to rise again for females between the ages of 15 and 19 in 2006 (CDC, 2009b). The CDC (2004) estimates that nearly 19 million new STD infections occur each year, with nearly half occurring among youth and young adults ages 15 to 24.

Sex education is very much related to these statistics. As of 2002, two out of three public school districts in the United States required some education about human sexuality. The great majority, 86%, of school districts that have sex education policies require that abstinence be promoted, and 35% require that abstinence be taught as the *only option*. The remaining school districts require that abstinence be taught as the *preferred option* and permit content on contraception and STDs. Ninety percent of sex education teachers believe that students should receive instruction on contraception, but one in four reports that they are prohibited from providing such instruction. At least 75% of parents report that sex education should include information about abstinence, abortion, sexual orientation, pressures to have sex, emotional reactions to having sex, and how to use condoms and other forms of birth control (Alan Guttmacher Institute, 2002a).

If adolescents are to make responsible decisions about their sexuality, they would be wise to develop an understanding of the structures and functions of the reproductive system as well as a value base. For some individuals, this information may come from the home; for others, from their schools or community activity centers; and for others, from family planning centers where social workers may work. The discussion that follows focuses on the interior environmental aspects of heterosexual sexuality and reproduction, but before beginning this discussion we raise several important points.

Social constructionist perspective

First, recent theory and research have advanced concepts that suggest that gender and sexuality are multifaceted. Some theorists identify ways in which culture influences gender definitions, beliefs, and attitudes about sexuality, as well as sexual behaviors (Rathus, Nevid, & Fichner-Rathus, 1998). Second, many contemporary definitions of gender, and thus of sexuality, move beyond the binary of male and female to the assertion that experience itself is a major element in ascribing gender. Moreover, experience does not have to be consistent with one's biology (Davies, 2006; Siragusa, 2001). Third, according to progressive approaches, rather than being a biological phenomenon, gender is considered by some to be a function of comfort as a member of a particular gendered group (Siragusa, 2001).

Finally, although we may typically think of gender as male or female, more recently the number of biologically described genders has expanded to five (heterosexual male, heterosexual female, homosexual male, homosexual female, and transsexual) (Davies, 2006), and six (McDermott, 1997): the feminine, masculine, androgynous, transsexual, cross-dresser, and culturally specific genders (DePoy & Gilson, 2007). It is possible for a person to be a chromosomal male with female genitals and vice versa. Chromosomal, genetic, anatomical, and hormonal aspects of sex are sometimes not aligned (Rudacille, 2005).

Let us now return to our discussion of the interior environment of heterosexual sexuality and gender. In humans, the reproductive system comprises internal and external structures. After conception, the sex-determining chromosome produced by the father unites with the mother's egg, and it is this configuration that determines the child's sex. At birth, boys and girls are distinguished by the presence of specific genitalia.

As Exhibit 3.8 shows, the external male organs are the penis and scrotum. Internal organs consist of the testes, the tubes and ducts that serve to transfer the sperm through the reproductive system, and the organs that help nourish and activate sperm and neutralize some of the acidity that sperm encounter in the vagina. The penis functions as a conduit for both urine and semen.

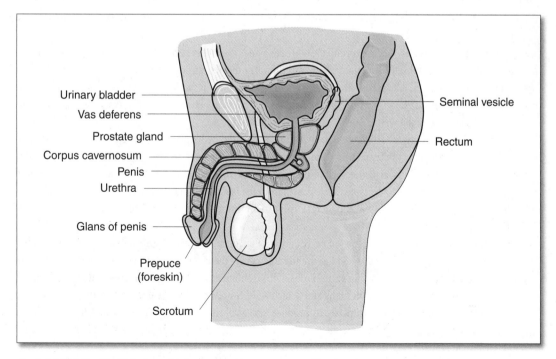

▲ **Exhibit 3.8**   The Male Reproductive System

Externally, one can view the shaft and the glans (often referred to as the head or tip) of the penis. The shaft contains three cylinders. The two largest are called the corpa cavernosa (singular: corpus cavernosum). During sexual arousal, these become engorged with blood and stiffen. The corpus spongiosum, the third cylinder, contains the urethra. It enlarges at the tip of the penis to form a structure called the glans. The ridge that separates the glans from the shaft of the penis is called the corona. The frenulum is the sensitive strip of tissue connecting the underside of the glans to the shaft. At the base of the penis is the root, which extends into the pelvis.

Three glands are part of the feedback loop that maintains a constant level of male hormones in the bloodstream. The primary functions of the **testes,** or male gonads, are to produce sperm (mature germ cells that fertilize the female egg) and to secrete male hormones called *androgens. Testosterone* is one of the most important hormones in that it stimulates the development of the sex organs in the male fetus and the later development of secondary sex characteristics such as facial hair, male muscle mass, and a deep voice. The two other glands in the feedback loop are the hypothalamus and the pituitary gland. Both secrete hormones that serve a regulatory function, primarily maintaining a constant testosterone level in the blood.

In the early stages of their development, sperm cells are called spermatocytes. Each contains 46 chromosomes, including both an X and a Y chromosome that determine sex. As the spermatocytes mature and divide, chromosomes are reduced by half, and only one (either the X or Y) sex-determining chromosome is retained. The mature sperm cell is called the spermatozoan. This cell fertilizes the female egg (ovum), which contains only X chromosomes. Thus, the spermatozoan is the determining factor for the child's sex. (Females have two X chromosomes, and males have one X and one Y chromosome.)

Before ejaculation, the sperm pass through a number of tubes and glands, beginning with a testis, proceeding through a maze of ducts, and then to an epididymis, which is the convergence of the ducts and serves as the storage facility for sperm in a testicle. Each epididymis empties into the vas deferens, which brings the mature sperm to the seminal vesicles, small glands that lie behind the bladder. In these glands, a nourishing and activating fluid combines with the sperm before the mixture is carried through the urethra to the outside of the penis. The *prostate gland,* through which the urethra passes, produces and introduces the milky fluid that preserves the sperm and neutralizes the alkalinity that is found in the female reproductive system. Cowper's glands also make their contribution to the seminal fluid before it leaves the male.

However, even if there is early ejaculation and the Cowper's glands do not have time to secrete fluid, viable sperm exist in the ejaculate and can fertilize the female egg. Early withdrawal of the penis from a woman's vagina therefore does not prevent the passage of some viable sperm cells. It is also important to know that sperm only compose about 1% of the ejaculate (3 to 5 milliliters of fluid total), but that this small percentage contains between 200 million and 400 million sperm. The number of sperm decreases with frequent ejaculation and advancing age.

Exhibit 3.9 shows the external female sex organs. They include the pudendum, also called the vulva, which consists of the mons veneris, the fatty tissue below the abdomen that becomes covered with hair after puberty; the labia majora and minora; the clitoris; and the vaginal opening. Unlike the male, the female has a physical separation between excretion and reproductive organs. Urine passes from the bladder through the urethra to the urethral opening, where it is expelled from the body. The urethra is located immediately in front of the vaginal opening and is unconnected to it.

The labia majora, large folds of skin, contain nerve endings that are responsive to stimulation and protect the inner genitalia. Labia minora join the prepuce hood at the top that covers the clitoris. These structures, when stimulated, engorge with blood and darken, indicating sexual arousal. Resembling the male penis and developing from the same embryonic tissue, the clitoris is about 1 inch long and ¼ inch wide. However, unlike the penis, the clitoris is not directly involved in reproduction but serves primarily to produce sexual pleasure. The vestibule located inside the labia minora contains openings to the urethra and the vagina. It is also a site for arousal because it is rich in nerve endings that are sensitive to stimulation.

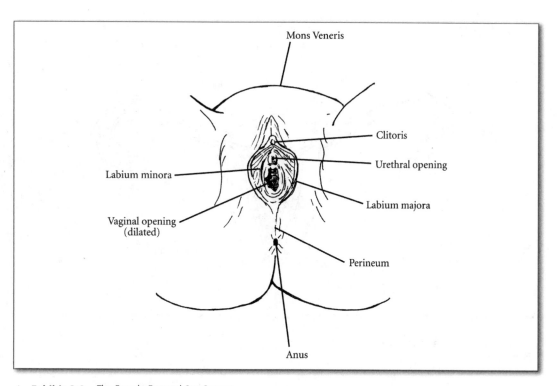

Mons Veneris

Clitoris

Urethral opening

Labium minora

Labium majora

Vaginal opening
(dilated)

Perineum

Anus

▲ **Exhibit 3.9**   The Female External Sex Organs

Internal structures of the female reproductive system, which are shown in Exhibit 3.10, include the vagina, ovaries, fallopian tubes, cervical canal (cervix), and uterus. The vagina is the structure that connects with the external sexual structures. Composed of three layers and shaped cylindrically, the vagina both receives the penis during intercourse and functions as the birth canal through which the child passes from the uterus to the world outside the mother. Because of its multiple functions, the vagina is flexible in size and changes climate from dry to lubricated. The cervix is the lower end of the uterus and protrudes into the vagina. It maintains the chemical balance of the vagina through its secretions.

The **uterus,** also called the womb, serves as the pear-shaped home for the unborn child for the 9 months between implantation and birth. The innermost of its three layers, the endometrium, is the tissue that builds to protect and nourish the developing fetus. If pregnancy does not occur, the endometrium is shed monthly through the process of menstruation. If pregnancy does occur, the well-muscled middle layer of the uterus produces the strong contractions necessary at birth to move the fetus out of the uterus, into the vaginal canal, and then into the world. The external layer protects the uterus within the body.

The fallopian tubes connect the ovaries to the uterus and serve as a conduit for the ova (egg cells) from the ovaries to the uterus. Located on either side of the uterus, the ovaries have two major functions: the production of ova and the production of the female sex hormones, progesterone and estrogen.

Unlike males, who produce an unlimited number of sperm throughout their lives, females are born with the total number of ova that they will ever possess. Less than half of the 2 million ova mature sufficiently to be maintained in the ovaries past puberty. Of the approximately 400,000 that remain, only about 400 are released in the monthly cycle.

Estrogen facilitates sexual maturation and regulates the menstrual cycle in premenopausal women. The benefits of estrogen in postmenopausal women, who can only obtain it from taking a supplement, are debatable. Some argue that estrogen maintains cognitive function and cardiac well-being in older women. However, estrogen supplements (also called

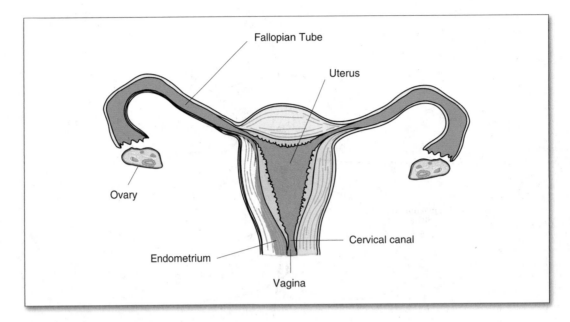

▲ **Exhibit 3.10**   The Female Internal Sex Organs

hormone replacement therapy [HRT]) have been associated with increasing breast and uterine cancer risk, among other problems. Progesterone, though less discussed in the popular media, is critically important in preparing the uterus for pregnancy. It also is a regulator of the menstrual cycle.

Women's breasts are considered to be secondary sex characteristics because they do not have a direct function in reproduction. Mammary glands contained in the breast produce milk that is discharged through the nipple. The nipples are surrounded by the aureoles and become erect when stimulated. The size of the mammary glands is incidental to breast size and milk production. Rather, breast size is a function of the fatty tissue within the breast.

The social worker who is knowledgeable about interior environment mechanisms can clarify the specifics of male and female sexuality for Juan and Belinda. In the school setting or a local community agency, youth may come to talk about their feelings for each other and ask questions regarding sexual and emotional intimacy. Young people in the United States often have inaccurate information about heterosexual and other types of sexuality and the biological aspects of sexual intimacy. Accurate information about sexuality could provide a basis for Juan and Belinda to make informed decisions about exercising their options related to sexuality.

While it is beyond the scope of this chapter to discuss sexual activity among diverse genders, we urge you to consider this important area of knowledge and social work practice.

Critical Thinking Questions 3.2

What are the available sources of information about the reproductive system in contemporary societies? What sources of information have you used to learn about the reproductive system? At what age did you begin to gather information about the reproductive system? How did you sort out accurate from inaccurate information? How would you like your little sister or brother to learn about the reproductive system?

EXTERIOR SOCIOECONOMIC ENVIRONMENT/
INTERIOR HEALTH ENVIRONMENT

Public health experts have long noted the association of poor health outcomes, in all body systems, with low income, low education, unsanitary housing, inadequate health care, unstable employment, and unsafe physical environments (Auerbach & Krimgold, 2001; Engels, 1892). Until recently, however, researchers have made little attempt to understand the reasons behind this empirically supported connection of SES and health.

But by the mid-1990s, researchers in several countries began to try to understand how health is related to SES. In the United States, that research effort became much more focused in 1997, when the MacArthur Foundation established the Network on Socioeconomic Status and Health (N. Adler, 2001). This network is interdisciplinary, including scholars from the fields of anthropology, biostatistics, clinical epidemiology, economics, medicine, neuroscience, psychoimmunology, psychology, and sociology. Beginning in 2000, there was a big jump in research on health inequalities related to SES, oppression, and discrimination in the United States (N. Adler, 2006).

The relationship between SES and health is turning out to involve complex interactions of interior and exterior environments, and researchers are finding some surprises. For example, immigrants to the United States have a longer life expectancy than native U.S.-born persons, and this difference increased between 1979 and 2003 (G. Singh & Hiatt, 2006). This increase may be at least partially explained by U.S. immigration policies, which have been favoring immigrant populations with skill sets that are well suited for contemporary global capitalism.

One of the most consistent, but also most controversial, findings is that the level of income inequality in a country, and not purely SES, is associated with health (N. Adler, 2001). Residents in more egalitarian countries, like Sweden and Japan, are healthier on average than residents in countries like Great Britain and the United States, where disparities between the incomes of the poor and the rich are larger (Wilkinson, 2001).

Conflict perspective

Likewise, within the United States, residents in states with the greatest levels of inequality are 25% more likely to report their health to be fair or poor than residents in states with less inequality (Kawachi & Kennedy, 2001). High levels of perceived inequality are particularly associated with heart attack, cancer, homicide, and infant mortality. A significant body of empirical inquiry has suggested that individuals in the lowest SES group are those hardest hit with the negative health effects of inequality (J. Chen et al., 2006).

Recent research is indicating that the mechanisms of this health-and-wealth connection involve a complex interaction of biological, psychological, and social factors. Several factors are consistently showing up in the research, however, including the following:

• *Persons with lower income engage in disproportionately high-risk health behaviors and lifestyles.* Persons with low income may be more likely than higher-SES individuals to smoke, use alcohol excessively, and eat high-fat diets. There is some evidence that these behaviors are used as coping strategies in the face of stress (J. Jackson, 2006). Researchers are also noting that people with low income who live in geographic areas with a high concentration of low-income families are less likely than those who live in more affluent areas to have access to health-related information, to health clubs and other facilities that foster good health, and to safe places to walk or jog. They are more likely than their affluent counterparts to be targeted by advertisers for fast food restaurants and to work in jobs with less flexibility. For example, one study of health among a sample of bus drivers found that many with hypertension did not take prescribed medications because the diuretics would increase the frequency of their need to visit a bathroom. Their rigid bus schedules did not allow for bathroom breaks (Ragland, Krause, Greiner, & Fisher, 1998).

• *Persons with lower income are more likely than those with more substantial incomes to be exposed to carcinogens, pathogens, and other hazards in the physical environment.* There is evidence that toxic waste sites are most likely to

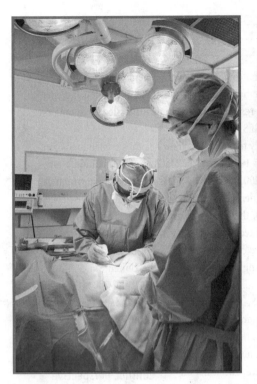

▲ **Photos 3.2a & 3.2b**   Biological health and illness greatly impact human behavior. Here, contrast how medical care is delivered in two very different situations, one in a high-tech operating room in the United States and the other in a temporary clinic in Haiti.

be located in neighborhoods with a high concentration of low-income residents (Kozol, 2000). Rapid urbanization in Africa and some parts of Asia is producing a number of hazards in the physical environment, including crowding, poor sanitation, and unsafe water (Curtis, 2004).

● *Persons with lower income, as compared to their wealthier counterparts, are exposed to more stressors, and have fewer resources for coping with stress.* Persons with low income often have less control over their work situations, a circumstance that has been found to have a powerful negative impact on health (Wilkinson, 2001). It is well documented that stress increases as SES decreases, and recent research indicates that high levels of stress are associated with cellular aging (Epel et al., 2006). It has also been found that "subjective social status," or an individual's evaluation of where he or she stands in the social hierarchy, is strongly related to health status (Sapolsky, 2005; Singh-Manoux, Marmot, & Adler, 2005). The subjective experience of being disadvantaged has been found to be highly correlated with endocrine response to stressors and with respiratory illness when exposed to a virus. These findings are in line with the emerging idea that the degree of the difference in wealth among a population has a greater effect than low SES alone. In addition, perceived racism is associated with ill health (Paradies, 2006).

The research so far supports the notion that the health care system alone cannot offset the effects of other external environment forces on health. Therefore, an important social work domain is public health research and practice. One recent study found that governmental policies aimed at reducing social inequalities result in lowering infant mortality rates and increasing life expectancy at birth (Navarro et al., 2006).

An additional critical factor in health status (positive and negative) involves health literacy. In *Healthy People 2010,* health literacy was defined by the U.S. Department of Health and Human Services as "The degree to which individuals have the capacity to obtain, process, and understand basic health information and services needed to make appropriate health decisions" (quoted in National Network of Libraries of Medicine, 2008, p. 1). Health literacy involves much more than simply translating health information into multiple languages. It also involves consideration of reading and listening skills; analytic and decision-making skills; and the freedom to be able to engage in dialogue, questioning, and critical evaluation of health information and health care options.

Critical Thinking Questions 3.3

What could be some reasons that the incidence of heart attack, cancer, homicide, and infant mortality increases as the level of societal inequality increases? What are the implications of this for public health policies?

IMPLICATIONS FOR SOCIAL WORK PRACTICE

This discussion of the interior biological person suggests several principles for social work assessment and intervention:

- Develop a working knowledge of the body's interior environmental systems, their interconnectedness, and the ways they interact with other dimensions of human behavior.

- In assessments and interventions, recognize that interior environmental conditions of health and illness are influenced by the exterior environmental social, political, cultural, and economic context.

- Recognize that the exterior environmental meanings attached to health and illness may influence not only the physical experience, but also the values and socio-emotional response assigned to health and illness.

- In assessment and intervention activities, look for the ways that behavior affects biological functions and the ways biological systems affect behaviors.

- In assessment and interventions, evaluate the influence of health status on cognitive performance, emotional comfort, and overall well-being.

- In assessment and intervention, consider the ways in which one person's interior environment health status is affecting other people in the person's exterior environment.

- Where appropriate, incorporate multiple social work roles into practice related to the health of the biological system, including the roles of researcher, clinician, educator, case manager, service coordinator, prevention specialist, and policy advocate.

KEY TERMS

acquired immunodeficiency syndrome (AIDS)	cardiovascular system	neuron
antibodies	diabetes mellitus	neurotransmitters
antigens	endocrine system	nonspecific immunity
assistive devices	feedback control mechanism	post-poliomyelitis syndrome (PPS)
atria	high blood pressure	specific immunity
autoimmune disease	human immunodeficiency virus (HIV)	synapse
axon	immune system	testes
blood pressure	lymphocytes	uterus
brain injury (BI)	musculoskeletal system	ventricles
	nervous system	

ACTIVE LEARNING

1. You have been asked by the local public middle school to teach youth about the experiences of living with one of the following conditions: brain injury, diabetes, HIV, high blood pressure, or post-polio syndrome. Locate literature and web resources on your chosen topic, select the material that you wish to present, and prepare a presentation in lay terms that will be accessible to the youth audience.

2. Working in small groups, prepare two arguments, one supporting and one opposing sex education in public school. Give some consideration to content that should or should not be included in sex education programs in public school and the ages at which such education should occur. Provide evidence for your arguments.

WEB RESOURCES

American Diabetes Association
www.diabetes.org
Site contains basic diabetes information as well as specific information on type 1 diabetes, type 2 diabetes, community resources, and healthy living.

American Heart Association
www.americanheart.org

Site contains information on diseases and conditions, healthy lifestyles, health news, and a heart and stroke encyclopedia.

Centers for Disease Control and Prevention (CDC) Division of HIV/AIDS Prevention
www.cdc.gov/hiv

Site contains basic science information on HIV/AIDS, basic statistics, fact sheets, and links to other resource sites.

Guttmacher Institute
www.guttmacher.org

Site presented by the Guttmacher Institute (formerly the Alan Guttmacher Institute), a nonprofit organization that focuses on sexual and reproductive health research, policy analysis, and public education, contains information on abortion, law and public policy, pregnancy and birth, pregnancy and disease prevention and contraception, sexual behavior, sexually transmitted infections and HIV, and sexuality and youth.

MacArthur Research Network on SES & Health
www.macses.ucsf.edu

Site has overviews of questions of interest to four working groups: a social environment group, psychosocial group, allostatic load (physiological wear and tear on the body resulting from chronic stress) group, and developmental group.

National Center for Health Statistics
www.cdc.gov/nchs

Site contains FASTATS on a wide range of health topics as well as news releases and a publication listing.

Neuroscience for Kids
http://faculty.washington.edu/
chudler/introb.html

Site maintained by faculty at the University of Washington presents basic neuroscience information, including brain basics, the spinal cord, the peripheral nervous system, the neuron, sensory systems, effects of drugs on the nervous system, and neurological and mental disorders.

Post-Polio Syndrome Central
www.skally.net/ppsc

Site maintained by a group of volunteers contains a post-polio syndrome (PPS) survey and links to other web resources about PPS.

4

The Psychological Person

Cognition, Emotion, and Self

Joseph Walsh

OPENING QUESTIONS

- How is human behavior influenced by cognitions and emotions?

- How do humans develop a sense of self?

KEY IDEAS

As you read this chapter, take note of these central ideas:

1. Cognition and emotion are different but interrelated internal processes, and the nature of their relationship has long been debated.

2. Cognition includes the conscious thinking processes of taking in relevant information from the environment, synthesizing that information, and formulating a plan of action based on that synthesis. Cognitive theory in social work practice asserts that thinking, not emotion, should be the primary focus of intervention.

3. Moral development is related to cognitive development, because it proceeds from stages of egocentrism through abstract principles of justice and caring. However, the stages of moral development differ among men and women and people of different cultures.

4. Emotions can be understood as feeling states characterized by appraisals of a stimulus, changes in bodily sensations, and displays of expressive gestures.

5. The symptoms of psychological problems may be primarily cognitive or emotional, but both cognition and emotion influence the development of problems.

6. The self may be conceptualized as a soul, organizing activity, cognitive structure, verbal activity, experience of cohesion, or flow of experience.

Case Study

Sheila's Difficult Transition to University Life

Sheila, age 22 and in her first semester at the state university, experienced a crisis during the 7th week of classes. It was the midpoint of the semester, when instructors were required to give interim grades so that students would clearly understand their academic status before the final date for course drops passed. Sheila knew that she was having trouble in all four of her courses but was shocked to receive two Cs and two Ds. She realized that she was at risk of failing two courses! Her chronic sense of sadness became worse; she started having the occasional thoughts of suicide that she had experienced in the past. Sheila knew that she needed to study that weekend, but instead she made the 5-hour drive to her parents' home, feeling a need to be around familiar faces. She had no close friends at school. Distraught, Sheila considered dropping out, but her parents convinced her to talk to her academic adviser first.

Sheila has told the social worker at the university counseling center that she had been quiet during her only previous meeting with the adviser, but this time she vented much emotion. Her adviser learned that Sheila had been a troubled young woman for quite some time. In fact, Sheila said that she had felt depressed and inferior to her peers since childhood. The patterns of negative thinking and feeling that influenced Sheila's current crisis had been in place for 10 years. At this moment, Sheila believed that she simply did not have the intelligence to succeed in college. She did, in fact, have a diagnosed learning disability, a type of dyslexia that made it difficult for her to read and write. A special university adviser was helping her manage this problem, although not all her professors seemed sympathetic to her situation. Sheila also did not believe she had the social competence to make friends, male or female, or the strength of will to overcome her negative moods and outlook. She believed her depression was a basic part of her personality. After all, she couldn't recall ever feeling different.

Sheila grew up in a rural county in Virginia, several miles from the nearest small town. She was accustomed to spending time with her family and relatives, including her sister, Amy, who is 2 years older. During the previous 2 years, Sheila had commuted from her family home to a nearby community college. She had stayed home and worked for a year after high school graduation, without the motivation or direction to continue with schooling.

Amy was, in contrast, the star child who attended a major university to pursue a career in commercial art after winning academic awards throughout her high school years. Sheila watched Amy, so polished and popular, make her way easily and independently into the world. Sheila, by comparison, knew that she could not function so well. Eventually, she decided to enroll in the community college for general education studies. She felt awkward around the other students, as usual, but liked the small size of the school. It was peaceful and kept Sheila near her parents.

When Sheila completed her studies at the community college, she applied for admission to the state university. She decided to major in art preservation, an area of study similar to Amy's. Sheila's adjustment to the state university had been difficult from the beginning. She was intimidated by the grand scale of the institution: the size of the classes, the more distant and formal manner of her professors, the large numbers of students she saw on the campus streets, and the crowds in the student union. The university seemed cold and the students unfriendly. Sheila was a White, middle-class student like the majority at her campus, but she believed that the other students saw her as a misfit. She didn't dress in the latest styles, was not interesting or sophisticated, and was not intelligent enough to stand out in her classes. Even as she sat in the back of her classrooms, she believed that others were thinking of her, in her own words, as a geek. Sheila even felt out of place in her off-campus living quarters. A cousin had found her a basement apartment in a house in which a married couple resided. The walls were thin, and Sheila felt that she lacked privacy. She enjoyed perusing Facebook, the social networking website, but admitted that she felt a marginal connection to her few dozen "friends" there.

Many students experience a difficult transition to college. The counseling center social worker, however, was struck by several family themes that seemed to contribute to Sheila's low self-esteem. Sheila's paternal grandmother, a powerful matriarch, had always lived near the family. She disapproved of much of her grandchildren's behavior, and was frequently critical of them to the point of cruelty. She had good social graces, and thus was particularly unhappy with Sheila's lack of social competence. Sheila's mother was always reluctant to disagree with her mother-in-law or defend her children. This passivity made Sheila angry at her mother, as did the fact that her mother argued with her father quite often and was known to have had several affairs.

Sheila was closer to her father, who was also fond of her, but he maintained a strict work ethic and believed that productive people should have no time for play. He felt that his children showed disrespect to him when they "wasted time" with recreation. Amy seemed able to take her father's admonitions in stride and was closer in spirit and personality to her exuberant mother. Sheila, however, felt guilty when violating her father's wishes. They did have a special relationship, and her father tended to confide in Sheila, but he sometimes did so inappropriately. He told her on several occasions that he was thinking of divorcing his wife, and that in fact Sheila might have been fathered by one of his wife's boyfriends.

(Continued)

(Continued)

Thus, during her transition to the university, Sheila was faced with the task of making her way with a learning disability, a work ethic that did not permit her to enjoy college life and young adulthood, a personal history of being criticized with little balancing support, and even a lack of identity. Sheila was also living in an unfamiliar cultural environment, vastly different from the quiet rural community in which she was raised. Now, in her 7th week, Sheila is depressed and vaguely suicidal—an outsider among her peers, without acknowledged strengths, and feeling all alone. She has come to the counseling center for help, on her academic adviser's suggestion.

COGNITION AND EMOTION

Sheila's difficult transition to college life reflects her personal **psychology**, which can be defined as her mind and her mental processes. Her story illustrates the impact on social functioning of a person's particular patterns of cognition and emotion. **Cognition** can be defined as our conscious or preconscious thinking processes—the mental activities of which we are aware or can become aware with probing. Cognition includes taking in relevant information from the environment, synthesizing that information, and formulating a plan of action based on that synthesis (Ronen & Freeman, 2007). *Beliefs,* key elements of our cognition, are ideas that we hold to be true. Our assessment of any idea as true or false is based on the synthesis of information. Erroneous beliefs, which may result from misinterpretations of perceptions or from conclusions based on insufficient evidence, frequently contribute to social dysfunction.

Emotion can be understood as a feeling state characterized by our appraisal of a stimulus, by changes in bodily sensations, and by displays of expressive gestures (Parkinson, Fischer, & Manstead, 2005). The term *emotion* is often used interchangeably in the study of psychology with the term **affect,** but the latter refers only to the physiological manifestations of feelings. Affect may be the result of *drives* (innate compulsions to gratify basic needs). It generates both conscious and **unconscious** feelings (those of which we are not aware but which influence our behavior). In contrast, emotion is always consciously experienced. Likewise, emotion is not the same as **mood,** a feeling disposition that is more stable than emotion, less intense, and less tied to a specific situation.

The evolution of psychological thought since the late 1800s has consisted largely of a debate about the origins of cognition and emotion, the nature of their influence on behavior, and their influence on each other. The only point of agreement seems to be that cognition and emotion are complex and interactive.

THEORIES OF COGNITION

Theories of cognition, which emerged in the 1950s, assume that conscious thinking is the basis for almost all behavior and emotions. Emotions are defined within these theories as the physiological responses that follow our cognitive evaluations of input. In other words, thoughts produce emotions.

Cognitive Theory

Jean Piaget's cognitive theory is the most influential theory of cognition in social work and psychology (Lightfoot, Lafonde, & Chandler, 2004). In his system, our capacity for reasoning develops in stages, from infancy through adolescence and early adulthood. Piaget saw the four stages as sequential and interdependent, evolving from activity without thought, to thought with less emphasis on activity—from doing, to doing knowingly, and finally to conceptualizing. He saw physical and neurological development as necessary for cognitive development.

A central concept in Piaget's theory is that of schema (plural: schemata), defined as an internalized representation of the world or an ingrained and systematic pattern of thought, action, and problem solving. Our schemata develop through *social learning* (watching and absorbing the experiences of others) or *direct learning* (our own experiences). Both of these processes may involve assimilation (responding to experiences based on existing schemata) or accommodation (changing schemata when new situations cannot be incorporated within an existing one). As children, we are motivated to develop schemata as a means of maintaining psychological *equilibrium,* or balance. Any experience that we cannot assimilate creates anxiety, but if our

> Developmental perspective

schemata are adjusted to accommodate the new experience, the desired state of equilibrium will be restored. From this perspective, you might interpret Sheila's difficulties in college as an inability to achieve equilibrium by assimilating new experience within her existing schemata. As a shy person from a rural background, Sheila was accustomed to making friends very slowly in environments where she interacted with relatively small numbers of peers. She could not easily adjust to the challenge of initiating friendships quickly in a much larger and more transient student population.

Another of Piaget's central ideas is that cognitive development unfolds sequentially. Infants are unable to differentiate between "self" and the external world; the primary task in early cognitive development is the gradual reduction of such egocentricity, or self-centeredness. The child gradually learns to perform cognitive operations—to use abstract thoughts and ideas that are not tied to situational sensory and motor information. Piaget's four stages of normal cognitive development are summarized in Exhibit 4.1.

Stage	Description
Sensorimotor stage (birth to 2 years)	The infant is egocentric; he or she gradually learns to coordinate sensory and motor activities and develops a beginning sense of objects existing apart from the self
Preoperational stage (2 to 7 years)	The child remains primarily egocentric but discovers rules (regularities) that can be applied to new incoming information. The child tends to overgeneralize rules, however, and thus makes many cognitive errors.
Concrete operations stage (7 to 11 years)	The child can solve concrete problems through the application of logical problem-solving strategies.
Formal operations stage (11 to adulthood)	The person becomes able to solve real and hypothetical problems using abstract concepts.

▲ **Exhibit 4.1**   Piaget's Stages of Cognitive Operations

Information Processing Theory

Social behavioral perspective; systems perspective

Cognitive theory has been very influential, but, as you might guess, it leaves many aspects of cognitive functioning unexplained. Whereas Piaget sought to explain how cognition develops, **information processing theory** offers details about how our cognitive processes are organized (G. Logan, 2000). This theory makes a clear distinction between the thinker and the external environment; each is an independent, objective entity in the processing of inputs and outputs. We receive stimulation from the outside and code it with sensory receptors in the nervous system. The information is first represented in some set of brain activities and is then integrated (by accommodation or assimilation) and stored for purposes of present and future adaptation to the environment. All of us develop increasingly sophisticated problem-solving processes through the evolution of our cognitive patterns, which enable us to draw attention to particular inputs as significant.

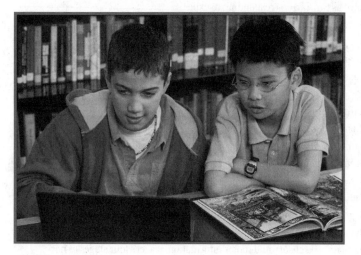

▲ **Photo 4.1** Information processing theory would suggest that the information these children are receiving from the computer flows through their senses to their minds, which operate much like computers.

Information processing is a *sensory theory* in that it depicts information as flowing passively from the external world inward through the senses to the mind. It views the mind as having distinct parts—including the sensory register, short-term memory, and long-term memory—that make unique contributions to thinking in a specific sequence. Interestingly, information processing theory has become important in designing computer systems! In contrast, a *motor theory* such as Piaget's sees the mind as playing an active role in processing—not merely recording, but actually constructing the nature of the input it receives. In Sheila's case, information processing theory would suggest that she simply has not experienced a situation like her current one and thus lacks the schemata required to adapt. Cognitive theory would suggest that a faulty processing of input established somewhere in Sheila's past is making her adjustment difficult.

Social Learning Theory

Social behavioral perspective; developmental perspective

According to *social learning theory,* we are motivated by nature to experience pleasure and avoid pain. Social learning theorists acknowledge that thoughts and emotions exist but understand them as behaviors in need of explaining rather than as primary motivating factors. Social workers should be aware that there are many ways in which adults may learn, even in the context of social learning theory (Kunkel, Hummert, & Dennis, 2006). People continue to experience cognitive development in adulthood, with age- and experience-related changes in memory, cognition, and the brain. The basic principles of social learning theory continue to apply, however.

Social learning theory relies to a great extent on social behavioral principles of conditioning, which assert that behavior is shaped by its reinforcing or punishing consequences (operant conditioning) and antecedents (classical conditioning). Albert Bandura (1977b) added the principle of vicarious learning, or *modeling,* which puts forth that behavior is also acquired by witnessing how the actions of others are reinforced.

Social learning theorists, unlike other social behavioral theorists, assert that thinking takes place between the occurrence of a stimulus and our response. They call this thought process **cognitive mediation.** The unique patterns we learn for evaluating environmental stimuli explain why each of us may adopt very different behaviors in response to the same stimulus—for example, why Sheila's reaction to the crowds in the student union is very different from the reactions of some of her peers. Bandura (1977b, 1986, 2001) takes this idea a step further and asserts that we engage in self-observations and make self-judgments about our competence and mastery. We then act on the basis of these self-judgments. Bandura (2001) criticizes information processing theory for its passive view of human agency, arguing that it omits important features of what it means to be human, including subjective consciousness, deliberative action, and the capacity for self-reflection. It is clear that Sheila made very negative self-judgments about her competence as she began her studies at the university.

Theory of Multiple Intelligences

Howard Gardner's (1999, 2006) theory of **multiple intelligences** constitutes a major step forward in our understanding of how people come to possess different types of cognitive skills and how the same person is able to effectively use cognitive skills in some areas of life but not others. In this theory, intelligence is defined as a "biopsychosocial potential to process information that can be activated in a cultural setting to solve problems or create products that are of value in a culture" (Gardner, 1999, p. 23). Intelligence includes the following:

- The ability to solve problems that one encounters in life
- The ability to generate new problems to solve
- The ability to make something or offer a service that is valued within one's culture

In this theory, the brain is understood not as a single cognitive system but as a central unit of neurological functioning that houses relatively separate cognitive faculties. During its evolution, the brain has developed separate organs, or modules, as information- processing devices. Thus, all people have a unique blend of intelligences derived from these modules. Gardner has delineated eight intelligences, which are overviewed in Exhibit 4.2, although in his ongoing research he is considering additional possibilities. You may be interested to note that in one recent study, social work educators rated intrapersonal, interpersonal, and linguistic intelligences as the most important for social work practice, and the same educators rated bodily-kinesthetic, musical, and spatial intelligences as important for culturally sensitive practice (Matto, Berry-Edwards, Hutchison, Bryant, & Waldbillig, 2006).

Systems perspective

Two intelligences, the *linguistic* (related to spoken and written language) and the *logical-mathematical* (analytic), are consistent with traditional notions of intelligence. The six others are not, however. Gardner (2006) has considered spiritual and existential intelligences as other possibilities.

One of the most positive implications of the theory of multiple intelligences is that it helps us see strengths in ourselves that lie outside the mainstream. For example, Sheila, who is so self-critical, might be encouraged to consider that she has a strong spatial intelligence that contributes to her artistic sensibilities. She needs help, however, in further development of both her intrapersonal and interpersonal intelligences.

Humanistic perspective

Linguistic Intelligence: The capacity to use language to express what is on your mind and to understand other people. Linguistic intelligence includes listening, speaking, reading, and writing skills.

Logical/Mathematical Intelligence: The capacity for mathematical calculation, logical thinking, problem solving, deductive and inductive reasoning, and the discernment of patterns and relationships. Gardner suggests that this is the type of intelligence addressed by Piaget's model of cognitive development, but he does not think Piaget's model fits other types of intelligence.

Visual-Spatial Intelligence: The ability to represent the spatial world internally in your mind. Visual-spatial intelligence involves visual discrimination, recognition, projection, mental imagery, spatial reasoning, and image manipulation.

Bodily-Kinesthetic Intelligence: The capacity to use your whole body or parts of your body to solve a problem, make something, or put on some kind of production. Gardner suggests that our tradition of separating body and mind is unfortunate because the mind can be trained to use the body properly and the body trained to respond to the expressive powers of the mind. He notes that some learners rely on tactile and kinesthetic processes, not just visual and auditory processes.

Musical Intelligence: The capacity to think in musical images, to be able to hear patterns, recognize them, remember them, and perhaps manipulate them.

Intrapersonal Intelligence: The capacity to understand yourself, to know who you are, what you can do, what you want to do, how you react to things, which things to avoid, which things to gravitate toward, and where to go if you need help. Gardner says we are drawn to people who have a good understanding of themselves because those people tend not to make mistakes. They are aware of their range of emotions and can find outlets for expressing feelings and thoughts. They are motivated to pursue goals and live by an ethical value system.

Interpersonal Intelligence: The ability to understand and communicate with others, to note differences in moods, temperaments, motivations, and skills. Interpersonal intelligence includes the ability to form and maintain relationships and to assume various roles within groups, and the ability to adapt behavior to different environments. It also includes the ability to perceive diverse perspectives on social and political issues. Gardner suggests that individuals with this intelligence express an interest in interpersonally oriented careers, such as teaching, social work, and politics.

Naturalist Intelligence: The ability to recognize and categorize objects and processes in nature. Naturalist intelligence leads to talent in caring for, taming, and interacting with the natural environment, including living creatures. Gardner suggests that naturalist intelligence can also be brought to bear to discriminate among artificial items such as sneakers, cars, and toys.

▲ **Exhibit 4.2** Gardner's Eight Intelligences

SOURCE: Based on Gardner (1999, 2006).

Theories of Moral Reasoning

Morality is our sensitivity to, and knowledge of, what is right and wrong. It develops from our acquired principles of justice and ways of caring for others. Theories of moral reasoning are similar to those of cognitive development in that a sequential process is involved. Familiarity with these theories can help social workers understand how clients make decisions and develop preferences for action in various situations. Both of these issues are important in our efforts to develop goals with clients. The best-known theories of moral reasoning are those of Lawrence Kohlberg and Carol Gilligan. In reviewing these theories, it is important to keep in

Developmental perspective

mind that they are based on studies of men and women in the United States. It is likely that moral development unfolds differently in other cultures, although more research is needed to investigate these differences (Gardiner & Kosmitzki, 2008).

Kohlberg (1969) formulated six stages of moral development, which begin in childhood and unfold through adolescence and young adulthood (see Exhibit 4.3). The first two stages represent **preconventional morality** in which the child's primary motivation is to avoid immediate punishment and receive immediate rewards. **Conventional morality** emphasizes adherence to social rules. A person at this level of morality might be very troubled, as Sheila is, by circumstances that make him or her different from other people. Many people never move beyond this level to **postconventional morality**, which is characterized by a concern with moral principles transcending those of their own society.

One limitation of Kohlberg's theory is that it does not take into account gender differences (his subjects were all male). In fact, he claims that women do not advance through all six stages as often as men. Addressing this issue, Gilligan (1982, 1988) notes that boys tend to emphasize independence, autonomy, and the rights of others in their moral thinking, using a *justice-oriented* approach. Girls, on the other hand, develop an ethic of care that grows out of a concern for the needs of others rather than the value of independence. To account for this difference, Gilligan proposed the three stages of

> Conflict perspective

moral development listed in Exhibit 4.4. Her stages place greater emphasis than Kohlberg does on the ethic of care and are meant to more accurately describe the moral development of females. We see in the next chapter how Gilligan's work has influenced feminist psychology.

The research findings on gender differences in moral reasoning are inconsistent. Some research indicates that boys do tend to emphasize justice principles, whereas girls emphasize caring, but these differences are not great (e.g., Malti, Gasser, & Buchmann, 2009). Other researchers find no differences in the ways that males and females reason about moral dilemmas (e.g., Hauser, Cushman, Young, Mikhail, & Jin, 2007; M. Ryan, David, & Reynolds, 2004). It is possible that gender differences in moral reasoning, when they do occur, are related to power differences and differences in the typical ethical dilemmas faced by males and females. In one revealing study, a sample of men and women were asked to respond to a set

Stage	Description
Preconventional	
Heteronomous morality Instrumental purpose	Accepting what the world says is right Defining the good as whatever is agreeable to the self and those in the immediate environment
Conventional	
Interpersonal experiences The societal point of view	Seeking conformity and consistency in moral action with significant others Seeking conformity and consistency with what one perceives to be the opinions of the larger community
Postconventional	
Ethics Conscience and logic	Observing individual and group (societal) rights Seeking to apply universal principles of right and wrong

▲ **Exhibit 4.3**   Kohlberg's Stages of Moral Development

Stage	Description
Survival orientation	Egocentric concerns of emotional and physical survival are primary.
Conventional care	The person defines as right those actions that please significant others.
Integrated care	A person's right actions take into account the needs of others as well as the self.

▲ **Exhibit 4.4**   Gilligan's Three Stages of Moral Development

of hypothetical scenarios in which they needed to assume positions of limited power as well as take on caregiving roles (Galotti, 1989). Under these conditions, the moral responses of men and women were similar. Researchers have also found evidence that culture may have a greater influence on moral reasoning than gender does, with Anglo-Americans putting less emphasis on an ethic of care than members of other ethnic groups (Al-Ansari, 2002; Gardiner & Kosmitzki, 2008; Gump et al., 2000). Further, Afrocentric theory, discussed in Chapter 5, sees the pursuit of morality as a collective human-istic experience.

Both Kohlberg's and Gilligan's stages of moral reasoning, like Piaget's cognitive theory, assume an increasing ability to think abstractly as the person progresses through adolescence. With her great concern about what her parents and grandmother want her to do, Sheila seems to fall into Kohlberg's stage of conventional morality and Gilligan's stage of conventional care.

Gardiner and Kosmitzki (2008) argue that moral development may not follow a universal script across cultures and suggest that the ecological system in which early social interactions occur shapes moral thought and behavior. For understanding moral reasoning across cultures, they recommend a social constructionist theory of moral develop-ment proposed by Norma Haan (1991) in which she suggests that moral reasoning comes from the understanding of the interdependence of self and others that develops through social interactions. She proposes that the most mature moral reasoner is the one who makes moral decisions that balance the person's own needs and desires with those of others who are affected by the issue at hand. Haan found that people who are able to control their own emotions in order to think about possible solutions engage in higher levels of moral action than people who are not able to control their emotions. In this view, moral reasoning would take different forms in different cultures, based on different defi-nitions of needs and desires.

Theories of Cognition in Social Work Practice

When theories of cognition first emerged, they represented a reaction against psychodynamic theories, which focused on the influence of unconscious thought. Many practitioners had come to believe that although some mental processes may be categorized as unconscious, they have only a minor influence on behavior. Rather, conscious think-ing is the basis for almost all behavior and emotions (J. Walsh, 2010).

Piaget's cognitive theory postulates that we develop mental schemata, or general information-processing rules that become enduring, from past experiences. Schemata are the basis for the way individuals screen, discriminate, and code stimuli; categorize and evaluate experiences; and make judgments. Cognition is viewed as active—our minds do not merely receive and process external stimuli but are active in constructing the reality they seek to apprehend. We are "rational" to the extent that our schemata, the basis for our perceptions, accommodate available environmental evidence and our decisions do not rely solely on preconceived notions of the external world.

So long as a person's cognitive style helps to achieve his or her goals, it is considered healthy. However, a person's thinking patterns can become distorted, featuring patterns of bias that dismiss relevant environmental information from judgment, which can lead in turn to the maladaptive emotional responses described in Exhibit 4.5. These *cognitive errors* are habits of thought that lead people to distort input from the environment and experience psychological distress (A. T. Beck, 1976; J. S. Beck, 1995).

As a social worker, you could use cognitive theory to surmise that Sheila feels depressed because she subjectively assesses her life situations in a distorted manner. For example, *arbitrary inferences* may lead her to conclude that because the university students do not approach her in the crowded student union, they are not friendly. Because she mistakenly concludes that they are not friendly, she may also conclude that she will continue to be lonely at the university, and this thought produces her emotional response of sadness.

To adjust her emotions and mood, Sheila needs to learn to evaluate her external environment differently. She needs to change some of the beliefs, expectations, and meanings she attaches to events, because they are not objectively true. She might conclude, for example, that the student union is simply not an appropriate place to meet people because it is crowded and students tend to be hurrying through lunch and off to classes. Sheila can either change her perceptions or change the troubling environments by seeking out new situations. In either case, cognitive theorists would make Sheila's thinking the primary target of change activity, assuming that cognitive change will in turn produce changes in her emotional states.

Cognitive theory is a highly rational approach to human behavior. Even though the theory assumes that many of a person's beliefs are irrational and distorted, it also assumes that human beings have great potential to correct these beliefs in light of contradictory evidence. In clinical assessment, the social worker must assess the client's schemata, identify any faulty thinking patterns, and consider the evidence supporting a client's beliefs. During intervention, the social worker helps the client adjust his or her cognitive process to better facilitate the attainment of goals. As a result, the client will also experience more positive emotions. It is important to emphasize at the same time that clients are

Cognitive Error	Description
Absolute thinking	Viewing experiences as all good or all bad, and failing to understand that experiences can be a mixture of both
Overgeneralization	Assuming that deficiencies in one area of life necessarily imply deficiencies in other areas
Selective abstraction	Focusing only on the negative aspects of a situation, and consequently overlooking its positive aspects
Arbitrary inference	Reaching a negative conclusion about a situation with insufficient evidence
Magnification	Creating large problems out of small ones
Minimization	Making large problems small, and thus not dealing adequately with them
Personalization	Accepting blame for negative events without sufficient evidence

▲ **Exhibit 4.5** Common Cognitive Distortions

not encouraged to rationalize all of their problems as involving faulty assumptions, as many challenges people face are due to oppressive external circumstances. Still, Sheila's belief that her peers in the busy student union have critical thoughts about her as she passes by is an arbitrary inference, based on her own inclination to think poorly of herself. To help her overcome this cognitive error, the social worker could review the available evidence, helping Sheila to understand that the other students probably did not notice her at all.

Social learning theory takes the tendency in cognitive theory to deemphasize innate drives and unconscious thinking even further. Some practitioners in the social learning tradition make no attempt to understand internal processes at all and avoid making any inferences about them. Social workers who practice from the behavioral approach conceptualize thoughts and emotions as behaviors subject to *reinforcement contingencies* (Thyer, 2005). That is, we tend to behave in ways that produce rewards (material or emotional) for us. Thus, behaviors can be modified through the application of specific action-oriented methods, such as those listed in Exhibit 4.6. If Sheila is depressed, the social worker would help to identify the things that reinforce her depressed behavior and adjust them so that her emotional states (as revealed in behaviors) will change in response. Through desensitization and behavioral rehearsal, for example, Sheila could learn step-by-step to approach a small group of students at a lunch table and ask to join them. Her positive reinforcers might include success in these measured experiences, a new sense of efficacy, reduced anxiety, and the affirmation of her social worker.

The combination of assessing and intervening with a person's thought processes, and then helping the client to identify and develop reinforcers for new ways of thinking and behaving, is known as *cognitive-behavioral therapy* (CBT). Most cognitive practitioners actually use cognitive-behavioral methods because it is important to help the client experience rewards for any changes he or she risks.

Strategy	Description
Desensitization	Confronting a difficult challenge through a step-by-step process of approach and anxiety control
Shaping	Differentially reinforcing approximations of a desired but difficult behavior so as to help the person eventually master the behavior
Behavioral rehearsal	Role-playing a desired behavior after seeing it modeled appropriately and then applying the skill to real-life situations
Extinction	Eliminating a behavior by reinforcing alternative behaviors

▲ **Exhibit 4.6**   *Four Behavioral Change Strategies*

Critical Thinking Questions 4.1

Why do you think social work educators rated intrapersonal, interpersonal, and linguistic intelligences as the most important for social work practice? Would you agree with that? Why or why not? Why do you think the same educators rated bodily-kinesthetic, musical, and spatial intelligences as important for culturally sensitive practice? Would you agree with that? Why or why not? Shouldn't all social work practice be culturally sensitive?

THEORIES OF EMOTION

Emotion is physiologically programmed into the human brain (see Chapter 3). Its expression is primarily mediated by the hypothalamus, whereas the experience of emotion is a limbic function. But emotion also involves a cognitive labeling of these programmed feelings, which is at least partially a learned process. That is, some emotional experience is an interpretation, and not merely given by our physiological state. For example, two students might feel anxious walking into the classroom on the first day of a semester. The anxiety would be a normal reaction to entering a new and unfamiliar situation. However, one student might interpret the anxiety as a heightened alertness that will serve her well in adjusting to the new students and professor, whereas the other student might interpret the same emotion as evidence that she is not prepared to manage the course material. The first student may become excited, but the second student becomes distressed.

Many theorists distinguish between primary and secondary emotions (Parkinson et al., 2005). The **primary emotions** may have evolved as specific reactions with survival value for the human species. They mobilize us, focus our attention, and signal our state of mind to others. There is no consensus on what the primary emotions are, but they are usually limited to anger, fear, sadness, joy, and anticipation (Panksepp, 2008). The **secondary emotions** are more variable among people and are socially acquired. They evolved as humans developed more sophisticated means of learning, controlling, and managing emotions to promote flexible cohesion in social groups. The secondary emotions may result from combinations of the primary emotions (Plutchik, 2005), and their greater numbers also imply that our processes of perception, though largely unconscious, are significant in labeling them. These emotions include (but are not limited to) envy, jealousy, anxiety, guilt, shame, relief, hope, depression, pride, love, gratitude, and compassion (Lazarus, 2007).

The autonomic nervous system is key to our processing of emotion (Bentley & Walsh, 2006). This system consists of nerve tracts running from the base of the brain, through the spinal cord, and into the internal organs of the body. It is concerned with maintaining the body's physical homeostasis. Tracts from one branch of this system, the sympathetic division, produce physiological changes that help make us more alert and active. These changes are sustained by the release of hormones from the endocrine glands into the bloodstream. As part of the feedback control mechanism, parasympathetic system nerve tracts produce opposite, or calming, effects in the body. The two systems work together to maintain an appropriate level of physical arousal.

> Systems perspective

Still, psychologists have debated for more than a century the sources of emotion. Theories range from those that emphasize physiology to those that emphasize the psychological or the purely social context, and they give variable weight to the role of cognition.

Physiological Theories of Emotion

A theory of emotion developed over a century ago by the psychologist William James (1890) speculated that our bodies produce automatic physiological reactions to any stimulus. We notice these reactions after the fact and then attempt through cognition to make sense of them. This "making sense" involves labeling the emotion. Thus, emotion follows cognition, which itself follows the physiological reaction to a stimulus. The original theory stated that a distinct emotion arises from each physiological reaction.

A few decades later, another theory was developed (Cannon, 1924) that argued that physiological arousal and the experience of emotion are unrelated. Our physiological responses to a stimulus are nonspecific and only prepare us for a general *fight-or-flight response* (to confront or avoid the stimulus). This response in itself has nothing to do with the experience of emotion because any particular physiological activity may give rise to different emotional states and may not even involve our emotions at all. Thus, a separate process of perception produces our feeling of emotion. Emotion derives from the associations we make based on prior attempts to understand the sensation of arousal.

Physiology-based theories of emotion lost favor in the mid-20th century, but recent brain research is once again suggesting a strong link between physiological processes and emotion. This **differential emotions theory** (Magai, 2001) asserts that emotions originate in our neurophysiology and that our personalities are organized around "affective biases." All of us possess five primary human emotions: happiness, sadness, fear, anger, and interest/excitement. These emotions are instinctual, are in a sense hardwired into our brains, and are the source of our motivations. When our emotions are activated, they have a pervasive influence on our cognition and behavior. A key theme in this theory is that emotions influence cognition, a principle opposite to that stressed in cognitive theory.

For example, Sheila has a persistent bias toward sadness, which may reflect some personal or material loss that occurred long before she started college. Her sadness has a temporary physical response: a slowing down and a decrease in general effort. It also leads her to withdraw in situations where her efforts to recover the loss would likely be ineffective. The sadness thus allows Sheila time to reevaluate her needs and regain energy for more focused attempts to reach more achievable goals. It is also a signal for others to provide Sheila with support. The sadness of others promotes our own empathic responses. Of course, it is likely that "appearing sad" may have been more functional for Sheila in her home community, where she was more consistently around people who knew and took an interest in her. In contrast, anger tends to increase a person's energy and motivate behavior that is intended to overcome frustration. Furthermore, it is a signal to others to respond with avoidance, compliance, or submission so that the person may resolve the problem.

Social constructionist perspective

Researchers have speculated for decades about the precise locations of emotional processing in the brain. Much has been learned about structures that participate in this process, and it is clear that many areas of the brain have a role (LeDoux & Phelps, 2008). Furthermore, it is now widely accepted that cultural patterns shape the ways in which environmental input is coded in the brain (Kagan, 2007).

As suggested in Chapter 3, the brain may be conceived as having three sections: hindbrain, midbrain, and forebrain. The *hindbrain* is the oldest of these and is sometimes called the reptilian brain. It consists of the brain stem and cerebellum and is responsible for involuntary life support functions. The *midbrain* is located just above the brain stem. It represents a second level of brain evolution, more advanced than the hindbrain. It includes the limbic system, a group of cell structures and the center of activities that create emotions. The *forebrain* is more focused on the external environment and on "rational" functions. It is the center of emotion, memory, reasoning, abstract thought, and judgment, and it integrates diverse brain activities. All of these sections have a role in the processing of emotion that researchers are only beginning to understand in depth.

The physiology of emotion begins in the *thalamus,* a major integrating center of the brain. Located in the forebrain, the thalamus is the site that receives and relays sensory information from the body and from the environment to other parts of the brain.

▲ **Photo 4.2** Here a boy experiences joy from the kiss of his mother.

Any perceived environmental event travels first to the thalamus and then to the sensory cortex (for thought), the basal ganglia (for movement), and the hypothalamus (for feeling). The *amygdala,* part of the limbic system, is key in the production of emotional states. There are in fact two routes to the amygdala from the thalamus. Sensations that produce the primary emotions described above may travel there directly from the thalamus, bypassing any cognitive apparatus, to produce an immediate reaction that is central to survival. Other inputs first travel through the cortex, where they are cognitively evaluated prior to moving on to the limbic system and amygdala to be processed as the secondary emotions.

Culture and the characteristics of the individual may influence the processing of stimulation because the cognitive structures (schemata) that interpret this stimulation may, through feedback loops to the thalamus, actually shape the neural pathways that will be followed by future stimuli. In other words, neural schemata tend to become rigid patterns of information processing, shaping subsequent patterns for making sense of the external world.

> Systems perspective

Psychological Theories of Emotion

Perhaps the most contentious debates about the role of cognition in emotion have taken place among psychological theorists. As Exhibit 4.7 shows, some psychologists have considered emotion as primary, and others have considered cognition as primary. Psychological theories in the social behavioral perspective, somewhat like physiology-based theories, assume an automatic, programmed response that is then interpreted as emotion, perhaps first consciously but eventually (through habit) unconsciously.

Psychoanalytic Theory

Freud's landmark work, *The Interpretation of Dreams*, first published in 1899, signaled the arrival of **psychoanalytic theory.** Freud's theories became prominent in the United States by the early 1900s, immediately influencing the young profession of social work, and were a dominant force through the 1950s. Psychoanalytic thinking continues to be influential in social work today, through the theories of ego psychology, self psychology, and object relations, among others.

The basis of psychoanalytic theory is the primacy of internal drives and unconscious mental activity in human behavior. Sexual and aggressive drives are not "feelings" in themselves, but they motivate behavior that will presumably gratify our impulses. We

> Psychodynamic perspective

experience positive emotions when our drives are gratified and negative emotions when they are frustrated. Our conscious mental functioning takes place within the **ego,** that part of the personality responsible for negotiating between internal drives and the outside world. It is here that cognition occurs, but it is driven by those unconscious thoughts that are focused on drive satisfaction.

In psychoanalytic thought, then, conscious thinking is a product of the drives from which our emotions also spring. By nature, we are pleasure seekers and "feelers," not thinkers. Thoughts are our means of deciding how to gratify our drives. Defense mechanisms result from our need to indirectly manage drives when we become frustrated, as we frequently do in the social world, where we must negotiate acceptable behaviors with others. The need to manage drives also contributes to the development of our unconscious mental processes. According to psychoanalytic theory, personal growth cannot be achieved by attending only to conscious processes. We need to explore all of our thoughts and feelings to understand our essential drives. Change requires that we uncover unconscious material and the accompanying feelings that are repressed, or kept out of consciousness.

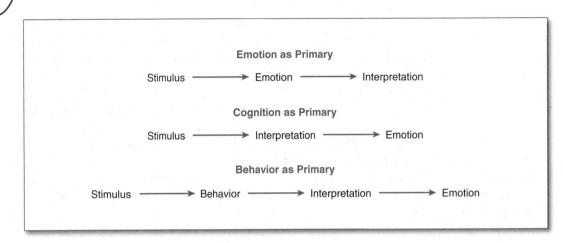

Emotion as Primary

Stimulus ──────→ Emotion ──────→ Interpretation

Cognition as Primary

Stimulus ──────→ Interpretation ──────→ Emotion

Behavior as Primary

Stimulus ──────→ Behavior ──────→ Interpretation ──────→ Emotion

▲ **Exhibit 4.7**   *Psychological Views of the Source of Emotion*

SOURCE: Adapted from Ellsworth (1991).

Psychodynamic perspective

Let us grant, for example, that Sheila has a normal, healthy drive for pleasure. She may thus be angry with her father for the manner in which he discourages her from developing a social life and also burdens her with his personal problems. This feeling of anger might be repressed into unconsciousness, however, because Sheila is close to her father in many ways and may believe that it is not permissible for a daughter to be angry with a well-meaning parent. Sheila's unconscious anger, having been turned inward at herself, may be contributing to her depression. A psychoanalytically oriented social worker might suspect from Sheila's presentation that she experiences this anger. The social worker might try to help Sheila uncover this by having her reflect on her feelings about her father in detail, in a safe clinical environment. With the insights that might result from this reflection, Sheila's feeling may become conscious, and she can then take direct measures to work through her anger.

Ego Psychology

Ego psychology, which emerged in the 1930s (E. Goldstein, 2008), shifted to a more balanced perspective on the influences of cognition and emotion in social functioning. As an adaptation of psychoanalytic theory, it signaled a reaction against Freud's heavy emphasis on drives and highlighted the ego's role in promoting healthy social functioning. Ego psychology represents an effort to build a holistic psychology of normal development. It was a major social work practice theory throughout much of the 20th century because of its attention to the environment as well as the person, and it continues to be taught in many schools of social work.

In ego psychology, the ego is conceived of as present from birth and not as derived from the need to reconcile drives within the constraints of social living, as psychoanalytic theory would say. The ego is the source of our attention, concentration, learning, memory, will, and perception. Both past and present experiences are relevant in influencing social functioning. The influence of the drives on emotions and thoughts is not dismissed, but the autonomy of the ego, and thus conscious thought processes, receives greater emphasis than in psychoanalytic theory. The ego moderates internal conflicts, which may relate to drive frustration, but it also mediates the interactions of a healthy person with stressful environmental conditions.

If we experience sadness, then, it is possible that we are having conflicts related to drive frustration that are internal in origin. However, it is also possible that we are experiencing person–environment conflicts in which our coping efforts are not effective; the negative emotion may result from a frustration of our ability to manage an environmental stressor and thus may arise from cognitive activities. Sheila may be experiencing both types of conflict. Her anger at the lack of adequate nurturance in her early family history may have been turned inward and produced a depression that has persisted in all of her environments. At the same time, the mismatch between her personal needs for mastery and the demands of this particular academic environment may be contributing to her frustration and depression.

> Social behavioral perspective

Attribution Theory: A Cognitive Perspective

Attribution theory was the first of the psychological theories of emotion to give primacy to cognition as a producer of emotions (Schacter & Singer, 1962). **Attribution theory** holds that our experience of emotion is based on conscious evaluations we make about physiological sensations in particular social settings. We respond to situations as we understand them cognitively, which leads directly to our experience of a particular emotion. For example, Sheila has often experienced anxiety, but she interprets it differently in dealing with her strict father (who makes her feel guilty about enjoying life) and her fellow students (who make her feel ashamed of who she is). Attribution theory also notes that the social setting determines the type of emotion experienced; the physiological response determines the strength of the reaction. In other words, the nature of the social setting is key to the process of emotional experience.

A further refinement of attribution theory states that our initial reactions to any stimulus are limited to the sense of whether it will have positive or negative consequences for us (Weiner, 2008). This is an automatic, preconscious process. Afterward, we consider what has caused the event, which leads to modification of the emotion we feel. The less we understand about the physiological nature of a sensation, the less likely we are to perceive it as physiological, and the more likely it is that we will be influenced by external cues in determining its cause and labeling the emotion. Thus, our perceptions of internal versus external cause determine in part the type of emotion that we experience. For example, if we experience frustration, the emotion of shame may emerge if we decide that it is due to our own behavior. However, we may experience anger if we decide that the frustration is due to the actions of someone else.

Richard Lazarus (2001) has proposed a three-part psychological theory of emotion based on appraisals of situations. He suggests that emotion develops when we assess a situation as somehow relevant to a personal value or life concern. First, we make an unconscious appraisal of whether a situation constitutes a threat. This appraisal is followed by coping responses, which may be cognitive, physiological, or both, and may be conscious or unconscious. Once these coping mechanisms are in place, we reappraise the situation and label our associated emotion. This process implies that our feelings originate with an automatic evaluative judgment. We decide whether there is a threat, take immediate coping action to deal with it, and then take a closer look to see exactly what was involved in the situation. At the end of this process, we experience a specific emotion.

A major life concern for Sheila is feeling secure in her interpersonal environments. She feels secure in familiar environments (such as her hometown) but feels threatened in unfamiliar places. When she walks into a new classroom, she experiences anxiety. The feeling seems to Sheila to be automatic, because her need for security is threatened in the situation. Her means of coping is to ignore the other students, neither speaking to nor making eye contact with them, and to sit in a relatively isolated area of the room. Sheila then makes at least a partly conscious appraisal that the room is not only occupied with strangers, but that they will also quickly judge her in negative ways. Sheila labels her emotion as shame because she concludes (erroneously, we would think) that her classmates are correct in perceiving her as socially inferior.

Theory of Emotional Intelligence

Emotional intelligence is a person's ability to process information about emotions accurately and effectively, and consequently to regulate emotions in an optimal manner (Goleman, 2005). It includes self-control, zest and persistence, ability to motivate oneself, ability to understand and regulate one's own emotions, and ability to read and deal effectively with other people's feelings. This is a relatively new concept in psychology. The idea of integrating the emotional and intellectual systems was considered contradictory for many years. Emotions deal with narrow informational content and specific events that are seen as changeable and unique. The intellect is related to patterns and regularities, but recently, psychologists have determined that emotional stimulation is necessary for activating certain schematic thought patterns.

> Systems perspective

Emotional intelligence involves recognizing and regulating emotions in ourselves and other people. It requires emotional sensitivity, or the ability to evaluate emotions within a variety of social circumstances. A person who is angry but knows that certain expressions of anger will be counterproductive in a particular situation, and as a result constrains his or her expressions of anger, is emotionally intelligent. On the other hand, a person with this same knowledge who behaves angrily in spite of this awareness is emotionally unintelligent.

People are not necessarily equally emotionally intelligent about themselves and other people. We may be more emotionally intelligent about other people than we are about ourselves, or vice versa. The first possibility helps to explain why some people, social workers included, seem to be better at giving advice to others than to themselves.

Emotional intelligence requires an integration of intellectual and emotional abilities. Recognizing and regulating emotions requires emotional self-awareness and empathy, but it also necessitates the intellectual ability to calculate the implications of different behavioral alternatives. To understand how and why we feel as we do, and other people feel as they do, demands emotional awareness and intellectual reasoning. Emotional intelligence is more important to excellence in many aspects of life than pure intellect because it includes intellect plus other capacities.

There is no necessary relationship between emotional intelligence and emotional intensity. Emotional intelligence includes the capacity to regulate and use emotions, which may in fact favor a type of detachment that is not typical of emotionally expressive people. For example, one of Sheila's great assets, and one that she herself can "own," is her sensitivity to preadolescent children. She likes them and is always attuned to the nuances of their thoughts and emotions. Sheila functions exceptionally well as a sitter for her friends and neighbors because children pick up on her sensitivity and reciprocate those positive feelings. On the other hand, as we have already seen, Sheila generally lacks emotional self-awareness and intensity. It seems that her negative moods and attitudes contribute to her generally flat emotional style with most people. In fact, her wariness of others may contribute in an odd way to her sensitivity to their emotional states. She is able to engage emotionally with children because, unlike her peers and older persons, they do not constitute any kind of threat to her.

Social Theories of Emotion

Social theories of emotion also take the view that perception, or the interpretation of a situation, precedes emotion. These interpretations are learned, and as such they become automatic (unconscious or preconscious). Social theories emphasize the purpose of emotion, which is to sustain shared interpersonal norms and social cohesion. Two social theories are considered here.

James Averill's (1997) theory states that emotions can be understood as socially constructed, transitory roles. They are socially constructed because they originate in our appraisals of situations. They are transitory in that they are time limited. Finally, emotions are roles because they include a range of socially acceptable actions that may be performed in a certain social context. We organize and interpret our physiological reactions to stimuli with regard to the social norms involved in the situations where these reactions occur. Emotions permit us, in response to these stimuli, to

> Social constructionist perspective

step out of the conventional social roles to which people not experiencing the emotion are held. For example, in our culture, we generally would not say that we wish to harm someone unless we were feeling anger. We would generally not lash out verbally at a friend or spouse unless we felt frustrated. We would generally not withdraw from certain personal responsibilities and ask others for comfort unless we felt sad. Because of the social function of emotions, we often experience them as passions, or feelings not under our control. Experiencing passion permits unconventional behavior because we assume that we are somehow not "ourselves," not able to control what we do at that moment. Our society has adopted this mode of thinking about emotions because it allows us to distance ourselves from some of our actions. Emotions are thus legitimized social roles or permissible behaviors for persons when in particular emotional states.

George Herbert Mead (1934), the originator of symbolic interaction theory, took a somewhat different view. He suggested that emotions develop as symbols for communication. He also believed that humans are by nature more sensitive to visual than to verbal cues. Emotional expressions are thus particularly powerful in that they are apprehended visually rather than verbally. Our emotional expression is a signal about how we are inclined to act in a situation, and others can adjust their own behavior in response to our perceived inclinations. Sheila's lack of eye contact, tendency to look down, and physical distancing from others are manifestations of her sadness. Other persons, in response, may choose either to offer her support or, more likely in a classroom setting, to avoid her if they interpret her expressions as a desire for distance. Sheila was accustomed to people noticing her sadness at home, and responding to it in helpful ways, but in the faster-paced, more impersonal context of the university culture, this was not happening.

Theories of Emotion in Social Work Practice

The preceding theories are useful in assessment and intervention with clients because they enhance the social worker's understanding of the origins of emotional experiences and describe how negative emotional states may emerge and influence behavior. The social worker can help the client develop more positive emotional responses by providing insight or corrective experiences. What follows, however, is a theory that is even more precise in identifying the processes of emotional experience.

L. S. Greenberg (2008) has offered an emotion-focused practice theory, similar to psychoanalytic theory, that promises to help in social work interventions. Greenberg asserts that all primary emotions—those that originate as biologically based rapid responses—are adaptive. Every primary emotion we experience has the purpose of helping us adjust our relationship with an environmental situation to enhance coping. Secondary emotions emerge from these primary emotions as a result of cognitive mediation. Problems in social functioning may occur in one of four scenarios, summarized in Exhibit 4.8.

1. A primary emotion may not achieve its aim of changing our relationship with the environment to facilitate adaptation.

2. We may, prior to awareness of a primary emotion, deny, distort, avoid, or repress it and thus become unable to constructively address our person–environment challenge.

3. We may develop cognitive distortions, or irrational "meaning construction" processes, that produce negative secondary emotions.

4. We may regulate our appropriate emotional experiences poorly, by either minimizing or not maintaining control over them.

▲ **Exhibit 4.8**   Four Sources of Emotion-Based Problems in Social Functioning

From this perspective, it is the unconscious or **preconscious** (mental activity that is out of awareness but can be brought into awareness with prompting) appraisal of situations in relation to our needs that creates emotions. Furthermore, as George Herbert Mead (1934) pointed out, we experience our emotions as images, not as verbal thoughts. Emotions are difficult to apprehend cognitively, and in our attempts to do so, we may mistake their essence. The bad feelings that trouble us come not from those primary emotional responses, which, if experienced directly, would tend to dissipate, but from defensive distortions of those responses. We tend to appraise situations accurately with our primary emotions, but our frustration in achieving affective goals can produce distortions. Thus, in contrast to the assumptions of cognitive theory, distortions of thought may be the *result* of emotional phenomena rather than their cause.

Consider Sheila's depression as an example. Perhaps she is interpersonally sensitive by nature and accurately perceives aloofness in others. Her affective goals of closeness are threatened by this appraisal, and the intensity of her reaction to this frustration becomes problematic. Her emotional patterns evoke tendencies to withdraw temporarily and to become less active in response to discouragement or sadness. To this point, the process may be adaptive, as she may be able to rest and regain energy during her temporary withdrawal. This particular feeling state, however, may become a cue for negative thoughts about herself, which then prevent her from actively addressing her frustrations.

Personal reality, then, may be as much a product of emotion as cognition. In any situation, the meaning we construct may automatically determine our conscious responses. It is when we directly experience primary emotions that we are functioning in an adaptive manner.

In emotion-focused practice, the social worker would attempt to activate the person's primary emotional reactions, making them more available to awareness within the safety of the social worker–client relationship and making secondary emotional reactions amenable to change when necessary. Emotional reactions, cognitive appraisals, and action tendencies may then be identified more clearly by the client. Affective needs can be identified, the sequencing of the emotional-cognitive process can be clarified, and a new sense of self may emerge along with an improved capacity for self-direction.

From this perspective, a social worker could help Sheila understand that she carries much anger at her family because of their long-term lack of adequate support for her emotional development. Sheila could be encouraged within the safety of the social worker–client relationship to experience and ventilate that anger, and gain insight into her pattern. Once Sheila can consciously identify and experience that negative emotion, she may be less incapacitated by the depression, which is a secondary emotion resulting from her suppression of anger. She would then have more energy to devote to her own social and academic goals and to develop new ways of interacting with others in the university setting.

COGNITIVE/EMOTIONAL "DISORDERS"

As social workers, we are reluctant to label people as having cognitive or emotional "disorders." Instead, we conceptualize problems in social functioning as mismatches in the fit between person and environment. Still, in our study of the psychological person, we can consider how problems are manifested in the client's cognitive and emotional patterns.

Many social workers are employed in mental health agencies and use the *Diagnostic and Statistical Manual of Mental Disorders* (*DSM-IV-TR*; American Psychiatric Association [APA], 2000) to make diagnoses as part of a comprehensive client assessment. The *DSM* has been the standard resource for clinical diagnosis in the United States for more than half a century. The purpose of the manual is to "provide clear descriptions of diagnostic categories in order to enable clinicians and investigators to diagnose, communicate about, study, and treat people with various mental disorders" (APA, 2000, p. xi). The *DSM* includes 16 chapters that address, among others, disorders diagnosed in infancy, childhood, or adolescence; cognitive disorders; substance-related disorders; psychotic disorders; mood disorders; anxiety disorders; sexual disorders; eating disorders; personality disorders; and adjustment disorders. The diagnostic system includes five categories, or "axes," for each client. Axis I includes clinical or mental disorders, Axis II includes personality disorders and mental retardation, Axis III lists any medical conditions the client may have, Axis IV pertains to psychosocial and environmental problems, and Axis V includes a global assessment of functioning.

It is important to recognize that the *DSM* provides a medical perspective on human functioning. There is tension between the social work profession's person-in-environment perspective and the requirement in many settings that social workers use the *DSM* to "diagnose" mental, emotional, or behavioral disorders in clients (Corcoran & Walsh, 2006). This will be discussed further in Chapter 5.

With this brief introduction, we can consider four examples of disorders selected from the *DSM* to illustrate how either cognitive or emotional characteristics may predominate in a client's symptom profile, even though both aspects of the psychological person are always present:

- Two disorders that feature cognitive symptoms are obsessive-compulsive disorder and anorexia nervosa. Obsessive-compulsive disorder is an anxiety disorder that, when featuring obsessions, is characterized by persistent thoughts that are experienced as intrusive, inappropriate, unwelcome, and distressful. The thoughts are more than excessive worries about real problems, and the person is unable to ignore or suppress them. In anorexia nervosa, an eating disorder, the person becomes obsessive about food, thinking about it almost constantly. The person refuses to maintain a reasonable body weight because of distorted beliefs about physical appearance and the effects of food on the body.

- Two disorders that feature emotional symptoms are dysthymia and agoraphobia. Dysthymia, a mood disorder, is characterized by a lengthy period of depression. It features the emotion of sadness, which persists regardless of external events. Agoraphobia is an anxiety disorder characterized by fear. The person is afraid to be in situations (such as crowds) or places (such as large open areas) from which escape might be difficult or embarrassing. The person must restrict his or her range of social mobility out of fear of having a panic attack (being overwhelmed by anxiety) for reasons that are not consciously clear.

As a social worker, you might note that Sheila is depressed and also has a mild form of agoraphobia. She feels uncomfortable and insecure on the large, crowded campus, and developed fears of having panic attacks when in the student union. This building includes several large open areas that are highly congested at certain times of the day. Sheila is concerned that people there look at her critically. You might thus conclude that Sheila's problems are primarily emotional. However, Sheila's cognitive patterns have contributed to the development of her negative emotions. Her overall negative self-assessment sustains her depression, and her distorted beliefs about the attitudes of others contribute to her fears of being in the crowded student union. It is rarely the case that only cognitive factors or only emotional factors are behind a client's problems.

Critical Thinking Questions 4.2

Some research suggests that emotional intelligence is more important to career success than intelligence measured as IQ. Does that make sense to you? Why or why not? How can we enhance our own emotional intelligence? How could you help Sheila enhance her emotional intelligence?

THE SELF

It remains for us to integrate cognition and emotion into a cohesive notion of the self. This is a difficult task—one that may, in fact, be impossible to achieve. All of us possess a sense of self, but it is difficult to articulate. How would you define *self*? Most of us tend to think of it as incorporating an essence that is more or less enduring. But beyond that, what would you say? Thinkers from the fields of philosophy, theology, sociology, psychology, and social work have struggled to identify the essence of the self, and they offer us a range of perspectives: self as a soul, as an organizing activity, as a cognitive structure, as a verbal activity, as an experience of cohesion, or as a flow of experience (Levin, 1992; see Exhibit 4.9 for a summary of these perspectives). Cultural psychologists suggest that all of these perspectives assume an independent self, but in many cultures of the world, the self is an interdependent one that cannot be detached from the context of human relationships (Markus & Kitayama, 2009).

The Self as a Soul

Humanistic perspective

Understanding the self as a soul appeals to those who see their essence as constant throughout life and perhaps transcending their physical lives. The soul may be identical with the conscious self, or the soul may be separate from (but intimately connected with) the self. This idea is based on certain spiritual traditions (see Chapter 6), and though widely shared, it does not easily lend itself to examination in terms of changing configurations of person and environment. If the self as soul is constant, that is, it may not be substantively influenced by interactions with the environment. This self can be conceived as existing apart from its material environment.

Concept	Definition
The self as soul	A constant, unchanging self, existing apart from its material environment and material body, perhaps transcending the life of the physical body
Organizing activity	The initiator of activity, organizer of drives, and mediator of both internal and person/environment conflicts; an evolving entity in the synthesizing of experiences
Cognitive structure	The thinker and definer of reality through conscious activities that support the primacy of thought
Verbal activity	The product of internal monologues (self-talk) and shared conversation with others; the product of what we tell ourselves about who we are
Experience of cohesion	The sense of cohesion achieved through action and reflection; the three-part self (grandiose, idealized, and twinship components)
Flow of experience	The self-in-process, the changing self

▲ **Exhibit 4.9** Six Concepts of the Sense of Self

The Self as Organizing Activity

The notion of self as an organizing activity incorporates the notions of action, initiative, and organization. We certainly experience ourselves as capable of initiating action, and the sense of organization emerges as we synthesize our activities and experiences.

Psychoanalytic theory and ego psychology are consistent with these ideas, as they conceptualize the ego as the organizer of drives and mediator of internal and external conflicts. In both theories, the ego organizes the drives in response to external restrictions on their satisfaction. The ego is neither thought nor emotion, but a coordinator of both. In ego psychology, this self is present from birth and

> Psychodynamic perspective

includes a drive to mastery and competence. In traditional psychoanalytic theory, the ego is not present from birth and must develop, and the drives thought to motivate human behavior do not include mastery and competence. In both theories, the ego is responsible for defensive functions, judgment, rational thinking, and reality awareness.

The ego is largely, although not entirely, conscious, whereas the other portions of the mind—including the id (the source of drives) and the superego (our sense of ideal behavior)—remain outside awareness and thus cannot be apprehended as part of our sense of self. Healthy human behavior is enhanced by bringing unconscious mental activity into conscious awareness, so we can have more choices and solve problems more rationally.

The Self as Cognitive Structure

The self as a cognitive structure is accepted as at least a part of most accounts of the self. All of us are in touch (although to varying degrees) with our conscious thinking processes and may come to accept them as representing our essence. This cognitive structure includes self-representations that develop within our schemata. The self as thinker implies that action and emotion originate in thought.

This self may be consistent with the view of reality as a human construction. As thinkers, our sense of self evolves as we actively participate in processing stimuli and define our realities in accordance with our perceptions. The cognitive self is thus interactional and dynamic, not static.

> Humanistic perspective

The Self as Verbal Activity: Symbolic Interactionism

The self can be understood as the product of symbols that we negotiate and share with other people in our culture. The theory of **symbolic interactionism** seeks a resolution to the idea that person and environment are separate and opposite (Blumer, 1998; Denzin, 2001; G. H. Mead, 1934). It stresses that we develop a sense of meaning in the world through interaction with our physical and social environments, which include other people but also all manifestations of cultural life. The mind represents our capacity to respond subjectively to external stimuli through conceptualizing, defining, symbolizing, valuing, and reflecting. This activity is not

> Social constructionist perspective

mechanical, but a creative and selective construction. Through social interaction, interpretation of symbols (objects and ideas with shared cultural meanings), and the filtering processes of the mind, we acquire meaning about the world and ourselves. The sense of self develops from our perceptions of how others perceive us. It is a role-taking process at odds with the psychoanalytic view that the self involves internal drives. Symbolic interactionism suggests that we define ourselves through the attitudes and behavior of others toward us and ultimately from the standards of our society. Our sense of self changes with the changing expectations of others about how we should behave, think, and feel.

The medium through which these processes occur is language. Words are symbols, and language is a product of the shared understandings of people within a culture. Thus, social interaction involves an ongoing negotiation of the meanings of words among persons. Consciousness and the sense of self become possible through language as we learn to talk to ourselves, or think, using these symbols.

Communicators must share an understanding of the cultural norms and rules governing conduct for their interaction to proceed coherently. Symbolic interactionism suggests that socialization is a highly dynamic process that continues throughout life and consists of the creation of new meanings, understandings, and definitions of situations through social interaction (Handel, Cahill, & Elkin, 2007). We change as we bring structure to ambiguous social situations to solve problems.

This concept of self includes both the *I* and the *me* (Vryan, Adler, & Adler, 2003). The *I* is the conscious self—what we are aware of in self-reflection and what actively processes information and solves problems. This self emerges as we become objects of our own thoughts. It develops through the influence of *significant others*—persons who have immediate influence on our self-definitions. The *me,* on the other hand, incorporates thoughts, feelings, and attitudes that we have internalized over time and that are beneath the level of ready awareness. The *me* is influenced by *generalized others*—the types of people whose expectations have come to guide our behavior over time.

Significant others can shape our sense of self (the *I*), even if other acquaintances (family and friends) have already made their mark on us. Sheila's sense of herself as unattractive, unintelligent, and socially incompetent may have originated in critical messages she received from her family, neighbors, teachers, and peers early in life. They may have acted toward her in ways that encouraged her to assume dependent and subservient roles. But interacting with other people who have more positive expectations for Sheila might influence her to enact different behaviors and may lead eventually to greater social competence. If these alternative social actions became prevalent in her life, Sheila's *me* would experience change as well. She might come to think of herself as more independent, competent, and attractive. By guidance and example, an individual may become involved in a community of supportive individuals whose role expectations strengthen the self-concept. The sense of self as competent in specific situations may improve, and the sense of having a substantial role as a member of a social group may also develop.

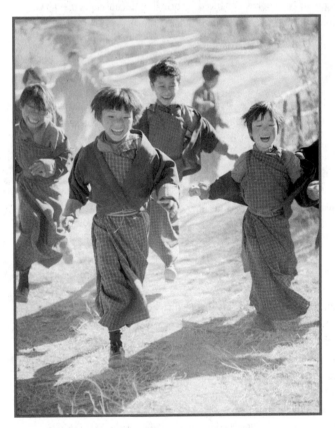

▲ **Photo 4.3** Some see the self as an ongoing process of experience. The play and exploration of these school girls in Bhutan contribute to their developing self-concepts.

The Self as the Experience of Cohesion: Self Psychology

Self psychology, which derives from psychoanalytic theory, conceives of the self as experienced cohesion through action and reflection (L. M. Flanagan, 2008b; E. Goldstein, 2001). Essentially, the self is the self-image, or what each of us perceives when we look into the mirror. It is not fundamentally cognitive or affective, but a mixture of both elements of the psychological self.

Self psychology proposes that the self has three parts, and our sense of cohesion results from their mutual development:

1. *Grandiose self* arises from the positive affirmations we internalize from others; it gives rise to our ambitions and enthusiasm.

2. *Idealized parent image* represents guidance from others, which results in our ability to be self-directed and to set goals.

3. *Twinship* represents our natural social propensities to connect with others and, through this process, to develop our individual talents and skills.

Significant others are essential parts of the self in this view. They provide us with emotional stability, energy, and an internal sense of cohesion. We all require the affirmation and support of others to feel competent and internally cohesive. We always try to achieve higher levels of coherence, improve our capacity to regulate self-esteem, and integrate new relationships with our older ones. Our psychological growth occurs primarily through empathic understanding from others.

> Psychodynamic perspective

Persons who experience problems in functioning may be experiencing situational stress or "disorders" of the self. Such problematic self-states may be characterized by understimulation or overstimulation in transactions with the environment, excessive external stress, or fragmentation (a feeling of incompleteness due to insufficient affirmation, idealization, or twinship experiences). Change is contingent on restoring self-esteem through corrective interpersonal experiences.

Consider Sheila's case. She is depressed and has a poor self-image. Perhaps she did not receive adequate affirmations from her family while she was growing up, did not receive sufficient direction from other adults and mentors to develop mature self-direction, or did not develop the social skills required to form and maintain the relationships that would help her mature in age-appropriate ways. Her self may thus be incomplete, or fragmented, which would be the source of her negative affect. Corrective experience in any of these three areas—perhaps through supportive relationships with her academic adviser (affirmation), teachers and employers (idealized parent image), and student peers on campus (twinship)—might enhance her sense of self.

The Self as a Flow of Experience

The concept of self as an ongoing process of experience may be closer to what we actually live than any of the other concepts. The sense that the flow is the actuality is incorporated in the philosophy and practice theory of *existentialism* (Burston & Frie, 2006; Krill, 1996). People who assume the existential viewpoint hold that there is no standard or "correct" human nature; we are all unique and unable to be categorized. What we are is a subjective and ever-changing notion. The self is never any "thing" at a single point in time because we are defined by the process

> Humanistic perspective

of becoming, a process for which there is no end point. The self is always in process. Our essence is defined by our freedom to make choices and our need to discover or create meaning (sometimes called *will* or *drive*) for ourselves. The self unfolds as we make commitments to ideals outside ourselves (Frankl, 1988).

Existential philosophy is often seen as a pessimistic view of reality because it emphasizes human loneliness, but it does remind us of our uniqueness and the idea that we can always make choices about the directions our lives will take. However negatively Sheila sees herself, for example, she need not necessarily maintain that self-image. She can and will always make choices that will make her a different person—that is, a different self. If Sheila can be helped to recognize her free will, she can perhaps make those choices that will enable her to define herself differently.

The self as a flow of experience is also consistent with **narrative theory**, a relatively new approach to social work practice. Its major premise is that all of us are engaged in an ongoing process of constructing a life story, or personal narrative, that determines our understanding of ourselves and our positions in the world (Herman, 2003). The self is the product of the stories we tell ourselves about who we are, who we were, and how we became who we are. We change by changing the stories we tell ourselves.

Narrative theory holds that human development is inherently fluid, that there are no developmental "milestones" that we should experience to maximize our chances for a satisfying life. Instead, it is the words we use, and the stories we learn to tell about ourselves and about others, that create our psychological and social realities. These life narratives are co-constructed with the narratives of significant people in our family, community, and culture.

According to narrative theory, all personal experience is fundamentally ambiguous, and we must arrange our lives into stories to give them coherence and meaning. These stories do not merely reflect our lives—they shape them! As we develop a dominant "story line" (and self-concept), our new experiences are filtered in or out depending on whether they are consistent with the ongoing life narrative. Many problems in living that we experience are related to life narratives that exclude certain possibilities for future action.

An ultimate value of narrative practice is that of empowering clients, helping them to gain greater control over their lives and destinies. Narrative theory is unique in its conceptualization of problems as, at least in part, by-products of cultural practices that are oppressive to the development of functional life narratives. In this sense, it is a "therapy of advocacy." While some argue that narrative interventions may not be well suited for client problems related to basic needs such as food, shelter, safety, and physical health, they are certainly suitable for issues related to self-concept, interpersonal relationships, and personal growth. From this perspective, we might want to help Sheila understand that her sense of self is being affected by certain oppressive practices related to her "minority" (rural) status in the university culture. Sheila seems to feel inadequate when she is merely different and unique, and her self-deprecating thoughts may reflect prevailing urban norms that are sometimes biased against persons with rural backgrounds. Understanding this may be an important step toward Sheila's gaining pride in herself and then using her strengths to make her way at school.

The above theories of the self represent only a partial overview. Many people believe that the self can only be defined in relation to others, and while this theme has been addressed here, it will receive more attention in the next chapter.

Critical Thinking Questions 4.3

How important is culture in influencing the nature of the self? Does religion or spirituality play a role in the development of self? If so, how?

IMPLICATIONS FOR SOCIAL WORK PRACTICE

The study of the psychological person as a thinking and feeling being and as a self has many implications for social work practice:

- Be alert to the possibility that practice interventions may need to focus on any of several systems, including family, small groups, organizations, and communities. The person's transactions with all of these systems affect psychological functioning.

- During assessment, remember that developmental theories have limited applicability to members of diverse populations, and be open to interpersonal differences with regard to patterns of thinking, feeling, and morality.

- Where appropriate, help individual clients to develop a stronger sense of competence through both ego-supportive and ego-modifying interventions.

- Where appropriate, help individual clients to enhance problem-solving skills through techniques directed at both cognitive reorganization and behavioral change.

- Where appropriate, help individual clients strengthen their sense of self by bringing balance to emotional and cognitive experiences.

- Help clients consider their strengths in terms of the unique sets of intelligences they may have, and show how these intelligences may help them address their challenges in unique ways.

- Where appropriate, encourage clients to become involved in small-group experiences that assist them to understand and change their thoughts, emotions, and behaviors.

- Help clients assess their transactions with formal organizations and the effects of these transactions on their psychological functioning.

- Help clients assess and make necessary changes in their transactions with the community. A person's perspective on his or her community may be influenced by its spatial organization, the conflicts between different groups, the relative harmony of the overall social system, the potential for bonding and meeting spiritual needs, and the community's networks of organizations.

KEY TERMS

accommodation (cognitive)
affect
assimilation (cognitive)
attribution theory
cognition
cognitive mediation
cognitive operations
conventional morality
differential emotions theory
ego

ego psychology
emotion
emotional intelligence
information processing theory
mood
multiple intelligences
narrative theory
postconventional morality
preconscious
preconventional morality

primary emotions
psychoanalytic theory
psychology
schema (schemata)
secondary emotions
self
self psychology
symbolic
    interactionism
unconscious

ACTIVE LEARNING

1. Reread the case study at the beginning of this chapter. As you read, what do you see as the driving force of Sheila's behavior as she makes the transition to the university? Is it cognition? Is it emotion? What patterns of thinking and feeling might Sheila have developed from her rural background? What theories presented in the chapter are most helpful to you in thinking about this, and why?

2. Howard Gardner has proposed a theory of multiple intelligences and suggests that each profession must decide which intelligences are most important to its work. Working in small groups, discuss which of Gardner's eight intelligences are most important for doing social work. Are some intelligences more important in some social work settings than in others? Develop a list of criteria for admission to your social work program based on multiple intelligences.

3. What is your own perspective on the nature of the self? How does this affect your work with clients when you consider their potential for change?

WEB RESOURCES

The Consortium for Research on Emotional Intelligence in Organizations
www.eiconsortium.org
Site contains recent research and model programs for promoting the development of emotional intelligence in the work setting.

Lawrence Kohlberg's Stages of Moral Development
www.xenodocy.org/ex/lists/moraldev.html

Site maintained by Ralph Kenyon, contains an overview and critique of Kohlberg's stage theory of moral development.

Multiple Intelligences for Adult Literacy and Education
http://literacyworks.org/mi/home.html

Site presented by Literacyworks, contains a visual overview of Howard Gardner's theory of multiple intelligences, guidelines

for assessment, and suggestions for putting the theory into practice in adult literacy programs.

Narrative Therapy Centre of Toronto
www.narrativetherapycentre.com/index_files/Page1733.htm

Site contains information on narrative therapy, events and training, articles and books, and links to other websites on narrative therapy.

Piaget's Developmental Theory
www.learningandteaching.info/learning/piaget.htm

Site maintained by James Atherton of the United Kingdom, overviews Jean Piaget's key ideas and developmental stages.

Self Psychology Page
www.selfpsychology.com

Site maintained by David Wolf, contains a definition of the self psychology of Heinz Kohut, bibliography, papers, discussion groups on self psychology, and links to other Internet sites.

5

The Psychosocial Person

Relationships, Stress, and Coping

Joseph Walsh

OPENING QUESTIONS

- How do relationships help us cope with stress?
- What are some different approaches to coping with stress?

KEY IDEAS

As you read this chapter, take note of these central ideas:

1. Understanding the nature of a person's relationship patterns is important for evaluating his or her susceptibility to stress and potential for coping and adaptation. A variety of psychological (object relations, relational, and feminist) and social (Afrocentric, social identity development) theories are useful toward this end.

2. The quality of one's relationships with primary caregivers in infancy and childhood affects neurological development and has lasting effects on the capacity for mental and physical health in later life.

3. Stress, an event that taxes adaptive resources, may be biological, psychological, or social in origin; psychological stress can be categorized as harm, threat, or challenge.

4. Traumatic stress refers to events that are so overwhelming that almost anyone would be affected—events such as natural and technological disasters, war, and physical assault.

5. Our efforts to master the demands of stress are known as coping.

6. All people rely on social supports as means of dealing with stress.

7. Classification of human behavior as normal or abnormal differs among the helping professions. Psychiatry focuses on personal inadequacy in goal attainment and in social presentation from a context of disease or disorder. Psychology focuses on personal inadequacy in a developmental context and often deemphasizes the idea of disease. Sociology considers abnormality, or deviance, as an inability to fulfill a significant social role within a range of accepted behaviors as assessed by significant others in the community. Social work is reluctant to label persons as abnormal because all behavior is conceptualized as interactional and related to the nature of the social context.

Case Study

Sheila's Coping Strategies for College

Midway through her first semester at the state university, Sheila (whom you met in Chapter 4) had reached a crisis point. It was bad enough that she was having trouble academically. But even worse, she was feeling isolated from her fellow students and thinking of herself as hopelessly incompetent at making friends. She missed what she perceived to be the simpler routines of her rural lifestyle. She was depressed, and she expected no better for the foreseeable future. Fortunately, Sheila's parents convinced her to talk with her academic adviser. The adviser immediately became more involved in helping Sheila manage her dyslexia. Sheila learned to become more assertive with her instructors so that they understood her special challenges with the course work.

The academic adviser also encouraged Sheila to begin seeing a counselor. Over several months, the social worker at the university counseling center helped Sheila focus her thoughts and feelings in ways that were productive for her problem solving. First, Sheila found an apartment that afforded her some privacy and personal space. Then, she got a part-time job at a shop on the campus perimeter to help keep busy and involved with people. With the social worker's encouragement, Sheila also joined some small university clubs focused on academic topics as a way for her to feel more comfortable on campus and to begin interacting with other students. She made a couple of good friends whose attention helped her believe that she was a person of worth. The social worker also helped her learn not to bury her emotions by escaping to her apartment, into her work, or back to her parents' home; rather, Sheila learned to experience her emotions as valid indicators that she was feeling threatened. This new way of coping was frightening to Sheila, but the social worker's support was helping her develop a greater sense of competence to manage stress.

By the end of her first year at the university, Sheila was still mildly depressed but feeling significantly better than she had been a few months before. She felt surer of herself, had more friends, and was looking forward to her second year at the university.

THE SELF IN RELATIONSHIPS

In this chapter, we focus on how the psychological person manages challenges to social functioning, particularly stress. Sheila was fortunate: In addition to her personal strengths, she had access to support systems that helped her confront and begin to overcome the stress she was experiencing. We look at the common processes by which we all try to cope with the stresses we experience in life. As Sheila learned, the ability to form, sustain, and use significant relationships with other people is a key to the process of successful coping and adaptation. With this theme in mind, we begin by considering several theories that address the issue of how we exist in the context of relationships, including the object relations, feminist, relational, Afrocentric, and social identity theories, and evidence demonstrating the importance of early nurturing in the ability to build relationships throughout life.

Object Relations Theory

The basic assumption of object relations theory is that all people naturally seek relationships with other people. The question is how well an individual forms interpersonal relationships and how any deficiencies in social functioning might have arisen. The term *object relations* is synonymous with *interpersonal relations*. An "object" is another person but may also be the mental image of a person that we have incorporated into our psychological selves.

Object relations theory is a psychodynamic theory of human development that considers our ability to form lasting attachments with others to be based on early experiences of connection with and separation from our primary caregivers. Many social workers see this theory as an advance over psychoanalytic theory because it

▲ **Photo 5.1** Relationships with significant others are resources for coping with stress.

Psychodynamic
perspective

considers people in the context of relationships rather than as individual entities. We internalize our early relationship patterns, meaning that our first relationships make such an impression on us that they determine how we approach relationships from that point on. These early relationships are a primary determinant of our personality and the quality of our interpersonal functioning (L. M. Flanagan, 2008a; E. Goldstein, 2001).

The ideal is to be raised by caregivers who help us gradually and appropriately move away from their physical and emotional supervision while communicating their availability for support. In such conditions, we acquire the capacity to form trusting attachments with others. This is known as *object constancy*. If, on the other hand, we learn (because of loss or negative caregiver behavior) that we cannot count on others for support as we take risks to move away, we might "internalize" an emotional schema that other people cannot be counted on. Stable object relations result in our ability to form stable relationships, to trust others, and to persist in positive relationships during times of conflict. This idea of internalization is very important, as it implies that we carry our attachments with us. Those significant others in our lives not only exist as memories but are also part of our psychological makeup—they are a part of who we are.

Object relations theorists have suggested a variety of stages in this process of developing object constancy, but we need not get into that level of detail. Suffice it to say that, in addition to the process of developing object relations in early childhood, we also experience a second such process in early adolescence. At that time (at least in Anglo-American society), we begin to move away from the pervasive influence of our families and test our ability to develop our own identity. This is another time of life in which we need to feel that we can trust our primary caregivers as we experiment with independence.

If you are concerned that your own early relationships might have been problematic, don't worry. Object relations theorists do not assert that caregivers need to be perfect (whatever that might be), only that they communicate a sense of caring and permit the child to develop a sense of self (Winnicott, 1975). Even if early object relations are problematic, a person's ability to develop trusting relationships can always be improved, sometimes with therapy.

It may be useful for us to consider one model of parent–child attachment here (Shorey & Snyder, 2006). All children seek close proximity to their parents, and they develop attachment styles suited to the types of parenting they encounter. Ainsworth and her colleagues (Ainsworth, Blehar, & Waters, 1978) identified three infant attachment styles—secure, anxious-ambivalent, and avoidant types. A fourth attachment style has been identified more recently—the disorganized type (Madigan, Moran, & Pederson, 2006).

Securely attached infants act somewhat distressed when their parent figures leave, but greet them eagerly and warmly upon return. Parents of secure infants are sensitive and accepting. Securely attached children are unconcerned about security needs and are thus free to direct their energies toward nonattachment-related activities in the environment. Infants who are not securely attached must direct their attention to maintaining their attachments to inconsistent, unavailable, or rejecting parents, rather than engaging in exploratory behaviors. Because these children are only able to maintain proximity to the parents by behaving as if the parents are not needed, the children may learn not to express needs for closeness or attention.

Anxious-ambivalently attached infants, in contrast, are distraught when their parent figures leave. Upon their parent's return, these infants continue to be distressed even as they want to be comforted and held. These children employ "hyperactivation" strategies. Their parents, while not overtly rejecting, are often unpredictable and inconsistent in their responses. Fearing potential caregiver abandonment, the children maximize their efforts to maintain close parental attachments and become hypervigilant for threat cues and any signs of rejection.

Avoidantly attached infants seem to be relatively undisturbed both when their parent figures leave and when they return. These children want to maintain proximity to their parent figures, but this attachment style enables the children to maintain a sense of proximity to parents who otherwise may reject them. Avoidant children thus suppress expressions of overt distress, and rather than risk further rejection in the face of attachment figure unavailability, may give up on their proximity-seeking efforts.

The *disorganized attachment* style is characterized by chaotic and conflicted behaviors. These children exhibit simultaneous approach and avoidance behaviors. Disorganized infants seem incapable of applying any consistent strategy to bond with their parents. Their conflicted and disorganized behaviors reflect their best attempts at gaining some sense of security from parents who are perceived as frightening. When afraid and needing reassurance, these children have no options but to seek support from a caregiver who is frightening. The parents may be either hostile or fearful and unable to hide their apprehension from their children. In either case, the child's anxiety and distress are not lessened, and one source of stress is merely traded for another.

Although the children with disorganized attachments typically do not attain senses of being cared for, the avoidant and anxious-ambivalent children do experience some success in fulfilling their needs for care.

Relational Theory

In recent years, there has been an integration of the psychoanalytic, object relations, and interpersonal theoretical perspectives, and this is broadly termed **relational theory** (Borden, 2009). In relational theory, as with object relations, the basic human tendency (or drive) is for relationships with others, and our personalities are structured through ongoing interactions with others in the social environment. In this theory, however, there is a strong value of recognizing and supporting diversity in human experience, avoiding the pathologizing of differences, and enlarging traditional conceptions of gender and identity. It is assumed that all patterns of human behavior are learned in the give-and-take of relational life and thus they are all adaptive, reasonable ways of our negotiating experience in the context of circumstances and our need to elicit care from others. Also consistent with object relations concepts, serious problems in living are seen as self-perpetuating because we all have a tendency to preserve continuity, connections, and familiarity in our interpersonal worlds. Our problematic ways of being and relating are perpetuated because they preserve our ongoing experience of the self. What is new is threatening because it lies beyond the bounds of our experience in which we recognize ourselves as cohesive, continuous beings. That is, problematic interpersonal patterns are repeated because they preserve our connections to significant others in the past.

The relational perspective provides contexts of understanding for social workers in their ongoing efforts to connect biological, psychological, and social domains of concern and to enlarge conceptions of persons in their environments. If this sounds to the reader like social work's long-standing focus on person-in-environment, it should! It seems in this sense that social work was ahead of some other disciplines, although this connection is not often made in the literature. Relational theory differs from social work's overarching perspective in that it preserves analytic and object relations concepts while enlarging the scope of environmental concerns. Nonetheless, the similarity is striking, and relational practitioners encourage a variety of activities familiar to social workers including brief intervention, case management, environmental development, and advocacy.

The relational approach enriches the concept of practitioner empathy by adding the notion of mutuality. The ability to participate in a mutual relationship through the use of empathic communication is seen as a goal for the client's growth and development, as well as a mechanism that allows for change in the worker–client relationship and beyond. Current social work literature reflects different views regarding the degree to which workers should remain emotionally detached from clients, but the general consensus calls for the worker to maintain a neutral, objective persona and a sense of separateness. In relational theory, the more the social worker expends energy on keeping parts of himself or herself out of the process, the more rigid, and less spontaneous and genuine, he or she will be in relating to the client system. The worker–client relationship runs the risk of becoming organized into dominant and subordinate roles.

Cultural psychologists argue that most Western psychological theories assume an independent, autonomous self as the ideal self-in-relationship (see Markus & Kitayama, 2009). They suggest that in many cultures of the world, including Asian, African, Latin-American, and Southern European cultures, the ideal self is an interdependent self that recognizes that one's behavior is influenced, even determined, by the perceived thoughts, expectations, and feelings of others in the relationship. Markus and Kitayama (2003) note that in U.S. coverage of the Olympics, athletes are typically asked about how they personally feel about their efforts and their success. In contrast, in Japanese coverage, athletes are typically asked, "Who helped you achieve?" This idea of an interdependent self is consistent with relational theory, as well as feminist and Afrocentric perspectives on relationships.

Feminist Theories of Relationships

The term *feminism* does not refer to any single body of thought. It refers to a wide-ranging system of ideas about human experience developed from a woman-centered perspective. Feminist theories may be classified as liberal, radical, Marxist, socialist, existential, postmodern, multicultural, or ecofeminist (Lengermann & Niebrugge-Brantley, 2007). Among the psychological theories are psychoanalytic feminism (Angers, 2008) and gender feminism (Marecek, Kimmel, Crawford, & Hare-Mustin, 2003). We focus on these two as we consider how feminism has deepened our capacity for understanding human behavior and interaction. All of these theorists begin from the position that women and men approach relationships differently, and that patriarchal societies consider male attributes to be superior.

> Conflict perspective

Psychoanalytic feminists assert that women's ways of acting are rooted deeply in women's unique ways of thinking. These differences may be biological, but they are certainly influenced by cultural and psychosocial conditions. Feminine behavior features gentleness, modesty, humility, supportiveness, empathy, compassion, tenderness, nurturance, intuitiveness, sensitivity, and unselfishness. Masculine behavior is characterized by strength of will, ambition, courage, independence, assertiveness, hardiness, rationality, and emotional control. Psychoanalytic feminists assert that these differences are largely rooted in early childhood relationships. Because women are the primary caretakers in our society, young girls tend to develop and enjoy an ongoing relationship with their mothers that promotes their valuing of relatedness as well as the other feminine behaviors. For young boys, on the other hand, the mother is eventually perceived as fundamentally different, particularly as they face social pressures to begin fulfilling male roles. The need to separate from the mother figure has long-range implications for boys: They tend to lose what could otherwise become a learned capacity for intimacy and relatedness.

> Psychodynamic perspective

Gender feminists tend to be concerned with values of separateness (for men) and connectedness (for women) and how these lead to a different morality for women. Carol Gilligan (1982; see also the section on theories of moral reasoning in Chapter 4 of this book) is a leading thinker in this area. She elucidated a process by which women develop an ethic of care rather than an ethic of justice, based on the value they place on relationships. Gender feminists believe that these female ethics are equal to male ethics, although they have tended in patriarchal societies to be considered inferior. Gilligan asserts that all of humanity would be best served if both ethics could be valued equally. Other gender feminists go further, however, arguing for the superiority of women's ethics. For example, Noddings (2002, 2005) asserts that war will never be discarded in favor of the sustained pursuit of peace until the female ethic of caring, aimed at unification, replaces the male ethic of strenuous striving, aimed at dividing people.

All psychological feminist theories promote the value of relationships and the importance of reciprocal interpersonal supports. They encourage us to note that Sheila's father raised her to be achievement- and task-oriented. These are admirable characteristics, but they represent male perspectives. Sheila's inclinations for interpersonal experience may have been discouraged, which was harmful to her overall development.

Afrocentric Relational Theory

The origins of Afrocentric relational theory (which can be considered a type of the broader relational theory discussed above) are in traditional Africa, before the arrival of European and Arabian influences. The Afrocentric worldview values cultural pluralism and, in fact, values difference in all of its forms. It does not accept hierarchies based on social differences, however. Eurocentric thinking, emphasizing mastery rather than harmony with the environment, is seen as oppressive. The three major objectives of Afrocentric theory are to provide an alternative perspective that reflects African cultures; to dispel negative distortions about African people held by other cultures; and to promote social transformations that are spiritual, moral, and humanistic.

> Humanistic perspective

Afrocentric relational theory assumes a collective identity for people rather than valuing individuality (Y. R. Bell, Bouie, & Baldwin, 1998; R. L. Jackson, 2004). It places great value on the spiritual or nonmaterial aspects of life, understood broadly as an "invisible substance" that connects all people. It values an affective approach to knowledge, conceptualizing emotion as the most direct experience of the self. This is of course in contrast to the Western emphasis on cognition and rationality. In its emphasis on the collective, Afrocentrism does not distinguish between things that affect the individual and things that affect larger groups of people, and it sees all social problems as related to practices of oppression and alienation. Personal connection and reciprocity are emphasized in helping relationships such as the social worker–client relationship. Like feminism, Afrocentrism counters the object relations emphasis on individuality and independence with attention to collective identity and human connectedness.

Social Identity Theory

Social identity theory is a stage theory of socialization that articulates the process by which we come to identify with some social groups and develop a sense of difference from other social groups (Hornsey, 2008; Nesdale, 2004). Social identity development can be an affirming process that provides us with a lifelong sense of belonging and support. I might feel good to have membership with a Roman Catholic or Irish American community. Because social identity can be exclusionary, however, it can also give rise to prejudice and oppression. I may believe that my race is more intelligent than another, or that persons of my cultural background are entitled to more benefits than those of another.

> Developmental perspective

Social identity development proceeds in five stages. These stages are not truly distinct or sequential, however; people often experience several stages simultaneously.

1. *Naïveté.* During early childhood, we have no social consciousness. We are not aware of particular codes of behavior for members of our group or any other social group. Our parents or other primary caregivers are our most significant influences, and we accept that socialization without question. As young children, we do, however, begin to distinguish between ourselves and other groups of people. We may not feel completely comfortable with the racial, ethnic, or religious differences we observe, but neither do we feel fearful, superior, or inferior. Children at this stage are mainly curious about differences.

2. *Acceptance.* Older children and young adolescents learn the distinct ideologies and belief systems of their own and other social groups. During this stage, we learn that the world's institutions and authority figures have rules that encourage certain behaviors and prohibit others, and we internalize these dominant cultural beliefs and make them a part of our everyday lives. Those questions that emerged during the stage of naïveté are submerged. We come

to believe that the way our group does things is normal, makes more sense, and is better. We regard the cultures of people who are different from us as strange, marginal, and perhaps inferior. We may passively accept these differences or actively do so by joining organizations that highlight our own identity and (perhaps) devalue others.

3. *Resistance.* In adolescence, or even later, we become aware of the harmful effects of acting on social differences. We have new experiences with members of other social groups that challenge our prior assumptions. We begin to reevaluate those assumptions and investigate our own role in perpetuating harmful differences. We may feel anger at others within our own social group who foster these irrational differences. We begin to move toward a new definition of social identity that is broader than our previous definition. We may work to end our newly perceived patterns of collusion and oppression.

4. *Redefinition.* Redefinition is a process of creating a new social identity that preserves our pride in our origins while perceiving differences with others as positive representations of diversity. We may isolate from some members of our social group and shift toward interactions with others who share our level of awareness. We see all groups as being rich in strengths and values. We may reclaim our own group heritage but broaden our definition of that heritage as one of many varieties of constructive living.

5. *Internalization.* In the final stage of social identity development, we become comfortable with our revised identity and are able to incorporate it into all aspects of our life. We act unconsciously, without external controls. Life continues as an ongoing process of discovering vestiges of our old biases, but now we test our integrated new identities in wider contexts than our limited reference group. Our appreciation of the plight of all oppressed people, and our enhanced empathy for others, is a part of this process. For many people, the internalization stage is an ongoing challenge rather than an end state.

The Impact of Early Nurturing

> Psychodynamic perspective; developmental perspective

We have been looking at theories that deem relationships to be important throughout our lives. Turning to the empirical research, we can find evidence that, as suggested by object relations theory, the quality of our *early* relationships is crucial to our lifelong capacity to engage in healthy relationships, and even to enjoy basic physical health.

There is a large body of research devoted to studying the links between early life experiences and physical and mental health risks (e.g., Gerhardt, 2004; Gunnar, Broderson, Nachimas, Buss, & Rigatuso, 1996; Stansfeld, Head, Bartley, & Fonagy, 2008). This work demonstrates that negative infant experiences such as child abuse, family strife, poverty, and emotional neglect correlate with later health problems ranging from depression to drug abuse and heart disease. Relational elements of our early environments appear to permanently alter the development of central nervous system structures that govern our autonomic, cognitive, behavioral, and emotional responses to stress.

Animal models are common in this research, tracing the physiological aspects of rat and monkey stress responses all the way to the level of gene expression (Bredy, Weaver, Champagne, & Meaney, 2001; Kempes, Gulickx, van Daalen, Sterck, & Louwerse, 2008; Lupien, King, Meaney, & McEwen, 2000). It has been found that highly groomed young rats (pups) develop more receptors in their brains for the substances that inhibit the production of corticotropin-releasing hormone (CRH), the master regulator of the stress response. As a result of the tactile stimulation they received from mothers, the pups' brains develop in a way that lowers their stress response—not only while being groomed, but also throughout life! When the rats are switched at birth to different mothers, the pups' brain development matched the behavior of the mother who reared them, not their biological mothers. Furthermore, high-licking and high-grooming (nurturing) mother rats change their behavior significantly when given a substance that stimulates the hormonal effects of chronic stress, raising their CRH and lowering oxytocin, a hormone related to the equanimity many human mothers feel after giving birth. That is, under the influence of these stress hormones, the high-nurturing mothers behaved like the low-nurturing mothers, and their offspring grew up to have the same stress responses.

Some of you may be familiar with the tradition of research on the nurturing practices of rhesus monkeys. Research continues in this area (Barrett et al., 2009; Suomi, 2005; S. J. Webb, Monk, & Nelson, 2001). In some of these experiments, monkeys are separated from their mothers at age intervals of 1 week, 1 month, 3 months, and 6 months and raised in a group of other monkeys that includes a different mother monkey. The infants who are separated later (3 or 6 months) exhibit normal behavior in the new setting. Those separated earlier, however, show a variety of abnormalities. The monkeys separated at 1 month initially exhibit a profound depression and refuse to eat. Once they recover, they show a deep need for attachments with other monkeys and also show great anxiety during social separation whenever they feel threatened. The monkeys separated at 1 week showed no interest in social contact with other monkeys, and this behavior did not change as they grew older. Autopsies of these monkeys showed changes in brain development. The timing of separation from the primary caregiver seems to be significant to their later development. These findings in monkeys may have a sad counterpart in human children who are separated at early ages from their mothers.

Although much of this research is being conducted on rats, monkeys, and other animals, it has clear implications for human development. The concept of **neural plasticity,** which refers to the capacity of the nervous system to be modified by experience, is significant here (Knudsen, 2004; Nelson, 2000). Humans may have a window of opportunity, or a critical period for altering neurological development, but this window varies, depending on the area of the nervous system. Even through the second decade of life, for example, neurotransmitter and synapse changes are influenced by internal biology but perhaps by external signals as well.

There is also much current research underway that is exploring the relationship between the processes of attachment and specific neurological development in young persons (Schore, 2001, 2002). Persistent stress in the infant or toddler results in an overdevelopment of areas of the brain that process anxiety and fear, and the underdevelopment of other areas of the brain, particularly the cortex. Of particular concern to one leading researcher (Schore, 2002) is the impact of the absence of nurturance on the orbital frontal cortex (OFC) of the brain. Chronic levels of stress contribute to fewer neural connections between the prefrontal cortex and the amygdala, a process that is significant to psychosocial functioning. The OFC is particularly active in such processes as our concentration and judgment as well as our ability to observe and control internal subjective states. Further, the frontal cortex is central to our emotional regulation capacity and our experience of empathy. The amygdala, part of the limbic system (as discussed in the previous chapter), is attributed with interpreting incoming stimuli and information and storing this information in our implicit (automatic) memory. The amygdala assesses threat and triggers our immediate responses to it (the fight, flight, or freeze behaviors). A reduction in neural connections between these two areas suggests that the frontal cortex is not optimally able to regulate the processing of fear, resulting in exaggerated fear responses.

Stress can clearly affect brain development, but there is little evidence that the first 3 years of life are all-important (Nelson, 1999). A study of 2,600 undergraduate students found that even in late adolescence and early adulthood, satisfying social relationships were associated with greater autonomic activity and restorative behaviors when confronting acute stress (Cacioppo, Bernston, Sheridan, & McClintock, 2000). Higher CRH levels characterized chronically lonely individuals.

In summary, the research evidence indicates that secure attachments play a critical role in shaping the systems that underlie our reactivity to stressful situations. At the time when infants begin to form specific attachments to adults, the presence of caregivers who are warm and responsive begins to buffer or prevent elevations in stress hormones, even in situations that distress the infant. In contrast, insecure relationships are associated with higher CRH levels in potentially threatening situations. Secure emotional relationships with adults appear to be at least as critical as individual differences in temperament in determining stress reactivity and regulation (Eagle & Wolitzky, 2009).

Still, there is much to be learned in this area. Many people who have been subjected to serious early-life traumas become effective, high-functioning adolescents and adults. Infants and children are resilient and have many strengths that can help them overcome these early-life stresses. Researchers are challenged to determine whether interventions such as foster care can remedy the physical, emotional, and social problems seen in children who have experienced poor nurturing and early problems with separation.

Critical Thinking Questions 5.1

Give some thought to social identity theory. With what social groups do you identify? How did you come to identify with these groups? How might your social identities affect your social work practice?

THE CONCEPT OF STRESS

One of the main benefits of good nurturing is, as you have seen, the way it strengthens the ability to cope with stress. **Stress** can be defined as any event in which environmental or internal demands tax the adaptive resources of an individual. Stress may be biological (a disturbance in bodily systems), psychological (cognitive and emotional factors involved in the evaluation of a threat), and even social (the disruption of a social unit). Sheila experienced psychological stress, of course, as evidenced by her troublesome thoughts and feelings of depression, but she also experienced other types of stress. She experienced biological stress because, in an effort to attend classes, study, and work, she did not give her body adequate rest. As a result, she was susceptible to colds and the flu, which kept her in bed for several days each month and compounded her worries about managing course work. Sheila also experienced social stress, because she had left the slow-paced, interpersonally comfortable environments of her rural home and community college to attend the university.

Three Categories of Psychological Stress

Psychological stress, about which we are primarily concerned in this chapter, can be broken down into three categories (Lazarus, 2007):

1. *Harm:* A damaging event that has already occurred. Sheila avoided interaction with her classmates during much of the first semester, which may have led them to decide that she is aloof and that they should not try to approach her socially. Sheila has to accept that this rejection happened and that some harm has been done to her as a result, although she can learn from the experience and try to change in the future.

2. *Threat:* A perceived potential for harm that has not yet happened. This is probably the most common form of psychological stress. We feel stress because we are apprehensive about the possibility of the negative event. Sheila felt threatened when she walked into a classroom during the first semester because she anticipated rejection from her classmates. We can be proactive in managing threats to ensure that they do not in fact occur and result in harm to us.

3. *Challenge:* An event we appraise as an opportunity rather than an occasion for alarm. We are mobilized to struggle against the obstacle, as with a threat, but our attitude is quite different. Faced with a threat, we are likely to act defensively to protect ourselves. Our defensiveness sends a negative message to the environment:

We don't want to change; we want to be left alone. In a state of challenge, however, we are excited, expansive, and confident about the task to be undertaken. The challenge may be an exciting and productive experience for us. In her second year at the university, Sheila may feel more excited than before about entering a classroom full of strangers at the beginning of a semester. She may look forward with more confidence to meeting people who may become her friends.

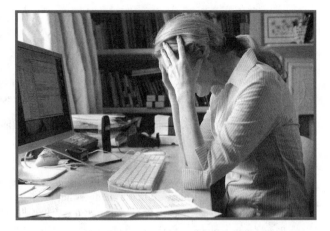

▲ **Photo 5.2** This woman is experiencing psychological stress; she is challenged by the task at hand, but she feels equal to the task.

Stress has been measured in several ways (Aldwin & Yancura, 2004; Lazarus, 2007). One of the earliest attempts to measure stress consisted of a list of *life events,* uncommon events that bring about some change in our lives—experiencing the death of a loved one, getting married, becoming a parent, and so forth. The use of life events to measure stress is based on the assumption that major changes involve losses and disrupt our behavioral patterns.

More recently, stress has also been measured as **daily hassles,** common occurrences that are taxing—standing in line waiting, misplacing or losing things, dealing with troublesome coworkers, worrying about money, and many more. It is thought that an accumulation of daily hassles takes a greater toll on our coping capacities than do relatively rare life events.

Sociologists and community psychologists also study stress by measuring **role strain**—problems experienced in the performance of specific roles, such as romantic partner, caregiver, or worker. Research on caregiver burden is one example of measuring stress as role strain (Bowman, 2006).

Social workers should be aware that as increasing emphasis is placed on the deleterious effects of stress on the immune system, our attention and energies are diverted from the project of changing societal conditions that create stress and toward the management of ourselves as persons who respond to stress (D. Becker, 2005). With the influence of the medical model, we should not be surprised when we are offered individual or biomedical solutions to such different social problems as working motherhood, poverty, and road rage. It may be that the appeal of the stress concept is based on its diverting attention away from the environmental causes of stress. This is why social workers should always be alert to the social nature of stress.

Stress and Crisis

A **crisis** is a major upset in our psychological equilibrium due to some harm, threat, or challenge with which we cannot cope (R. K. James & Gilliland, 2001). The crisis poses an obstacle to achieving a personal goal, but we cannot overcome the obstacle through our usual methods of problem solving. We temporarily lack either the necessary knowledge for coping or the ability to focus on the problem, because we feel overwhelmed. A crisis episode often results when we face a serious stressor with which we have had no prior experience. It may be biological (major illness), interpersonal (the sudden loss of a loved one), or environmental (unemployment or a natural disaster such as a flood or fire). We can regard anxiety, guilt, shame, sadness, envy, jealousy, and disgust as stress emotions (Zautra, 2003). They are the emotions most likely to emerge in a person who is experiencing crisis.

Crisis episodes occur in three stages:

1. Our level of tension increases sharply.

2. We try and fail to cope with the stress, which further increases our tension and contributes to our sense of being overwhelmed. We are particularly receptive to receiving help from others at this time.

3. The crisis episode ends, either negatively (unhealthy coping) or positively (successful management of the crisis).

Crises can be classified into three types (Lantz & Walsh, 2007). *Developmental* crises occur as events in the normal flow of life create dramatic changes that produce extreme responses. Examples of such events include going off to college, college graduation, the birth of one's child, a midlife career change, and retirement from work. People may experience these types of crises if they have difficulty negotiating the typical challenges outlined by Erikson (1968) and Gitterman (2009). *Situational* crises refer to uncommon and extraordinary events that a person has no way of forecasting or controlling. Examples include physical injuries, sexual assault, loss of a job, major illness, and the death of a loved one. *Existential* crises are characterized by escalating inner conflicts related to issues of purpose in life, responsibility, independence, freedom, and commitment. Examples include remorse over past life choices, a feeling that one's life has no meaning, and a questioning of one's basic values or spiritual beliefs.

Sheila's poor midterm grades during her first semester illustrate some of these points. First, she was overwhelmed by the negative emotions of shame and sadness. Then, she retreated to her parents' home where she received much-needed support from her family. With their encouragement, she sought additional support from her academic adviser and a counselor. Finally, as the crisis situation stabilized, Sheila concluded that she could take some actions to relieve her feelings of loneliness and incompetence (a positive outcome).

Traumatic Stress

Although a single event may pose a crisis for one person but not another, some stressors are so severe that they are almost universally experienced as crisis. The stress is so overwhelming that almost anyone would be affected. The term **traumatic stress** is used to refer to events that involve actual or threatened severe injury or death, of oneself or significant others (APA, 2000). Three types of traumatic stress have been identified: natural (such as flood, tornado, earthquake) and technological (such as nuclear) disasters; war and related problems (such as concentration camps); and individual trauma (such as being raped, assaulted, or tortured) (Aldwin, 2007). People respond to traumatic stress with helplessness, terror, and horror.

Some occupations—particularly those of emergency workers such as police officers, firefighters, disaster relief workers, and military personnel in war settings—involve regular exposure to traumatic events that most people do not experience in a lifetime. The literature about the stress faced by emergency workers refers to these traumatic events as *critical incidents* (CIs) and the reaction to them as *critical incident stress* (Prichard, 2004). Emergency workers, particularly police officers and firefighters, may experience threats to their own lives and the lives of their colleagues, as well as encounter mass casualties. Emergency workers may also experience *compassion stress,* a feeling of deep sympathy and sorrow for another who is stricken by misfortune, accompanied by a strong desire to alleviate the pain (Figley, 2002). Any professionals who work regularly with trauma survivors are susceptible to compassion stress. Many social workers fall into this category.

Vulnerability to Stress

Our response to stress is in part related to our individual biological constitutions and our previous experiences with stress. Research from the field of mental illness underscores this point. In an attempt to understand the causes of many mental disorders, several researchers have postulated **stress/diathesis models** of mental illness (Ingram & Luxton, 2005). These models are based on empirical data indicating that certain disorders (psychotic and mood disorders, for example) develop from the interaction of environmental stresses and a *diathesis,* or vulnerability, to the disorders. The diathesis may be biological (a genetic or biochemical predisposition), environmental (history of severe stressors), or both. Most models, however, emphasize biological factors.

Stress/diathesis models suggest that all persons do not have an equal chance of developing mental disorders because it depends in part on one's chemical makeup. A person at risk may have an innate inability to manage high levels of stimulation from the outside world. For example, one model postulates that the onset of schizophrenia is 70% related to innate predisposition and 30% related to external stress (Jones & Fernyhough, 2007).

The stress/diathesis view highlights a probable interaction between constitutional and environmental factors in our experience and tolerance of stress. It suggests that a single event may pose a crisis for one person but not another. In its broadest versions, it also suggests that vulnerability to stress is related to one's position in the social structure, with some social positions exposed to a greater number of adverse situations—such as poverty, racism, and blocked opportunities—than others (Ingram & Luxton, 2005).

Critical Thinking Questions 5.2

Why do you think we easily get diverted from thinking about societal conditions that create stress, and come, instead, to focus on helping individuals cope with stress? How does such an approach fit with social work's commitment to social justice?

COPING AND ADAPTATION

Our efforts to master the demands of stress are referred to as **coping.** Coping includes the thoughts, feelings, and actions that constitute these efforts. One method of coping is **adaptation,** which may involve adjustments in our biological responses, in our perceptions, or in our lifestyle.

Biological Coping

The traditional biological view of stress and coping, developed in the 1950s, emphasizes the body's attempts to maintain physical equilibrium, or **homeostasis,** which is a steady state of functioning (Selye, 1991). Stress is considered the result of any demand on the body (specifically, the nervous and hormonal systems) during perceived emergencies to prepare for fight (confrontation) or flight (escape). A stressor may be any biological process, emotion, or thought.

In this view, the body's response to a stressor is called the **general adaptation syndrome.** It occurs in three stages:

1. *Alarm:* The body first becomes aware of a threat.

2. *Resistance:* The body attempts to restore homeostasis.

3. *Exhaustion:* The body terminates coping efforts because of its inability to physically sustain the state of disequilibrium.

The general adaptation syndrome is explained in Exhibit 5.1.

In this context, *resistance* has a different meaning than is generally used in social work: an active, positive response of the body in which endorphins and specialized cells of the immune system fight off stress and infection. Our immune systems are constructed for adaptation to stress, but cumulative wear and tear of multiple stress episodes can gradually deplete our body's resources. Common outcomes of chronic stress include stomach and intestinal disorders, high blood pressure, heart problems, and emotional problems. If only to preserve healthy physical functioning, we must combat and prevent stress.

This traditional view of biological coping with stress came from research that focused on males, either male rodents or human males. Since 1995, the federal government has required federally funded researchers to include a broad representation of both men and women in their study samples. Consequently, recent research on stress has included female as well as male participants, and gender differences in responses to stress have been found.

Research by Shelley Taylor and colleagues (S. E. Taylor et al., 2002; S. E. Taylor & Stanton, 2007) found that females of many species, including humans, respond to stress with "tend-and-befriend" rather than the "fight-or-flight" behavior described in the general adaptation syndrome. Under stressful conditions, females have been found to turn to protecting and nurturing their offspring and to seeking social contact. The researchers suggest a possible biological basis for this gender difference in the coping response. More specifically, they note a large role for the hormone oxytocin, which plays a role in childbirth but also is secreted in both males and females in response to stress. High levels of oxytocin in animals are associated with calmness and increased sociability. Although males as well as females secrete

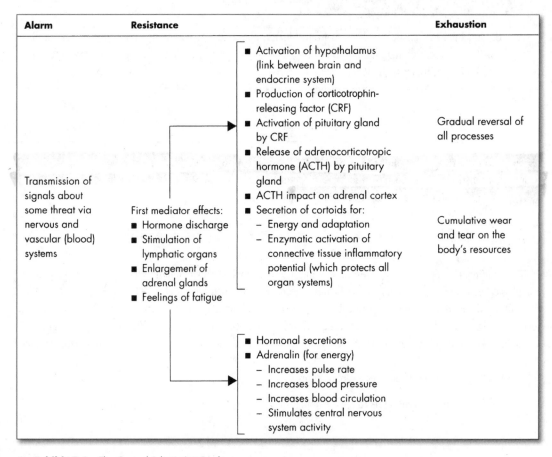

▲ **Exhibit 5.1**   The General Adaptation Syndrome

oxytocin in response to stress, there is evidence that male hormones reduce the effects of oxytocin. Taylor and colleagues believe this in part explains the gender differences in response to stress.

Psychological Coping

The psychological aspect of managing stress can be viewed in two different ways. Some theorists consider coping ability to be a stable personality characteristic, or **trait**; others see it instead as a transient **state**—a process that changes over time, depending on the context (J. Y. F. Lau, Eley, & Stevenson, 2006).

Those who consider coping to be a *trait* see it as an acquired defensive style. **Defense mechanisms** are unconscious, automatic responses that enable us to minimize perceived threats or keep them out of our awareness entirely. Exhibit 5.2 lists the common defense mechanisms identified by ego psychology (discussed in Chapter 4). Some defense mechanisms are considered healthier, or more adaptive, than others. Sheila's denial of her need for intimacy, for example, did not help her meet her goal of developing relationships with peers. But through the defense of sublimation (channeling the need for intimacy into alternative and socially acceptable outlets), she has become an excellent caregiver to a friend's child.

Psychodynamic perspective

Those who see coping as a *state*, or process, observe that our coping strategies change in different situations. After all, our perceptions of threats, and what we focus on in a situation, change. The context also has an impact on our perceived and actual abilities to apply effective coping mechanisms. From this perspective, Sheila's use of denial would be adaptive at some times and maladaptive at others. Perhaps her denial of loneliness during the first academic semester helped her focus on her studies, which would help her achieve her goal of receiving an education. During the summer, however, when classes are out of session, she might become aware that her avoidance of relationships has prevented her from attaining interpersonal goals. Her efforts to cope with loneliness might also change when she can afford more energy to confront the issue.

Systems perspective

The trait and state approaches can usefully be combined. We can think of coping as a general pattern of managing stress that allows flexibility across diverse contexts. This perspective is consistent with the idea that cognitive schemata develop through the dual processes of assimilation and accommodation, described in Chapter 4.

Systems perspective

Coping Styles

Another way to look at coping is based on how the person responds to crisis. Coping efforts may be problem-focused or emotion-focused (Sideridis, 2006). The function of **problem-focused coping** is to change the situation by acting on the environment. This method tends to dominate whenever we view situations as controllable by action. For example, Sheila was concerned about her professors' insensitivity to her learning disability. When she took action to educate them about it and explain more clearly how she learns best in a classroom setting, she was using problem-focused coping. In contrast, the function of **emotion-focused coping** is to change either the way the stressful situation is attended to (by vigilance or avoidance) or the meaning to oneself of what is happening. The external situation does not change, but our behaviors or attitudes change with respect to it, and we may thus effectively manage the stressor. When we view stressful conditions as unchangeable, emotion-focused coping may dominate. If Sheila learns that one of her professors has no empathy for students with learning disabilities, she might avoid taking that professor's courses in the future, or decide that getting a good grade in that course is not as important as being exposed to the course material.

U.S. culture tends to venerate problem-focused coping and the independently functioning self and to distrust emotion-focused coping and what may be called relational coping. **Relational coping** takes into account actions that maximize the survival of

Conflict perspective

Defense Mechanism	Definition	Example
Denial	Negating an important aspect of reality that one may actually perceive.	A woman with anorexia acknowledges her actual weight and strict dieting practices, but firmly believes that she is maintaining good self-care by dieting.
Displacement	Shifting feelings about one person or situation onto another.	A student's anger at her professor, who is threatening as an authority figure, is transposed into anger at her boyfriend, a safer target.
Intellectualization	Avoiding unacceptable emotions by thinking or talking about them rather than experiencing them directly.	A person talks to her counselor about the fact that she is sad but shows no emotional evidence of sadness, which makes it harder for her to understand its effects on her life.
Introjection	Taking characteristics of another person into the self in order to avoid a direct expression of emotions. The emotions originally felt about the other person are now felt toward the self.	An abused woman feels angry with herself rather than her abusing partner, because she has taken on his belief that she is an inadequate caregiver. Believing otherwise would make her more fearful that the desired relationship might end.
Isolation of affect	Consciously experiencing an emotion in a "safe" context rather than the threatening context in which it was first unconsciously experienced.	A person does not experience sadness at the funeral of a family member, but the following week weeps uncontrollably at the death of a pet hamster.
Projection	Attributing unacceptable thoughts and feelings to others.	A man does not want to be angry with his girlfriend, so when he is upset with her, he avoids owning that emotion by assuming that she is angry at him.
Rationalization	Using convincing reasons to justify ideas, feelings, or actions so as to avoid recognizing true motives.	A student copes with the guilt normally associated with cheating on an exam by reasoning that he was too ill the previous week to prepare as well as he wanted.
Reaction formation	Replacing an unwanted unconscious impulse with its opposite in conscious behavior.	A person cannot bear to be angry with his boss, so after a conflict he convinces himself that the boss is worthy of loyalty and demonstrates this by volunteering to work overtime.
Regression	Resuming behaviors associated with an earlier developmental stage or level of functioning in order to avoid present anxiety. The behavior may or may not help to resolve the anxiety.	A young man throws a temper tantrum as a means of discharging his frustration when he cannot master a task on his computer. The startled computer technician, who had been reluctant to attend to the situation, now comes forth to provide assistance.

Repression	Keeping unwanted thoughts and feelings entirely out of awareness.	A son may begin to generate an impulse of hatred for his father, but because the impulse would be consciously unacceptable, he represses the hatred and does not become aware of it.
Somatization	Converting intolerable impulses into somatic symptoms.	A person who is unable to express his negative emotions develops frequent stomachaches as a result.
Sublimation	Converting an impulse from a socially unacceptable aim to a socially acceptable one.	An angry, aggressive young man becomes a star on his school's debate team.
Undoing	Nullifying an undesired impulse with an act of reparation.	A man who feels guilty about having lustful thoughts about a coworker tries to make amends to his wife by purchasing a special gift for her.

▲ **Exhibit 5.2** Common Defense Mechanisms

SOURCE: Adapted from Goldstein (1995).

others—such as our families, children, and friends—as well as ourselves (Zunkel, 2002). Feminist theorists propose that women are more likely than men to employ the relational coping strategies of negotiation and forbearance, and Taylor's recent research (S. E. Taylor et al., 2002; Taylor & Stanton, 2007) gives credence to the idea that women are more likely than men to use relational coping. As social workers, we must be careful not to assume that one type of coping is superior to another. Power imbalances and social forces such as racism and sexism affect the coping strategies of individuals (Lippa, 2005). We need to give clients credit for the extraordinary coping efforts they may make in hostile environments.

Richard Lazarus (1999) has identified some particular behaviors typical of each coping style:

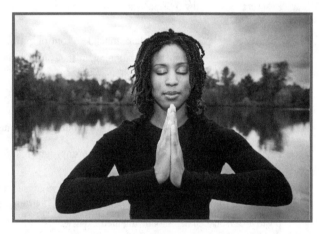

▲ **Photo 5.3** Meditation is an emotion-focused method for dealing with stress. This woman is using meditation to change the way she attends to stress.

- *Problem-focused coping:* confrontation, problem solving

- *Emotion-focused coping:* distancing, escape or avoidance, positive reappraisal

- *Problem- or emotion-focused coping (depending on context):* self-control, search for social support, acceptance of responsibility

Lazarus emphasizes that all of us use any or several of these mechanisms at different times. None of them is any person's sole means of managing stress.

Using Lazarus's model, we might note that Sheila did not initially employ many problem-focused coping strategies to manage stressors at the university, and she overused emotion-focused methods. For example, she accepted responsibility (that is, blamed herself) for her difficulties at first and tried without success to control her moods through force of will. Later, she distanced herself from her emotions and avoided stressors by spending more time away from campus working, and she was in fact quite skilled at this job. When she began seeking social support, she became more problem-focused.

I probably don't need to tell you that college students face many predictable stressors when attending to the demands of academic work. A few years ago, I wanted to learn more about how students use both problem- and emotion-focused coping strategies in response to stress. I surveyed social work students in two Human Behavior in the Social Environment courses at a large urban university, at the beginning of an academic year, about their anticipated stressors and the ways they might cope with them. The results of this informal survey are outlined in Exhibit 5.3. The students chose problem- and emotion-focused coping strategies almost equally—a healthy mix (although they may not have been forthcoming about some socially "unacceptable" strategies).

Coping and Traumatic Stress

People exhibit some similarities between the way they cope with traumatic stress and the way they cope with everyday stress. For both types of stress, they use problem-focused action, social support, negotiation skills, humor, altruism, and prayer (Aldwin, 2007). However, coping with traumatic stress differs from coping with everyday stress in several ways (Aldwin & Yancura, 2004):

- Because people tend to have much less control in traumatic situations, their primary emotion-focused coping strategy is emotional numbing, or the constriction of emotional expression. They also make greater use of the defense mechanism of denial.

- Confiding in others takes on greater importance.

- The process of coping tends to take a much longer time. Reactions can be delayed, for months or even years.

- A search for meaning takes on greater importance, and transformation in personal identity is more common.

Although there is evidence of long-term negative consequences of traumatic stress, trauma survivors sometimes report positive outcomes as well. Studies have found that 34% of holocaust survivors and 50% of rape survivors report positive personal changes following their experiences with traumatic stress (Burt & Katz, 1987; Kahana, 1992).

However, many trauma survivors experience a set of symptoms known as **posttraumatic stress disorder (PTSD)** (APA, 2000). These symptoms include the following:

- *Persistent reliving of the traumatic event:* intrusive, distressing recollections of the event; distressing dreams of the event; a sense of reliving the event; intense distress when exposed to cues of the event

- *Persistent avoidance of stimuli associated with the traumatic event:* avoidance of thoughts or feelings connected to the event; avoidance of places, activities, and people connected to the event; inability to recall aspects of the trauma; loss of interest in activities; feeling detached from others; emotional numbing; no sense of a future

- *Persistent high state of arousal:* difficulty sleeping, irritability, difficulty concentrating, excessive attention to stimuli, exaggerated startle response

Problem-Focused Coping

Confrontation
- Learn to say no.

Problem Solving
- Exercise.
- Work with other students.
- Talk with professors.
- Go to the beach (for relaxation).
- Manage time.
- Undertake self-care.
- Reserve time for oneself.
- Stay ahead.
- Use relaxation techniques.
- Walk.
- Clean the house.
- Carry own lunch (save money).
- Aim for good nutrition.
- Take breaks.
- Look for "free" social activities.
- Pursue art interest.
- Organize tasks.
- Carefully budget finances.
- Plan for a job search.

Self-Control
- Bear down and "gut it out."
- Take on a job.

Search for Social Support
- Talk.
- Network with others.
- Demand support from others.
- Reserve time with family.

Emotion-Focused Coping

Distancing
- Deny that problem exists.
- Procrastinate.

Escape or Avoidance
- Drink.
- Smoke.
- Drink too much caffeine.
- Overeat, undereat.
- Give up.
- Vent on others.
- Curse other drivers.
- Neglect others.
- Watch too much television.
- Neglect other important concerns.
- Use charge cards.

Positive Reappraisal
- Think of money produced by job.
- Maintain perpective.
- Maintain flexibility.
- Reframe frustrations as growth opportunities.

Self-Control
- Push too hard.
- Study all night.

Search for Social Support
- Seek intimacy.
- Engage in sex.
- Participate in therapy.

Acceptance of Responsibility
- Cry.

▲ **Exhibit 5.3**   Coping Styles Among Social Work Students

Symptoms of posttraumatic stress disorder have been noted as soon as 1 week following the traumatic event, or as long as 30 years after (Sadock & Sadock, 2007). It is important to understand that the initial symptoms of post-traumatic stress are normal and expectable, and that PTSD should only be considered a disorder if those symptoms do not remit over time and result in serious, long-term limitations in social functioning (D. Becker, 2004). Complete recovery from symptoms occurs in 30% of the cases, mild symptoms continue over time in 40%, moderate symptoms continue in 20%, and symptoms persist or get worse in about 10%. Children and older adults have the most trouble coping with traumatic events. A strong system of social support helps to prevent or to foster recovery from posttraumatic stress disorder. Besides providing support, social workers may be helpful by encouraging the person to discuss the traumatic event and by providing education about a variety of coping mechanisms.

Social Support

In coping with the demands of daily life, our social supports—the people we rely on to enrich our lives—can be invaluable. **Social support** can be defined as the interpersonal interactions and relationships that provide us with assistance or feelings of attachment to persons we perceive as caring (Hobfoll, 1996). Three types of social support resources are available (J. Walsh, 2000):

1. *Material support:* food, clothing, shelter, and other concrete items

2. *Emotional support:* interpersonal support

3. *Instrumental support:* services provided by casual contacts such as grocers, hairstylists, and landlords

Some authors add "social integration" support to the mix, which refers to a person's sense of belonging. That is, simply belonging to a group, and having a role and contribution to offer, may be an important dimension of support (Wethington, Moen, Glasgow, & Pillemer, 2000). This is consistent with the "main effect" hypothesis of support, discussed below.

Our **social network** includes not just our social support, but all the people with whom we regularly interact and the patterns of interaction that result from exchanging resources with them (Moren-Cross & Lin, 2006). Network relationships often occur in *clusters* (distinct categories such as nuclear family, extended family, friends, neighbors, community relations, school, work, church, recreational groups, and professional associations). Network relationships are not synonymous with support; they may be negative or positive. But the scope of the network does tend to indicate our potential for obtaining social support. Having supportive others in a variety of clusters indicates that we are supported in many areas of our lives, rather than being limited to relatively few sources. Our **personal network** includes those from the social network who, in our view, provide us with our most essential supports (Bidart & Lavenu, 2005).

Exhibit 5.4 displays Sheila's social network. She now has two close friends at the university with whom she spends much time. She met both Christine and Ben in her classes. Christine has a young child, Tiffany, for whom Sheila frequently babysits. Sheila feels a special closeness to the infant, who makes her feel unconditionally accepted and worthwhile. Ironically, Sheila finds herself doing much advice-giving and caregiving for these friends while wanting (but lacking) nurturing for herself. Still, Sheila feels good about the nature of these relationships because she does not want to confide too much in her friends. She is concerned that they might reject her if they get to know her too well. Sheila feels some instrumental connection with several coworkers because they represent consistency in her life and affirm her competence as a worker. She is also supported emotionally as well as materially by her family members, with whom she keeps in regular contact. Sheila particularly looks to her sister for understanding and emotional

Network Cluster	Network Member*	Type of Support
Family of origin	Mother*	Material and emotional
	Father*	Material and emotional
	Sister*	Emotional
Extended family	Grandmother*	Emotional
Intimate friends	Christine*	Emotional
	Tiffany*	Emotional
	Ben*	Emotional
Neighborhood	Landlord	Instrumental
Informal community relations	None	
School	Barbara	Instrumental
	Terri	Instrumental
	Academic adviser	Instrumental
	Instructor	Instrumental
	Paul* (counselor)	Emotional
Work	Kim	Instrumental
	Thomas	Instrumental
	Laura	Instrumental
Church/religion	None	
Recreation	None	
Associations	None	

▲ **Exhibit 5.4**   Sheila's Social Network

support, and she uses her sister as a model in many ways. She has always enjoyed seeing her parents and, ironically, even the grandmother who can be so critical of her. They make her feel more "whole" and reinforce her sense of identity, even though, like many young adults working toward independence, she has mixed feelings about spending more than a few days at a time with them. At school, Sheila has casual relationships with two classmates, her academic adviser, and a couple of faculty members, although she does not identify them as significant. They qualify as instrumental support.

In total, Sheila has 16 persons in her social support system, representing 6 of a possible 10 clusters. She identifies 8 of these people as personal, or primary, supports. It is noteworthy that half (8) of her network members provide only instrumental support, which is an important type but the most limited. Because people in the general population tend to identify about 25 network members (Uchino, Holt-Lunstad, Smith, & Bloor, 2004), we can see that Sheila's support system, on which she relies to cope with stress, is still probably not adequate for her needs at this time in her life.

Systems perspective; psychodynamic perspective

Based on one recent research report, Sheila is not alone in having an inadequate support network. McPherson, Smith-Lovin, and Brashears (2006) found that 43.6% of their 2004 sample reported that they have either no one or only one person with whom they discuss important matters in their lives, in contrast to an average of three such persons reported in a 1985 sample. These findings raise several important questions for further exploration: Is it possible that people today have larger, but less intimate networks? How is the level of intimate exchange affected by time spent in electronic communication? Do the trends in the United States toward increased time spent at work and in commuting have a negative impact on social support networks?

How Social Support Aids Coping

The experience of stress creates a physiological state of emotional arousal, which reduces the efficiency of cognitive functions (Caplan & Caplan, 2000). When we experience stress, we become less effective at focusing our attention and scanning the environment for relevant information. We cannot access the memories that normally bring meaning to our perceptions, judgment, planning, and integration of feedback from others. These memory impairments reduce our ability to maintain a consistent sense of identity.

Social support helps in these situations by acting as an "auxiliary ego." Our social support—particularly our personal network—compensates for our perceptual deficits, reminds us of our sense of self, and monitors the adequacy of our functioning. Here are 10 characteristics of effective support (Caplan, 1990; Caplan & Caplan, 2000):

1. Nurtures and promotes an ordered worldview

2. Promotes hope

3. Promotes timely withdrawal and initiative

4. Provides guidance

5. Provides a communication channel with the social world

6. Affirms one's personal identity

7. Provides material help

8. Contains distress through reassurance and affirmation

9. Ensures adequate rest

10. Mobilizes other personal supports

> Systems perspective

Some of these support systems are formal (service organizations), and some are informal (such as friends and neighbors). Religion, which attends to the spiritual realm, also plays a distinctive support role (Caplan, 1990). This topic is explored in Chapter 6.

Two schools of thought have emerged around the question of how we internalize social support (Bal, Crombez, & Oost, 2003; Cohen, Gottlieb, & Underwood, 2001):

1. *Main effect model.* Support is seen as related to our overall sense of well-being. Social networks provide us with regular positive experiences, and within the network a set of stable roles (expectations for our behavior) enables us to enjoy stability of mood, predictability in life situations, and recognition of self-worth. We simply don't experience many potential stressors as such, because with our built-in sense of support, we do not perceive situations as threats.

> Systems perspective; social constructionist perspective

2. *Buffering model.* Support is seen as a factor that intervenes between a stressful event and our reaction. Recognizing our supports helps us to diminish or

prevent a stress response. We recognize a potential stressor, but our perception that we have resources available redefines the potential for harm or reduces the stress reaction by influencing our cognitive, emotional, and physiological processes.

Most research on social support focuses on its buffering effects, in part because these effects are more accessible to measurement. Social support as a main effect is difficult to isolate because it is influenced by, and may be an outcome of, our psychological development and ability to form attachments. The main effect model has its roots in sociology, particularly symbolic interaction theory, in which our sense of self is said to be shaped by behavioral expectations acquired through our interactions with others. The buffering model, more a product of ego psychology, conceptualizes social support as an external source of emotional, informational, and instrumental aid.

> Psychodynamic perspective

How Social Workers Evaluate Social Support

There is no consensus about how social workers can evaluate a client's level of social support. The simplest procedure is to ask for the client's subjective perceptions of support from family and friends (Procidano & Smith, 1997). One of the most complex procedures uses eight indicators of social support: available listening, task appreciation, task challenge, emotional support, emotional challenge, reality confirmation, tangible assistance, and personal assistance (Richman, Rosenfeld, & Hardy, 1993). One particularly useful model includes three social support indicators (Uchino, 2009):

1. *Listing of social network resources:* The client lists all the people with whom he or she regularly interacts.

2. *Accounts of supportive behavior:* The client identifies specific episodes of receiving support from others in the recent past.

3. *Perceptions of support:* The client subjectively assesses the adequacy of the support received from various sources.

In assessing a client's social supports from this perspective, the social worker first asks the client to list all persons with whom he or she has interacted in the past 1 or 2 weeks. Next, the social worker asks the client to draw from that list the persons he or she perceives to be supportive in significant ways (significance is intended to be open to the client's interpretation). The client is asked to describe specific recent acts of support provided by those significant others. Finally, the social worker asks the client to evaluate the adequacy of the support received from specific sources, and in general. On the basis of this assessment, the social worker can identify both subjective and objective support indicators with the client and target underused clusters for the development of additional social support.

Sheila's support network is outlined in Exhibit 5.4. From a full assessment of her social supports, a social worker might conclude that her personal network is rather small, consisting only of her sister, counselor, and three friends. Sheila might report to the social worker that she does not perceive many of her interactions to be supportive. The social worker might explore with Sheila her school, neighborhood, and work clusters for the possibility of developing new supports.

NORMAL AND ABNORMAL COPING

Most people readily assess the coping behaviors they observe in others as "normal" or "abnormal." But what does "normal" mean? We all apply different criteria. The standards we use to classify coping thoughts and feelings as normal or abnormal are important, however, because they have implications for how we view ourselves and how we behave toward those different from us. For example, Sheila was concerned that other students at the university perceived her as abnormal because of her social isolation and her inadequacy. Most likely, other students did not notice her at all. It is interesting that, in Sheila's view, her physical appearance and her demeanor revealed her as abnormal. However, her appearance did not stand out, and her feelings were not as evident to others as she thought.

Social workers struggle just as much to define *normal* and *abnormal* as anybody else, but their definitions may have greater consequences. Misidentifying someone as normal may forestall needed interventions; misidentifying someone as abnormal may create a stigma or become a self-fulfilling prophecy. To avoid such problems, social workers may profitably consider how four different disciplines define normal.

The Medical (Psychiatric) Perspective

One definition from psychiatry, a branch of medicine, states that we are normal when we are in harmony with ourselves and our environment. Normality is characterized by conformity with our community and culture. We can be deviant from some social norms, so long as our deviance does not impair our reasoning, judgment, intellectual capacity, and ability to make personal and social adaptations (Bartholomew, 2000).

The current definition of *mental disorder* used by the American Psychiatric Association (2000), which is intended to help psychiatrists and many other professionals distinguish between normality and abnormality, is a

significant behavioral or psychological syndrome or pattern that occurs in an individual and that is associated with present distress (e.g., a painful symptom) or disability (i.e., impairment in one or more important areas of functioning) or with significantly increased risk of suffering death, pain, disability, or an important loss of freedom. (p. xxiii)

The syndrome or pattern "must not be an expectable and culturally sanctioned response to a particular event" (p. xxiii). Whatever its cause, "it must currently be considered a manifestation of behavioral, psychological, or biological dysfunction in the individual" (p. xxiii). Neither deviant behavior nor conflicts between an individual and society are to be considered mental disorders unless they are symptomatic of problems within the individual.

In summary, the medical model of abnormality focuses on underlying disturbances within the person. An assessment of the disturbance results in a diagnosis based on a cluster of observable symptoms. This is sometimes referred to as the *disease model of abnormality*. Interventions, or treatments, focus on changing the individual. The abnormal person must experience internal, personal changes (rather than induce environmental change) in order to be considered normal again. Exhibit 5.5 summarizes the format for diagnosing mental disorders as developed by psychiatry in the United States and published in the *Diagnostic and Statistical Manual of Mental Disorders* (4th ed., text revision; APA, 2000), generally referred to as *DSM-IV-TR*. Many people in the helping professions follow this format, including social workers in some service settings.

Psychological Perspectives

One major difference between psychiatry and psychology is that psychiatry tends to emphasize biological and somatic interventions to return the person to a state of normalcy, whereas psychology emphasizes various cognitive, behavioral, or reflective interventions for individuals, families, or small groups.

The field of psychological theory is quite broad, but some theories are distinctive in that they postulate that people normally progress through a sequence of life stages. The time context thus becomes important. Each new stage of

| Axis I | Clinical or mental disorders |
| | Other conditions that may be a focus of clinical attention |

Axis I — Clinical or mental disorders
Other conditions that may be a focus of clinical attention

Axis II — Personality disorders
Mental retardation

Axis III — General medical conditions

Axis IV — Psychosocial and environmental problems

Primary support group	Economic
Social environment	Access to health care services
Educational	Interaction with the legal system
Occupational	Other psychosocial and
Housing	environmental problems

Axis V — Global assessment of functioning (based on the clinician's judgment):

| 90–100 | Superior functioning in a wide range of activities |
| 0–10 | Persistent danger of severely hurting self or others, persistent inability to maintain personal hygiene, or serious suicidal acts with clear expectation of death |

▲ **Exhibit 5.5** *DSM-IV* Classification of Mental Disorders

SOURCE: *Diagnostic and Statistical Manual of Mental Disorders,* copyright © 2000 American Psychiatric Association. Reprinted with permission

personality development builds on previous stages, and any unsuccessful transitions can result in abnormal behavior—that is, a deviant pattern of coping with threats and challenges. An unsuccessful struggle through one stage implies that the person will experience difficulties in mastering subsequent stages.

> Developmental perspective

One life-stage view of normality very well known in social work is that of Erik Erikson (1968), who proposed eight stages of normal *psychosocial development* (see Exhibit 5.6). Sheila, although 22 years old, is still struggling with the two developmental stages of adolescence (in which the issue is identity vs. diffusion) and young adulthood (in which the issue is intimacy vs. isolation). Common challenges in adolescence include developing a sense of one's potential and place in society by negotiating issues of self-certainty versus apathy, role experimentation versus negative identity, and anticipation of achievement versus work paralysis. Challenges in young adulthood include developing a capacity for interpersonal intimacy as opposed to feeling socially empty or isolated within the family unit. According to Erikson's theory, Sheila's difficulties are related to her lack of success in negotiating one or more of the four preceding developmental phases or challenges.

From this perspective, Sheila's experience of stress would not be seen as abnormal, but her inability to make coping choices that promote positive personal adaptation would signal psychological abnormality. For example, in her first semester at the university, she was having difficulty with role experimentation (identity vs. identity diffusion).

Life Stage	Psychosocial Challenge	Significant Others
Infancy	Trust versus mistrust	Maternal persons
Early childhood	Autonomy versus shame and doubt	Parental persons
Play age	Initiative versus guilt	Family
School age	Industry versus inferiority	Neighborhood
Adolescence	Identity versus identity diffusion	Peers
Young adulthood	Intimacy versus isolation	Partners
Adulthood	Generativity versus self-absorption	Household
Mature age	Integrity versus disgust and despair	Humanity

▲ **Exhibit 5.6**   Erikson's Stages of Psychosocial Development

She lacked the necessary sense of competence and self-efficacy to allow herself to try out various social roles. She avoided social situations such as study groups, recreational activities, and university organizations in which she might learn more about what kinds of people she likes, what her main social interests are, and what range of careers she might enjoy. Instead, she was stuck with a negative identity, or self-image, and could not readily advance in her social development. From a stage theory perspective, her means of coping with the challenge of identity development would be seen as maladaptive, or abnormal.

The Sociological Approach: Deviance

Social constructionist perspective

The field of sociology offers a variety of approaches to the study of abnormality, or deviance. As an example, consider one sociological perspective on deviance derived from symbolic interactionism. It states that those who cannot constrain their behaviors within role limitations that are acceptable to others become labeled as deviant. Thus, *deviance* is a negative label that is assigned when one is considered by a majority of significant others to be in violation of the prescribed social order (Downes & Rock, 2003). Put more simply, we are unable to grasp the perspective from which the deviant person thinks and acts; the person's behavior does not make sense to us. We conclude that our inability to understand the other person's perspective is due to that person's shortcomings rather than to our own rigidity, and we label the behavior as deviant. The deviance label may be mitigated if the individual accepts that he or she should think or behave otherwise and tries to conform to the social order.

From this viewpoint, Sheila would be perceived as abnormal, or deviant, only by those who had sufficient knowledge of her thoughts and feelings to form an opinion about her allegiance to their ideas of appropriate social behavior. She might also be considered abnormal by peers who had little understanding of rural culture. Those who knew Sheila well might understand the basis for her negative thoughts and emotions and in that context, continue to view her as normal in her coping efforts. However, it is significant that Sheila was trying to avoid intimacy with her university classmates and work peers so that she would not become well known to them. Because she still views herself as somewhat deviant, she wants to avoid being seen as deviant (or abnormal) by others, which in her view would lead to their rejection of her. This circular reasoning poorly serves Sheila's efforts to cope with stress in ways that promote her personal goals.

The Social Work Perspective: Social Functioning

The profession of social work is characterized by the consideration of systems and the reciprocal impact of persons and their environments (the bio-psycho-social-spiritual perspective) on human behavior. Social workers tend not to classify individuals as abnormal. Instead, they consider the person-in-environment as an ongoing process that facilitates or blocks one's ability to experience satisfactory social functioning. In fact, in clinical social work, the term *normalization* refers to helping clients realize that their thoughts and feelings are shared by many other individuals in similar circumstances (Hepworth, Rooney, Rooney, Strom-Gottfried, & Larsen, 2010).

> Social systems perspective

Three types of situations are most likely to produce problems in social functioning: stressful life transitions, relationship difficulties, and environmental unresponsiveness (Gitterman, 2009). Note that all three are related to transitory interactions of the person with other persons or the environment and do not rely on evaluating the client as normal or abnormal.

Social work's **person-in-environment (PIE) classification system** formally organizes the assessment of individuals' ability to cope with stress around the four factors shown in Exhibit 5.7: social functioning problems, environmental problems, mental health problems, and physical health problems. Such a broad classification scheme helps ensure that Sheila's range of needs will be addressed. James Karls and Maura O'Keefe (2008), the authors of the PIE system, state that it "underlines the importance of conceptualizing a person in an interactive context" and that "pathological and psychological limitations are accounted for but are not accorded extraordinary attention" (p. x). Thus, the system avoids labeling a client as abnormal. At the same time, however, it offers no way to assess the client's strengths and resources.

With the exception of its neglect of strengths and resources, the PIE assessment system is appropriate for social work because it was specifically developed to promote a holistic biopsychosocial perspective on human behavior. For example, at a mental health center that subscribed to psychiatry's *DSM-IV* classification system, Sheila might be given an Axis I diagnosis of adjustment disorder or dysthymic disorder, and her dyslexia might be diagnosed on Axis III. In addition, some clinicians might use Axis IV to note that Sheila has some school adjustment problems. With the PIE system, the social worker would, in addition to her mental and physical health concerns, assess Sheila's overall social and occupational functioning, as well as any specific environmental problems. For example, her problems with the student role that might be highlighted on PIE Factor I include her ambivalence and isolation, the high severity of her impairment, its 6 months' to a year's duration, and the inadequacy of her coping skills. Her environmental stressors on Factor II might include a deficiency in affectional support, of high severity, with a duration of 6 months to a year. Assessment with PIE provides Sheila and the social worker with more avenues for intervention, which might include personal, interpersonal, and environmental interventions.

Critical Thinking Questions 5.3

What biases do you have about how people should cope with discrimination based on race, ethnicity, gender, sexual orientation, and so on? How might the coping strategy need to change in different situations, such as receiving service in a restaurant, being interviewed for a job, or dealing with an unthinking comment from a classmate?

Factor I: Social Functioning Problems

A. Social role in which each problem is identified
   1. Family (parent, spouse, child, sibling, other, significant other)
   2. Other interpersonal (lover, friend, neighbor, member, other)
   3. Occupational (worker/paid, worker/home, worker/volunteer, student, other)

B. Type of problem in social role
   1. Power   4. Dependency   7. Victimization
   2. Ambivalence   5. Loss   8. Mixed
   3. Responsibility   6. Isolation   9. Other

C. Severity of problem
   1. No problem   4. High severity
   2. Low severity   5. Very high severity
   3. Moderate severity   6. Catastrophic

D. Duration of problem
   1. More than five years   4. Two to four weeks
   2. One to five years   5. Two weeks or less
   3. Six months to one year

E. Ability of client to cope with problem
   1. Outstanding coping skills   4. Somewhat inadequate
   2. Above average   5. Inadequate
   3. Adequate   6. No coping skills

Factor II: Environmental Problems

A. Social system where each problem is identified
   1. Economic/basic need   4. Health, safety, social services
   2. Education/training   5. Voluntary association
   3. Judicial/legal   6. Affectional support

B. Specific type of problem within each social system

C. Severity of problem

D. Duration of problem

Factor III: Mental Health Problems

A. Clinical syndromes (Axis I of DSM)

B. Personality and developmental disorders (Axis II of DSM)

Factor IV: Physical Health Problems

A. Disease diagnosed by a physician

B. Other health problems reported by client and others

▲ Exhibit 5.7   The Person-in-Environment (PIE) Classification System

IMPLICATIONS FOR SOCIAL WORK PRACTICE

Theory and research about the psychosocial person have a number of implications for social work practice, including the following:

- Always assess the nature, range, and intensity of a client's interpersonal relationships.

- Help clients identify their sources of stress and patterns of coping. Recognize the possibility of particular vulnerabilities to stress, and to social and environmental conditions that give rise to stress.

- Help clients assess the effectiveness of particular coping strategies for specific situations.

- Where appropriate, help clients develop a stronger sense of competence in problem solving and coping. Identify specific problems and related skill-building needs, teach and rehearse skills, and implement graduated applications to real-life situations.

- Where appropriate, use case management activities focused on developing a client's social supports through linkages with potentially supportive others in a variety of social network clusters.

- Recognize families as possible sources of stress as well as support.

- Recognize the benefits that psychoeducational groups, therapy groups, and mutual aid groups may have for helping clients cope with stress.

- Where appropriate, take the roles of mediator and advocate to attempt to influence organizations to be more responsive to the needs of staff and clients. Where appropriate, take the roles of planner and administrator to introduce flexibility into organizational policies and procedures so that agency–environment transactions become mutually responsive.

- For clients who experience stress related to inadequate community ties, link them to an array of formal and informal organizations that provide them with a greater sense of belonging in their communities.

- When working with persons in crisis, attempt to alleviate distress and facilitate a return to the previous level of functioning.

- Assess with clients the meaning of hazardous events, the precipitating factors, and potential and actual support systems. When working with persons in crisis, use a here-and-now orientation, and use tasks to enhance support systems. Help clients to connect current stress with patterns of past functioning and to initiate improved coping methods. As the crisis phase terminates, review with the client the tasks accomplished, including new coping skills and social supports developed.

KEY TERMS

adaptation	defense mechanisms	object relations theory
Afrocentric relational theory	emotion-focused coping	personal network
coping	general adaptation syndrome	person-in-environment (PIE)
crisis	homeostasis	classification system
daily hassles	neural plasticity	posttraumatic stress disorder

problem-focused coping	social identity theory	stress
relational coping	social network	stress/diathesis models
relational theory	social support	trait
role strain	state	traumatic stress

ACTIVE LEARNING

1. You have been introduced to four ways of conceptualizing normal and abnormal coping: mental disorder, psychosocial development, deviance, and social functioning. Which of these ways of thinking about normality and abnormality are the most helpful to you in thinking about Sheila's situation? For what reasons?

2. Think of your own social support network. List all persons you have interacted with in the past month. Next, circle those persons on the list who you perceive to be supportive in significant ways. Describe specific recent acts of support provided by these significant others. Finally, evaluate the adequacy of the support you receive from specific sources and in general. What can you do to increase the support you receive from your social network?

3. Consider several recent situations in which you have utilized problem-focused or emotion-focused coping strategies. What was different about the situations in which you used one rather than the other? Were the coping strategies successful? Why or why not?

WEB RESOURCES

Institute of Contemporary Psychotherapy and Psychoanalysis
www.icpeast.org/index.html

Site contains information on conferences, training, and links to other resources on contemporary self and relational psychologies.

MedlinePlus: Stress
www.nlm.nih.gov/medlineplus/stress.html

Site maintained by the National Institute of Mental Health, includes links to latest news about stress research; coping; disease management; specific conditions; and stress in children, seniors, teenagers, and women.

National Center for Posttraumatic Stress Disorder
www.ptsd.va.gov

Site presented by the National Center for PTSD, a program of the U.S. Department of Veterans Affairs, contains facts about PTSD, information about how to manage the traumatic stress of terrorism, and recent research.

Object Relations Theory and Therapy
www.objectrelations.org

Site maintained by Thomas Klee, PhD, clinical psychologist, contains information on object relations theory, a method of object relations psychotherapy, and current articles on object relations theory and therapy.

Stone Center
www.wcwonline.org

Site presented by the Stone Center of the Wellesley Centers for Women, the largest women's research center in the United States, contains theoretical work on women's psychological development and model programs for the prevention of psychological problems.

Stress Management
http://mentalhealth.about.com/od/stress/stress_management.htm

Site presented by About.com, which is owned by the *New York Times,* includes a large number of articles and links about topics related to stress management in a variety of contexts.

CHAPTER

6

The Spiritual Person

Michael J. Sheridan

OPENING QUESTIONS

- How does the inclusion of the spiritual dimension in the existing biopsychosocial framework expand and enhance our understanding of human behavior? What challenges does it bring to this understanding?

- How can social workers effectively tap into the universals (e.g., love, compassion, service, justice) found in most spiritual perspectives—both religious and nonreligious—while recognizing and honoring diversity among various spiritual paths?

KEY IDEAS

As you read this chapter, take note of these central ideas:

1. Spirituality, a universal and fundamental aspect of human existence, is a broad concept that includes a search for purpose, meaning, and connections among oneself, other people, the universe, and the ultimate reality.

2. Religion refers to a set of beliefs, practices, and traditions experienced within a specific social institution over time.

3. There is a rich diversity of religious and spiritual beliefs and expression in the United States and the world that needs to be understood and taken into account in the current climate of globalization.

4. Spiritual development can be conceptualized as moving through a series of stages—each with its own particular characteristics—similar to physical, cognitive, or psychosocial development.

5. Two theories of spiritual development are Fowler's theory of stages of faith and Wilber's integral theory of consciousness; both models envision an endpoint in human development that is beyond a mature ego and self-actualization, allowing humans to transcend the body, ego, and social roles to experience a wider and deeper connection with all beings and the universe.

6. Social work's relationship to religion and spirituality in North America has changed over time—beginning in a land that already possessed rich, Indigenous spiritual traditions; initially emerging as a profession from strong Judeo-Christian religious or moral foundations; moving to increased professionalization and secularization; experiencing a resurgence of interest and attention; and reaching the current period of expansion and transcending boundaries.

7. A growing body of literature explores the relevance of spirituality to both human diversity and the human condition, with implications for all levels of social work practice.

Case Study 6.1

Caroline's Challenging Questions

Caroline, who grew up in a large, close-knit family in North Carolina, is in her first year of college at a university in another state where she is encountering all kinds of new experiences. A devout Christian, Caroline is a member of a Baptist church back home, where her family has attended for generations. She was very involved in her home church, singing in the choir and actively engaged in several youth programs. Most of her high school friends attended her church, so she was more than a little uncomfortable when she learned that her roommate, Ruth, was Jewish. Caroline has met a number of other students who are from different faiths or who say that they don't belong to a church at all. This has been a new and challenging experience for her.

At first she tried to stay away from anyone who wasn't Christian, but she struggled with this because so many of her non-Christian classmates seemed like nice people and she really wanted to have friends. All sorts of questions began to emerge in her mind, like "How can they not believe in Jesus Christ?" and "I wonder what they *do* believe?" and "What will happen to them in the afterlife if they are not saved?" These questions only grew as she took a Comparative Religions class where she learned about faiths that she had never heard of before. In one class exercise, she was paired with another student from Turkey who said she was Muslim. At first, Caroline was anxious about talking with her, but as they moved through the exercise, she began to feel that they were more alike than different. They both were from very religious families, their faith was important to them personally, and they both were struggling with all the different perspectives that they were encountering in college. Later on that day, Caroline realized that if she had been born in Turkey, she would probably be a Muslim, too. This thought both intrigued and unsettled her. More and more, she is asking herself, "What *do* I really believe and why?"

Case Study 6.2

Naomi's Health Crisis

Naomi is a 42-year-old mother of three children who are 10, 7, and 3 years old. Naomi discovered a lump in her breast a couple of weeks ago and she and her husband, David, have been anxiously awaiting news regarding test results. When the diagnosis of cancer finally comes, they are both stunned and frightened, but pull themselves together for the sake of the children. Naomi begins the long journey of doctors, surgery, chemotherapy, and radiation treatments while simultaneously trying to maintain family life and a part-time job as best she can. David takes on new duties as a more active parent and homemaker while still going to his full-time job. He struggles with his own fears and anger about what is happening, initially not sharing these with Naomi because he is determined to be her "rock."

Naomi and David are members of Temple Shalom, a local Reform Jewish congregation, which they joined after their first child was born. When they were growing up, Naomi's family were members of a Reform congregation, while David's family expressed their Jewish heritage in more secular and cultural terms, gathering annually for a Passover Seder but not attending services except occasionally on Yom Kippur. Naomi had not regularly attended services after her bat mitzvah, but both she and David decided that they wanted to be part of a spiritual community for their children. They had heard good things about the temple in their neighborhood and decided to explore it. They liked its open, welcoming atmosphere; its liberal viewpoints on social issues; and its active engagement in social action in the community. They both enjoy the weekly connection with other adults and are happy with the religious classes that their children attend. Recently, Naomi and David have been engaged in weekly Shabbat Torah study sessions, to deepen their understanding of Jewish sacred texts.

(Continued)

(Continued)

Now that Naomi is facing this health crisis, both she and David are feeling a bit lost and are searching for answers. Although friends have been supportive, both of their families live far away and their short visits and phone calls only provide minimal comfort. One night, when they both can't sleep, Naomi and David begin to share their doubts and fears with one another, even admitting that they feel angry with God and are wondering if there is such a thing as God at all. Naomi finally suggests, "I think it would help to talk with Rabbi Shapiro and some of the people we've met at Temple Shalom." David agreed and added that they should also explore the Jewish Healing Network that was described in the bulletin last week.

Case Study 6.3

Mathew's Faith Journey

Matthew will be 70 next month—a fact that is hard for him to believe. He's been a widower for 5 years now since he lost his wife, Betty, who died of a sudden heart attack. The first few years following her death were rough, but Matthew made it through with the help of his sons and their families, and members of his Catholic parish, which he has been attending for 40 years. His faith has always been very important to him, even though he has struggled with periods of doubt and confusion—the latest following Betty's death. At one point when he was younger, he considered leaving the church, when disagreements about doctrine and rumblings about the new priest were causing uproar in the congregation. He even visited several other denominations to see if they were a better fit for him. But after much reflection and conversation with Betty, Matthew decided to stick with his commitment to the Catholic faith and his parish saying, "No church is perfect and this is where I truly belong."

For the past couple of years, he has been actively involved with the outreach activities of the church, working on the Food Bank and Affordable Housing committees. Recently, he has been a member of the Interfaith Dialogue Program, which promotes respect and mutual understanding across religious and cultural perspectives. Matthew finds the panel discussions, conferences, and interfaith community projects both challenging and invigorating. He's particularly looking forward to an upcoming conference on the role of interfaith dialogue in advancing world peace. He's also been involved with the National Religious Partnership for the Environment (NRPE), a Judeo-Christian association composed of many faiths that focuses on environmental stewardship. As a result of all of these activities, Matthew has also been reading a number of books on different religions and is struck with the similar themes that are reflected in the teachings of very diverse traditions. He is beginning to feel a new sense of purpose for his life, which both surprises and delights him as he heads into his seventies. Some of his friends have asked him if his involvement with the Interfaith Dialogue Program is making him question his own religion, but Matthew says, "No, quite the opposite. I feel more deeply connected to my faith as I understand more about other religions. It's not that I think mine is right and theirs is wrong, but I appreciate and respect other religions, while still knowing that mine is right for me."

Trudy's Search for the Sacred

Trudy is a 35-year-old single woman living in Berkeley, California—which is a long way from the little town in Arkansas where she lived until she left home at 18. She's lived in several places since then, searching for a new home that feels right to her. She thinks she may have finally found it. A new job in a health food store; a small, but comfortable and affordable apartment; a great yoga class; and a welcoming Buddhist Sangha (community) of like-minded people all make her feel like she's finally found what she's been looking for.

Trudy's early years were not easy ones. Her father was an alcoholic who flew into rages when drunk, which happened more often as the years went by. It was not an unusual event for someone in her family to be physically hurt during these episodes. Trudy, her mother, and her two sisters were afraid of her father and "walked around on eggshells" most of the time to avoid triggering his angry spells. Trudy found refuge in the woods in back of her house and in books, which she devoured as they took her to places beyond her current reality. She could stay curled up in a nook of her favorite tree for hours, transporting herself to somewhere else—anywhere else. She promised herself she would leave as soon as she finished high school.

Life since then has not been easy either. Trudy was briefly married in her twenties to a man who also had a hard time controlling his anger and began to drink more and more as problems in the marriage began to emerge. Trudy even found herself turning to alcohol as a way of numbing her pain, which really scared her. With the support of some friends, she finally left the marriage and was off again, searching for a new home. After a couple of other relationships that didn't work out, Trudy decided to avoid men and increasingly became isolated from all social ties. But in her new home in Berkeley, she finds that she likes the people who attend her Sangha and likes even more the fact that they don't share a lot of personal information, focusing more on spiritual practices. She loves the group meditation and the dharma talks and has made a commitment to increased periods of solitary meditation when she is at home. Trudy is now rising at 4:00 AM to meditate for 3 hours before she has to get ready for work, and she meditates an additional 2 hours most evenings. Her reading is now totally focused on books about spirituality, which support her quest to rise above personal concerns and her ego to become an enlightened being. Although Trudy was not exposed to a particular religious tradition during childhood, the search for spiritual development is now her highest priority.

Leon's Two Worlds

Leon is a 23-year-old man who is feeling torn in two. He is the oldest son in a family with five kids and the mainstay of his mother's life. Regina became a widow 8 years ago when her husband, Rodney, was killed in an accident at the mill yard where he worked. Since then, she's leaned heavily on Leon for help with his

(Continued)

(Continued)

brothers and sisters and as a major contributor to the family's finances. He is also the one she confides in the most, sharing things with him that she once shared with her husband. The whole family also relies heavily on their African Methodist Episcopal (AME) church for both social support and spiritual nurturance.

Leon has grown up in the church and loves the fellowship and the joyous feeling that comes over him as he sings and worships on Sundays. But it is also a place that increasingly troubles him, as he has finally admitted to himself that he is gay. He has denied this for years, trying hard to follow church teachings about homosexuality being a sin and something that can be overcome with the help of God. He has prayed and prayed to God to change him, but this has not worked. Leon is now battling despair, as he fears that he will always be caught between his love for his faith and his church and a longing to be who he truly is. The idea of telling his mother about his sexual orientation seems unthinkable, but he's not sure how long he can go on living a lie. He knows he will have to leave the church if it ever becomes known that he is gay. That possibility also seems unthinkable. He has been feeling more and more depressed, to the point where his mother keeps asking him what's wrong. He's even had thoughts of suicide, which frighten him. In his nightly prayers to God he asks, "Why must I lose you to be who I am?"

Case Study 6.6

Jean-Joseph's Serving the Spirits

Jean-Joseph is a 50-year-old man, originally from Haiti, who came with his family to the United States 10 years ago. He and his family were adherents of the Roman Catholic faith in Haiti and now attend a Catholic church near their new home. Jean-Joseph's family are also believers in Vodoun (known by most Westerners as Voodoo), which is widely practiced in Haiti and often integrated with belief in Catholicism. Most Roman Catholics who are active in this spiritual tradition refer to it as "serving the spirits." Although this belief system holds that there is only one God, Bondje, who created the universe, he is considered to be too far away for a personal relationship with humans. Instead, believers in Vodoun center on *Loa,* or spirits of ancestors, animals, natural forces, and good and evil spirits. Family Loa are spirits who are seen to protect their "children"—the Haitian people—from misfortune. Jean-Joseph and his family regularly participate in rituals to feed the Loa food and drink, and offer them other gifts.

Recently, a Loa visited Jean-Joseph in a dream, telling him that his youngest son was ill and needed healing. His son Emmanuel had indeed been listless for days, not wanting to eat or play, and his parents were very worried about him. Jean-Joseph decided that they needed to take him to a *Mambo*, a Vodoun priestess, who could mediate between the human and spirit worlds to diagnose and treat Emmanuel's illness. The Mambo agreed to perform a healing ceremony, which was held at a *hounfour*, or Vodoun temple around a *poteau-mitan*; a center pole where the spirits can communicate with people. A *veve*, or pattern of cornmeal unique to the Loa who was the focus of the ceremony, was created on the floor, and an altar was decorated with candles, pictures of Christian saints, and other symbolic items. A goat was also sacrificed for the ceremony. The Mambo and her assistants began to chant and dance, accompanied by the shaking of rattles and beating of drums. Finally, the Mambo was possessed by the Loa and fell down. The Lao then spoke through the Mambo and told the family how to treat the distressed spirit that was causing Emmanuel's illness. After the ceremony, the Mambo gave Jean-Joseph an herbal remedy to give to his son and instructions on how to continue feeding the spirit of the Lao until Emmanuel was healed. The family also prayed to the Christian God and Catholic saints to bring healing to Emmanuel.

THE SPIRITUAL DIMENSION

All of the stories presented in the six case studies could be viewed through many different lenses. Social work's biopsychosocial framework would be helpful in understanding many facets of these cases. Knowledge of the biological components of health certainly would be useful in understanding the circumstances of Naomi's health crisis and Jean-Joseph's attempts at healing his son's illness. Psychological perspectives would shed light on Caroline's discomfort with encountering different beliefs, Matthew's deepening faith perspective, Trudy's search for a home

> Systems perspective

and a different sense of self, and Leon's despair at being torn between his faith and his sexual identity. Social theories on family dynamics, ethnicity and culture, social movements, socioeconomic class, and social institutions would yield invaluable information about all of the cases, providing a wider frame for understanding their individual lives.

However, the biopsychosocial framework omits an important dimension of human existence: spirituality. This omission seems antithetical to social work's commitment to holistic practice. What would be gained if we added a spiritual lens in our attempt to understand Caroline's challenging questions, Naomi's health crisis, Matthew's faith journey, Trudy's search for the sacred, Leon's two worlds, and Jean-Joseph's serving of the spirits? And how would this perspective help you as a social worker provide holistic and effective service in working with them? Keep these questions and all of the stories in mind as you read the rest of the chapter.

The Meaning of Spirituality

The concept of spirituality is often confused with religion, and writers in social work and related fields point to a number of attempts to delineate these terms and distinguish them from one another (Bullis, 1996; Canda, 1997; Carroll, 1998; D. MacDonald, 2000; Sheridan, 2004; Wuthnow, 2003; Zinnbauer et al., 1997). Canda and Furman (2010) provide a detailed discussion of how the two terms are understood in social work and related fields, including medicine, nursing, and psychology. They also report findings from a series of national studies they have conducted in the United States, the United Kingdom, Norway, and New Zealand, which show relative consistency across countries. Specifically, the top six descriptors of *spirituality* across geographic locales were "meaning, personal, purpose, values, belief, and ethics." Similar congruence was found for the term *religion*, where the top six descriptors selected in all of the countries were "belief, ritual, community, values, prayer, and scripture" (p. 67). Drawing from these studies and additional research in the helping professions, Canda and Furman propose the following definitions for these two concepts.

Spirituality is "a process of human life and development

- Focusing on the search for a sense of meaning, purpose, morality, and well-being;

- *In relationship* with oneself, other people, other beings, the universe, and ultimate reality however understood (e.g., in animistic, atheistic, nontheistic, polytheistic, theistic, or other ways);

- Orienting around centrally significant priorities; and

- Engaging a sense of the transcendence (experienced as deeply profound, sacred, or transpersonal)." (Canda & Furman, 2010, p. 75)

Religion is "an institutionalized (i.e., systematic and organized) pattern of values, beliefs, symbols, behaviors, and experiences that involves

- Spirituality

- A community of adherents

- Transmission of traditions over time and

- Community support functions (e.g., organizational structure, material assistance, emotional support, or political advocacy) that are directly or indirectly related to spirituality." (Canda & Furman, 2010, p. 76)

Thus, the term *spirituality* is generally used in the social work literature to mean a broader concept than religion in that spiritual expression may or may not involve a particular religious faith or religious institution. But some writers have pointed out that for persons affiliated with certain faith perspectives, the two terms cannot be separated from one another, or religion is considered to be the broader construct, subsuming spirituality (Pals, 1996; Praglin, 2004). Others propose that the separation of the two terms in social work has resulted in discrimination against particular religious worldviews, especially those of evangelical or conservative faiths (Hodge, 2002, 2003; Ressler & Hodge, 2003). Clearly, there is a need for continued exploration and dialogue about definitional issues. Regardless of how the scholarly definition of these terms evolves, it is important as social workers to always inquire about and honor the client's definition of spirituality and religion, and use the term that is most acceptable and relevant for that person, family, or community.

For the sake of clarity, it should be noted that when the term *spirituality* is used in the current chapter, it is meant to convey spirituality as the broader concept, inclusive of both religious and nonreligious expressions. Occasionally, the two terms are used together in the same sentence (e.g., "gathering religious or spiritual information"). In this case, the reader should recognize that both are included in order to be applicable regardless of whether persons identify themselves as primarily religious, primarily spiritual, both religious and spiritual, or neither.

▲ **Photo 6.1** Spirituality is understood and expressed differently by individuals but is generally associated with a person's search for meaning.

Regardless of the precise words that are used to capture the meaning of spirituality, the term brings to mind many related themes. Exhibit 6.1 lists 20 symbolic themes of spirituality identified by Patrick O'Brien (1992). Which themes do you think are most applicable to the six case studies presented at the beginning of this chapter?

Spirituality in the United States and Globally

The current spiritual landscape in the United States reveals both common threads and a colorful array of unique patterns. A number of polls have consistently reported that between 92% and 96% of people in the United States say they believe in God or a universal spirit, and 80% report that religion is either "very important" or "fairly important" in their life (Gallup, 2008). In another intriguing survey of how Americans experience spirituality in everyday life, George Gallup and Timothy Jones (2000) asked participants about their activities during the previous 24 hours. Two thirds said that they had prayed, and almost half stated that they had experienced "a strong sense of God's presence" (p. 17).

1. Morality, ethics, justice, and right effort

2. The nature and meaning of self and the intention and purpose of human existence

3. Interconnection; wholeness; alignment; and integration of persons, place, time, and events

4. Creativity, inspiration, and intuition

5. Altruistic service for the benefit of others

6. The mystery and wonder that are woven into nature, the universe, and the unknown

7. Sociocultural-historical traditions, rituals, and myths

8. Virtues (such as compassion, universal love, peace, patience, forgiveness, hope, honesty, trust, faith)

9. Mystical, altered states of consciousness

10. Sexuality

11. Openness, willingness, surrender, and receptivity

12. The power of choice, freedom, and responsibility

13. Special wisdom or revealed knowledge

14. Prayer, meditation, and quiet contemplation

15. Answers to pain, suffering, and death

16. Identity and relation to the metaphysical ground of existence, ultimate reality, and life force

17. The relationship of cause and effect regarding prosperity or poverty

18. Beliefs or experiences related to intangible reality or the unobstructed universe

19. The path to enlightenment or salvation

20. Sensitive awareness of the earth and the nonhuman world

▲ **Exhibit 6.1** Symbolic Themes of Spirituality

SOURCE: Adapted from O'Brien (1992).

These statistics indicate a strong thread of spirituality in the United States. However, expressions of both religious and nonreligious spirituality have become increasingly diverse, making the United States likely the most religiously diverse country in the world today, with more than 1,500 religious groups (Parrillo, 2009; Pew Forum on Religion & Public Life, 2008).

This diversity is due, in part, to ongoing schisms and divisions among many of the organized religions historically present within the United States. For example, the number of Christian denominations alone grew from 20 to more than 900 from 1800 to 1988 (Melton, 1993). In addition, there has been a significant rise in other spiritual traditions with each new influx of immigrants from other parts of the world. They have brought not only faiths that are recognized as major religions (e.g., Islam, Buddhism, Confucianism, Hinduism), but also various forms of spiritualism, folk healing, and shamanism (e.g., Santeria, *espiritismo*, Vodoun, *curanderismo, krou khmer, mudang*). This trend is further augmented by a growing interest in Eastern and Middle Eastern religions (e.g., Islam, Buddhism, and Hinduism) and earth-based spiritualities (e.g., neo-paganism, goddess worship, and deep ecology). There has also been a revived or more visible involvement in traditional spiritual paths within Indigenous communities, as increasing numbers of Native Americans or First Nations peoples explore their tribal traditions or combine these traditions with Christianity. Many of these "new" religions are among the fastest growing in the United States, although their overall numbers are still relatively small. Exhibit 6.2 shows the top 10 religions in the United States as of 2001, along with their growth rates since 1990.

Religion	1990 Estimates	2001 Estimates	Percentage of U.S. Population in 2001	% Change 1990–2001
Christianity	151,225,000	159,030,000	76.5%	+5%
Judaism	3,137,000	2,831,000	1.3%	−10%
Islam	527,000	1,104,000	0.5%	+109%
Buddhism	401,000	1,082,000	0.5%	+170%
Hinduism	227,000	766,000	0.4%	+237%
Unitarian-Universalist	502,000	629,000	0.3%	+25%
Wiccan/Pagan/Druid		307,000	0.1%	
Spiritualist		116,000	<0.1%	
Native American Religion	47,000	103,000	<0.1%	+119%
Baha'i	28,000	84,000	<0.1%	+200%

▲ **Exhibit 6.2**   Top 10 Religions in the United States: 1990–2001

SOURCES: Based on data drawn from the 1990 National Survey of Religious Identification (NSRI) and the 2001 American Religious Identification Survey (ARIS). Published online at www.gc.cuny.edu/faculty/research_studies/aris.pdf.

It should be noted that estimates of members of any particular religious group vary widely depending on the source, data collection methods, and definition of "adherents" (e.g., self-identified, formal membership, regular participant). For example, in the United States, figures for adherents of Islam range from 1 million to 8 million, adherents of Judaism from 1 million to 5 million, adherents of Buddhism from 1 million to 5 million, and adherents of neo-paganism from 10,000 to 770,000 (Canda & Furman, 1999; *Major Branches of Religion*, 2005; Parrillo, 2009).

As tempting as it is to make overarching statements based on statistics concerning belief in God and religious identification—for example, that the U.S. population is highly religious—we must be cautious in drawing specific conclusions, as the picture changes depending on the particular indicator. During generally same time period, 1990–2001, the percentage of U.S. adults who regularly attend religious services decreased from 49% to 36%, reflecting a worldwide trend among industrialized countries (Reeves, 1998). More recent data drawn from Gallup Polls (2008) reveal only 30% reporting that they attend religious services on a weekly basis. Furthermore, the 2001 American Religious Identification Survey (Kosmin, Mayer, & Keysar, 2001) reports that respondents who did not subscribe to any religious identification showed the greatest increase in both absolute numbers and percentages of the U.S. population. Specifically, this group grew from 14.3 million (8%) in 1990 to 20.4 million (over 14%) in 2001. More recent data from the Pew Forum on Religion & Public Life (2008; hereafter, "Pew Forum") reveal that 16.1% of adults report being unaffiliated, making them a substantial category, second only to Christians in the United States.

In addition, there appears to be increasing fluidity in religious affiliation. Data on changes from one major religious tradition to another (e.g., from Protestantism to Catholicism, or from Judaism to no religion) show that 28% of U.S. adults have changed their affiliation from that of their childhood. When changes *within* affiliations are examined (e.g., from Baptist to Methodist), an even larger percentage (44%) of American adults report shifts in religious affiliation. The two affiliations showing the greatest net gains are the unaffiliated, increasing from 7.3% to 16.1%, and non-denominational Protestantism, increasing from 1.5% to 4.5% (Pew Forum, 2008).

Groups that show a net loss due to changes in affiliation include Baptists, Methodists, and other Protestant groups, which show decreases ranging from less than 1 percentage point to 3.7 percentage points. Judaism also shows a small loss due to changing affiliations (0.2 percentage points). But the group that has experienced the greatest decrease is the Catholic Church, with 31.4% reporting being raised as Catholic, but only 23.9% identifying as Catholic today, a net loss of 7.5 percentage points (Pew Forum, 2008). It should be noted, however, that the overall proportion of the U.S. population that is Catholic is roughly the same as it was in the early 1970s. This can be explained in part by the number of converts, but the greatest contributor to replacing those who have left the Catholic Church has been immigrants coming into the United States who are adherents of this faith.

Overall, it is noteworthy that the percentage of respondents moving from "some" religious affiliation to "none" (12.7%) was greater than that of people moving from "none" to "some" religious affiliation (3.9%) (Pew Forum, 2008). All of this suggests that the current phenomenon of "religion switching" may be a reflection of deeper cultural changes within our society, perhaps in part explained by what Roof (1993) calls the "generation of seekers," referring to the substantial numbers of the baby boomer cohort in the United States.

Interestingly, these figures concerning shifts and declines in organized religious affiliation or identification emerge at a time when people in the United States are expressing an unprecedented interest in spirituality in general. In 1994, an estimated 58% of the U.S. population said they "feel the need . . . to experience spiritual growth in their lives"; in 1998, just 4 years later, 82% made the same claim (Gallup & Lindsay, 1999, p. 1). It is apparent that this interest in spiritual growth may or may not be expressed within traditional religious institutions and is increasingly focused on a spirituality that is more subjective, experiential, and personalized (Roof, 1993, 1999). This reflects Ulrich Beck's (1992) understanding of spirituality as attending to the development of positive human qualities—such as generosity, gratitude, a capacity for awe and wonder, an appreciation of the interconnectedness among all beings, and deeper awareness and insight—as much as or even more than a search for any divine form of transcendence.

It is important to consider all of these data within the context of global statistics (see Exhibit 6.3). Although adherents of Christianity remain the highest proportion of the population in the United States, worldwide they comprise only 33% of all religious adherents, with the remainder being composed of those who self-identify with some other perspective, including Islam (21%); Hinduism (14%); nonreligious (16%); Buddhism, Chinese traditional, and primal-Indigenous faiths (6% each); and Sikhism and Judaism (less than 1% each) (*Major Religions of the World*, 2005).

It is important to understand the impact of globalization on religious or spiritual diversity both within and outside of the United States. *Globalization* is used here to refer to "the worldwide diffusion of practices, expansion of relations across continents, reorganization of social life on a global scale, and a growth of a shared global consciousness" (Lechner, as quoted in Swatos, 2005, p. 320). Simply put, it is our growing sense of the world being "a single place" (Robertson, 1992). As with other aspects of human life, globalization is also increasing our awareness of the many different religious and spiritual traditions in the world and the role they play in various conflicts, both between and within countries.

Lester Kurtz (2007) posits that there are three factors—modernism, multiculturalism, and modern technologies of warfare—that are significant in understanding religious conflict today. First, modernism, based on scientific, industrial, and technological revolutions, has had an ongoing contentious relationship with religious perspectives and institutions beginning in the 17th century, when Church authorities charged Galileo with heresy because he had stated that the earth revolved around the sun. Present-day examples include debates regarding evolution versus creationism and intelligent design; the question of when life begins and ends; the ethics of stem-cell

Conflict perspective

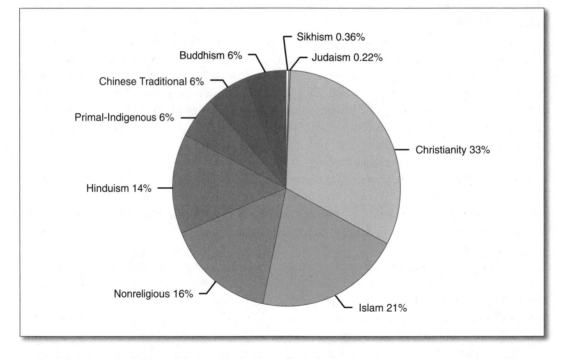

▲ **Exhibit 6.3**   *Major Religions of the World Ranked by Number of Adherents*

SOURCE: Data drawn from www.adherents.com.

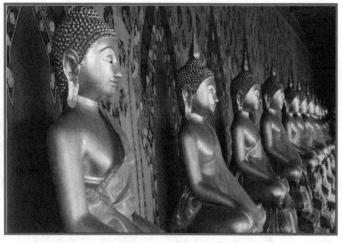

▲ **Photos 6.2a & 6.2b**   Religion involves the patterning of spiritual beliefs and practices into social institutions; different cultures focus their beliefs around different central figures.

research and genetic manipulation; the proper codes of behavior, especially sexual behavior; the rightful roles of women in society and the correct way to raise children; and the appropriate place of religion in the political sphere. Thus, this tension between science and religion continues during our current postmodern times as scientific and secular thought competes with religious traditions and doctrine as the authority for both "truth" and moral guidelines for contemporary life.

Second, multiculturalism increasingly requires us to recognize that there are myriad worldviews and ways of life, both within the United States and globally. This pluralistic reality stands in contrast to unilateral belief systems, both religious and cultural, that have historically provided what Peter Berger (1969) calls a "sacred canopy," or the security and certainty of one view of the universe, one answer to profound and mundane questions, and one approach to organizing individual and collective life. Such a unified perspective is difficult to maintain, as individuals and whole cultures are increasingly exposed to a religious and spiritual "marketplace" (Warner, 1993) of diverse belief systems and practices, which often challenge the basic tenets previously held as absolute.

The potential for conflict is inherent in both modernism and multiculturalism, conflict that becomes especially deadly when combined with the third aspect of globalization—the dispersion of modern technological advances in warfare. Violent conflict, often intertwined with religious issues, has been part of human history for thousands of years. But in the current period of globalization, the cost of such conflict has grown unimaginably high in that our arsenal now includes nuclear, biological, and chemical weapons of mass destruction as opposed to stones, clubs, and other primitive weapons. As Lester Kurtz (2007) succinctly states, "Given the destructive capabilities of modern weaponry and the consequent necessity for peaceful coexistence, the potential for religious traditions to promote either chaos or community becomes a crucial factor in the global village" (p. 243).

Given this complex and ever-changing picture, social workers gain very little real understanding of a person by simply knowing his or her primary religious affiliation. First, religious affiliation may or may not hold great significance for the person, and identification with a religion alone does not indicate depth of involvement. Second, belief, practice, and involvement can be quite varied, even among adherents of the same spiritual tradition or among members of the same family, kinship group, or faith community—even if they all self-identify as Methodist or Muslim or Wiccan. Third, some people feel connected to multiple spiritual perspectives simultaneously, such as a combination of Judaism and Buddhism or traditional Indigenous spiritual beliefs and Christianity. Fourth, the meaning of religious or spiritual affiliation may change across the life course; a person may feel more or less connected to a particular tradition at different points in his or her life. And finally, the meaning of a person's religious or spiritual affiliation must be understood within his or her broader historical, sociopolitical, and cultural context in order for its full significance to be realized. It is important to understand the range of spiritual influences (both religious and nonreligious) that may contribute to anyone's life story and the larger collective realities that impact that story at any particular point in time.

Critical Thinking Questions 6.1

At the beginning of the chapter, you read about the spiritual and religious beliefs of six people. With which of the stories were you most comfortable? For what reasons? With which of the stories were you least comfortable? For what reasons? How comfortable are you with the idea of including the spiritual person in social work's understanding of human behavior? What do you like about the idea? What don't you like about the idea?

TRANSPERSONAL THEORIES OF HUMAN DEVELOPMENT

Psychodynamic perspective

Developmental perspective

The idea that spirituality is an important dimension of human behavior is not a new one in social work or in other helping professions. Although Sigmund Freud (1928) asserted that all religious and spiritual beliefs were either illusions or projections of unconscious wishes, many other early behavioral science theorists viewed the role of spirituality differently.

Notably, Carl Jung, who had been a student of Freud's, differed with his former teacher and mentor in regard to the topic of spirituality. Jung's (1933) theory of personality includes physical, mental, and spiritual selves, which all strive for unity and wholeness within each person. In Jung's (1959/1969) view, an important archetype (a universal unconscious idea) is "the Spirit." Jung further proposed that the evolution of consciousness and the struggle to find a spiritual outlook on life were the primary developmental tasks in midlife. If this task is successfully accomplished, the result is *individuation*, which he defined as "the moment when the finite mind realizes it is rooted in the infinite" (quoted in Keutzer, 1982, p. 76).

Robert Assagioli (1965, 1973) also emphasized the spiritual dimension in his approach known as *psychosynthesis*. His understanding of the human psyche included the constructs of "higher unconscious" or "superconscious" as the source of creativity and spirituality. In Assagioli's view, some psychological disturbances are best understood as crises of spiritual awakening rather than symptoms of psychopathology. In such cases, the responsibility of the therapist is to facilitate the client's exploration of spiritual possibilities while dealing with the difficulties that such awakenings can engender. As Assagioli (1989) defined it, "'spiritual' refers not only to experiences traditionally considered religious but to *all* the states of awareness, all the human functions and activities which have as their common denominator the possession of *values* higher than average" (p. 30, emphasis original).

A third major contributor to early formulations on spirituality and human behavior was Abraham Maslow, founding father of humanistic psychology. Maslow (1971) described spirituality as an innate and key element in human nature. In his study of optimally functioning people, he characterized people at the top of his hierarchy as "transcendent self-actualizers" and described them as having (among other traits) a more holistic view of life; a natural tendency toward cooperative action; a tendency to be motivated by truth, goodness, and unity; a greater appreciation for peak experiences; an ability to go beyond their ego self to higher levels of identity; and more awareness of the sacredness of

> Humanistic perspective

every person and every living thing. Maslow later came to believe that even this definition was not adequate to explain the highest levels of human potential. Near the end of his life, he predicted the emergence of a more expansive understanding of human behavior: "a still 'higher' Fourth psychology; transpersonal, trans-human, centered in the cosmos, rather than in human needs and interests, going beyond humanness, identity, self-actualization, and the like" (quoted in Wittine, 1987, p. 53).

Describing this evolution of forces within psychology, Au-Deane Cowley (1993, 1996) delineates four major therapeutic approaches that have emerged over the past century, each developed in response to our understanding of human behavior and human needs at the time:

1. **First Force therapies** are based on dynamic theories of human behavior. The prime concern of these therapies is dealing with repression and resolving instinctual conflicts by developing insight.

> Psychodynamic perspective

2. **Second Force therapies** evolved from behavioral theories. These therapies focus on learned habits and seek to remove symptoms through various processes of direct learning.

> Social behavioral perspective

3. **Third Force therapies** are rooted in existential/ humanistic/experiential theories. They help the person deal with existential despair and seek the actualization of the person's potential through techniques grounded in immediate experiencing.

> Humanistic perspective

4. **Fourth Force therapies,** based on transpersonal theories, specifically target the spiritual dimension. They focus on helping the person let go of ego attachments—external identifications with the mind, body, and social roles—and transcend the self through various spiritually based practices. (Cowley, 1996)

The Fourth Force builds upon the previous three forces and thus incorporates existing knowledge concerning human behavior within its framework. What differentiates the Fourth Force—the **transpersonal approach**—from other theoretical orientations is the premise that some states of human consciousness and potential go beyond our traditional views of health and normality. These states explicitly address the spiritual dimension of human existence (Cowley & Derezotes, 1994).

The term *transpersonal* literally means "beyond" or "through" the "persona" or "mask" (Wittine, 1987). When applied to theories of human behavior, transpersonal means going beyond identity tied to the individual body, ego, or social roles to include spiritual experience or higher levels of consciousness. A major focus of transpersonal theory is on "humanity's highest potential, and with the recognition, understanding and realization of intuitive, spiritual and transcendent states of consciousness" (Lajoie & Shapiro, 1992, p. 91). Increasingly, there has been recognition of the relevance of a transpersonal orientation to the realm of everyday life as well, including the "lower end" of human functioning. Thus, transpersonal practice approaches must "include the whole—not just the high end of human experience but the very personal realm of ordinary consciousness as well" (Cortright, 1997, p. 13). There are several branches of transpersonal thought that are currently recognized, including Jungian psychology; depth or archetypal psychology; spiritual psychology; positive psychology; psychosynthesis; and approaches based on the writings of Abraham Maslow, Stanislav Grof, Ken Wilber, Michael Washburn, Frances Vaughan, Roger Walsh, Jorge Ferrer, and Charles Tart, among others. A major objective of all transpersonal theories is to integrate spirituality within a larger framework of human behavior. One key application of transpersonal theory is as a conceptual underpinning for theories that address spiritual development.

Two theorists who have developed comprehensive perspectives on spiritual development are James Fowler and Ken Wilber. Although these two theorists are not the only contributors to this area, they have produced two of the best-known approaches in the field today. The following sections provide an overview of these two theories of spiritual development, providing key concepts and discussion of their respective models. Along the way, we will consider the people you read about in the case studies at the beginning of this chapter and see how these two perspectives enhance our understanding of their current life situations and spiritual journeys.

Fowler's Stages of Faith Development

Developmental perspective

James Fowler's (1981, 1995) theory of faith development grew out of 359 in-depth interviews conducted between 1972 and 1981 in Boston, Chicago, and Toronto. The sample was overwhelmingly White (97.8%), largely Christian (over 85%), evenly divided by gender, and widely distributed in terms of age (3.5 years to 84 years). Each semi-structured interview consisted of more than 30 questions about life-shaping experiences and relationships, present values and commitments, and religion. After the responses were analyzed, interviewees were placed in one of six **faith stages** (see Exhibit 6.4). Fowler found a generally positive relationship between age and stage development; as age increased, so did the tendency for persons to be in higher stages. However, only a minority of persons revealed characteristics of Stages 5 or 6, regardless of age.

To Fowler (1996), **faith** is broader than religious faith, creed, or belief. It can, in fact, be expressed even by people who do not believe in God. Instead, faith is viewed as a universal aspect of human existence,

> an integral, centering process, underlying the formation of beliefs, values, and meanings that (1) gives coherence and direction to people's lives, (2) links them in shared trusts and loyalties with others, (3) grounds their personal stances and communal loyalties in a sense of relatedness to a larger frame of reference, and (4) enables them to face and deal with the limited conditions of life, relying upon that which has the quality of ultimacy in their lives. (p. 56)

Thus, Fowler's definition of faith is more aligned with the definition of spirituality given at the beginning of this chapter and is clearly distinguished from more specific notions of particular beliefs or religious traditions.

Another important concept in Fowler's theory is the **ultimate environment** (also known as the ultimate reality or simply the ultimate)—the highest level of reality. Faith is not only your internal image of the ultimate environment, but also your relationship with that image. Your view of the ultimate environment—as personal or impersonal, trustworthy or not dependable, capable of dialogue or silent, purposeful or based on chance—and your relationship with it, is an evolving, dynamic process that is strongly influenced by your experiences throughout the life course. Thus, Fowler's faith is best understood as a verb, or a way of being, versus a noun, or a thing that is unchangeable.

Fowler's stages of faith development should not be viewed as goals to be achieved or as steps necessary for "salvation." Rather, they help us understand a person's values, beliefs, and sense of meaning, and help us better appreciate the tasks, tensions, and challenges at various points in life. They also reveal increasing capacity in terms of cognitive functioning; moral reasoning; perspective taking; critical reflection and dialectical thought; understanding of symbols, myths, and rituals; deeper faith commitments; and openness and acceptance of difference.

Now let us consider the stories revealed in the six case studies through the lens of Fowler's faith stages, based on both his early research and later theoretical refinements. (Fowler offered more accessible names to most of his stages in his later writings; both the original and revised names are included here.) As you read through these descriptions, refer to Exhibit 6.4, which summarizes some of the features of each faith stage and correlates Fowler's stages with Piaget's stages of cognitive development and Kohlberg's stages of moral development (both described in Chapter 4).

In Fowler's model, our early experiences set the stage for later faith development. Given what we know about our six people described in the case studies, it is probably safe to assume that most of them were able to develop at least a "good enough" fund of basic trust and mutuality during the *Pre-stage: Primal Faith* for later development of a relationship with the ultimate. A possible exception to this is Trudy, whose early years were marked by parental substance abuse and violence. It would be important to know when these problems first appeared within her family and how much they interfered with her initial bonding with her mother and father, as these factors would be influential in both her ability to trust and her internal sense of the ultimate as she moves through her life.

None of the six case studies tells us much about the development of early images of the ultimate environment during *Stage 1: Intuitive-Projective Faith* (Magical World). However, we can speculate that these images were probably drawn from each person's particular faith affiliation. For Caroline, Matthew, and Leon, these initial conceptions of the divine would have been grounded within their particular Christian denominations, while Naomi would have developed her sense of the ultimate as it was reflected in her Jewish faith. Caroline's partner in the Comparative Religions class exercise would most likely have developed her sense of the divine based on examples, modes, actions, and stories that she experienced in her family's belief in Islam. Jean-Joseph's sense of the ultimate would have been influenced by a combination of Catholic symbols, narratives, and rituals and the spiritual beliefs and practices of Vodoun. Trudy was not raised in any particular faith tradition, but found her solace in nature. It would be important to talk with her about how these early experiences affected her sense of the sacred and to not assume that her lack of exposure to organized religion meant that she had no early images or experiences with the ultimate, as spirituality is experienced and expressed through both religious and nonreligious means. In working with all six people, we would want to understand how this process of image making was handled by their families and others in their lives, and how much support they were given for their own intuition and imagination during this time.

If Fowler had interviewed any of the six during middle childhood, they more than likely would have reflected many of the aspects of *Stage 2: Mythic-Literal Faith* (Concrete Family). It would be important to understand the role of their childhood spiritual communities in shaping each person's sense of the world and his or her place in it. It would be particularly useful to explore the stories and narratives that they remember from that time, especially as they transmitted values, attitudes, and norms for behavior. For example, discussing with Leon what he understood as his church's core principles relative to sin and redemption would be invaluable in comprehending his current struggle. It would also be important to understand the messages that Caroline received regarding her own religion as the only true faith. For Naomi and Jean-Joseph, it would be key to talk about how their communities handled being believers of a nondominant (or "other") religion, in a culture where Christianity is the dominant faith and is generally seen as "the norm." For all six people, it would be vital to explore what helped create a sense of order and meaning at this stage of life and what provided a sense of guidance and belonging.

Faith Stage	Life Stage	Major Characteristics	Form of Logic (Piaget)	Form of Moral Judgment (Kohlberg)
Pre-stage: Primal Faith	Infancy	Learn to trust (or not trust) immediate environment, develop sense of object permanence, and form first pre-images or sense of the ultimate. If consistent nurturance is experienced, develop a sense of trust and safety about the universe and the divine. Conversely, negative experiences produce images of the ultimate as untrustworthy, punitive, or arbitrary. Sets the stage for further faith development. Transition to next stage begins with integration of thought and languages, which facilitates use of symbols in speech and play.		
Stage 1: Intuitive-Projective Faith (Magical World)	Early childhood	Generally emerges in children aged 2 to 7, who have new tools of speech and symbolic representation. Thought patterns are generally fluid and magical, and ways of knowing are based in intuition and imagination. Awareness of self is egocentric, with little ability to take the perspective of others. Have first awareness of death and sex and learn familial and cultural taboos. Faith is fantasy-filled and imitative and can be powerfully influenced by examples, modes, actions, and stories of significant others. Because faith images at this stage can be long-lasting, it is important to honor the child's own process of faith development. Stage normally ends at age 6 or 7, but may be found in adolescents or adults experiencing psychological difficulties. Transition to next stage is facilitated by emergence of concrete operational thinking and resolution of Oedipal issues.	Preoperational	Punishment/ reward
Stage 2: Mythic-Literal Faith (Concrete Family)	Middle childhood and beyond	Generally begins between ages 7 and 8, when child takes on stories, beliefs, and practices that symbolize belonging to his or her community. High level of conformity (reciprocal fairness) to community beliefs and practices, and symbols are seen as one-dimensional and literal in meaning. Authority and tradition are very powerful influences as the child incorporates moral rules and attitudes of community. Ability to engage in concrete operations allows distinction between fantasy and reality, which reorders imaginative picture of the world developed in Stage 1. Narrative and story are very important as the major way of gaining coherence and meaning of experiences; thus, child can be deeply affected by symbolic and dramatic presentations concerning the ultimate reality. Increased capacity to take perspective of others, and ideas about reciprocity and fairness become central. Majority of persons in this stage are in elementary school, but some are adolescents and adults. Transition to next stage occurs with breakdown of literalism, disillusionment with previous teachers, and clashes or conflicts between accounts by various authority figures (e.g., creation story vs. theory of evolution). Movement into Piaget's	Concrete operational	Instrumental hedonism (reciprocal fairness)

Stage	Age	Description		
		formal operational thought and development of capacity for mutual perspective taking allows for deeper reflection and creates need for more personal relationship with the ultimate in the next stage.		Interpersonal expectations and concordance
Stage 3: Synthetic-Conventional Faith (Faith Community)	Adolescence and beyond	Capacity for abstract thinking and manipulation of concepts affects process of developing both overall identity and faith. Environment broadens, and there is increased influence of peers, school and work associates, and media and popular culture. Authority perceived as external and is found in traditional authority figures (parents, teachers) or valued groups (peers). Images of the ultimate reflect qualities experienced in personal relationships (e.g., compassion exhibited by parent or teacher). Beliefs and values often deeply felt, but are primarily tacit rather than critically examined. Person has an ideology, or outlook, but has not systematically reflected on it and is largely unaware of having it. Differences in outlook between people understood as differences in "kinds" of people. Symbols are not perceived as literally as in Stage 2, but symbols that evoke deep meaning and loyalty are not seen as separate from what they represent. Although this stage is most evident in adolescence, a considerable number of adults also fall within this stage, and it can become long-lasting or permanent. Factors leading to transition to next stage include serious clashes or contradictions between authority figures, changes in previously sanctioned religious practices or policies, experiences that lead to critical reflection about one's own beliefs and values, or experience of "leaving home"—physically or emotionally.	Early formal operations	
Stage 4: Individuative-Reflective Faith (Rational Constructs)	Young adulthood and beyond	Stage of increased responsibility for one's commitments, lifestyle, beliefs, and attitudes. Constructs an individual self (identity) and outlook (ideology) from previously held conventional faith. Requires struggling with unavoidable tensions (e.g., individuality vs. being defined by group membership; subjectivity and unexamined feelings vs. objectivity and critical reflection; self-fulfillment and self-actualization vs. service to and being for others; commitment to the absolute vs. struggle with the possibility of the relative). Previously held creeds, symbols, and stories are demythologized through critical analysis. The ultimate becomes more explicit and personally meaningful, and symbols are reshaped into more powerful conceptualizations. Goal is to create a rational, workable, and personal worldview or faith. Ideal time for movement into Stage 4 is early to mid-20s, but for many this transition occurs during the 30s or 40s (if at all). Process creates significant upheaval and can last for 5 to 7 years or longer. Transition to the next stage begins with a growing awareness of the paradoxes and complexities of life and increased attention to inner voices and images that have previously been submerged or set aside.	Formal operations (dichotomizing)	Societal perspective: reflective relativism or class-biased universalism

(Continued)

(Continued)

Stage 5: Conjunctive Faith (Numinous [Supernatural/ Mysterious] Universe)	Midlife and beyond	Most people do not reach Stage 5; only one of six interviewees in Fowler's sample fit the characteristics of this stage, and no one prior to midlife. Involves the integration of what has been suppressed or unrecognized during rational certainty of Stage 4. Must rework the past and be open to voices of the "deeper self." Requires capacity for "both/and" vs. "either/or" thinking; polarities are not seen as problems but as realities to be accepted (e.g., both determinism and free will play a role in life; the ultimate is experienced as both personal and abstract; humanity is understood as both good and evil). Symbolic power reunited with conceptual meaning at deeper level (e.g., cross is both a symbol of the crucifixion of Christ and representation of sacrifice or death and rebirth). Person strives to unify opposites in mind and in experience. Increased openness to the truths of those who are "other" and critical examination of one's social constructions (e.g., myths, ideal images, and prejudices internalized as a result of membership in certain social class, religious tradition, ethnic group, etc.). Definition of "community" expands beyond own immediate environment and faith community to encompass all human beings and, sometimes, the natural world. Recognition that one's personal faith, however defined, is of supreme value, and commitments based on this faith must be carried out despite consequences. Ready to expend energies in service of generating identity and meaning within the lives of others. Transition to next stage (experienced by very few) comes when person can no longer live with the paradoxical and divided world of Stage 5 and is willing to make sacrifices required of Universalizing Faith.	Formal operations (dialectical)	Prior to society: principled higher law (universal and critical)
Stage 6: Universalizing Faith (Selfless Service)		Able to confront dilemmas faced in Stage 5 because of ability to truly embrace paradox. Injustice seen more clearly because of enlarged awareness of demands of justice. Partial truths recognized because of expanded vision of truth. Symbols, myths, and rituals appreciated and cherished at deeper level because of knowledge of depth of reality that symbols, myths, and rituals reflect. Divisions within human family felt with vivid pain because of recognition of possibility of inclusive union of all beings. Stage 6 persons move beyond these universalizing understandings to action, regardless of threats to self, to primary groups, or to institutional arrangements of society. They become a disciplined, activist embodiment of imperatives of love and justice. They live a sacrificial life aimed at transformation of humankind. Very few persons reach this stage; Fowler identifies Gandhi, Mother Teresa, and Martin Luther King Jr. Although universalizers are not "perfect," they shake up notions of normalcy and call into question the compromise arrangements that most people accept. As such, universalizers "lean into the future of God for all being" (p. 211).	Formal operations (synthetic)	Loyalty to being

▲ **Exhibit 6.4** Fowler's Faith Stages

SOURCE: Fowler (1981).

The events that occur during adolescence generally have a significant effect on faith development during *Stage 3: Synthetic-Conventional Faith* (Faith Community), as this is the point where people are heavily engaged in the process of identity development, including spiritual identity. It is also a time when the person's world is greatly expanded, bringing diverse and complex ideas and experiences regarding all of life. Adolescents must make coherent meaning from all of the different messages that they receive from family, school, work, media, and the larger sociocultural realm. A person's faith understanding can help synthesize various values and viewpoints and provide a basis for forming a stable identity and worldview. There is a tendency to construct one's faith through conforming to a set of values and beliefs that are most familiar and to defer to whatever authority is most meaningful. As the two people most recently in this life stage, both Caroline and Leon illustrate the strong impetus to form a faith identity that provides a solid sense of self and a feeling of belonging to a particular group. For both of them, the faith of their families and their home churches were highly instrumental in this process. And for both of them, entry into the next stage of life brought questions regarding the beliefs and values of these key social institutions and an urge to explore beyond what they had previously known.

If we look at Caroline's and Leon's lives as they move into *Stage 4: Individuative-Reflective Faith* (Rational Constructs), we see young people grappling with key questions about themselves and their belief systems. Caroline's experiences at college have opened the door to considering different worldviews, which she handles with an approach/avoidance strategy. On the one hand, she is troubled by her experience with others who believe and practice differently than she does, but on the other hand, she is increasingly curious about these differences. For Leon, the struggle is more difficult, as he is attempting to live with values, attitudes, and beliefs that tell him that a core aspect of his identity is unacceptable. For both of these young adults, the task ahead is to construct a unique, individual self (identity) and outlook (**ideology**) from previously held conventional beliefs and develop an approach to faith that is both personal and workable. This requires a level of critical reflection and a capacity to struggle with conflicts and tensions that were not yet fully developed in the previous stage. As a social worker, you would want to facilitate this process while being mindful of the social work principles of self-determination and empowerment.

Naomi and David provide another example of *Individuative-Reflective Faith*, even though they are considerably older than Caroline and Leon. When they were in their late teens and early twenties, their identity formation led them to a more secular worldview, as Naomi lessened her involvement with her faith and David continued to base his identity and outlook on more humanistic understandings of self and the world. But the creation of a family caused them both to reconsider the role of Judaism in their lives as they realized their desire for a spiritual community. As their children grew, their involvement with their temple has provided the personal and workable framework that is characteristic of this phase. That framework is now being challenged by Naomi's illness and is leading both her and David to a deeper reflection of their faith. Social work with this couple would involve supporting this reflection, as well as exploring with them possible supports they could receive from their Rabbi and larger faith community in dealing with Naomi's health crisis.

Fowler reports that *Stage 5: Conjunctive Faith* (Numinous [Supernatural/ Mysterious] Universe) generally emerges in midlife and is not seen in most adults. According to Lownsdale (1997), only one in six adults reflects characteristics of this stage. Of our six life stories, only Matthew's provides glimpses of this faith stage. Although there is not much information about Matthew's internal reflection on the paradoxes of life (a key criterion of *Conjunctive Faith*), we do know that he was able to work through the loss of his wife, and other losses that inevitably come with aging, to embrace a new chapter in his life. As a social worker, it would be useful to explore with Matthew his understanding of life's paradoxes (such as God being both personal and abstract, and life being both rational and mysterious), and talk with him about any previously unrealized parts of himself that are now emerging. What is apparent in Matthew's story is his enthusiastic willingness to acknowledge and honor multiple faith perspectives, while being open to new depths within his own spirituality. We also see him engaging in service for others and concern for the natural world. All of these activities suggest a perspective that goes beyond egocentric and ethnocentric views to a more **worldcentric** (identification with the entire global human family) and **ecocentric** (identification with the whole ecosphere, of which humans are only one part) way of being in the world. As a result of these commitments, he is experiencing a renewed sense of purpose, meaning, and connection in his life. All of these are characteristic of persons of *Conjunctive Faith*, which brings a broader social consciousness, a passion for social justice, and a wider and deeper understanding of the sacred.

It is clear that none of the six people reflects Fowler's *Stage 6: Universalizing Faith* (Selfless Service). These persons are exceedingly rare, perhaps two to three individuals per thousand (Lownsdale, 1997). Persons at this stage are deeply committed to universal values of peace and justice and live sacrificial lives aimed at the transformation of humankind. Given the exceptional nature of such persons, it is not surprising that the six case studies do not reveal examples of this faith stage. Some might point to Trudy's total immersion in spiritual practices as evidence of this stage, but another perspective on her development will be offered later in this chapter during discussion of the second theorist, Ken Wilber, and his *integral theory of consciousness.*

Finally, we must address Jean-Joseph's spiritual path, which includes a syncretism of Catholicism and Vodoun, or "serving the spirits." If a social worker embedded in dominant Western culture assessed his faith development solely from the standpoint of this context, he or she may determine that Jean-Joseph falls within an early stage, either *Mythic-Literal* (Concrete Family) or perhaps even *Intuitive-Projective* (Magical World). This determination would no doubt lead to a conclusion that this 50-year-old man is an example of underdeveloped faith and may lead to interventions aimed at helping him give up his "primitive and immature" beliefs and practices for a worldview seen as more appropriate for mature adults. If this was the stance taken by a practitioner, he or she would be showing ethnocentric and religiocentric bias, as well as cultural insensitivity. Viewed within his sociocultural context, Jean-Joseph is exhibiting a faith stage that could be more accurately determined to be at least *Synthetic-Conventional* (Faith Community), given its congruence with the spiritual beliefs and practices of his Haitian culture. Upon further exploration with him—with an open mind, respect, and humility for the limits of one's knowledge about his religion—a social worker may discover that Jean-Joseph displays characteristics of higher stages of faith development. This highlights the need for social workers to constantly be aware of their own lack of knowledge and their internalized biases when working with religious and spiritual traditions that are unfamiliar to them, in order to engage in culturally sensitive service that is respectful of those traditions (Weaver, 1999).

Wilber's Integral Theory of Consciousness

Ken Wilber first published his transpersonal theory of development in 1977 in *The Spectrum of Consciousness*, but has continued to develop and refine his model in numerous writings. His work reflects a unique integration of biology, history, psychology, sociology, philosophy, and religion. It is rooted in both conventional Western knowledge and contemplative/mystical traditions of Eastern religions and other spiritual perspectives. Wilber currently refers to his approach as an "integral theory of consciousness" (2006). He identifies it as "integral" because it explores human development across **four quadrants** or vantage points (interior-individual, exterior-individual, interior-collective, and exterior-collective), as well as through *three levels of consciousness* (pre-personal, personal, and transpersonal). He posits that to fully understand human development, it must be understood through the lenses of subjective awareness of *personal meaning and sense of self* (the interior of individuals), objective knowledge of the *physical body and observable behaviors* (the external of individuals), intersubjective understanding of *sociocultural values and shared meanings* (the internal of collectives), and interobjective knowledge of *institutional structures and systemic forces* (the external of collectives). Within each quadrant, the three levels of consciousness unfold in a way that reflects the unique properties of that particular quadrant (see Exhibit 6.5). According to Wilber, integrated knowledge of all of these areas is required for an accurate and complete understanding of human behavior.

Developmental perspective

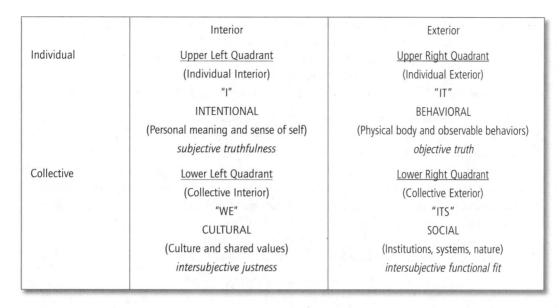

	Interior	Exterior
Individual	<u>Upper Left Quadrant</u> (Individual Interior) "I" INTENTIONAL (Personal meaning and sense of self) *subjective truthfulness*	<u>Upper Right Quadrant</u> (Individual Exterior) "IT" BEHAVIORAL (Physical body and observable behaviors) *objective truth*
Collective	<u>Lower Left Quadrant</u> (Collective Interior) "WE" CULTURAL (Culture and shared values) *intersubjective justness*	<u>Lower Right Quadrant</u> (Collective Exterior) "ITS" SOCIAL (Institutions, systems, nature) *intersubjective functional fit*

▲ **Exhibit 6.5**   Wilber's Integral Theory: Four Quadrants & Three Levels of Consciousness

SOURCES: Wilber (1996, 2006).

Wilber sees the ultimate goal of human development (at the individual and collective levels) as being to evolve to a higher, nondual level of consciousness that is well-integrated into personal and societal functioning. This requires movement through the three stages of spiritual development, marked by increasingly complex, comprehensive, and inclusive understandings of spirituality and expanded consciousness about reality. We will look closer at Wilber's description of transpersonal levels within the *interior of individuals,* as this is a major contribution of his model to theories of spiritual development. But first we need to review some key concepts underpinning integral theory.

As already noted, Wilber (1995, 2000a, 2000b, 2006) agrees with other transpersonal theorists that consciousness spans from pre-personal to personal to transpersonal. This overall spectrum is reflected in the world's major spiritual traditions and is referred to as the "great chain of being" (matter to body to mind to soul to spirit). Wilber points out that because this process is not strictly a linear one, it is best understood as a "great nest of being" in that it is really a series of enfolding and unfold-

Systems perspective

ing spheres or spirals. In other words, spirit transcends but includes soul, which transcends but includes mind, which transcends but includes body, which transcends but includes matter. This process of incorporation is rooted in the concept of a *holon,* or "that which, being a *whole* in one context, is simultaneously a *part* in another" (Wilber, 1995, p. 18, emphasis original). Thus, Wilber refers to his spectrum of consciousness as a *holarchy* (rather than a hierarchy), because it reflects an ordering of holons (or increasing levels of complexity and wholeness) throughout the developmental process. It may be helpful to visualize this as a set of Russian nesting dolls, with each larger doll both including and going beyond the smaller ones. With each larger level (or doll), one expands his or her awareness of reality and develops a larger repertoire of individual and social functioning.

There are five major components relative to the development of interior individual consciousness in Wilber's theory. The following gives an overview of each of these components, leading to a more detailed discussion of the higher or transpersonal levels of consciousness.

1.   **Levels** (or waves) **of consciousness** refers to various developmental milestones that unfold within the human psyche. As our discussion of holarchy suggests, this is not a strictly linear process. Rather, it involves "all sorts of regressions, spirals, temporary leaps forward, peak experiences, and so on" (Wilber, 1996, p. 148). A person does

not have to master all the competencies of one level to move into the next; in fact, most people at any given level will often respond about 50% from one level, 25% from the level above, and 25% from the level below. However, levels cannot be skipped over, as each level incorporates the capacities of earlier levels. Drawing from various cross-cultural sources, Wilber posits several major levels of consciousness, all of which are *potentials*—but not *givens*—at the onset of development. We will consider these in more detail following introduction of the other major components.

2.   Multiple **lines** (or streams) **of consciousness** flow through the basic levels of consciousness. Wilber identifies the following developmental lines as areas for which we have empirical evidence: "morals, affects, self-identity, psychosexuality, ideas of the good, role taking, socio-emotional capacity, creativity, altruism, several lines that can be called 'spiritual' (care, openness, concern, religious faith, meditative stages), joy, communicative competence, modes of space and time, death-seizure, needs, worldviews, logico-mathematical competence, kinesthetic skills, gender identity, and empathy" (Wilber, 2000a, p. 28). He proposes that these lines or streams are relatively independent of one another in that they can develop at different rates within the same individual. Thus, a person can be at a relatively high level of development in some lines (such as cognition), medium in others (such as morals), and low in still others (such as spirituality). Although most *individual* lines unfold sequentially, *overall development* does not, and can be a relatively uneven process.

3.   Wilber also includes in his model **states of consciousness,** which include both ordinary (e.g., waking, sleeping, dreaming) and non-ordinary experiences (e.g., peak experiences, religious experiences, altered states, and meditative or contemplative states). He points out that research has shown that a person at virtually any *level* of consciousness can have an altered *state* of consciousness, including a peak or spiritual experience. For example, a person might experience a sense of oneness with nature, extraordinary feelings of expansion or compassion, or communion with a transcendent or divine being. Whatever the actual experience, individuals can only interpret these experiences at their current level of consciousness and may have to grow and develop further to really accommodate the full depth or meaning of the experience. As Wilber (1996) puts it, "They still have to go from acorn to oak if they are going to become one with the forest" (p. 152). In other words, in order for these *temporary* experiences or states to become *permanent* aspects of a person's level of consciousness, they must become fully realized through continual development.

4.   Wilber proposes that levels, lines, and states of consciousness are all navigated by the self or **self-system.** He posits that there are at least two parts to the self: (a) an observing self (an inner subject or watcher) and (b) an observed self (the object that is watched and can be known in some way). The first self is experienced as "I" (the "proximate" or closer self); the second is experienced as "me" or "mine" (the "distal self" that is farther away). The distinction is important according to Wilber (2000a) because, during development, "the 'I' of one stage becomes a 'me' at the next" (p. 34). As a person negotiates each unfolding *level* and various *lines* of consciousness, and integrates experiences from various *states* of consciousness, he or she moves from a narrower to a deeper and wider sense of self and self-identity.

5.   At each point of development, the self goes though a **fulcrum,** or switch point. Specifically, each time the self moves to a different level on the developmental spiral, it goes through a three-step process. First, the self becomes comfortable and eventually identifies with the basic functioning of that level. Second, new experiences begin to challenge the way of being at this level, and the self begins to differentiate or "dis-identify" with it. Third, the self begins to move toward and identify with the next level while integrating the functioning of the previous basic structure into one's sense of self. If the person is able to negotiate these fulcrum points successfully, development is largely nonproblematic. However, disturbances at different fulcrum points tend to produce various pathologies, although Wilber (1996) cautions that there are "no pure cases" (p. 107), and various internal and external factors need to be taken into account.

Exhibit 6.6 depicts Wilber's 10 basic levels of consciousness, along with their corresponding fulcrums, pathologies, and treatment modalities. As noted earlier, Wilber's spectrum of consciousness can be further categorized into the three phases of development: the Pre-personal (Pre-egoic) phase, the Personal (Egoic) phase, and the Transpersonal

Nondual

Phase of Development	Level	Level of Consciousness	Corresponding Fulcrums	Characteristic Pathologies	Treatment Modalities
Transpersonal or Transegoic	9	Causal	F-9	Causal pathology	Formless mysticism
	8	Subtle	F-8	Subtle pathology	Deity mysticism
	7	Psychic	F-7	Psychic disorders	Nature mysticism
Personal or Egoic	6	Centauric or Vision-Logic	F-6	Existential pathology	Existential therapy
	5	Formal-Reflexive Mind (formal operations)	F-5	Identity neuroses	Introspection
	4	Rule-Role Mind (concrete operations)	F-4	Script pathology (problems with roles or rules)	Script analysis
Prepersonal or Pre-egoic	3	Representational Mind	F-3	Psychoneuroses	Uncovering techniques
	2	Phantasmic-Emotional	F-2	Narcissistic-borderline	Structuring/building techniques
	1	Sensoriphysical	F-1	Psychoses	Physiological/pacification techniques
	0	Primary Matrix	F-0	Perinatal pathology	Intense regressive therapies

Nondual

▲ **Exhibit 6.6**   Wilber's Integral Theory of Consciousness

SOURCES: Robbins, Chatterjee, and Canda (2006); Wilber (1996).

(Trans-egoic) phase. The specific levels of consciousness at both the Pre-personal and Personal phases in Wilber's theory are very similar to the first five of Fowler's faith stages and will not be presented in detail here. (See Wilber [1995, 1996, 1997a, 1997b] for a detailed discussion of these levels.) A review of the levels of Pre-personal and Personal phases of consciousness should sound familiar to students of conventional approaches to human development. In contrast, the levels of the Transpersonal phase (and the language used to describe them) are most likely unfamiliar to those who are not well versed in contemplative Eastern ideas about human development. However, this synthesis of both conventional and contemplative approaches and the inclusion of higher-order levels of development is Wilber's primary contribution to our attempts to understand human behavior.

As one moves into the Transpersonal or Trans-egoic phase, the world and life in general is perceived in more holistic and interconnected terms. There is movement from an egocentric and ethnocentric perspective to a worldcentric and ecocentric grasp of the complete interdependence of all things in the cosmos. There is also the realization that the self is more than a body, a mind, and culture-bound social roles, and awareness that there is a self that exists beyond time/space limits or ego boundaries. This realization facilitates a growing awareness of how all beings are unified within a singular or nondual ultimate reality. As people move further into the Transpersonal or Trans-egoic phase, they retain all the capacities developed during previous levels and incorporate these functions into expanded consciousness experienced at higher levels. The three Transpersonal levels are described below. As you read through each one, focus on what the descriptions are saying about a person's *level of consciousness* at each level. In other words, what are they perceiving or what are they aware of beyond the ordinary states of reality (waking, sleeping, dreaming) that are common to most people?

1. *Level 7* (Psychic) is characterized by a continuing evolution of consciousness as the observing self develops more and more depth. Wilber refers to this evolving inner sense as the *Witness,* because it represents an awareness that moves beyond ordinary reality (sensorimotor, rational, existential) into the transpersonal (beyond ego) levels. A distinguishing spiritual experience at this level is a strong interconnectedness of self with nature. For example, a person may temporarily become one with a mountain or bird or tree. This type of experience is not psychotic fusion—the person is still very clear about his or her own personal boundaries—but it is a strong awareness of communion with the natural world. At this point, one's higher self becomes a World Soul and experiences nature mysticism. Because of this powerful experience of connection and identification, there is a natural deepening of compassion for all living things, including nature itself.

2. *Level 8* (Subtle) is characterized by an awareness of more subtle processes than are commonly experienced in gross, ordinary states of waking consciousness. Examples of such processes are interior light and sounds; awareness of transpersonal archetypes; and extreme states of bliss, love, and compassion. At this point, even nature is transcended, yet it is understood as a manifest expression of the ultimate. One's sense of connection and identification is extended to communion with the Deity, or union with God, by whatever name. Thus, consciousness at this level is not just nature mysticism—union with the natural world—but gives way to deity mysticism. This level of consciousness can be experienced in many forms, often rooted in the person's personal or cultural history. For example, a Christian may feel union with Christ, while a Buddhist might experience connection with the Buddha.

3. *Level 9* (Causal) transcends all distinctions between subject and object (even self and God). The Witness is experienced as pure consciousness and pure awareness, prior to the manifestation of anything. Thus, this level is said to be timeless, spaceless, and objectless. As Wilber (1996) describes it, "Space, time, objects—all of those merely parade by. But you are the Witness, the pure Seer that is itself pure Emptiness, pure Freedom, pure Openness, the great Emptiness through which the entire parade passes, never touching you, never tempting you, never hurting you, never consoling you" (p. 224). This level is pure *formless mysticism,* in that all objects, even God as a perceived form, vanish into pure consciousness. This level of consciousness is sometimes referred to as "full Enlightenment, ultimate release, pure nirvana" (p. 226). But it is still not the final story.

Wilber also proposes a *Level 10 (Nondual),* so to speak, which is characterized by dis-identification with even the Witness. (This level is represented in Exhibit 6.6 by the word "Nondual" in the space surrounding the other levels.) The interior sense of *being* a Witness disappears, and the Witness turns out to be everything that is witnessed. Emptiness as part of awareness at the Causal level (awareness of pure consciousness without form) becomes different at the Nondual level. At this level, Emptiness becomes pure Consciousness itself. There is no sense of two; there is only one (hence the name Nondual). Essentially, the person's awareness has moved beyond nature, Deity, and formless mysticism to *nondual mysticism.* Furthermore, it is not really a level among other levels but is rather the condition or reality of *all* levels. It is simultaneously the source, the process, and the realization of consciousness. Wilber (1995) describes it as "the Ground or Suchness or Isness of *all* levels, at all times, in all dimensions: the Being of all beings, the Condition of all conditions, the Nature of all Natures" (p. 301, emphasis original). Wilber does not depict the Nondual as a separate level in his illustration of the structures of consciousness because it represents the ground or origin of all the other levels—the paper on which the figure is drawn.

With this model, Wilber is proposing that the Personal phase of development, with its achievement of strong ego development and self-actualization, is not the highest potential of human existence, although a necessary point along the way. Rather, the ultimate goal of human development is the Transpersonal or Trans-egoic phase—beyond ego or self to self-transcendence and unity with the ultimate reality. The capacity for attaining the highest levels of consciousness is innate within each human being, although Wilber acknowledges that very few people reach the higher transpersonal levels. He describes these individuals as "a rather small pool of daring men and women—both yesterday and today—who have bucked the system, fought the average and the normal, and struck out toward the new and higher spheres of awareness" (Wilber, 1996, p. 198).

As for the characteristic pathologies, or problems in development at each level, all the disorders or conditions listed in Exhibit 6.6 for the lower phases of development are well recognized within conventional diagnostic approaches (albeit with different labels). It is again at the Transpersonal phase that Wilber strikes new ground, by including what he calls psychic disorders and subtle or causal pathologies. Examples of such problems in living include unsought spiritual awakenings, psychic inflation, split life goals, integration/identification failure, pseudo nirvana, and failure to differentiate or integrate. Wilber (1996) states that although these conditions are not well known, because most people do not reach these higher levels of development, they must be understood in order to be treated properly when they do occur.

Again, the treatment modalities listed in Exhibit 6.6 at the Pre-personal and Personal phases are well known to most social workers. However, the approaches that Wilber proposes for Transpersonal phase disorders—nature mysticism, deity mysticism, and formless mysticism—are largely unknown (and sound a bit strange) to the majority of helping professionals. But they have been used in non-Western cultures for centuries. Furthermore, they are becoming more widely accepted in the United States as effective, complementary treatment approaches (e.g., prayer and meditation, yoga, visualization and spiritual imagery, focusing, dreamwork, dis-identification techniques, body work, acupuncture, journaling, intuition techniques). Wilber (1996, 2000a) stresses that practitioners should be able to correctly identify the level of development in order to provide the most appropriate treatment. If not correctly identified, there is the probability of what Wilber (1995, 2000b) calls the "pre/trans fallacy," which occurs when a problem at a Transpersonal level (such as a spiritual awakening) may be treated as if it were a Pre-personal or Personal disorder (a psychotic episode or existential crisis), or vice versa.

Let's revisit Trudy's story to better understand what Wilber is talking about here. Trudy is currently focusing most of her time and energy toward developing her spiritual self in order to achieve enlightenment. She is meditating 5 hours a day, is engaged with a daily yoga practice, and limits her reading and interpersonal contacts to those that she identifies as spiritual. Given that most transpersonal theorists and spiritual leaders would agree that engagement in some type of spiritual practice is necessary for spiritual growth, one might characterize Trudy's behavior as that of a disciplined spiritual seeker. But there is evidence in her story that Trudy is caught up in **spiritual bypassing,** a term first coined by John Welwood (2000), which he describes as "the tendency to use spiritual practice to bypass or avoid dealing with certain personal or emotional 'unfinished business'" (p. 11). He states that persons who are struggling with life's developmental challenges are particularly susceptible to spiritual bypassing, as they attempt to *find themselves* by *giving themselves up*—or prematurely trying to move beyond their ego to self-transcendence, ignoring their personal and emotional needs. This attempt to create a new "spiritual" identity in order to avoid the pain of working through unresolved psychosocial issues does not work and frequently causes additional problems. As Trudy's social worker, you would want to do a thorough assessment, taking into account the substantial unresolved trauma and losses in her life. To ignore these issues and focus only on supporting her quest for enlightenment would be to commit Wilber's "pre/trans fallacy." As a responsible and ethical social worker, you would help her address these unresolved issues at the personal, and perhaps even pre-personal, levels while maintaining respect for her spiritual perspective. You would also help her discern the appropriate role of her spiritual practices in support of her overall growth and development. Consulting with a spiritual teacher or a transpersonal practitioner, with Trudy's permission, also might be helpful in this case.

Likewise, if a practitioner dismisses spiritual practices as signs of a serious problem simply because they are unfamiliar or seem "strange," he or she would be moving to the other side of the pre/trans fallacy—treating potentially spiritual or transpersonal experiences as if they were psychological disorders. The potential for this type of error is evident in the case of Jean-Joseph and his family. If this family sought conventional health care services, while also following traditional spiritually based healing processes, as a social worker your task would be to help the family and the medical professionals find a way to work together. This is not always an easy task, as is poignantly illustrated in Anne Fadiman's book, *When the Spirit Catches You and You Fall Down* (1998), which tells the tragic story of a Hmong child with epilepsy who becomes brain dead because of the failure of professionals to understand unfamiliar spiritual worldviews and negotiate cultural differences. This true account highlights the critical need for social workers to develop the knowledge, values, and skills of spiritually sensitive practice in order to serve clients from diverse spiritual traditions.

Summary and Critique of Fowler's and Wilber's Theories

Both Fowler's and Wilber's models of individual spiritual development reflect Fourth Force theory in that they incorporate the first three forces (dynamic, behavior, and existential/humanistic/experiential theories). In fact, both Fowler and Wilber use many of the same theorists as foundations for their own work (e.g., Piaget, Kohlberg, Maslow). And both are delineating higher and more transcendent levels of human development than have been previously proposed by Western theorists; namely Fowler's *Universalizing Faith* and Wilber's *Psychic, Subtle, Causal,* and *Nondual* levels. In later writings, both theorists also offer additional conceptual formulations at the larger sociocultural levels (Fowler, 1996; Wilber, 2000b).

The major difference between the two models in terms of individual development is that Wilber provides more substance and specification than Fowler does about what Transpersonal levels of development look like and how they evolve. Wilber also provides more detailed descriptions of the potential pitfalls of spiritual development than Fowler, who offers only a general overview of the possible dangers or deficits of development at each of his faith stages. However, Fowler provides more specification about the content and process of spiritual development at the Pre-personal and Personal phases. In terms of their utility for social work practice, we could say that Fowler's model is more descriptive and Wilber's more prescriptive. Both theories have been critiqued in a number of areas. An overview of these critiques is presented next.

> Conflict perspective

First, as developmental models, Fowler's and Wilber's models are open to the criticisms of all developmental perspectives, including charges of dominant group bias. Such perspectives do not pay enough attention to social, economic, political, and historical factors and the role of power dynamics and oppression in human development. Developmental perspectives are also said to convey the idea that there is only one right way to proceed down the developmental path and thus display an ethnocentrism often rooted in middle-class, heterosexual, Anglo-Saxon male life experience.

Both Fowler and Wilber might counter by pointing out that familial, cultural, and historical contexts are considered in their models. Wilber, in particular, would highlight the extensive use of cross-cultural knowledge in the development of his theory and point to the cessation of ethnocentrism as a major characteristic of his later stages of consciousness. He would also stress the integral nature of his more current theoretical developments, which pay equal attention to *exterior* impacts on spiritual development and to *interior* aspects (Wilber, 2000b, 2001, 2006). Both theorists would also support the notion that there are many paths to spiritual development, although they would say that these paths have common features in their evolution.

A second critique of both theories is their relative lack of attention to the spiritual capacities and potentialities of children, focusing more on the emergence of spiritual issues in adulthood. This is due to the assertion that higher levels of cognitive functioning (capacity for formal operations and abstract thought) are necessary to fully understand and incorporate spiritual experience. A number of writers have contested this assertion, proposing that childhood is a unique time of enhanced, not diminished, spiritual awareness (Coles, 1990; Hay, Nye, & Murphy, 1996; S. Levine, 1999; R. Nye & Hay, 1996). They base this viewpoint on in-depth interviews with children, which often revealed a richness and depth regarding spirituality that is generally not expected of people so young. They point to a variety of spiritual experiences and epiphanies that the children shared with them, including archetypical mythical dreams; visionary experiences; profound insights about self-identity, life, and death; and heightened capacities for compassion for all living things.

An example of this research is a study conducted by Hay and Nye (2006), which involved in-depth interviews with children ranging in age from 6 to 11. These interviews revealed children's capacity for a relational consciousness that encompassed relations not only with people, but with all things, including being in relationship with oneself, the world, and a transcendent force. They also reported that these children maintained and nurtured their spirituality through various means, such as removing themselves physically or mentally from the everyday rhythms of life, developing and sustaining a connection with the divine through prayer, philosophical musing about the origins of the world and the nature of God, and purposefully seeking altered states of consciousness. Interestingly, results from a recent national survey of seasoned social workers who work with children and adolescents reveal that practitioners generally see the relevance of religion and spirituality in the lives of children and that they encounter youth who present spiritual issues in their practice (Kvarfordt & Sheridan, 2007).

Wilber (2000a) concedes that children can have a variety of spiritual experiences, including peak experiences that provide glimpses of the transpersonal realm, but states that these incidents are experienced and incorporated within the child's pre-personal or personal stage of development. Regardless of the particular developmental level, there clearly is a need for further exploration of children's spirituality in order to understand their unique spiritual experiences, developmental processes, and needs. Similarly, there is also a need to revisit assumptions about the spiritual experiences and capacities of adults who have lower cognitive functioning, either congenitally or as a result of injury.

A third critique concerns empirical investigation of the theories. Although Fowler's model was developed through an inductive research process and Wilber's formulations are grounded in a synthesis of many lines of research, there is a need for empirical verification of both models. Limited empirical exploration of Fowler's faith stages has provided partial support for his framework (Das & Harries, 1996; Furushima, 1983; Mischey, 1981; Swenson, Fuller, & Clements, 1993), while a number of research projects are currently underway as part of Wilber's Integral Institute. The fact that such research is still in its beginning stages is somewhat understandable, given the difficulties of empirical investigation in such an abstract realm. It is difficult enough to operationalize and measure such concepts as formal operational cognition or self-esteem; the challenge of investigating transcendence is even more daunting. Nonetheless, strategies from both positivist and constructivist research approaches are currently available to study interior states and subjective experiences of meaning as well as biophysical manifestations of different states of consciousness. (See Chapters 1 and 2 for a review of positivist and constructivist research approaches.) As is true for all theories of human behavior, transpersonal models such as Fowler's and Wilber's need to be specifically tested and refined through the research process. This research also must be replicated with different groups (defined by sex and gender, age, race, ethnicity, socioeconomic status, geopolitical membership, and the like) in order to explore the universality of the models.

In conclusion, both Fowler and Wilber provide perspectives beyond our traditional biopsychosocial framework that allow us to better understand human development and functioning, and suggest a direction for working with people from diverse spiritual perspectives. Their theories are major contributions to human behavior theory. However, we also need viable practice theories and practice models that explicitly address the spiritual dimension. There have been promising developments in this area. Examples include E. D. Smith's (1995) trans-egoic model for dealing with death and other losses; Cowley's (1999) transpersonal approach for working with couples and families; Hickson and Phelps's (1998) model for facilitating women's spirituality; and J. L. Clark's (2007) model for working with spirituality, culture, and diverse worldviews. There are also practice models that directly integrate spirituality within biopsychosocial approaches. Examples are Almaas's (1995, 1996) Diamond approach, which incorporates object relations and body sensing within Sufism, and Grof's (1988, 2003; Grof & Bennett, 1992) holotropic breathwork model, which combines bodywork and altered states of consciousness to address unresolved psychological issues from earlier points in development. Finally, Cortright (1997) provides a good overview of how a transpersonal orientation can be generally incorporated within psychoanalytic and existential therapies, and Mikulas (2002) offers a practice approach that integrates a transpersonal perspective with behavioral approaches. All of these developments reflect a synthesis of transpersonal with earlier therapeutic modalities (First, Second, and Third Force therapies). As with human behavior theories of spiritual development, these practice theories and models also must be tested and continually refined to determine their utility and applicability for a wide range of client situations.

Critical Thinking Questions 6.2

Fowler and Wilber both think of spirituality in terms of development to higher levels of faith over time. Do you think this is a helpful way to think about spirituality? Is it a helpful way to think about your own spiritual life? Do you see any cultural biases in either of the theories?

THE ROLE OF SPIRITUALITY IN SOCIAL WORK

Canda and Furman (2010) outline five broad historical phases that trace the development of linkages between spirituality and social work in the United States. An overview of these phases is presented next.

1. *Indigenous Pre-Colonial Period:* This period includes the thousands of years when Indigenous cultures in North America employed a variety of spiritually based approaches to healing and mutual support. These practices focused beyond human welfare to include the well-being of other living things and the earth itself. Although there are few written accounts for the majority of this period, there are certain characteristics that can be surmised from archeological evidence, oral traditions, current practices of contemporary Indigenous peoples, and the records that do exist for the later years of this period. These characteristics include a high value on "(1) individual development of harmony between spiritual, emotional, physical, and mental aspects of persons; (2) a strong web of family, clan, and community relations; (3) family, clan, and community-based identity; (4) a sense of respect for and interdependency with all of nature; (5) rootedness in particular places and special relationship with the sacred beings thereof; and (6) a sense of sacredness and connectedness of person, family, clan, nation, world, mother earth, and universe" (Canda & Furman, 2010, pp. 109–110). Many of these traditional ways continue into the present, both outside of and within social work (Baskin, 2006; Brave Heart, 2001; Bucko & Iron Cloud, 2008; Deloria, 1994).

2. *Sectarian Origins:* This phase began with the colonial period and lasted through the first 20 years of the 20th century. Early human services, institutions, and social welfare policy were significantly influenced by Judeo-Christian worldviews on charity, communal responsibility, and social justice (Fauri, 1988; Leiby, 1985; Lowenberg, 1988; Marty, 1980; Popple & Leighninger, 2005). At this time, there were also competing explanations of human behavior: on the one hand, an emphasis on distinguishing individual moral blame or merit (e.g., the worthy vs. unworthy poor), and on the other hand, a focus on social reform and social justice (e.g., Jewish communal service and Christian social gospel). This period also included human service providers who had a strong

spiritual foundation for their work, but offered service through non-sectarian means (e.g., Jane Addams and the settlement house movement). Finally, Indigenous, African American, and Spanish and French Catholic spiritual perspectives also contributed to the evolution of social work during this time frame (E. P. Martin & Martin, 2002; Van Hook, Hugen, & Aguilar, 2001).

3. *Professionalization and Secularization:* Beginning in the 1920s and continuing through the 1970s, social work began to distance itself from its early sectarian roots. This movement mirrored a shift within the larger society, which began to replace moral explanations of human problems with a scientific, rational understanding of human behavior. The social work profession increasingly relied on scientific empiricism and secular humanism as the major foundations for its values, ethics, and practice approaches (Imre, 1984; Siporin, 1986). This period also witnessed social work's reliance on a variety of emerging psychological and sociological theories (such as psychoanalytic, behavioral, and social functionalism), which did not recognize the spiritual dimension as significant for either understanding human behavior or as a focus for practice. As this stage has been described, "Religion and spirituality were increasingly viewed, at best, as unnecessary and irrelevant, and, at worst, as illogical and pathological" (Russel, 1998, p. 17). However, several religiously affiliated agencies continued to provide social services (e.g., Catholic Social Services, Jewish Family Services, Lutheran Social Services, Salvation Army). Nonsectarian spiritual influences were also felt, including principles of 12-step programs; humanistic, existential, and Jungian thought; and ideas about human development drawn from Eastern religions (Robbins, Chatterjee, & Canda, 2006a).

4. *Resurgence of Interest in Spirituality:* A renewed interest in the spiritual dimension began in the 1980s and continued through 1995 (Canda, 1997; Russel, 1998). Indicators of this new phase within the profession included a marked increase in the numbers of publications and presentations on the topic; the development of a national Society for Spirituality and Social Work (SSSW); and the first national conference on spirituality and social work, held in 1994. As part of this substantial activity, there was infusion of new and diverse perspectives on spirituality that influenced the profession, including Buddhism, Confucianism, Hinduism, Shamanism, Taoism, and transpersonal theory. This period differed from the earlier sectarian era in that it emphasized the need to address spirituality in a way that recognizes the value of diverse spiritual traditions and respects client self-determination (Canda, 1988; Sheridan, Bullis, Adcock, Berlin, & Miller, 1992). This trend toward reexamination and reintegration of spirituality within the profession corresponded with increased interest within the larger culture (Gallup & Lindsay, 1999).

5. *Transcending Boundaries:* From 1995 to the present, the profession has witnessed an elaboration and expansion of prior trends. This includes the reintroduction of references to religion and spirituality in the Council on Social Work Education's (CSWE) 1995 Curriculum Policy Statement and 2000 Educational Policy and Accreditation Standards after an absence of more than 20 years. The first international conference of the SSSW was held in 2000, with other national and international conferences increasingly including presentations on spirituality (e.g., National Association of Social Workers [NASW], CSWE's Annual Program Meeting, International Federation of Social Workers [IFSW], International Association of Schools of Social Work [IASSW]). The Canadian Society for Spirituality and Social Work was established in 2002 and cohosts conferences with the United States. New postmodern perspectives on spirituality have also entered the arena, including feminist, ecophilosophical, postcolonial, and expanded transpersonal frameworks, which have broadened the focus of spirituality to include all peoples, all nations, all beings, and the planet itself, with special concern for the marginalized and oppressed (Besthorn, 2001; Canda, 2005; Coates, 2003; Meinert, Pardeck, & Murphy, 1998). There has also been exponential growth in empirical work during this period, including over 50 studies on social work practitioners, faculty, and students (see Sheridan, 2004 and 2009, for reviews of this literature) and growing numbers of studies on social work clients (see, for example, Beitel et al., 2007; Margolin, Beitel, Shuman-Olivier, & Avants, 2006; Nelson-Becker, 2006; C. Stewart, Koeske, & Pringle, 2007). Clearly, the focus has shifted from *whether* the topic should be included in the profession to *how* to integrate spirituality within social work practice in an ethical, effective, and spiritually sensitive manner (Canda & Furman, 2010; Canda, Nakashima, & Furman, 2004; Derezotes, 2006; Sheridan, 2009; Van Hook, Hugen, & Aguilar, 2001).

In regard to social work education, two major rationales have been proposed for including content on spirituality within undergraduate and graduate studies. These include the important roles it plays in both human diversity and overall human experience and behavior. Studies of social work educators (Sheridan, Wilmer, & Atcheson, 1994) and students (Sheridan & Amato-von Hemert, 1999) reveal general endorsement of these two rationales, as reflected in the following statements:

- Religious and spiritual beliefs and practices are part of multicultural diversity. Social workers should have knowledge and skills in this area in order to work effectively with diverse client groups (90% of educators "strongly agree/agree"; 93% of students "strongly agree/agree").

- There is another dimension of human existence beyond the biopsychosocial framework that can be used to understand human behavior. Social work education should expand this framework to include the spiritual dimension (61% of educators "strongly agree/agree"; 72% of students "strongly agree/agree").

A number of publications address the relevance of spirituality for the profession in these two domains and this literature has become extensive. Thus, the following sections provide examples of writings that examine the role of spirituality relative to human diversity or the human condition. Readers are encouraged to use these as a starting place for further exploration.

Spirituality and Human Diversity

Commitment to issues of human diversity and to oppressed populations is a hallmark of the social work profession. At various times in history, some branches of organized religion have played a negative or impeding role in the attainment of social justice for various groups. Examples include the use of religious texts, policies, and practices to deny the full human rights of persons of color; women; and gay, lesbian, bisexual, and transgendered persons. At the same time, organized religion has a rich heritage of involvement in myriad social justice causes and movements, including the civil rights movement, the peace movement, the women's movement, the gay rights movement, abolition of the death penalty, the antipoverty movement, and the deep ecology movement.

Conflict perspective

It is beyond the scope of this chapter to do an overall analysis of the role of religion in the struggle for social and economic justice. However, the following sections provide examples of the impact of both religious and nonreligious spirituality in the lives of oppressed groups as defined by race and ethnicity, sex and gender, sexual orientation, and other forms of human diversity.

Race and Ethnicity

Spirituality expressed in both religious and nonreligious forms has been pivotal in the lives of many persons of color and other marginalized ethnic groups. This brief discussion of spirituality and race/ethnicity emphasizes common experiences and themes in order to provide a general overview. However, remember that a great deal of diversity exists within these groups and that every person's story will be unique.

1. *African Americans.* Religious affiliation for African Americans is generally high, and this racial group is most likely to report a specific affiliation. Data from the General Social Surveys from 1972–2004 show the majority of African Americans as Protestant (75.7%), followed by Catholic (6.5%), and Jewish (less than 1%). Seven percent reported some other type of affiliation, and 10.6% do not identify with a religious group (*A Guide to African Americans and Religion,* 2007). African Americans comprise about one-fourth of adherents to Islam in the United

States (Pew Forum, 2008), including membership in Sunni Islam or other mainstream Islamic denominations, the Nation of Islam, and smaller Black Muslim sects (Haddad, 1997). Black churches, in particular, have historically been a safe haven for African Americans facing racism and oppression, as well as an important source of social support, race consciousness and inspiration, leadership training, human services, and empowerment and social change (R. M. Franklin, 1994; S. L. Logan, 2001; R. J. Taylor, Ellison, Chatters, Levin, & Lincoln, 2000). The legacy of slavery and the integrated heritage of African and African American spiritual values have emphasized collective unity and the connection of all beings: "I am because we are, and because we are, therefore, I am" (Nobles, 1980, p. 29). Afrocentric spirituality stresses the interdependence among God, community, family, and the individual. Its central virtues include beneficence to the community, forbearance through tragedy, wisdom applied to action, creative improvisation, forgiveness of wrongs and oppression, and social justice (Paris, 1995). *Kwanzaa* is an important nonsectarian Afrocentric spiritual tradition, which was developed by author and activist Maulana Karenga in the 1960s as a mechanism for celebrating and supporting African and African American strengths and empowerment. Seven principles represent the core values of Kwanzaa: Umoja (Unity), Kujichagulia (Self-Determination), Ujima (Collective Work and Responsibility), Ujamaa (Collective Economics), Nia (Purpose), Kuumba (Creativity), and Imani (Faith) (Karenga, 1995). Many writers stress the importance of paying attention to the role of spirituality in its various forms when working with African American clients, families, and communities (see, for example, Banerjee & Canda, 2009; Burke, Chauvin, & Miranti, 2005; D. R. Freeman, 2006; Stewart, Koeske, & Pringle, 2007).

2. *Latino(a) Americans.* This category includes people with ties to 26 countries in North, South, and Central America; the Caribbean; and Europe (Spain). Thus, the labeling of these peoples under a reductionist label such as Latino(a) or Hispanic denies the considerable diversity within this population. Keeping this in mind, the majority (58%) of Latino(a) Americans are Roman Catholic, but there is also a large and growing number (23%) of Protestants among this group. Almost 5% report other religious affiliations, including Muslim and Jewish, and 14% are unaffiliated (Pew Forum, 2008). In addition, many Latino(a) people follow beliefs and practices that represent a blending of Christian, African, and Indigenous spiritual traditions (Castex, 1994; Canda & Furman, 2010). Latino(a) American spirituality has been strongly affected by factors related to colonialism (Costas, 1991). This history includes military, political, economic, cultural, and religious conquest, forcing many Indigenous peoples to take on the Catholicism of their conquerors. Many traditional places of worship, spiritual texts, beliefs, and practices were destroyed, repressed, or blended with Catholic traditions (Canda & Furman, 2010). Today, Christian Latino(a) faith has several central features: a personal relationship with God that encompasses love and reverence as well as fear and dread; an emphasis on both faith and ritual behavior; belief in the holiness of Jesus Christ as savior, king, and infant God; special reverence shown to Mary as the mother of God; recognition of saints as models of behavior and as benefactors; significance of sacred objects as both symbols of faith and transmitters of luck or magic; and special events and celebrations, such as saints' feast days, Holy Week, Christmas Eve, feasts of the Virgin, and life passages (e.g., baptisms, first communions, confirmations, coming-of-age ceremonies, weddings, and funerals) (Aguilar, 2001; Ramirez, 1985). In addition to mainstream religions, a number of African and Indigenous spiritual healing traditions continue to be practiced by some Latino(a) groups today, including curanderismo, santiguando, espiritismo, Santeria, and Vodoun (Delgado, 1988; Paulino, 1995; Torrez, 1984). Social workers need to understand the importance of both religious institutions and folk healing traditions when working with Latino(a) populations. These various expressions of spirituality serve as important sources for social support, coping strategies, means of healing, socialization and maintenance of culture, and resources for human services and social justice efforts (Burke et al., 2005; Delgado & Humm-Delgado, 1982; Faver & Trachte, 2005; Paulino, 1998).

3. *Asian Americans and Pacific Islanders.* This population represents many different cultures, including Chinese, Filipino, Japanese, Korean, Asian Indian, Vietnamese, Hawaiian, Cambodian, Laotian, Thai, Hmong, Pakistani, Samoan, Guamanian, Indonesian, and others (Healey, 2010). These different peoples are affiliated with a wide range of spiritual traditions, including Hinduism, Buddhism, Islam, Confucianism, Sikhism, Zoroastrianism, Jainism, Shinto, Taoism, and

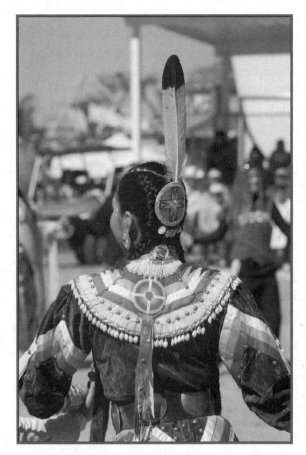

▲ **Photo 6.3** Native American dance is a cultural and highly spiritual form of expression.

Christianity (Tweed, 1997). In the United States, recent data show that 27% of this group is Protestant, 17% Catholic, 14% Hindu, 9% Buddhist, and 4% Muslim. Approximately 6% report other religious affiliations, and 23% are unaffiliated (Pew Forum, 2008). There is much diversity within these various religious traditions as well, making it particularly difficult to discuss common elements of spiritual beliefs or practices. However, several themes can be discerned: the connection among and the divinity of all beings; the need to transcend suffering and the material world; the importance of displaying compassion, selflessness, and cooperation; the honoring of ancestors; a disciplined approach to life and spiritual development; and a holistic understanding of existence (Canda & Furman, 1999; D. K. Chung, 2001; R. Singh, 2001). Both religious institutions and traditional practices have been helpful to a variety of Asian and Pacific Islander immigrants and refugees and their descendants. For example, many Southeast Asian refugee communities have established Buddhist temples and mutual assistance associations, which provide social, physical, mental, and spiritual resources (Canda & Phaobtong, 1992; Morreale, 1998; Timberlake & Cook, 1984), and the Korean church has been an essential provider of social services (Choi & Tirrito, 1999). Some Asian Americans and Pacific Islanders also use Indigenous healers, such as the Cambodian krou khmer, the Korean mudang, the Hmong spirit medium, and the Hawaiian kahuna (Canda & Furman, 1999; Canda, Shin, & Canda, 1993; D. E. Hurdle, 2002). As with other groups, there is an emerging literature stressing the importance of attending to spirituality in practice with clients from this large and diverse cultural population (Canda, 2001; D. K. Chung, 2001; Hodge, 2004; D. E. Hurdle, 2002; R. Singh, 2001; Tan, 2006). In addition, several writers have proposed incorporating concepts and practices from Asian spiritual traditions into mainstream social work practice, including meditation (Keefe, 1996; S. L. Logan, 1997), Zen-oriented practice (Brandon, 1976), and yoga (Fukuyama & Sevig, 1999).

4. *Native Americans:* Native Americans, or First Nations people, originally numbered in the millions and were members of hundreds of distinct tribes or nations, each with its own language, heritage, and spiritual traditions (Healey, 2010; Swift, 1998). As part of the effort to "humanize and civilize" First Nations people, the U.S. Congress regularly appropriated funds for Christian missionary efforts, beginning in 1819 (U.S. Commission on Human Rights, 1998). American Indian boarding schools were a major component of these efforts, where children were forbidden to wear their native attire, eat their native foods, speak their native language, or practice their traditional religion, and were often severely punished for failure to adhere to these prohibitions (Haig-Brown, 1988; Snipp, 1998). Through a long history of resistance and renewal, however, Indigenous spiritual traditions have persisted and currently are being restored and revitalized (Swift, 1998). Various expressions of First Nations spirituality have several common themes: the inseparability of spirituality from the rest of life; connection to and responsibility for the Earth and all her creatures; the sacredness of all things, including animals, plants, minerals, and natural forces; the values of balance, harmony, and connectedness; the importance of extended family and community; and the use of myth, ritual, and

storytelling as spiritual practices (Duran & Duran, 1995; Matheson, 1996; Yellow Bird, 1995). Many of these values are of increasing appeal to non-Indigenous people, producing great concern among First Nations people regarding appropriation of their customs, ceremonies, rituals, and healing practices (Kasee, 1995; LaDue, 1994). This cross-tradition borrowing of spiritual practices requires sensitivity, respect, competence, and permission (Canda & Yellow Bird, 1996). Many service providers also call for sensitivity and awareness of the effects of historical trauma on Native Americans and recommend the integration of traditional practices for more effective service delivery (Brave Heart, 2001; Burke et al., 2005; French & White, 2004; Limb & Hodge, 2008; Skye, 2002; Weaver, 1999). In addition, Indigenous worldviews and spiritual practices have application to social work in general (Canda, 1983; R. W. Voss, Douville, Little Soldier, & Twiss, 1999).

It is important to remember the experience of other groups that have been more extensively assimilated into the dominant culture of the United States (e.g., Irish, Italian, and Jewish Americans). Many of these groups also have histories of discrimination and religious intolerance, the effects of which are felt by succeeding generations. Currently, in the aftermath of the terrorist attacks on September 11, 2001, we in the United States have witnessed increased discrimination and oppressive acts against Muslim Americans, especially those of Middle Eastern descent (Crabtree, Husain, & Spalek, 2008; New York City Commission on Human Rights, 2003). At the time of the writing of this chapter, we are seeing increased suspicion and calls for racial profiling of people assumed to be Muslim as a result of a failed attempt to down a U.S. plane headed for Detroit on Christmas Day. Given this atmosphere and the growing Muslim population within the United States, it is imperative that social workers develop sensitivity and competence in working with Muslim clients (Carolan, Bagherinia, Juhari, Himelright, & Mouton-Sanders, 2000; Hodge, 2005a). Indeed, social workers must be sensitive to the particular history and spiritual traditions of all racial and ethnic groups.

Sex and Gender

Women are more likely than men to report that they are religious, church-affiliated, and frequent users of prayer; are certain in their belief of God; feel close to God; hold a positive view of their church; and are more religiously engaged (Cornwall, 1989; Felty & Poloma, 1991; Pew Forum, 2008). Women also are the majority of members in most religious bodies in the United States and play important roles in the life of many religious communities (Braude, 1997).

However, in several denominations, women's participation has been significantly restricted, prohibiting women from holding leadership positions or performing certain religious rites and ceremonies (Burke et al., 2005; Holm & Bowker, 1994; Reilly, 1995). In addition, women members of traditional Judeo-Christian-Islamic faiths generally experience conceptualizations and symbols of the divine as masculine, suggesting that men are closer to (and thus more like) God than women (Reuther, 1983). In response to this, some scholars are calling for increased ordination of women and more women in leadership positions in order to create a more woman-affirming environment within religious institutions (K. A. Roberts, 2004).

Although most women who belong to mainstream denominations report being generally satisfied with their affiliations (Corbett, 1997), some struggle with the patriarchal aspects of their faith. One study conducted in-depth interviews of 61 women between the ages of 18 and 71 who were affiliated with Catholic, United Methodist, Unitarian Universalist, or Jewish congregations (Ozorak, 1996). Most (93%) perceived gender inequality within their religions. Sixteen percent viewed these inequalities as appropriate, and thus accepted them; 8% left their faith in reaction to this issue and others. The remainder coped by using either behavioral strategies (e.g., requesting equal treatment; requesting gender-inclusive language; substituting feminine words, images, or interpretations; participating in feminist activities), cognitive strategies (e.g., focusing on positive aspects of the religion, comparing their faith favorably to others, emphasizing signs of positive change), or a combination of both behavioral and cognitive mechanisms.

Christian and Jewish feminist theologians have made efforts to emphasize the feminine heritage of conventional faiths, and some Christian and Jewish denominations have increased opportunities for women in both lay leadership roles and clerical positions (Canda & Furman, 1999). There also has been a movement toward alternative women's spiritualities. Some women have become involved in spiritual support groups or explored other religious traditions such as Buddhism (Carnes & Craig, 1998; Holm & Bowker, 1994). Others have pursued feminist-identified theology, such as goddess worship (Bolen, 1984; Christ, 1995; Kruel, 1995), Wicca (Starhawk, 1979; Warwick, 1995), Jewish feminism (Breitman, 1995), or Christian womanist spirituality (M. A. Jackson, 2002). These spiritual traditions emphasize the feminine aspect of the divine; the sacredness of women's bodies, rhythms, and life cycles; the power and creativity of women's spirituality; a connection to earth-centered practices; and the care of all people and the planet (Kidd, 1996; J. G. Martin, 1993; Ochshorn & Cole, 1995; Warwick, 1995). Some men are also turning to alternative spiritual traditions to overcome religious experiences and conceptions of God and masculinity that they feel have been detrimental to them (Kivel, 1991; Warwick, 1995).

Sexual Orientation

Nonheterosexual persons are often linked together as the GLBT community (gay, lesbian, bisexual, and transgendered persons). It should be noted, however, that transgendered persons may identify themselves as heterosexual, bisexual, or homosexual; therefore, transgendered status is a matter of sex and gender, not sexual orientation. However, as a group, transgendered persons have much in common with gay, lesbian, and bisexual persons when it comes to experiences with oppression, and thus will be included with these groups in this discussion of spirituality.

As an oppressed population, GLBT persons have suffered greatly at the hands of some groups affiliated with organized religion. Some egregious examples are the pronouncement by certain religious leaders that AIDS is a "punishment for the sins" of GLBT persons and the picketing of the funeral for Matthew Shepard (victim of an antigay hate crime) by religiously identified individuals. More pervasively, many GLBT members of various faiths have had to struggle with religious teachings that tell them their feelings and behaviors are immoral or sinful.

Every major religious and spiritual tradition has GLBT adherents. Furthermore, there are religious rationales within Christianity, Islam, Judaism, Buddhism, Confucianism, and Taoism for tolerance of nonheterosexual orientations, even though historically these religions have privileged heterosexuality (Ellison & Plaskow, 2007). There are also associations within every major religion that go beyond tolerance to work for full inclusion of GLBT persons. Examples include Affirmation—United Methodists for Lesbian, Gay, Bisexual & Transgender Concerns; Association of Welcoming & Affirming Baptists; Integrity (Episcopal); Lutherans Concerned; More Light Presbyterians; United Church of Christ Coalition for Lesbian, Bisexual, Gay and Transgender Concerns; World Congress of Gay, Lesbian, Bisexual, and Transgender Jews: Keshet Ga'avah; Al-Fatiha (Muslim); Gay Buddhist Fellowship; The Gay and Lesbian Vaishnava Association (Hindu); and Seventh Day Adventist Kinship. There are also denominations that generally identify themselves as "open and gay-affirming," including Dignity (Catholic), Metropolitan Community Church (Protestant), Society of Friends (Quakers), United Church of Christ, Unitarian Universalism, and Reform and Reconstructionist branches of Judaism.

GLBT persons who grow up in less tolerant religious communities experience considerable tension between their faith and their sexuality. They, and others close to them, must decide how to respond to this tension. Canda and Furman (2010) identify four alternative ideological responses that are evident within Christianity, but are applicable to other faiths as well. The first three refer to the faith's stance on nonheterosexual orientation, and the fourth refers to a possible stance that GLBT persons or their allies may take regarding organized religion:

1. Condemn homosexuality and homosexual persons.

2. Accept homosexual persons but reject homosexual behavior.

3. Affirm and accept GLBT persons at every level.

4. Reject the faith's position relative to GLBT persons and depart from the faith.

These four responses have implications for both GLBT persons and social work practitioners. For GLBT persons, involvement with religious institutions characteristic of the first response exacerbates both the direct and internalized oppression that most experience as a result of living in a society that privileges heterosexual orientation and views any other sexual expression as deviant or "less than." At the other end of the spectrum, involvement with congregations that display the third response of affirmation and acceptance would allow GLBT persons to honor both their sexual identity and their faith commitments. The middle position of accepting the person but rejecting the behavior would most likely maintain the tension and internal conflict that a GLBT person experiences when an important part of his or her identity is "not welcome at the table." The final reaction, leaving one's faith, is unsatisfactory for many GLBT persons who want to be involved with communal religious experiences and desire a spiritual community that is welcoming of their whole self. For others, it represents a choice that is self-affirming and liberating.

In regard to social work practitioners, Canda and Furman (2010) point out that the first response is clearly antithetical to social work values and ethics, while the third position is congruent with ethical standards of practice. The second response brings up questions concerning how this stance will affect the practitioner's work with GLBT clients. It is challenging enough to affirm a positive self-identity and possess confidence and assurance as a GLBT person in a heterosexist and homophobic society without experiencing negative attitudes from one's social worker. If the practitioner cannot transmit the level of empathy and respect for GLBT persons and their sexual orientation that is required by the NASW Code of Ethics, referral to another practitioner is warranted. Furthermore, the practitioner needs to engage in a process of reflection and self-examination in order to be able to move toward a more positive and ethical response to GLBT clients. Social workers who themselves have left a faith tradition (the fourth response) due to disagreement with teachings on sexual orientation, or any other issue, also need to be vigilant that they are not transmitting negative and disrespectful attitudes toward religious clients, whether they are GLBT or heterosexual.

It also is important to respect the unique spiritual journeys that individual GLBT persons may take. If you were working with Leon as he struggles with the conflict between his church and his sexual identity, it would be important to work collaboratively with him to discern what option was best for him, providing him information about alternatives while maintaining respect for his self-determination. As Barret and Barzan (1996) point out, regardless of the individual decisions that GLBT persons make regarding religion, the process of self-acceptance is a spiritual journey unto itself. Speaking of the pain and joy of this journey, one deeply religious man describes his growing self-acceptance during a spiritual retreat, exclaiming that he "did not believe anyone, including God, could love me for myself" (McNeill, 1995, p. 35).

Other Aspects of Diversity

The issues and implications relative to spirituality that pertain to race and ethnicity, sex and gender, and sexual orientation apply to other forms of human diversity as well. For example, some religious teachings have interpreted disability as a punishment for the sins of the person or family (Miles, 1995; Niemann, 2005) or as a means for nondisabled persons to acquire spiritual status through expressions of pity and charity (J. Fitzgerald, 1997). Conversely, spirituality has been noted as both a significant means of coping and a vehicle toward positive self-definition for persons with disabilities (J. Fitzgerald, 1997; Hurst, 2007; Niemann, 2005; Parish, Magana, & Cassiman, 2008; Swinton, 1997).

Spirituality and age is another area that has been widely addressed. Both religious and nonreligious forms of spirituality are an important source of social support for older persons and a pathway for coping, ongoing development, and successful aging (Burke et al., 2005; Hedberg, Brulin, & Alex, 2009; Yoon & Lee, 2004). In addition, spirituality is viewed as an essential foundation for healthy development among young people (Hay & Nye, 2006; B. K. Myers, 1997; Roehlkepartain, King, Wagener, & Benson, 2006). Research has shown spirituality to be a significant protective factor against substance abuse, premature sexual activity, and delinquency for children and adolescents (Holder et al., 2000; Johnson, Jang, Larsen, & De Li, 2001; Miller, Davies, & Greenwald, 2000; C. Smith & Denton, 2005). As our understanding of the interaction between religious and nonreligious spirituality and other forms of human diversity increases, social work will be in a better position to work sensitively, competently, and ethically with many diverse groups and communities.

Spirituality and the Human Experience

Social workers deal with every aspect of the human experience. They simultaneously focus on solving problems in living while supporting optimal human functioning and quality of life. The literature regarding spirituality in these two areas is immense, with significant development in social work, psychology, nursing, medicine, rehabilitation counseling, pastoral counseling, marital and family counseling, and other helping disciplines. The following discussion highlights examples of this continually evolving knowledge base. Similar to the previous discussion of spirituality and diversity, readers can use this brief overview as an entry point to this expanding literature.

Problems in Living

It is difficult to find an area related to problems in living in which spirituality is not being explored. For example, much has been written about the link between spirituality and mental health. Various indicators of spirituality—such as religious commitment, involvement in spiritual or religious practices, level of religiosity or spirituality—have been shown to have an inverse relationship with depression, anxiety, hopelessness, suicide, and other mental health problems while showing a positive relationship with self-esteem, self-efficacy, hope, optimism, life satisfaction, and general well-being (Koenig, 2005; Mueller, Plevak, & Rummans, 2001; Pargament, 1997).

Similar relationships are found between spirituality and physical health, with spirituality linked to a variety of better health outcomes (C. G. Ellison & Levin, 1998; Koenig, 2001a; Koenig, McCullough, & Larson, 2000; Matthews et al., 1998). Various propositions have been investigated to explain the exact mechanisms of this relationship. Findings suggest that religion and spirituality benefit physical health through their support of health-promoting behaviors and discouragement of risk behaviors, while others indicate possible biological processes that mediate the negative impacts of stress and support healthy immune functioning (Koenig, 1999; Mueller et al., 2001; O. Ray, 2004; Segerstrom & Miller, 2004). Specific spiritual practices, such as mindfulness-based stress-reduction techniques, have shown positive outcomes in several areas, including chronic pain, anxiety disorders, recurrent depression, psoriasis, and general psychological well-being (Grossman, Niemann, Schmidt, & Walach, 2004; Williams, Teasdale, Segal, & Kabat-Zinn, 2007), as well as benefits to the immune system (Davidson et al., 2003).

For both mental and physical health problems, religion and spirituality have been noted as major means of coping (Koenig, 2005; Koenig, Larson, & Larson, 2001; Koenig, McCullough, & Larson, 2000; Pargament, 1997). In an extensive review of the social and behavioral science literature, Oakley Ray (2004) cites spirituality as one of four key factors that are significantly linked to positive coping, along with knowledge, inner resources, and social support. The specific benefits of spiritually based coping include relieving stress, retaining a sense of control, maintaining hope, and providing a sense of meaning and purpose in life (Koenig, 2001b, 2005).

Higher levels of social support through religious and spiritual networks also play a significant role in positive coping with health issues (C. G. Ellison & Levin, 1998; B. G. F. Perry, 1998; Reese & Kaplan, 2000). Both religious and nonreligious forms of spirituality have proven helpful to persons coping with caregiving demands related to health problems of family members (Koenig, 2005; Sanders, 2005; Tolliver, 2001; Vickrey et al., 2007). Similar effects are noted for coping with poverty (Black, 1999; Greeff & Fillis, 2009; Parish et al., 2008) and homelessness (Ferguson, Wu, Dryrness, & Spruijt-Metz, 2007; E. W. Lindsey, Kurtz, Jarvis, Williams, & Nackerud, 2000).

Still another body of scholarship explores spirituality and substance abuse. Both religiosity and spirituality have been noted as protective factors in this area for adults and children (Kendler, Gardner, & Prescott, 1997; Hodge, Cardenas, & Montoya, 2001; C. Smith & Denton, 2005; Wills, Yaeger, & Sandy, 2003). In addition, the spiritual dimension as a key factor in recovery from substance abuse has long been recognized in self-help groups such as Alcoholics Anonymous, Narcotics Anonymous, and other treatment approaches (Hsu, Grow, Grow, Marlatt, Galanter, & Kaskutas, 2008; Pardini, Plante, Sherman, & Stump, 2000; Streifel & Servaty-Seib, 2009).

There is also a growing literature addressing the role of spirituality in understanding and dealing with the effects of various types of trauma—including physical abuse and violence (Garbarino & Bedard, 1997; Parappully, Rosenbaum, van den Daele, & Nzewi, 2002; P. L. Ryan, 1998); sexual abuse and sexual assault (Galambos, 2001; Robinson, 2000; Walker, Reid, O'Neill, & Brown, 2009); severe accidents and serious injury (Ashkanani, 2009; Johnstone, Yoon, Rupright, & Reid-Arndt, 2009); incarceration (O'Brien, 2001; Redman, 2008; Sheridan, 1995); and ethnic trauma, war, displacement, and terrorism (Drescher et al., 2009; Markovitzky & Mosek, 2005; Meisenhelder & Marcum, 2009; Schuster et al., 2001). Certain spiritually oriented interventions, such as the use of ceremony and ritual, appear to have particular utility in helping persons recover from trauma and loss (M. J. Barrett, 1999; Cairns, 2005; Lubin & Johnson, 1998).

Finally, nowhere has spirituality been viewed as more relevant than in the area of death and dying. Religious and spiritual issues often arise at the end of life, and thus practitioners need to be able to deal with these issues effectively (G. R. Cox, 2000; MacKinlay, 2006; J. P. Morgan, 2002; Nelson-Becker, 2006). Spiritual sensitivity and competence are also needed in working with those who are grieving the loss of loved ones (Angell, Dennis, & Dumain, 1998; Golsworthy & Coyle, 1999; Winston, 2006) or facing other kinds of loss, such as divorce (Nathanson, 1995; E. D. Smith & Gray, 1995).

Individual and Collective Well-Being

Spirituality also has a role to play in regard to the second major focus of social work: supporting and enhancing optimal human functioning and quality of life. This role is evident at all levels of human systems, including the individual, family, community, organizational, and societal spheres. The following identifies key points of this influence on well-being at both individual and collective levels.

At the individual level, interest in wellness, holistic health, and the mind–body connection has exploded in recent years, as evidenced by increasing numbers of workshops and retreats, weekly groups, self-help books, and media reports on the topic. Furthermore, there has been a marked increase in the use of complementary and alternative medicine (CAM), defined as "a group of diverse medical and healthcare systems, practices, and products that are not generally considered to be part of conventional medicine" (National Center for Complementary and Alternative Medicine [NCCAM], n.d., ¶2). These approaches, which often are grounded in spiritual traditions and a holistic understanding of the human condition, include homeopathy and naturopathic medicine; traditional Chinese and Ayurvedic medicine; chiropractic and osteopathic manipulation; massage and other relaxation techniques; acupuncture and acupressure; herbal therapy; yoga and Tai Chi; energy medicine such as Qi Gong, Reiki, and healing touch; reflexology; and bioelectromagnetic-based therapies (NCCAM, n.d.).

Over 1,200 research projects have been funded by NCCAM, which is the lead agency under the National Institutes of Health (NIH) charged with investigating the efficacy of these approaches for both physical and mental health. Many of these studies have found positive effects of various CAM modalities, while also identifying approaches that are ineffective. Regardless of the scientific results, Americans are increasingly using CAM processes and products. Findings from a 2007 national survey reveal that approximately 50% of Americans (38% of adults and 12% of children) used some form of alternative or complementary medicine (P. M. Barnes, Bloom, & Nahin, 2008), compared to 34% in 1990 (Williamson & Wyandt, 2001). There is a rise in the use of CAM by physical health and mental health practitioners, as well. In a study of social work practitioners, over 75% of the sample reported either direct use or referral to mind–body techniques or community health alternatives in work with their clients (Henderson, 2000).

In related research, investigations are uncovering the specific mechanisms of the mind–body connection. In a meta-analysis of 30 years of research, findings show clear linkages between psychological stress and lowered functioning of the immune system, the major biological system that defends the body against disease (Segerstrom & Miller, 2004). In another review of 100 years of research, Oakley Ray (2004) reports mounting evidence that stressors that affect the brain are harmful to the body at both a cellular and molecular level and that they diminish a person's health and quality of life. In addition, intriguing results are coming out of research on the "neurobiology of consciousness." Several studies have shown demonstrable links between subjective experiences reported during meditation and noted alterations in brain function (e.g., EEG patterns, gamma activity, phase synchrony), as well as evidence of neuroplasticity (transformations of the brain) in long-term meditators (Lutz, Dunne, & Davidson, 2007). Taken together, these investigations suggest that many of our core mental and emotional processes are not only pivotal in maintaining optimal health, but also affect our capacity for personal happiness and compassion for others. Results from the consciousness studies suggest that positive workings of the mind are trainable skills through practices such as meditation. This possibility has significant implications for both individual and communal well-being.

As a result of this research, a growing number of articles in the professional literature also promote the use of wellness or mind–body approaches for both clients and practitioners. Examples include the development of specialized wellness programs (C. C. Clark, 2002; Kissman & Maurer, 2002; Neufeld & Knipemann, 2001; Plasse, 2001; A. H. Scott et al., 2001), the use of stress management and relaxation techniques (Finger & Arnold, 2002; McBee, Westreich, & Likourezos, 2004; Payne, 2000), and the use of mindfulness meditation and yoga (L. Bell, 2009; Brantley, Doucett, & Lindell, 2008; Lee, Ng, Leung, & Chan, 2009; Vohra-Gupta, Russell, & Lo, 2007; Wisniewski, 2008). Many of these approaches are rooted in spiritual traditions, especially Eastern traditions.

There also has been a great deal of recent development concerning spirituality and work. Much of this literature focuses on the search for "right livelihood," or the conscious choice of work that is consistent with one's spiritual values and supportive of ongoing spiritual growth (Bloch & Richmond, 1998; M. Fox, 1994; Hansen, 1997). Other writers exploring the role of spirituality in the workplace discuss such issues as use of power, management style, workplace environment, and integrating spiritual values with overall work goals (DePree, 1997; Natale & Neher, 1997; Roberson, 2004; N. R. Smith, 2006).

The social work enterprise itself has been the subject of such interest. Edward Canda and Leola Furman (2010) identify 15 principles for spiritually sensitive administration of human service organizations. They include such activities as formulating a "spiritually attuned mission, goals, and objectives"; limiting the size and complexity of the organization in order to maintain a "human scale"; facilitating "preparedness for spiritually sensitive practice"; supporting the "holistic satisfaction of personnel aspirations"; ensuring "participatory decision making" by staff members and clients; creating a "spiritual diversity innovation planning group"; paying attention to "work environment aesthetics"; and building "social and cultural environmental rapport" within the community, including collaboration with religious and spiritual leaders and helpers (pp. 237–239).

The connection between spirituality and creativity is another area being addressed by a variety of writers. Much of this writing emphasizes the potential that linking spirituality and creativity has for healing as well as nurturing self-expression and optimal development. Examples include use of the visual arts (Cohn, 1997; Farrelly-Hansen, 2009); journaling, poetry, and creative writing (Cameron, 1992; Wright, 2005); music and sound (D. Campbell, 1997; Goldman, 1996); and movement and dance, drama, and other performing arts (J. Adler, 1995; Pearson, 1996; Wuthnow, 2001). Engaging in the creative process seems to facilitate spiritual growth and well-being by encouraging the person to go beyond ego limitations, surrender to process, and tap into spiritual sources of strength and self-expression (Fukuyama & Sevig, 1999; K. R. Mayo, 2009).

Spirituality is also emerging as an important factor in the optimal functioning of various human collectives. In social work with couples and families, paying attention to the spiritual dimension of family life is viewed as important not only for the religiously affiliated, but for the nonaffiliated as well (Dosser, Smith, Markowski, & Cain, 2001; Duba & Watts, 2009; F. Walsh, 2009a). It has been identified as an important component in working with couples and families relative to a wide range of problems, including discord (Cowley, 1999; Derezotes, 2001; Hunler & Gencoz, 2005), challenges of adoption and parenting (Belanger, Copeland, & Cheung, 2009; C. J. Evans, Boustead, & Owens, 2008), health issues (Cattich, & Knudson-Martin, 2009), death and loss (F. Walsh, 2000b), and other issues that arise as part of family functioning (H. Anderson, 2009; Gale, 2009; Hames & Godwin, 2008).

The literature also notes the role of spirituality in community-based initiatives. Examples include community health-promotion programs (K. A. Brown, Jemmott, Mitchell, & Walton, 1998; C. C. Clark, 2002), collective action and social justice efforts (A. V. Perry & Rolland, 2009; Staral, 2000; Tripses & Scroggs, 2009), services to rural communities (Furman & Chandy, 1994; S. K. Johnson, 1997), and other types of community-focused practice (D. R. Garland, Myers, & Wolfer, 2008; Obst & Tham, 2009; Pargament, 2008; Tangenberg, 2008). Social workers are also becoming acquainted with the newly emerging "spiritual activism" movement, which goes beyond a focus on political and economic forces as primary mechanisms for social change to incorporate a spiritual framework for activism. Emerging principles of this new model include such themes as "awareness, compassion, and love"; "interdependence"; "mindfulness and presence"; "paradox and mystery"; "seeking balance"; and "living our values" (C. Goldstein, n.d., ¶6). This more holistic approach is viewed as having greater potential for achieving liberation and social justice than previous efforts embedded in a conflict perspective.

Attention to religious and spiritual resources is also being identified in organizational practice. President Obama announced the newly configured White House Office of Faith-Based and Neighborhood Partnerships on the 17th day of his new administration. This office is charged with four priorities: "involving faith-based and neighborhood groups in the economic recovery, promoting responsible fatherhood, fostering interfaith cooperation, and building common ground to reduce unintended pregnancies and the need for abortion" (Office of Faith-based and Neighborhood Partnerships, 2009, ¶3). The proliferation of congregational and faith-based social services, which began with the George W. Bush administration in 2001, is being closely followed and evaluated by social work scholars. Some note positive opportunities and outcomes as a result of this trend, while others point to negative and unanticipated consequences (Belcher, Fandetti, & Cole, 2004; Boddie & Cnaan, 2006; Netting, O'Connor, & Singletary, 2007; M. L. Thomas, 2009). NASW's (2002) response to the federal faith-based initiative remains cautious, stressing the need for services to be delivered in a way that makes them clearly voluntary and emphasizing the central role and responsibility of government in providing social services. There is a need for ongoing research on the impact of the faith-based services for both clients and social workers employed in such agencies.

At the larger policy and societal levels, both conservative and progressive religious perspectives have a significant voice in a host of issues that impact the well-being of individuals, families, and communities. The Pew Forum (n.d.) has identified four arenas where religion plays a role in public life, often creating controversy and debate due to differing visions of the common good:

1. Religion and politics (e.g., the influence of religion and religious organizations on political behavior, including political campaigns and voting)

2. Religion and the law (e.g., church–state controversies, such as legal battles over the Ten Commandments and public displays of nativity scenes, the Pledge of Allegiance, suicide, the death penalty, and school vouchers)

3. Religion and domestic policy (e.g., issues such as abortion; gay rights, including marriage and adoption; stem-cell research, genetic engineering, and cloning; and faith-based initiatives)

4. Religion and world affairs (e.g., appropriate role for religion in foreign policy, international initiatives, and climate change and environmental issues)

Social workers should keep abreast of these issues, particularly as they impact the client populations they serve.

Finally, spirituality is being increasingly identified as a needed force in nurturing and sustaining life beyond the circle of the human family to include all living beings and our planet that is home to all. Growing numbers of religious congregations, both conservative and progressive, are identifying "stewardship of the planet" as part of their religious commitment (National Religious Partnership for the Environment, n.d.). Many writers are pointing to the critical link between our capacity to view all of nature as sacred and the mounting issues of environmental degradation, climate change, and eco-justice for vulnerable and marginalized populations (Berry, 2009; Coates, 2003, 2007; W. Jenkins, 2008; McFague, 2001). This spiritually grounded perspective challenges us to redefine the meaning of community and reimagine our rightful place in the "sacred hoop" of life.

In sum, spirituality in both its religious and nonreligious forms holds much potential for promoting well-being and quality of life at all levels of the human experience, as well as for helping the profession address the problems and possibilities inherent in the human condition.

Spiritual Assessment

Given the important role of spirituality in understanding both human diversity and human experience, it has become evident that gathering information about a client's religious or spiritual history and assessing spiritual development and current interests are as important as learning about biopsychosocial factors. Assessment needs to go beyond the surface features of faith affiliation (such as Protestant, Catholic, Jewish, or Muslim) to include deeper facets of a person's spiritual life (Sheridan, 2002). For example, talking with Caroline about where she is in her unfolding spiritual development would be helpful in supporting her exploration of different faith perspectives. Asking Matthew what brings him meaning, purpose, and connection right now would be valuable in assisting him in the next chapter of his life. And in working with Leon, it would be useful to know what aspects of his current religious affiliation are the most important and meaningful to him as he struggles with the conflicts regarding his faith and his sexual identity. None of this knowledge would be gleaned by a simple response to "What is your current religious affiliation?"

Social workers also need to assess both the positive and negative aspects of clients' religious or spiritual beliefs and practices (Canda & Furman, 2010; Joseph, 1988; Lewandowski & Canda, 1995; Sheridan & Bullis, 1991). For example, Naomi and David's understanding of the meaning of illness may be either helpful or harmful in dealing with Naomi's health crisis. Trudy's current spiritual practices may be supportive or detrimental to her physical, emotional, and social well-being. And Jean-Joseph's synthesis of Catholic and Vodoun beliefs and practices may be very positive for his personal and family life, but may be problematic in his interactions with the wider social environment. Assessing the role and impact of all of these factors would be important areas for exploration in developing a spiritually sensitive relationship with any of these individuals.

A growing number of assessment instruments and approaches are available to help social workers. These include brief screening tools, which can provide an initial assessment of the relevance of religion or spirituality in clients' lives. Examples include the HOPE (Anandarajah & Hight, 2001), the FICA (Puchalski, & Romer, 2000); the MIMBRA (Canda & Furman, 2010), and the Brief RCOPE (Pargament, Koenig, & Perez, 2000). There are also several more comprehensive assessment tools that focus on religious/spiritual history and current life circumstances. For example, Bullis (1996) developed a spiritual history survey that includes questions about individuals, their parents or guardians, and their spouses or significant others. Canda and Furman (2010) provide a discussion guide for a detailed spiritual assessment, which covers spiritual group membership and participation; spiritual beliefs activities, experiences, and feelings; moral and value issues; spiritual development; spiritual sources of support and transformation; spiritual well-being; and extrinsic/intrinsic styles of spiritual propensity.

There are also examples of more implicit assessment approaches, which do not directly include a reference to "religion" or "spirituality," but are composed of open-ended questions that tap into spiritual themes, such as those identified by Titone (1991) and Canda and Furman (2010) (see Exhibit 6.7 for examples of these kind of questions). A number of other creative, nonverbal strategies for gathering such information have also been developed, including the use of spiritual timelines (Bullis, 1996); spiritual lifemaps, genograms, ecomaps, and ecograms (Hodge, 2005b); and spiritual trees (Raines, 1997). Finally, Lewandowski and Canda (1995) and Canda and Furman (2010) provide questions for assessing the helpful or harmful impacts of participating in spiritual groups or organizations (e.g., satisfaction with leadership style, methods of recruitment, response to members leaving the group).

Assessment must also be able to distinguish between a religious/spiritual problem and a mental disorder. The fourth edition of the *Diagnostic and Statistical Manual of Mental Disorders, Text Revised* (*DSM-IV-TR*) (APA, 2000) provides guidance in this area. "Religious or spiritual problem" is now included as a condition (*not* a mental disorder) that is appropriate for clinical attention. Types of religious problems under this category include difficulties resulting from a change in one's denomination or conversion to a new religion, intensified adherence to beliefs or practices, loss or questioning of faith, guilt, or involvement in destructive religious groups. Spiritual problems may include distress due to mystical experiences, near-death experiences, spiritual emergence/emergency, or separation from a spiritual teacher (Turner, Lukoff, Barnhouse, & Lu, 1995). This framework would be helpful in understanding any extraordinary or mystical experiences that Trudy, Jean-Joseph, or any of the other people in the case studies might share with you. Accurate assessment of such an occurrence can help determine whether the experience needs to be integrated and used as a stimulus for personal growth or whether it should be recognized as a sign of mental instability.

Assessment is just one component of spiritually sensitive social work practice. Other aspects include the use of transpersonal theory, the goals and context for practice, the nature of the helping relationship, spiritually based interventions and ethical guidelines for their use, referral to and collaboration with religious or spiritual leaders and helping systems, and the practitioner's own spiritual development (Sheridan, 2002). The field is accumulating a number of publications that provide more comprehensive discussion of spiritually sensitive practice (see, for example, Bullis, 1996; Frame, 2003; Canda & Furman, 2010; Derezotes, 2006; Mijares & Khalsa, 2005; Pargament, 2007; Scales et al., 2002; Sheridan, 2002).

---

1. What nourishes you spiritually—for example, music, nature, intimacy, witnessing heroism, meditation, creative expression, sharing another's joy?

2. What is the difference between shame and guilt? What are healthy and unhealthy shame and guilt?

3. What do you mean when you say your spirits are low? Is that different from being sad or depressed?

4. What is an incident in your life that precipitated a change in your belief about the meaning of life?

5. What helps you maintain a sense of hope when there is no immediate apparent basis for it?

6. Do you need forgiveness from yourself or someone else?

7. What currently brings a sense of meaning and purpose to your life?

8. Where do you go to find a sense of deep inspiration or peace?

9. For what are you most grateful?

10. What are your most cherished ideals?

11. In what way is it important or meaningful for you to be in this world (or in this situation)?

12. What are the deepest questions your situation raises for you?

▲ **Exhibit 6.7**   Examples of Questions for Implicit Spiritual Assessment

SOURCES: Canda and Furman (2010); Titone (1991).

Critical Thinking Questions 6.3

With globalization, we have more regular contact with people of diverse religious and spiritual beliefs. How much religious and spiritual diversity do you come in contact with in your everyday life? How comfortable are you with honoring different religious and spiritual beliefs? How have you seen religious and spiritual beliefs used to discriminate against some groups of people? How have you seen religious and spiritual beliefs used to promote social justice?

IMPLICATIONS FOR SOCIAL WORK PRACTICE

Spiritually sensitive social work practice involves gaining knowledge and skills in the areas discussed in this chapter, always keeping in mind that this approach must be grounded within the values and ethics of the profession. The following practice principles are offered as guidelines for effective and ethical social work practice in this area.

- Maintain clarity about your role as a spiritually sensitive practitioner, making a distinction between being a social worker who includes a focus on the spiritual dimension as part of holistic practice and being a religious leader or spiritual director.

- Be respectful of different religious or spiritual paths, and be willing to learn about the role and meaning of various beliefs, practices, and experiences for various client systems (individuals, families, groups, communities).

- Critically examine your own values, beliefs, and biases concerning religion and spirituality, and be willing to work through any unresolved or negative feelings or experiences in this area that may adversely affect your work with clients.

- Inform yourself about both the positive and negative role of religion and spirituality in the fight for social justice by various groups, and be sensitive to this history in working with members of oppressed and marginalized populations.

- Develop a working knowledge of the beliefs and practices frequently encountered in your work with clients, especially those of newly arriving immigrants/refugees or nondominant groups (for example, Buddhist beliefs of Southeast Asian refugees, spiritual traditions of First Nations peoples).

- Conduct comprehensive spiritual assessments with clients at all levels, and use this information in service planning and delivery.

- Acquire the knowledge and skills necessary to employ spiritually based intervention techniques appropriately, ethically, and effectively.

- Seek information about the various religious and spiritual organizations, services, and leaders pertinent to your practice, and develop good working relationships with these resources for purposes of referral and collaboration.

- Engage in ongoing self-reflection about what brings purpose, meaning, and connection to your own life, and make disciplined efforts toward your own spiritual development, however you define this process.

ecocentric

faith

faith stages

First Force therapies

Four quadrants

Fourth Force therapies

fulcrum

ideology (personal)

levels of consciousness

lines of consciousness

religion

Second Force therapies

self-system

spiritual bypassing

spirituality

states of consciousness

Third Force therapies

transpersonal approach

ultimate environment

worldcentric

ACTIVE LEARNING

1. Consider any of the case studies presented at the beginning of the chapter. Using either Fowler's stages of faith development or Wilber's integral theory of consciousness as the conceptual framework, construct a timeline of the person's spiritual development. Trace the overall growth patterns through the different stages, including any ups and downs as well as plateau periods. Identify the significant points or transitions that you consider as pivotal to the person's spiritual development.

   • How would this information help you to better understand the person's story and overall development? How would this information help you, as a social worker, work with the person at various points in his or her life?

   • What would your own spiritual timeline look like, including patterns throughout various stages and significant points or transitions that were particularly significant for your own growth and development?

2. Select a partner for this exercise. This chapter provides a brief overview of the spiritual diversity present within the United States. Given both your knowledge and experiences with different spiritual traditions, both religious and nonreligious, address the following questions. Take a few moments to reflect on each question before answering it. Partners should take turns answering the questions.

   • To which spiritual perspectives do you have the most positive reactions (e.g., are in the most agreement with, feel an appreciation or attraction toward, are the most comfortable with, find it easiest to keep an open mind and heart about)? What is it about you that contributes to these reactions (e.g., previous knowledge, personal experiences, messages from family or larger culture)?

   • To which perspective do you have the most negative reactions (e.g., are in the most disagreement with, feel a repulsion or fear about, are the most uncomfortable with, find it most difficult to keep an open mind and heart about)? What is it about you that contributes to these reactions (e.g., previous knowledge, personal experiences, messages from family or larger culture)?

   • What impact(s) might your reactions (both positive and negative) have on work with clients (especially with those who may hold different spiritual perspectives from yourself)? What personal and professional "work" on yourself is suggested by your positive or negative reactions?

3. Select a partner for this exercise. Together select one of the open-ended questions listed in Exhibit 6.7 to consider as it applies to your own lives. After a few moments of quiet reflection, write your response to the question, allowing yourself to write freely, without concern for the proper mechanics of writing (e.g., spelling, grammar).

Then sit with what you've written, reading it over with fresh eyes. When you're ready, share this experience with your partner, sharing as much or as little of what you've written as you feel comfortable with. Then talk together about the following questions:

- What was the experience like of answering this question and then reading the response to yourself? (e.g., easy, difficult, exciting, anxiety-producing, confirming)
- Are there previous times in your life in which you have considered this question? Did you share your thoughts about it with others? If so, what was that like? What is it like to do that now with your partner?
- Can you see yourself asking this kind of question with a client? What do you think that experience might be like for both the client and yourself?

WEB RESOURCES

Adherents.com
www.adherents.com

Site not affiliated with any religious, political, educational, or commercial organization. Contains a comprehensive collection of over 41,000 statistics on religious adherents, geography citations, and links to other major sites on diverse religious and spiritual traditions.

Association of Religion Data Archives
www.thearda.com

Site sponsored by the Lilly Endowment, the John Templeton Foundation, and Pennsylvania State University. Provides over 350 data files on U.S. and international religion using online features for generating national profiles, maps, overviews of church memberships, denominational heritage trees, tables, charts, and other summary reports.

Canadian Society for Spirituality and Social Work
http://w3.stu.ca/stu/sites/spirituality/ index.html

Site includes information about the activities of this society, links to other websites, and other resources. The Canadian SSSW is under the directorship of Dr. John Coates of St. Thomas University.

Pew Forum on Religion & Public Life
http://pewforum.org/

Site sponsored by the larger Pew Research Center. Functions as both a clearinghouse for research and other publications related to issues at the intersection of religion and public affairs, and also as a virtual town hall for discussion of related topics.

Religious Tolerance
www.religioustolerance.org

Site presented by the Ontario Consultants on Religious Tolerance, an agency that promotes religious tolerance as a human right. Contains comparative descriptions of world religions and diverse spiritual paths, from Asatru to Zoroastrianism, and links to other related sites.

Society for Spirituality and Social Work
http://ssw.asu.edu/spirituality/sssw/

Site includes information about joining the U.S. Society for Spirituality and Social Work, a selected bibliography, and other resources. The directorship of the society is currently in transition from Dr. Ann Weaver Nichols of Arizona State University to Dr. Helen Land of the University of Southern California.

Virtual Religion Index
www.virtualreligion.net/vri/
Site presented by the Religion Department at Rutgers University. Contains analysis and highlights of religion-related websites and provides links to major sites for specific religious groups and topics.

The Multiple Dimensions of Environment

Social workers have always recognized the important role the environment plays in human behavior and, equally important, have always understood the environment as multidimensional. The social work literature has not been consistent in identifying the significant dimensions of environment, however. Although all dimensions of environment are intertwined and inseparable, social scientists have developed specialized literature on several specific dimensions. Both the environment and the study of it become more complex with each new era of technological development, making our efforts to understand the environment ever more challenging.

The purpose of the eight chapters in Part III is to provide you with an up-to-date understanding of the multidisciplinary theory and research about dimensions of environment. It begins with Chapter 7 on an important dimension that is often overlooked in the social work literature, the physical environment. Next comes Chapter 8, which reviews our historical attempts to understand culture and presents a contemporary framework to help us become more competent social workers in a multicultural world. Chapter 9 explores the macro environment, focusing on contemporary trends in social structure and social institutions, placing U.S. trends in a global context. Chapters 10 and 11 cover the smaller-scale configurations of families and small groups. Part III ends with Chapters 12, 13, and 14 on the moderate-size configurations of formal organizations, communities, and social movements. In Part II, you learned about the multiple dimensions of persons. When you put that together with the knowledge gained about multiple dimensions of environments, you will be better prepared to understand the situations you encounter in social work practice. This prepares you well to think about the changing configurations of persons and environments across the life course—the subject of the companion volume to this book, *The Changing Life Course*.

7

The Physical Environment

Elizabeth D. Hutchison

OPENING QUESTIONS

- What is the relationship between the physical environment and human behavior?

- What are some implications of the research on the relationship between the physical environment and human behavior for social work practice?

KEY IDEAS

As you read this chapter, take note of these central ideas:

1. To better understand the relationship between the physical environment and human behavior, social workers can draw on multidisciplinary research from the social sciences and design disciplines.

2. Eleven key concepts for the study of the physical environment and human behavior are accessibility, activity, adaptability, comfort, control, crowding, legibility, meaning, privacy, sensory stimulation, and sociality.

3. Three broad categories of theories about human behavior and the physical environment are stimulation theories, control theories, and behavior settings theories.

4. Researchers have found a strong human preference for elements of the natural environment and positive outcomes of time spent in the natural environment.

5. Built environments may promote health, healing, and social interaction.

6. A recent recognition that built physical environments can be disabling has led to legislation to protect the civil rights of persons with disabilities.

7. Children, adolescents, and elderly adults have special needs with respect to the built environment, particularly for control, privacy, and stimulation.

Case Study

Ben Watson's Changing Experience With the Physical Environment

I finished my final semester in the Bachelor of Architecture Program and a couple of friends and I decided to spend a few days doing some rock climbing before graduation. I already had a job lined up with a small architecture firm down in North Carolina. Things were looking good.

It doesn't take but a minute to change things forever. I fell 500 feet and knew, as soon as I came to, that something was very wrong. My legs were numb, I couldn't move them, and I had terrific pain in my back. My friends knew not to move me, and one stayed with me while the other went for help.

(Continued)

(Continued)

I don't remember much about the rescue, the trip to the nearest hospital, or the medivac to the closest trauma center. In my early days at the trauma hospital, I saw lots of medical people, but I vividly remember the doc who told me that I had an incomplete spinal cord injury, that I would have some sensation below my lesion but no movement. I didn't really believe it. Movement was what I was all about. I spent 5 months in the hospital and rehabilitation center, and I gradually began to understand that my legs were not going to move. I was depressed, I was angry (furious, really), and for one week I wanted to give up. My parents and my brothers pulled me through. They showered me with love but were firm when I tried to refuse rehabilitation treatments. Oh yeah, some of my friends were terrific also. When things get rough, you learn who your real friends are. I also appreciated a chance to talk with the rehab social worker about my grief over this unbelievable turn in my life. It was good to talk with him because he wasn't dealing with his own grief about my situation the way my family and friends were.

I left rehab with my new partner, a sophisticated titanium wheelchair, and went home to live with my parents. They rearranged the house so that I could have the first floor bedroom and bath. I appreciated the assistance from my parents and brothers, and my friends made heroic efforts to get me out of the house. As we did so, I began to learn the importance of the word *access*. The first time my friends took me out, we wanted to go to a bar; after all, that's what twenty-something guys do. My friends called around to find a nearby bar that would be accessible to me and my wheelchair. That turned out to be tougher than they thought. Did you ever notice how many bars require dealing with stairs? Finally, they were assured that one bar was accessible—well, actually, nobody wanted to say their place wasn't accessible, given the law and all, plus most folks haven't given any thought to what that really means. So, my friends had to run through a set of questions about stairs, ramps, size of doors, etc., to make their own determination about accessibility. One question they didn't think to ask was whether there were stairs leading to the bathroom. So we went out drinking, but I was afraid to drink or eat because I couldn't get to the bathroom.

After several months at home, I began to get restless and wanted to get on with my life. After my accident, the architecture firm down in North Carolina had told my parents that they would still be interested in having me work for them when I was strong enough. So I began to talk with my parents about making the move to North Carolina. They understood that I needed to get on with my life, but they worried about me moving 350 miles away. I was still dependent on them for a lot of personal care, but I was gradually learning to do more for myself.

I knew from my interviews that the architecture firm was accessible by wheelchair—it was in a relatively new building with a ground-level entrance, spacious elevator, wide doors, and accessible bathrooms. With some trepidation, my dad drove me down to look for housing. There were plenty of new apartment complexes, but we found that everybody, not just people with disabilities, wants ground-floor apartments with the open architectural features that make wheelchair mobility so much easier. After a lot of calls, we found a one-bedroom apartment that I could afford. I immediately loved the location, in a part of the city where there was a lot happening on the streets, with shops, restaurants, and a movie theater. The apartment was attractive, convenient, and accessible, but most important it was mine. I was finally beginning to feel like an adult. I would have my privacy, but the open floor plan would allow me to have friends over without feeling cramped. And, I loved the abundance of windows that would allow for good natural lighting from the sun. I couldn't afford to get my own car with hand controls yet, but the apartment luckily was only a short cab ride from my office.

My father and brothers helped me make the move, and my grandmother came for a visit to add some charming decorating touches. I hired a personal assistant to help me get ready in the mornings—well, actually, my parents paid him for the first few months, until I could get my finances worked out.

Given my profession, it is good that I still have excellent function of my upper body, particularly my hands. My colleagues at work turned out to be good friends as well as good colleagues. And, I never paid much attention to issues of accessibility in my design studios at school, but I have become the local expert on accessible design.

I learned a lot about accessible design from some of my own frustrating experiences. I have been lucky to develop a close set of friends, and we have an active life. My friends and I have learned where the streets are that don't have curb cuts, which bars and restaurants are truly accessible, places where the "accessible" entry is really some dark alley back entrance, and to watch out for retail doorways blocked by displays of goods.

My friends and I travel, and I find some airline personnel handle me and my wheelchair well and some are disastrous—imagine being rolled over on the ramp, and with an audience, no less. The natural environment was always an important part of my life—it provides beauty and serenity—and my friends and I could write a book about all the wonderful hiking trails that are wheelchair accessible. Hey, that's a good idea!

THE RELATIONSHIP BETWEEN THE PHYSICAL ENVIRONMENT AND HUMAN BEHAVIOR

As with most stories we hear as social workers, Ben Watson's story provides multidimensional information about changing configurations of person and environment. It presents issues of life course development, family and friend relationships, physical disability, and a struggle for emotional well-being. And, of course, a supremely impor-

> Systems perspective

tant dimension of this unfolding story is the physical environment. Ben's story reminds us that all human behavior occurs in a physical context.

Perhaps the most obvious aspect of Ben's relationship with his physical environment is *accessibility*—the amount of ease with which Ben can act in his environment. But accessibility is only one relevant aspect. Gerald Weisman (1981) has identified 11 key concepts that unify the multidisciplinary study of the relationship between human behavior and the physical environment. (A slightly revised version of these concepts appears in Exhibit 7.1.) In addition to accessibility, Ben's story addresses another 7 of Weisman's 11 concepts: *activity* (a lot happening on the streets), *adaptability* (house rearranged to provide a first-floor bedroom and bath), *comfort* (attractive; charming decorating touches), *control* (It was *mine*), *crowding* (friends can come over without feeling cramped), *privacy* (I would have my privacy), and *sensory stimulation* (good natural lighting from the sun). We are also aware that the physical environment of the new apartment may hold very different *meanings* for the storyteller, for his parents, and for friends who visit. *Sociality* will be discussed later in the chapter. *Legibility* refers to the ease with which people can find their way in the environment. Legibility can be especially challenging in large regional hospitals, like the one where Ben was treated for his injury.

When we as social workers make person-in-environment assessments, we ought to pay attention to the physical environment, which has an inescapable influence on human behavior. Unfortunately, the social work literature includes only scant coverage of the physical environment. A handful of social work scholars (Germain, 1978, 1981; Gutheil, 1991, 1992; M. Kahn & Scher, 2002; Resnick & Jaffee, 1982; Seabury, 1971) have provided most of the existing analyses of the implications for social work of theory and research related to the physical environment. The relationship between human behavior and the physical environment is a multidisciplinary study that includes contributions from the social and behavioral sciences of psychology, sociology, geography, and anthropology as well as from the design disciplines of architecture, landscape architecture, interior design, and urban and regional planning. Recently, it has also included contributions from neuroscience research (Sternberg, 2009; Zeisel, 2006) and

Concept	Definition
Accessibility	Ease in movement through and use of an environment
Activity	Perceived intensity of ongoing behavior within an environment
Adaptability	Extent to which an environment and its components can be reorganized to accommodate new or different patterns of behavior
Comfort	Extent to which an environment provides sensory and mobility fit and facilitates task performance
Control	Extent to which an environment facilitates personalization and conveys territorial claims to space
Crowding	Unpleasant experience of being spatially cramped
Legibility	Ease with which people can conceptualize key elements and spatial relationships within an environment and effectively find their way
Meaning	Extent to which an environment holds individual or cultural meaning(s) for people (e.g., attachment, challenge, beauty)
Privacy	Selective control of access to the self or to one's group
Sensory stimulation	Quality and intensity of stimulation as experienced by the various sensory modalities
Sociality	Degree to which an environment facilitates or inhibits social interaction among people

▲ **Exhibit 7.1**   Key Concepts for Understanding Physical Environment–Behavior Relationships

SOURCE: Adapted from Weisman (1981). Reproduced with permission of the author.

public health (H. Frumkin, 2003; Northridge & Sclar, 2003). This chapter gives you some ways of thinking about the relationship between human behavior and the physical environment as you begin to consider the role it plays in the stories of the people you encounter in practice.

Most theorists start from an assumption that person and physical environment are separate entities and emphasize the ways in which the physical environment influences behavior. Some theorists, however, start from an assumption of person-environment unity and propose interlocking and ongoing processes of coexistence between people and physical environments—people shape their environment just as the physical environment influences them—an approach called **transactionalism** (see Minami & Tanaka, 1995; Wapner, 1995; Werner & Altman, 2000; Werner, Brown, & Altman, 2002). This transactional approach is consistent with the assumption of person–environment unity in this book.

Systems perspective

Three broad categories of theory about human behavior and the physical environment are introduced in this chapter: stimulation theories, control theories, and behavior settings theories. The first two categories originated in the theoretical approach that assumes separation of person and physical environment, but they have increasingly recognized the interrelatedness of person and physical environment. Behavior settings theories have always been based in transactionalism. Each of these categories of theory, and the research they have stimulated, provides useful possibilities for social

Theories	Key Ideas	Important Concepts
Stimulation theories	The physical environment is a source of sensory information essential for human well-being. Patterns of stimulation influence thinking, emotions, social interaction, and health.	Stimulus overload Stimulus deprivation
Control theories	Humans desire control over their physical environments. Some person–environment configurations provide more control over the physical environment than others.	Personal space Territoriality Crowding Privacy
Behavior settings theories	Consistent, uniform patterns of behavior occur in particular settings. Behaviors of different persons in the same setting are more similar than the behaviors of the same person in different settings.	Behavior settings Programs Staffing

▲ **Exhibit 7.2**   Three Categories of Theories About the Relationship Between the Physical Environment and Human Behavior

workers to consider as they participate in person-environment assessments, although stimulation theories and control theories have been more widely used than behavior settings theories. Exhibit 7.2 presents the key ideas and important concepts of these three types of theories.

Stimulation Theories

Have you thought about how you would react to the abundance of sunlight in Ben Watson's new apartment or the activity on his street? That question is consistent with **stimulation theories,** which focus on the physical environment as a source of sensory information that is essential for human well-being. The stimulation may be light, color, heat, texture, or scent, or it may be buildings, streets, and parks. Stimulation theorists propose that patterns of stimulation influence thinking, feelings, social interaction, and health.

Stimulation varies by amount—intensity, frequency, duration, number of sources—as well as by type. Stimulation theories that are based on theories of psychophysiological arousal assume that moderate levels of stimulation are optimal for human behavior (Gifford, 2007). Thus, both *stimulus overload* (too much stimulation) and *restricted environmental stimulation* (once called *stimulus deprivation*) have a negative effect on human behavior. Theorists interested in the behavioral and health effects of stimulus overload have built on Han Selye's work regarding stress (see Chapter 5).

Some stimulation theories focus on the direct, concrete effect of stimulation on behavior; others focus on the meanings people construct regarding particular stimuli (Gifford, 2007). In fact, people respond to both the concrete and the symbolic aspects of their physical environments. A doorway too narrow to accommodate a wheelchair has a concrete effect on the behavior of a person in a wheelchair; it will also have a symbolic effect, contributing to the person's feelings of exclusion and stigma. You

Social behavioral perspective; social constructionist perspective

probably will have a very different emotional reaction to a loud bang if it occurs during a street riot versus at a New Year's Eve party; your understanding of the meaning of the noise has a strong influence on your reactions. In this case, your response is primarily symbolic. Stimulation theories alert social workers to consider the quality and intensity of sensory stimulation in the environments where their clients live and work.

Environmental design scholars have begun to incorporate recent advances in neuroscience research to understand how people's brains respond to different types of stimulation in physical environments. Their goal is to use this knowledge to design environments that support brain development and functioning for the general population as well as for groups with special needs, such as premature newborns and persons with Alzheimer's disease (Zeisel, 2006). Neuroscientists are also working with architects and environmental psychologists to learn what aspects of the physical environment stimulate emotional and physical healing (Sternberg, 2009).

Control Theories

Psychodynamic perspective; social behavioral perspective

The ability to gain control over his physical environment is a central theme of Ben Watson's story. In that way, the story is a good demonstration of the ideas found in control theories. **Control theories** focus on the issue of how much control we have over our physical environments and the attempts we make to gain control (Gifford, 2007). Four concepts are central to the work of control theorists: privacy, personal space, territoriality, and crowding. Personal space and territoriality are **boundary-regulating mechanisms** that we use to gain greater control over our physical environments.

Privacy

Altman (1975) defines privacy as "selective control of access to the self or to one's group" (p. 18). This definition contains two important elements: Privacy involves control over information about oneself as well as control over interactions with others. Virginia Kupritz (2003) has extended Altman's work by making a distinction between speech or conversational privacy (being able to hold conversations without being overheard) and visual

Psychodynamic perspective

privacy (being free of unwanted observation). Contemporary innovations in communication technologies have introduced new concerns about having control over information with respect to oneself and one's group and about how to balance national security with rights to privacy (Friedman, Kahn, Hagman, Severson, & Gill, 2006).

Some of us require more privacy than others, and some situations stimulate privacy needs more than others. Ben Watson was accustomed to sharing a house with his university pals and didn't mind the lack of privacy that came with that situation. He felt differently about lack of privacy in his parents' home after rehab and was eager for a more private living situation, even though his privacy in some areas would be compromised by his need for a personal care assistant.

Social constructionist perspective

It appears that people in different cultures use space differently to create privacy. Susan Kent (1991) theorizes that the use of partitions, such as walls or screens, to create private spaces increases as societies become more complex. She particularly notes the strong emphasis that European American culture places on partitioned space, both at home and at work (see Duvall-Early & Benedict, 1992). More recent research supports this idea; for example, college students in the United States have been found to desire more privacy in their residence halls than Turkish students in their home country (Kaya & Weber, 2003).

Kupritz (2003) is interested in the physical attributes of workplace offices that satisfy the privacy needs of the U.S. workforce. She argues that in recent decades, employers have limited personal space of employees, using open-plan cubicles, based on the belief that such arrangements will facilitate communication among employees. Her research indicates that often the open cubicles have the opposite impact, because employees tend to communicate less when they feel they cannot control the privacy of communications.

Have you given much thought to your need for private space? Do you have sufficient privacy in your home and work environments to feel some sense of control over who has access to you and your interpersonal interactions? Do the clients at your field agency have private space? Personal space and territoriality are two mechanisms for securing privacy.

Personal Space

Personal space, also known as interpersonal distance, is the physical distance we choose to maintain in interpersonal relationships. Robert Sommer (1969) has defined it as "an area with invisible boundaries surrounding a person's body into which intruders may not come" (p. 26). More recent formulations (Gifford, 2007) emphasize that personal space is not stable, but contracts and expands with changing interpersonal circumstances and with variations in physical settings. The distance you desire when talking with your best friend is likely to be different from the distance you prefer when talking with a stranger, or even with a known authority figure like your social work professor. The desired distance for any of these interpersonal situations is likely to expand in small spaces (Sinha & Mukherjee, 1996). We will want to recognize our own personal space requirements in different work situations and be sensitive to the personal space requirements of our coworkers and clients.

Variations in personal space are also thought to be related to age, gender, attachment style, previous victimization, and culture. The need for personal space has been found to increase with age until early adulthood (Gifford, 2007). One recent research project found that, in shopping malls in the United States and Turkey, adolescents interacting with other adolescents kept the largest interpersonal distance of any age group (Ozdemir, 2008). When encountering strangers, personal space has been found to increase again in late adulthood if there are declines in mobility (J. Webb & Weber, 2003). Males have often been found to require greater personal space than females, but research indicates that the largest interpersonal distances are kept in male–male pairs, followed by female–female pairs, with the smallest interpersonal distances kept in male–female pairs (Akande, 1997; Kilbury, Bordieri, & Wong, 1996; Ozdemir, 2008). One research project found no gender differences in personal space among children ages 7 to 9 (Vranic, 2003). There is also evidence that adults with insecure attachment style require a larger personal space than children and adults with secure attachments (Kaitz, Bar-Haim, Lehrer, & Grossman, 2004). Physically abused children have also been found to keep significantly larger personal space than nonabused children, suggesting that personal space provides a protective function for these children (Vranic, 2003).

> Social constructionist perspective; developmental perspective

In *The Hidden Dimensions,* Edward Hall (1966) reported that his field research indicated that members of contact-oriented, collectivist cultures (e.g., Latin, Asian, Arab) prefer closer interpersonal distances than members of noncontact-oriented, individualist cultures (e.g., Northern European, North American). More recent research has supported this suggestion; for example, pairs in Turkish malls have been observed to interact more closely than pairs in U.S. malls (Ozdemir, 2008), but within-culture differences in interpersonal distance preferences have also been noted (G. Evans, Lepore, & Allen, 2000). Hirofumi Minami and Takiji Yamamoto (2000) suggest that communal space is more important than personal space in Japan and other Asian cultures that value intimate community life, a preference that should be considered when designing built environments.

Previous research (Langer, Fiske, Taylor, & Chanowitz, 1976; Stephens & Clark, 1987) found that people maintain larger interpersonal distances when interacting with people with disabilities. However, a more recent study found that research participants sat closer to a research assistant in a wheelchair than to one without a visible disability (Kilbury et al., 1996). These researchers conjectured that recent legislation is reducing the stigma of disability. Some of this legislation will be discussed later in this chapter.

Sommer (2002) has recently updated his discussion of personal space by raising questions about how personal space is affected by digital technology. Perhaps you have been interested, as I have been, in how people define their personal space while talking on their cell phones. It seems that we are still negotiating what is appropriate interpersonal distance while using our cell phones, but I have been surprised to sit very close to strangers in public spaces who are using cell phones to "break up" with a partner or to try to straighten out a credit problem. Sommer also raises questions about the impact of the computer on personal space, noting that at work people sometimes communicate by e-mail with coworkers sitting beside them in the same office. Other researchers have examined how much personal space people need when using automatic teller machines and other technology where private information is stored and found that people report larger desired space than the space actually provided (Shu & Li, 2007).

Territoriality

Personal space is a concept about individual behavior and about the use of space to control the interpersonal environment. **Territoriality** refers primarily to the behavior of individuals and small groups as they seek control over physical space (R. Taylor, 1988), but recently, the concept has also been used to refer to attempts to control objects, roles, and relationships (G. Brown, Lawrence, & Robinson, 2005). For example, Robert Gifford (2007) recently defined territoriality as "a pattern of behavior and attitudes held by an individual or group, based on perceived, attempted, or actual ownership or control of a definable physical space, object, or idea" (p. 166). Territoriality leads us to mark, or personalize, our territory to signify our "ownership," and to engage in a variety of behaviors to protect it from invasion. The study of animal territoriality has a longer history than the study of human territorial behavior. For humans, there is much evidence that males are more territorial than females, but there is also some contradictory evidence (Kaya & Burgess, 2007; Kaya & Weber, 2003). For example, in crowded living conditions in Nigerian university residence halls, female students appeared to use more territorial strategies to cope, while male students used more withdrawal strategies (Amole, 2005). Other research shows that by their mid-teens, many youth in the United States want some territory of their own, as is sometimes demonstrated with graffiti, tagging, and gang behavior (Childress, 2004).

Irwin Altman (1975) classifies our territories as primary, secondary, and public. A **primary territory** is one that evokes feelings of ownership that we control on a relatively permanent basis and that is vital to our daily lives. For most of us, our primary territory would include our home and place of work. **Secondary territories** are less important to us than primary territories, and control of them does not seem as essential to us; examples might be our favorite table at Starbucks or our favorite cardio machine at the gym. **Public territories** are open to anyone in the community, and we generally make no attempt to control access to them—places such as public parks, public beaches, sidewalks, and stores. For people who are homeless and lack access to typical primary territories, however, public territories may serve as primary territories.

Systems perspective; conflict perspective

Much of the literature on territoriality draws on the functionalist sociological tradition (discussed in Chapter 2), emphasizing the positive value of territorial behavior to provide order to the social world and a sense of security to individuals (R. Taylor, 1988). We know, however, that territorial behavior can also be the source of conflict, domination, and oppression. Recently, it has been suggested that globalization is reducing territoriality among nation states (Raustiala, 2005). Indeed, globalization does blur national boundaries, but current national conversations about "securing our borders" are prime examples of territorial behaviors.

Crowding

The term *crowding* has sometimes been used interchangeably with *density,* but environmental psychologists make important distinctions between these terms. **Density** is the ratio of persons per unit area of a space. Crowding is the subjective feeling of having too many people around. **Crowding** is not always correlated with density; the feeling of being crowded seems to be influenced by an interaction of personal, social, and cultural as well as physical factors. For example, in one study, the perception of crowding was associated with density among older adults living with extended families in India, but perceived social support in high-density environments buffered the perception of crowding and decreased personal space requirements (Sinha & Nayyar, 2000). Researchers (G. Evans et al., 2000) have compared different ethnic groups that live in high-density housing in the United States. They found that Latin American and Asian American residents tolerate more density before feeling crowded than Anglo Americans and African Americans. These researchers also found, however, that all four ethnic groups experienced similar psychological distress from crowding. Another research team found that Middle Eastern respondents were less likely to perceive high-density retail situations as crowded than their North American counterparts (Pons, Laroche, & Mourali, 2006).

> Social constructionist perspective

Research has also found gender differences in response to crowding. Women living in crowded homes are more likely to be depressed, while men living in crowded homes demonstrate higher levels of withdrawal and violence (Regoeczi, 2008). In crowded elementary school classrooms, girls' academic achievement and boys' classroom behavior are adversely affected (Maxwell, 2003).

Crowding has been found to have an adverse effect on child development (G. Evans & Saegert, 2000), and to be associated with elevated blood pressure and neuroendocrine hormone activity (Gifford, 2007), poor compliance with mental health care (Menezes, Scazufca, Rodrigues, & Mann, 2000), increased incidence of tuberculosis (Baker, Das, Venugopal, & Howden-Chapman, 2008; Wanyeki et al., 2006), and aggressive behavior in prison inmates (Lawrence & Andrews, 2004).

Behavior Settings Theories

Would you expect to observe the same behaviors if you were observing Ben Watson in different settings—for example, his parents' home, his apartment, running errands in his neighborhood, at work, at a party with friends, or on an outing in the natural environment? My guess is that you would not. A third major category of theories about the relationship between human behavior and the physical environment is **behavior settings theories.** According to these theories, consistent, uniform patterns of behavior occur in particular places, or **behavior settings.** Behavior is *always* tied to a specific place, and the setting may have a more powerful influence on behavior than characteristics of the individual (Bechtel, 2000; M. Scott, 2005).

> Social behavioral perspective; systems perspective

Behavior settings theory was developed by Roger Garlock Barker (1968), who was searching for the factors that influence different individuals to behave differently in the same environment. He and his colleagues studied human behavior in public settings, rather than in the laboratory, where individual differences were usually studied. They unexpectedly noted that observations of different persons in the same setting, even when substantial time elapsed between the observations, were more similar than those of the same person in different settings, even when there was only a short time between observations. For example, your behavior at a musical festival is more similar to the behavior of other festival attendees than it is to your own behavior in the classroom or at the grocery store.

R. G. Barker (1968) suggested that **programs**—consistent, prescribed patterns of behavior—develop and are maintained in many specific settings. For example, when you enter a grocery store, you grab a cart, travel down aisles collecting items and putting them in the cart, and take the cart to a checkout counter where you wait while store employees tabulate the cost of the items and bag them. In some stores, a store employee will take the groceries to the car for you, but in other stores you take your groceries to the car yourself. Imagine how surprised you would be if you went into the grocery store to find everybody kicking soccer balls! You might argue that behavior settings theory is more about the social environment than the physical environment—that behavioral programs are socially constructed, developed by people in interaction, and not determined by the physical environment. As suggested earlier, however, R. G. Barker (1968) takes a transactional approach to person in environment; physical and social elements are combined in behavior settings (Gifford, 2007; M. Scott, 2005). Behavioral programs are created conjointly by individuals and their inanimate surroundings, and behavior settings are distinctive in their physical-spatial features as well as their social rules. You won't see a soccer goal in the grocery store, and you won't see aisles of groceries at a soccer game. The relationships of the social and physical environments to behavior can be summarized in these words: "*It is the social situation that influences people's behavior, but it is the physical environment that provides the cues*" (Rapoport, 1990, p. 57, emphasis original).

However, in recent years, behavior settings theory has been extended to explain behavior in nonplace settings, more specifically to explain behavior in *virtual behavior settings* such as chat rooms and blogs (Stokols & Montero, 2002). This line of inquiry is interested in how interaction in such virtual behavior settings is integrated, or not, with the place-based settings in which it occurs, such as home, workplace, or Internet café.

Behavior settings as conceptualized by Barker had a static quality, but Allan Wicker (1987) has more recently written about the changing nature—the life histories—of behavior settings. In other words, behavior settings themselves are now seen as changing configurations of person and environment. Some settings disappear (Have you been to a barn raising lately?), and some become radically altered. The high school prom that my neighbor attended in 2009 was a different setting, with a very different behavioral program, from the high school prom that I attended in 1963. And, these days, that trip to the grocery store often involves getting your own reusable grocery bags from the car before entering the store (or making a trip back to the car to get them when you are almost at the store door).

Behavior settings theory has implications for social work assessment and intervention. It suggests that patterns of behavior are specific to a setting and, therefore, that we must assess settings as well as individuals when problematic behavior occurs. Ben Watson was feeling restless at his parents' home, but we do not see behaviors that suggest he was feeling the same way once he got settled in North Carolina. The behavior setting may not be the only factor involved in this change, but it should be considered as one possible factor. Behavior settings theory also suggests that the place where we first learn a new skill helps recreate the state necessary to retrieve and enact the skill. When we are assisting clients in skill development, we should pay particular attention to the discontinuities between the settings where the skills are being "learned" and the settings where those skills must be used.

Another key concept in behavior settings theory is the level of **staffing** (R. G. Barker, 1968; L. Brown, Shepherd, Wituk, & Meissen, 2007; Wicker, 1979). Different behavior settings attract different numbers of participants, or staff. It is important to have a good fit between the number of participants and the behavioral program for the setting. Overstaffing occurs when there are too many participants for the behavioral program of a given setting; understaffing occurs when there are too few participants. Roger G. Barker and Paul Gump's (1964) study of the optimal high school size is a classic piece of research about optimal staffing for particular behavior settings. This research will be addressed later in the chapter, when we discuss the physical environment and the life course. A growing body of research also suggests that larger settings tend to exclude more people from action, and smaller settings put pressure on more people to perform (Bechtel, 2000). The issue of appropriate staffing, in terms of number of participants, for particular behavioral programs in particular behavior settings has great relevance for the planning of social work programs. Indeed, behavior settings theory and the issue of optimal staffing have been used to understand the benefits of member participation in consumer-run mental health organizations (L. Brown et al., 2007). These researchers suggest that behavior settings theory be extended by integrating role theory (see Chapter 2 for discussion of roles) to examine the different roles played within a behavior setting.

Critical Thinking Questions 7.1

Have you noticed ways that your behavior is affected by the physical environment? Have you given much thought to the impact of the physical environment on your behavior and the behavior of others? How well do any of the theories discussed above—stimulation theory, control theory, or behavior settings theory—account for the influence of the physical environment on your behavior?

THE NATURAL ENVIRONMENT

Do you find that you feel refreshed from being in the natural environment—walking along the beach, hiking in the mountains, or even walking in your neighborhood? Research findings suggest that you may, and that you should consider the benefits of time spent in the **natural environment**—the portion of the environment influenced primarily by geological and nonhuman biological forces—for both you and your clients. The natural environment has always been a place of serenity for Ben Watson. Most of the research on the relationship between human behavior and the natural environment has been in the stimulation theory tradition—looking for ways in which aspects of the natural environment affect our thinking, feeling, social interaction, and health. In general, this research identifies a strong human preference for elements of the natural world and finds many positive outcomes of time spent in the natural environment (H. Frumkin, 2001, 2003; P. Kahn, 1999; R. Kaplan & Kaplan, 1989). These benefits are summarized in Exhibit 7.3. The findings are not surprising, given the distinctive place accorded to the natural environment in the cultural artifacts—music, art, literature—of all societies. Sociobiologists propose that humans have a genetically based need to affiliate with nature; they call it **biophilia** (Kellert & Wilson, 1993; E. Wilson, 1984, 2007). They argue that humans have a 2 million year history of evolving in natural environments and have only lived in cities for a small fraction of that time; therefore, we are much better adapted to natural environments than built environments.

In a study of Israeli adults and children, Rachel Sebba (1991) found that almost all the adults retrospectively identified an outdoor setting as the most significant place in their childhood. This finding held for both men and women and for adults from different generations and different environmental and social backgrounds. Similarly, a cross-cultural study of adults from Senegal, Ireland, and the United States found that 61% of the participants named a setting in the natural environment as their favorite place (Newell, 1997). Sebba also found features of the natural environment to be more effective than features of the built environment in engaging children's interest and stimulating their imaginations. Natural features also stimulated them to action, an outcome related to the concept of *activity,* as defined in Exhibit 7.1.

- Engaging children's interest
- Stimulating children's imagination
- Stimulating activity and physical fitness
- Increasing productivity
- Enhancing creativity
- Providing intellectual stimulation
- Aiding recovery from mental fatigue
- Improving concentration
- Enhancing group cohesiveness and community cooperation
- Fostering serenity
- Fostering a sense of oneness or wholeness
- Fostering a sense of control
- Fostering recovery from surgery
- Improving physical health
- Improving emotional state

▲ **Exhibit 7.3**   Benefits of Time Spent in the Natural Environment (Based on Stimulation Theory Research)

In recent years, practitioners in various disciplines have taken the age-old advice of poets, novelists, and philosophers that natural settings are good for body, mind, and spirit and have developed programs that center on activities in both wilderness and urban natural settings. Researchers who have studied the effects of such programs have found some positive gain and no evidence of negative effects (see Burton, 1981; P. Kahn, 1999; R. Kaplan & Kaplan, 1989). Studies on the impact of wilderness programs have reported three positive outcomes: recovery from mental fatigue with improved attention (Hartig, Mang, & Evans, 1991; R. Kaplan & Kaplan, 1989), enhanced group cohesiveness (Cumes, 1998; Ewert & Heywood, 1991), and spiritual benefits such as serenity and a sense of oneness or wholeness (Cumes, 1998; R. Kaplan & Kaplan, 1989). But it may not be necessary to travel to wilderness areas to benefit from activity in natural settings. Urban community gardening projects have been found to contribute to the development of cooperation and to improved self-esteem among the participants (Lewis, 1979, 1996). The presence of trees and grass in the neighborhood has been found to stimulate social activity in common spaces (Sullivan, Kuo, & DePooter, 2004). Research with individuals involved in both community gardening and backyard gardening indicates benefits that include a sense of tranquility, sense of control, and improved physical health (R. Kaplan, 1983; S. Kaplan, 1995). Spending 120 minutes a week in the natural environment has been found to improve concentration among women in their third trimester of pregnancy (Stark, 2003). Playing in outdoor green spaces has been found to improve attention among children and adolescents with attention deficit/hyperactivity disorder (ADHD) (Kuo & Faber Taylor, 2004). Opportunities to walk in outdoor urban green spaces have been found to increase longevity in a sample of older adults in Tokyo, even when controlling for social class, age, gender, marital status, and functional status (Takano, Nakamura, & Watanabe, 2002).

One does not have to be active in the natural environment to derive benefits from it. Surgery patients with views of nature from their hospital windows have been found to recover more quickly than patients whose window views have no nature content (Ulrich, 1984). Two studies in prison settings found that inmates who had views of nature from their cells sought health care less often than those without such views (Moore, 1981; West, 1986). In a psychiatric ward renovation project that included changes in or additions of paint, wallpaper, carpet, lighting, furniture, curtains, plants, and bathtubs, staff rated the addition of plants to be the most positive change (Devlin, 1992). Patients in a short-term psychiatric hospital were found to respond favorably to wall art that involved nature but negatively to abstract wall art (Ulrich, 1993). For 7- to 12-year-old girls living in inner-city high-rise apartments, having a view of nature from the home was associated with greater self-discipline; this association was not found for boys in the same environments, and the researchers speculate that boys spend more time in more distant green spaces than girls do (A. Taylor, Kuo, & Sullivan, 2002). University students with a view of nature while taking a test scored better on the test than students who did not have a view of nature (Tennessen & Cimprich, 1995). Commuter drivers with nature-dominated drives demonstrate quicker recovery from stress than those whose drives have minimal nature scenery (Parsons, Tassinary, Ulrich, Hebl, & Grossman-Alexander, 1998). Several recent research projects report that views of natural settings stimulate recovery from stress (Hartig, Evans, Jamner, Davis, & Gärling, 2003; Hartig & Staats, 2006; Staats, Kieviet, & Hartig, 2003). Office workers have been found to experience less anger and stress when art posters with nature paintings are present (Byoung-Suk, Ulrich, Walker, & Tassinary, 2008).

Three features of the natural environment have been found to be particularly influential on emotional states:

1. *Water:* Cross-cultural comparisons of preferences for landscape elements find water to be the preferred element among Korean, Australian, and U.S. participants (Herzog, Herbert, Kaplan, & Crooks, 2000; Yang & Brown, 1992).

2. *Trees:* When viewing line drawings and slides of urban streets with and without trees and shrubs, the participants in one study reported more positive feelings when viewing the tree-lined streets (Sheets & Manzer, 1991). They reported feeling friendlier, more cooperative, less sad, and less depressed. Another study found that having well-maintained trees and grass increased the sense of safety of residents of a large inner-city housing project (Kuo, Bacaicoa, & Sullivan, 1998). Finally, another study found that children in inner-city neighborhoods engage in more creative play in settings with trees than in settings without trees (A. Taylor, Wiley, Kuo, & Sullivan, 1998).

3.   *Sunlight:* Ben Watson made special note of the ample sunlight in his apartment. Design innovations for older adults, particularly those with Alzheimer's disease, are emphasizing the benefit of natural light over artificial light (Brawley, 2006). However, the relationship between sunlight and human behavior is curvilinear, with benefit coming from increasing amounts until a certain optimum point is reached, after which increasing amounts damage rather than benefit. Excessive sunlight can have negative impacts, such as glare and overheating, and inadequate sunlight has been identified as a contributor to depression, sometimes referred to as seasonal affective disorder (SAD), in some persons (Sadock & Sadock, 2007; Westrin & Lam, 2007). One research team found that sunlight penetration in indoor spaces was related to feelings of relaxation, with patches of sunlight as the optimum situation and both too little and too much penetration decreasing the feeling of relaxation (Boubekri, Hull, & Boyer, 1991).

Given the growing evidence of the psychological benefits of time spent in nature, there is a growing call for **ecotherapy,** exposure to nature and the outdoors as a component of psychotherapy, as a major agenda for mental health promotion and treatment (see Buzzell, 2009; Jordan, 2009; Maller, Townsend, Pryor, Brown, & St. Leger, 2005; Mind, 2007). The combination of green spaces with physical exercise has been found to be a particularly potent program for mood elevation in people with major depression (Mind, 2007). This is important in light of estimates that major depression will constitute one of the largest health problems worldwide by 2020 (Maller et al., 2005). Ecotherapy includes time spent with domestic and companion animals.

Although the natural environment can be a positive force, it also has the potential to damage mental, social, and physical well-being. The relationship between sunlight and human behavior provides a clue. The natural environment provides sensory stimulation in an uncontrolled strength, and the patterns of stimulation are quite unstable. Extremely stimulating natural events are known as natural disasters, including such events as hurricanes, tornadoes, floods, earthquakes, volcanic eruptions, landslides, avalanches, tsunamis, and forest fires. Natural disasters are considered to be cataclysmic events—a class of stressors with great force, sudden onset, excessive demands on human coping, and large scope. These events are considered to be almost

▲ **Photo 7.1**   The physical environment (both natural and humanmade) impact our behavior. Researchers have found a strong preference for elements of the natural environment and positive outcomes of time spent in nature.

universally stressful (Kobayashi & Miura, 2000). Most of us still have vivid memories of horrific television images after the South Asian tsunami on December 26, 2004, and the aftermath of Hurricane Katrina hitting New Orleans in late August 2005. Social workers play active roles in providing services to communities that have experienced natural disasters.

There is currently great international concern about the damage that is being done to the natural environment by human endeavors and about the need to protect the natural environment. In 2000, United Nations Secretary-General Kofi Annan called for an assessment of "the consequences of ecosystem change for human well-being" (Millennium Ecosystem Assessment, 2005, p. ii). The report, presented in 2005, included four major findings:

1.   In response to growing demands for food, fresh water, timber, and fuel, humans have changed ecosystems more over the last 50 years than in any other historical period. The unfortunate result is a sizable and mostly irreversible loss of diversity of life.

2.   Although there are, to date, net gains for human well-being from these changes, they have exacerbated poverty for some groups of people. In addition, many costs of the changes will be deferred to future generations.

3. It is likely that the degradation of world ecosystems will grow significantly worse in the first half of the 21st century.

4. Reversing the degradation of ecosystems will require major changes in policies across the globe.

Social scientists are interested in understanding how people perceive their relationships with the natural environment and what motivates them to be concerned about protecting it (Clayton & Opotow, 2003). Gabriel Ignatow (2006) proposes two different cultural models of nature–human relationships that can predispose people to be concerned about protecting nature. The first model, a *spiritual model,* sees nature as sacred in its own right and threatened by human activity. The second model, an *ecological model* based in science, sees humans as interconnected with nature, and looks to science and technology to find ways for humans to live in balance with nature. Although the track record of environment policy implementation is not good to date, there is evidence that the international environmental movement has slowed the pace of degradation of the natural environment to some extent (Schofer & Hironaka, 2005).

The National Association of Social Workers (NASW; n.d.) has recognized the effect of the natural environment on human behavior and developed an environmental policy statement that argues that

> social workers have a professional interest . . . in the viability of the natural environment, including the noxious effect of environmental degradation on people, especially oppressed individuals and communities, and they have a professional obligation to become knowledgeable and educated about the precarious position of the natural environment. (n.p.)

THE BUILT ENVIRONMENT

It is the uncontrollable quality of the natural environment that humans try to overcome in constructing the **built environment**—the portion of the physical environment attributable solely to human effort. The built environment is intended to create comfort and controllability, but unfortunately, technological developments often have negative impacts as well. The toxic waste problem is but one example of the risks we have created but not yet learned to control. Social workers have called attention to the fact that the risks of environmental hazards are falling disproportionately on minority and low-socioeconomic communities (M. Kahn & Scher, 2002; Rogge, 1993). A very current concern is the dumping of electronic waste on developing nations. The Environmental Protection Agency estimates that the United States produces 300 million tons of electronic waste (e-waste) each year, and about 80% of it ends up in landfills overseas in conditions that are hazardous (Bennion, 2009).

Research on the relationship between human behavior and the built environment draws heavily on control theories as well as stimulation theories. Some researchers study stimulation exclusively, others study control exclusively, but most researchers study both—providing a good example of research that attempts to integrate ideas from different theoretical perspectives to achieve a more comprehensive understanding of changing person–environment configurations. This integration of theoretical perspectives is increasingly common.

For several decades, environmental psychologists have been studying the impact of the physical environment on such factors as mood, problem solving, productivity, and violent behavior. They have examined physical designs that encourage social interaction, **sociopetal spaces,** and designs that discourage social interaction, **sociofugal spaces.** As Exhibit 7.1 shows, Weisman refers to this social interaction aspect of the physical environment as *sociality.* Researchers have studied design features of such institutional settings as psychiatric hospitals, state schools for persons with cognitive disabilities, college dormitories, and correctional facilities. Exhibit 7.4 summarizes some of the key results of this line of inquiry. Late 20th- and early 21st–century developments in biomedical science, particularly new understandings of the brain and the immune system, have allowed more sophisticated analysis of how the built environment affects physical and mental health and can be a source of healing (see Sternberg, 2009; Ulrich, 2006; Ulrich & Zimring, 2005).

Healing Environments

By many accounts, Roger Ulrich (1984) was the first researcher to measure the effects of the physical environment on physical health of hospital patients. He studied patients who had undergone gallbladder surgery and had rooms with one of two different types of views out their hospital windows. One group had views of a brown brick wall, and the other group had views of a small stand of trees. On average, the patients who had views of the trees left the hospital almost a day sooner than the patients with views of a brick wall. They also required less pain medication, received fewer negative comments from the nurses, and had slightly fewer postoperative complications.

The idea that nature is important to healing is not new; indeed, it has been around for thousands of years (Sternberg, 2009). Furthermore, there is a long tradition in architecture that proposes that nature and architecture are connected to health (Joye, 2007). In the 19th century, hospitals were built with large windows, even skylights, and often in beautiful natural settings (Joye, 2007; Sternberg, 2009). Clinics and hospitals were particularly designed to take advantage of natural light because it was thought that sunlight could heal. Some public health scholars argue, however, that as medical technology became more sophisticated, design of hospital space began to focus more on care of the equipment than on care of the patient (Maller et al., 2005; Sternberg, 2009). These public health scholars are calling attention to biomedical research that links physical environments and human health.

Based on his early research, Roger Ulrich, a behavioral scientist, has collaborated with architects, environmental psychologists, and public and private agencies and foundations to develop a field called **evidence-based design,** which uses physiological and health-outcome measures to evaluate the health benefits of hospital design features (Ulrich, 2006). Following on the earlier work of Ulrich, researchers use such measures as length of stay; amount of pain medication; rates of health complications; and patient satisfaction, stress, and mood to evaluate design innovations. By 2006, a total of 700 rigorous studies had been identified (Ulrich, 2006), and the Center for Health Design (2006) had been established to engage in ongoing hospital design innovations and evaluations. Two foci of this research are discussed here: noise and sunlight.

A great deal of international research has focused on hospital noise as an impediment to healing. This research consistently finds that hospital noise exceeds the guidelines recommended by the World Health Organization (Sternberg, 2009). Hospital noise comes from a variety of sources, for example, overhead paging, moving of bedrails, medical equipment, and staff shift changes. The problem is exacerbated in hospitals that have hard, sound-reflecting floors and ceilings. It is also intensified in multi-bed rooms because of the activity of caring for multiple patients. Noise has been associated with high blood pressure and elevated heart rates, sleep loss, slower recovery from heart attack, and negative physiological responses such as apnea and fluctuations in blood pressure and oxygen saturation in infants in neonatal intensive care (G. Brown, 2009; Hagerman et al., 2005; Ulrich, 2006; Ulrich & Zimring, 2005). Preterm infants exposed to prolonged high levels of noise are at risk for hearing loss, impaired brain development, and speech and language problems (G. Brown, 2009). Excessive noise also contributes to hospital staff fatigue (Ulrich, 2006). A number of design innovations have been found to be effective in reducing hospital noise. These include single-bed rooms, replacing overhead paging with a noiseless system, covering neonatal incubators with blankets, and installing high-performance sound-absorbing ceiling tiles and floor carpets (G. Brown, 2009; Ulrich, 2006). These innovations have been found to be related to improved health outcomes and fewer rehospitalizations for patients as well as improved staff satisfaction and home sleep quality (Sternberg, 2009).

There is also growing evidence that 19th-century hospital designers were accurate in their belief that sunlight can heal. Beauchemin and Hays (1998) found that patients recovering from heart attacks in sunny hospital rooms had significantly shorter hospital stays than patients recovering in rooms without natural light. Another research team studied

Therapeutic Design Features	Positive Behaviors
Tables with chairs instead of shoulder-to-shoulder and back-to-back seating Large spaces broken into smaller spaces Flowers and magazines placed on tables	Increase in both brief and sustained interaction
Special activity centers with partitions Sleeping dormitories divided into two-bed rooms with table and chairs Long hallways broken up Sound baffles added to high ceilings Improved lighting, bright colors, and large signs added	Increase in social interaction Decrease in passive and inactive behavior
Painted walls replacing bars Carpeted floors Conventional furniture with fabric upholstery Visually interesting public areas Private rooms with outside windows Solarium with exercise equipment	Decrease in violent behavior in correctional facilities
Open sleeping wards and dayroom turned into personal living spaces and a lounge	Increase in social interaction
Places for personal belongings provided Personalized decorations	Decrease in stereotypical behavior Increase in alert, purposive behavior
Institutional furniture replaced with noninstitutional furniture Rugs, lamps, and draperies added Control over lighting	Decrease in intrusive behaviors Increase in use of personal space

▲ **Exhibit 7.4**   Selected Research Findings About the Therapeutic Use of Architecture

▲ **Photo 7.2**   There is a long tradition in architecture that proposes that nature and architecture are connected to healing.

patients recovering from spinal surgery in one hospital and compared the experiences of patients in sunny rooms with the experiences of patients in rooms without sunlight. Patients in sunny rooms took 22% less pain medication and had 21% lower medication costs than similar patients recovering in rooms without sunlight (Walch, Day, & Kang, 2005). The patients in the sunny rooms also reported less stress than patients in the rooms without sunlight. Hospital rooms with morning sunlight have also been found to reduce the hospital stay of patients with unipolar and bipolar depression (Beauchemin & Hays, 1996; Benedetti, Colombo, Barbini, Campori, & Smeraldi, 2001).

Roger Ulrich and Craig Zimring (2005) have reviewed the large array of evidence-based design research and proposed a list of hospital design changes that have been found to promote healing. These are overviewed in Exhibit 7.5. Ulrich (2006) reports that these design upgrades would increase initial construction cost by 5.4%, but those costs would be recaptured in only one year.

Urban Design and Health

Prior to the early 20th century in the United States, public health experts focused on what they called "the urban penalty" for health and mortality: As city size increased, so did the death rate. Infectious diseases such as tuberculosis, measles, small pox, and influenza were the main cause of the urban penalty. Such diseases spread quickly in high-density environments. By the 1920s, improved sanitation and other public health measures had eliminated the urban penalty in the United States and other wealthy nations, but it still exists in very large cities in poorer nations, and in the poorest sections of cities in wealthy nations. The biggest threats to urban populations in the United States at the current time are violent crime and pollution, the latter of which contributes to high rates of asthma (Sternberg, 2009).

In recent years, some public health officials have begun to suggest an increasing rural and suburban penalty, and an urban advantage (see Vlahov, Galea, & Freudenberg, 2005). To illustrate, in 2007, public health data indicated that New York City (NYC) was the healthiest location in the United States as indicated by longevity. Life expectancy increased there by 6.2 years between 1990 and 2007, compared to 2.5 years for the rest of the country. NYC was considered the healthiest based on longevity (the most commonly used measure of a geographical area's health) (Sternberg, 2009). Other wealthy cities, particularly those that are designed to encourage walking, show a similar urban advantage. The current rural health disadvantage is thought to stem from such factors as isolation and economic disadvantage.

Considerable research has focused in recent years on urban sprawl and design features of suburban built environments that contribute to decreased physical activity. The researchers note the long distances that suburban dwellers need to travel to work and to amenities, requiring more time spent in the car. These researchers have been particularly interested in whether suburban built environments contribute to obesity and the related health

---

Single-occupancy rooms

Sound-absorbing ceiling tiles and floors

Improved air quality and ventilation

Better lighting and access to natural light

Pleasant and comfortable patient rooms

Gardens

Nature views

Rooming-in spaces for families

Artwork on walls

Soothing music

Soothing colors

Spaces for family members to congregate for mutual support

Clearer signage to assist with wayfinding

▲ **Exhibit 7.5**   Evidence-Based Design for Health Care Settings

SOURCE: Based on Ulrich and Zimring (2005).

problems of cardiovascular disease and diabetes. The evidence is mixed on this question. Some researchers have found that urban sprawl is associated with weight problems and obesity (Ewing, Schmid, Killingsworth, Zlot, & Raudenbush, 2003; L. Frank, Andresen, & Schmid, 2004; Garden & Jalaludin, 2009; Lopez, 2004). The Centers for Disease Control and Prevention (CDC; 2006b) has mapped obesity across the United States and found that it is a perfect match for the map of urban sprawl, both of which are greatest in the southeast and midwest. Others have found that aspects of the built environment contribute to neighborhood walkability, but no conclusive evidence that these design features contribute to obesity (Berke, Koepsell, Moudon, Hoskins, & Larson, 2007). The new urbanist designers are designing suburban towns with several features that are known to contribute to walkability: houses with front porches; neighborhood spots for congregation; sidewalks; short blocks; good lighting; amenities that are accessible by foot; public transportation; mixed-used areas, including residences, businesses, offices, and recreation centers; and bike paths, tennis courts, parks, and gold courses (WebUrbanDesign, 2009). The hope is that these design features will contribute to resident activity and health.

Lopez and Hynes (2006) enter this conversation with a more complicated story. They report that although it is true that obesity is associated with urban sprawl, inner-city populations have higher rates of obesity and inactivity than suburban dwellers. They suggest that different aspects of the physical environment are contributing to ill health for inner-city residents and making their neighborhoods unwalkable. Inner-city neighborhoods have some of the design features recommended by the new urbanist designers, features such as sidewalks, short blocks, and public transportation, but they have a set of barriers to walking that do not exist in suburbs, such as hazardous waste sites, abandoned buildings, decaying sidewalks, disappearing tree canopies, and dilapidated school playgrounds and parks. For example, one study found that low-income neighborhoods are 4 times as likely as high-income neighborhoods to have hazardous waste facilities, power plants, and polluting industrial plants, and low-income *minority* neighborhoods are 20 times as likely as high-income neighborhoods to have these facilities (Faber & Krieg, 2005, cited in Lopez & Hynes, 2006). Public health officials also warn that with the new types of infectious diseases whose spread is fueled by global warming, dense cities contribute to contagion (Sternberg, 2009).

Defensible Space and Crime Prevention

Applying the concept of territoriality to crime prevention, Oscar Newman (1972, 1980) developed his theory of **defensible space**. This theory suggests that residential crime and fear of crime can be decreased by means of certain design features that increase residents' sense of territoriality and, consequently, their motivation to "watch out" for the neighborhood. The recommended design features are listed in Exhibit 7.6.

This theory has been influential but also controversial. It has spawned the development of "crime prevention by design" programs in several European countries, and evaluation research has found a number of cases where redesign of the physical environment has contributed to a significant decrease in crime (Reynald & Elffers, 2009). The findings suggest that design features help reduce crime and the fear of crime because criminals, as well as residents, perceive the redesigned spaces to be under greater control of the residents.

However, the defensible space theory has also been criticized for vagueness in definition of concepts, and some researchers have found that physical design can deter crime but not to the extent suggested by Newman (see B. Hillier, 2004). These researchers argue that social factors, as well as physical environment features, play a considerable role in territoriality to guard against crime. They suggest that without a strong sense of community, which creates a motivation for neighbors to work together, territoriality breaks down (Schweitzer, Woo Kim, & Mackin, 1999). This idea that aspects of both the social and physical environment play a role in neighborhood control of crime is consistent with the multidimensional model proposed in this book, and, indeed, was acknowledged by Oscar Newman in his later work (Newman & Franck, 1980).

- Real and symbolic barriers, such as fences, walls, or shrubs, to divide the residential environment into smaller, more manageable sections

- Opportunities for surveillance of both interior spaces and exterior spaces by residents

- Opportunities for personalizing both interior and exterior spaces

- Spaces that encourage social interaction and community building

- Strengthening of potential targets of crime, such as raising fire escapes to get them out of reach and having doors in vulnerable spots open outward

▲ **Exhibit 7.6**   Design Features to Create Defensible Space

SOURCES: Based on O. Newman (1980) and Katyal (2002).

Behavior Settings and Addictions

An emerging line of research suggests that behavior settings are an important element in substance addiction. For instance, Winifred Gallagher (1993) reports that large numbers of American soldiers who used heroin during the Vietnam conflict left the drug behind when they returned to an environment that they did not associate with heroin. Shepard Siegel's research (Kim, Siegel, & Patenall, 1999; Ramos, Siegel, & Bueno, 2002; S. Siegel, 1991, 2001, 2005; S. Siegel & Allan, 1998; S. Siegel, Hinson, Krank, & McCully, 1982) also supports the idea that behavior settings play an important role in substance addiction. Siegel and colleagues found that when a person with a heroin addiction takes a customary dose of heroin in an environment where he or she does not usually take the drug, the reaction is much more intense, and an overdose may even occur. This consistent finding over time has led Siegel to suggest that *tolerance*—the ability to take increasing amounts of the drug without feeling increased effects—is embedded in the environment in which the drug is usually taken. He has also found that behavior settings stimulate craving, even when the person has been in recovery for some time. Siegel recommends that treatment include systematic exposure to cues from the behavior setting, with no reinforcement of drug ingestion, to provide environmental deconditioning. You may recognize that this approach to treatment comes from classical conditioning.

Social behavioral perspective

Maybe the concept of behavior setting also explains why many people with addictions attempt to shake them by moving to a new environment. Siegel reports that "studies from all over the world show that after a year, most of those who don't relapse after drug treatment have relocated" (cited in W. Gallagher, 1993, p. 138).

Critical Thinking Questions 7.2

How might social workers incorporate ecotherapy into their practice in different settings? Have you seen examples of this being done? Which do you think are the healthiest type of communities in which to live: rural, small town, suburban, or urban? What do you think are the costs and benefits of living in each of these types of communities?

PLACE ATTACHMENT

Have you ever been strongly attached to a specific place—a beloved home, a particular beach or mountain spot, or a house of worship? **Place attachment**—the process in which people and groups form bonds with places—is the subject of a growing literature (Devine-Wright, 2009; Hidalgo & Hernandez, 2001; Kyle, Graefe, Manning, & Bacon, 2004; Manzo & Perkins, 2006). Although place attachment is usually discussed in terms of emotional bonding, an interplay of emotions, cognitions, and behaviors and actions is what forges the people–place bond (Low & Altman, 1992). Consider the role of behaviors and actions, laboring and sweating, in the attachment to the lost home described by a survivor of the 1972 Buffalo Creek flood:

> I have a new home right now, and I would say that it is a much nicer home than what I had before. But it is a house, it is not a home. Before, I had a home. And what I mean by that, I built the other home. I took a coal company house, I remodeled it, I did the work on it myself. I put many a drop of sweat and drove many a nail into it, and I labored and sweated and worried over it. And it was gone. I left home Saturday morning and I had a home. On Saturday evening I didn't have nothing. (Quoted in K. Erikson, 1976, p. 175)

This example focuses on attachment to home, but researchers have looked at attachment to places of different scale, including outdoor recreational areas (Kyle et al., 2004). We will run into the concept of place attachment again in Chapter 13 when we discuss community as a dimension of environment.

In the context of place attachment, *place* is defined as a "space that has been given meaning through personal, group, or cultural processes" (Low & Altman, 1992, p. 5). The literature on place attachment emphasizes emotional bonding to environmental settings that are satisfying in terms of one or more of the aspects of physical environment–behavior relationships presented in Exhibit 7.1, with different researchers focusing on different aspects. Those who focus on sociality remind us that attachment to places may be based largely on our satisfying relationships with people in those places—once again reminding us of the inseparability of people and environments.

> Psychodynamic perspective; social behavioral perspective

When a strong place attachment develops, it has been suggested that the place has become an important part of the self, that we can't think of who we are without some reference to the place (Gifford, 2007). When a particular place becomes an important part of our self-identity, this merger of place and self is known as **place identity**. Place identity can develop where there is strong negative, as well as positive, place attachment, as a boy named Kareem observes:

> It's strange, but I really like when the lights go off in the movies because then I'm no longer a "homeless kid." I'm just a person watching the movie like everyone else. A lot of the children at the hotel believe that they are "hotel kids." They've been told by so many people for so long that they are not important, that they live up to what is expected of them. It gets so some children have no dreams and live in a nightmare because they believe that they are "hotel kids." It's worse than being in jail. In jail you can see the bars and you know when you're getting out. In the hotel you can't see the bars because they're inside of you and you don't know when you're getting out. (Quoted in Berck, 1992, p. 105)

Home and work are the settings most likely to become merged with our sense of self, but recent research has focused on attachment to the neighborhood (Altman, 1993; Devine-Wright, 2009; Manzo & Perkins, 2006). Place attachment can also play a strong role in group and cultural identity (Low & Altman, 1992). One recent study found that many Cambodian American and Filipino American older adults expressed a desire to die in their homelands (G. Becker, 2002).

Researchers have been particularly interested in what happens to people when a place of identity is lost. Certainly, we should pay attention to issues of place identity when we encounter people who have relocated, particularly when working with immigrant and refugee families. We should also consider the long-term consequences of early experiences, such as homelessness or frequent movement between foster homes, in which no stable place attachment forms, or that result in a negative place attachment.

HOMELESSNESS

As suggested above, place attachment can be quite problematic for people without homes. The official U.S. definition of homelessness is found in Exhibit 7.7. The National Coalition for the Homeless (NCH, 2009b) points out that this definition does not apply as well in rural areas as it does in urban areas, because there are few shelters in rural areas. Many homeless rural people live in crowded situations with relatives or in substandard housing.

It is difficult to count the number of people who are homeless in the United States and worldwide, but there are generally accepted estimates of both. In 2005, a United Nations (UN) report estimated 100 million homeless people worldwide and 1.6 billion inadequately housed people (National Alliance to End Homelessness, 2005). Economic globalization, poverty, and lack of affordable housing are thought to be the major causes of global homelessness. The UN report emphasized the contributing role of inequality in home ownership, noting that, worldwide, almost 75% of private land is controlled by 2.5% of landowners.

There are several national estimates of the number of people who are homeless in the United States and different methods for deriving such estimates (NCH, 2009a). Some researchers count the number of people who are homeless at a given point in time, on a given day or during a given week, and others count the number of people who have a spell of homelessness over a given period of time, usually over a year. One problem in counting the number of homeless persons is that many people without homes stay in places where researchers cannot easily find them, for example, in automobiles or campgrounds. In 2009, the National Alliance to End Homelessness (NAEH, 2009) estimated that over a month's time, there are 671,859 homeless people in the United States. The NCH (2009a) estimates that between 2.3 and 3.5 million people are homeless in the United States each year. In most cases, homelessness is temporary, and the average stay in an emergency shelter is 70 days for families, 69 days for single men, and 51 days for single women.

In 2008 and 2009, housing foreclosures, eroding work opportunities, and the declining value of public assistance increased the number of people who experience homelessness in the United States (NCH, 2009c). A 2007 survey found

---

An individual is homeless if he or she

1. Lacks a fixed, regular, and adequate nighttime residence; and

2. Has a primary nighttime residence that is

   • A supervised publicly or privately operated shelter designed to provide temporary living accommodations (including welfare hotels, congregate shelters, and transitional housing for the mentally ill);

   • An institution that provides temporary residence for individuals intended to be institutionalized; or

   • A public or private place not designed for, or ordinarily used as, a regular sleeping accommodation for human beings

---

▲ **Exhibit 7.7**   Official U.S. Federal Definition of Homelessness

SOURCE: U.S. Department of Housing and Urban Development (2009).

that half of the cities surveyed had to turn people away from emergency shelters (U.S. Conference of Mayors, 2007). About 75% of homeless people in the United States are from urban areas (NAEH, 2009). Families with children are one of the fastest growing segments of the homeless population, comprising 23% in 2007. Males comprise 68% of the single segment of the homeless population but are represented in only 35% of homeless families with children. Approximately half of all women and children experiencing homelessness are escaping from domestic violence. Twenty-six percent of sheltered homeless persons have severe mental illness, and among surveyed homeless persons, sheltered and unsheltered, 38% report an alcohol problem and 26% report problems with other drugs. African Americans are overrepresented, accounting for 42% of the sheltered homeless population (NCH, 2009b).

ACCESSIBLE ENVIRONMENTS FOR PERSONS WITH DISABILITIES

Accessibility is one of the key concepts for the study of human behavior and the physical environment (see Exhibit 7.1). In recent years, we have been reminded that environments, particularly built environments, can be disabling because of their inaccessibility to many persons, including most people with disabilities. Ben Watson provides us with several examples of how the physical environment curtailed his activity at times, and he is now in a professional position to try to minimize the barriers that people with disabilities experience in the world. The *social model of disability* emphasizes the barriers that people with impairments face as they interact with the physical and social world, arguing that disability is a result of the relationship between the individual and the environment (see Swain, French, Barnes, & Thomas, 2004).

Conflict perspective

▲ **Photo 7.3** The kitchen room in the "Michael Ciravolo Jr. Wheelchair Suite," the suite that the Hotel Delmonico in New York City dedicated specifically to accommodating people with disabilities.

This way of thinking about disability was the impetus for development of Disabled Peoples' International (2005), a network of national organizations that promotes the rights of people with disabilities worldwide. In the United States, the social model of disability led to legislation at all levels of government during the 1970s and 1980s, most notably two pieces of federal legislation (Gilson, 1996). The Rehabilitation Act of 1973 (Public Law 93–112) was the first federal act to recognize the need for civil rights protection for persons with disabilities. It required all organizations receiving federal assistance to have an affirmative action plan to ensure accessibility of employment to persons with disabilities. The Americans With Disabilities Act of 1990 (ADA) (Public Law 101–336) extended the civil rights of persons with disabilities to the private sector. It seeks to end discrimination against persons with disabilities and promote their full participation in society.

The five titles of the ADA seek to eliminate environmental barriers to the full participation of persons with disabilities. You will want to be aware of the legal rights of your clients with disabilities. Ben Watson has discovered that, in spite of the law, he still encounters many physical barriers to his full participation in society.

- Title I addresses discrimination in the workplace. It requires reasonable accommodations, including architectural modification, for disabled workers.

- Title II requires that all public services, programs, and facilities, including public transportation, be accessible to persons with disabilities.

- Title III requires all public accommodations and services operated by private organizations to be accessible to persons with disabilities. It specifically lists 12 categories of accommodations: hotels and places of lodging; restaurants; movie and live theaters auditoriums and places of public gathering; stores and banks; health care service providers, hospitals, and pharmacies; terminals for public transportation; museums and libraries; parks and zoos; schools; senior centers and social service centers; and places of recreation.

- Title IV requires all intrastate and interstate phone companies to develop telecommunication relay services and devices for persons with speech or hearing impairments to allow them to communicate in a manner similar to that of persons without impairments.

- Title V covers technical guidelines for enforcing the ADA.

Under industrial capitalism, wages are the primary source of livelihood. People who cannot earn wages, therefore, tend to be poor. Research by staff at the World Bank indicates that, around the world, poverty and disability are inextricably linked (Elwan, 1999). In the United States, people with disabilities are disproportionately represented in poverty statistics. In 2000, a total of 17.6% of people with disabilities were poor, compared to 10.6% of people without disabilities (U.S. Census Bureau, 2005). In January 2010, an estimated 15.2% of adults with disabilities were unemployed, compared to an overall unemployment rate of 9.7% (U.S. Department of Labor, 2010). People with disabilities who lobbied for passage of the ADA argued that government was spending vast sums of money for what they called "dependency programs," but was failing to make the investments required to make environments accessible so that people with disabilities could become employed (M. Johnson, 1992; Roulstone, 2004).

Social workers need to keep in mind the high prevalence of disabilities among older persons, the fastest growing group of the United States. More accessible environments may be an important way to buffer the expected deleterious effects of a large elderly population. As the baby boomers age, they will benefit from the earlier activism of the disability community.

Exhibit 7.8 lists some of the elements of environmental design that improve accessibility for persons with disabilities. It is important to remember, however, that rapid developments in assistive technology are likely to alter current guidelines about what is optimal environmental design. For example, the minimum space requirements in the ADA's guidelines for wheelchairs are already too tight for the new styles of motorized wheelchairs.

- Create some close-in parking spaces widened to 8 feet to accommodate unloading of wheelchairs (1 accessible space for every 25 spaces).
- Create curb cuts or ramping for curbs, with 12 inches of slope for every inch of drop in the curb.
- Make ramps at least 3 feet wide to accommodate wheelchairs and provide a 5-by-5-foot square area at the top of ramps to entrances to allow space for door opening.
- Remove high-pile carpeting, low-density carpeting, and plush carpeting, at least in the path of travel. Put nonslip material on slippery floors.
- Avoid phone-in security systems in entrances (barriers for persons who are deaf).
- Make all doorways at least 32 inches wide (36 is better).
- Use automatic doors or doors that take no more than 5 pounds of force to open.
- Use door levers instead of doorknobs.

Exhibit 7.8 *(Continued)*

- Create aisles that are at least 3 feet wide (wider is better). Keep the path of travel clear.
- Connect different levels in buildings with ramps (for small level changes) or a wheelchair-accessible elevator.
- Place public phones no higher than 48 inches (35–42 is optimal)
- Place other things that need to be reached at this optimal height.
- Brightly light foyers and areas with directories to assist persons with low vision. Use 3-inch-high lettering in directories.
- Install Braille signs about 5 feet off the ground.
- Make restroom stalls at least 3 feet deep by 4 feet wide (5 feet by 5 feet is optimal).
- Install toilets that are 17–19 inches in height. Provide grab bars at toilets.
- Hang restroom sinks with no vanity underneath, so that persons in wheelchairs can pull up to them.
- Avoid having low seats, and provide arm supports and backrests on chairs.
- Apply nonslip finish to tub and shower. Install grab bars in tub and shower.
- Use both visual and audible emergency warning systems.

▲ **Exhibit 7.8**   Elements of Accessible Environments for Persons With Disabilities

SOURCES: Based on Brawley (2006); M. Johnson (1992).

THE PHYSICAL ENVIRONMENT AND HUMAN BEHAVIOR ACROSS THE LIFE COURSE

Developmental perspective

People have different physical environment needs at different ages and may respond to features of the physical environment in different ways as they progress through the life course. Some of these differences have been discussed earlier in this chapter. Because the built environment is designed, for the most part, to accommodate the needs and responses of adults, this section calls attention to some of the special needs and responses of children, adolescents, and elderly adults.

Children

In infancy and early childhood, home is the primary physical environment, but day care centers and early childhood education programs constitute a major environment for increasing numbers of young children. As children grow older, their neighborhood and school become important environments.

Research indicates that the physical environment can have both positive and negative effects on child development. Thomas David and Carol Weinstein (1987) suggest that the physical environments of children should be designed to serve five common functions of child development:

1. *Personal identity:* Children need "personalized furnishings and individual territories" (David & Weinstein, 1987, p. 8) to assist in the development of personal identity. Place identity is essential to the development of personal identity.

2. *Sense of competence:* A sense of competence is supported when children have physical spaces and furnishings of a size and scale that allow them to meet their personal needs with minimal assistance. Thus, storage areas, furniture, and fixtures should be at the appropriate height and of the appropriate size for children.

3. *Intellectual, social, and motor development:* Development of intellectual, social, and motor skills is supported by the opportunity to move, explore, and play with interesting materials. Environments that restrict movement inhibit development in all domains.

4. *Security and trust:* Familiar, comfortable, and safe physical environments support the development of security and trust.

5. *A balance of social interaction and privacy:* Physical environments should support social interaction but also provide private spaces that allow children the opportunity to retreat from overstimulating situations. Crowding, clutter, and high noise levels have been found to have negative effects on child development. Research shows that children who come from crowded homes and attend crowded day care centers are more likely to exhibit withdrawal, aggression, competitiveness, and hyperactivity than children for whom crowding is present in neither or only one of these environments (G. Evans, 2006). Constant exposure to high noise levels has been found to have a negative effect on memory, reading and language development, and blood pressure (G. Evans, 2006). Research has found that the negative effects of residential crowding are greatest for children who live in families where there is a lot of interpersonal turmoil (G. Evans & Saegert, 2000). This is a reminder that the physical environment interacts with the social environment to influence behavior.

Neuroscientists have called attention to the physical environment needs of prematurely born babies, noting the competing needs of these vulnerable babies and the medical staff that care for them in neonatal intensive care units (NICUs). The medical staff needs bright light, noisy equipment, and alarms to alert them to physiological distress of their patients. The vulnerable baby needs a physical environment that more nearly approximates the uterus, without bright lights and stressful noise stimulation (Graven et al., 1992; Zeisel, 2006). NICUs are currently being modified to accommodate the neurological needs of the vulnerable newborns.

Adolescents

After the rapid physical growth of puberty, adolescents have outgrown the need for physical environments with reduced scale and size. They have not outgrown the need for personalized furnishings and individual territories, however. Research indicates that privacy needs increase in adolescence (Blumberg & Devlin, 2006; Sinha, Nayyar, & Mukherjee, 1995). At the same time, with the increased emphasis on peer relationships, adolescents have a special need for safe gathering places and recreational opportunities.

Since the 1964 publication of R. G. Barker and Gump's *Big School, Small School: High School Size and Student Behavior,* considerable attention has been given to the question of optimal high school size. As Paul Gump (1987) suggests, high schools need to be larger than elementary schools for the following reasons. First, high schools provide more varied curricular offerings than elementary schools to assist students in sorting out their interests and competencies, which requires a larger and more specialized faculty. Second, high schools offer a varied set of extracurricular activities to meet the need for safe gathering places and recreational opportunities, which requires sufficient numbers of students to "staff" each activity and sufficient faculty sponsors. There is some agreement that high schools of fewer than 500 students will result in "understaffing" (too few participants). On the other hand, as high schools grow larger, they lose some of the continuity and intimacy of small schools, and very large student populations result in "overstaffing," with meaningful opportunities for participation unavailable to many students.

Elderly Adults

As the population in the United States and other advanced industrial societies is aging, there is increasing attention to the special needs of elderly adults in relation to the physical environment. There is general agreement that home and neighborhood are the primary physical environments for elderly adults, but housing of elderly adults has become a major social policy issue (Brawley, 2006).

Because there are more differences among elderly adults than among children and adolescents, it is difficult to make definitive statements about their needs in relation to the physical environment. To assist in assessing the needs of individual clients who are elderly, however, you may find it helpful to adapt the previous list of five ways that the physical environment supports child development:

1. *Personal identity:* As they attempt to hold onto personal identity in the midst of multiple losses, elderly adults will benefit from personalized furnishings and personal territories.

2. *Sense of competence:* Elderly adults are more likely to maintain a sense of competence when the demands of the physical environment match the capabilities of the person. Few modifications are needed for those elderly adults with no disabilities, but for those with one or more disabilities, modifications such as the ones listed in Exhibit 7.8 may be appropriate. Chronic conditions are common among older adults: Over 50% older adults in the United States have arthritis, and smaller but significant percentages have hypertension, hearing impairment, heart disease, cataracts, and other vision problems (Brawley, 2006). Researchers have found that, because of the costs involved, many elderly adults who need modifications in the home environment do not make them (Pyroos & Nishita, 2003).

3. *Intellectual, social, and motor skills:* Maintenance and development of intellectual, social, and motor skills will be supported by opportunities to read, think, reflect, explore, and work with interesting materials; by opportunities for social interaction; and by opportunities for movement.

4. *Security and trust:* Safe homes and neighborhoods are essential for a sense of security and trust.

5. *A balance of social interaction and privacy:* Home environments, private or institutional, should provide private spaces as well as opportunities for social interaction.

Neuroscientists are recognizing that people with Alzheimer's disease benefit from specially planned environments to compensate for the several parts of the brain that are damaged by the disease (Brawley, 2006; Zeisel, 2006). Zeisel summarizes existing research on the brain changes that occur in Alzheimer's and the recommended environmental design features that support the functioning of people with the disease (see Exhibit 7.9).

Affected Brain Structures	Functional Deficits/Capabilities	Recommended Design Features
Parietal and occipital lobes	Loss of ability to hold a cognitive map; remaining ability to be in the present	Environments that provide all the information needed to find one's way around (because residents can't keep this information in mind)
Anterior occipital lobe and hippocampus	Out of sight, out of mind; lack of safety without enclosure	Camouflaged exit doors, electronically locked doors, windows with safety latches, high garden fences impossible to climb
Frontal lobe	Loss of sense of self; memories can be primed	Furniture and decorations that evoke memories of a person's culture, personal history, family, and achievements
Hippocampal loss and amygdala strength	Loss of ability to remember places visited in the recent past; remaining ability to hold onto moods, feelings, emotions	Varied common areas, each decorated to evoke a different mood and emotion

Hippocampus	Difficulty perceiving and processing new places, remaining hardwired memories of home and hearth	Homelike residential elements such as fireplace, eat-in country kitchen, view of garden
Frontal lobe and motor cortex of the parietal lobe	Lack of self-awareness of physical disabilities, natural sense of self control and independence	Residential elements such as hallway rails, raised toilet seats, soft materials on the floor to cushion falls
Anterior and medial temporal lobe and parietal lobe losses, sensory cortex strengths	Loss of receptive and expressive language centers; remaining senses of smell, touch, hearing	Environments in which smells of food, sounds of music, comforting soft materials, etc., indicate time for certain activities
Supra chiasmatic nuclei (SCN)	Loss of sense of time and circadian rhythms; remaining ability to sense nature, the passage of time, and the seasons out of doors	Gardens with clear pathways, lively planting areas, hard surfaces to walk on, benches to sit down, shady areas, trees, and plants

▲ **Exhibit 7.9**   Brain Deficits of Alzheimer's Disease and Recommended Design Features for the Physical Environment

SOURCE: "Table: Alzheimer's Design Performance Criteria Responsive to Cognitive Neuroscience," from *Inquiry by Design: Environment/Behavior/Neuroscience in Architecture, Interior, Landscape, and Planning* by John Zeisel. Copyright © 2006 by John Zeisel, 1984 by Cambridge University Press. Copyright © 1981 by Wadsworth, Inc. Used by permission of W. W. Norton & Company, Inc.

Critical Thinking Questions 7.3

How much thought have you given to what makes an accessible environment for people with the type of mobility impairment that Ben Watson has? How easy would it be for Ben to visit your home, your favorite restaurant, or your classroom?

IMPLICATIONS FOR SOCIAL WORK PRACTICE

This discussion of the relationship between human behavior and the physical environment suggests several practice principles:

- Where appropriate, collaborate with design professionals to ensure that specific built environments are accessible, adaptable, and comfortable; provide adequate privacy and control; provide an optimal quality and intensity of stimulation; and facilitate social interaction.

- Assess the physical environment of your social service setting. Do clients find it accessible, legible, and comfortable? Do they find that it provides adequate privacy and control? Does it provide optimal quality and intensity of sensory stimulation? If it is a residential setting, does it promote social interaction?

- Routinely evaluate the physical environments of clients—particularly those environments where problem behaviors occur—for accessibility, legibility, comfort, privacy and control, and sensory stimulation. Check your evaluation against the clients' perceptions. If you have no opportunity to see these environments, have the clients evaluate them for you. Provide space on the intake form for assessing the physical environments of clients.

• Know the physical environments of the organizations to which you refer clients. Assist referral agencies and clients in planning how to overcome any existing environmental barriers. Maximize opportunities for client input into design of their built environments.

• Be alert to the meanings that particular environments hold for clients. Recognize that people have attachments to places as well as to other people.

• When assisting clients to learn new skills, pay attention to the discontinuities between the setting where the skills are learned and the settings where they will be used.

• When designing social service programs, consider issues of optimal staffing, for both staff and clients, in particular behavior settings.

• When planning group activities, ensure the best possible fit between the spatial needs of the activity and the physical environment where the activity will occur.

• Keep the benefits of the natural environment in mind when planning both prevention and remediation programs. When possible, help clients gain access to elements of the natural environment, and where appropriate, help them plan activities in the natural environment.

• Assist clients to use cues from the physical environment (such as neighborhood landmarks, or carpet color in institutions) to simplify negotiation of that environment.

• Become familiar with technology for adapting environments to make them more accessible.

KEY TERMS

behavior settings	density	public territory
behavior settings theories	ecotherapy	secondary territory
biophilia	evidence-based design	sociofugal spaces
boundary-regulating mechanisms	natural environment	sociopetal spaces
built environment	personal space	staffing
control theories	place attachment	stimulation theories
crowding	place identity	territoriality
defensible space	primary territory	transactionalism
	programs	

ACTIVE LEARNING

1. Compare and contrast Ben Watson's place of his own with your own living space using the 11 concepts found in Exhibit 7.1.

2. Take a walking tour of your neighborhood. Does the neighborhood include defensible space design characteristics found in Exhibit 7.6? Do you note any of the design features to improve accessibility for persons with disabilities noted in Exhibit 7.8? What effects do you think the physical environment of the neighborhood might have on children, adolescents, and elderly adults?

3. Work with a small group of classmates to develop examples of primary territories, secondary territories, and public territories in your lives. What attempts do you make to protect each of these territories?

WEB RESOURCES

Academy of Neuroscience for Architecture
www.anfarch.org/

Site contains information about the academy and its projects, upcoming workshops on neuroscience and specific design environments, and links to neuroscience and architecture organizations.

American Association of People With Disabilities
www.aapd.com

Site maintained by the American Association of People With Disabilities, a national nonprofit cross-disability organization, contains information on benefits, information on disability rights, news, and links to other disability-related sites.

The Center for Health Design
www.healthdesign.org/

Site maintained by the Center for Health Design, a research and advocacy organization committed to using architectural design to transform health care settings into healing environments.

Environmental Justice in Waste Programs
http://www.epa.gov/oswer/ej/index.html

Site maintained by the U.S. Environmental Protection Agency, contains special topics in environment justice, an action agenda, resources, laws and regulations, and news and events.

Job Accommodation Network (JAN)
www.jan.wvu.edu

Site maintained by the Job Accommodation Network of the Office of Disability Employment Policy of the U.S. Department of Labor, contains ADA statutes, regulations, guidelines, technical sheets, and other assistance documents.

National Alliance to End Homelessness
www.endhomelessness.org/

Site contains facts and policy issues related to homeless families, chronic homelessness, rural homelessness, homeless youth, homeless veterans, domestic violence, and mental health and physical health; also contains case studies and best practices for ending homelessness.

CHAPTER

8

Culture

Linwood Cousins

OPENING QUESTIONS

- How does culture produce variations in human behavior?
- How does culture produce and maintain social inequality?
- How do members of nondominant groups respond to the dominant culture?

KEY IDEAS

As you read this chapter, take note of these central ideas:

1. In contemporary society, culture refers to a people's ethos (how people feel about the world around them) and worldview (how people perceive the world around them), all of which is encoded in how people construct and employ meanings that guide their perceptions and behavior in multiple contexts.

2. Features of life such as ethnic customs, traditions, values, beliefs, and notions of common sense are not static entities, but neither are they changing very rapidly.

3. Our understandings of others are always based on the understandings we have constructed both about ourselves and about how the world does and should operate. We can easily misunderstand others by using our own categories and rankings to order such realities.

4. A practice orientation is a contemporary approach to understanding culture by thinking of human action as a product, producer, and transformer of history and social structures.

5. Members of nondominant groups may respond to the dominant culture with different processes, including assimilation, accommodation, acculturation, and bicultural socialization.

6. A multidimensional understanding of culture is necessary to grasp the increasing complexity of the construction and employment of meaning regarding identities and the distribution of resources, remembering that both identities and resources are based in political, social, and economic structures and processes.

Case Study

Stan and Tina at Community High School

Community High School in Newark, New Jersey, has approximately 1,300 students, the majority of whom are Black (African American, Afro-Caribbean, and West African). Most of the students live in the community of Village Park, which has a total population of approximately 58,000 people, also predominantly Black. Village Park has a distinct social history and identity as well as distinct physical boundaries that distinguish it from less prosperous communities and schools in Newark.

Village Park evolved from a middle- and working-class Jewish community that centered around its academic institutions, such as Community High. The school generated a national reputation for academic excellence as measured by the number of graduates who went on to become doctors, lawyers, scientists, professors, and the like. But after the Newark riots of the late 1960s, Jews and other Whites started moving out. By the early 1970s, upwardly mobile middle- and working-class Black families had become the majority in Village Park. The same process has occurred in other communities, but what's interesting about Village Park is that its Black residents, like the Jewish residents who preceded them, continued to believe in the ethic of upward mobility through schooling at Community High.

(Continued)

(Continued)

Since the mid-1980s, however, Village Park and Community High have undergone another transformation. Slumps in the economy and ongoing patterns of racial discrimination in employment have reduced the income base of the community's families. Many families who were able to maintain a middle-class income moved to the suburbs as crime and economic blight encroached on the community. Increasingly, Village Park was taken over by renters and absentee landlords, along with the social problems—drug abuse, crime, school dropout—that accompany economically driven social despair.

By 1993, the population profile of Newark reflected an ethnic mix that was simultaneously Black and multiethnic. In the 1990s, the majority of Newark's residents were African American, but the city had a considerable population of other ethnic groups: Hispanics (Puerto Ricans, Colombians, Mexicans, Dominicans, etc.), Italians, Portuguese, Africans (from Nigeria, Sierra Leone, Liberia, Ghana, and other countries), Polish, and small groups of others. At the same time, the governing bodies of the city, the school system, and Community High in particular were predominantly composed of Black people. With an estimated population of 278,000 in 2008, Newark remains an ethnically diverse urban community.

The intermingling of such history and traditions has had an interesting impact on the students at Community High. Like many urban high schools all over the nation, Community High has suffered disproportionate levels of dropouts, low attendance, and violence. Yet a few parents, teachers, school staff, and community officials have tried hard to rekindle the spirit of academic excellence and social competence that are the school's tradition.

In this context, many of the students resist traditional definitions of academic success, but value success nonetheless. Consider the behaviors of Stan and Tina, both students at Community High. Stan is the more troubled and academically marginal of the two students. He is 17 years old, lives with his girlfriend who has recently had a baby, and has made a living selling drugs (which he is trying to discontinue). Stan was arrested (and released) for selling drugs some time ago. He was also under questioning for the drug-related murder of his cousin, because the police wanted him to identify the perpetrator. However, Stan has considerable social prestige at school and is academically successful when he attends school and is focused. Stan's mother—who has hammered into his head the importance of education—is a clerical supervisor, his stepfather works in a meat factory, and his biological father sells drugs. Stan has three brothers, and his mother and biological father were never married.

Among his male and female peers, Stan is considered the epitome of urban maleness and style. He is an innovator. He mixes and matches the square-toe motorcycle boots normally associated with White bikers with the brand-name shirts and jeans commonly associated with urban, rap-oriented young people of color. At the same time, Stan is respected by teachers and administrators because he understands and observes the rules of conduct preferred in the classroom and because he can do his work at a level reflecting high intelligence. Before the end of his senior year, Stan visited Howard University in Washington, D.C., and was smitten by the idea that young Black men and women were participating in university life. He said he will try very hard to go to that school after he graduates, but the odds are against him.

Tina is also 17 years old, but she is more academically successful than Stan. She ranks in the top 25 of her senior class and has been accepted into the premed program of a historically Black university. Tina talks about the lower academic performance of some of her Black peers. She sees it as a manifestation of the social distractions that seem to preoccupy Black youths—being popular and cool. On the other hand, Tina sees her successful academic performance, level of motivation, and assertive style of interacting in the classroom as part of being Black, too—taking care of business and trying to make it in this world.

Tina is an only child. Her father is an engineer, and her stepmother is a restaurant manager. Tina has never known her biological mother, and she was raised primarily by her father until about 6 years ago. They moved to Village Park from Brooklyn, New York, around that time. Tina's is the kind of family that is likely to leave Village Park, not for the suburbs but for a more productive and less hostile urban community. Tina has been raised in a community that, despite its ills, centers around Black identity and culture.

Like Stan, Tina is an innovator. She adopted modes of language, demeanor, and clothing that are seen by some as decidedly mainstream in their origins. In reality, Tina mixes the aesthetics of Black and mainstream White culture as well as the contemporary urban flavor that textures the lives of many youths today. Perhaps the results are most apparent in the way Tina mixes and matches hip-hop–influenced clothing, attitudes, and hairstyles with mainstream clothing styles and the mannerisms associated with the norms and standards of professional, middle-class occupations.

However, anyone who would approach Tina as an ally of "the system"—defining the system as the White establishment—would meet with disappointment. They would discover that in Tina's view, and perhaps in Stan's, there is nothing generally wrong with Black people and their behavior. But there is something wrong with Black individuals who do things that are not in their own best interest and consequently not in the best interest of the Black community.

Furthermore, they would hear Tina, Stan, and other students at Community High describe academic success and failure not just in terms of students' actions. They would hear these students indict uninterested and complacent teachers and staff and schools that do not understand "how to educate Black people."

SOURCE: Based on an ethnographic study of culture, race, and class during the 1992–1993 academic year in Cousins (1994). See Fordham (1996) and Ogbu (2003) for similar studies of Black high school students that confirm the persistence of the characteristics described here.

THE CHALLENGE OF DEFINING CULTURE

The case of Tina and Stan has been selected because it makes a point we often miss in the United States in general and in social work and human services in particular: Culture is right under our noses and therefore often concealed from our awareness. We are more likely to think of immigrants and non-Americans as the real examples of culture because they represent peoples who appear to be more different from us than perhaps they are. Indeed, it is much easier to think of Tina and Stan as more like you (or people you know) and me than perhaps they are. As such, the case example highlights not only race and ethnicity, but also social class, power relations, gender, popular culture, and other significant features of interactions between people and environments. Consequently, I ask you to pay attention to the subtleties of the case example as you read the presentation of the evolution and variation in the definitions of culture, including its history as a concept. If you conclude that we should not be as confident about some concepts and ideas as we are, then you get one of the main points of this chapter and of the move in social work toward evidence-based practice. In our everyday lives, we think we know what we see, but our life experiences lead us to see some things and not others. It is incredibly hard for us to take a detached viewpoint about our person–environment interactions.

The U.S. Census Bureau (2009b) tells us that there are now over 7 billion people in the world. Just over 300 million of them live in the United States. The United States is the third most populated country, behind China (just over 1.3 billion) and India (just over 1 billion), with the smallest population being in Montserrat, a small Caribbean island of 5,097 people. The U.S. population includes 199 million White (non-Hispanic) people of various ancestries, just over 46 million Hispanics/Latinos, just over 37 million African Americans/Blacks, more than 13 million Asians, and over 3 million American Indians and Alaskan Natives, with Native Hawaiian and other Pacific Islanders and other peoples constituting the rest (U.S. Census Bureau, 2009a). Finally, approximately 34.2 million, or 12% of the civilian, non-institutionalized U.S. population, are foreign born (U.S. Census Bureau, 2004).

Much diversity is concealed in this numerical portrait, but it is a good place to begin our discussion of the diverse society we live in. Given this scenario, how should we as social workers interpret the multifaceted contexts of Tina's and Stan's lives? Economics, race/ethnicity, traditions and customs, gender, political processes, immigration, popular culture, psychology, academic processes, and a host of other factors are all involved. All this and more must be considered in our discussion of culture.

> Social constructionist perspective

Over 40 years ago, Peter Berger and Thomas Luckmann (1966) stated the following: "Society is a human product. Society is an objective reality. Man is a social product" (p. 61). If you replace "society" with "culture," you get the following: Culture is a human product, culture is an objective reality, and man (or humankind) is a cultural product. These restatements suggest the enormous span of human behavior we try to make intelligible through the concept of culture.

In this chapter, you will learn how the concept of culture evolved and how it applies to the puzzle of human diversity that is so dominant in public discussions today about our multicultural society. Understanding culture as a concept and a process can help you interpret changes in what people believe and value within families, and it can help you deal with communities with large immigrant populations.

But let me caution you: Defining culture is a complex and arbitrary game. It is a word we use all the time but have trouble defining (Gardiner & Kosmitzki, 2008; Griswold, 2008). Long ago, Alfred Kroeber and Clyde Kluckhohn (1963, 1952/1978), two renowned anthropologists, cataloged more than 100 definitions of culture (see Exhibit 8.1). Definitions and discussions of culture tend to reflect the theoretical perspectives and purposes of the definers.

Like other views of culture, the one presented here has its biases. In keeping with the emphasis in this book on power arrangements, a view of culture is presented that will expose not only social differences or human variation, but also the cultural bases of various forms of inequality. This chapter looks at the ways in which variations in human behavior have led to subjugation and have become the basis of, among other things, racial, ethnic, economic, and gender oppression and inequality.

Enumeration of Social Content

- That complex whole that includes knowledge, belief, art, morals, law, custom, and any other capabilities and habits acquired by humans as members of society; the sum total of human achievement

Social Heritage/Tradition

- The learned repertory of thoughts and actions exhibited by members of a social group, independently of genetic heredity from one generation to the next
- The sum total and organization of social heritages that have acquired social meaning because of racial temperament and the historical life of the group

Rule or Way of Life

- The sum total of ways of doing and thinking, past and present, of a social group
- The distinctive way of life of a group of people; their complete design for living

Psychological and Social Adjustment and Learning

- The total equipment of technique—mechanical, mental, and moral—by use of which the people of a given period try to attain their ends

- The sum total of the material and intellectual equipment whereby people satisfy their biological and social needs and adapt themselves to their environment
- Learned modes of behavior that are socially transmitted from one generation to another within a particular society and that may be diffused from one society to another

Ideas and Values

- An organized group of ideas, habits, and conditioned emotional responses shared by members of a society
- Acquired or cultivated behavior and thought of individuals; the material and social values of any group of people

Patterning and Symbols

- A system of interrelated and interdependent habit patterns of response
- Organization of conventional understandings, manifest in act and artifact, that, persisting through tradition, characterizes a human group
- Semiotics—those webs of public meaning that people have spun and by which they are suspended
- A distinct order or class of phenomena—namely, those things and events that are dependent upon the exercise of a mental ability peculiar to the human species—that we have termed symboling; or material objects (such as tools, utensils, ornaments, amulets), acts, beliefs, and attitudes that function in contexts characterized by symboling

▲ **Exhibit 8.1** Categorical Definitions of Culture

SOURCE: Adapted from Kroeber and Kluckhohn (1952/1978), pp. 40–79.

A Preliminary Definition of Culture

Culture as we have come to know it today is rooted in definitions based on behavioral and material inventions and accomplishments. The late 19th-century German intellectual tradition, for example, distinguished between peoples who had or did not have art, science, knowledge, and social refinement (Stocking, 1968). These aspects of culture were thought to free humans from the control of nature and give them control *over* nature. The word *culture* also derives from the Latin verb *colere*—to cultivate. Note that this sense of the concept is associated with tilling the soil and our agricultural origins (Wagner, 1981, p. 21)—another way of controlling nature.

But is culture simply the opposite of nature? According to Raymond Williams (1983), "Culture is one of the two or three most complicated words in the English language" (p. 87), partly because of its intricate historical development in several European languages, but also because it is used as a concept that sometimes has quite different meanings in several incompatible systems of thought. For example, early German intellectual traditions merged with English traditions to define culture as general processes of intellectual, spiritual, and aesthetic development. A modified version of this usage is found in the contemporary field of arts and humanities, which describes culture in terms of music, literature, painting, sculpture, and the like. By contrast, U.S. tradition has produced the use of culture as we know it in contemporary social sciences to describe a particular way of life of a people, a period of time, or humanity in general. But even in this tradition, anthropologists have used the concept to refer to the material production of a people, whereas historians and cultural studies have used it to refer to symbolic systems such as language, stories, and rituals. Currently, and with the rise of postmodern theorizing, these uses of the concept overlap considerably.

A more useful definition for a multidimensional, postmodern approach to human behavior sees culture as "a set of common understandings, manifest in act and artifact. It is in two places at once: inside somebody's head

> Systems perspective;
> psychodynamic
> perspective

as understandings and in the external environment as act and artifact. If it isn't truly present in both spheres, it is only incomplete culture" (Bohannan, 1995, p. 47). **Culture,** in other words, includes both behavior (act or actions) and the material outcomes of that behavior (artifacts, or the things we construct from the material world around us—such as houses, clothing, cars, nuclear weapons, jets, and the like). It both constrains and is constrained by nature, biology, social conditions, and other realities of human existence. But at the same time, it is "inside our heads," or part of our thoughts, perceptions, and feelings. It is expressed through our emotions and thought processes, our motivations, intentions, and meanings as we live out our lives.

It is through culture that we construct meanings associated with the social and material world. Art, shelter, transportation, music, food, and clothing are material examples. The meanings we give these products influence how we use them. For example, some women's clothing is considered provocative, and pork for some people is considered "polluted." In interaction with the social world of things around us, we construct religion, race and ethnicity, family and kinship, gender roles, and complex modern organizations and institutions.

▲ **Photo 8.1** These dancers take part in a cultural festival to increase awareness of their traditions.

Here's an example from U.S. history of how human beings construct meaning in a cultural context. Slaves of African descent tended to interpret their plight and quest for freedom in terms of Judeo-Christian religious beliefs, which were pressed on them by their slaveholders but which were also adapted for better fit with their oppressive situations. They likened their suffering to that of the crucifixion and resurrection of Jesus Christ. Just like the biblical "children of Israel" (the Jews) who had to make it to the Promised Land, so it was that slaves had to find freedom in the promised land of northern cities in the United States and Canada. The association of the plight of Christians and Jews in the Bible with racial oppression lives on today in the lives of many African Americans.

You may encounter clients who believe that their social, economic, and psychological difficulties are the result of God's will, or issues of spirituality, rather than of the biopsychosocial causes we study and apply as social workers. How would you apply a multidimensional approach to human behavior in this context? Should a social work assessment include the various meanings that people construct about their circumstances? Applying a cultural perspective that considers these questions will help you find more empowering interpretations and solutions to issues you face as a social worker, especially when working with members of oppressed communities.

Here is another example. Disability in our culture seems to be about its opposite: being normal, competent, and "properly human" (R. Jenkins, 1998, p. 2). It is also about the "assumption or desirability of equality"—that is, sameness or similarity (Ingstad & Whyte, 1995, pp. 7–8). But deciding what is normal is embedded in culture. We may think that physical, mental, or cognitive disabilities are purely biological or psychological and therefore real in a scientific sense. But like race and gender, what they mean to the person possessing them and to those looking on and judging is a matter of the meanings that individuals assign to differing abilities (S. Snyder & Mitchell, 2001; Thomson, 1996). These meanings play out in social, economic, and political relations that determine the distribution of resources and generate various types of inequality.

What are your emotional responses to seeing a child in a wheelchair? How do you suppose that child feels? Can you imagine the sexual attractiveness of people whose legs dangle freely below them as they walk with metal crutches? Do you suppose they see themselves as sexual beings? What are the bodily images we hold for being "handsome" or "beautiful"? Do they correspond with the images that others hold? The point is that if the culturally diverse people who reside in the United States see life in various ways, we must expect no less regarding those with different types and levels of ability. Here again, we as social workers must use a multidimensional conceptualization of culture to guide our actions.

The above examples about African Americans and disability occur in a historical context. But history is about more than dates, names, inventions, and records of events. Rather, history is an ongoing story about the connections among ideas, communities, peoples, nations, and social transformations within the constraints of the natural world (Huynh-Nhu et al., 2008; McHale, Updegraff, Ji-Yeon, & Cansler, 2009). Think about how the historical plight of Native Americans, Asian Americans, or Hispanic Americans in the United States influences how they perceive their lives today. Think about the historical development of the terms and ideas associated with disability: "crippled," "handicapped," "disabled," "differently abled," and so on.

Now consider the history of social work. It is about more than mere dates and events. Think of the people involved in social work, such as Mary Richmond, a leader in the early charity movement, and Jane Addams, a leader in the early settlement house movement. Think about the philosophy and social practices they espoused in working with the disadvantaged people of their time. What do you know about the ethnic identity, socioeconomic status, gender, and living conditions of these social work pioneers? What about the dominant thinking and political, social, and economic trends of their time? What do you know about what may have influenced their

Conflict perspective

very different conceptions of social work and how those influences connect to the ideas and practices of contemporary social work? Now, think about Ida B. Wells-Barnett, former slave, contemporary of Jane Addams, and founder of an African American settlement house. How much do you know about her achievements? This line of thought reveals a lot about U.S. culture and how it has interacted with the development of social work.

To sum up, culture includes multiple levels of traditions, values, and beliefs, as well as social, biological, and natural acts. These processes are driven by the meanings we give to and take from them. These meanings are fortified or changed in relations between people, as history unfolds. Culture so defined is therefore not limited to the elite. It affects all of us.

Among those who are affected by culture are the students and staff at Community High School. Culture affects the social and academic process of schooling by influencing what curriculum is delivered, how, and by whom. A cultural interpretation would reveal competition and *strain,* or unequal power relations, in this process. For example, many Village Park residents and Community High students have cultural frames of reference that give adversarial meanings to requirements that students act "studiously and behave a certain way" in class. These community members and students do not necessarily dismiss education and classroom rules, but they may see education and some of its rules as part of a system of mainstream institutions that have been oppressive and insensitive toward Blacks. They see schools as dismissing their norms and points of view, and the power to change things eludes them. When a teacher at Community High asks Black students like Stan and Tina to stop talking out of turn in class, these students hear more than an impartial and benign request. Of course, any adolescent student might resent being told to stop talking by an adult authority. However, the interpretation of that request by Black students is likely to reflect their understanding about what it means to be "put down" or "dissed" in front of one's peers by an "outsider" who represents the dominant White society and does not respect the Black community.

These are complex issues, but they are part of the everyday problems social workers encounter. Further examination of what culture is and how its meaning has varied over time helps in our quest for multidimensional knowledge and skills.

TRADITIONAL UNDERSTANDINGS OF CULTURE AND VARIATION IN HUMAN BEHAVIOR

Ideas about culture have changed over time, in step with intellectual, social, economic, and political trends. Understanding these changes is integral to understanding current definitions of culture. As you learned earlier, the concept of culture has a lengthy history. But for our purposes, we will summarize some of the ideas and concepts that

Time Period	Ideas and Human Processes
18th and 19th centuries: Enlightenment and Romanticism	Rankings of logic, reason, art, technology Culture seizing nature Psychic unity of humankind
19th and 20th centuries: Variation in human behavior and development	Cultural relativism Culture as patterns and structures Culture and personality Symbols as vehicles of culture
Contemporary understandings: Integration and synthesis of processes of human development and variation since 1950s	Cultural psychology (cognitive psychology and anthropology) Meaning, ecology, and culture Political and economic systems and culture Culture as private and public Physical environment, biology, and culture Ideology, history, common sense, tradition as cultural systems

▲ **Exhibit 8.2**   Ideas and Processes Influencing the Evolution of Culture as a Concept

have become a part of our understanding of culture today. Exhibit 8.2 provides an overview of the evolution of culture as a concept since the 18th century.

Some of the influential ideas that have remained with us from the past come from the Enlightenment and Romantic intellectual traditions, dating back to the 18th century. A result of Enlightenment thinking in the early 18th century was that cultures and civilizations could be ranked according to their developed logic, reason, and technology (or mastery and use of the physical environment). Africans and Native Americans, for example, were seen as less civilized and less valuable than Europeans because their technology was not on the same scale as some European countries. Can you think of situations that demonstrate Enlightenment biases today? Is this the same framework that justifies interpreting the actions of Tina and Stan as less developed, less mature, and less rational than the actions of more mainstream students?

Another set of ideas comes from a Romantic orientation dating from the late 18th century. This orientation suggests that all people and their cultures are relatively equal in value. Differences in culture reflect different frameworks of meaning and understanding and thus result in different lifestyles and ways of living (Benedict, 1946, 1934/1989; Shweder, 1984/1995). From this tradition comes the idea of **cultural relativism** that frames contemporary multiculturalism. For example, at some point you may have been asked which is superior, Islam or Christianity, Black culture or White culture, African culture or European culture. These religions and cultures differ in content and meaning, but is one better than the other? If so, what is the standard of measure, and in whose interest is it developed and enforced?

Conflict perspective

Some today dismiss cultural relativism as "politically correct" thinking, but it does have practical value. For instance, as a social worker, you could contrast the behavior of Tina and Stan with that of successful White students to identify differences between them. How will doing so help Tina, Stan, or the successful White students—or any other students, for that matter? In the context of the recent conflict between the United States and Iraq, one may question the value of Islam compared to Christianity or Eastern culture compared to Western. Perhaps it is more productive to measure each of these against some mutually relevant standard, such as how well the students will be able to succeed in their own communities, or how well a religion or culture serves humanity. The point here is not that we should apply different standards to different people. Rather, in social work at least, to start where individuals are, to understand their points of view and the context of their lives, has been an effective method of helping them gain control of their lives.

In the United States today, we still see conflicts between Enlightenment thinking and the cultural relativism of Romanticism. Romanticism is reflected by those who call for respect for diversity in our multicultural society. But the premises of Enlightenment thinking have a great influence on our everyday understanding of culture. Again, consider recent public debates over crime, welfare, health insurance, Islam, and other issues that associate historical and contemporary social problems with people's race/ethnicity, religion, and socioeconomic status. Some social scientists and the popular media frequently express mainstream, Enlightenment-oriented values, attitudes, and morals in examining these issues, assigning more value to some things than to others (Huntington, 1996; Lakoff, 2006; McWhorter, 2000; C. Murray & Herrnstein, 1994; O'Reilly, 2007; J. Q. Wilson, 1995).

Another outcome of such thinking is **biological determinism**—the attempt to differentiate social behavior on the basis of biological and genetic endowment. One form of biological determinism is based on racial identity. For example, a person's intellectual performance is associated with brown skin and other physical differences believed to be related to race. *Race,* however, is a social construction based on biological differences in appearance. No relationship between differences in racial identity and differences in cognitive and intellectual capacities has been proved as biologically based. There is no verifiable evidence that the fundamental composition and functioning of the brain differs between Blacks and Whites, Asians and Hispanics, or whatever so-called racial groups you can identify and compare (S. Gould, 1981; Mullings, 2005). Yet many still believe that race makes people inherently different. Such false associations are a vestige of Enlightenment thinking.

As a social work student, you can recognize the maligned power and influence of such tendencies. Thinking in terms of natural, ordained, and inevitable differences based on race reinforces the social tendency to think in terms of "we-ness" and "they-ness," which often has unfortunate effects (Jandt, 2010). It leads to what has come to be called **othering**, or labeling people who fall outside of your own group as abnormal, inferior, or marginal. In your personal and professional lives, pay attention to the images and thoughts you use to make sense of the economic, social, and behavioral difficulties of Black people or other ethnic groups. Pay attention to the characterizations of English-speaking and non–English-speaking immigrants, or of legal and illegal immigrants.

CONTEMPORARY/POSTMODERN UNDERSTANDINGS OF CULTURE AND VARIATION IN HUMAN BEHAVIOR

Twentieth- and twenty-first century scholars of culture inherited both advances and limitations in thought from scholars of previous centuries. With these challenges in mind, anthropologist Franz Boas (1940/1948) encouraged us to understand cultural differences as environmental differences interacting with the accidents of history. Boas's ideas, along with those developed by others, have led to the basic axioms about culture found in Exhibit 8.3 (Kottak, 1994, 2008).

- Culture is learned through social interaction.
- A society may have customary practices, but not all members have the same knowledge of them or attach the same significance to them.
- Culture seizes nature. That is, humans seek to control nature (in the form of climate, oceans and rivers, etc.) and shape it according to their own needs and interests.
- Culture is patterned, culture is symbolic, and culture is both adaptive and maladaptive.

▲ **Exhibit 8.3** Basic Axioms About Culture

SOURCE: Based on Kottak (1994, 2008).

Before we go further, it is important to note that many contemporary culture scholars suggest that environmental differences interacting with accidents of history have produced three major types of cultures in recent centuries (see Griswold, 2008; Leeder, 2004). They suggest the name *traditional culture,* or *premodern culture,* to describe preindustrial societies based on subsistence agriculture. They argue that this type of culture was markedly different from *modern culture,* which arose with the 18th-century Enlightenment and is characterized by rationality, industrialization, urbanization, and capitalism. **Postmodernism** is the term many people use to describe contemporary culture. They suggest that global electronic communications are the foundation of postmodern culture, exposing people in advanced capitalist societies to media images that span place and time, and allow them to splice together cultural elements from these different times and places (Griswold, 2008). Exhibit 8.4 presents the primary characteristics usually attributed to these three types of culture. While culture scholars who make these distinctions often present these three types as a historical timeline, running from traditional to modern to postmodern culture, traits of all three types of culture can in fact be found in advanced capitalist societies today, and often become the source of contemporary culture wars within societies. Furthermore, many nonindustrial and newly industrializing societies can be characterized as either traditional or modern cultures.

> Social constructionist perspective; social behavioral perspective

Let's return now to Boas's axioms (Exhibit 8.3). Why are these axioms important for social workers? Three things come to mind if we are going to work effectively and sensitively with people like Stan and Tina and communities whose norms vary from mainstream norms:

Characteristic	Traditional Culture	Modern Culture	Postmodern Culture
Role of rationality	Positive value for irrational aspects of life; religious traditions superior to reason	Supreme value of rationality; rational control of nature	Questions the limits of rationality
Status	Status based on blood line; hierarchy as natural order; patriarchy	Status based on achievement; egalitarianism	Emphasis on difference, not power
Source of authority	Religious authority	Nation-state; science	Globalization; national authority breaks down
Stability and change	Stability and order valued; order based on religion	Progress valued	Unpredictability and chaos
Unit of value	Communal values	Individualism	Diversity: multiplicity of perspectives and voices
Life structure	Agrarian, subsistence agriculture	Industrialization, urbanization, capitalism, commodity fetishism, specialization of function	Electronic communications, simulation, mass consumption

▲ **Exhibit 8.4** Characteristics of Traditional, Modern, and Postmodern Culture

1. We must be able to understand how mainstream beliefs, customs, traditions, values, and social institutions, comprising "normal" social behavior, fit into the lives of our clients, especially those whose behaviors and traditions are considered "abnormal."

2. We must recognize that beliefs, customs, values, traditions, and social institutions vary in degrees of complexity from one society to another. People have a tendency to consider cultures other than their own to be aberrations from a universal norm or standard that all people should meet. For example, human service norms and standards in Canada differ from U.S. norms and standards. Two questions evolve from this point: Which norms and values are acceptable as universal, and what criteria are these norms based on? Are these universals adaptive, or functional, under all social, economic, political, and environmental conditions?

3. Finally, we must pay attention to the development of emotional and cognitive frameworks as elements of society and culture. We must avoid the trap of confounding emotional and cognitive capacities with hierarchies of race, ethnicity, gender, and other ways of ranking humankind.

A few additional concepts help round out our discussion of past and present conceptions of culture:

- *Ideology:* **Ideology** is the dominant idea about the way things are and should work. Problems of inequality and discrimination arise when ideological aspects of the social, economic, and political structures of society support the exploitation and subjugation of people. Institutionalized gender bias, for example, is the systematic incorporation into the culture's structures of ideologies that directly and indirectly support the subordination of women (most typically) or men. These subordinating elements are built into the everyday, taken-for-granted way the culture's members live their lives.

> Conflict perspective

- *Ethnocentrism:* Through cross-cultural comparisons, anthropologists have demonstrated that Western culture is not universal. They have exposed our tendency to elevate our own ethnic group and its social and cultural processes over others, a tendency known as **ethnocentrism.** For instance, theories of personality development are based on Western ideals of individuality and reliance on objective science rather than Eastern ideals of collective identity and reliance on subjective processes such as spirituality (Kottak, 2008; Matsumoto, 2007; Shweder & LeVine, 1984/1995; Whiting & Whiting, 1975).

> Social constructionist perspective; psychodynamic perspective

- *Cultural symbols:* A **symbol** is something, verbal or nonverbal, that comes to stand for something else. The letters *d-o-g* have come to stand for the animal we call *dog;* golden arches forming a large *M* stand for McDonald's restaurants or hamburgers; and water in baptism rites stands for something sacred and holy, which moves a person from one state of being to another (D'Andrade, 1984/1995; Kottak, 2008). But as Conrad Kottak (1996) points out, "Water is not intrinsically holier than milk, blood or other liquids. A natural thing has been arbitrarily associated with a particular meaning for Catholics" and other religious groups (p. 26). Race, ethnicity, and gender are symbols that can be thought of in this way as well. For instance, beyond biological differences, what comes to mind when you think of a girl or woman? What about a boy or man? How do the images, thoughts, and feelings you possess about gender influence how you interact with boys and girls, men and women? Gendered thinking undoubtedly influences your assessment of persons, even those you have not actually met. In short, symbols shape perception, or the way a person sees, feels, and thinks about the world, and they communicate a host of feelings, thoughts, beliefs, and values that people use to make sense of their daily lives (Ortner, 1973; Wilkin, 2009). They are vehicles of culture that facilitate social action. The role of symbols in culture raises questions that social workers face all the time: Do we really know what's going on inside people's heads—what they mean and intend when, for example, they use concepts such as "discipline," "being on time," "budgeting," or "love"? The idea that symbols express meaning within a culture is part of many recent models of practice in social work and psychology. For example, social constructionists focus on how narratives and stories can bring about emotional and behavioral changes in clinical social work practice.

- *Worldview and ethos:* A **worldview** is an idea of reality, a "concept of nature, of self, of society" (Geertz, 1973, p. 126). **Ethos** is the "tone, character, and quality of [people's] life, its moral and aesthetic style and mood; it is the underlying attitude toward themselves and their world that life reflects" (Geertz, 1973, p. 126). Worldview is associated with the cognitive domain, what we think about things; ethos is associated more with the emotional or affective and stylistic dimensions of behavior—how we feel about things (Ortner, 1984, p. 129). Like Stan and Tina, recent Hispanic/Latino and African immigrants are adept at using symbols such as clothing, language, and music to convey specific feelings and perceptions that express their worldview and ethos. Exhibit 8.5 compares some additional symbols that convey differences in worldview and ethos.

- *Cultural innovation:* Culture is not static; it is adapted, modified, and changed through interactions over time. This process is known as **cultural innovation.** For example, Stan and Tina were described earlier as innovators. Both restyle mainstream clothing to fit with their sense of meaning and with the values of their peers and their community. In addition, in the classroom and with peers, Stan and Tina can switch between Standard English and Black English. The mode of language they use depends on the social and political message or identity they want to convey to listeners. We see economic cultural innovation with immigrants, both recent and in the past. Many focus on and successfully exploit areas of the U.S. economy that are relatively underutilized by native populations—for example, engineering; computer science; and for better or worse, lawn care and maintenance.

- *Cultural conflict:* The symbols we use are arbitrary. They can mean one thing to you and something different to others. Therefore, **cultural conflict** over meanings can easily arise. For example, jeans that hang low on the hips of adolescents and young adults generally signify an ethos of hipness, toughness, and coolness. This is the style, mood, and perspective of a particular generation. (Some of us who are professionals, or soon will be, have a similar need to fit in with the particular ethos and worldview that is important to us and to the people with whom we interact. We are likely to choose an entirely different style of clothing.) However, the clothing, music, and language of politically and economically disadvantaged Black and Hispanic/Latino adolescents convey a different symbolic meaning to law enforcers, school officials, parents, and even social workers. In today's sociopolitical climate, these authority figures are likely to perceive low-slung jeans not only as signs of hip-hop culture, but also as signs of drug and gang culture or as a form of social rebellion, decadence, or incivility.

> Conflict perspective

In sum, culture is both public and private. It has emotional and cognitive components, but these play out in public in our social actions. Symbols are a way of communicating private meaning through public or social action. Furthermore, people's actions express their worldview (how they think about the world) and their ethos (how they feel about the world)—just as Tina and Stan do when they alternate between Black and mainstream styles.

These concepts have great relevance to social work. For example, arguments accompanying welfare reform legislation in the United States in the late 1990s represented shifting meanings regarding poverty, single parenting, and work. During the 1960s, it was considered society's moral duty to combat poverty by assisting the poor. Today, poverty does not just mean a lack of financial resources for the necessities of life; to many people, it symbolizes laziness, the demise of family values, and other characteristics that shade into immorality. Thus, to help people who are poor is now often purported to hurt them by consigning them to dependency and immoral behavior.

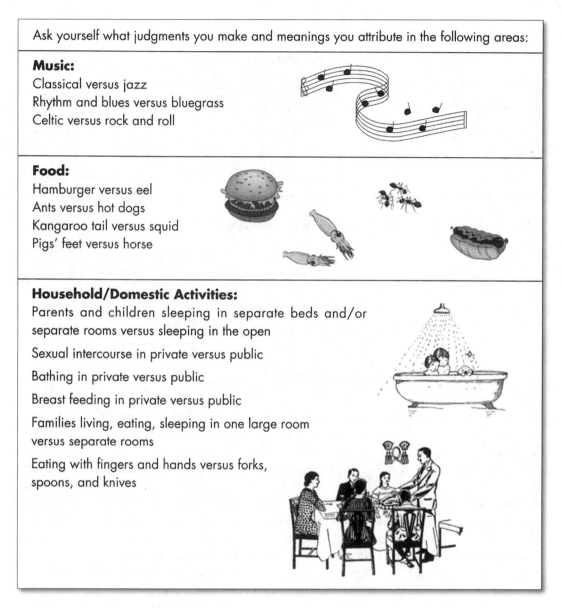

Ask yourself what judgments you make and meanings you attribute in the following areas:

Music:
Classical versus jazz
Rhythm and blues versus bluegrass
Celtic versus rock and roll

Food:
Hamburger versus eel
Ants versus hot dogs
Kangaroo tail versus squid
Pigs' feet versus horse

Household/Domestic Activities:
Parents and children sleeping in separate beds and/or separate rooms versus sleeping in the open

Sexual intercourse in private versus public

Bathing in private versus public

Breast feeding in private versus public

Families living, eating, sleeping in one large room versus separate rooms

Eating with fingers and hands versus forks, spoons, and knives

▲ **Exhibit 8.5**   Sociocultural Creations

As social workers, we depend on the NASW Code of Ethics for professional guidance in negotiating these shifts. But what is the source of the values and beliefs that guide our personal lives? And what happens when what we believe and value differs from our clients' beliefs and values? These questions raise the issue of how we form and act on meanings derived from our private cultural leanings that are part of our professional lives. Exhibit 8.6 demonstrates several cultural conflicts that may arise as our personal social habits confront the principles, values, and ethics of professional social workers.

Critical Thinking Questions 8.1

When you think of your day-to-day life, do you think you live in a traditional, modern, or postmodern culture? Explain. What do you see as the benefits and costs of each of these types of culture?

What are your beliefs about the following interactions with clients and colleagues?

Continuum

Most Professional (Formal) .... Least Professional (Informal)

Greetings by handshake .... hugging .... kissing

Use of last name/title .... first name .... nickname
(Mr., Ms., Dr.)

Authority by credentials .... age, experience, ... religion/politics
(BSW, MSW, etc.)   gender, marital status

Sharing no personal .... pertinent information .... open-ended,
information   mutual sharing

Confidentiality .... sharing with professionals/ .... sharing with friends/
                           family   community members

▲ **Exhibit 8.6**   Customary Social Habits Interacting With Social Work Principles, Values, and Ethics on a Continuum

A POSTMODERN, HOLISTIC APPLICATION OF CULTURE

The discussion to this point has attempted to assist social workers in expanding their understanding of the multidimensional nature of human behavior by examining what culture is and how thinking about culture has evolved. What follows is a discussion of how to apply a multidimensional concept of culture.

To increase our understanding of culture and human behavior, we might ask how it is that Tina's and Stan's ways of living are different from our own. We can apply the same question to immigrants and other groups that differ from the mainstream norm. We need to recognize that their lives may be based on values, beliefs, and rationalizations that we don't fully understand. We could try to understand them, but would we succeed by applying our own cultural frame of reference, our own worldview and ethos? If we limit our quest to our own terms, to our authority and power as social workers to define who they are, what do we achieve? We are likely to learn more about ourselves and our standards than about people like Stan and Tina. The most we can learn about these students by looking at them from our own frame of reference is how they compare to us. The comparison, however, is in our terms, not theirs. For example, we may well say that Stan is at greater than average risk of failing socially and academically. But he might say that he is more successful than most at negotiating the oppressive structures of school and society.

Ask yourself what would happen if we as social workers compared the views and feelings of clients regarding their lives and problems with our own views and feelings. What would we have to give up and what would we and our clients gain? We need a multidimensional perspective of diversity and human behavior to ground our professional actions in this way. But what should a multidimensional approach to a culture analysis consist of, and what would it be trying to explain? These are important questions for social workers.

A Practice Orientation

Forty or more years ago, the problems of Village Park and Community High School would have been explained largely in terms of a culture of poverty. The term **culture of poverty** was originally used to bring attention to the way of life developed by poor people to adapt to the difficult circumstances of their lives. Proponents of this theoretical orientation twisted it to suggest that Black schools and communities were impoverished because of Black people's own beliefs, values, traditions, morals, and frames of reference. Mainstream culture's racism and discrimination were not considered to be decisive factors. That Black people faced *redlining*, a practice that forced them to buy or rent homes only in Black communities, was not considered to be a factor. That Black people were working in low-income jobs despite qualifications for better ones was likewise not considered to be a factor. That major colleges and universities were denying admission to qualified Black applicants was not considered to be a factor either. The list could go on. The culture of poverty orientation was used to argue both for and against publicly financed social programs. From time to time, some of my students even today use a culture of poverty line of reasoning to explain people on welfare, poor single parents, and other problems of inner cities.

Contemporary and postmodern culture scholars (anthropologists, sociologists, psychologists, political scientists, social workers, economists) have also adopted some of the tenets of past theorizing. However, they have taken the better parts of it to develop what has come to be called postmodern and **practice orientations** (Berger & Luckmann, 1966; Bourdieu, 1977; Giddens, 1979; Ortner, 1989, 1996, 2006; Sahlins, 1981). *Practice* as used here is different from its use in social work. This theoretical orientation seeks to explain what people do as thinking, intentionally acting persons who face the impact of history and the restraints of structures that are embedded in our society and culture. It asks how social systems shape, guide, and direct people's values, beliefs, and behavior. But it also asks how people, as human actors or agents, perpetuate or shape social systems. The underlying issues, in sum, are about understanding two things:

1. How, through culture, human beings construct meaning, intentionality, and public behavior

2. How human beings produce systemic cultural change or adapt to and maintain the culture

The hope of the practice orientation is that—by reflection on history, structure, and agency—we can develop a deeper understanding of inequalities based on race, ethnicity and social class, and gender relations, among other sociocultural processes.

> Social constructionist perspective; conflict perspective

The issue of poverty offers one example of how the practice orientation can be applied. The practice orientation would not blame poverty's prevalence and influence in Tina's and Stan's community solely on the failings of individuals. Rather, it would seek to identify the structural factors—such as low-income jobs, housing segregation, and racism—that impede upward mobility. It would also seek to understand how poor African Americans perceive and contribute to their conditions; how nonpoor, non-Black Americans perceive and contribute to the conditions of poor African Americans; and how all of these perceptions and actions shape the lives and influence the upward mobility of poor African Americans. Thus, this perspective would ask, are poor African Americans as different in values, beliefs, and attitudes as other people think they are? Is there a "culture" of poverty, or do people in dire circumstances adapt their values and beliefs to the demands of survival? These are matters of considerable importance and complexity.

Other examples of the types of questions fruitfully addressed through the practice orientation apply to Stan's situation: How have Stan's family and community influenced his behavior in general and his response to racism and classism in school in particular? How have Stan's own responses contributed to his subordination as a Black youth, thereby leaving certain oppressive structures in society unchanged? Likewise, how have the values and beliefs encoded through the rules and regulations in public schools like Community High served to perpetuate or reproduce various forms of structural or systemic subjugation? What are the symbolic meanings of school and education, and what role do they play in Stan's behavior? From our position as educated Americans with many mainstream values, we would tend to see schools as intrinsically good because they are largely about academic growth rather than social and cultural relations. But is this the whole, multidimensional picture?

The same questions apply to social work. How have the values, beliefs, and practices of the profession helped to maintain the profession and society as they are? When we label a person or group as having a social problem or dysfunction, are we perpetuating or reproducing subjugation in creating a truth or fact? For better or worse, when social science categorizes human functioning, it does just that. When we label the people we have failed to help as resistant, unmotivated, and pathological, are we carelessly overlooking the ineffectiveness of our modes of understanding and intervention? Are we blaming the victim and reproducing his or her victimization? These and other questions are important for all of us to ponder.

History, social structure, and human agency are key elements in a practice orientation. This chapter has tried to demonstrate how some life events reflect the intertwined influences of history, social structure, and human agency. These kinds of interactions sometimes reflect social strain and sometimes social solidarity. Sometimes they reflect a conflict between the objective and the subjective nature of what we do and believe. In any case, the relationship between human action and social systems is never simple in a political world.

Systems perspective

History, Social Structure, and Human Agency

History is made by people, but it is made within the constraints of the social, economic, political, physical, and biological systems in which people are living. History includes, but is not totally defined by, chains of events and experiences to which people simply react. However, to understand human diversity and to unearth sociocultural forms of oppression, exploitation, and subjugation, we must take into account people's diverse motives and actions as they make and transform the world in which they live. We must listen to the memories of official and unofficial observers. We must hear those voices that are represented in the official records and those that are not. We must listen to clients as much as to social workers.

Social Structure implies the ordered forms and systems of human behavior existing in public life (e.g., capitalism, kinship, public education). It also includes cognitive, emotional, and behavioral frameworks that are mapped onto who we are as people. Structure influences how we construct ourselves—that is, what we make of ourselves based on what things mean to us. We carry forth meanings, values, and beliefs through social, economic, and political practices in our everyday, personal lives and the institutions in which we participate. We reproduce structures when we assume the rightness of our values, beliefs, and meaning and see no need to change them. When this process dominates, **cultural hegemony** results—the dominance of a particular way of seeing the world. Most observers of culture in the United States would agree that it is based on the hegemony of a Euro-American, or Anglo, worldview. People in many other parts of the world have observed the hegemony of the U.S. worldview. As the artist Diego Rivera said in 1931 and Mike Davis (2000, p. ix) reiterates in his book on Latino influences on U.S. cities, "When you say 'America' you refer to the territory stretching between the icecaps of the two poles. So to hell with your barriers and frontier guards!" As the quote implies, those whose cultures are overtaken by another culture often resent the hegemony. Chapter 9 will deal with trends and patterns in contemporary social institutions and social structures, at the national and global levels.

Human agency asserts that people are not simply puppets, the pawns of history and structure; people are also active participants, capable of exercising their will to shape their lives. Thus, although racism is structured into society, it is not so completely dominant over Tina and Stan that they have no room for meaningful self-expression in their social and political lives.

Humanistic perspective

Human agency helps to counteract cultural hegemony as well. Consider the influence of African American urban youth culture. Rap music and clothing styles that originated with Black teens like Tina and Stan have become popular with White, middle-class young people. This is a way individuals and groups exercise agency by constructing culture. They invest the world with their own subjective order, meaning, and value. They rely on their frame of mind or worldview to consciously and unconsciously make choices and take action. They construct social and political identities that help them resist and contest cultural hegemony.

However, no individual or group is a fully free agent. All are constrained by external factors such as climate, disease, natural resources, and population size and growth—although we may be able to modify these constraints through technology (Diamond, 1999). Examples of technologies that modify facts of biology and nature are medicines, agricultural breakthroughs, climate-controlled homes, telecommunications, transportation, and synthetic products that replace the use of wood in furniture and related items.

A contemporary example of the interface of culture and technology is the cell or mobile phone. Scholars are still not sure of its impact, but they have begun to identify the aesthetic or fashion value of the phone on the one hand—the styles and colors and what they mean to and convey about the owner (Goggin, 2008). Its practical function, on the other hand, points to enhanced communication, invasiveness, and annoyance due to its ubiquity. Add to this the role of the camera in the phone in documenting personal events such as family reunions, and misconduct of, say, the police against citizens. But to raise prior questions, does the technology shape us—our culture—or does our culture shape the technology? How has cell phone technology shaped social work, for example? Is a practitioner assisted by the phone as a security device, or is the practitioner's workload unnecessarily extended by being available relatively endlessly? If core practices of social work change as a result of this technology, what does that mean for clients?

In sum, human agents are "skilled and intense strategizers" (Ortner, 1996, p. 20). We are constantly stretching the process by which we live and define ourselves. But we do so within the constraints of structures or forces that can never wholly contain us. Human agency is a major source of hope and motivation for social workers who encounter people, organizations, and systems that seem unable to break away from the constraints of daily life.

Cultural Maintenance, Change, and Adaptation

Tina's and Stan's experiences with mainstream schooling provide a good example of how cultural structures are maintained, how they change, and how they adapt. School systems are centered on the norms, values, and beliefs

---

Politics and Law

Legislation, laws, and regulations regarding attendance and social behavior; educational content; segregation/desegregation; school funding

Family

Socialization regarding gender roles and relations; sex; discipline; health/hygiene/nutrition; recreation; emotional support and development

Religion

Prayer; holidays; family and personal morality and ethics

Social Structure and Economics

Status, opportunities, and rewards associated with knowledge, grades, and credentials; individual versus collective achievement; appropriate versus inappropriate behavior and social skills; media, market, and popular cultural trends and factors

Community

Ethnic representation and attitudes; economic resources and stability; levels of crime

---

▲ **Exhibit 8.7**   Sociocultural Factors in the Construction of Education and Schooling

preferred by those who have had the power to decide what is or is not appropriate to learn and use in our lives. Some things we learn in school fit well with the needs of industry. Other things we learn fit well with the needs of our social and political institutions. These include the values and workings of family and community life and of local, state, and national governing bodies. From the outside looking in, schools look like benign or innocent institutions that are simply about academics and education. Yet which academic subjects are taught, how they are taught, who teaches them, and how they are to be learned involve an assertion of someone's values and beliefs, whether right or wrong, whether shared by many or few. Exhibit 8.7 lists some of the factors involved in the cultural construction of schooling. As you can see, schooling's influence extends far beyond reading, writing, and arithmetic.

Even in the face of evidence that schools do not work for many of us, they persist. Education is strongly correlated with economic and social success. Therefore, ineffective schools play a role in the persistent poverty we have faced in this country. In addition, if you examine how girls are treated in schools, you will discover correlations with women's subjugation in other domains as well. The experiences of immigrants in schools also raise issues regarding cultural processes in schools and beyond.

Culture provides stability to social life, but it changes over time. It does not change rapidly, however. First, we will look at some ideas about how culture produces stability, and then we will turn to how culture changes over time through immigration and processes of negotiating multicultural community life.

Common Sense, Tradition, and Custom

Over time, the ways in which families, schools, cities, and governments do things in the United States have come to seem natural to us. They seem to fit with the common sense, traditions, and customs of most people who live here.

Keep in mind, however, that **common sense** is a cultural system. It is what people have come to believe everyone in a community or society should know and understand as a matter of ordinary, taken-for-granted social competence. It is based on a set of assumptions that are so unself-conscious that they seem natural, transparent, and an undeniable part of the structure of the world (Geertz, 1983; Swidler, 1986). For example, rain is wet; fire burns; and, as I hear more and more in the general population, as well as from many Community High students, "one can't make it without an education!" In addition, "Common sense tells you that you gotta speak English to make it in America," you might overhear a citizen of Charlotte, North Carolina, say about the Mexicans who have recently come to the city.

Yet not everyone—especially not members of oppressed, subjugated, or immigrant groups within a society—is likely to share these common schemes of meaning and understanding. Thus, common sense becomes self-serving for those who are in a position of power to determine what it is and who has it. We believe common sense tells us what actions are appropriate in school or in any number of other contexts. But, as a part of culture, common sense is subject to historically defined standards of judgment related to maleness and femaleness, parenting, poverty, work, education, and mental and social (psychosocial) functioning, among other categories of social being. For better or worse, common sense helps to maintain cultures and societies as they are.

We need to approach traditions and customs with the same caution with which we approach common sense. Traditions are cultural beliefs and practices so taken for granted that they seem inevitable parts of life (Swidler, 1986). **Customs,** or cultural practices, come into being and persist as solutions to problems of living (Goodenough, 1996). **Tradition** is a process of handing down from one generation to another particular cultural beliefs and practices. In particular, it is a process of ratifying particular beliefs and practices by connecting them to selected social, economic, and political practices. When this is done well, traditions become so taken for granted that they seem "natural" parts of life, as if they have always been here and as if we cannot live without them (Hobsbawm, 1983; Swidler, 1986; R. Williams, 1977). Some traditions and customs are routine; others, such as special ceremonies, are extraordinary. They are not necessarily followed by everyone in the culture, but they seem necessary and ordained, and they stabilize the culture. They are, in a sense, collective memories of the group. They reflect meanings at a particular moment in time and serve as guides for the present and future (I. W. Chung, 2006; McHale et al., 2009).

Traditions and customs are selective, however. They leave out the experiences, memories, and voices of some group members while highlighting and including others. African American students generally do not experience schooling as reflecting their traditions and customs. In many cases, Latino or Hispanic immigrants in Charlotte will not, either. Stan, Tina, and their peers often raised this point in their classes at Community High, and several residents of Village Park have been raising similar issues for many years. Latino/Hispanic families express similar concerns.

To reflect Village Park residents' traditions and customs, Community High would have to respect and understand the use of Nonstandard English as students are learning Standard English. Literature and history classes would make salient connections between European traditions and customs and those

▲ **Photo 8.2** These mothers from different cultural backgrounds may have some different traditions and customs regarding child rearing, but they find their toddlers have much in common.

of West Africans, Afro-Caribbeans, and contemporary African Americans. In addition, processes for including a student's family in schooling would include kinship bonds that are not based on legalized blood ties or the rules of state foster care systems. What would a school social worker have to learn to assist schools and immigrant families in having a more successful experience in school?

Traditions and customs, moreover, play a role in the strain that characterizes shifts from old patterns and styles of living to new ones in schools and other institutions in society. To survive, groups of people have to bend their traditions and customs without letting them lose their essence. Nondominant ethnic, gender, religious, and other groups in the United States often have to assimilate or accommodate their host culture if they are to share in economic and political power. In fact, the general survival of the traditions and customs of nondominant groups requires adaptability.

Traditions and customs are parts of a cultural process that are changing ever so subtly and slowly but at times abruptly. Sometimes groups disagree about these changes, and some members deny that they are occurring because they believe they should still do things the old way. Social workers have to understand a group's need to hold onto old ways. They do this to protect their worldview about what life means and who they are as a people.

Immigration

It would be foolish to deny that the United States is a nation of immigrants (Parrillo, 2009). Immigration to this land began with the gradual migration of prehistoric peoples that anthropologists envision, and picked up speed when Columbus and other Europeans arrived from across the Atlantic Ocean. It continued with the involuntary arrival of Africans and the voluntary and semi-voluntary arrivals of various European ethnic groups. Later came Asian peoples and others. Forceful extension of the nation's borders and political influence incorporated Hispanics and Pacific Islanders. There have been many subsequent waves of immigration, with a great influx late in the 20th century and continuing today. Now, more than ever, people are coming to the United States from all over the world. Today, we define cultural diversity as a relatively new issue. But the nation's fabric has long included a rich diversity of cultures (Hing, 2004).

Although diversity has been a feature of life in the United States for centuries, immigration is an especially prominent feature of society today. According to U.S. Census estimates, 34.2 million foreign-born residents now reside in the United States (U.S. Census Bureau, 2002a, 2002b, 2004). They represent 12% of the total U.S. population of 300 million. Over 53% of these immigrants were born in Latin America in general, and 37.7% were born in Central America in particular. They are agents of what the media have called the "browning" of the United States. As for the remaining immigrants, 25.4% of all foreign-born U.S. residents were born in Asia, 13.6% in Europe, and 7.5% in other regions of the world. One of every three foreign-born is a naturalized citizen (U.S. Census Bureau, 2002a, 2002b).

These population profiles represent relatively recent immigration trends. For example, 18% of immigrants alive today entered the United States since 2000—39.5% in the 1990s, 28.3% entered in the 1980s, 16.2% in the 1970s, and the remaining 16.0% arrived before 1970 (U.S. Census Bureau, 2002a, 2002b). Each group brings with it its own cultural traditions and languages, which influence its worldview; ethos; and social, economic, and political beliefs and values. Nevertheless, foreign-born people have a few characteristics in common. For example, they are more likely to live in central cities of metropolitan areas and to live in larger households than nonimmigrants, those age 25 and over are roughly 67% as likely as nonimmigrants to have graduated from high school, and 6 million (17.1%) are in poverty (U.S. Census Bureau, 2002a, 2002b, 2004).

Although many immigrants realize their dream of economic opportunity, many also (but not all) encounter resistance from the native-born. Let us consider the case of immigrants from Latin American countries (Central and South America and the Caribbean). This group recently surpassed African Americans as the largest minority in the United States and is therefore the group that social workers are increasingly likely to encounter. New York City, Los Angeles, Chicago, San Antonio, Houston, and other southwestern cities are traditional sites for the settlement of Hispanic/Latino immigrants. However, they are also settling in increasing numbers in growing metropolitan areas such as Charlotte, where I formerly resided. Charlotte is centered in a metropolitan region of over a million residents. Prior to the financial crisis of 2007–2010, it had a vibrant economy and was the second-largest banking center in the nation (home to Bank of America). People came to Charlotte because economic opportunities abound.

Like other Americans, Hispanic/Latino immigrants come to Charlotte to get a piece of the economic pie. However, Hispanic/Latino immigrants face a unique set of circumstances. One often hears complaints in Charlotte about "foreigners taking our jobs." African Americans and Latinos/Hispanics face social conflicts over lifestyles in the low-income neighborhoods they share. Social service and law enforcement agencies scramble for Spanish-language workers and interpreters. Banks decry the fact that many new Spanish-language residents don't trust banks and consequently don't open checking and savings accounts.

This situation can be thought of from different perspectives. Is immigration, or are immigrants, inherently a problem? Or are they perceived as a problem because of what they mean in the economic, political, and social context of these cities? Who should be more concerned about losing cultural ground: Hispanic/Latino immigrants or long-term U.S. residents? Notions of common sense, tradition, and custom apply in this situation. An understanding of cultural processes also helps social workers interpret the issues they encounter in practice.

Processes of Cultural Change

In multicultural societies, cultural change can be understood in terms of four processes: assimilation, accommodation, acculturation, and bicultural socialization. They describe the individual's or group's response to the dominant culture and may have implications for clients' well-being.

- *Assimilation:* **Assimilation** is the process in which the cultural uniqueness of the minority group is abandoned, and its members try to blend invisibly into the dominant culture (Kottak, 2008). Some culture scholars have noted a prevailing assimilation ideology that asserts the ideal of Anglo conformity (Gordon, 1964). In keeping with this view, some people have argued that the root of the problems faced by African Americans and by economically marginal immigrants is that they have not assimilated successfully. This argument is oversimplified. First, to the extent that discrimination is based on obvious features such as skin color or lack of facility with Standard English, the ability to assimilate is limited. Second, capitalist economies and societies arbitrarily select different group characteristics as desirable at different times. Historically, we have done this in part through immigration policies that admit some groups but not others. Many minorities, especially first-generation immigrants, often resist giving up parts of their ethnic identity in order to protect their sense of meaning and purpose in life.

- *Accommodation:* **Accommodation** is more common than assimilation in multicultural, multiethnic society in the United States. Accommodation is the process of partial or selective cultural change. Nondominant groups follow the norms, rules, and standards of the dominant culture only in specific circumstances and contexts. When Punjabi Sikh children attended school in Stockton, California, in the 1980s, they generally followed the rules of the school (Gibson, 1988). They did not, however, remove their head coverings, socialize with peers of both sexes as is normal in mainstream U.S. society, or live by U.S. cultural standards at home. Some of the Muslim students at Community High could be compared to the Punjabis. Black Muslim girls at Community High, for example, refuse to remove their head coverings or customary long gowns to attend school, even though the school asks them to do so. Increasingly, Latino/Hispanic immigrants and native citizens are refusing to give up Spanish in many settings, even though they can and will speak English when necessary. Similar stories continue to turn up in local and national newspapers about students whose Islamic religious attire conflicts with school norms and rules, especially in light of the conflict between the United States and terrorists who claim an Islamic background.

- *Acculturation:* As mentioned in Chapter 1, acculturation is the other side of accommodation. It, too, is a more likely outcome when groups with multiple cultural backgrounds interact. Acculturation is a mutual sharing of culture (Kottak & Kozaitis, 2008). Although cultural groups remain distinct, certain elements of their culture change, and they exchange and blend preferences in foods, music, dance, clothing, and the like. As cities and towns grow in diversity, Mexican, Vietnamese, Asian Indian, and other cuisines are becoming more common in the United States. At the same time, these diverse cultural groups are incorporating parts of regional cultures into their lives. Similarly, the refrigerators of many nonimmigrant families in the United States now contain salsa and soy sauce, as well as ketchup.

- *Bicultural socialization:* The process of **bicultural socialization** involves a nonmajority group or member mastering both the dominant culture and his or her own (Robbins, Chatterjee, & Canda, 2006b). Bicultural socialization is necessary in societies that have relatively fixed notions about how a person should live and interact in school, work, court, financial institutions, and the like. A person who has achieved bicultural socialization has, in a sense, a dual identity. Mainstream economic, political, and social success (or "crossing over") requires nonmajority musicians, athletes, intellectuals and scholars, news anchors, bankers, and a host of others to master this process of cultural change and adaptation.

Social workers who conduct a multidimensional cultural analysis should seek to uncover the processes by which culture is being maintained, changed, and adapted in the lives of the individuals and groups with whom they work. We must also be alert to the fact that the process of cultural change is not always voluntary, or a free and open exchange of culture. We must also pay attention to the political, social, and economic practices that undergird institutional norms and values. If these processes are harmful and oppressive for some people, we have a professional obligation, through our code of ethics, to facilitate change.

Women, people of color, immigrants, and poor people have historically not had a significant say in how cultural change proceeds. But having a limited voice does not eliminate one's voice altogether. Predominantly Black schools and institutions sometimes seek to preserve and strengthen elements of African American culture. Organizations dominated by women and feminists, such as NOW (National Organization of Women), give women a voice in a male-dominated culture. Other examples of different cultures being expressed include the aisles of ethnic foods in many grocery stores, ethnic and "world" music in music stores, a significant presence of Black literature in bookstores, and the influence of Latino/ Hispanic/Chicano culture on the social, economic, and political life in cities such as Los Angeles and Houston.

Conflict perspective

As social workers, we must comprehend the process of cultural change affecting our clients and act in accord with such knowledge. We cannot accept only the dominant notions about the meaning of the actions of people of color and poor people. We cannot look only to mainstream culture and traditions of knowledge to determine the actions we take with nonmajority people. If we do, we are merely reproducing inequality and subjugation and limiting our effectiveness as human service providers.

Critical Thinking Questions 8.2

How much human agency do you think you have to take charge of your life? Do all people have the same level of human agency? What factors make a difference in how much human agency people have?

Diversity

The *practice orientation* is a model for conceptualizing, organizing, and analyzing cultural processes. It helps us to explore different meanings for things we take for granted. It is especially useful for interpreting variation in the social environment. Such variables as race, ethnicity, social class, gender, and family are important symbols in the U.S. psyche and express a host of feelings, beliefs, thoughts, and values about the world around us. Lakoff (2004) demonstrates the use of symbols in the form of metaphors in a discussion of the 2000 and 2004 U.S. presidential elections and their aftermath. He says that metaphors work powerfully by framing how we see the world. He describes how the phrase "permission slip"—as in the United States does not need to "ask for a permission slip" (p. 11) from the United Nations to act against rogue nations such as Iraq—was used in President G. W. Bush's 2004 State of the Union address to justify war against Iraq. The use of permission slip in this context frames the metaphor of an adult–child relationship and suggests that, as an adult nation, the United States has the authority to act like a grown-up and make independent decisions. The concepts that follow have been similarly employed as symbols—indeed, as metaphors—across centuries and continents to generate meaning and power in society. Let's examine them.

Race

Race is first and foremost a system of social identity. It has been constructed over many years through cultural, social, economic, and political relations. Social and cultural meanings have been mapped onto physical or biological aspects of human variation such as skin color, hair texture, and facial characteristics. Race has become a fundamental principle of social organization, even though it has no validity as a biological category (Mullings, 2005; Winant, 2004). The physical or biological characteristics—*phenotypes*—we associate with race are in fact variations resulting from human adaptation to different geographic environments over thousands of years. Some phenotypes have been publicly categorized as European (White), African (Black), Asian, Latino/Hispanic, or Native American (to see a visual representation of this, go to the website www.understandingrace.org/home.html). However, the physical attributes of each group have no intrinsic or natural relationship to emotional, cognitive, or social capacities. **Racism** is the term for thinking and acting as if the phenotype (or as we like to say, the "genes") and these other capacities are related and imply inferiority or superiority.

The meanings and uses of race shift, depending on the social, economic, and political context. In one context, for example, being Black or African American is an asset, whereas in another it is a deficit. Even among Black students and communities, these meanings shift. This variability is a result of the social, political, and economic advantages or disadvantages associated with a Black racial identity at a particular moment in time. Race relations and identity issues in the 1960s were somewhat different from what they were in the 1990s because the social, economic, and political climates were very different.

Consider the issue of racial identity among Community High students. Today's Black students experience less conflict among themselves about "acting White" than did the Black students who attended Community High a decade ago (Cousins, 2008; Fordham, 1996; Fordham & Ogbu, 1986). *Acting White* is the term used to identify behavior that fits with the norms of speech, demeanor, dress, and so on that are preferred and valued by mainstream European American society. "White" norms are perceived to be at play in school activities such as doing homework, carrying books, and speaking in Standard English when answering questions in the classroom. Today, as a decade ago, Black students who do "act White" possess "cultural capital" and are therefore likely to receive more social, economic, and political acceptance within the larger society. They will also be given more privilege and prestige than those who act in accord with what is perceived as distinctly "Black" behavior. These judgments are made by both Blacks and non-Blacks. In addition, the demands of survival require adaptability. Therefore, many families of Black students at Community High and the Black residents of that community are allowing a greater range of flexibility in defining "Black" behavior.

Stan and Tina offer examples of the current blurring of distinctions between behaviors that have historically been defined as Black and those defined as White. Both students borrow from mainstream norms as they shape their ethnic identity. Stan redefines the mainstream meaning of brand-name shirts and biker boots. Tina can speak directly and assertively in class using mainstream Standard English, but her attitude and demeanor are perceived as distinctly Black. Both of these students maintain an ethos and worldview seated in the experience of their Black community. But at the same time, they are relatively bicultural and accommodating toward mainstream standards. Such changes in meaning and practice are likely to continue in their community in predictable and unpredictable ways.

Ethnicity

Ethnicity is often associated with static traditions, customs, and values that reflect a deep and enduring cultural identity and a desire to keep that identity intact. Ethnic identity has traditionally been asserted through preferences in food, clothing, language, and religion. It is also often tied up with blood relations, geographic location, and nationality. Conflict between Bosnians and Serbs in the 1990s—a matter of nationality and land against a backdrop of religion—is a case in point. Ethnic conflicts in African countries such as Rwanda and Burundi provide further examples. In the United States, ethnic conflict includes more than Black–White relations. We see conflict between Koreans and Blacks, Hispanics/Latinos and Blacks, Whites and Hispanics/Latinos, Arabs and Blacks, Arabs and Whites, and so forth.

Ethnic identity is how ethnic groups define themselves and maintain meaning for living individually and as a group. In contemporary industrial societies, ethnic identity is part of a person's social identity (which also includes occupational roles, gender roles, individual and family mobility, and family rituals—regarding meals, for instance). Ethnic identity also includes methods of solving family problems and social conflicts with schools and other institutions. The meaning of a person's identity shifts, however subtly and slowly, as a result of economic, social, and political processes interacting with individual and collective beliefs and values. Consequently, people do not end up practicing the exact particulars of what they espouse about their values, customs, traditions, and other things that make up ethnic identity (I. W. Chung, 2006; McHale et al., 2009). Think back to the process of acculturation discussed earlier.

Such a dilemma of ideal versus real ethnic identity might be thought of as the difference between upholding the spirit (intentions) versus the letter (exact meaning or interpretation) of the law. Ethnic groups in complex societies such as the United States often are better able to uphold the spirit rather than the letter of their values, customs, and beliefs. It is less a matter of truth or fact than one of process, change, and adaptation. When change and adaptation do not occur, ethnic culture may become a trap in an inflexible society. A group that is not willing or able to adapt is left economically, socially, and politically disenfranchised (Bohannan, 1995). Societies and their institutions could be thought of as trapped as well when they do not support the kind of changes that foster equality among all peoples.

Conflict perspective

The rejection and disdain that members of some ethnic groups experience in the United States take a toll on identity (Zuniga, 1988). The result is that people of color or members of ethnic groups may need help to sort out their identities. Stan and Tina were able to develop relatively positive identities because they live in communities and families that celebrate and affirm being Black or African American. Likewise, Puerto Rican youth in some communities see themselves positively and tend to achieve highly in school (Flores-Gonzales, 1999). However, those whose ethnicity is not so well supported may need help. Three steps social workers can take are to (1) teach clients about the effects of the political realities of racism, (2) teach clients how to use the strengths and resources of their own culture in rearing their children, and (3) organize ethnic communities to seek cultural democracy in dealing with institutions such as schools (Crocetti, Rubini, & Meeus, 2008; Zuniga, 1988).

Social Class

Social class (which includes **socioeconomic status,** or **SES**) is a dirty phrase among people in the United States, who generally believe that any class differences that may exist are of one's own making. But class differences do exist, and they document another form of cultural inequality, as well as imperfections in our capitalist economic system. Social class is a way of ascribing status, prestige, and power. It is based on education, income, and occupation. Each of these indices—how much education one has, how much money one makes or has, and what one does for a living—carries poignant meanings. These meanings are derived from subjective values and beliefs in interaction with dominant customs, traditions, and notions of common sense. Social scientists do not fully know how or why, but the meanings associated with social class get condensed into our society's fascination with lifestyles.

The terms we commonly use to categorize class status are upper class, middle class, working class, and lower class or underclass. We also talk in terms of jobs that are blue collar (working class), pink collar (supervisory, especially in traditionally female occupations), and white collar (managerial and professional). These categories and their meanings become infused into identities such as race and ethnicity. For instance, Stan's and Tina's identities as African Americans automatically tend to reduce their social class status to the category of lower- or underclass. The income, occupation, and education of Stan's and Tina's families, however, would generally place them in the middle class.

To understand the power of class or socioeconomic status, think about the class status of your family of origin when you were living at home. Why was that status assigned? What did it mean in social terms? When did you first recognize that your social class status differed in significant ways from that of some other people? That background of experience with social class colors our values and beliefs throughout life. What do you think of today when a person is referred to as lower class? What are your thoughts about clients who are on welfare? What about disparities in health care? Do poor people and members of ethnic minority groups receive health care on par with higher-income White citizens?

Gender

Along with race, gender has been and remains a controversial concept. Gender is what our culture symbolizes and means by maleness and femaleness. These terms are further defined through the prescribed roles of men and women, boys and girls, and husbands and wives. The physical characteristics of male and female bodies, combined with their sexual and reproductive functions, carry strong symbolic meanings. Physical differences between males and females are perceived by many as an indisputable basis for assigning different gender roles. That is, some believe that "anatomy is destiny."

Conflict perspective

Natural differences translate into inequitable power and opportunity for men and women, as seen in social, economic, and political arenas. In other words, natural differences translate into differences in rank, power, and prestige. This plays out at home and at work; in churches, mosques, or synagogues; and in school and at play.

No doubt, meanings surrounding gender involve historical processes. Gender meanings are also the product of dominant structures reinforced by traditions, customs, and our dominant notions of common sense. A thorough understanding of gender is hindered without consideration of these factors. However, gender meanings are currently in flux in our society.

At Community High, for example, aggressive behavior by boys toward girls has generated a provocative response from girls. Girls have re-gendered some of their social practices by adopting the aggressive language and posturing of boys as a defense against them (Cousins & Mabrey, 2007). Many of Tina's female peers have abandoned ascribed characteristics such as passivity, weakness, and inactivity (lack of agency), which are part of the traditional meanings assigned to female gender roles (Ortner, 1996). One consequence, in school and beyond, is that these girls have been defined as unladylike and "loud" (Fordham, 1993). By contrast, the aggressiveness and loudness of boys have been defined in school and beyond as "toughness" and "boys being boys"—being who they naturally are and doing what they naturally do as males. In the domain of sexual activity, strong traditions and entrenched frames of reference among school staff and some students still define the girls as the polluted or promiscuous participants in sexual liaisons. Sexual activity becomes a social problem for a boy only if the boy gets a venereal disease or the girl gets pregnant. Underlying these gender relations are traditions and customs that have shaped how girls' and boys' bodies and activities are defined. The process of girls redefining themselves in response to social and cultural forces, however, is a good example of human agency, structure, and history in action.

Family

Family and kinship are key symbols in U.S. life. Family may be defined as a set of relationships among two or more people to carry out various social and biological functions, such as support, nurturance, sexual mating, procreation, and child rearing. Family is also an ideological construct on which we impose ideas about intimacy, love, morality, and kinship connections and obligations. Issues of contemporary versus traditional family values, structure, and change can serve as one last example of how culture works as a process, as well as how cultural change and adaptation proceed (Mason, Skolnick, & Sugarman, 2003).

We have been bombarded in recent years by scholarly and public dialogue about the demise of "family and cultural values" ("The Moynihan Report Revisited," 2009). Many believe this demise leads to the destruction of family life and thereby society (M. Gallagher, 1996; Popenoe, 1996; Whitehead, 1997). Recent debates about family life and its role in the maintenance of society at large have been fueled by both research and the opinions of

▲ **Photo 8.3** Family life is structured by meanings, values, and beliefs that fit our desires and imaginations about what is right and appropriate.

influential politicians. On one side is the argument that increases in single parenting, divorce, and out-of-wedlock births are a reflection and a source of moral malaise. They reflect beliefs about misplaced or absent values and the social instability and demise of U.S. society. Families of the past have been presented as the model for families of the present and future. On the other side are arguments attempting to counter the "hysteria" about family values. John Gillis (1996), in particular, notes that neither family change nor anxiety about such change is new. In fact, "diversity, instability, and discontinuity have been part of the European experience of family at least since the late Middle Ages, and continued into the new world" (Skolnick, 1997, p. 87).

At the heart of these debates is a process addressed differently by both sides: If we value family coherence in the form of a stable household consisting of mother, father, and children, why do we have such a high divorce rate, an increase in single parenting, and an increase in nontraditional types of relationships? One side claims that recent trends reflect the absence of morals and virtue in our society; if we punish those who don't have morals and reward those who do, we can fix things. The other side argues that a host of medical and economic changes—including birth control and women working outside the home—have fueled social and cultural changes. At particular issue is the disagreement between the two sides about how women fit into society and family life.

The process of family change and adaptation is complex. Much of it reflects the values we *want* our families to live by versus the values families actually *practice* (G. H. Albrecht, 2002; Erera, 2002; Stuening, 2002). Family life is structured by meanings, values, and beliefs that fit our desires and imaginations about what is right and appropriate. But family life is also constructed and lived in a world of competing and interacting meanings and material realities. People do not always do what they intend. They do construct and author their lives, so to speak, but they do so with a host of choices among very real constraints.

Rational choice perspective

Social workers who want to understand and assist families have to understand the processes that create these realities. For instance, Stan and his parents intended for him to be successful in school and avoid criminal behavior. So far, however, Stan's life has not turned out that way. But his experience cannot be reduced solely to psychological, economic, or social factors outside the cultural contexts that shape his life: history, social structure, human agency, common sense, traditions, customs, and the like. All of us, and these processes, are in the embrace of constantly changing social, economic, and political realities of life in society.

THE MEANING OF CULTURE

Social workers must not limit themselves to understanding culture only in the terms provided by other academic, scholarly, and professional traditions. We must position ourselves to understand what culture means and how it works in our own terms and in a multidimensional context. Such an understanding of culture challenges simplistic psychological analyses of individual and collective human practices that claim to adequately explain child abuse and neglect, poverty, academic failure, parent–child problems, substance abuse, school dropouts, and a host of other psychosocial and social policy issues. We want to know how our world and the worlds of our clients are constructed in all their complexity. Even though this knowledge will inevitably remain incomplete due to the motion of life and the complex world of nature impinging on us and we on it, we must try. Indeed, tools are available for just such an activity: a practice orientation and a multidimensional conceptualization of culture.

Ann Swidler's (1986) definition of culture summarizes what this chapter has tried to explain. She sees culture as a tool kit of symbols, stories, rituals, and worldviews that people may use in varying configurations to solve different kinds of problems. Culture works by suggesting strategies of action or persistent ways of ordering or patterning action through time, rather than only shaping ultimate ends or values toward which action is directed (Rosaldo, 1993; Swidler, 1986). Corresponding with Ortner's notion of human agents—our clients and ourselves included—as intense strategizers, Swidler's succinct description does not dismiss the challenges to maintain a coherent concept of culture that adequately explains the "mixing up" of ways people know themselves and others and the ways they develop and express meanings (Abu-Lughod, 1999; Ortner, 1999, 2006).

In the case of Community High students like Stan and Tina, who they have become and how they perform depend on a complex maze of social and psychological processes embedded in European American and African American cultures. The interaction of these processes contributes to Stan's and Tina's ethos and worldview. The extent to which these processes limit and restrain their overall academic and social success is an important issue. Neither Stan nor Tina can live outside the meaning of their blackness or their gender in the strained social world they inhabit. Their individual human agency is a factor, however, and it gives them flexibility to interpret or act on such meanings. Tina has managed to transcend culturally insensitive school processes without giving up her ethnic identity. Stan is still finding his way. Still, their interpretations of life events could serve either as motivation to succeed in terms they define or as a source of debilitating anxiety and despair. Their interpretations could also generate indignation and ethnic zealotry in the fight for equality in the mainstream United States. If they do, will Tina or Stan respond by becoming a race leader? Or will their interpretations result in a loss of self-worth and personal value, leading to a fatalistic dependence on drugs and alcohol to soften the reality of not being powerful and White? Members of immigrant groups face similar questions.

Clearly, U.S. culture and society have a role in this experience. Earlier, the concept of cultural hegemony was discussed, referring to the way dominant social, economic, and political processes subjugate those who do not comply or fit in. Cultural hegemony skews our search for problems and solutions. If a person has an interpersonal or psychologically oriented social problem, we tend to look to the individual for the cause and answer rather than also considering culture and society.

What will your interpretations be as a social worker encountering people who differ from the norm? Will you accept the fact that people experience strain and contradictions between the meanings in their heads and the social, economic, and political realities of everyday public life? Will you interpret social and economic problems as largely personal deficits? Will you misinterpret personal functioning due to a one-dimensional understanding of culture? Will your cultural understanding leave out issues of inequality in society and their role in the oppression of people of color; women; poor people; immigrants; older adults; people who are physically, mentally, or cognitively disabled; or gay and lesbian people?

In summarizing a contemporary paradox of family life, Arlene Skolnick (1997) offers us insight into a host of practice and policy issues for social work: "Americans have still not come to terms with the gap between the way we think our families ought to be and the complex, often messy realities of our lives" (p. 86). Insert *traditions, customs, values,* and so on for the word *families,* and we have a succinct formulation of the simplicity and complexity of culture as a lived process in postindustrial societies.

Critical Thinking Questions 8.3

How important is gender in your life today (or how important was it yesterday)? What about ethnicity? How important has that been in your life in the past 2 days? What factors can make a difference in how important gender and ethnicity are in people's lives?

IMPLICATIONS FOR SOCIAL WORK PRACTICE

I learned how the practice orientation works when I was an ethnographer at Community High, conducting research largely to describe the students' culture from their point of view as well as mine as a researcher. As a social worker, you may be doing ethnographic inquiry without knowing it. Here are a few principles you can follow:

- Recognize the categories of knowledge—social science theories and perspectives; folk or common, everyday theories and perspectives—that you rely on to understand human behavior in the social environment.

- Embrace the traditions, customs, values, and behaviors of disparate groups identified by race, ethnicity, sexual orientation, gender, physical differences, age, nationality, and religion. Avoid approaching these groups in a cookbook, stereotyped, or one-size-fits-all fashion.

- Appreciate the tension between the force of social structure and the resiliency and intentionality of human agency in complex societies such as ours.

- Attempt to understand both personal and social acts of making meaning, and realize how such acts give substance to and obscure our own lives as well as those of our clients.

- Examine culture through the lens of the practice orientation using a "strengths" and person-in-environment perspective that allows you to assess the simultaneous forces of history, social structure, and human agency, and the political context in which all of these forces work themselves out in the lives of your clients.

- Use the practice orientation to frame the actions of those who resist being mainstream Americans. This perspective will help you see the creativity and hope, as well as the ugliness and pain, of their resistance.

- Pay attention to processes of cultural change, including assimilation, accommodation, acculturation, and bicultural socialization, in the lives of individuals and groups with whom you work.

- Work to ensure that members of nondominant groups have a significant say in how cultural change proceeds.

KEY TERMS

accommodation (cultural)	culture	practice orientation
assimilation (cultural)	culture of poverty	race
bicultural socialization	customs	racism
biological determinism	ethnic identity	socioeconomic status (SES)
common sense	ethnocentrism	symbol
cultural conflict	ethos	traditions
cultural hegemony	ideology	worldview
cultural innovation	othering	
cultural relativism	postmodernism	

ACTIVE LEARNING

1. *The cultural construction of schooling.* Compare and contrast Stan's and Tina's experiences at Community High School with your own high school experience, considering the following themes:
   - Material and behavioral cultural symbols
   - Processes of cultural change (assimilation, accommodation, acculturation, bicultural socialization)
   - Ways in which race, ethnicity, social class, and gender play out in the school setting
   - Cultural conflict

   Next, imagine that you spend a day as a student at Community High, and Stan and Tina spend a day at your high school. How do you think you might react to the cultural symbols at Community High? How might Stan and Tina react to the cultural symbols at your high school? How do you account for these reactions?

2. *Cultural change* (Adapted from an exercise in Bradshaw, Healey, & Smith, 2001). Either by telephone or face-to-face, interview an adult over the age of 60 for the purpose of learning about cultural change over time.

- Ask the respondent to reflect on his or her childhood. What favorite activities can the respondent recall from early childhood? What were the person's favorite toys? What types of clothing were worn? What values were stressed? How was family life structured? What kind of relationship did the respondent have with his or her parents? What type of discipline was used in the family? What was the nature of peer relationships?

- Ask the respondent to think about the one most important technological change since he or she was a child (e.g., television, the Internet, medical technologies). Ask the respondent whether this innovation has been good or bad for children and for family life, and to think about exactly how it has changed the lives of children and families.

- Ask the respondent to think about the one most important change in customs and traditions of how people go about their everyday lives since he or she was a child (e.g., mothers working outside the home, smaller families). Again, ask the respondent whether this change has been good or bad for children and families, and to talk about exactly how it has changed the lives of children and families.

Write a brief paper to summarize the thoughts of your respondent, and your analysis of the responses, based on concepts from this chapter.

WEB RESOURCES

Electronic Magazine of Multicultural Education
www.eastern.edu/publications/emme

An open-access e-journal published twice a year by Eastern University, St. Davids, Pennsylvania, includes articles on multicultural education for an international audience.

Internet Resources for Ethnic Studies
http://www2.lib.udel.edu/subj/ethst/internet.htm

Site maintained by University of Delaware Library, contains links to information on a wide range of materials on ethnic issues.

Multicultural Pavilion
www.edchange.org/multicultural/

Site maintained by Paul C. Gorski at Hamline University, contains resources, research, awareness activities, and links to multicultural topics.

CHAPTER

9

Social Structure and Social Institutions

Global and National

Elizabeth D. Hutchison

OPENING QUESTIONS

- What are the key social institutions that give pattern to social life?

- What are the major global and U.S. trends in each of these social institutions?

- What are the positions in the contemporary debate about social inequality?

KEY IDEAS

As you read this chapter, take note of these central ideas:

1. Social structure is a set of interrelated social institutions developed by human beings to impose constraints on human interaction for the purpose of the survival and well-being of the society.

2. Social institutions are patterned ways of solving the problems and meeting the requirements of a particular society.

3. Social institutions are relatively stable but also changing. Most of the major global and U.S. social institutions have undergone extraordinary changes from 1970 to the present.

4. Since 1974, income inequality has grown substantially in the United States.

5. Eight key social institutions in societies around the world are government and politics, economy, education, health care, social welfare, religion, mass media, and family and kinship. Each of these institutions plays a role in the creation and maintenance of social inequality.

6. Over time, societies have vacillated between a conservative thesis that inequality is the natural order and the radical antithesis that equality is the natural order to answer the question, is social inequality a good thing or a bad thing?

Case Study

The Meza Family's Struggle to Make It in the United States

The Meza family had been getting along well in the United States until the birth of their daughter, Minerva, now age 2, who was born premature and experienced some developmental delays. In 1986, Mr. and Mrs. Meza applied to the amnesty program to legalize their immigrant status. They had been in the United States for many years, and their three oldest children, Enrique, age 17, Myra, age 15, and Jesus, age 11, are all U.S. citizens, having all been born here. During the application process, Mrs. Meza's mother, in the interior of Mexico, became very ill, and Mrs. Meza returned to Mexico to stay with her mother until her death 6 months later. Because of this visit, Mrs. Meza was not able to get her legal documents processed, although her husband was able to develop legal status.

Mr. Meza is grateful for the health insurance coverage he receives from the construction company that employs him; it covered much of the extensive hospitalization expense demanded by Minerva's premature

(Continued)

(Continued)

birth. However, Mrs. Meza is not covered because she is not documented. Her lack of legal status often causes stress both for her and her family, especially when she becomes ill and they have to pay for all her medical expenses. Also, the children are aware of other situations where parents are forced to return to Mexico due to lack of legal immigration status, and in many cases children are left in the United States with relatives. They fear that their mother can be deported if Citizenship and Immigration Services (USCIS) finds out. The family also has been afraid to report unethical landlords who did not return rental deposits as agreed or who had failed to address hazardous plumbing problems that violated housing codes and jeopardized family health. They were afraid that the landlords would report them to the USCIS.

Mrs. Meza, 42, worked until Minerva's birth at a dry cleaning establishment, where she was exposed to the fumes of toxic cleaning fluids. She feels that she should have obtained a safer job when she discovered she was pregnant. However, her undocumented status prevented her from easily finding other employment. In addition, her employer knew about her lack of documentation, yet paid her as well as others who worked there and were citizens. Moreover, the family had just recently purchased their first home and she was hesitant to seek new employment because she felt that no one would hire a pregnant woman.

Minerva has been hospitalized several times this year, just recently due to pneumonia. The doctor has also recently informed Mrs. Meza that Minerva very likely has cerebral palsy, and Mrs. Meza needs to attend meetings of the multidisciplinary team that oversees Minerva's care, which includes a social worker. Mrs. Meza feels that this disability is a way for God to punish her for not placing the health of her unborn child over her concern about meeting new house payments. Although she took good care of herself—took vitamins regularly, watched her diet, and tried not to work too hard—she only saw a doctor twice during her pregnancy.

Two months ago, Mrs. Meza returned to work because the family desperately needed her income. Mr. Meza's mother, age 65, came from Mexico to babysit Minerva and help out with housework and meals. Although Grandma has really helped to lift the caregiving burden from Mom, there have been communication issues and conflicts about methods of child care between Mrs. Meza and her mother-in-law. These problems are now causing marital conflict between Mr. and Mrs. Meza because he often sides with his mother. His mother raised 10 children, all of whom are healthy, according to her health care beliefs, so he argues that she knows what she is doing.

Recently, a real problem arose when Mom picked up Minerva from Grandma, who had been asked to bathe and ready Minerva for a late afternoon appointment Mom had scheduled with the doctor, so she would not lose too much work. When the nurse asked Mom to undress Minerva, Mom discovered Minerva's chest had been wrapped in a poultice that smelled quite strongly. When the doctor asked what the poultice consisted of, Mom was embarrassed that she could not tell him. When the mustard-like substance was wiped away, the physician noted bruising on Minerva's rib cage. Mom was just as surprised as the physician and was not able to explain how the bruising occurred. A referral to Child Protective Services (CPS) resulted in a home call to the Meza household. Both Mr. and Mrs. Meza stayed home from work to try to sort out this embarrassing situation and to explain what had happened.

When Mrs. Meza returned from the doctor's office, she nervously grilled the grandmother about the poultice. She discovered that the senior Mrs. Meza had taken it upon herself to take Minerva to a huesero in a nearby barrio. This man is essentially a masseur. The grandmother felt that if Minerva's chest was massaged, the phlegm that was causing so much congestion would be loosened and Minerva could breathe more easily. Mr. and Mrs. Meza went to visit the huesero, and he explained that he had only rubbed her chest as he normally would any client. He claimed that the child's lack of weight resulted in the bruising.

When all this information was shared with the CPS worker, he informed the family that they could never use this huesero again, and if they did, they would be charged with child abuse. Mr. Meza has informed his mother that she cannot undertake any kind of intervention without his knowledge. Mrs. Meza fears that more interactions with CPS might cause her to be identified as undocumented.

Although Mr. Meza is now more supportive of his wife, Mrs. Meza is constantly fearful about the care of Minerva. She calls home several times during the day and has demanded that both Enrique and Myra come home immediately after school each day to attend to Minerva's care. Enrique is a top student and is hoping that his grades and extracurricular activities, including his membership in the Science Club, will result in scholarship opportunities for college. He has a Saturday job tutoring children, which provides a little income. He understands his parents' concerns about Minerva but feels it should be enough if Myra takes care of Minerva after school. He feels that he has been a good son and has not caused any problems for his parents. He also feels that his parents are not concerned about intruding on his college plans, and he has become irritable and almost disrespectful to his parents and to his grandmother.

Myra, on the other hand, is scared to take care of Minerva by herself, especially when Minerva is ill. She feels that she cannot depend on her grandmother to make correct choices about Minerva's care, particularly if Minerva starts to cough a lot. She also feels that Enrique is trying to dump all responsibility on her and that her parents have always let him get away from doing household chores because he is a boy. She has always had to do more around the house, like care for her younger brother, Jesus. She feels it is really unfair that Mexican families do that with their children. The one time she voiced this sentiment, her father told her she was acting like she no longer wanted to be Mexican.

Mrs. Meza has lost 8 pounds in the 6 weeks since the child abuse report. She has noticed that the night sweats she was already experiencing have increased; she wakes up three to four times a night soaked with perspiration and finds herself exhausted at work the next day. She also feels overwhelmed and has had crying spells both at work and at home. She has tried to hide her feelings from her husband, but he is concerned that something is wrong with her. He wants her to see a doctor, but she does not want to call any attention to herself after what happened with the child abuse report. Often when she wakes up at night, she thinks about what would happen to her family if she were forced to return to Mexico. She feels that this would destroy her family. Meanwhile, the visitor's permit the grandmother has used to come to the United States will expire soon. Should they try to renew it? Should Mrs. Meza stop working? How will they pay their expenses with less income, especially now, with the extracurricular activities of the two oldest children costing more money? Maybe buying their home was a bad decision. Maybe the family is becoming too Americanized.

—Maria E. Zuniga

PATTERNS OF SOCIAL LIFE

As you read this story, you are probably aware of both the people and the environments involved. A number of people are involved in the story, and you may be observing how they are interacting with each other and what each contributes to the current situation. Although you do not want to lose sight of the personal dimensions of the Mezas' story, in this chapter we consider the broad patterns of social life that they have encountered and continue to encounter. I want you to see the connections between the personal troubles of the Meza family and social conditions.

A good way to begin to think about broad patterns of social life is to imagine that you and 100 other people have made a space journey to a new planet that has recently, thanks to technological breakthroughs, become inhabitable by humans. You are committed to beginning a new society on this new frontier. How will you work together to be successful in this endeavor? What will you need to do to ensure your survival? Now imagine that your society of 100 has grown to include almost 7 billion people, spread across six continents, with news and ideas being carried around the globe instantly through multiple media outlets, billions of dollars moving across continents with the click of the computer mouse, and products being manufactured and services being provided by a dispersed global labor force. How would you suggest that people work together to ensure the survival of this global society? One way to think about the Meza family story is to think of it as a globalization story. In Chapter 1, we defined globalization as a process by which the world's people are becoming more interconnected economically, politically, environmentally, and culturally.

Sociologists and anthropologists have given much thought to how people work together to try to ensure the survival of a society. They have identified two concepts—social structure and social institutions—as central to understanding those endeavors. Social structure and social institutions are among the more abstract concepts used by sociologists. In the broadest sense, social structure is another term for *society*, or simply an acknowledgment that social life is patterned, not random. It provides the framework within which individual behavior is played out in daily life. **Social structure** is a set of interrelated social institutions developed by human beings to impose constraints on human interaction for the purpose of the survival and well-being of the collectivity. Certainly, we can see some of the constraints that various social institutions impose on members of the Meza family.

Systems perspective

Our understanding of social institutions is complicated by the casual, everyday use of the term *institution* to cover a variety of meanings. In this book, however, we use the definition of **social institutions** as "patterned ways of solving the problems and meeting the requirements of a particular society" (D. Newman, 2008, p. 27). To provide stability, social institutions organize rights and duties into statuses and roles and the expected behaviors that accompany them. **Statuses** are specific social positions; roles, as suggested in Chapter 2, are the behaviors of persons occupying particular statuses. Sociologists have identified a set of interrelated social institutions—such as family, religion, government, economy, and education—with each institution organizing social relations in a particular sector of social life. We see evidence of each of these institutions in the lives of the Meza family.

Sociological treatment of social structure and social institutions emphasizes the ways in which they persist and contribute to social stability. But often they persist despite unintended consequences and evidence that they are ineffective. In addition, although social institutions are relatively stable, they also change—whether by accident, by evolution, or by design (McMichael, 2008; W. R. Scott, 2008). Social institutions persist only when they are carried forward by individual actors and only when they are actively monitored. This view of social structure and social institutions as relatively stable but also changing is consistent with the multidimensional perspective of this book. This perspective seems justified, given the extraordinary changes in several major social institutions since 1970 in societies around the world (McMichael, 2008).

W. Richard Scott (2008) suggests that there are three different types of processes that contribute to the stability of social institutions: regulatory processes, normative processes, and cultural-cognitive processes. Different types of processes are at work in different social institutions. *Regulatory processes* involve rules, monitoring, and enforcement through rewards and punishment. *Normative processes* involve values and norms about how things should be done. *Cultural-cognitive processes* involve beliefs, internalized understandings about the world and how to behave it.

Eight interrelated social institutions will be discussed in this chapter: government and politics, economy, education, health care, social welfare, religion, mass media, and family and kinship. We can see how important each of these institutions is in the current lives of the Meza family. Exhibit 9.1 presents these social institutions and the major functions that they perform for society.

Social Institution	Functions Performed
Government and politics	Making and enforcing societal rules Resolving internal and external conflicts Mobilizing collective resources to meet societal goals
Economy	Regulating production, distribution, and consumption of goods and services
Education	Passing along formal knowledge from one generation to next Socializing individuals
Health care	Promoting the general health
Social welfare	Promoting interdependence Dealing with issues of dependence
Religion	Answering questions about meaning and purpose of life Socializing individuals Maintaining social control Providing mutual support
Mass media	Managing the flow of information, images, and ideas
Family and kinship	Regulating procreation Conducting initial socialization Providing mutual support

▲ **Exhibit 9.1**   Key Social Institutions and the Functions They Perform

CONTEMPORARY TRENDS IN GLOBAL AND U.S. SOCIAL INSTITUTIONS

You have plans to become a social worker, so it is probably safe to assume that you have been at least a casual observer of trends in social institutions. As casual observers, we all keep abreast of trends by making personal observations, listening to stories of people in our social network, and consuming the output of the mass media. In our casual observations about trends in social life, we make comparisons between the contemporary social world as we understand it and some past social world as we understand it. This type of comparison provides many opportunities for error. We may view the contemporary world through a lens that is biased by age, gender, social status, religion, or political persuasion, and we may tend to either romanticize or devalue the past. To avoid these errors, social workers must become professional, not casual, observers of trends in the social world. As planners and administrators, we must design and implement programs that are responsive to trends in social life. Those of us who engage clients directly, to ameliorate problems of living, must understand the changing social situations in which those problems have developed and are being maintained. The purpose of this chapter is to help you observe trends in a more professional way so that you can function more effectively as a social worker.

As Philip McMichael (2004) suggests, when speaking about U.S. society, "we can no longer understand the changes in our society without situating them globally" (p. xxxiii). Indeed, the process of globalization has been stimulating changes in all eight of the social institutions for several decades, but in a pronounced way for the past two decades. The discussion that follows positions trends in U.S. social institutions within a global context. Doing so illuminates how U.S. society is both different from and the same as other societies, and it aids critical thinking about the question, why do we do things the way we do?

Perhaps the most important and troubling trend in contemporary life is the continued extremely high level of social inequality, both between nations and within nation-states. Although globalization has brought some improvements in literacy, health, and living standards for many, we pay particular attention to trends in social inequality because the profession of social work has historically made a commitment to persons and groups that are disadvantaged in the distribution of resources by social institutions. To carry out this commitment, we must have a way of understanding social inequality and its influence on human behavior. Throughout this chapter, we demonstrate how social inequality is created and maintained in eight major interrelated social institutions. But first we take a closer look at inequality globally and in the United States.

> Conflict perspective

There are many debates about whether globalization is leading to increased or decreased global inequality, and the answer depends on how the question is asked. McMichael (2008) argues that global inequality is deepening; he reports that the gap between the richest 20% of the world's people and the poorest 20% has doubled since 1970, now standing at 89 to 1. He further reports that in 2000, there were 3 people in the world whose combined wealth was more than the total of the wealth of the people in the 48 poorest countries. The best available data indicate that the average gap in income among peoples of the world has closed slightly since 1980, with the estimated decrease ranging from 4% to 24% (Firebaugh & Goesling, 2004; Melchior & Telle, 2001; United Nations Development Program, 2005). This reverses a trend of increasing global inequality that began in the 1820s, but leaves us with much greater global income inequality than existed 200 years ago. It is estimated that average incomes in the world's richest regions were 3 times greater than average incomes in the poorest regions 200 years ago, 9 times greater 100 years ago, and 20 times greater in 1998 (Firebaugh & Goesling, 2004). Although different data sources report different numbers, there is agreement that we are talking about comparatively huge disparities in the contemporary world.

It is clear that not all regions of the world have shared equally in the benefits of globalization. One analysis suggests that the regions of the world can be divided into three groups with different recent income trends (Firebaugh & Goesling, 2004):

- Group 1: Rich regions that have been growing richer (Western Europe, Northern America, and Japan)

- Group 2: Regions with lower-than-average per capita but rapidly growing income (South Asia, East Asia, and China)

- Group 3: Poor regions with slower-than-average growth, or decline, in average income (Latin America, Middle East and North Africa, Eastern Europe and Russia, and sub-Saharan Africa)

Because 40% of the world's population lives in China and South Asia, the rapid increase in incomes in these areas carries great weight in calculating overall global inequality and produces the decline noted above. During a time of massive income growth worldwide, average incomes fell in most of sub-Saharan Africa, leading to a growing disparity between this region and the rest of the world. For example, the average U.S. resident was 38 times richer than the average Tanzanian in 1990 and 61 times richer in 2005 (United Nations Development Program, 2005). That same report estimated that if incomes in high-income countries were to stop growing in 2005, and incomes in Latin America and sub-Saharan Africa were to continue at their current rate, Latin America would not catch up with high-income countries until 2177, and sub-Saharan Africa would not catch up until 2236. So, while available data show a slight average decline in global inequality, they also indicate that income inequality is growing between the poorest 10% and the richest 10% of the world's people (Melchior & Telle, 2001).

Although most of the global inequality is due to inequality *between* countries, it is important to understand the patterns of inequality *within* a given country. In the period 1947 to 1973, income inequality in the United States declined slightly. Since 1974, however, income inequality has grown substantially (Burtless, 2001; DeNavas-Walt, Proctor, & Hill Lee, 2006). The most commonly used measure of income inequality is the **Gini index,** which measures the extent to which the distribution of income within a country deviates from a perfectly equal distribution. Gini index scores range from 0 (perfect equality) to 100 (perfect inequality). As Exhibit 9.2 shows, the Gini index in the United States grew from 39.4 in 1970 to 46.9 in 2005, with most of that growth occurring between 1980 and 2000 (DeNavas-Walt et al., 2006). U.S. Census data show no change in the U.S. Gini index between 2005 and 2008 (DeNavas-Walt, Proctor, & Smith, 2009). Emmanuel Saez (2009) reports that the incomes of the top 1% of earners in the United States captured half of the overall economic growth in the country in the period from 1993–2007. As this is being written, in February 2010, there is much controversy about the very large bonuses being paid to financial companies that received government aid in the economic crisis that began in December 2007. Unfortunately, there is a 2-year lag in the most reliable data on income inequality, and it is too early to tell what impact the current recession, with its high rate of unemployment, is having on income inequality, in either the short term or the long term.

When per capita income is adjusted for cost of living, the United States is the highest-income country in the world (Sernau, 2006), but in recent years it has earned the distinction of the most unequal society in the advanced industrial world. Exhibit 9.3 shows the ranking of 19 advanced industrialized countries in terms of income inequality, based on the Gini index, moving from the country with the least inequality at the bottom (Denmark) to the country with the greatest inequality at the top (United States).

Of course, the United States does not have more inequality than all countries in the world. In a general sense, highly industrialized, high-income countries have much lower levels of inequality than nonindustrial or newly industrializing countries. As demonstrated in Exhibit 9.4, the rate of inequality is much lower in the United States than in many low- to middle-income countries. Overall, the highest rates of inequality can be found in some Latin American countries and African countries, but the rate of inequality is not consistent within these regions.

The Mezas came to the United States to escape brutal poverty in Mexico. In recent years, Mexico has developed trade agreements with a number of other countries and has moved from being the world's 26th largest economy to

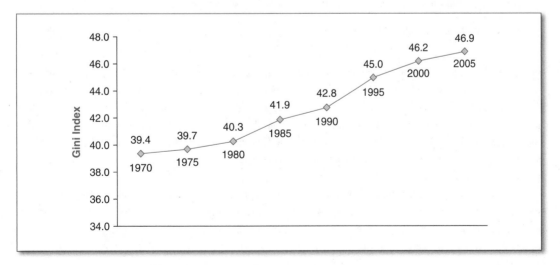

▲ **Exhibit 9.2** Gini Index of Inequality in the United States 1970–2005

SOURCE: DeNavas-Walt, Proctor, and Hill Lee (2006).

Most Inequality

Least Inequality

United States

United Kingdom, Italy

Ireland

Israel

Australia

Switzerland, Canada

France

Spain

Netherlands

Austria

Germany

Finland

Norway

Belgium

Sweden

Japan

Denmark

▲ **Exhibit 9.3**   Ranking of Social Inequality in 19 Advanced Industrial Countries

SOURCE: United Nations Development Program (2005).

being the 9th largest. However, real wages in Mexico have declined by about 20% in this period of growth. A large percentage of workers, about 40% of Mexico's workforce, are poorly paid and have few employment options (McMichael, 2008; Sernau, 2006). Half of Mexican families live in poverty, a rate that has not changed since the early 1980s. Half of the country's rural population earns less than $1.40 per day (McMichael, 2008). You can see from Exhibit 9.4 that Mexico's ratio of inequality is lower than that of Brazil and Guatemala, but it is still much higher than that of most advanced or postindustrial countries. Although the Mezas are struggling for economic survival in the United States, they do not wish to return to Mexico.

Some social analysts argue that social inequality is the price of economic growth and suggest that the poorest families in the United States enjoy a much higher standard of living than poor families in other countries (Rector & Hederman, 1999). In other words, as the saying goes, "A rising tide lifts all boats." Indeed, the growing number of immigrant families taking great risks to come to the United States from the Latin American countries would seem to support this idea.

But a comparison of the United States with other advanced industrialized countries suggests that societal health is best maintained when economic growth is balanced with attention to social equality. A growing international research literature suggests that high levels of inequality are bad for the social health of a nation. Let's look at three

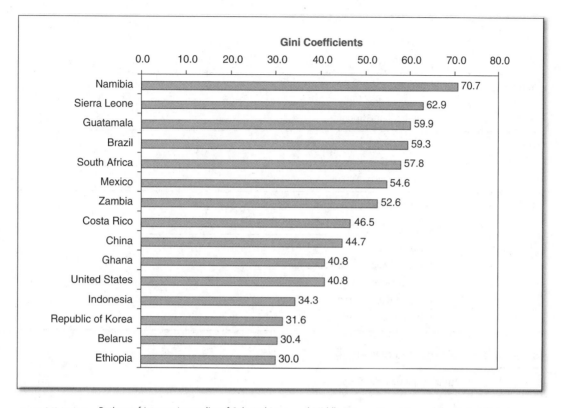

Gini Coefficients

▲ **Exhibit 9.4**   Ratings of Income Inequality of Selected Low- and Middle-Income Countries and the United States

SOURCE: United Nations Development Program (2005).

social indicators for the 19 industrialized countries in Exhibit 9.3: childhood mortality (probability of dying before age 5), life expectancy, and secondary school enrollment. In 1960, the United States had a lower childhood mortality rate than 10 of the other countries listed in Exhibit 9.3. By 2008, the United States had the highest childhood mortality rate of the 19 countries. Indeed, the cross-national continuum for childhood mortality looks almost exactly like the continuum of inequality. All but two of the advanced industrialized countries have longer life expectancies than the United States, and 10 have higher rates of completion of secondary education, with data unavailable for four of the countries (UNICEF, 2009).

Observers have noted that a culture of inequality develops in countries with high rates of inequality. The interests of the rich begin to diverge from the interests of the average family. There is good cross-national evidence that societies with high levels of inequality make smaller investments in public education and other social supports. These societies also have higher levels of violence, less trust and more hostility, and lower levels of involvement in community life (Wilkinson, 2001).

Marc and Marque-Luisa Miringoff and colleagues (M. L. Miringoff, Miringoff, & Opdycke, 1996; M. L. Miringhoff & Miringhoff, 1999; M. Miringhoff, 2003; M. L. Miringoff & Opdycke, 2008) developed an index that can be used to monitor the social health of the United States. They suggest that we in the United States are highly attentive to economic performance and have access to minute-by-minute reports on the economic health of the country through the Dow Jones Industrial Average. However, it is much harder to get indicators of social health. Although there has been some revision of their index over time, Miringoff and colleagues most recently recommend the 16 indicators found in Exhibit 9.5, and they suggest that these indicators should not be measured against

Children	Infant mortality Child abuse Child poverty
Youth	Teenage suicide Teenage drug abuse High school dropouts
Adults	Unemployment Wages Health care coverage
Older adults	Poverty, ages 65 and older Out-of-pocket health costs, ages 65 and older
All ages	Homicides Alcohol-related traffic fatalities Food stamp coverage Affordable housing Income inequality

▲ **Exhibit 9.5**   Indicators of Social Health

SOURCE: Based on Miringoff and Opdycke (2008).

an ideal standard, but rather in comparison to the best year this nation has achieved, a model year. In their research covering the years from 1970 to 2005, they found five main phases in the social health of the nation (M. L. Miringoff & Opdycke, 2008):

1970–1976: social health at a record high

1976–1983: social health declined rapidly

1983–1993: social health stagnated at low level

1993–2000: period of progress, highest score since 1978

2000–2005: social health stalled again

Between 1970 and 1976, the Index of Social Health was 65 or higher for every year but one, with the record level of 70 in 1973. From 1976 to 1983, the index lost 21 points, hitting a new low during the 1982 recession. The index changed little between 1983 and 1993, ending the period with a score of 43. The mid- to late 1990s brought a spurt of progress, and the index climbed 17 points to 60. No progress was made between 2000 and 2005, and the score in 2005 was 53 (M. L. Miringoff & Opdycke, 2008). It is too early to know what happened to the social health of the nation during the recession that began in December 2007, but the preliminary evidence is not good.

Until the mid-1970s, the Index of Social Health tracked well with the Dow Jones Industrial Average. After the mid-1970s, however, the social health of the United States stagnated while the economic health began a rapid upturn. From 1970 to 2001, the gross domestic product (GDP) in the United States grew by 158%, and the nation's social health declined by 38% (M. Miringoff, 2003).

Poverty rates in the United States, one measure of social inequality, demonstrate that social inequality is related to race and ethnicity, age, gender, family structure, and geographic location (DeNavas-Walt et al., 2009). The overall poverty rate in 2008 was 13.2%, up from 12.5% in 2007. Unfortunately, there are no available official data to describe how the deep recession that began in December 2007 affected the poverty rate. Although the majority of people living below the poverty level are White, and people of color can be found in all income groups, Blacks and Hispanics are almost three times as likely as Whites to be poor. The poverty rate in 2008 was 24.7% for Blacks, 23.2% for Hispanics, 11.8% for Asians, and 8.6% for non-Hispanic Whites. The good news is that the differential between Whites and groups of color has decreased in recent years. The bad news is that the differential remains quite large. For example, in the 1940s, the median income of Black families was about 50% of that of White families, and in 2005, the median income of Black families was 61% of that of non-Hispanic White families (Bradshaw et al., 2001; DeNavas-Walt et al., 2006). Foreign-born noncitizens have a higher poverty rate (23.3%) than natives (12.2%), but foreign-born citizens have a lower poverty rate (10.2%) than natives (12.1%) (DeNavas-Walt et al., 2009). You can see from the Mezas' story how lack of citizenship makes people particularly vulnerable in the labor market.

Over the past 50 years, vulnerability to poverty has shifted from older adults to children. Between 1959 and 2008, the percentage of the U.S. population 65 years and older living in poverty decreased from about 35% to about 9.7% (DeNavas-Walt et al., 2006, 2009). The proportion of the population under 18 years living in poverty showed a smaller decrease in this same period, from about 27% to about 19%. Since 1974, the poverty rate for persons under 18 has been higher than for those 65 and over.

Women are more likely than men to be poor in the United States as well as globally. In the United States, women's poverty rate (12.9%) is higher than men's (10.4%), and this difference continues to grow across the life course, rising to 12.4% of women 65 and over compared to 7.0% of men of the same age (U.S. Census Bureau, 2002). Single-parent, mother-only families are more likely to live in poverty (28.7%) than two-parent families (5.5%) or single-parent father-only families (13.8%) (DeNavas-Walt et al., 2009).

In 1970, poverty was primarily a rural problem in the United States. By 1990, poverty was much more of an urban problem. In 2000, an estimated 17.0% of people living inside principal cities were poor, compared to 14.5% of people in rural areas and 9.3% of people in suburbs (DeNavas-Walt et al., 2006). Poverty rates also vary by geographical region in the United States, with 11.6% in the Northeast, 12.4% in the Midwest, 13.5% in the West, and 14.3% in the South living in poverty in 2008 (DeNavas-Walt et al., 2009).

We turn now to analysis of trends in eight major social institutions, both globally and in the United States. We look for the good news in these trends, but we also pay close attention to how social inequality and social conflict are created or maintained in each institution.

Trends in Government and Politics

At the current time, Mrs. Meza lives in fear of agents of the government, whether they come from the U.S. Citizenship and Immigration Services or Child Protective Services. She sees the government as a coercive force rather than a supportive one in her life. The **government and political institution** is responsible for how decisions get made and enforced for the society as a whole. It is expected to resolve both internal and external conflicts and mobilize collective resources to meet societal goals.

> Systems perspective; conflict perspective

Political systems around the world vary widely, from authoritarian to democratic. Authoritarian systems may have a hereditary monarchy or a dictator who seized power; sometimes democratically elected leaders become dictators. Leaders in democratic systems are elected by their citizens and are accountable to them; they must govern in the context of written documents (Ballantine & Roberts, 2009). Evidence suggests that the

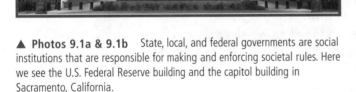

▲ **Photos 9.1a & 9.1b**   State, local, and federal governments are social institutions that are responsible for making and enforcing societal rules. Here we see the U.S. Federal Reserve building and the capitol building in Sacramento, California.

government institution is in a transition period globally as well as in the United States. There is much complexity in global trends in government and politics, but three historical factors are supremely important for beginning to understand current complexities.

1. *Colonialism:* The contemporary global political landscape must be understood in the historical context of **colonialism** (L. Kurtz, 2007; McMichael, 2008). Eight European countries (Belgium, Britain, France, Germany, Italy, the Netherlands, Portugal, and Spain) were involved over several centuries in setting up colonial empires, which allowed them to strengthen their own economies by exploiting the raw materials and labors of the colonized countries. Colonial governments took power away from local governance and prevented the localities from establishing stable political systems. Most of these empires came to a rather abrupt end after World War II, but they left a disorganizing political legacy in their wake in much of Africa, Central and South America, and parts of Asia and the Middle East (McMichael, 2008; T. R. Reid, 2004). After the colonized countries established their independence, the United States and other Western powers advanced a new institutional framework that called for free trade and transformation of the formerly colonized countries into democracies (Aronowitz, 2003). This new institutional framework, sometimes referred to as **neocolonialism,** is promoted by such international organizations as the World Bank, the International Monetary Fund (IMF), and the World Trade Organization (WTO). These organizations, which are led by the United States and Western Europe, regulate relations between countries, and this role carries much power over political and economic institutions. The United States and Western Europe also played a major role in coercing former colonies to organize into nation-states, and imposed national boundaries that were inconsistent with age-old ethnic divisions. This has resulted in ongoing ethnic clashes throughout the former colonies (McMichael, 2008).

2. *Aftermath of hot and cold wars:* Two bloody world wars in the 20th century, both initiated between European countries, left Europe weakened and wary of war as a viable solution to conflicts between nations. With the European states weakened after World War II, the United States and the Soviet Union emerged as competing superpowers. These two superpowers became competing spheres of influence, each trying to promote its political and economic interests around the

world in a struggle known as the Cold War. The collapse of the Soviet Union in 1989 produced political instability in the former Soviet Union, and that country is no longer considered a superpower. In the meantime, after World War II, the nations of Europe began a process of unification, a process that has not always been smooth but has produced the European Union (EU), with "a president, a parliament, a constitution, a cabinet, a central bank, a bill of rights, a unified patent office, and a court system," as well as a currency system (the euro) used by 12 countries to date (T. R. Reid, 2004, p. 2). T. R. Reid suggests that the EU has become a second superpower and may well be joined by China as a third superpower in the near future.

3. *Economic globalization:* Changes in the government institution are very intertwined with changes in the economic institution, and these changes taken together are playing a large role in global inequality. Beginning in the 1970s, economic globalization started to present serious challenges to nationally based democracies (McMichael, 2008). For a number of centuries, political and economic life had been organized into nation-states with bureaucracies for maintaining order and mobilizing resources to meet societal needs. Starting in the 1970s, however, new information and transportation technologies made possible the development of **transnational corporations (TNCs),** which carry on production and distribution activities in many nations. These corporations cross national lines to take advantage of cheap labor pools, lax environmental regulations, beneficial tax laws, and new consumer markets. It is hard for any nation-state to monitor or get control over the TNCs (Alperovitz, 2005; McMichael, 2008). Under these circumstances, around 1970, governments began to retrench in their efforts to monitor and control the economic institution. A **neoliberal philosophy** that governments should keep their hands off the economic institution took hold, perhaps nowhere more than in the United States. Neoliberalism led to the abolition of many government regulations that attempted to control actions in the economic system, a process known as *deregulation.* Neoliberalism also promotes transferring control of many government functions from the public to the private sector, with the belief that privatization will result in more efficient government and improve the economic health of the nation. It also promotes trade liberalization, or free trade across national boundaries.

Countries around the world have attempted to adapt to the challenges of economic globalization by changing the way that government does business. One common adaptation is to make changes in the level of government that assumes power in particular situations. Three common adaptations have been to move federal power downward, upward, and outward (Bradshaw et al., 2001).

1. *Upward movement:* The United States played a leadership role in the development of several transnational political and economic organizations and policies at the end of World War II. These organizations and policies have been significant in helping to move power upward from nation-states. The United Nations (UN) was developed to ensure international peace and security. The World Bank was developed to promote reconstruction in war-torn nations but has, in recent years, taken on a concern for poverty. The World Bank president is appointed by the U.S. president. The IMF was developed to promote international monetary cooperation and a fair balance of trade. The managing director of the IMF is appointed by the United Kingdom, France, and Germany. The General Agreement on Tariffs and Trade (GATT) was designed to provide an international forum for developing freer trade across national boundaries; the World Trade Organization (WTO) was developed under GATT in 1995 to regulate the global economy according to principles of free trade. More recently, the United States, Canada, and Mexico signed the North American Free Trade Agreement (NAFTA) in 1994. European nations joined together as the EU, adopting a common currency, a set of common legal and economic structures, and other joint endeavors. Similar organizations are in various stages of development in Latin America, Asia, and Africa.

These trends are not without controversy. In recent years, there have been conflicts among rich and poor nations at meetings of the WTO and IMF as well as activist demonstrations at their meetings. The last decade has seen growth of a number of antiglobalization social movements that are challenging neoliberal principles and the ways they are being enforced around the world. The World Bank, IMF, and WTO, all governed by unelected officials, have become very powerful in dictating how nation-states should govern. For example, when making loans, the World Bank requires that borrowing nations follow the principles of neoliberalism, including reducing their social welfare programs, privatizing their public services, and becoming more open to imports. The IMF has enforced these principles, sometimes overriding decisions made at the national level. The deliberations of the WTO are secret; members can lodge complaints, but the decision of the WTO's dispute settlement program is binding unless every member of the WTO votes to reverse it. There is much evidence that the decisions of the World Bank, IMF, and WTO have been more favorable to some nations than others (McMichael, 2008).

2. *Downward movement:* In a period of rising doubt about the ability of nation-states to govern, many of them, including the United States, have been passing policy responsibilities down to regional and local governments. In the United States, **devolution** became the code word for passing responsibilities to state and local governments. This downward movement has also been called the **new federalism.** The stated intent of devolution is to improve the responsiveness and efficiency of government. The U.S. federal government has used several different mechanisms for devolution, including block grants (large grants to regional, state, or local governments) and increased flexibility for states in complying with federal mandates. As pressures increase on states, some are beginning to devolve responsibilities to local governments. On the other hand, some states are beginning to tackle tough issues like immigration and environmental policy that are not being addressed by federal policy.

3. *Outward movement:* Growing faith across the world in the wisdom and efficiency of the economic institution led many nation-states to withdraw from direct control of activities that they have hitherto controlled. They do this in several ways:

- *Privatization:* The government sells enterprises that produce goods or deliver services to the private sector. This can be done at any level of government. Between 1986 and 1992, monetary policies of the World Bank and IMF required former colonial countries to engage in massive privatization in exchange for rescheduling their debts (McMichael, 2008).

- *Contracting out:* The government retains ultimate control over a program but contracts with private organizations for some activities. The most notable example of this type of government retrenchment is state contracts with the private prison industry that has grown up in recent years in the United States, but also in other countries such as Australia (Wettenhall, 1999). Governmental social service agencies also contract out many social service programs to both nonprofit and for-profit organizations. Some school systems have experimented with contracting out public schools to the private sector, in the hopes that the result will be more effective schools.

- *Deregulation:* Governments give up their claims to the right to regulate particular activities that they have previously regulated but not controlled. The expectation is that deregulation will lead to greater economic growth and lower cost to the consumer. Deregulation of the telephone system is often credited with the proliferation of new services, including wireless telephones. States of the United States followed the global trend to deregulate electricity and other utilities. As the financial system in the United States and other countries began to collapse in late 2007, much attention was paid to the lax regulation of the financial system, particularly the U.S. system, and the role that deregulation played in the crisis.

The future of the neoliberal philosophy is not clear. For a number of decades, it served wealthy nations and wealthy individuals well. However, the global economic crisis that began in late 2007 has called its principles into question and begun to chip away at its primary premise that the market has its own wisdom and should not be interfered with. The wisdom of deregulation is getting another review. For some time now, poor nations and social justice advocates have engaged in growing resistance to the neoliberal philosophy and its implementation by the World Bank, IMF, and WTO. There has been much concern about the unfair advantage given to wealthy nations and the exploitation of labor and natural resources in poor nations. However, there is also much resolve by rich and powerful individuals and societies to hold onto neoliberal principles.

Economic globalization combined with war and political strife has produced mass cross-national migration. Most of this migration has occurred within regions; for example, most refugees fleeing Iraq have gone to other Middle Eastern countries. But there is also a trend of migration from low-wage to high-wage countries (McMichael, 2008). This has led to considerable political attention to immigration issues around the globe. In the United States and Europe, immigration issues are the source of intense political debate, and more restrictive immigration policies are being proposed across these two regions.

As we think about the trials of the Meza family, we are reminded of this increased attention to immigration issues. Some observers (Teeple, 2000) have suggested that nation-states compensate for their inability to control the business processes that cross their borders by heightening their attempts to control the human movement across their borders. By controlling borders, a nation-state can get some control of the flow of labor across national boundaries.

> Rational choice perspective

Although the United States and the EU share a commitment to democracy and a free market economy, they have some important differences in political theory that come out of their different experiences in the 20th century. The United States puts much more emphasis on military power than the EU does, or any other part of the world, for that matter. European countries devote more of their GDP to overseas development aid (ODA) to poor nations than the United States does. European countries also devote more of their GDP to social welfare programs than does the United States. The EU's European Convention on Human Rights is more expansive than the U.S. Bill of Rights. The EU also has been more willing than the United States to regulate TNCs. In recent years, the EU has enacted policies for greater personal privacy at the same time that the United States has enacted policies like the Patriot Act that added limitations to personal privacy (T. R. Reid, 2004).

Michael Reisch (1997) reminds us that social work has been "at the mercy of political forces throughout its history" (p. 81). He argues that social workers cannot afford to ignore processes and trends in the political arena. In the United States, social workers must be attuned to the important role that money plays in providing access to government and politics, and to continuing underrepresentation of women and people of color among elected officials.

Trends in the Economy

As you read the Mezas' story, their economic struggles seem paramount, and yet, both Mr. and Mrs. Meza are employed full time and working hard to provide for their family. The **economic institution** has the primary responsibility for regulating the production, distribution, and consumption of goods and services. In a capitalistic market economy, like the one in the United States, what one is able to consume is dependent on how much one is paid for selling goods and services in the economic marketplace. Most people, if they are not self-employed or independently wealthy, exchange labor for wages, which they then use for consumption. The nature of the economy has been ever changing since premodern times, but the rate of change has accelerated wildly since the beginning of the industrial revolution, particularly in recent decades under neoliberalism and economic globalization.

Before further discussion, we should have some clarity about what we mean by *economic globalization.* The primary ingredients are a global production system, a global labor force, and global consumers. Much of what we wear, eat, and use has global origins. If you look around your room, you will see many examples of economic globalization, but much of the global process will be invisible to you. A few examples, taken from the work of Philip McMichael (2008), will demonstrate some of the complexity of current globalization. First, let's look at the U.S.-based athletic shoe industry. The design and marketing of the shoes are typically done at headquarters in the United States by workers earning relatively high wages. The materials are produced, dyed, cut, stitched, and assembled, and then packed and transported in work sites in South Korea, Taiwan, China, Indonesia, and the Philippines, primarily by women earning low wages. The shoes are sold globally, but disproportionately to consumers in wealthy advanced industrialized countries.

A second example involves the food we eat. In wealthy countries, we have become accustomed to having our favorite fruits and vegetables available year round. We can have this because of the global food market. During the winter months, if we live in the United States, we can get grapes, apples, pears, apricots, cherries, peaches, and avocados from Chile; and tomatoes, broccoli, bell peppers, cucumbers, and cantaloupe from Mexico. If we live in Japan, we might get pineapples and asparagus from Thailand; and if we live in Europe, we can buy strawberries, mangoes, and chilies grown in Kenya as well as organic fruits and vegetables from China. For a final example, we can look at the production of the Ford Escort car, which uses parts from 14 countries and is assembled at work sites in several different countries.

The global economy is driven by corporate desire for the bigger profits that come from cheap raw materials and cheap labor, and by consumer desire for cheap and novel products. Corporations are constantly seeking cheaper labor sites to stay competitive. Much of the global economy is controlled by TNCs, also called multinational corporations, which are very large companies with production and marketing departments in multiple countries. TNCs have become very powerful over the past several decades; in fact, UN data indicate that TNCs account for two thirds of world trade and hold most product patents (cited in McMichael, 2008). Most TNCs are headquartered in France, Germany, the United Kingdom, or the United States.

Conflict perspective

Proponents of economic globalization argue that in time it will bring modernity and prosperity to all regions of the world. Critics argue that it is just an unsustainable pyramid scheme that must end because prosperity of victors is always paid for by the losses of latecomers, or because the physical environment can no longer sustain the economic activities (Sernau, 2006). This is a good place to point out that not all peoples of the world put a high value on consumerism and chasing economic growth, values that are central to globalization. Unfortunately, however, policies of the World Bank, IMF, and WTO have made it impossible to make a living on subsistence farms and small craft enterprises. The future of globalization is not certain, but several trends can be identified at its current stage of development.

1. *Regional disparities.* Rich nations have been getting richer, a few nations have made impressive gains, most poor nations have made few gains, and the poorest nations have lost ground. Consumers in high-income countries benefit from the cheap labor of workers in newly industrializing countries. For example, much of the clothing in the stores in the United States has "Made in China" on its labels, and this clothing is often produced by people working 12-hour shifts and 7-day work weeks (McMichael, 2008). Current regional disparities must be put into historical context. Globalization gained speed just as European colonialism collapsed, at the end of World War II. Formerly colonized countries began the global era in a compromised position created by colonial exploitation. The newly created World Bank made large loans to the former colonies to improve their infrastructures, and much of the money was used to import technology from wealthy industrialized countries. In the 1980s, a combination of factors,

including recession in the United States and other wealthy Western nations, produced a debt crisis in many previously colonized countries. They began taking out new loans to pay for previous loans. The World Bank and IMF imposed austerity measures, which resulted in social service cuts, as a condition for restructuring the loans. Some countries have not been able to recover from the debt crisis, especially those facing a massive AIDS crisis. More recently, beginning in late 2007, low-income countries have been severely affected by the global economic recession, which originated in the financial systems of the wealthy countries of the world. Poor countries entered the recession in already weak fiscal positions, and there have been several negative impacts of the recession on their fragile economies: a decline of foreign aid, restricted access to credit, lost trade, and loss of remittances from family members who have migrated to wealthy countries (UNESCO, 2010). Sub-Saharan Africa has been the most vulnerable global region to these economic losses, but low-income countries in Eastern Europe, Asia Pacific, and Latin America have also been at risk.

2. *Labor force bifurcation.* As globalization progressed, wage labor began to **bifurcate,** or divide into two branches. One branch is the *core* of relatively stable, skilled, well-paid labor. The other branch is the *periphery* of periodic or seasonal (often referred to as casual), low-wage labor. The upper tier of jobs is found disproportionately in the wealthy advanced industrialized countries, and the lower tier of jobs is found disproportionately in the previously colonized countries. The

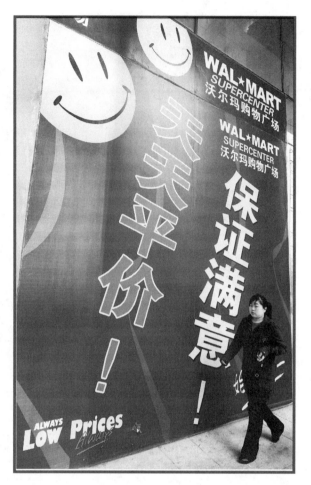

▲ **Photo 9.2** Walmart is a growing symbol of economic globalization.

athletic shoe industry provides one of the most extreme examples of this bifurcation: Vietnamese workers earn about US$400 a year stitching the sneakers, and celebrity athletes in the United States are paid US$10–$20 million to market them. According to a UN report, the world's richest 20% had 30 times the income of the world's poorest 20% in 1960, but this difference was about 74 to 1 by 1997 (cited in McMichael, 2004). Recently, bifurcation of labor has occurred all over the world, in advanced industrial societies as well as in poor, newly industrializing societies (McMichael, 2008). Work in the *core* is usually full time and comes with nonwage compensation such as sick leave, health insurance, and retirement benefits. Work in the *periphery* is usually part time and/or temporary, with many working on a contract basis, and it provides few if any nonwage benefits. Use of such casual, irregular low-wage labor provides employers with a lot of flexibility as they try to stay competitive. Workers in the *periphery* often work very long hours in crowded and unsafe workplaces, and, if they are women, they may cope with sexual harassment on the job. Women have been reported to comprise 70% to 90% of the temporary workers in advanced industrial societies, but, recently, many jobs historically performed by

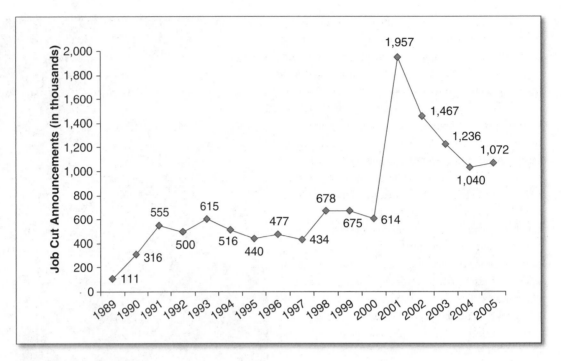

▲ **Exhibit 9.6**   U.S. Job Cut Announcements

SOURCE: Based on Challenger, Gray, and Christmas, Inc. (2006).

middle-class men are being filled by contract workers who do not receive the nonwage benefits once associated with these jobs (McMichael, 2008).

3. *Corporate downsizing.* Another way that corporations in advanced industrial societies have responded to global competition is by **downsizing** for greater efficiency. Increasingly, high-wage workers are almost as vulnerable to layoffs as low-wage workers. Exhibit 9.6 demonstrates the large increase in downsizing in the United States since 1990. This trend, coupled with the increasing use of casual labor discussed above, has resulted in low job security for many workers. This situation was exacerbated by the recession that began in December 2007. It is estimated that 2.6 million jobs were lost in the United States in 2008, and the unemployment rate rose to 10% by December 2009. The rates of unemployment vary by major worker groups. In January 2010, an estimated 10% of adult men and 7.9% of adult women were unemployed; the unemployment rate was 16.5% among Blacks, 12.6% among Hispanic Americans, 8.7% among Whites, and 8.4% among Asian Americans. The unemployment rate for veterans from the Gulf War era II (since September 2001) was 12.6%, and the unemployment rate for persons with disabilities was 15.2%. The unemployment rate for the foreign born was 11.8%, compared to 10.3% for the native born (U.S. Department of Labor, Bureau of Labor Statistics [hereafter BLS], 2010). Unfortunately, the unemployment rate is predicted to stay at a high level, at least through 2011.

4. *Work intensification.* J. Walsh and Zacharias-Walsh (2008) suggest that since the beginning of capitalism, there has been a constant struggle between workers and employers over the length of the workday, with a constant pressure from employers to increase it. They provide evidence that in the contemporary global era, the length of the working day is increasing, but there is also much evidence that the length of the working day varies across national lines as well as within national borders. For example, migrant workers in some settings reportedly work 12- to 16-hour days,

7 days a week. In sweatshops around the world, workers have been found to work as many as 84 hours a week, and sometimes 22 hours a day, at very low wages, producing products for major U.S. retailers such as Nordstrom, Gymboree, and J. Crew (McMichael, 2008; J. Walsh & Zacharias-Walsh, 2008). But it is not just in newly industrializing countries that such long workweeks can be found. J. Walsh and Zacharias-Walsh argue that there was a "return of the 12-hour day" in the United States in the 1990s, with a number of major U.S. corporations instituting the 12-hour shift and enforced overtime during that period. By some reports, the average workweek increased in the United States between 1990 and 2000 (Berg, Appelbaum, Bailey, & Kalleberg, 2004), and by other reports it remained essentially steady (Mishel, Bernstein, & Alegretto, 2006). At any rate, the trend toward longer workweeks is not universal. In some European and Scandinavian countries, and in Japan, the workweek grew shorter rather than longer during the 1990s (Berg et al., 2004). Exhibit 9.7 compares the changes in the average annual hours worked in a number of rich industrialized countries from 1979 to 2006. In interpreting the trends, it is helpful to note that workers worked an average of 1,786 hours annually in the United States in 1969, well below the number of hours worked since 1979 (J. Walsh & Zacharias-Walsh, 2008). The average annual work hours do not tell the full story about the intensification of work in contemporary societies, however. The increased labor force participation of women in recent decades has resulted in a significant increase in family work hours (Crompton, 2006). For example, the average middle-class family with two wage earners worked a total of 3,932 hours in 2000 (Berg et al., 2004). This extra time spent in the economic institution has a major impact on the family and kinship institution as well as community life. The Mezas are a good example of a family struggling to balance their work life with family needs.

5. *Limited protection by organized labor.* Since the beginning of industrial capitalism, labor unions have been the force behind governmental protection of workers' rights, fighting successfully for such protection as workplace

	1979	1989	2000	2006
United States	1,834	1,855	1,841	1,804
Japan	2,126	2,070	1,821	1,784
Germany	–	–	1,473	1,436
France	1,949	1,899	1,591	1,564
Italy	1,697	1,654	1,861	1,800
United Kingdom	1,818	1,786	1,711	1,669
Canada	1,832	1,801	1,768	1,738
Australia	1,823	1,785	1,777	1,714
Finland	1,869	1,802	1,750	1,721
Norway	1,580	1,511	1,455	1,407
Spain	2,022	1,822	1,815	1, 764
Sweden	1,530	1,565	1,625	1,583

▲ **Exhibit 9.7**   Average Annual Hours Worked in Select Affluent Industrial Countries, 1979–2006

safety, a minimum wage, a reduced workweek, and pensions. Economic globalization has seriously weakened the bargaining power of nationally based labor unions, because companies can always threaten to take their business somewhere else. However, labor unions are still strong in some countries, and this helps to explain much of the differences in annual work hours across national lines. For example, 13.5% of the workers in the United States are union members, compared to 30.4% of the workers in the EU and 80% in Sweden (Berg et al., 2004). Keep this in mind as you review the statistics in Exhibit 9.7. In addition, labor unions play a strong role in negotiating working conditions in India (Rai, 2006), but there is a ban on independent labor unions in China (Pan, 2002). South Korea accomplished much of its economic growth in the contemporary era by suppressing unions. Unionization has been on the decline in Mexico, where 1 in 3 workers held union membership in 1984, but only 1 in 5 in 1998 (Hilger, 2003). A growing international labor movement is currently attempting to forge networks of labor organizations across national lines (McMichael, 2008) (see discussion of this social movement in Chapter 14).

Social workers who participate in policy development must be informed about the serious challenges to job security in the contemporary era. They are also called on to deal with many of the social problems arising out of these changes in the economic institution—problems such as inadequate resources for family caregiving, domestic violence, substance abuse, depression, and anxiety. Social workers attached to the workplace need to be skillful in influencing organizational policy and linking the work organization to the wider community, as well as in assessing specific work situations affecting their clients.

Trends in Education

As young as they are, Enrique and Myra Meza understand that educational attainment is becoming increasingly important in the labor market, but Myra complains that their parents take Enrique's education more seriously than hers. Traditionally, the primary purpose of the **educational institution** has been to pass along formal knowledge from one generation to the next—a function that was largely performed by the family, with some help from the church, until the 19th century. Formal education, schooling that includes a predetermined curriculum, has expanded dramatically around the world in the past several decades. In the process, there has been a trend toward convergence in educational curricula, especially in mathematics and science (Ballantine & Roberts, 2009).

The Education for All movement is an international effort to meet the basic learning needs of all children, youth, and adults of the world. In 2000, this movement established six goals to be accomplished by 2015 (UNESCO, 2010):

Goal 1: To expand and improve comprehensive early childhood care and education (EECE), especially for the most disadvantaged children

Goal 2: To ensure that all children, particularly girls and ethnic minority children, have access to free primary education of good quality

Goal 3: To ensure that all youth and adults have access to appropriate learning and life-skills programs

Goal 4: To achieve a 50% improvement in adult literacy, especially for women

Goal 5: To achieve gender equality in education

Goal 6: To improve all aspects of the quality of education

There has been some progress on these goals. The number of the world's children who are out of school has dropped by 33 million since 1999. The share of girls who are out of school dropped from 58% to 54% in this same period, and the gender gap in primary education is narrowing in many countries. The world adult literacy rate has increased by 10% since 1994 (UNESCO, 2010).

However, in an era of a knowledge-based global economy, there continue to be large global gaps in opportunities for education. In both low-income and wealthy nations, children from low-income families have less access to early childhood education than other children (UNESCO, 2010). Although educational participation is almost universal between the ages of 5 and 14 in affluent countries, 115 million of the world's children, most residing in Africa or South Asia, do not receive even a primary education (United Nations Development Program, 2005). This situation

> Conflict perspective

was worsened by conditions the World Bank set on debt refinancing in the late 1980s, which mandated reductions in education expenditure. The result was reduced educational levels in Asia, Latin America, and Africa, and a widening gap in average years of education between rich and poor countries (McMichael, 2008). The global financial crisis that began in late 2007 is also having an impact; both nations and families are finding it necessary to cut back on education spending. This is happening in wealthy nations like the United States, but the impact is greatest in low-income nations (UNESCO, 2010). The average child born in Mozambique in 2005 will receive 4 years of formal education, compared to the child in South Asia who will receive 8 years, and the child in France who will receive 15 years (United Nations Development Program, 2005). About 40% of college-age people in affluent countries go to college, but this opportunity is afforded to only 3% in poor countries (D. Newman, 2006). There are gender disparities in educational attainment across the globe, but there is a difference in the direction of this disparity between poor and affluent nations. Females still receive 1 year less education than males in African and Arab countries, and 2 years less in South Asia (United Nations Development Program, 2005), but females receive higher levels of education than males in most affluent industrialized countries (Sen, Partelow, & Miller, 2005). Women still make up nearly two thirds of the world's adults who lack literacy (UNESCO, 2010).

There are also inequalities in the resources available for schooling across the world. In low-income countries, and also in impoverished neighborhoods in the United States, children attend schools with leaking roofs, poor sanitation, bad ventilation, and inadequate materials, or go to school under a tree in some parts of the world. There is a shortage of trained teachers in many areas around the globe. In countries such as Madagascar, Mozambique, Sierra Leone, and Togo, the pupil-to-teacher ratio is 80:1 (UNESCO, 2010).

In this era of global economic competition, the U.S. Department of Education (DOE) has been interested in tracking how education in the United States compares to that in other affluent industrialized countries. The DOE's most recent comparisons focus on the United States, Canada, France, Germany, Italy, Japan, the Russian Federation, and the United Kingdom (England, Scotland, Wales, and Ireland) (Sen et al., 2005). There are some similarities and some differences in the education institutions in these countries. All of these countries have compulsory education, and participation in formal education is high until the end of the compulsory period, which is age 18 in Germany; age 17 in the United States; age 16 in Canada, France, and the United Kingdom; and age 15 in Italy, Japan, and the Russian Federation (Sen et al., 2005). China's compulsory education law requires 9 years of education rather than stipulating a compulsory age, but also indicates age 6 as the age of school entry. This would make the age of completion of compulsory education in China closer to the age of 15, as in Italy, Japan, and Russia, rather than to the higher end, as in Germany and the United States (China Education and Research Network, 2000).

Universal early childhood enrollment, defined as a 90% enrollment rate, begins later in the United States than in several other countries: age 5 in the United States, compared to age 3 in France and Italy and age 4 in Japan and the United Kingdom. In France, a large number of children below the age of 3 are enrolled in formal education.

The ratio of the average annual teacher salary to GDP per capita, a measure of how teachers are paid relative to other salaried employees, is lower in the United States than it is in England, Germany, Japan, and Scotland, and on par with

▲ **Photos 9.3a & 9.3b**   The contrast between these two classrooms—one in a well-resourced suburban school in the United states and the other on a footpath in Ahmedabad, India—demonstrates global inequality in resources for education.

France and Italy, where primary and secondary education are funded primarily at the federal level: A total of 74% of education funding comes from federal sources in France, and 81% does in Italy. In contrast, very little of education at this level is funded federally in the United States (8%), Germany (8%), Canada (4%), and the Russian Federation (1%). In the United States, individual states provide 51% of primary and secondary education funds, and local governing entities provide 41%. A somewhat different picture emerges for funding of higher education, where the federal government plays a very large role in several countries, including the United Kingdom, where the government provides 100% of higher education funding; Italy (92%); France (91%); and Japan (84%) (Sen et al., 2005).

In the 20th century, average educational attainment increased spectacularly in the United States. For a time after the 1954 *Brown v. Board of Education* Supreme Court ruling that "separate but equal" has no place in public education, there was a serious attempt to desegregate many urban school systems, and racial and ethnic differences in educational attainment were reduced (Kozol, 2005). In the past 15 years, however, courts at both the state and federal level have been lifting desegregation orders, arguing that separate *can* be equal or at least "good enough," and African American and Latino/Hispanic students are now more segregated than they were 30 years ago (D. Newman, 2008). Jonathan Kozol, a long-time equal education advocate, describes the current situation as "the restoration of apartheid schooling in America" in the subtitle of his 2005 book.

Conflict perspective

In the current climate, the education institution is becoming a prime force in perpetuating, if not exacerbating, economic inequalities. A 2006 report by Kati Haycock of the Education Trust indicates that current trends in the education institution are the principal reason that there is less upward mobility in the social class structure in the United States today than there was 20 years ago, and less mobility in the United States than in any European nation except England. Trends at every educational level are involved in this situation.

Before summarizing some of those trends, it is important to note that the stated goal of the No Child Left Behind (NCLB) Act of 2001 was to raise academic achievement for all students, out of concern that U.S. students were falling behind those in other wealthy nations, and to close the achievement gaps that divide low-income students and students of color from their peers. There has been much state-level opposition to aspects of this federal legislation across the political spectrum, and some negotiated changes to the law over time (Sunderman, 2006). In November 2006, the U.S. Department of Education proclaimed NCLB to be a major success, but a 2006 study by the Civil Rights

Project (which was then at Harvard University) reported that NCLB had not improved reading and mathematical achievement, nor had it reduced achievement gaps (J. Lee, 2006). Some critics argue that NCLB relies heavily on testing to accomplish its goals without providing the increased resources necessary for schools serving low-income and minority youth to raise test scores or to approximate the education provided in wealthy communities (Kozol, 2005).

Let's return now to discussion of some of the trends in education that perpetuate societal inequalities:

1. *Trends in early childhood education.* As noted earlier, the United States has no universal early childhood education program, and there is much evidence that low-income and racial minority students have less access to quality early childhood education than their White and higher-income peers (Education Trust, 2006b). Many poorer school districts do not provide prekindergarten programs, and many low-income children are placed on a waiting list for Head Start programs. Some low- to middle-income districts are canceling full-day kindergarten, and some public school districts have begun to provide for-pay preschool and full-day kindergarten, a practice that clearly disadvantages low-income children. Wealthy families are competing for slots for their young children in expensive preschool programs, nicknamed the "baby ivies," that provide highly enriched early learning environments, further advancing the opportunities for children in privileged families (Kozol, 2005).

2. *Trends in primary school education.* In 35 states, school districts that educate the greatest number of low-income and minority children receive much less state and local money per pupil than other school districts (Education Trust, 2006b; Habash Rowan, Hall, & Haycock, 2010). Nationally, the average difference is $1,100 per child, but in some states the difference is much larger. Kozol (2005) reports that a high-poverty elementary school with 400 students in New York receives over $1 million less per year than a school of equal size in a district where there are few poor children. The result is usually poor building infrastructures, lower salaries for teachers, and less technology in the lower-funded schools. Although NCLB requires equity in teacher quality for poor and minority students, very few states have developed methods to evaluate progress on this requirement, and much evidence suggests that these students are disproportionately taught by inexperienced and poorly qualified teachers (Education Trust, 2006a; Habash Rowan et al., 2010). In addition, parents in affluent communities often supplement public funds to enhance the school library, to provide art and music programs, and even to hire extra teachers to reduce class size. There is little wonder that the longer children of color stay in school, the larger their achievement gap becomes (Education Trust, 2006b).

3. *Trends in secondary education.* High school graduation rates are a key measure of whether schools are making adequate yearly progress (AYP) under the provisions of NCLB. As it turns out, most school districts do not have a system for calculating graduation rates, and there are major holes in their reported data (Habash, 2008). Furthermore, researchers at Education Trust have analyzed the reported state data and found that all states inflated their graduation rates, ranging from a 1% to a 33% inflation rate (as reported in D. Hall, 2005). These researchers estimate that graduation rates for students who entered high school in 2000 ranged from 51% in South Carolina to 86% in New Jersey. More than half of the nongraduates were African American, Latino, or Native American, indicating an overrepresentation because these groups together comprise about one third of students in public school nationally. African Americans have made gains in high school completion in the past 30 years, however. In 2008, an estimated 94% of Whites age 25–29 had completed high school, compared to 88% of Blacks, and 68% of Hispanics (Habash Rowan, Hall, & Haycock, 2010). Even when students in impoverished rural and urban neighborhoods graduate, their high schools may not have offered the types of courses that college admissions departments require (Habash Rowan et al., 2010; Kozol, 2005). There is also a critical shortage of teachers who are trained to teach English language learners, who often must navigate very large high school settings (Hood, 2003).

4. *Trends in higher education.* The costs to attend college have been escalating rapidly in recent years, and financial aid for low-income students has not been keeping pace. Consequently, the rate of completion of a bachelor's degree by age 24 for students from the top income quartile increased from 40% in the 1970s to 75% in 2003, compared to an increase from 6% to 9% for low-income students. Between 1970 and 2008, the race and ethnic gap in college education declined but remains quite high, as demonstrated in Exhibit 9.8. There are many factors that

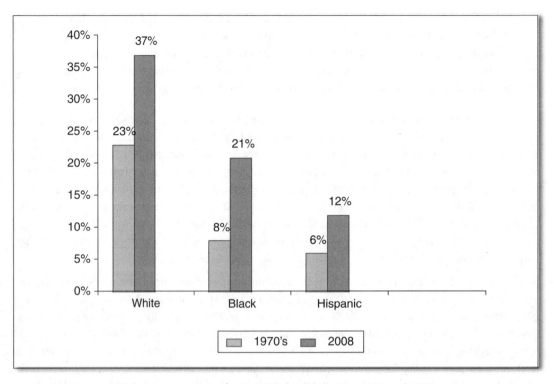

▲ **Exhibit 9.8**   Bachelor's Degree Attainment for 25 to 29-Year-Olds by Race, 1970s and 2008

SOURCE: Based on Child Trends Data Bank (2010); Haycock (2006).

contribute to these disparities, including rising tuition, but changes in the pattern of financial aid distribution are important. There was a strong increase in financial aid over the past 20 years, but the biggest increases went to affluent students rather than to low-income students. By 2005, a total of 34% of federal financial aid went to families with annual incomes over $100,000. Between 1995 and 2005, state need-based grants increased by 95%, while state non–need-based grants increased by 350%. In that same period, private colleges and universities increased their grants to low-income students by 52% and their grants to students from families with incomes over $100,000 by 254% (Haycock, 2006). Some colleges and universities are doing better than others in improving the graduation rate of minority students (see Engle & Theokas, 2010).

It is important to remember that many immigrants, like Mr. and Mrs. Meza, had limited education in their home country but manage to instill in their children the value of a college education. Social workers should become active partners in efforts at educational reform, particularly those that equalize educational opportunities. To be effective in these efforts, we need to be informed about trends in the educational institution.

Trends in Health Care

Health and health care costs are important issues for the Meza family. Mrs. Meza didn't receive much prenatal care, which is relatively inexpensive, when she was pregnant with Minerva because she lacked health insurance. Luckily, Mr. Meza had insurance coverage for Minerva's long postnatal care, which was very expensive. Health is important to this family, but health is also important to a society. Child development, adult well-being, and family stability are all affected by health. The **health care institution** is the primary one for promoting the general health of a society. At one time, health care was addressed primarily in the home, by families. Today, in wealthy countries, health care is a major social institution and health care organizations are major employers (Ballantine & Roberts, 2009).

Unfortunately, there is much disparity in the global health care institution, both between and within countries (WHO, 2008b). Global inequalities in child and adult mortality are large and growing. They are highly influenced by factors in the economic institution and the health care institution, but also by factors in the education institution and the family institution (Ruger & Kim, 2006). Almost 10 million children in the world die each year before they are 5 years old (UNICEF, 2009). Every 2 minutes, four people in the world die from malaria, three of them children. Almost all (98%) of the children who die each year live in poor countries. The sad story is that these children "die because of where they are born" (United Nations Development Program, 2005, p. 24).

Conflict perspective

In poor countries, basic health prevention and treatment services are almost nonexistent. The World Health Organization (2006d) reports that the African Region has 24% of the world's health burden but only 3% of the world's health workers, and it attracts only 1% of world health expenditure. People living in extreme poverty typically lack access to safe drinking water, adequate housing, adequate sanitation, adequate nutrition, health education, and professional health care. Infectious and parasitic diseases are rampant; they account for 77% of child deaths in Africa and 57% of those in Southeast Asia, compared to about 5% of child deaths in the United States and Western Europe. And yet, only 1% of the drugs introduced by pharmaceutical companies between 1975 and 1999 target the tropical diseases that kill or disable millions of people in Africa, Asia, and South America each year (D. Newman, 2008). In sub-Saharan Africa, only 17% of those in need of antiretroviral therapy for HIV/AIDS had access to it in December 2005, even though there was an eightfold increase in coverage between December 2003 and December 2005. In the Sudan, less than 1% of those in need had access (WHO, 2006b).

Within-country health disparities are very prominent in the United States, where deep inequalities are related to socioeconomic status, race, and ethnicity, and poverty is seen as the driving force behind the growing health disparities (J. Chen et al., 2006). A baby born to a family in the top 5% of the U.S. income distribution has an average life expectancy that is 25% longer than a baby born to a family in the bottom 5% (United Nations Development Program, 2005). As a result of poor health, impoverished children are at risk for poor school attendance and thus low educational attainment, increasing the odds of poor health and its consequences across the life course (L. Bauman, Silver, & Stein, 2006). However, it is clear that race as well as social class critically impact health disparities in the United States. Even at the higher ends of education, there are large health gaps between African Americans and Whites (J. Jackson, 2006).

Although much of the health disparities are related to factors in other social institutions, aspects of the health care institution play a large role. The United States is currently the only affluent country with no universal health plan. In 2008, an estimated 46.3 million people in the United States (15.4% of the population) were without health insurance coverage (DeNavas-Walt et al., 2009). Between 2007 and 2008, there was a slight decline in the percentage of people covered by private health insurance and a slight increase in the percentage covered by government health insurance. It is likely that the number of uninsured grew during the recession that began in December 2007, as the rate of unemployment grew. The uninsured rate varied by race and ethnicity for the 3-year period 2006–2008. American Indians/Alaska Natives (31.7%) and Latinos (30.7%) were about three times as likely to be uninsured as Whites/Not Hispanic (10.7%); and Native Hawaiian and Other Pacific Islanders (18.5%), Asian Americans (16.6%), and African Americans (19.7%) were close to twice as likely (DeNavas-Walt et al., 2009). Over 40% of the uninsured have no usual source of health care, and almost half (49%) of uninsured adults with chronic conditions reported going without needed health care because of the cost in 2003 (Davidoff & Kenney, 2005; United Nations Development Program, 2005).

The level of uninsured individuals and families is only part of the story. Recent research indicates that bankruptcies related to health care costs have been increasing, and one study found that 62.1% of all bankruptcies in the United

States in 2007 were caused by illness and medical bills, up 49.6% since 2001. Three-quarters of the people involved in medical bankruptcies had health insurance. Many faced bankruptcy because they lost income due to illness or mortgaged their home to pay for medical bills. Most people facing medical bankruptcy owned their own homes, were well educated, and had middle-class occupations (Himmelstein, Thorne, Warren, Woolhandler, 2009).

Jeanne Ballantine and Keith Roberts (2009) suggest that the United States has both the best and the worst health care system in the industrialized world. It is one of the best in terms of quality of care, trained practitioners, facilities, and technology. But it is the worst in terms of costs, inefficiency, equality of access, and fragmentation. As demonstrated in Exhibit 9.9, the United States spends a greater percentage of its GDP on health care than any other industrialized country and has the greatest concentration of advanced medical technology. Even so, the World Health Organization ranks the United States 37th among all nations in performance of its health care system (Auerbach & Krimgold, 2001). Public satisfaction with the health care system does not seem to reflect the percentage of the national GDP spent on health. In 1999–2000, public satisfaction was highest in Austria, with 83% of the public reporting that they were fairly or very happy with their health care system. This compares to 40% in the United States. Indeed, satisfaction levels were lower than those in the United States in only three countries—Italy, Portugal, and Greece (Organisation for Economic Co-operation and Development [OECD], 2006a). The major causes of dissatisfaction in the United States relate to costs and system fragmentation. One solution that some U.S. patients are choosing is to become what is called "medical tourists." They are traveling to countries such as India, Thailand, Singapore, and Malaysia for surgery and other procedures, where the costs are typically 20% to 25% of what they are in the United States (Kher, 2008).

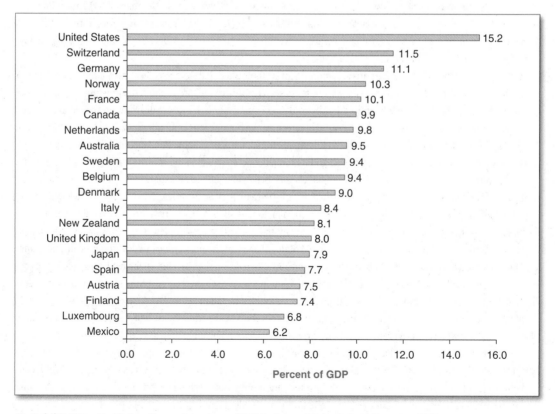

▲ **Exhibit 9.9**   Health Spending as Percentage of GDP in Selected Industrialized Countries, 2003

SOURCE: Based on World Health Organization (2006a).

The reasons why the health care institution is so costly in the United States are quite complex, but two contributing factors are discussed here. First, compared to the health care systems in other countries, the U.S. approach to financing health care is extremely complex, and the administrative cost of this complex system is greater than in the more streamlined universal systems in other industrialized countries (Reinhardt, Hussey, & Anderson, 2004). Second, the health care institution is influenced by culture. Health care in the United States reflects the aggressive, can-do spirit of the mainstream culture (H. W. Gardiner & Kosmitzki, 2008; D. Newman, 2008). For example, compared to European physicians, U.S. physicians recommend more routine examinations and perform many more bypass surgeries and angioplasties than European doctors. These are both examples of a more aggressive approach to treatment that could be attributed to a reimbursement system that rewards such aggressiveness as much as to a cultural bias toward aggressive treatment (Reinhardt, Hussey, & Anderson, 2002). The rapid growth in **therapeutic medicine**—diagnosing and treating disease—has drained resources from the U.S. *public health system,* which focuses on disease prevention and health promotion (Coombs & Capper, 1996). Researchers in the United States and the United Kingdom agree that the impressive decline in mortality in the 20th century was more the result of improvements in the social and physical environments in which people lived than of advances in medical treatment. They note that medical advancements such as therapeutic drugs, immunizations, and surgical procedures were introduced several decades after significant declines in the diseases that they targeted (Auerbach & Krimgold, 2001).

Societies around the world struggle with health care costs, quality and access to care, and medical technology. Most governments in Europe made a decision in the late 1800s and early 1900s to support health care as a human right and put some form of national health care system into place. It appears that they were operating out of a belief that maintaining a healthy population was necessary to maintain a strong society. In contrast, the health care system in the United States developed with less direction and made piecemeal policies over time. Medical research has been a major strength in the developing health care system, but the two biggest challenges in the past three decades have been lack of universal access to care and continuously escalating costs. Several attempts were made to develop federal legislation to address these problems for a number of decades, but these efforts failed because politicians had different philosophical positions on the role of government in health care delivery and because of considerable opposition from private insurance companies, physicians, and pharmaceutical companies.

After a year-long contentious debate, the U.S. Congress passed the Patient Protection and Affordable Care Act and the Health Care and Education Reconciliation Act of 2010, and both bills were signed into law in March 2010. It is projected that 95% of people in the United States will be covered by the new health reform plan once the plan is fully implemented by the end of 2018 (Whitehouse.gov, 2010). As this is book is being prepared for production, some states are challenging the new health reform legislation, and its impact once it is fully implemented remains to be seen. Proponents of the legislation argue that it will make health insurance more affordable (whitehouse.gov, 2010).

Like many other families, the Meza family may need social work assistance to navigate the very complex, quite fragmented health care system as they seek ongoing care for Minerva. Social workers need to be particularly sensitive to the situation of immigrant families who try to integrate traditional healing traditions with global North, technology-oriented medical practices.

Critical Thinking Questions 9.1

What have you heard about the benefits of economic globalization? What have you heard about harms from economic globalization? What do you make of the controversy about whether economic globalization is a good thing or a bad thing? How is economic globalization affecting the government institution and the education institution?

Trends in Social Welfare

The Meza family is facing a number of stressors that are beginning to overwhelm them and tear at their relationships with one another. Although Mrs. Meza is becoming desperate about her situation, because of her undocumented immigrant status she is fearful about trusting anyone outside the family. Her understanding of what social workers do is that they "take children away," and her social worker will have a challenge to win her trust. A good understanding of the special stressors of undocumented immigrants will be essential. As social workers, we are well aware of the network of social welfare agencies and programs that could help the Meza family; we are also aware of the gaps in the contemporary social welfare institution.

Different writers have presented various definitions of the **social welfare institution,** but the definition provided by Philip Popple and Leslie Leighninger (2001) is particularly compatible with the one used in this chapter: The social welfare institution functions to promote *interdependence* and to deal with issues of *dependence*. Individuals are interdependent with institutions, as well as with other individuals, for survival and for satisfactory role performance. We depend on our doctors, day care centers, families, friends, neighbors, and so on, and they depend on us. Sometimes, situations occur that increase our need for assistance or decrease the assistance available to us. For example, we may become sick or injured, lose our job, or take on a caregiving role for a newborn infant or a frail parent. In these situations, our ability to successfully fulfill role expectations is jeopardized—a situation that Popple and Leighninger refer to as dependence. In analyzing such problematic situations, social workers must pay attention not only to the behavior of individuals, but also to how well social institutions are supporting people in their role performance.

> Systems perspective

In the contemporary era, there are several major challenges facing the social welfare institution around the globe.

- *Aging population.* The prosperous advanced industrialized societies in the United States, Europe, and Japan face a crisis involving aging populations produced by recent trends of mass longevity and low fertility, a situation commonly referred to as the "graying" of the population. In the United States, that has translated into policy debates about "tightening" our Social Security and Medicare programs. Japan, the world's most rapidly graying nation, has begun to respond by cutting back its safety net for older adults (Faiola, 2006).

- *Labor market insecurities.* Global labor market insecurities are undermining the ability of families, even those with middle incomes, to avoid dependence. This situation intensified during the deep economic recession that began in December 2007.

- *Debt in low-income countries.* The World Bank and IMF have required many impoverished countries to reduce social spending as a condition for rescheduling their debt during a time when these countries face rising numbers of orphans of the AIDS pandemic (McMichael, 2008).

- *Increasing evidence of the importance of the early years.* Behavioral science research is finding increasing evidence of the important role that early social environment plays in long-term physical and mental health.

The social welfare institution developed in all industrialized countries in the 19th and 20th centuries as these nations tried to cope with the alienation and disruption caused by social inequalities of industrial capitalism (Teeple, 2000). However, the social welfare institution, like any other social institution, reflects the culture of the society. Exhibit 9.10 demonstrates that public expenditure on social welfare (including old age, survivors, disability, health, family, unemployment, housing, and other policies), as a percentage of GDP, varies among affluent societies. It also demonstrates that expenditures on social welfare increased in most affluent societies between 1980 and 2003. It is important to note, however, that as societies gray, expenditures on old-age benefits are increasing at a much faster

Country	Percentage Change 1980–2003	Percentage of GDP in 2003
Ireland	−5%	15.9
United States	+22%	16.2
Canada	+23%	17.3
Japan	+72%	17.7
Australia	+64%	17.9
New Zealand	+5%	18.0
United Kingdom	+21%	20.1
Spain	+31%	20.3
Switzerland	+47%	20.5
Netherlands	−14%	20.7
Greece	+85%	21.3
Luxembourg	-6%	22.2
Finland	+22%	22.5
Portugal	+118%	23.5
Italy	+34%	24.2
Norway	+49%	25.1
Austria	+15%	26.1
Belgium	+13%	26.5
Denmark	+10%	27.6
Germany	+20%	27.6
France	+38%	28.7
Sweden	+9%	31.3

▲ **Exhibit 9.10**   Public Social Expenditures on Social Welfare as a Percentage of GDP in 2003

SOURCE: Based on OECD (2006b).

rate than those in other social welfare sectors. Consequently, in many affluent countries, there was an increase in child poverty rates, but not older adult poverty rates, in the 1990s (UNICEF, 2005). Given what we are learning about the long-term negative health consequences of early deprivation, this may pose serious challenges for the social welfare institution in the future (N. Adler, 2006).

The differences in cultural attitudes toward social welfare are best illustrated by the approaches of the United States and Europe. In the United States, the neoliberal political philosophy led to a diminishing sense of public responsibility and an increasing emphasis on individual responsibility for the social well-being of the nation. U.S. officials have boasted in recent years about how much the welfare rolls have been reduced since the passage of welfare reform in 1996. In a period of declining security in the labor market, the governmental welfare safety net for families with children has become more short term (Sennett, 2006). The overall goal of U.S. policy is to prevent dependency.

In contrast, European officials tend to speak with pride about their "European Social Model" and their "welfare state" (T. R. Reid, 2004). Their goal is to promote interdependence and social inclusion, rather than preventing dependence, and paying for the social health of the society is seen as everyone's responsibility. Indeed, the expansive cradle-to-grave programs in the European welfare states are expensive and paid for by high taxes, particularly high sales taxes, which run from a low of 16% in Germany to a high of 25% in Denmark and Sweden (T. R. Reid, 2004). European countries have higher minimum wages and more generous unemployment compensation than the United States. A worker who becomes unemployed in the United States will receive an average of 50% wage replacement from public assistance. In Europe, a laid-off worker receives a housing benefit, heat and light benefit, food benefit, child care benefit, as well as a monthly unemployment payment, in addition to continued access to public health care. This results in the family of an unemployed person in France receiving approximately 86% of the former earnings, while the family of an unemployed person in Sweden or the Netherlands receives approximately 90% of the former earnings. European countries provide birth or maternity grants, family allowances, and generous paid parental leave to care for children. Many European countries treat the monthly payment to parents as a salary, withholding income and social security taxes as would happen with any paycheck (T. R. Reid, 2004).

The European countries are not alone in providing more generous public support to families than is offered in the United States. Parental leave policies are a good example. The United States and Australia are the only affluent countries of the world that do not offer some *paid* parental leave at the time of birth and adoption. Australia does, however, provide families with a universal, flat-rate maternity grant of $5,000 for each new child to assist with the costs of birth or adoption (Australian Government, 2006). Many low- and middle-income countries also offer paid parental leave; for example, Afghanistan offers 3 months at 100% of wages, the Bahamas offers 13 weeks at 60% of wages, Brazil offers 17 weeks at 100% of wages, Congo offers 15 weeks at 50% of wages, and Libya offers 3 months at 100% of wages (Clearinghouse on International Developments on Child, Youth and Family Policies, 2004). If the Mezas lived in Sweden, they might have made use of a family policy that allows one year of parental leave at 80% of wage replacement as well as up to 60 days of sick child leave at the same wage-replacement level. The sick child leave could give them time to work with the multidisciplinary team to stabilize the situation at home.

The social welfare institution in the United States has been influenced by the call to move federal power both downward and outward. The Personal Responsibility and Work Opportunity Reconciliation Act (PRWORA) of 1996 devolved to the states most of the responsibility for public assistance to needy families and children. The Temporary Assistance to Needy Families (TANF) block grant gives states more flexibility to design their own public assistance programs (Urban Institute, 2006). This is a downward movement of power. However, in 2006, the Congress and the George W. Bush administration wrote new rules that tightened the federal reins on state definitions of work requirements for people on welfare, demonstrating some continued negotiations about the role of federal and state governments (A. Goldstein, 2006).

Since the 1970s, there has also been a growing global trend for government at all levels to develop "purchase of service" contract agreements with private, nonprofit organizations to provide social welfare services in "public–private partnerships." These nonprofit organizations are coming to be known as *nongovernmental organizations* (NGOs). This trend has accelerated since the 1980s, particularly in affluent societies. In recent natural disasters, such as the Asian Tsunami caused by an Indian Ocean earthquake in December 2004 and the earthquake in Haiti in January 2010, large numbers of NGOs provided aid, but coordination among them was a major challenge. In 2004, it was estimated that 2 million NGOs operate in the United States, with 70% of them established since the 1970s (Roff, 2004).

Historically, the social welfare institution has had a mix of governmental and nongovernmental monies and activities, but the nature of this mix has changed over time. The government is now playing a smaller role in delivering social service programs, but it continues to play a large role in the funding of services through contract agreements (Schmid, 2004). In the late 1990s, nonprofit organizations in the United States received 43% of their revenues from government, while those in France received 58% from government, those in Britain received 47%, and those in Israel, 55% (Salamon, Anheier, List, Toepler, & Sokolowski, 1999). The nonprofit sector is larger in affluent countries than in low- and middle-income countries, and it is most highly developed in Western Europe (Roff, 2004; Salamon et al., 1999). Increasingly, NGOs are becoming multinational organizations, and there is some evidence that social welfare is higher in poor countries when multinational NGOs are involved (Aldashev & Verdier, 2009).

There is also a long history of faith-based organizations providing social welfare services in the United States. Currently, much controversy exists about the "charitable choice provision" of PRWORA, which allows states to contract with religious organizations, as well as other private organizations, for service provision. President George W. Bush (2000–2008) introduced a "faith-based initiative" to expand the role of faith-based organizations in social service delivery. When he took office in 2009, President Barack Obama developed the White House Office of Faith-Based and Neighborhood Partnerships to build bridges between the federal government and both secular and faith-based nonprofits. Some critics have been concerned that the religious freedom of clients would not be honored with such arrangements. However, a 2009 public opinion poll showed that 69% of the U.S. public favors allowing religious organizations to apply for government funding to provide social services, but 63% oppose allowing groups that encourage religious conversion to seek such funding (Pew Research Center, 2009).

The most controversial trend in the social welfare institution is the entrance of for-profit organizations into the mix of public–private partnerships, beginning in the 1980s. The for-profit share of social welfare services continued to grow, and by the early 1990s, nearly half of social welfare agencies in the United States were for-profit, and they accounted for 22% of all social service employees (P. Frumkin, 2002; L. Lynn, 2002). The for-profit organizations continue to expand their business lines into new service sectors. America Works, Maximus, Children's Comprehensive Services, and Youth Services International are just a few of the large, for-profit social welfare organizations on the contemporary scene. Among the serious questions that have been raised by the entrance of for-profit organizations into the social welfare institution is whether these organizations will choose to serve only "easy to serve" client groups, avoiding those with entrenched problems related to poverty (L. Lynn, 2002; W. Ryan, 1999). For-profit agencies have greater access to capital and can take advantage of efficiencies of scale if they are part of a national chain (S. Smith, 2010).

The Meza family is struggling to reorganize itself to cope with Minerva's special needs. They could use help in this effort, but to date, they have experienced the social welfare institution only as a coercive institution, one that tries to control their behavior rather than provide compassionate support. Indeed, the social welfare institution in the United States has always played a social control function as well as a social reform function (Hutchison, 1987). In recent times, it has moved toward greater attention to social control than to social reform (Hutchison & Charlesworth, 2000; Teeple, 2000). Social workers cannot be active participants in moving that balance back to social reform unless they clearly understand trends in the interrelated social institutions discussed in this chapter.

> Conflict perspective

Trends in Religion

Mrs. Meza believes that Minerva's health problems are God's way of punishing her for not placing the health of her unborn child over other concerns. This is how she makes meaning of the situation. The **religious institution** is the primary one for addressing spiritual and ethical issues. It also serves important socialization, social control, and mutual support functions.

Although there is a long history of conflict and adaptation as the major world religions confronted each other in the same political and geographic areas, globalization has urgently increased the need for religious communities to find ways to coexist globally as well as locally. A religious belief system helps people to feel secure, and exposure to different belief systems can be unsettling and sometimes perceived as a threat to the integrity of one's own beliefs and identity. Today, however, it is almost impossible for believers in one religious tradition to be isolated from other religious traditions. We are increasingly exposed to the beliefs, rituals, and organizations of diverse religious groups, and this is not a trend that is likely to be reversed. There are few choices about how to cope with this trend. We can attempt to impose one belief system on the world and commit genocide if that doesn't work. Or we can attempt to find a unified ethical code that is consistent with all religious traditions, and respectfully agree to disagree if that doesn't work, giving legal protections to all groups. In the past, both these choices have been put into practice at one time or another.

We are living in a time of much religious strife. Serbian Orthodox Christians recently engaged in ethnic cleansing of Muslims in the former Yugoslavia. Catholics and Protestants have waged a long and often violent battle in Northern Ireland. The Ku Klux Klan in the United States has used religious arguments to vilify and sometimes persecute Jews, African Americans, and other groups. Terrorists have killed and injured thousands in the name of Islam. The United States has called on the name of God, and the language of good and evil, to justify the war on terror and the invasion of Iraq. Hindus and Muslims kill each other in India. When religious differences are woven with other forms of struggle, such as social class, ethnic, or political struggle, the conflict is likely to be particularly intense (L. Kurtz, 2007).

On the other hand, there are also historical and current stories of peaceful coexistence of religious groups. In 1893, representatives of a wide range of religions were brought together to create the Parliament of the World's Religions. The second meeting of the Parliament did not convene until a century later, in 1993 (L. Kurtz, 2007). It met again in 1999, 2004, and 2009. The mission of the parliament is "to cultivate harmony among the world's religious and spiritual communities and foster their engagement with the world and its other guiding institutions in order to achieve a just, peaceful and sustainable world" (Council for a Parliament of the World's Religions, 2010). Among the issues discussed and debated at the 2009 parliament were healing the earth, reconciling with Indigenous peoples, overcoming poverty in a patriarchal world, increasing social cohesion in village and city, sharing wisdom in search for inner peace, securing food and water for all people, and building peace in pursuit of justice. Many predict that access to safe water will become the next major battle over scarce resources (McMichael, 2008).

It is not surprising that both violence and nonviolence have been used in the name of religion. The texts of all of the major world religions include what Lester Kurtz (2007) calls both a "warrior motif" and a "pacifist motif" (p. 247). All major religions justify violence on occasion, but no religion justifies terrorism. They also include norms of mercy, compassion, and respect. In the contemporary era, Islam is sometimes characterized as a violent religion, but Christianity was seen as the most violent world religion during the Crusades and the Inquisition. All of the major world religions have proven that they are capable of perpetrating violence in the name of religion, and all have demonstrated compassion and tolerance.

It is good to get a sense of the global religious landscape. Consider a group of 10 people that represent the distribution of world religions. Three will be Christian, two will be Muslim, two will be unaffiliated or atheists, one will be Hindu, one will be Buddhist or from another East Asian religion, and the remaining one will represent every other religion of the world (L. Kurtz, 2007). This landscape includes two Eastern religions (Hinduism and Buddhism) and three Western religions (Judaism, Christianity, and Islam). The Western religions are *monotheistic,* believing that there is only one God, while the Eastern religions are either *polytheistic,* believing in multiple Gods (e.g., Hinduism, some forms of Buddhism) or not believing in a deity (e.g., some forms of Buddhism). Eastern religions are less insistent on the primacy of their "Truth" than the Western religions and are more likely to embrace nonviolence. Eastern religions have also tended to be less centrally organized than the Western religions.

Each of the major world religions has changed over time and place and become more diverse, a "patchwork of contradictory ideas stitched together over the centuries" (L. Kurtz, 2007, p. 190). Lester Kurtz suggests that we should speak of all of the major world religions in the plural: Hinduisms, Buddhisms, Judaisms, Christianities, and Islams. He also argues that some of the most violent contests occur *within* these religious traditions and not *between* them, as experienced by the Christian Catholics and Protestants in Northern Ireland, and the Muslim Sunnis and Shias in Iraq.

Each of the major world religions, but especially the Western religions, has an internal struggle, sometimes called a culture war (J. D. Hunter, 1994), between a branch of traditionalists and a branch of modernists (L. Kurtz, 2007). The *traditionalists* believe that moral obligations are rigid, given, and absolute. The *modernists* believe that moral commitment is voluntary, conditional, and fluid. These two branches often engage in a struggle for the heart and soul of the religious tradition, sometimes using violence to press their case.

> Conflict perspective

Although many religious peoples around the world fear that modernism and postmodernism are destroying religion, there is clear evidence that the religious institution is quite resilient. Public opinion polls consistently report that religion is important in the lives of a great majority of people in the United States (Gallup, 2008). International data indicate that people in the United States have much higher weekly attendance at religious services than Europeans; they spend more time in private devotions and more money on religious activities than residents of other advanced industrialized countries. This is an aspect of U.S. life that has been very appealing to the Meza and many other immigrant families. In the 1990s, about 60% of the U.S. population were church members, compared with about 10% in 1776 (L. Kurtz, 2007). As suggested in Chapter 6, diversity is the hallmark of the religious institution in the United States today, with between 1,500 and 2,000 religious groups represented, about half of them Christian (L. Kurtz, 2007; Parrillo, 2009). Indeed, the United States might be the most religiously diverse country in the world today.

Christianity remains dominant within the United States, but there are intense culture wars between the traditionalists and the modernists, with the conflict centering on such issues as the definition of family, the role of women, the beginning and end of life, same-sex relationships, prayer in school, and theories of the creation of the world. Both the traditionalists and the modernists base their arguments on their understanding of biblical texts, but each tends to see the other as immoral.

> Conflict perspective

Some examples will help to clarify the competing moral precepts regarding some of these questions. Traditionalists see the push for women's rights as destructive to the traditional family and motherhood. Modernists see women's rights as necessary in a just society. Likewise, traditionalists see the gay rights movement as a particularly vicious attack on the traditional family, and modernists see it as a struggle for dignity. Traditionalists argue that school prayer is essential to help students develop a moral code, and modernists argue that it is an intrusion on religious freedom and tolerance. The culture wars are intense because both groups wish for dominance in the political institution.

On the global scale, Lester Kurtz (2007) suggests that each of the world's major religions has something to offer to the effort to find a way for religious groups to peacefully coexist:

Hinduism: The idea that there are many paths to the same summit

Buddhism: The idea that the way to escape suffering is to treat all creatures with compassion

Judaism: The idea that we should be a light for others

Christianity: The ideas of loving one's enemies and bringing good news to the poor

Islam: The call for intensity of commitment

Given the clear evidence of the central importance of religion in the lives of billions of people in the world, social workers must become comfortable in assessing the role of religion and spirituality in the lives of their

▲ **Photos 9.4a & 9.4b**   Mass media technology is the engine of globalization, and people around the world are saturated with images from multiple media forms. In photo 9.4a, a man sits next to a billboard promoting Chinese wine in Chengdu. In Photo 9.4b, a woman logs in to her Facebook page.

client systems at the individual, family, and community levels. Certainly, we cannot be helpful to Mrs. Meza without understanding the role religion plays in the way she views her situation or her connectedness to a religious community. We should not assume that all persons of a religious group hold the same beliefs regarding social issues. But we must be aware of religious beliefs—both our own and those of clients—when working with controversial social issues.

Trends in Mass Media

The **mass media institution** is the primary institution for managing the flow of information, images, and ideas among all members of society. Mass media serves an entertainment role for society, but it also influences how we understand ourselves and the world. Mass media technology is the engine of globalization, giving people worldwide immediate access to other cultures and other markets. Rapid advances in electronic communication technology since the 1950s have resulted in widespread access to multiple forms of mass communication—"old media" such as newspapers, magazines, books, radio, television, and film, and "new media" such as the Internet, digital television and radio, MP3 players, ever more elaborate multifunctional cellular telephones, and video games. Electronic media now allow two-way as well as one-way communication, and they can store and manipulate vast amounts of information. The mass media is thoroughly embedded in our daily lives and a larger focus of our leisure time than any other social institution (Devereau, 2008).

Like other families around the world, the Meza family is saturated with images from these media. Some of these images are negative portrayals of Mexican immigrants, which add to the family's distress, but others, like those shown on the television networks Univision and Telemundo, allow them to be in touch with their Latino heritage, and Telemundo (a U.S. network that broadcasts in Spanish with closed captions in both English and Spanish) can help make connections between the English and Spanish languages.

There are several important trends in the mass media landscape:

1. *Growth in media outlets and media products.* For much of the latter half of the 20th century, U.S. households had access to 3 television channels, but by 2002, the average number of television channels receivable by U.S. families

reached over 100, and some predict that we may well be coming into an era of over 500 cable channels (Croteau & Hoynes, 2006). New media products have been coming at a very fast clip for more than a decade.

2. *More time and money spent on media products.* There were 650,000 cable television subscribers in the United States in 1960, but the number had grown to 74 million by 2003. In an even newer media sector, the number of cellular telephone subscribers in the United States was 5 million in 1990, and by 2010, an estimated 83% of adults reported having a cell phone. (There are over 220 million adults in the United States, and some own more than one cell phone [Croteau & Hoynes, 2006; Rainie, 2010].) Indeed, by the end of 2007, half of the world's people had a mobile phone, including 1 out of 4 in Africa and 1 out of 3 in Asia (International Telecommunications Union, 2008). Widespread use of the Internet did not begin until the early 1990s, but by 2010, the Pew Internet & American Life Project found that 74% of U.S. adults over the age of 18 used the Internet (Rainie, 2010).

3. *Integration of media functions.* Increasingly, one media product is expected to provide several functions. Computers can be used to word process; surf the Internet; communicate by e-mail, instant message, social networking sites, or Skype; participate in chat rooms and blogs; shop; play music; watch DVDs; or read online newspapers. Cellular phones can now send text messages, take and transmit photographs, browse the Internet, and communicate by e-mail or on social networking sites. Newspapers have stagnated or lost readership, but large newspapers are developing online versions (Oates, 2008).

4. *Globalization.* Media companies are increasingly targeting a global market to sell products. For example, by 2006, the Viacom corporation reported that it had been able to export the MTV (Music Television) network to 175 countries and territories, to 480 million households, in more than 25 languages, making it the most widely distributed television network in the world (Croteau & Hoynes, 2006; Viacom, 2006). The great majority of households receiving MTV are outside the United States. The Arabic news channel, Al-Jazeera, is based in Qatar, but its broadcasts are carried worldwide (D. Newman, 2006). Some critics suggest that the global reach of media companies based in North America and Europe, particularly in the United States, is a form of cultural imperialism through which U.S. cultural values are spread around the world (Devereux, 2008).

5. *Concentration of ownership.* The mass media institution has been experiencing a merger mania. In 1983, the majority of all media products in the United States were controlled by 50 media companies. By 2004, although there were many new media products, five global conglomerates controlled the media business in the United States: Time Warner (U.S.), Disney (U.S.), News Corporation (Britain), Viacom (U.S.), and Bertelsmann (Germany) (Bagdikian, 2004). News Corporation CEO Rupert Murdoch argues that his company, News Corp, is the most international mass media provider in the world. News Corp owns several movie studios, including Twentieth Century Fox, and has released such blockbusters as *Star Wars* and *Titanic.* It owns satellite systems and television channels in North America, Europe, and Asia. News Corp is the leading publisher of English-language newspapers, owning more than 100 in the United States, the United Kingdom, Australia, Fiji, Papua New Guinea, and across Europe and Asia. The *Wall Street Journal* was bought by News Corp in 2007. HarperCollins Publishers, with more than 20 imprints, is News Corp's book publishing division. In addition, News Corp owns MySpace, the social networking site. It also owns the Australian National Rugby League, it has owned the British soccer club Manchester United and the Los Angeles Dodgers baseball club, and it has been a minority owner of the New York Knicks basketball team and the New York Rangers hockey team (News Corporation, 2006, 2010).

In totalitarian societies, like North Korea, the flow of information, images, and ideas is controlled by the government. In the United States, we have a long tradition of freedom of the press—a belief that the media must be free to serve as a public watchdog. Traditionally, the emphasis has been on the watchdog role in relation to the government and political institution—in other words, a press that is not controlled by the government. Exposure of the Watergate cover-up during the Richard M. Nixon presidency is considered a high point in U.S. media history. However, the relationship between government and media is controversial, with some groups calling for more government censorship (e.g., to limit young people's access and exposure to pornography) and other groups calling for strict adherence to freedom of the press. In the current era of media mergers and acquisitions, concerns have centered on media censorship by the economic institution (Bagdikian, 2004; Croteau & Hoynes, 2006). Critics suggest that powerful multinational media corporations censor the coverage of news to protect their economic or political interests. Organizations that analyze freedom of the press report that after two decades of improvement around the world, there was a decline in press freedom in 2009, with only 17% of the world's population living in countries with a free press. These organizations rated the United States as 21st in freedom of the press in 2009. The highest marks went to the Nordic countries (Freedom House, 2010; Reporters Without Borders, 2010).

Social psychologists have been interested in the effects of the media on human behavior, focusing particularly on the effects of television, which has become the dominant form of mass media communication globally. Research on the effects of the media on human behavior is difficult to design, because it is hard to isolate the effects of specific media forms in changing person-environment configurations and to capture the cumulative effect of multiple forms. Although it is possible for the media to influence human behavior in both positive and negative ways, the research has focused, for the most part, on negative effects. Social workers and other professionals have been particularly concerned that television provides more models of antisocial than prosocial behavior. Feminists have been concerned about the influence of gender role stereotypes presented in the media. Members of racial and ethnic minority groups; the disability community; and the gay, lesbian, bisexual, and transgender community have also been concerned about stereotypical media presentations of their groups (D. Newman, 2008). The Mezas have grown increasingly concerned about the negative portrayal of immigrant issues on U.S. television.

Conflict perspective

Mass media critics also suggest that control of the media by political and economic elites results in control of cultural meanings to benefit elites and silence dissident views. The mass media has historically been controlled by White, middle- and upper-class men, who have presented their worldviews. Mass media owners are interested in attracting affluent consumers and choose content with this aim in mind (Croteau & Hoynes, 2006). As a partial corrective, Croteau and Hoynes argue that privately owned media should be required to provide a minimum amount of substantive public affairs programming. Social work advocates can collaborate with other professionals toward this goal.

It is estimated that there were 1.7 billion Internet users around the world in September 2009, but they are concentrated in the wealthy industrialized nations. The latest cross-national data indicate that the largest number of users (738 million) are in Asia, with 418 million in Europe, 252 million in North America, 179 million in Latin America/Caribbean, 67 million in Africa, 57 million in the Middle East, and 20 million in Oceania/Australia. Although Asia has the most Internet users, North America has the highest percentage of its population online (74.2%), compared to 60.4% in Oceania/Australia, 52.0% in Europe, 30.5% in Latin America/Caribbean, 28.3% in the Middle East, 19.4% in Asia, and 6.8% in Africa (Internet World Stats, 2010). When interpreting these data, it is important to note that the European data include both wealthy Western European countries and the less wealthy Eastern European countries. Unequal access perpetuates advantage and disadvantage in life chances. Writing about the United States, Croteau and Hoynes (2006) argue that we must work toward publicly funded universal access to the Internet to prevent "hardening of the digital divide" (p. 239). They suggest that Internet services should be made available to schools, community centers, and libraries, particularly in low-income neighborhoods. Increasing access to the Internet has also raised new questions about the need to prevent minors from gaining access to sexually explicit material and from being exploited by predators on the Internet. These are issues that call for social work advocacy.

Trends in Family and Kinship

You undoubtedly would agree that family and kinship relationships are a very important part of the unfolding story of the Meza family. Family and kinship is the most basic social institution, and in simple societies it fulfills many of the functions assigned to other social institutions in complex societies. Although the functions of family and kinship have been the subject of some controversy in the contemporary era, most societies generally agree that the **family and kinship institution** is primarily responsible for the regulation of procreation, for the initial socialization of new members of society, and for mutual support.

As the primary unit of every society, families are altered as the result of social change, and globalization is changing family life in some extraordinary ways around the world (Adams & Trost, 2005; Leeder, 2004). There are many ways of being a family that are evident around the globe, and there seems to be an exception for almost every family trend that can be identified. However, we can identify three global trends in family life.

1. *Modified extended family form.* Historically, the extended family has been more important in Latin America, Asia, and Africa than in Europe and North America. Globalization appears to be leading to some convergence toward a *modified extended family,* a family system in which family members are highly involved with each other but maintain separate dwellings (Leeder, 2004). This is the current family form for the Meza family, where family members maintain households across national lines, making them one of the growing numbers of *transnational families.* Within this general pattern, there are many variations. In wealthy advanced industrialized societies, governmental programs augment the care of dependent family members, but such programs are not typically available in nonindustrial or newly industrializing societies. Marriages continue to be arranged by the elders in many parts of the world, particularly in African and Asian societies, but they are based on love matches in Western societies. *Monogamy,* or marriage to one person at a time, is the norm in Western societies, but *polygamy,* or marriage to multiple partners, is still followed in some parts of the world.

2. *Mass migration.* Migration for a better life is not new; indeed, it is the history of the United States. Between 1810 and 1921, a total of 34 million people emigrated from Europe to the United States (McMichael, 2008). With economic globalization, many rural peasants in nonindustrialized and newly industrializing countries have been displaced by large agricultural corporations, many headquartered in the United States; some move to the cities in their own countries, and others immigrate to countries with greater economic opportunities. Many migrate because their labor became obsolete in a constantly reorganizing global market. Still others migrate to escape war or political persecution. By one account, 75% of refugees and displaced persons are women and children (McMichael, 2008). Often families are separated, with some members migrating and others staying behind, sometimes to migrate at a later stage. Migrants seek to earn money for families back home, and it is estimated that 100 million people globally depend on the remittances from family members who have migrated (McMichael, 2008). Indeed, the Mezas regularly send money to relatives in Mexico. In affluent societies, like the United States, corporations welcome the cheap labor of undocumented immigrants, and wealthy households welcome the access to cheap household servants. Yet there is ongoing backlash and political fear campaigns against immigrants from low-income nations. Anti-immigrant sentiment has been particularly strong in Europe in recent years (Klapper, 2006).

3. *Feminization of wage labor.* In many parts of the world, women are increasingly involved in wage labor, in newly industrializing as well as highly industrialized societies (Leeder, 2004). For example, women make up 80% of the labor force in the export processing zones of Taiwan, the Philippines, Sri Lanka, Mexico, and Malaysia. In these export zones, women typically work longer hours at lower wages than men (McMichael, 2008). In the United States, both parents currently work outside the home for wages in 78% of married-couple families with children, up from 32% in 1976 (D. Newman, 2008). And yet, there is a global gender wage gap. In the United States, women involved in

full-time wage labor earn about 76 cents for every dollar earned by men. In other late industrial societies, such as Australia, Denmark, France, New Zealand, and the United Kingdom, women earn 80% to 90% of what men earn (D. Newman, 2008). In many parts of Latin America, Africa, and Asia, women earn 25% or less of what men earn (McMichael, 2008). Multinational corporations often pay female factory workers in newly industrializing countries as little as half of what they pay men (D. Newman, 2008).

Two other trends are more characteristic of the United States and other late industrial societies than of the preindustrial and newly industrializing societies, but are occurring, nevertheless, in societies around the world (Adams & Trost, 2005).

1. *A rise in divorce rates.* Increase in divorce and separation are well documented in Argentina, China, Cuba, India, Iran, Kenya, and Kuwait. The divorce rate in the United States is nearly twice what it was in 1960. The divorce rate peaked in 1981, began to decline slightly, and leveled off at the high rate of nearly 50% for first marriages. Divorce rates are highest for couples who married as teens, for high school dropouts, and for the nonreligious (National Marriage Project, 2006). There has been an increase in the divorce rate in almost every advanced industrialized nation since 1960, but the United States leads most others in divorce (Adams & Trost, 2005).

2. *Declining fertility.* Declining fertility has been documented in Argentina, India, Iran, Kenya, Kuwait, South Africa, and Turkey (Adams & Trost, 2005). The birthrate in the United States dropped from 23.7 births per 1,000 population in 1960 to 14.3 in 2007 (B. Hamilton, Martin, & Ventura, 2009; U.S. Department of Health and Human Services, n.d.). People are waiting longer to have children and are having fewer children. In 1970, a total of 73.6% of women between the ages of 25 and 29 had given birth to at least one child; this had fallen to 48.7% by 2000. In 1976, an estimated 1 in 10 women over 40 was childless; this had increased to almost 1 in 5 by 2004. Fertility decreases with education; in 2004, it is estimated that 24% of college-educated women between the ages of 40 and 44 were childless, compared to 15% of women of the same age who lacked a high school education (National Marriage Project, 2006). This means that those with the fewest economic resources are raising a disproportionate number of children in the United States. Another important trend is for more children to be raised in single-parent families; the percentage of children being raised in such families increased from 9% of children in the United States in 1960 to 28% in 2005. Although the total fertility rate in the United States was slightly below the replacement level of 2.1 in 2004, it is one of the highest birthrates in advanced industrialized societies (National Marriage Project, 2006). In China, a one-child policy, initiated in 1979, has resulted in low birthrates.

Two other long-term trends in family relationships are likely to continue: greater valuing of autonomy and self-direction in children, as opposed to obedience and conformity, and equalization of power between men and women. These trends have been found to be almost universal, but they are more problematic in some societies than in others (Adams & Trost, 2005). Not all people agree that these trends are good, and some point to them as causes of the weakening of the family. Other people see these trends as providing possibilities for stabilizing the family in a time of great change in all major social institutions.

The average life expectancy is increasing in all of the advanced industrialized societies. In the United States, it increased from 68.2 years in 1950 to 77.7 years in 2009 (CDC, 2009b). This increase in longevity, added to the decrease in fertility, is changing the shape of families in the late industrial societies. Families now have more generations but fewer people in each generation. The increase in longevity has also led to an increase in chronic disease and the need for families to provide personal care for members with disabilities.

Social service programs serving families, children, and older adults need to be responsive to these changing trends. The confluence of declining family size, increasing numbers of single parents, increasing numbers of women in the paid labor force, and an aging population calls for a reexamination, in particular, of our assumptions about family caregiving for dependent persons. Social workers should lead the way in discussions about social policies that can strengthen families and alleviate family stressors. We must pay particular attention to the needs of immigrant families like the Mezas. These issues receive greater attention in Chapter 10.

| Critical Thinking Questions 9.2 |

What would life be like without the mass media? How would you find out about national and global events? Where would you get your ideas about social welfare, religion, and family? How would your daily life be different?

THEORIES OF SOCIAL INEQUALITY

Throughout this chapter, we have presented information on how social inequality is created and maintained in eight interrelated major social institutions. Social class is the term generally used by sociologists to describe contemporary structures of inequality. Perhaps no question regarding the human condition has generated more intense and complex controversies and conflicts than the related issues of inequality and distributive justice. Unequal distribution of resources is probably as old as the human species and certainly has existed in all complex societies. Long before the discipline of sociology arose, thoughtful people constructed explanations and justifications for these inequalities (Lenski, 1966; Sernau, 2006). Although social class has been an important topic for sociology, by no means do sociologists agree about the role that social class plays in human behavior.

The contributing authors and I have presented inequality as a problem, but as you have probably noted, not everyone agrees with this view. Gerhard Lenski (1966) did a careful study of how societies over time have answered the question, is inequality a good thing or a bad thing? He divided the way that societies have responded to this question into a conservative thesis and a radical antithesis. In the conservative thesis, inequality is the natural, divine order, and no efforts should be made to alter it. In the radical antithesis, equality is the natural, divine order; inequality is based on abuse of privilege and should be minimized.

Classical Sociological Theories of Social Inequality

When social inequality is considered to be the natural order and divinely ordained, there is no need to search further for explanations of inequality. But as this traditional assumption gave way to a belief that human beings are born equal, persistent social inequalities required explanation and justification. Explanation of inequality and its relationship to human behavior became central questions for the emerging social and political sciences. Two classical theorists, Karl Marx (1818–1883) and Max Weber (1864–1920), have had lasting impact on the sociological analysis of social inequality.

Karl Marx was both a social theorist and a committed revolutionary. He was interested in explaining the social inequalities of industrial capitalism, but his interests went beyond explanation of inequality to promotion of a more just and equitable society. Marx (1887/1967) emphasized the economic determinants of social class relationships and proposed that class lines are drawn according to roles in the capitalist production system. Although he did not propose a strict, two-class system, he suggested a social class division based on a dichotomy of owners and controllers of production (bourgeoisie), on the one hand, and workers who must sell their labor to owners (proletariat), on the other. Marx saw the relationship between the classes to be based on exploitation and domination by the owners and controllers of production and on alienation among the workers. He saw social class as a central variable in human behavior and a central force in human history, and he believed that *class consciousness*—not only the awareness of one's social class, but also hostility toward other classes—is what motivates people to transform society.

In contrast to Marx, who was a revolutionary, Weber argued for a value-free social science. Weber differed from Marx in other ways as well. Marx saw a class division based on production roles (owners of production and workers); Max Weber (1947) saw a class division based on "life chances" in the marketplace. *Life chances* reflect the distribution of power within a community, including economic power, social prestige, and legal power. Instead of Marx's dichotomous class system, Weber proposed that life chances fall on a continuum, and that the great variability found along the continuum reflects the multiple sources of power. He suggested that social class is an important variable in human behavior, but not, as Marx believed, the *primary* variable.

This difference in perspective on the causal importance of social class reflects the theorists' disagreement about the inevitability of class consciousness or class action. Marx saw class consciousness and communal action related to class as inevitable. Weber saw social class as a possible, but not inevitable, source of identity and communal action.

The Contemporary Debate

Attempts to determine the cause of persistent social inequalities have led to debate among sociologists who embrace functional theories and sociologists who embrace conflict theories. *Functional theories* of social stratification present structural inequality (social classes) as necessary for society. According to this view, unequal rewards for different types of work guarantee that the most talented persons will work hard and produce technological innovation to benefit the whole society. *Conflict theorists* (see Chapter 2 for more discussion of conflict theories), on the other hand, emphasize the role of power, domination, and coercion in the maintenance of inequality. According to this view, persons with superior wealth and income also hold superior social and political power and use that power to protect their privileged positions.

Sociological functionalism was dominant in U.S. sociology during the 1940s and 1950s, but it faded in importance after that. However, functionalism was the root for *modernization theory,* which attempted, in the 1960s, to explain on the global level why some countries are poor and others are rich (Rostow, 1990). These theorists suggested that poverty is caused by traditional attitudes and technology—by the failure to modernize. The conflict perspective counterargument to modernization theory was *dependency theory,* which argued that poor societies are created by worldwide industrial capitalism, which exploits natural resources and labor (A. Frank, 1967). These theorists emphasized the tremendous power of foreign multinational corporations to coerce national governments in poor nations. They called attention to colonial imperialism as the historical context of contemporary global inequalities (Sernau, 2006).

The most recent debate has been between neoliberalism and the world systems perspective. *Neoliberalism* is based in classic economics and argues that free trade and free markets, with limited government interference, will result in a fair distribution of resources. As suggested earlier, this philosophy has been dominant across the world for the past few decades, but is currently being challenged on several fronts. Economists at the World Bank and IMF have been strong voices in favor of neoliberalism, which informed the ideals of their structural adjustment program for dealing with the debts of impoverished nations. *Structural adjustment* called for poor countries to "clean house" by reducing government spending and bureaucracy and increasing exportation and entrepreneurship. To counter this view, the *world systems perspective* suggests that inequality is created and maintained by economic globalization (I. Wallerstein, 1974, 1980, 1989). Under this perspective, the world is divided into three different sectors: a *core sector* that dominates the capitalist world economy and exploits the world's resources, a *peripheral sector* that provides raw material to the core and is heavily exploited by it, and a *semiperipheral sector* that is somewhat independent but very vulnerable to the financial fluctuations of the core states. The core currently includes the United States, Western Europe, and Japan; the periphery includes much of Africa, South Asia, and Latin America; and the semiperiphery includes such places as Spain, Portugal, Brazil, Mexico, Venezuela, and oil-producing countries in the Middle East (Leeder, 2004; McMichael, 2008). According to the world systems perspective, the hegemony of the core sector is reinforced by neocolonial practices of such transnational institutions as the World Bank, the IMF, and the WTO.

Structural Determinism Versus Human Agency

Will knowledge of my social class position help you to predict my attitudes and behaviors? That question has become a controversial one for contemporary social science. Social scientists who see human behavior as highly determined by one's position in the social class structure *(structural determinism)* are challenged by social scientists who emphasize the capacity of humans to create their own realities and who give central roles to human actors, not social structures *(human agency).*

Macro-oriented sociologists have taken Émile Durkheim's lead in arguing that human action is a by-product of social institutions that are external to human consciousness. Micro-oriented sociologists have taken Max Weber's lead in the counterargument that humans are proactive agents who construct meaning in interaction with others. In a position that is more consistent with the multidimensional framework of this book, Anthony Giddens (1979) has proposed *structuration theory,* a theory of the relationship between human agency and social structure. Giddens notes that social practices repeat themselves in patterned ways over time and in space, structured by the rules and resources embedded in social institutions. While acknowledging the constraints that rules and resources place on human action, he also notes that human agents have the ability to make a difference in the social world. Human actions produce social structure, and at all times human action is serving either to perpetuate or to transform social structure. You may recognize that this is very similar to the practice approach to culture presented in Chapter 8. Some critics have suggested that Giddens is too optimistic about how much agency humans have, but Giddens acknowledges that those with the most power have a disproportionate opportunity to reinforce institutional arrangements that perpetuate their positions of power.

Structuration theory is a good framework for social workers. It calls our attention to power arrangements that constrain the behaviors of some actors more than others in a way that perpetuates social injustice. But it also calls our attention to the possibilities for human action to transform social institutions. Mary Ellen Kondrat (1999) suggests that structuration theory poses two questions that, when raised, provide critical consciousness, a necessary ingredient for progressive change agents. **Critical consciousness** can be defined as an ongoing process of reflection and knowledge seeking about mechanisms and outcomes of social, political, and economic oppression that requires taking personal and collective action toward fairness and social justice. The first question raised by Kondrat is, "How aware are we of the ways in which social institutions and social structure condition our behaviors?" The second question is, "How aware are we of the ways in which our day-to-day activities over time perpetuate or transform social structure?" Just as individual agency is essential for individual change, collective agency is essential for changing social institutions. That will be the central point of the final chapter in this book, the chapter on social movements.

Critical Thinking Questions 9.3

Which social institutions have the greatest impact on your day-to-day life? What are some ways that your day-to-day activities perpetuate the existing social structure? What are some ways that your day-to-day activities have a potential to change social structure?

IMPLICATIONS FOR SOCIAL WORK PRACTICE

The trends in social institutions and social structure discussed in this chapter suggest several principles for social work practice. These practice principles have greatest relevance for social work planning and administration, but some are relevant for direct social work practice as well.

- Develop adequate information-retrieval skills to keep abreast of trends in the interrelated social institutions and the impact of these trends on human interdependence and dependence.

- Monitor the impact of public policies on poverty and inequality.

- Learn to use political processes to promote social services that contribute to the well-being of individuals and communities.

- Be particularly aware of the impact of trends in the economic institution on client resources and functioning.

- Collaborate with other social workers and human service providers to advocate for greater equality of opportunity in the educational institution.

- Work to ensure that the voices of poor and other oppressed people are included in ongoing public dialogue about health care reform.

- Consider the extent to which contemporary social welfare programs, especially those with which you are personally involved, are "imperfect solutions to past problems" and how responsive they are to recent changes in the other major social institutions.

- Take the lead in public discourse about the fit between the current social welfare institution and trends in the other major social institutions.

- Be aware of the role that religious organizations play in social service delivery and the role that religion plays in the lives of clients.

- Collaborate with other social workers and human service providers to influence media coverage of vulnerable populations and patterns of social inequality.

- Review social service programs serving children, older adults, and other dependent persons to ensure that they are responsive to changes in the family and kinship institution as well as the economic institution.

KEY TERMS

bifurcate	Gini index	religious institution
colonialism	government and political	social class
conservative thesis	institution	social institution
critical consciousness	health care institution	social structure
devolution	mass media institution	social welfare institution
downsizing	neocolonialism	status
economic institution	neoliberal philosophy	therapeutic medicine
educational institution	new federalism	transnational
family and kinship institution	radical antithesis	corporation (TNC)

ACTIVE LEARNING

1. In the case study at the beginning of the chapter, Mr. and Mrs. Meza are eager to legalize their immigrant status to ensure that they can stay in the United States rather than return to their native Mexico. One way to begin to understand their motivation to stay in the United States is to do a comparative analysis of social indicators in the two countries. To do this, you can make use of some of the many web resources that contain statistics on global well-being, including the following:

   - *www.census.gov.* Official site of the U.S. Census Bureau. Under People & Households, click on International, which will take you to the International Programs Center. Click on International Data Base (IDB). Click on

World Population Information. Click on Data Access. You can select specific countries and years and get key summary information about the social health of the countries.

- www.unicef.org. Official site of the United Nations Children's Fund. By going to Info by Country and clicking on a specific country and Statistics under that country, you can access data on the status of children by country.

- www.undp.org. Site of the United Nations Development Program. Click on Regions, select Full List of Countries, and click on a specific country. You will get updated material on the country, including the latest report on efforts to meet the Millennium Development Goals.

Use these three resources, or other relevant resources, to prepare a statistical overview of the social health of the United States and Mexico. What are the areas of similarity? Main areas of difference? What indicators seem to be the most important in understanding Mr. and Mrs. Meza's motivation to stay in the United States?

2. We have looked at the conservative thesis and the radical antithesis in an ongoing debate about the role of inequality in social life. Talk to at least five people about this issue, including at least one member of your family and at least one friend. Ask each person the following questions:

- Is inequality a good thing for a society? If not, why not? If so, in what way, and good for whom?

- If we accept inequality as inevitable, how much is necessary? Should society try to maximize or minimize the amount of inequality?

- On what criteria do we measure inequality?

- If we seek equality, is it equality of opportunity or of outcomes?

What kinds of positions did people take? How did they support their arguments? Did you find more support for the conservative thesis or the radical antithesis in the responses you heard?

WEB RESOURCES

Center for Responsive Politics
www.opensecrets.org

Site maintained by the nonpartisan Center for Responsive Politics, contains information on the money collected and spent by major political candidates, major organizational and individual contributors, and political news and issues.

The Civil Rights Project
http://www.civilrightsproject.ucla.edu/
aboutus.php

Site presented by the Civil Rights Project, which was founded at Harvard University in 1996 and in 2007 moved to UCLA, presents data that track racial achievement gaps in the United States.

Pew Internet & American Life Project
www.pewinternet.org

Site presented by the Pew Research Center's Internet & American Life Project, presents reports on the impact of the Internet on families, communities, work and home, daily life, education, health care, and civic and political life.

United Nations Children's Fund
www.unicef.org

Site contains cross-national information on the well-being of children.

U.S. Census Bureau
www.census.gov

Official site of the U.S. Census Bureau contains statistics on a wide variety of topics, including race and ethnicity, gender, education, birthrates, disabilities, and many other topics.

World Health Organization (WHO)
www.who.int

Site contains information on the health and the health care institutions of countries around the world.

CHAPTER

10

Families

Elizabeth D. Hutchison

OPENING QUESTIONS

- What theoretical perspectives are available to help social workers understand family life and provide avenues for positive change in families?

- What competencies do social workers need for working with families from family structures and cultures different from their own?

KEY IDEAS

As you read this chapter, take note of these central ideas:

1. How we define family shapes our view of family membership and our approach to working with different types of families.

2. From the earliest days of the United States as a nation, there has been a diversity of family structures and customs.

3. There is general agreement that the most pronounced change in family life in the United States in the past 50 years has been the change in gender roles.

4. A number of theoretical "lenses" for understanding families have been proposed, including the psychodynamic perspective, family systems perspective, family life cycle perspective, feminist perspective, family stress and coping perspective, and family resilience perspective.

5. Social workers encounter a diversity of family structures in their work with families, including nuclear families, extended families, cohabiting heterosexual couples, couples with no children, lone-parent families, stepfamilies, same-sex partner families, and military families.

6. In their work with families, social workers must be sensitive to their economic and cultural influences, as well as their experiences with immigration where relevant.

7. Contemporary families face many challenges, including family violence, divorce, and substance abuse, and often need assistance to cope with these issues.

Case Study

The Sharpe Family Prepares for Deployment

Bobby Sharpe's Army National Guard Unit is preparing for a 12-month deployment to Afghanistan, and they have been spending more than the usual one weekend per month in drills and training. Bobby has 2 months to help his family prepare for his deployment, and then his unit will train in Texas for another 2 months before leaving for Afghanistan. This is not the first time his family has needed to prepare for Bobby's deployment to a war zone, but the preparations are more complicated this time.

Bobby Sharpe is a 36-year-old African American man who lives in a small southwestern town. He has been married to Vivian for 13 years, and they have a 12-year-old daughter, Marcie, and a 3-year-old son, Caleb, who has cerebral palsy. Back when Bobby finished high school, he served in the Army for four years.

(Continued)

(Continued)

He received some good training, enjoyed making friends with people from diverse backgrounds, and had two tours overseas but never served in a war zone. After 4 years, he was eager to return home to be near his close-knit family. Soon after returning home, he ran into Vivian who had grown up in his neighborhood, and they were soon spending a lot of time together. A year later, they were married, and a year after that, Marcie was born.

Bobby wasn't sure what work he could do after he left the Army, but a few months after he returned home, he got in touch with a high school friend who was working as a heating and air conditioning technician. After another technician was fired, Bobby got a job where his friend worked, and his friend helped him learn the technical aspects of the heating and air conditioning business. When Marcie was born, Vivian cared for her at home and also cared for her sister's small children while her sister, a single mother, worked. When Bobby's father had an automobile accident and had to miss work for 6 months, Bobby and Vivian provided some financial aid to Bobby's mother and younger siblings while his father was out of work. Finances were tight, and Bobby and Vivian were afraid they would not be able to keep up the mortgage on their house, which was a source of great pride to them. Bobby decided to join the Army National Guard to bring in some extra money. He also looked forward to the type of camaraderie he had experienced in the Army. He went to drills one weekend per month and took time off from work for a 2-week training each year. His unit was mobilized on two occasions to assist with floods in the state. The extra money helped to stabilize the family economics, and he enjoyed the friendships he developed, even though only one other person in his unit was from his small town. When Marcie entered public school, Vivian took a job in the cafeteria at her school, which allowed Bobby and Vivian to start a college fund for Marcie.

Bobby grew up in a close-knit family that included his mother and father and three younger sisters, as well as a maternal grandmother who lived with them. Several aunts, uncles, and cousins lived nearby. Both parents were hardworking people, and they created a happy home. Bobby's grandmother provided child care when the children were small and helped to keep the household running smoothly.

Vivian grew up a few blocks from Bobby. Her father died in Vietnam a few months before she was born, and her mother moved her two daughters back to the town where she had grown up. She struggled to raise her two daughters while working two jobs, with some help from her mother who lived in town but also worked two jobs. Vivian was lucky that another neighborhood couple became her godparents and played an active role in her life. This couple was never able to have children of their own, and they were happy to include Vivian in their leisure activities. Vivian often turned to them for support and encouragement, and she continues to consider them family.

During Bobby's deployment to Iraq 5 years ago, Vivian and Marcie were able to get along fine, with the love and support of Bobby's family; Vivian's mother, sister, and godparents; and Bobby's boss. They missed Bobby and worried about him, but Marcie was very good about picking up more responsibilities to help Vivian with the chores usually performed by Bobby. When the furnace broke, Bobby's boss was generous about doing the repair. One of Bobby's sisters helped Vivian juggle taking Marcie to her after-school activities and picking her up. Bobby was injured by shrapnel in his last week in Iraq and spent 2 weeks in the hospital in the nearest city when he returned home. The family and friend network took care of Marcie while Vivian juggled trips to the hospital with her work schedule.

But things are more complicated as Bobby and Vivian prepare for the impending deployment to Afghanistan. Bobby's beloved grandmother had a stroke 2 years ago, and his mother and father are working opposite shifts at the local nursing home so that someone is always home to care for her. Bobby's aunts, uncles, and cousins take turns providing a few hours of care so that his mom and dad can get a break and run errands. One of Bobby's sisters stayed in the city after she completed college and has a busy life there. Another sister, a single mother of a 2-year-old daughter, is serving in the Army in Iraq. Her daughter has been living with Bobby and Vivian while she is deployed. Bobby and Vivian's son Caleb is the joy of the family, but he requires extra care. Vivian's mother has moved in with Bobby and Vivian and cares for Caleb and the 2-year-old niece during the day while Vivian works, and then turns their care over to Vivian so that she can do a 6-hour shift caring for an older woman with dementia. Work has been very slow for Bobby lately, and his boss has talked about closing the business down and retiring, so there is some anxiety about whether Bobby will have work when he returns from Afghanistan. To help stabilize the family finances, Vivian recently accepted the offer to take a supervisory position in the school department's lunch program. She is excited about the new responsibilities but also concerned about whether the added stress is manageable in this time of great family upheaval. She is especially concerned about monitoring Marcie's after-school activities now that she is approaching adolescence. Her godparents have promised to help with that, just as they did for Vivian during her adolescent years. Vivian has heard that the National Guard has family support groups, but there is nothing in the small town where she lives.

FAMILY DEFINED

We know that families are one of the key institutions in almost every society, past and present. Perhaps no other relationships contribute as much to our identity and have such pervasive influence on all dimensions of our lives as our family relationships (Floyd & Morman, 2006). Families address personal needs, but they also contribute to the public welfare by caring for each other and developing responsible members of society (D. Newman, 2008).

Families in every culture address similar societal needs, but there are many variations in family structure, family customs, and power arrangements (D. Newman, 2008). Around the globe, families are expected to provide economic security, emotional support, and a place in society for each family member; they also fulfill the critical social roles of bearing, providing for, and socializing children and youth (Benokraitis, 2004). Families respond to these challenges in different ways, due in no small part to different cultures and different political and economic circumstances. Family situations and their access to resources differ as a function of their socioeconomic location. As suggested in Chapter 9, social, cultural, and economic globalization is changing families in the United States and around the world (Gardiner & Kosmitzki, 2008; Leeder, 2004).

> Social constructionist perspective

So, what is a family? We were all born into some sort of family and may have created a similar or different sort of family. Take a break from reading and think about who is family to you. Who is in your family and what functions does your family perform for you? We hear a lot of talk about family and family values, but family means different things to different people. Even family scholars struggle to define how family is different from other social groups. White and Klein (2002) argue that family differs from other social groups in degree only. They suggest that nonfamily groups such as friend networks and coworkers often have some of the same properties as families, but usually to a lesser degree. Family research is hampered by the lack of consensus about how to define family (Baxter & Braithwaite, 2006). This lack of consensus was consistent in family science throughout the 20th century (Chibucos & Leite, 2005).

The family literature includes many different definitions of family, but the many definitions center on three ways to form a family: biologically, legally, or socially (Floyd & Morman, 2006; Lepoire, 2006). *Biologically,* family refers to people who are related by blood and are genetically bound to each other, however distantly. Examples of biological family relationships include parents, children, aunts, uncles, second cousins, grandparents, and great-grandparents. Families are created *legally* by marriage, adoption, or formalized fostering. There are many ways that families can be created *socially*, by social interaction, when there is no biological or legal relationship. Sometimes neighbors, godparents, or longtime friends are considered "family." These have been called "fictive kin," but I prefer to refer to them as chosen family. Vivian Sharpe clearly thinks of her godparents as family. Family is increasingly being created by cohabiting romantic partners of either the opposite sex or same sex. Family may also be created by informal fostering.

Different definitions of family include different configurations of biological, legal, and social relationships. Exhibit 10.1 provides a selection of definitions that have been developed by family scholars in the United States, as well as the definition used by the U.S. Census Bureau. It is very difficult to develop one definition that includes all forms of families, but family scholars have attempted to develop inclusive definitions. As you can see, the Census Bureau definition includes families formed biologically and legally, but not those that are formed socially without legal sanction. Think about what types of family would not be considered family by this definition. In contrast to the Census Bureau, the definitions of family scholars Baxter and Braithwaite (2006); Galvin, Bylund, and Brommel (2003); and Seccombe and Warner (2004) include families formed socially along with families formed biologically and legally. Leeder (2004) goes even further with a purely social definition of family. Which of these definitions is the best fit for who you call family?

How do the definitions fit for Bobby and Vivian Sharpe's family? The Census Bureau definition would certainly include Bobby, Vivian, Marcie, and Caleb as they prepare for Bobby's deployment. It also can embrace Vivian's mother, now that she lives in the household. Would it still include Bobby once he is deployed and not living in the household? It is clear that he and other family members will think of him as family. But what about Bobby's 2-year-old niece? Is she family? Could Vivian sign permission forms if she needs medical care? Who do you think Bobby, Vivian, and Marcie consider to be family? How would they define family?

For the purposes of our discussion, I will use the Baxter and Braithwaite (2006) definition of family: **family** is "a social group of two or more persons, characterized by ongoing interdependence with long-term commitments that stem from blood, law, or affection" (p. 2). Increasingly, we exercise the freedom to use the word family to describe the

Braithwaite & Baxter (2006)	A social group of two or more persons, characterized by ongoing interdependence with long-term commitments that stem from blood, law, or affection
Galvin, Bylund, & Brommel (2003)	Networks of people who share their lives over long periods of time bound by ties of marriage, blood, or commitment, legal or otherwise, who consider themselves as family and who share a significant history and anticipated future of functioning in a family relationship
Leeder (2004)	A group of people who have intimate social relationships and have a history together
Seccombe & Warner (2004)	A relationship by blood, marriage, or affection, in which members may cooperate economically, may care for any children, and may consider identity to be intimately connected to the larger group
U.S. Census Bureau (2009a)	A group of two or more people who reside together and who are related by birth, marriage, or adoption

▲ **Exhibit 10.1**   Selected Definitions of Family

social group with whom we have emotional closeness (a social definition). However, our freedom to define our own families is limited (D. Newman, 2008). We must interact with organizations that have their own definitions of family and sometimes have the power to impose those definitions on us. Local, state, and federal governments have definitions of family and also have the power to enforce those definitions when providing goods, services, and legal sanctions. Examples include legal standards about who can marry, who inherits from whom, who can benefit from filing joint tax returns, who receives survivor benefits, and who can make medical decisions for another person.

Restricted definitions of family have been used by local governments to discourage some groups of immigrant residents. For example, in December 2005, the city of Manassas, Virginia, amended the definition of family in the City Code to include nuclear family only, essentially prohibiting extended families from living together. The stated

> Conflict perspective

purpose of the amendment was to combat overcrowding, but many critics saw it as a way to discourage Latino/Hispanic families from settling in the city. Under heavy criticism, the zoning amendment was suspended in 2006 (Equal Rights Center, 2009). In the United States, the most contentious and public struggle over the tension between legal definitions and social definitions of family involve families formed by same-sex couples, a topic that will be covered later in the chapter.

Many organizations in the private world also impose definitions of family. Health clubs define who can be included in a family membership, corporations decide which family members can receive health coverage, and hospitals decide who has visitation rights in intensive care units. As social workers, we should be most interested in who a person considers to be family, because that is where social resources can be tapped, but we must also be alert to situations where legal definitions do not recognize a given form of family and how enforcement of those definitions impinges on the lives of particular individuals and families. This is an area that calls for social work activism.

In the United States, *monogamy,* or partnering with one spouse at a time, is the legal way to start a biological family. But it is estimated that 75% of the world's societies prefer some type of *polygamy,* or having more than one spouse at a time (D. Newman, 2008). Polygamy can take the form of either polygyny (one man and multiple wives) or polyandry (one woman and multiple husbands). Polyandry is much less common than polygyny, however. Polygyny is found on every continent, but is most common in Islamic countries, African countries, and parts of Asia (Gardiner & Kosmitzki, 2008). All societies allow monogamy, and, indeed, most people of the world cannot afford to support multiple spouses.

There are cultural variations in the process of mate selection. In most societies, mate selection is governed by both exogamy and endogamy rules. *Exogamy rules* require that mates must be chosen from *outside* the group. Most societies have either formal or informal rules prohibiting mating with specified family members, often referred to as the "incest taboo," but there are differences across cultures about which family members are prohibited. In the United States, 24 states prohibit marriage of first cousins, but 6 states allow it under some circumstances where the couple cannot reproduce, and North Carolina allows first cousin marriage but prohibits double cousin marriage (such as a sister and brother marrying cousins who are brother and sister; National Conference of State Legislatures, 2009). There are also some informal exogamy taboos against mating with people within other groups, such as in the same university dorm (dormcest) and with people in the workplace (workcest) (D. Newman, 2008). *Endogamy rules,* on the other hand, require that mates should be selected from within the group on characteristics such as religion, race and ethnicity, and social class. Bobby and Vivian were honoring these rules when they chose each other, but endogamy rules are loosening in many places.

In the United States and other Western societies, mate selection is a culmination of romantic love, and it is often assumed that there is one true love in the world for each one of us. In many Eastern societies, marriages are arranged, and it is generally assumed that there are several possible mates with whom one can establish a successful long-term relationship. It is also assumed that parents will make wiser decisions than young people would make for themselves. In countries like Japan, however, love marriages are beginning to replace arranged marriages (Gardiner & Kosmitzki, 2008).

THE FAMILY IN HISTORICAL PERSPECTIVE

Social constructionist perspective; conflict perspective

I often hear people lament the demise of the family. Maybe you hear this as well. To understand whether there is reality in this lament, it is necessary to place the contemporary family in historical context. This is a daunting task, however. For one thing, the family has never been a monolithic institution. The structure and functions of families always varied according to race, ethnicity, religion, sexual orientation, social class, and so on. Most of what has been written about the family historically was written from the perspective of dominant members of society. It is only since the 1960s, when the discipline of social history began to describe the lives of women and other marginalized groups, that we have a more complete understanding of the varieties of ways that families have adapted to the challenges they've faced in their lives. When people in the United States talk about the "golden age of the traditional family," they are typically talking about one particular group of families: White, middle-class, heterosexual, two-parent families living in the 1950s. Social historians argue that the rosy picture usually painted about this group is really something that never existed. It is important to remember that a great diversity of family structures and functions has existed in the United States and around the world over time.

For another thing, in the United States, because we are a very young country, we tend to have a very short view of history. A tracing of the history of families worldwide over longer-term historical time would be the subject of multiple books. So, for the longer-term global view, I will simply note two important themes. First, it seems clear that

Rational choice perspective

families have adapted both their structures and their functions over time to cope with the changing nature of societies, as hunting and gathering societies gave way to horticultural societies, which gave way to agrarian societies, which gave way to industrial societies, and industrial societies are giving way to postindustrial societies focused on information, services, and technology. Second, a global understanding of the family in contemporary times must take account of the effects of colonialism. As the United States and European countries exploited local people in colonized countries, family life was directly impacted in both the colonizing and colonized countries. Most recently, families have been separated as some members relocate to find work, sometimes relocating from the rural areas to the cities within their own country, and other times, moving to wealthier countries where work is more plentiful. The case study in Chapter 13 provides an example of the impact of these relocations on both families and communities.

Any discussion of the history of the family in the United States should begin with the Native peoples who predated the White settlers from Europe. The Native peoples included over 2,000 cultures and societies, each with its own set of family customs and lifestyles (Leeder, 2004). There were some similarities across these societies, however. As with other societies, social life was organized around the family. Affection was lavished on children, and they were never spanked or beaten. There was a clear gender division of labor, with women growing crops, and caring for the home and property, and men hunting, fishing, and waging war. In many Native societies, women were afforded a great deal of respect and power (Colonial Williamsburg, n.d.).

The White settlers established small, privately owned agricultural enterprises, and families performed many of the functions that have since been turned over to other institutions such as hospitals, schools, and social welfare agencies. David Fischer's (1989) historical analysis, based on original sources, found that there were regional differences in the organization of family life among the White settlers. Between 1629 and 1775, four major waves of English-speaking immigrants settled in what became the United States of America. Each wave of immigrants came from a different part of what is now the United Kingdom and brought their own family customs with them. Fischer argues that in spite of later waves of immigration and much interregional mobility, these regional differences in family customs have endured to some degree over time. See what you think.

1. *The Puritans.* The Puritans came from the east of England to Massachusetts from 1629 to 1640. They condemned the pursuit of wealth and avoided wealth inheritance by *partible inheritance,* meaning that property was divided among heirs rather than being passed on to one person. Marriage was highly valued, and family life was organized around a strong nuclear family, but the Puritans approved of divorce if the marriage covenant had been broken. They expected marriage to be based on true love. There was some gender inequality in family life, but women and men worked together, and husbands and wives were involved in mutual decision making. Women were protected from domestic violence by law, and there were high expectations for marital peace and harmony. Small children were seen as evil, and child rearing was based on "will breaking."

2. *The Virginia Cavaliers and Indentured Servants.* From 1642 to 1675, royalist elite and large numbers of indentured servants came from the south of England to Virginia. Their society was marked by profoundly unequal distribution of wealth, and slavery was introduced to replace indentured servants who earned their freedom. Primogeniture inheritance, or inheritance of the full estate by the first-born son, ensured the continued concentration of wealth. There was a lot of intermarrying among a small elite group, with cousin marriage allowed. Family life was organized around a strong sense of extended family, and they lived in neighborhoods based on kin. Much effort went into protecting family reputations. Marriage was highly valued but was expected to be based on social position rather than love. Divorce was not allowed, but there is evidence of much marital discord. Family life was male dominant, and rape was less severely punished than petty theft. Elite men expected servant women to yield to them sexually. Elite children were expected to exercise their will, but children of servants were expected to yield to hierarchy.

3. *The Quakers.* The Quakers came from Wales and the North Midland area of England to the Delaware Valley from 1675 to 1725. They embraced religious freedom, cultural pluralism, and nonviolence. Family life was child-centered and nuclear. The Quakers had fewer children and more servants than the Puritans, but more children and fewer servants than the Cavaliers. Family life was more egalitarian than for the Puritans or Cavaliers, and there were stiff penalties for sex crimes against women. Marriage was based on love, and cousin marriage was forbidden. Children were seen as harmless and innocent, and child rearing was based on the use of rewards.

4. *The Appalachians.* From 1718 to 1775, families left the borderlands between England and Scotland, where they had been the victims of one invasion after another, and settled in the Appalachian backcountry. On the whole, they were an impoverished group of farmers who hoped to improve their economic situation in the new land, but there was a highly unequal distribution of wealth among them. The small population of elite among them intermarried. The Appalachians had a strong sense of extended family and a weak sense of individual privacy. Marriage ties were weaker than blood ties, and families grew into clans. Marriage was full of both love and violence. Family life was male dominant, and women were expected to be hardworking, patient, and submissive. Male children were raised to be willful with a warrior's courage, and female children were raised to be industrious, obedient, patient, sacrificial, and devoted. Child rearing was permissive but punctuated by acts of anger and violence.

As you can see, from the earliest days of the United States as a nation, there were differences in family customs along several dimensions, including gender power arrangements, child-rearing practices, appropriate marriage partners, and nuclear versus extended family. Different attitudes about social inequality were also transmitted through the family. Subsequently, new waves of immigration increased the diversity of family customs.

During the industrial revolution, the economy of the United States and other newly industrializing nations shifted from the family-based economy of small, privately owned farms to a wage-based economic system of large-scale industrial manufacturing. The functions of the family changed to accommodate the changes in the economic system. In the upper and middle classes, men went out to work and women ran the household, but less advantaged women engaged in paid labor as well as family labor. By 1900, one fifth of U.S. women worked outside the home (D. Newman, 2008). The great majority of African American women engaged in paid labor, often serving as domestic servants in

White households where they were forced to leave their own families and live in the employer's home. Women in other poor families took in piecework so they could earn a wage while also staying in the home. Poorer families also took in boarders to assist the family financially, something that also happened in the earlier agrarian period. Schools took over education, and family life began to be organized around segments of time: the workweek and weekends, and summers off from school for children (Leeder, 2004). Rather than the center of work, the family home became a place to retreat from economic activities, and the primary role of the family was to provide emotional support to its members. A new ideal of marriage developed, based on sexual satisfaction, companionship, and emotional support (Zimmerman, 2001). Family togetherness was never more emphasized than in the 1950s, a period of strong economic health in the United States.

Since the 1950s, personal fulfillment has become a major value in the United States and a number of other information/service/technology societies, but the great majority of people still view loving, committed relationships to be the most important source of happiness and well-being (Kamp Dush, & Amato, 2005; Snyder & Lopez, 2007). Family members are often scattered across state and national lines, but the new technologies allow for continued connection. Recently, work and family time is once again comingled in many families, as the new technologies allow more work from home. Unfortunately, this often means that the work day is expanded.

As the above discussion suggests, diversity of family structures is not new, but family forms have become increasingly varied in recent decades. Marriage and birthrates have declined, and more adults are living on their own. More children are born to unmarried parents. Divorce and remarriage are creating complex remarried families. Perhaps the biggest change in family structure in recent decades is the increase in dual-earner families, as women increased their involvement in paid labor (F. Walsh, 2006).

There is general agreement that the most pronounced change in family life in the United States in the past 50 years is the change in gender roles. By 1960, one-third of all workers were women (Gibbs, 2009), but employers typically paid women less than men performing the same job. In addition, as the current cable TV series *Mad Men* illustrates, women were often treated in a demeaning manner at work. Females were about half as likely as males to go to college, and less than 10% of students playing high school sports were girls (Gibbs, 2009). When women needed surgery or other medical treatment, they often had to secure the signed consent from husbands or fathers. In many settings, they were not allowed to wear pants in public. (For a comprehensive review of the changes in gender roles in the United States since 1960, see G. Collins, 2009.) By 2007, women made up 47% of the labor force, and in the midst of the 2008–2009 recession in which 82% of job losses affected men, women were expected to outnumber men in the labor force by the end of 2009, for the first time in U.S. history (Rampel, 2009). In 2008, women earned 80% of what men earned, on average, up from 62% in 1979, but in the midst of the current recession, women are increasingly the sole support of families (E. Galinsky, Aumann, & Bond, 2009; U.S. Department of Labor, 2008). In Bobby's family, as in many African American families, women have always been in the paid labor force, often working more than one job. In fact, research indicates that gender roles in African American families have typically been applied flexibly to manage work and family demands.

There is evidence that attitudes about women in the labor force are changing. In 1977, a total of 74% of men and 52% of women agreed with the statement that "men should earn the money and women should take care of the children and family"; in 2008, only 42% of men and 39% of women agreed with the statement (E. Galinsky et al., 2009, p. 9). The attitudes of men in dual-earner couples have changed the most. In 2008, an estimated 26% of women in dual-earner couples had annual earnings that were at least 10% higher than the earnings of their spouses/partners. In the 2005–2006 academic year, women earned 58% of all bachelor's degrees and 60% of master's degrees (E. Galinsky et al., 2009). The rate of girls participating in high school sports is also approaching that of males. In addition, women have a larger presence in the public arena, serving in leadership positions in both the private and public sectors. However, women are still underrepresented on university faculties, and in boardrooms and legislatures. They have also been charged higher insurance premiums than men, and this became a part of the debate about health care reform in 2009 (Gibbs, 2009). Although men are increasing their participation in child care and household labor, women still perform a larger share of this domestic work (E. Galinsky et al., 2009).

Unfortunately, business and government in the United States have been slow to respond to the changing needs of families who do not have a full-time mother at home. The Family and Medical Leave Act (FMLA) of 1993 requires employers with more than 50 employees to provide up to 12 weeks of *unpaid* sick leave per year for the birth or adoption of a child or to care for a sick child, parent, or spouse, excluding temporary and part-time workers. With the exemptions, about 40% of U.S. workers are not eligible for FMLA leave, but a good feature of the FMLA is that it covers both male and female workers (Ray, Gornick, & Schmitt, 2009). Compare this to the way that most other countries have responded to the increasing numbers of dual-earner families. One research project found that of 168 countries studied, 163 guarantee *paid* leave to women for childbirth and maternity, and 45 guarantee paid paternity leave (cited in D. Newman, 2008). The combined leave employers must provide for both mothers and fathers in the five most generous countries ranges from 18 to 47 weeks. It is important to note, however, that the number of weeks of paid leave offered to fathers ranges from 2–7 in these same five countries (Ray et al., 2009).

Not all people in the United States agree that the above-noted changes in gender roles are a good trend. Certainly, around the world, there are many societies that have not embraced these changes, even though economic globalization has depended on the cheap labor of women in poor societies working long hours in low-wage jobs (McMichael, 2008).

Critical Thinking Questions 10.1

Where have you gotten your ideas about what it means to be family? Have those ideas changed over time? If so, what influenced those changes? What beliefs do you have about appropriate gender relationships, child-rearing practices, appropriate marriage partners, and nuclear versus extended family? How might those beliefs affect your ability to work with different types of families and families facing different types of challenges?

THEORETICAL PERSPECTIVES FOR UNDERSTANDING FAMILIES

With an understanding of societal trends affecting families as background, you can use a number of theoretical "lenses" to understand family functioning and avenues for positive change. There are a number of theoretical perspectives on the family. This section introduces six of these: psychodynamic perspective, family systems perspective, family life cycle perspective, feminist perspective, family stress and coping perspective, and family resilience perspective.

Psychodynamic Perspective and Families

Psychodynamic approaches to thinking about families are a mix of ideas from psychodynamic and social systems perspectives. Social workers who approach family situations from this perspective assume that current personal and interpersonal problems are the result of unresolved problems in the **family of origin,** the family into which we were born and/or in which we were raised (Nichols & Schwartz, 2006; J. Walsh, 2010). They suggest that these unresolved problems continue to be acted out in our current intimate relationships. Patterns of family relationships are passed on from generation to generation, and intergenerational relationship problems must be resolved to improve current problems.

> Psychodynamic
> perspective

Some social workers who employ the psychodynamic perspective draw heavily on Murray Bowen's (1978) concept of differentiation of self. Bowen suggested that there are two aspects of **differentiation of self** in the family system (see Carter & McGoldrick, 2005a; J. Walsh, 2010):

1. *Differentiation between thinking and feeling.* Family members must learn to own and recognize their feelings. But they must also learn to think about and plan their lives rather than reacting emotionally at times that call for clear thinking. It is assumed that many family problems are based on family members' emotional reactivity to each other. This aspect of differentiation is very similar to Daniel Goleman's concept of emotional intelligence, which was discussed in Chapter 4.

2. *Differentiation between the self and other members of the family.* While recognizing their interdependence with other family members, individuals should follow their own beliefs rather than make decisions based on reactivity to the cues of others or the need to win approval. They should do this, however, without attacking others or defending themselves. A clear sense of self allows them to achieve some independence while staying connected to other family members. This aspect of differentiation is similar to Howard Gardner's concept of interpersonal intelligence, also discussed in Chapter 4.

Another key concept in the psychodynamic perspective on families is triangulation. **Triangulation** occurs when two family members (a family subsystem) inappropriately involve another family member to reduce the anxiety in the dyadic relationship. For example, if a couple is having marital problems, they may focus their energy on a child's school problems to relieve the tension in the marital relationship. The child's school problems then become the stabilizing factor in the marriage, and this problem will not improve until the parents look at their relationship problem (and the origins of it in their own families of origin). In recent years, proponents of this approach have noted that it is not always another family member that gets "triangulated in." It may be an addiction, an over-involvement in work, or an extramarital affair—all used to ease tension in a dyadic relationship.

The psychodynamic perspective has been criticized for its Anglo-American emphasis on individualism versus collectivism. To some, it pathologizes the value of connectedness that prevails in some cultures. There is some merit to this criticism if the theory is misused to interpret a strong sense of familial responsibility as seen in the Sharpe family, and many ethnic minority families, to be a sign of lack of differentiation. A strong separate self is not a value in many cultures. The psychodynamic perspective can alert us, however, to any problematic triangles that emerge when the parental subsystem is expanded in times of stress, such as when a parent in the military is deployed.

If you use a psychodynamic perspective for thinking about the Sharpe family, you might want to do a multigenerational **genogram,** or a visual representation of a family's composition and structure (see Exhibit 10.2), to get a picture of the multigenerational family's patterns of relationships. (Females are indicated by circles, males by squares; lines indicate marriages and births.) The Sharpe genogram helps you to visualize the extended family relationships in Bobby Sharpe's family and Vivian's more limited extended family system in her family of origin. It may lead you to think about whether Bobby's impending deployment will stir unresolved grief about the loss of her father for Vivian and the loss of her husband for Vivian's mother.

Family Systems Perspective

Systems perspective

A **family systems perspective** adds another lens—that of the family as a social system. As you might imagine, this approach requires a focus on relationships within the family rather than on individual family members. Persons are not thought of as

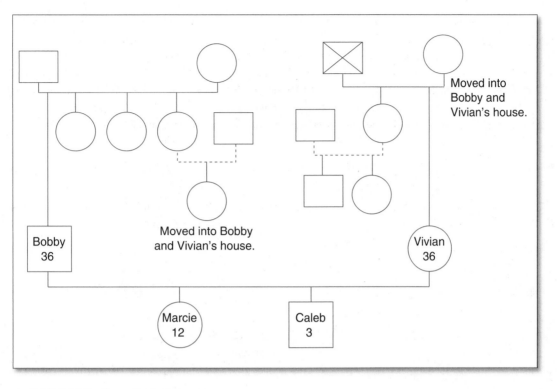

Moved into
Bobby and
Vivian's house.

Moved into Bobby
and Vivian's house.

Bobby
36

Vivian
36

Marcie
12

Caleb
3

▲ **Exhibit 10.2**   Sharpe Family Genogram

individuals but as parts of overall patterns of roles and interactions (Galvin, Dickson, & Marrow, 2006). All parts of the family system are interconnected. Family members both affect and are affected by other family members; when change occurs for one, all are affected. Certainly, we can see that Bobby's deployment, as well as that of his sister, and his grandmother's stroke, affect the entire extended kinship system.

From the family systems perspective, families develop boundaries that delineate who is in the family at any given time. In the Sharpe family, the boundaries have shifted over time to cope with stressors of various kinds. Among members, families develop organizational structures and roles for accomplishing tasks, commonly shared beliefs and rules, and verbal and nonverbal communication patterns (White & Klein, 2008d). Like all systems, families have subsystems, such as a parental subsystem, sibling subsystem, or parent–child subsystem. When problems occur, the focus for change is the family system itself, with the assumption that changing the patterns of interaction between and among family members will address whatever problem first brought a family member to the attention of a social worker. Intervention may focus on helping to open communication across subsystems, helping the family explore the stated and unstated rules that govern interactions, or teaching members to communicate clearly with each other (Vetere, 2005; J. Walsh, 2010).

The **multilevel family practice model** (Vosler, 1996) widens the social worker's theoretical framework to include the larger systems in which the family system is embedded—including the neighborhood, the local community, the state, the nation, and the current global socioeconomic system. Thus, the multilevel model is broadly focused, acknowledging the economic, political, and cultural factors that affect resources available to the family and how family members view their current situation and future challenges. This model recognizes, as suggested in Chapter 9, that the family institution is interrelated with other social institutions—religious, political, economic, educational, social welfare, health care, and mass media. Among other things, this perspective would call our attention to how the Sharpe family is affected by terrorism and war, the global economic meltdown, and health and social welfare policies related to elder care and children with disabilities. They are also influenced by mass media coverage of race issues and the U.S. involvement in war.

A *family ecomap* can be used to assess the way the Sharpe family is connected to larger social systems. The family ecomap uses circles, lines, and arrows to show family relationships and the strength and directional flow of energy and resources to and from the family (Hartman & Laird, 1983; see also Vosler, 1996). Ecomaps help the social worker and the family to identify external sources of stress, conflict, and social support. Exhibit 10.3 is an example of an ecomap for the Sharpe family. It shows that Bobby and Vivian's nuclear family has both external stressors and external resources.

Family Life Cycle Perspective

The family life cycle perspective expands the concept of family system to look at families over time (Carter & McGoldrick, 2005b). Families are seen as multigenerational systems moving through time, composed of people who

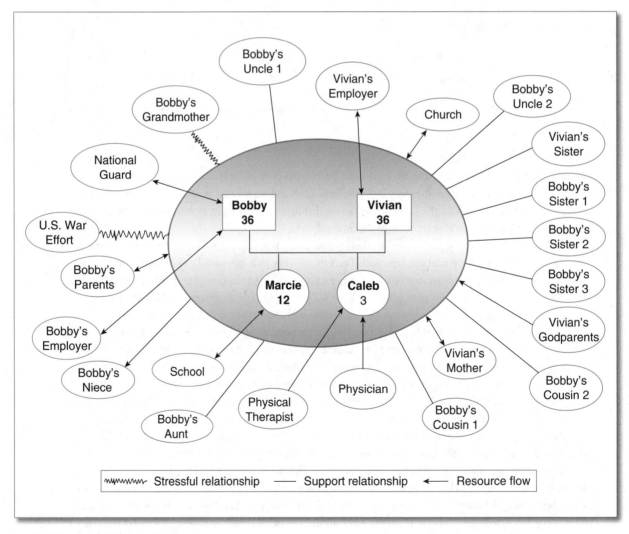

▲ **Exhibit 10.3**   Sharpe Family Ecomap

have a shared history and a shared future. Relationships in families go through transitions as they move along the life cycle; boundaries shift, rules change, and roles are constantly redefined. The family moving through time is influenced by cultural factors and by the historical era in which they live. The family life cycle perspective proposes that **transition points,** when the family faces a transition in family life stage or in family composition, are particularly stressful for families. Such transition points are especially stressful to those with a family or cultural history of trauma or disruption. Carter and McGoldrick recognize that contemporary families are undergoing changes and have many forms, but they delineate six stages that many U.S. families seem to pass through: single young adults, new couples, families with young children, families with adolescents, families launching children and moving on, and families in later life. Each of these stages involves normative changes and challenging tasks, both for individual family members and for the family system as a whole. In this view, change is inevitable in families, and transitions offer opportunities for positive adaptation and growth. The identified life stages may not fit many of the families in today's society, however, including divorced and remarried families and families without children.

> Developmental perspective

From the family cycle perspective, we can see that Bobby and Vivian's nuclear family will soon become a family with an adolescent and will need to open the family boundaries to allow for Marcie's growing relationships with peers. At the same time, they are a family with young children and need to focus inward to ensure adequate care for two young children, including one with special care needs. This is happening as the family must cope with the stressful transition of Bobby's deployment and the stress that will come with Vivian's new work responsibilities. The family life cycle perspective would alert us to the possibility that the family will struggle under the pressure of these stressful transitions.

Feminist Perspective and Families

Unlike the family systems perspective, the **feminist perspective on families** proposes that families should not be studied as whole systems, with the lens on the family level, because such attention results in failure to attend to patterns of dominance, subjugation, and oppression in families (Chibucos & Leite, 2005). As suggested in Chapter 2, the focus of the feminist perspective is on how patterns of dominance in major social institutions are tied to gender, with women devalued and oppressed. When applied to the family, the feminist perspective proposes that gender is the primary characteristic on which power is distributed and misused in the family (Allen, Lloyd, & Few, 2009). Although the Sharpe family, like many African American families, has relatively egalitarian approaches to enacting gender roles, they live in a world that gives men more power than women and are influenced by that bias. Men and women are both involved in nurturing care, but women are considered the primary caregivers. Bobby and Vivian have nieces and nephews whose fathers have taken no responsibility for their children, leaving the mothers to take full responsibility for their economic and emotional well-being.

> Conflict perspective

The feminist perspective makes a distinction between sex and gender: Sex is biologically determined, but gender is socially constructed and learned from the culture. The feminist perspective questions how society came to assign male and female characteristics; seeks understanding of women's and children's perspectives on family life; analyzes how family practices create advantages for some family members and disadvantages for others; raises questions about caregiving responsibilities in families; and questions why the state should decide who should marry and receive a range of financial, legal, and medical rights (J. Wood, 2006). It argues that a diversity of family forms should be recognized and that the strengths and weaknesses of each form should be thoughtfully considered. It calls attention to the family as a site of both love and trauma (Allen et al., 2009). Although gender is the starting point of the feminist perspective, most feminist theories focus on disadvantage based on other characteristics as well, including race, ethnicity, social class, sexuality, age, religion, nationality, and ability status (Lloyd, Few, & Allen, 2009).

The feminist perspective includes a variety of feminist theories—we should speak of *feminisms,* not feminism—such as liberal, radical, interpretive, critical, cultural, and postmodern feminism. These different varieties of feminism may disagree on important issues. For example, liberal feminists support the inclusion of women in all military positions, because of their focus on equality of opportunity, while the cultural feminists oppose women in the military because they see the valuing of life and nurturing, rather than destroying, as a central part of female culture (White & Klein, 2008b). Bobby Sharpe's sister does not consider herself a feminist, but she is among the many women who are taking advantage of career opportunities in the military.

The emerging **intersectionality feminist theory** is consistent with the multidimensional approach proposed in this book. Feminists of color introduced the concept of *intersectionality* to challenge the idea that gender is a monolithic category (P. H. Collins, 2000). They suggested that no single category is sufficient to understand social oppression, and categories such as gender, race, and class intersect to produce different experiences for women of various races and classes. Bobby Sharpe's sister could probably embrace this version of feminist theory, based on the observation that her e-mails from Iraq often include musings about what she is learning about how different her life experiences and life chances have been from other women in her unit, both White women and other African American women. She has also been shocked at the level of sexual harassment and sexual violence she is finding in the military.

Intersectionality theory has also been used to look at other intersections in women's lives—for example, those related to sexuality, religion, disability, age, and nationality. From this perspective, a person may experience oppression based on gender or some other attribute, but also experience privilege based on a different attribute. Some people may experience oppression related to several social categories. Intersectionality theory is being expanded to study transnational contexts, considering the consequences for women of colonialism and capitalism (Allen et al., 2009). Intersectionality theory would call attention to the ways that Bobby Sharpe and members of his family have experienced oppression related to race. But it would also suggest that Bobby has been able to build a middle-class life that has given him some class privilege compared to poor African American families. He also carries male privilege, heterosexual privilege, age privilege, and Christian privilege.

Family Stress and Coping Perspective

Systems perspective; psychodynamic perspective

You read about theories of individual stress and coping in Chapter 5, and research in this area is incorporated into theorizing about stress and coping at the family level. The primary interest of the family stress and coping perspective is the entire family unit (Price, Price, & McKenry, 2010). The theoretical foundation of this perspective is the **ABC-X model of family stress and coping,** based on Rueben Hill's (1949, 1958) classic research on war-induced separation and reunion. It theorizes that to understand whether an event in the family system (A) becomes a crisis (X), we also need to understand both the family's resources (B) and the family's definitions (C) about the event. The main idea is that the impact of stressors on the family (the X factor) is influenced by other factors, most notably the internal and external resources available and the meaning the family makes of the situation. With some updating, this theory continues to be the basis for examining family stress and coping (see Boss, 2006; Price et al., 2010).

Systems perspective

The ABC-X model describes a family transition process following a stressful event. A period of disequilibrium is followed by three possible outcomes: (1) *recovery* to the family's previous level of functioning; (2) *maladaptation,* or permanent deterioration in the family's functioning; or (3) *bonadaptation,* or improvement in the family's functioning over and above the previous level. Thus, under certain circumstances, a stressor event can actually be beneficial, if the family's coping process strengthens the family in the long term. They might, for instance, come together to deal with the stressors. Vivian and Marcie Sharpe often talk about how their relationship was strengthened by the way they pulled together during Bobby's earlier deployment.

A more complex, *double* ABC-X model incorporates the concept of **stress pileup** (McCubbin & Patterson, 1983). Over time, a series of crises may deplete the family's resources and expose the family to increasing risk of very negative outcomes (such as divorce, violence, or removal of children from the home). In this view, the balance of stressors and resources is an important consideration. Where there are significant numbers of stressors, positive outcomes depend on a significant level of resources being available to family members and the family as a whole. A **family timeline**, or chronology depicting key dates and events in the family's life (Satir, 1983; Vosler, 1996), can be particularly helpful in identifying times in the family's life when events have piled up. Family timelines can be used to begin to identify the resources that have been tapped successfully in the past, as well as resource needs in the present. Exhibit 10.4 presents a family timeline for the Sharpe family. It suggests that there has been a recent pileup of stressors for the family; consequently, they will need a significant number of resources in the coming year to allow for continued healthy individual and family functioning.

Two types of stressors are delineated in the ABC-X model (McCubbin & Figley, 1983). **Normative stressors** are the typical family life-cycle transitions, such as the birth of a first child. **Nonnormative stressors** are potentially catastrophic events, such as natural disasters, medical trauma, drug abuse, unemployment, and family violence. These nonnormative events can quickly drain the family's resources and may leave family members feeling overwhelmed and exhausted. Lower-level but persistent stress—such as chronic illness or chronic poverty—can also create stress pileup, resulting in instability within the family system and a sense of being out of control on the part of family members.

Family Resilience Perspective

The **family resilience perspective** extends the family stress and coping perspective by seeking to identify and strengthen processes that allow families to bear up under and rebound from distressing life experiences. From this perspective, distressed families are seen as challenged, not damaged, and they have the potential for

> Humanistic perspective

repair and growth (F. Walsh, 2006). In her book, *Strengthening Family Resilience*, Froma Walsh (2006) draws on existing research on risk and resilience to present a family resilience model for intervention and prevention, one that focuses on the family system as the target for intervention. She defines *resilience* as "the capacity to rebound from adversity strengthened and more resourceful" (p. 4). She describes this as "bouncing forward," rather than bouncing back. She assumes that all families face adversity, but resilient families "struggle well" and experience "both suffering and courage" (p. 6). She cautions social workers to avoid the tendency to pathologize the families that they encounter in the midst of transitional distress, assessing families, instead, in the context of the situations they face, and looking for family strengths.

Froma Walsh (2006) has taken the research on risk and resilience and organized the findings into a conceptual framework for targeting interventions to strengthen core processes of family resilience, whatever form the family takes. She organizes this framework into three dimensions: family belief systems, organizational patterns, and communication processes. Each dimension is summarized below:

- *Family belief systems.* How families view problems and possibilities is crucial to how they cope with challenges. Resilient families make meaning of adversity by viewing it as a shared challenge. They find a way to hold onto a shared confidence that they can overcome the challenge. They act on this shared hope by taking initiative and persevering. They draw on a spiritual value system to see their situation as meaningful, and to imagine future possibilities.

- *Organizational patterns.* Resilient families have organizational patterns that serve as shock absorbers. They maintain flexibility in family structure, and are able to make changes in roles and rules to respond to the demands of the moment, but in the midst of change, they hold onto some rituals and routines to provide stability and continuity. Strong family leaders provide nurturance and protection to children and other vulnerable family members,

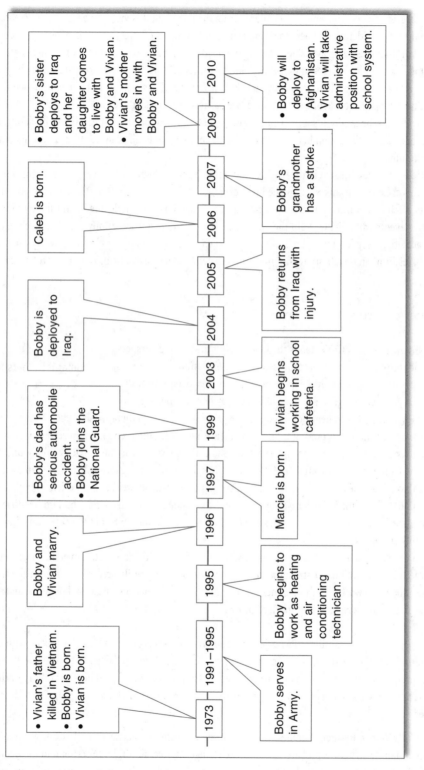

▲ **Exhibit 10.4** Sharpe Family Time Line

but they also leave some room to negotiate rules and roles, based on the situation at hand, and exercise leadership with warmth. Resilient families provide mutual support and commitment while honoring individual differences. They are able to mobilize extended kin and community resources.

- *Communication processes.* Good communication is vital to family resilience. Resilient families send clear, consistent, and genuine messages. They share a wide range of feelings and show mutual empathy and tolerance for differences. They can use humor to lighten threatening situations. They also engage in collaborative problem solving, identifying problems and possible solutions, sharing decision making, and taking concrete steps.

Froma Walsh (2003b) cautions that

the concept of family resilience should not be misused to blame families that are unable to rise above harsh conditions, by simply labeling them as not resilient. Just as individuals need supportive relationships to thrive, family resilience must be supported by social and institutional policies and practices that encourage the ability to thrive, such as flexible work schedules for parents and quality, affordable health, child-, and elder-care services. (pp. 412–413)

The Sharpe family has weathered a number of challenges along the way: health problems, war zone deployments for Bobby and his sister, the birth of a baby with special care needs, and intense elder care needs. According to Froma Walsh's model of family resilience, they are a resilient family. They view each adversity as a shared challenge for the extended kinship network, and they move forward with confidence that they can overcome each challenge. They take the initiative to devise plans for handling difficult situations, and they draw on a deeply held faith that makes meaning of their challenges. In terms of organizational patterns, they are flexible in the assignment of roles and resourceful in mobilizing extended care resources. They have not made similar use of community resources in the past, but may need to reach out more to the community during the coming highly stressful period. They communicate well, for the most part, often using humor to lighten stressful situations. Vivian, her sister, and her mother could benefit from more open communication about the struggles they had after Vivian's father was killed in Vietnam. They have never been able to talk about this, and it may well play a role in Vivian's sister's clinical depression and her mother's pervasive sadness.

Critical Thinking Questions 10.2

Which one of the above theoretical perspectives on families do you find most useful for thinking about the multigenerational Sharpe family? Which perspective do you think offers the least insight into this family? Which of the perspectives do you find most useful for thinking about your own family? The least useful?

DIVERSITY IN FAMILY LIFE

One question that must be asked about each of the above theoretical perspectives on families is how well it applies to different types of families. As suggested earlier, diversity has always existed in the structures and functions of families, but that diversity is clearly increasing, and the reality today is that a great deal of diversity exists among families, both in the United States and globally. There is diversity in family structures, as well as economic and cultural diversity.

Diversity in Family Structures

It is difficult, if not impossible, to catalog all of the types of family structures represented in the world's families. The discussion below is not meant to be exhaustive, but rather to overview some relatively common structures that social workers might encounter.

Nuclear Families

There is a worldwide trend toward the nuclear family structure as societies become more industrialized and more people live in urban areas where smaller families are more practical (Ballantine & Roberts, 2009). The nuclear family is an adaptation to industrialization and urbanization. Some of the White settlers in the United States preferred the extended family structure, and others preferred the nuclear family, but the nuclear family has been the preferred family structure throughout most of U.S. history. Consequently, we would expect nuclear family to be easy to define. Actually, the family literature presents different definitions of this family structure. Some definitions specify that the nuclear family is composed of two parents and their biological or adopted offspring (LePoire, 2006). Others specify that a nuclear family is composed of at least one parent and one child (Leeder, 2004; D. Newman, 2008). This definition would include a broader brush of families, including lone-parent families and same-sex partners with children. But for the purpose of this discussion, we will use the definition that the *nuclear family* is composed of two parents and their biological or adopted offspring, because we think it is important to distinguish this idealized family structure from other family structures. Although, as mentioned, the nuclear family has been the preferred model throughout U.S. history, it has always been an ideal that was difficult to accomplish (Hareven, 2000). Families in colonial days and later were often marked by unplanned pregnancies and untimely death. Early parental death led to remarriage and stepfamilies, and to children being placed with extended family, or in foster care or orphanages. Non-kin boarders were brought in to provide income and companionship.

In 2007, according to the U.S. Census Bureau (2009a), 22.5% of households in the United States were married couples with children, down from 40.3% in 1970. We don't know a lot about the functioning of nuclear families because they are not often studied, except to compare other types of families to them. For example, children in lone-parent families are often compared to children in two-parent families, with the finding that children benefit from the resources—material and social—that come with two parents (see Shore & Shore, 2009). Recent U.S. Census data indicate that adults in married-couple families are older, more likely to have a bachelor's degree, more likely to own their own homes, and have higher incomes than lone-parent families (U.S. Census Bureau, 2009a). Both government (through marriage initiative programs) and religious groups are actively involved in trying to promote more two-parent families. Some social scientists see risk in nuclear families as compared to extended families, suggesting that the family can easily become too isolated with too much pressure put on the spousal relationship to fill each other's needs (F. Walsh, 2003a; Williams & Nussbaum, 2001).

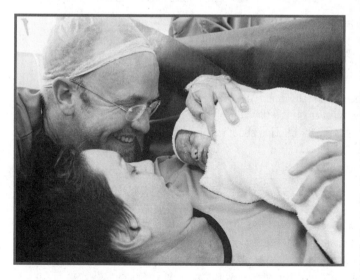

▲ **Photo 10.1**   The birth of a first child is a major transition for a family system, calling for new roles and the management of new tasks.

The often idealized nuclear family has a father in the labor force and a stay-at-home mother. That type of nuclear family peaked in the 1950s but was already beginning to decline by 1960. In 2007, a total of 66% of married couples with children under the age of 18 had two parents in the labor force (U.S. Census Bureau, 2009a). Having two parents in the labor force puts married couples at an economic advantage over single parents, but also raises concerns about who will provide child care and other domestic labor.

Nuclear families may include adopted children (as may lone-parent families, same-sex partner families, and step-families). The 2000 U.S. Census found that 2.5% of children under 18 were adopted, and 12.6% of those were foreign-born children (cited in Galvin, 2006). Adoptive families face the same challenges as other families, but they also face some additional ones. Every adopted child has two families, and disclosure about and navigation of this complexity must be addressed. The adoptive family must also develop a coherent story about how they came to be family and cope with issues of loss, grief, and attachment.

Extended Families

An *extended family* is one in which the parent–child nuclear family lives along with other relatives, such as grandparents, adult siblings, aunts, uncles, or cousins. This is a common pattern in agricultural societies around the world. In the United States, this pattern exists in some rural families, as well as in some ethnic groups, particularly among Mexican Americans and some Asian American groups. This is financially practical, and it also allows family groups to practice their ethnic traditions (Ballantine & Roberts, 2009). However, there are some downsides to the extended family. Sometimes family members exploit the labor of other family members. In other cases, the emotional and economic obligations to the extended family may come at the expense of individual development (Leeder, 2004).

At the moment, there is great debate about the appropriate role for extended family in the care of children orphaned by AIDS in southern Africa (see Mathambo & Gibbs, 2009). In societies where extended families share in the care of children, poor families are being challenged by the prolonged illness and death of family members who are at the prime working age. There is a growing interest in the capacity of the extended family to care for the increasing number of children orphaned by AIDS. Some argue, however, that the extended family network is collapsing under the strain of the devastation caused by AIDS. Where resources are scarce, both support and misery are shared.

Some family scholars suggest that it is more appropriate to speak of the contemporary family in the United States and other industrialized nations as a *modified extended family* than as a nuclear family (Leeder, 2004). Members of the extended family network may not reside together, but they are involved with each other in ongoing emotional and economic action. They stay connected. This is clearly the pattern in the Sharpe family. It is also the pattern in the current migrations across national lines. Family members are often separated across thousands of miles, but money is shared and the new technologies allow ongoing communication. Often immigrant groups travel together in kin networks and live very close to each other when not living together. The extended kin network is a source of support in times of crisis. For example, children may be transferred from one nuclear family to another within the extended kin network as need arises. The extended kin system also influences values and behaviors. For instance, Vivian Sharpe has expectations that her extended kinship system will have a positive influence on Marcie's values and behaviors as she grows into an adolescent. Extended family ties are usually stronger in Asian and Pacific Islander Americans, First Nations Peoples, African Americans, and Latino Americans than among middle-class White Americans (Ho, Rasheed, & Rasheed, 2004).

Cohabiting Heterosexual Couples

Cohabiting is living together without marriage. This method of forming a romantic partnership has been on the increase in the United States and other Western societies since 1960. Cohabitation is now recognized as a family form by family scholars. Sociologists Patrick Heuveline and Jeffrey Timberlake (2004) examined data from almost 70,000 women from 17 nations to learn how nonmarital cohabitation in the United States compares with that in 16 other industrialized nations. They examined the percentage of women in each of the nations estimated to experience at least one cohabiting relationship before the age of 45, and found a very large cross-nation range, from 4.4% in Poland to 83.6% in France. Spain and Italy were at the low end, with less than 15% of women in each country reporting cohabitation. The United States fell in the middle of the range, with about 50% of women estimated to ever cohabit before age 45. Heveline and Timberlake suggest that the cross-national differences in rates of cohabitation are influenced by a number of sociocultural factors, including religion, the economy, partnership laws and benefits, and availability of affordable housing. Besides differences in rates of cohabitation, they also found different types of cohabiting relationships occurring in different nations. For example, cohabitation can be a prelude to marriage or an alternative to marriage. Hueveline and Timberlake found that cohabiting relationships are less stable in the United States than in other countries.

Although the estimates vary, there is agreement that the rate of unmarried cohabiting partners in the United States has increased dramatically since the 1960s, and that, currently, a majority of couples getting married are already living in a cohabiting relationship (Bjorklund & Bee, 2008). The increase in cohabitation is related to the increasing age at marriage. In the United States and other Western industrialized countries, cohabitation is most frequent among young adults between the ages of 20 and 34 (OECD Family Database, 2008).

A number of researchers have found that cohabiting partners who marry are more likely to divorce than couples who married without cohabiting, and the first group also reports lower levels of marital satisfaction (see Kline et al., 2004; Phillips & Sweeny, 2005). Other researchers, however, have found that the increased risk of divorce applies only to those women who have cohabited with more than one partner. In other words, if a woman has cohabited with only her husband before marriage, she is no more likely to divorce than women who never cohabited before marriage (Teachman, 2003).

Two things are important to note about research on cohabitation. Because of the time that passes between data collection and publication of findings, the samples studied are typically people who cohabited in the late 1980s to the mid-1990s, and the nature of the cohabiting population appears to be changing. Second, the researchers are focusing on cohabiting women. Less is known about the relationship trajectory of cohabiting men, but some researchers find that cohabiting men report more time spent in domestic work than married men across 28 nations, a suggestion that traditional gender roles may be less common in cohabiting than in married romantic partnerships (S. Davis, Greenstein, & Marks, 2007; Kurdek, 2006). Lichter and Qian (2008) speculate that serial cohabitation by women may "reflect demographic shortages of men who are good providers or companions (e.g., men with good jobs, who are faithful, or who are drug free)" (p. 874).

Couples With No Children

Over the past three decades, the United States and other wealthy nations have seen an increase in the proportion of married couples who are childless. Interestingly, relatively high rates of childlessness were experienced in these same societies between 1890 and 1920, followed by the lowest recorded prevalence of childlessness during the 1950s and early 1960s (Abma & Martinez, 2006: Kohli & Albertini, 2009). Thus, the current high rates of childlessness are a return to a trend started in the late 19th century. Couples may be temporarily or permanently childless. Permanently childless couples may be voluntarily or involuntarily childless. Although childlessness is a growing type of family structure, there is very little research on childless couples; the research that has been done focuses on childless women, with little or no attention to childless men (fertility of men is much harder to study) or to the childless couple system, except in cases of infertility. The research often does not distinguish between married and unmarried women.

The most comprehensive study of childless women in the United States to date was conducted by Joyce Abma and Gladys Martinez (2006) at the National Center for Health Statistics. Their study examined three types of childlessness: temporarily childless, voluntarily childless, and involuntarily childless. They studied both married and unmarried women and did not make distinctions between these two groups. They found that from 1976 to 2002, the percentage of women aged 35–39 who were childless increased from 11% to 20%, and the percentage of women aged 40–44 who were childless increased from 10% to 18%. The voluntarily childless was the largest group of childless women in 2002, making up 42% of all childless women; 30% were temporarily childless, and 28% were involuntarily childless. As might be expected, given declining fertility between the ages of 35 and 44, women who were temporarily childless were more likely to be in the younger cohort, ages 35–39, and women who were involuntarily childless were more likely to be in the older group, ages 40–44.

All three groups of childless women were found to have more egalitarian views on family relationships than the women who were parents. There were some differences in the profiles of these three groups of childless women, however. Consistent with earlier research, the voluntarily childless women, compared to parenting women and other childless women, were disproportionately White, tended to be employed full time, had the highest incomes, and were more likely to be nonreligious. However, between 1995 and 2002, the percentage of Black women among the voluntarily childless increased to where it was equivalent to their share of the total population of women between the ages of 35 and 44. From 1976 to 2002, Hispanic women were consistently underrepresented among the voluntarily childless.

One finding from the Abma and Martinez (2006) study is that there was a slight downturn in the percentage of women who were voluntarily childless and a slight upturn in the percentage who were involuntarily childless between 1995 and 2002. They speculate that this change is probably related to the trend toward later marriage and childbearing, resulting in some couples discovering that they had fertility problems when they decided to become parents. Infertility can be caused by problems in the reproductive systems of the man, the woman, or both. It is a global problem, but in countries with low resources it is most likely to be caused by infection-related tubal damage. Although there are currently many assistive technologies for dealing with fertility problems, these are inaccessible to most women in low-resource countries (Sharma, Mittal, & Aggarwal, 2009). In many countries of the world, childlessness is often highly stigmatizing (Chachamovich et al., 2009).

Research on the emotional impact of infertility indicates that it is a major source of stress. Infertility has been consistently associated with decreased scores in quality of life, affecting mental health, physical vitality, and social functioning (Drosdzol & Skrzypulec, 2008; El-Messidi, Al-Fozan, Lin Tan, Farag, & Tulandi, 2004; J. T. Lau et al., 2008). When couples experience similar levels of distress, they are more able to communicate about it and support each other (Peterson, Newton, & Rosen, 2003). However, it is not unusual for husbands and wives to have different reactions to infertility. The stressors related to infertility may go on over a long period of time. Treatments can be very costly and are often unsuccessful.

Although attitudes are changing, some social stigma is still attached to childlessness. Little is known about the lives of childless couples. In a recent attempt to understand the life trajectories of childless adults, an entire issue of the journal *Ageing & Society* was devoted to research on childless older adults. One researcher (Wenger, 2009) found that by the time they reached old age, childless people in rural Wales had made adaptations to their childless situation and developed closer relationships with kin and friends. This is the way that Vivian Sharpe's godparents have adjusted to involuntary childlessness, and they draw great pleasure from being a part of the lively extended kin network in which Vivian and Bobby are embedded. On average, however, childless older adults in Wales entered residential care at younger ages than older adults who had children.

Lone-Parent Families

Lone-parent families are composed of one parent and at least one child residing in the same household. They are headed by either a divorced or an unmarried parent. Lone-parent families are on the increase in all wealthy industrialized nations, but nowhere more than in the United States (UNICEF, 2007). In 2007, nearly one-third (32%) of children in the United States lived with only one parent, 82% with the mother and 18% with the father (Shore & Shore, 2009). This compares with less than 10% in Greece and Italy (UNICEF, 2007). Around the world, lone mothers are the great majority of parents in lone-parent families. In the United States, 65% of non-Hispanic Black children, 49% of Native

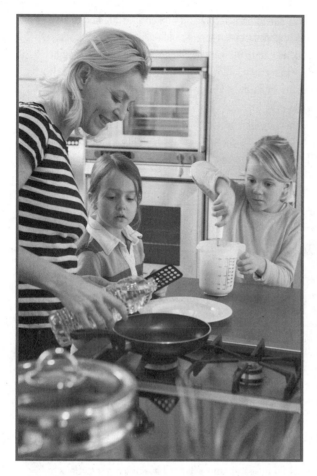

▲ **Photo 10.2** Family time: Mother spends quality time with her two daughters making breakfast.

American children, 37% of Hispanic children, 23% of non-Hispanic White children, and 17% of Asian American and Pacific Islander children live with one parent. The share of children living with one parent in the United States tripled since 1970 when the rate was 11% (Shore & Shore, 2009). It is important to exercise caution with these statistics, however. Sometimes families who get counted as being lone-parent families reside with other family members and/or may have the support of a romantic partner.

Single mothers around the world have some common challenges: They are playing the dual roles of mother and worker with no partner assistance, receive lower earnings than men, and receive irregular paternal support. If they became lone parents after divorce, they and their children must cope with loss and grief, may have to relocate, and face an average of 37% decline in their standard of living (Stirling & Aldrich, 2008). Lone-parent families headed by mothers are especially vulnerable to economic insecurity and poverty. Cross-national differences in government policies result in different circumstances for single mothers and their children, however. Some countries provide universal child allowances, paid maternity leave, and free child care. Children of single mothers have higher rates of poverty than children from two-parent families around the world, but the poverty rates among children of single parents are much lower in countries that provide such supports (D. Lindsey, 2004).

In 2000, the poverty rate for single-parent families in the United States was 55.4%, compared to 6.7% in Sweden (UNICEF, 2000). This is a very large range and primarily reflects differences in child and family policies in the two countries. Three other countries had poverty rates of over 45% for single-parent families: Canada, Germany, and the United Kingdom. At the other end of the continuum, three other countries had poverty rates of less than 15% for single-parent families: Denmark, Norway, and Hungary.

In the United States, social policy has focused on two priorities to improve the living situation of children in lone-parent families, as well as to decrease public expenditures on these families: improved child support payment by the nonresidential parent and marriage of the lone parent. The first of these priorities is to step up the enforcement of child support payment by the nonresidential parent. The research to date indicates that if nonresidential parents paid the child support required, the economic situation of residential children does indeed improve, although not to the level they would experience if both parents resided together. However, for impoverished families, the payment of child support is not sufficient to bring them out of poverty (see Stirling & Aldrich, 2008).

The second policy direction proposed in the United States in recent years is to encourage marriage of the lone parent. Some policy analysts conclude that this would, indeed, improve the economic situation of children currently being raised in lone-parent families (see Rector, Johnson, & Fagan, 2008). Others conclude that while this might be a good solution for some lone-parent families, male unemployment and marginal employment present serious barriers to marriage for many low-income couples (Edin & Reed, 2005; Gibson-Davis, Edin, & McLanahan, 2005). These latter researchers have found that men and women in impoverished neighborhoods often value marriage highly, but do not see themselves as economically stable enough to have a viable marriage. Impoverished lone mothers have reported that they do not have a pool of attractive marriage partners who are economically stable, not addicted to drugs and alcohol, not involved with the criminal justice system, and able to be loving and kind parents to their children (Edin, Kefalas, & Reed, 2004).

It is important to note that in the wealthy nations, the number of lone-parent families is growing across all socioeconomic groups, and in the United States, many affluent and well-educated women and men are choosing to become lone parents because they want to be a parent but do not have a partner with whom to share parenting (Anderson, 2005). These lone parents have the resources to afford full-time child care, private schools, and other domestic assistance.

One more point is important. Much of the research on lone-parent families has taken a deficit approach in looking at family interaction and functioning. Other researchers have attempted to look at lone parents from a strengths perspective and document how they function to adapt to the challenges they face. One example of this is a qualitative research project that asked low-income African American mothers and members of their families (who were sometimes not biologically related to them) to identify components of effective and ineffective family functioning (McCreary & Dancy, 2004). They found that all but 1 of the 40 respondents reported that they see or talk daily with at least one family member other than their children, a coping strategy that increases the effectiveness of family functioning by preventing isolation.

Stepfamilies

Stepfamilies have always been a relatively common family form in the United States, but they have changed over time. In colonial days, stepfamilies were typically the result of one parent dying and the other parent remarrying. Today, most stepfamilies are formed after biological parents divorce or dissolve their relationship, and go on to form new romantic partnerships. We don't have good current data on the number of stepfamilies in the United States, but it is estimated that between 10% and 20% of children under the age of 18 reside in stepfamilies (Saint Louis Healthy Marriage Coalition, 2009). The U.S. Census Bureau defines stepfamilies as those with two adults and children, where one adult is not the biological parent (cited in Pasley & Lee, 2010). Stepfamilies can be of several different types. The most common is the stepfather family in which the mother has children from a previous relationship in the household. Another type is the stepmother family in which the father has children from a previous relationship in the household. Some stepfamilies have children from both partners' prior relationships living in the household. Any of these family forms can become more complex when children are born to the new partnership. Stepfamilies are also formed by same-sex partners where one or both partners have children from prior relationships living in the household. Although not counted by the U.S. Census Bureau as living in stepfamilies, many children reside with a single mother and make visits to the biological father and his new wife.

Stepfamilies are complex family structures. They involve complicated networks of relationships that include biological parents; stepparents; perhaps siblings and step-siblings; and multiple sets of grandparents, aunts, uncles, and cousins. Children in stepfamilies may move back and forth between two homes and maintain connections with the nonresident parent. There are a number of subsystems in the stepfamily, including the new couple, the parent–child, the stepparent–stepchild, the child–nonresidential parent, the biological parents, the parent–stepparent–nonresidential parent, and sometimes the sibling or stepsibling subsystem. The parent–child subsystem is a more long-standing form than the new couple subsystem.

The new stepfamily must negotiate rules, roles, rituals, and customs. Things as simple as foods served in the households, bedtimes, chores, and methods of discipline may become points of tension. This works best when the issues and expectations are made explicit. It is quite common for loyalty conflicts to arise involving several subsystems, with family members feeling torn and caught between people that they love (Pasley & Lee, 2010). The biological parent often feels torn between loyalty to the child(ren) and love for the new spouse or partner. Children may aggravate this situation by testing the biological parent's loyalty to them. Children may feel a conflict between their loyalty to the nonresidential parent and the need to form a relationship with the stepparent. Children can easily get triangulated into conflict between the parent and stepparent, between the residential parent and the nonresidential parent, or between the stepparent and the nonresidential parent. Events such as Parent Night at school can become a knotty situation.

The more children there are in the stepfamily situation, the more complicated the negotiations can become. First-marriage couples report that the biggest source of stress is finances, followed by child rearing. For stepfamilies, the biggest sources of stress are reversed, with child rearing coming first, followed by finances (Stanley, Markman, & Whitton, 2002). Stepparents are often treated as outsiders by children, and this is a difficult position from which to attempt to parent. Research indicates that stepfathers are less likely than stepmothers to try to engage in active parenting of stepchildren, no doubt because of expectations of gendered behavior; consequently, stepfathers tend to be perceived more positively than stepmothers (Pasley & Lee, 2010). There is also evidence that stepdaughters are more difficult to parent than stepsons (Hetherington & Kelly, 2002).

Same-Sex Partner Families

Long-term relationships between same-sex partners are becoming more visible, if not more common, in the United States and around the world. It is possible for gay and lesbian partners to be married or to enter into other legally sanctioned partnerships in some countries and some parts of the United States. As of December 2009, seven countries have federal laws that legalize same-sex marriage: the Netherlands (2001), Belgium (2003), Spain (2005), Canada (2005), South Africa (2006), Norway (2009), and Sweden (2009). A number of other countries of the world have some sort of federal civil union laws that grant partner registration and some rights and benefits of marriage. In the United States, the Defense of Marriage Act, enacted in 1996, defines marriage as a legal union between one man and one woman and makes two stipulations: (1) States are not required to recognize same-sex marriages performed in other states; and (2) the federal government will not acknowledge same-sex marriages, even if they are recognized by states. In spite of this law, as of May, 2010, five states and the District of Columbia issue marriage licenses to same-sex couples: Massachusetts (2004), Connecticut (2008), Iowa (2009), Vermont (2009), New Hampshire (2010), and the District of Columbia (2010). New York (2008) and Maryland (2010), recognize marriages of same-sex couples legalized in other jurisdictions. Five states provide the equivalent of spousal rights to same-sex couples in the state: California, Nevada, New Jersey, Oregon, and Washington. Four other states have laws that provide some spousal rights to same-sex couples: Colorado, Hawaii, Maine, and Wisconsin (Human Rights Campaign, 2010).

But the issue of marriage equality for same-sex couples is still hotly debated in the United States at this time. Same-sex partnerships are openly condemned by some religious and political leaders as well as segments of society that think these partnerships are a threat to the family institution. Twenty-nine states have passed constitutional amendments restricting marriage to the union of one man and one woman. Eleven other states have state laws, instead of constitutional amendments, that similarly restrict marriage (Human Rights Campaign, 2009). Given the current state of debate about same-sex marriage, it is quite likely there will be other actions by nations and states by the time you read this.

Same-sex partnerships share many characteristics with heterosexual partnerships, but they also have some that are unique; the partners are of the same gender, they must navigate a social world that continues to stigmatize same-sex relationships, and in many places they lack legal recognition. Some researchers have found that same-sex partners report about the same frequency of arguments as heterosexual couples (Peplau & Fingerhut, 2007), but others have found that same-sex couples report less conflict than heterosexual couples, more relationship satisfaction, and better conflict resolution (Balsam, Beauchaine, Rothblum, & Solomon, 2008; Kurdek, 2004). There is evidence that both same-sex and heterosexual partners tend to disagree about similar topics, such as sex, money, and household tasks

(Kurdek, 2006). Some studies find that members of sex-same partnerships are more likely than married heterosexual couples to separate when they are unhappy, but the one longitudinal study that has followed the first same-sex partners to take advantage of Vermont's civil union laws found that same-sex couples in civil unions are less likely to separate than same-sex couples not in civil unions (Balsam et al., 2008). Same-sex partners have been found to engage in less traditional division of labor than heterosexual married couples with children, but this finding must be interpreted in the context of considerable research that shows that heterosexual couples become more traditional and less egalitarian when they become parents (Kurdek, 2006). Same-sex partners report receiving more support from friends and less support from biological family than heterosexual couples (Kurdek, 2006).

Many lesbians and gay men became parents in earlier heterosexual relationships, before coming out as gay or lesbian. Increasingly, lesbians and gay men are also becoming parents in the context of their same-sex partner relationships, with the assistance of reproductive technology or by adoption (Savin-Williams, 2008). The U.S. Census Bureau estimates that about 1 in 5 gay male couples and 1 in 3 lesbian couples were raising children in 2000 (cited in Gates & Ost, 2004). Lesbian couples may choose artificial insemination and gay male couples may choose to use a surrogate mother; each method results in the child sharing a bloodline with one partner but not the other. Some lesbian and gay couples become parents through adoption. Each of these options involves challenges and decisions.

Considerable research attention has been given to the question of how children fare in families of same-sex partners. This research consistently finds that children who grow up with same-sex parents do not differ in any important way from children raised in families of heterosexual couples. They have similar emotional and behavioral adjustment; no differences are found in self-esteem, depression, or behavioral problems (Wainright, Russell, & Patterson, 2004). This is remarkable, given the stigma that such families often have to face. Children of same-sex parents have also been found to be no more likely than the children of heterosexual couples to identify as homosexual. The school setting may present challenges, however; the children may face harassment, and their parents may find that they are not accepted on parent committees (Goldberg, 2010).

Thomas Johnson and Patricia Colucci (2005) argue that lesbians and gays are bicultural. They have been reared and socialized in the dominant heterosexual culture and have internalized the norms, values, and beliefs learned in that culture. For the most part, they are members of heterosexually oriented families, and they have heterosexual models of family life. At the same time, lesbians and gays participate in a gay culture that copes with homophobia and develops a set of norms and roles for the special circumstances of same-sex partnerships. They must often deal with family-of-origin reactivity to their sexual orientation and romantic relationships. Johnson and Colucci suggest that

> following this track, we believe that gays and lesbians are part of a complex multigenerational family system consisting of a family of origin, a multigenerational lesbian/gay community, and/or a family of choice that consists of friends, partners, and/or children. (p. 347)

Military Families

Military families may have any of the family structures discussed above. They are included in this discussion of diversity of family structures, however, because of some special challenges they face in times of deployment to war zones. In the United States, military members may serve in either the active-duty or reserve components of the military. Active-duty members serve in the U.S. Army, Navy, Marine Corps, or Air Force. Reservists serve either in the Army National Guard or Air National Guard. Compared to other recent conflicts, deployments to Afghanistan and Iraq have been more frequent and lengthier, usually lasting 12 to 15 months. Another dramatic difference is that reservists have made up almost one-third of the military force being deployed (Faber, Willerton, Clymer, MacDermid, & Weiss, 2008). Historically, the National Guard has been a domestic 911 force responding to local, state, and sometimes national emergencies. Since 2003, they have been an important component of the armed forces, fighting in two theaters of war. Reservist deployments are typically longer than active-duty deployments, because reservists usually must be away

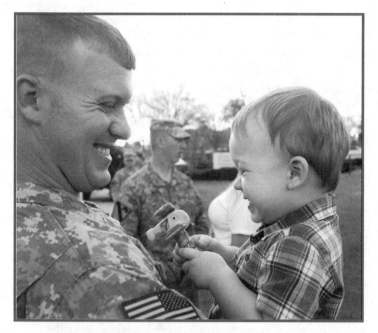

▲ **Photo 10.3** This father and son share a moment of joy during a welcome home ceremony when the Arkansas National Guard's 39th Infantry Brigade Combat Team returns from deployment to Iraq.

from home for predeployment training for as long as 3 months before deployment (J. Martin & Sherman, 2010).

Approximately one-third of both active-duty and reservist members have children; children of reserve members are a little older, on average, than children of active-duty members. The circumstances of reservist families are different in some ways from those of active-duty families. Active-duty military families typically live on or near military installations where the active-duty member receives daily military training. Reservist families live and work in a civilian community and receive military training one weekend per month (Faber et al., 2008).

Research indicates that active-duty families usually cope well with temporary separations during peacetime (Flake, Davis, Johnson, & Middleton, 2009). Active-duty military spouses are accustomed to managing as single parents for periods of time, and then readjusting to operating in their predeployment family structure again when the deployment ends. Reservists and their families, on the other hand, are accustomed to occasional brief deployments to respond to state, local, and even national emergencies. They are not as prepared to deploy quickly for long periods of time, and must deal with the break in civilian employment, as well as prepare the family for the coming separation. Consequently, active-duty families and reservist families face both similar and different challenges in the current system of deployment to Iraq and Afghanistan.

Spouses of both active-duty soldiers and reservists have reported loneliness, loss of emotional support, role overload, and worry about the safety and well-being of the deployed spouse (Faber et al., 2008). Parents who are spouses or partners of soldiers deployed to war zones report higher levels of stress than the national average for parents. Communication with the military member in the war zone is spotty at best, as the deployed soldier is in and out of the range of adequate communications systems. During his earlier deployment to Iraq, Bobby Sharpe was only able to have infrequent contact with his family, but his sister is much luckier and has been able to be in regular e-mail communication. Both the family members at home and the deployed family member may try to avoid alarming each other about what is happening in their worlds, and together they must gauge how involved the deployed family member can be in making decisions about what is happening at home. Bobby Sharpe did not know his furnace was broken until he returned home from his first deployment, because Vivian did not want to bother him with that kind of family problem.

As the end of the deployment draws near, family members report that they begin to worry about what to expect when the soldier returns, in terms of possible war wounds or personality or behavior changes (Faber et al., 2008). Marcie Sharpe had heard scary stories of parents coming home with completely changed personalities. She worried about this during Bobby's first deployment and has already begun to worry about it again. Although it is often a joyous time, the military member's return home can be very stressful for families. Family members have to readjust to one another and realign family roles. Three out of four military families report that the first 3 months after coming home can be the most stressful period of the deployment process (Flake et al., 2009). Soldiers have to reacclimate to life away from the war zone and renegotiate roles, responsibilities, and boundaries with family members who had made adjustments in their absence (Faber et al., 2008). This readjustment is particularly difficult when there have been physical or mental injuries, such as traumatic brain injury or posttraumatic stress disorder (J. Martin & Sherman, 2010). Families tend to stabilize over time, but many families must prepare for another deployment that can come as quickly as in one year.

Children of both active-duty and reservist families involved in the current wars have been found to be at increased risk for a range of problems in psychosocial functioning. In the time just before a parent's deployment, children may become withdrawn or engage in regressive behavior. Early in the deployment, they may be overwhelmed, sad, and anxious, and have more somatic (physical) symptoms, but these symptoms usually diminish once children adjust to the deployment. They are usually excited and relieved when the soldier parent comes home, but may experience conflict about the readjustments being made at home (Flake et al., 2009). A recent study of children of deployed National Guard members found that they reported missing their deployed parent as the biggest difficulty of the deployment. Their biggest worry was that their deployed parent would be injured or killed. The biggest change in their lives involved increased responsibility at home, more chores, and more responsibility for younger siblings. They reported concern about trying to avoid upsetting the parent at home. The children also described some positive aspects of deployment. Some reported being proud of what their deployed parents were doing for the country, although this pride was tempered when they heard talk from television, classmates, and other sources suggesting that the war is bad. Some children also reported pride in themselves for their ability to be more responsible while the deployed parent was away (Houston et al., 2009).

There is one important difference in the experiences of active-duty and reservist families. A large portion of active-duty military families continue to live in or near military installations during the family member's deployment. This allows them to have ongoing support from other military families as well as from military programs. Reservist families, on the other hand, are scattered across all 50 states and the U.S. territories, many of them living in rural communities. This is especially the case for National Guard members because the National Guard has a strong tradition in rural communities, where it serves as a point of pride as well as a supplement to the low wages often found in these communities (Martin & Sherman, 2010). Sometimes a National Guard family will be the only one in their area experiencing deployment at a given time. This is problematic because of the lack of access to other families facing similar experiences. Children of deployed reservists have reported that a chance to talk to other children with a deployed parent would be a big help (Houston et al., 2009). Likewise, the returning reservist soldier may be isolated from other returning soldiers, as well as from some of the medical and psychiatric resources available in and near military installations. Recognizing some of these challenges, the National Guard has instituted the Yellow Ribbon Program to provide support for families throughout the cycle of deployment. The challenge is to maintain the same level of services throughout each state.

As of December 2009, Operation Iraqi Freedom is winding down and Operation Enduring Freedom (the War in Afghanistan) is escalating. It is hard to say what the future of these wars is, but it is clear that the military families involved, both active-duty and reservist families, will experience multiple challenges in the aftermath of the wars. According to a large-scale study sponsored by the RAND Corporation, many service members from the Wars in Iraq and Afghanistan have undergone prolonged periods of combat stress (Tanielian & Jaycox, 2008). In the aftermath of the trauma, many service members and veterans are experiencing horrific combat injuries; others are experiencing substance abuse, PTSD, relationship problems, and work problems. Social workers in all practice settings should be alert to possibilities for engaging these families in supportive services.

Economic and Cultural Diversity

Family structure is influenced by economic and cultural patterns, as well as immigration status. As you read the following sections on economic diversity, cultural diversity, and immigrant families, think about how family structure is affected by the family's position in the economic structure; cultural heritage; and experience with immigration, where relevant.

Economic Diversity

Economic inequality exists in all societies, historical and contemporary, but the number of social classes and the amount of inequality vary from society to society. As indicated in Chapter 9, the United States has less inequality than some nations of the world, but it has more inequality than any other advanced industrialized nation. And, unfortunately, since 1970, the gap between the richest and poorest U.S. citizens has been growing. As I write this at the end of 2009, the worst recession in the United States since the Great Depression of the 1930s may be beginning to lift, but the national unemployment rate has climbed to 10%. A number of wealthy families have lost millions, even billions, of dollars in fraud schemes and investments gone bad. Middle-class families have been devastated by job cutbacks, home foreclosures, and high debt, with middle-class men over the age of 55 being particularly hard hit by job cutbacks. The poorest of families are barely surviving, not able to meet basic needs for food and shelter. Large numbers of U.S. families report feeling a sense of financial insecurity (Bartholomae & Fox, 2010).

The question to be addressed here is, what impact do economic resources have on family life? How do family economic circumstances affect parental relationships, parent–child relationships, and child development? A large volume of research has found that individual physical and mental health, marital relationships, parent–child relationships, and child outcomes decline as economic stress increases. Two theoretical models have been proposed to explain the connection between economic resources and individual and family functioning: the family economic stress model and the family investment model.

The family economic stress model is based on Glen Elder's (1974) research on the impact of the Great Depression on parents and children. This research found that severe economic hardship disrupted family functioning in ways that negatively affected marital quality, parenting quality, and child outcomes. Similar results have been found in more recent studies of Iowa farm families facing a severe downturn in the agricultural economy in the 1980s (Conger & Elder, 1994), and of economic pressure in African American families (Conger et al., 2002). In the **family economic stress model** based on this research, economic hardship leads to economic pressure, which leads to parent distress, which leads to disrupted family relationships, which leads to child and adolescent adjustment problems (see Exhibit 10.5; Conger & Conger, 2008).

There is a great deal of research to support the family economic stress model. Economic stress, such as unemployment, low income, and high debt, have been found to have negative effects on physical and mental health of parents (J. Kahn & Pearlin, 2006; Mckee-Ryan, Song, Wanberg, & Kinicki, 2005; Mistry, Vandewater, Huston, & McLoyd, 2002). Research has also found that psychological distress about economic pressures takes its toll on marital quality (Gudmunson, Beutler, Israelsen, McCoy, & Hill, 2007; Kinnunen & Feldt, 2004). Couple disagreements and fighting increase with financial strain. Parental psychological distress and marital conflict have been found to affect parenting practices, leading to less parental warmth and more inconsistent, punitive, and controlling discipline (Mistry, Lowe, Renner, & Chien, 2008; Waanders, Mendez, & Downer, 2007).

Family economic hardship has also been found to be associated with a number of child outcomes. Children in families experiencing economic hardship tend to have higher levels of depression and anxiety (Gutman, McLoyd, & Tokoyawa, 2005). They also have been found to demonstrate more aggressive and antisocial behaviors (Solantaus, Leinonen, & Punamaki, 2004). Economic disadvantage is associated with lower self-esteem and self-efficacy in children (Shek, 2003) and poorer school performance (Gutman et al., 2005). Adolescents who report worrying about the family's finances also report more somatic complaints, such as stomachaches, headaches, and loss of appetite (Wadsworth & Santiago, 2008).

Where the family economic stress model focuses on the impact of low income and economic hardship on family life, the **family investment model** focuses on the other end of the economic continuum, on how economic advantage affects family life and child outcomes. This theoretical model proposes that families with greater economic resources can afford to make large investments in the development of their children (M. Bornstein & Bradley, 2003; Bradley & Corwyn, 2002).

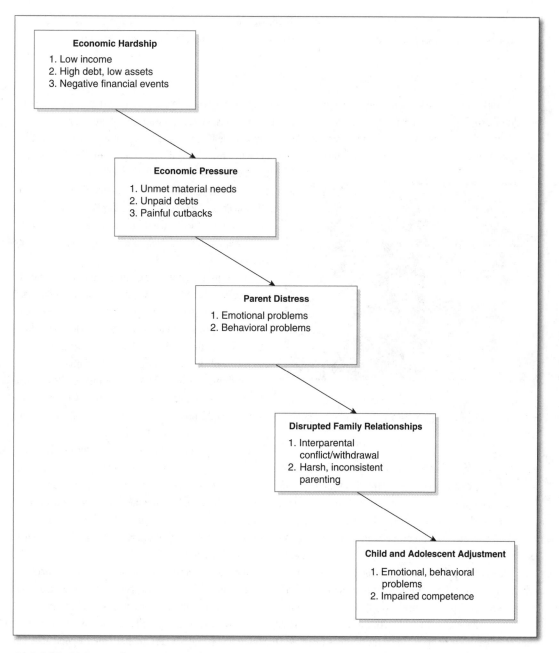

▲ **Exhibit 10.5**   Family Economic Stress Model

SOURCE: Conger and Conger, 2008. Reprinted with permission.

Families with abundant economic resources are able to make more learning materials available in the home; spend more time engaged in intellectually stimulating activities, such as visiting museums and traveling; secure education in enriched educational environments; secure outside assistance such as tutoring and specialized training; provide a higher standard of living in such areas as housing, clothing, nutrition, transportation, and medical care; and reside in a safe, clean, and roomy environment. They also are able to open doors to social networks that provide educational and career opportunities. This seems to go without saying, but there is empirical support for the proposal that family income affects the types of investments parents make in their children (Bradley & Corwyn, 2002), and this investment has been demonstrated to be positively associated with child cognitive development (Linver, Brooks-Gunn, & Kohen, 2002).

Cultural Diversity

The world over, we are living in a time when people are moving about from society to society and increasing the level of cultural diversity in small towns, suburbs, and cities. As suggested earlier, there has always been cultural diversity in the United States, but with the new waves of immigration in recent years, the United States has become a microcosm of the whole world in terms of the complex mix of ethnic heritages and religions. Across cultural groups, families differ in how they define family; in how they organize family life; and in their customs, traditions, and communication patterns (Hines, Preto, McGoldrick, Almeida, & Weltman, 2005). Social workers face a daunting challenge in responding sensitively and appropriately to each and every family they encounter.

▲ **Photo 10.4**   It is important for social workers to understand ethnic differences in family beliefs, rules, communication patterns, and organizational norms.

In the past, many of the clinical models for family practice were based on work with primarily middle-class and often two-biological-parent European American families. Working from these models often led to thinking of racial and ethnic minority families as deviant or deficient. One of the best examples of the damage that this way of thinking can do is Anne Fadiman's (1998) story about the experience of a Hmong family with the health care and child protective systems in California. (If you haven't read this book yet, I suggest you put it on your to-do list during your next break between terms.) In recent years, however, there has been a concerted call for social workers and other professionals to practice in a culturally sensitive manner that moves from culturally aware to culturally competent practice (Fong & Furuto, 2001; Lum, 2007; Rothman, 2008). I prefer to talk in terms of culturally sensitive practice, because I doubt that we can ever be truly competent in a culture other than the one in which we were raised, and certainly not in the multiple cultures we are likely to encounter in our work over time. In light of the great diversity in contemporary life, the goal should be to remain curious and open-minded, taking a stance of "informed not knowing" (Dean, 2001).

Consequently, I do not present a cookbook approach to working with cultural differences, but rather a process by which we can develop cultural awareness about the family groups with which we work. The first step, as suggested above, is to develop an intense understanding of the limitations of our own cultural perspective and a healthy respect for the integrity of all cultures. Starting from this position, we can set out to become as well informed as possible about the cultural groups represented by the families we serve. One thing that social workers are particularly good at, when we are at our best, is putting people and situations into context. We will want to use that strength to learn as much as possible about the context of the culturally variant families we encounter. Juliet Rothman (2008, p. 38) suggests the types of knowledge needed to practice in a culturally sensitive manner; they are presented in modified form here:

- The group's history prior to arriving in the United States, if relevant

- The group's experience with immigration, if relevant

- The group's experience with settlement in the United States, if relevant

- The group's experience with oppression, discrimination, bias, and prejudice

- The group's relationship to the country of origin, if relevant

- The group's relationship to the country of residence

- The group's worldviews and beliefs about child rearing, family relationships, dating and marriage, employment, education, recreation, health and illness, aging, death and bereavement, and other life course issues

- Variations and differences within the group, particularly those related to social class

- Generational issues about acculturation within the group, if relevant

Some of this information may be more important for specific practice situations. There are a number of ways to learn this information: through Internet research, history books, biographies and autobiographies of members of the group, films and documentaries about the group, conversations with friends or colleagues who are members of the group, attendance at cultural festivals, and by asking your clients what you need to know to be helpful to them.

Even though we want to learn as much as we can about the cultural group, we must realize that there are many variations within all cultural groups. When I need to avoid stereotypical application of knowledge about a cultural group, it helps me to think about how many variations there are within my own cultural group, and how well or poorly generalizations about my group apply to me. It is also helpful to hear different stories from members of the group, through books, videos, or personal conversations. It is particularly important to remember that there are social class differences among all cultural groups. You will want to consider whether the African American woman you are working with is middle class or working class, and know something about her experiences with oppression. You will want to keep in mind that over 500 distinct First Nations (or Native American) peoples exist within the United States, and they differ in language, religion, social structure, and many other aspects of culture (Weaver, 2007). You will want to know how a specific nation coped with attempts to eradicate their cultural practices. You will want to note whether the Latino immigrant family came from a rural or urban environment and what level of education they received in their home country; you will also want to note their country of origin and whether they are of documented or undocumented status. When working with an Asian or Pacific Island family, you will want to know not only the country of origin (out of 60 represented in the United States), but also the social class and education level of the family, religious beliefs, and when the family first immigrated to the United States. You will want to note how integrated the family from North Africa or the Middle East is into U.S. mainstream culture, as well as how traditional they are in religious and cultural beliefs. These are only a few examples of how you will need to individualize families while also putting them into cultural context.

Immigrant Families

The United States is built on successive waves of immigration. Recent census data indicate that approximately 37.5 million immigrants are currently living within the United States, making up 12.5% of the U.S. population (Bush et al., 2010). Immigrants are foreign-born people who plan to settle permanently in the United States. They may be economic migrants who are seeking better jobs and pay, family migrants who come to join family members already here, or refugees who are involuntarily fleeing political violence or extreme environmental distress. Current immigrants to the United States are more diverse than earlier immigrants in terms of country of origin, language, religion, and socioeconomic status. The places from which immigrants come has changed over time, influenced by immigration policies. For example, 1965 amendments to the Immigration and Nationality Act of 1952 created a "family reunification" category and gave preference to immigrants who had family members already in the United States. The 1986 Refugee Assistance

Extension Act made it easier for families facing political persecution and extreme environments in their home countries to enter the United States. The Immigration Act of 1990 shifted policy away from family reunification to individuals with specific education and credentials and to wealthy individuals who could invest in the U.S. economy (Bush et al., 2010).

Immigrants may be *first-generation* (moved from another country to the United States), *second-generation* (children of first-generation immigrants), or *third-generation* (grandchildren of first-generation immigrants). In general, first-generation immigrants will experience more loss and grief than second- and third-generation immigrants, but the reaction to immigration differs by the degree of choice about migration, accessibility to the country of origin, gender and age, stage of family life cycle, number of family members immigrating and left behind, community social supports, and experiences with discrimination in the country of origin and the country of adoption (Falicov, 2003). Many losses are involved with migration, including loss of the family members and friends left behind, loss of familiar language, and loss of customs and traditions. Involuntary immigrants often have been traumatized in their country of origin and have no option to visit home. Other immigrants are able to make frequent visits home and maintain transnational families who are in frequent contact. Families may migrate together or in sequential stages, whereby one or two family members immigrate first, followed by others at later times.

In cases of sequential migration, family roles and relationships must be reorganized over time. The first immigrating family member must now perform some roles not carried out in the home country, whether those were domestic chores, paid labor, or managing finances. Likewise, the spouse left in the home country must now take on roles that had been filled by the immigrating family member. If the trailing spouse later immigrates, the spousal roles will have to be renegotiated, as happens when military families reunite. One difference in the reunifications of immigrant and military families is that sequential immigration may happen over a period of years and have unexpected delays, and the separations can be much longer than for military families. When children are left behind for a number of years, they may have trouble reattaching to the parents.

Immigrant families face a number of challenges. If they come from a non–English-speaking country, the language barrier will be a serious impediment to becoming comfortable in the new country. They will be unable to read street signs, job announcements and applications, food labels, and communications from the children's schools, unless they live where language translations are commonly used. Because children learn new languages more easily than adults, parent and child roles often are reversed as children become the language and cultural brokers. Children also learn the new cultural norms more quickly than parents, and this causes intergenerational tension about the appropriate level of acculturation, how much of the old to maintain and how much of the new to adopt. Parents may not understand the new culture's norms about child rearing and find themselves at odds with the school system, and perhaps with the child protective system. Immigrant wives often come from cultures with traditional gender roles but need to engage in paid work in the United States to keep the family afloat. This often results in more independence and status for wives than they were accustomed to in their home countries, and can cause marital conflict if men want to hold onto the traditional gender hierarchy. Research has found increased male-to-female violence in Asian families when wives earn as much or more than their husbands (G. Chung, Tucker, & Takeuchi, 2008). Many immigrant families come from collectivist cultures where harmony is valued over individual ambition and may feel a great deal of tension about how to respond to cultural pressures toward individualism. They may have had both the support and control of the extended family in the home country and find themselves struggling to maintain family stability with a much more limited support network.

CHALLENGES TO FAMILY LIFE

Contemporary families of all types of family structures face many stressful situations that challenge their ability to provide nurturance and the necessary resources for healthy development of family members. Every historical era and every culture presents its own set of challenges to families. In the following sections, we discuss three challenges to contemporary families: family violence, divorce, and substance abuse.

Family Violence

The family is the social group from whom we expect to receive our greatest love, support, nurturance, and acceptance. And yet, family relationships are some of the most violent in many societies. It is estimated that wife beating occurs in about 85% of the world's societies, and husband beating occurs in about 27% (D. Newman, 2008). Children are even more vulnerable to violence within the family than adults. Children are abused by parents, but physical violence between siblings may be the most common form of family violence. Older adults are sometimes abused by their family caregivers, and teenage children sometimes abuse their parents, particularly their mothers (Gelles, 2010).

It is very difficult to produce accurate statistics about the amount of family violence in different categories because the family is the most intimate of social groupings; what happens in families is usually "behind closed doors," away from the watchful eyes of strangers, relatives, and neighbors. In addition, different definitions of violence are used by different researchers. The data presented here are the best available. According to the U.S. Bureau of Justice Statistics (Catalano, 2007), 510,970 women and 104,820 men in the United States were victims of physical or sexual assault by current spouses, former spouses, or other romantic partners in 2005. Other studies suggest higher estimates, but there is general agreement that intimate partner violence has in fact declined in the last 15 years (see Tjaden & Thoennes, 2000). In 2006, an estimated 905,000 children were judged to be victims of child maltreatment by parents or other caregivers; of these situations where the type of maltreatment is known, 64% involved child neglect, 16% involved physical abuse, and 9% involved sexual abuse (U.S. Department of Health and Human Services, 2008). National surveys find much higher numbers of child maltreatment than this (see Finkelhor, Ormrod, Turner, & Hamby, 2005). One research team found that 35% of 2,030 children in a national survey reported being physically assaulted by a sibling in the past year (Finkelhor et al., 2005). There are no national statistics on elder abuse, but in 2003, it was estimated that between 1 and 2 million Americans over age 65 had been abused in some way by a caregiver (Bonnie & Wallace, 2003). It is estimated that between 750,000 and 1 million violent acts are committed against parents by their adolescent children each year (Gelles, 2010).

How is it that the social group assigned the societal task of providing love and nurturance becomes a setting for so much violence? Research indicates that family violence is multi-determined and identifies a number of associated factors. Stress, social isolation, economic distress, substance abuse, mental health problems, and intergenerational modeling have all been found to increase the risk of family violence (Gelles, 2010; D. Newman, 2008). The United States is a relatively violent society, and violence is often seen as an appropriate way to resolve disputes (Hutchison, 2007). There are cultures of the world and subcultures in the United States that believe that men have the right to beat women and parents have the right to beat children.

> Conflict perspective

It can be argued that the very nature of family life makes it a breeding ground for conflict. Family members spend a great deal of time together and interact intimately in good times and bad. They tend to stir each other's most intense emotions, both positive and negative. If family members do not have good conflict resolution skills, they may not have a repertoire of behaviors other than violence to resolve conflicts.

Intervention in situations of family violence requires careful assessment, and even with the best assessment, it is difficult to predict future behavior. The decision that must be made is whether protective steps are necessary: Must children be removed, are restraining orders necessary, must the abused partner flee for safety? There are no ideal solutions. Removing children from abusive households may be necessary to protect them physically, but this solution carries its own risks. Children suffer emotional damage from the separation and loss, and may blame themselves for the family disruption. They may be vulnerable to further abuse in the foster home if they have intense care needs. There are also risks to leaving children in homes where they have been abused, including the risk that the child will be killed. Unfortunately, the available resources are not often sufficient to meet a distressed family's needs. Clearly, no one solution fits every situation of child abuse.

The literature on domestic partner violence has proposed some useful typologies for thinking about intervention in such situations (Holtzworth-Munroe & Stuart, 1994; M. Johnson, 1995). Domestic partner violence can be one-way or mutual; mutual violence can be mutual fighting, or involve self-defense or retaliation against a primary aggressor. It may be considered minor, involving shoving, pushing, grabbing, and slapping, or severe, involving choking, kicking, hitting with an object, beating up, or using a knife or gun. Mutual fighting tends to be less severe and more infrequent than other forms of intimate partner violence, and does not usually escalate. It involves both partners who use physical means to resolve conflicts. On the other hand, one-sided use of severe forms of violence, sometimes called intimate terrorism, typically occurs more frequently and escalates over time. Many of the perpetrators of this type of violence are involved in other antisocial behaviors as well.

Just as with child abuse, different types of intervention are required for different types of domestic partner violence. Protective removal is imperative for intimate terrorism or any form of escalating violence. On the other hand, systemic couples' work, in which couples are taught other methods of conflict resolution, may well be appropriate for couples who occasionally use mutual violence to resolve conflict. Support for this idea comes from a research project that looked at mutual and one-way spouse abuse in the Army. The researchers found about even rates of these two types of intimate violence in 1998. After 4 years of prevention and education programs, mutual abuse had decreased by 58%, while one-way abuse had decreased by only 13% (McCarroll, Ursano, Fan, & Newby, 2004). This finding suggests that further attention to matching the intervention to the specific situation may be fruitful. The typologies discussed above do not cover every type of intimate partner violence situation, but they do make a good start at thinking about the multiple factors involved in family violence.

Divorce

Most people who get married do not anticipate that they will divorce, and yet divorce is very common. Almost all societies have mechanisms for dissolving marriages, whether it is divorce, or civil or religious annulment. Worldwide, divorce rates tend to be higher in wealthier nations; for example, divorce rates are lower in the newly industrializing nations of Latin America and Asia than in the wealthy late-industrial nations of Western Europe and North America (D. Newman, 2008). In the United States, however, the divorce rate is highest among low-income families.

The divorce rate in the United States increased steadily from the mid-19th century through the 1970s, except for a sharp drop in the 1950s. It peaked in 1981 and has been dropping slightly since then, but remains high compared to other wealthy industrialized countries. Data from the 2004 U.S. Census survey indicates that African Americans are less likely to marry and more likely to divorce than other ethnic groups in the United States (U.S. Census Bureau, 2007). Exhibit 10.6 shows the percentage ever married and the percentage ever divorced by age 60 for different ethnic groups. At first glance, it appears that the divorce rate is higher for Whites than for African Americans, 41.1% compared to 39.3%. However, when you consider the low rate of marriage for African Americans, 72.7% compared to 92.8% for non-Hispanic Whites, that is not at all the case. By age 60, approximately 54% of African Americans who ever married have been divorced at least once, compared to 44% for non-Hispanic Whites. Asian Americans and Hispanic Americans have high marriage and relatively low divorce rates.

It is thought that economic factors contribute to divorce. Wages have stagnated for non-Hispanic White men and have declined for African American men. Millions of lower-income wage earners are receiving poverty-level wages and are vulnerable to layoffs. Although women still earn less than men, they are becoming more economically independent, and about two-thirds of divorces are initiated by women (Amato & Irving, 2006; M. Coleman, Ganong, & Warzinik, 2007). On the other hand, wives' earnings may reduce economic pressures and help to stabilize marriage (Fine, Ganong, & Demo, 2010).

There is a controversy in the empirical literature about the consequences of divorce for family members. Some researchers have found serious, long-term, post-divorce adjustment problems for both children and adults

Ethnic Group	Ever Married by Age 60	Ever Divorced by Age 60
African American	72.7%	39.3%
Asian American	95.0%	16.3%
Hispanic American	91.6%	27.8%
White Non-Hispanic American	92.8%	41.1%

▲ **Exhibit 10.6** Marital and Divorce History for Specific Ethnic Groups, 2004: Ever Married and Ever Divorced

SOURCE: U.S. Census Bureau (2007).

(J. Wallerstein & Blakeslee, 1990). Other researchers who use larger and more representative samples have found more modest and shorter-term effects for both adults and children (Barber & Demo, 2006; Braver, Shapiro, & Goodman, 2006).

Fine et al. (2010) suggest several reasons for the differences in findings. First, researchers tend to focus on one or two reactions to divorce and fail to measure other types of reactions. Second, few researchers have taken a longer-term longitudinal view of divorce adjustment, and consequently they are tapping reactions during the difficult acute adjustment phase. Third, researchers look for average reactions rather than for the variability of reactions to divorce. The feminist perspective, on the other hand, would emphasize that divorce is experienced and perceived differently by different family members and would be interested in these various perspectives. Fine et al. assert that the different conclusions about the effects of divorce on child and adult development may result partly from the fact that the effect sizes are often small and may vary with the nature and size of the sample, which would not happen if there was a stronger relationship between divorce and adjustment.

There is consistent evidence, however, that the economic well-being of women and children declines after divorce (Sayer, 2006). There are several reasons for this. Mothers devote more time to caring for children than fathers, and this restricts their time to devote to educational and occupational pursuits. Women do not earn as much as men. Moreover, many fathers do not comply fully with child support requirements (Pirog & Ziol-Guest, 2006), but even if they did, child support awards are typically too low to meet the costs of raising children (Stirling & Aldrich, 2008).

It seems clear that divorce is a crisis for most adults, lasting for approximately 2 years. Stress increases in the run up to the divorce, during the divorce, and in the immediate aftermath. However, the stress level typically subsides within a year after divorce as families adjust relationships and routines (Demo & Fine, 2010). There is also evidence that African American women get more support than White women following divorce (Orbuch & Brown, 2006).

After a careful review of the empirical evidence, Fine et al. (2010) agree with Emery (1999) on the following points about children's adjustment to divorce:

- Divorce is stressful for children.
- Divorce leads to adjustment and mental health problems for children.
- Most children are resilient and adjust well to divorce over time.
- Children whose parents divorce report pain, unhappy memories, and continued distress.

- Post-divorce family interaction has a great influence on adjustment to divorce.

- Children's adjustment is enhanced if they have a good relationship with at least one parent.

Substance Abuse

Substance abuse is often part of the fabric of family life and usually has an effect on the partner relationship and on child development. For the purposes of this discussion, substance abuse is defined as serious and persistent problems with alcohol and/or other substances, and does not refer specifically to a clinical diagnosis. Substance abuse is often described as a family problem, not only because of its effect on the entire family system, but also because of the growing evidence of a strong genetic component in the etiology of substance abuse (Sadock & Sadock, 2007). The effect of substance abuse on the partner relationship and the impact of adolescent substance abuse on the family are discussed briefly here, followed by a larger discussion of the impact of parental substance abuse on children.

Kenneth Leonard and Rina Eiden (2007) reviewed the evidence about the impact of alcohol abuse on marital satisfaction and marital violence. They conclude that alcohol abuse has an adverse effect on marital satisfaction and stability, especially among couples where one partner is abusing alcohol and the other partner is not. They also conclude that there is evidence of a strong association between excessive alcohol consumption and intimate partner violence. Interestingly, consistent with a family life cycle perspective, they found evidence that family transitions can affect patterns of alcohol use for both men and women, with excessive drinking declining in the transition to marriage and during pregnancy and increasing in the postnatal period. There is also strong evidence that excessive alcohol use increases after divorce, but may decrease for women divorcing from spouses with alcohol problems.

Some evidence also exists that adolescent substance abuse problems change the nature of parent–child relationships, with parents changing their discipline methods in response to the substance abuse (Mezzich et al., 2007). There is also evidence that adolescent substance abuse increases parental stress and sometimes results in increased use of alcohol among parents (Leonard & Eiden, 2007). Parents may need family support, training in coping responses, as well as social policies that allow family leave from work when they are faced with an adolescent with substance abuse problems (Deater-Deckard, 2004).

By one estimate, one in four children in the United States is exposed to a family member's alcohol abuse, and one in six children live with parents who abuse illicit drugs (VanDeMark et al., 2005). Although recent research finds that parental substance abuse does not always lead to an unacceptable level of parenting (Coyle et al., 2009; Street, Harrington, Chiang, Cairns, & Ellis, 2004), there is much empirical evidence that parental substance abuse often impairs parental functioning. Brynna Kroll (2004) reviewed the empirical literature on the experiences of children who grow up in families where adult use of alcohol and other substances is problematic. A number of negative effects on children were noted. In all of the reviewed studies, secrecy and denial about the substance abuse was an organizing feature of family life, cutting the family off from extended family and community supports. Children often become afraid and mistrustful of outsiders who try to help, fearing being taken from their parent(s), among other fears.

Adult children of alcoholics report pervasive loss and grief, including loss of feeling loved, loss of a reliable parent, loss of a "normal" lifestyle, and loss of childhood itself. And, while not all substance-abusing parents abuse their children, there is an increased risk of child maltreatment while using. Given that substance abuse is often characterized by cycles of relapse and recovery, parental substance abuse does not mean that everything falls apart, particularly during phases of abstinence or reduced use, but parental conflict and fighting do typically increase during periods of excessive substance use. Children's lives are often dominated by the needs, feelings, and behaviors of substance-abusing parents. The children sometimes become caregivers to their parents, putting them to bed when they are drunk, or cleaning up after a parent who urinates on the floor. There is considerable evidence that substance-abusing parents engage in less monitoring of their children's behavior.

Research has also found parental substance abuse to be a risk factor for child behavior problems as well as depression and anxiety (Barnard & McKeganey, 2004). School performance often suffers in children of substance-abusing parents, as do peer relationships. Parental substance abuse during childhood is also associated with young adult difficulties with romantic partnerships (J. Fischer, Lyness, & Engler, 2010).

Although parental substance abuse is a risk factor in child development, some substance-abusing parents are able to manage family life in a way that supports healthy child development. James Coyle and colleagues (2009) were interested in family functioning in families affected by parental alcohol abuse, particularly in the dimensions of family functioning that allowed these families to be resilient. Their statistical analysis identified families who were functioning at above-average, average, and below-average levels, according to standardized measures. Their research provides support for Froma Walsh's (2006) model of family resilience, in which aspects of belief systems, family organization, and communication processes allow families to be resilient in the face of adversity. They found that families who functioned well on one of these dimensions functioned well on all three. Levels of social functioning were not related to social class or parental education. They did find, however, that Black families with a substance-abusing parent were more likely to have above-average or average functioning than White and Native American families, even though the Black families were, overall, in the lower end of the range in terms of economic resources and reported more stressful life events.

Other research that has looked at the strengths of substance-abusing parents has focused on those parents in treatment. This research finds that these parents are self-critical about their abilities to parent while abusing substances, but also report making attempts to combine their substance abuse with efforts to ensure that the needs of their children were being met. The desire to look after their children properly or to get the children back from substitute care is a powerful motivator to stop using alcohol and/or other drugs (C. Fraser, McIntyre, & Manby, 2009; Tracy & Martin, 2007).

Some researchers report that substance-abusing mothers feel overwhelming guilt and shame about the impact their substance abuse has on their parenting (K. Cox, 2000). In a study of mothers in treatment, 68% of whom had "lost" children to substitute care, Tracy and Martin (2007) found that 90% of the mothers viewed their relationships with their children as close, and 84% reported that their children provide as much support for sobriety as the adults in their lives do. The emotional care provided by children of substance-abusing parents is often noted in the literature by such terms as "role reversal," "parental child," or "parentification," all of which suggest a negative impact on the child of providing such care. One research team (Godsall, Jurkovic, Emshoff, Anderson, & Stanwyck, 2004) examined the relationships between parental alcohol misuse, and parentification and children's self-concept. They found that African American child participants scored higher on self-concept than European American children. They suggest that the concept of parentification, and similar concepts, may not be applicable to African American families and other collectivist-oriented families where close kinship networks are valued. They further suggest that considerable caregiving responsibilities in the context of close kinship ties may not have negative effects for children who are also receiving support and caring. Caregiving by children may be a part of a pattern of "filial responsibility," and not interpreted as unjust by the children.

In interpreting their finding that African American families with alcohol-abusing parents score better on family functioning than other such families, Coyle et al. (2009) note that Froma Walsh's (2006) model of family resilience indicates that flexibility in family structure in times of adversity serves as a shock absorber and fosters family resilience. Walsh also identifies family belief systems as sources for resilience, and Coyle et al. note that other researchers have found that cultural pride, kinship, spirituality, and high expectations for children are common in African American families. Coyle et al. suggest that struggling families may best be helped by identifying possible cultural beliefs, locating resources outside the nuclear family, becoming more flexible in family roles, and improving communication. You may recognize this as consistent with Walsh's model of family resilience that identifies belief systems, organizational patterns, and communication as the ingredients for family resilience.

Critical Thinking Questions 10.3

Three challenges to family life were discussed in this chapter: family violence, divorce, and substance abuse. If you were to be my coauthor on this chapter for the 5th edition of the book, what advice would you give me about the most important challenges facing families today? Are family violence, divorce, and substance abuse new or enduring challenges for families in the United States? Do these challenges appear to occur across cultural lines—across traditional, modern, and postmodern cultures (review Chapter 8 for descriptions of these three types of culture)?

IMPLICATIONS FOR SOCIAL WORK PRACTICE

This discussion of families and family life, in the context of larger social systems, suggests several practice principles:

- Assess families from a variety of theoretical perspectives. Given recent economic shifts, be particularly aware of the impact of changes in larger systems on families' resources and functioning.

- Recognize the diversity of family structures represented by the families with whom you work, and be sensitive to the relative strengths and weaknesses of each of these family structures.

- Develop awareness of economic diversity among families and the different economic and other resources available to the families you serve.

- Develop awareness of cultural diversity among families and a commitment to culturally sensitive practice that involves ongoing learning both about and from families that are different from your own.

- Use appropriate family assessment tools, including the genogram, ecomap, and timeline to help you develop a more comprehensive understanding of families with which you work.

- Give families credit for struggling well in adverse circumstances.

- Understand policies and changes at state and national levels and the ways they affect both your own work and the lives of all families—particularly lower-income, stressed families.

- Where appropriate, encourage family members to become involved in neighborhood, local, state, and national efforts for positive change.

- As appropriate, work toward your agency's becoming involved in policy and advocacy work on behalf of families, including development of needed programs and services.

KEY TERMS

ABC-X model of family
   stress and coping
cohabiting
differentiation of self
family
family economic stress model
family investment model
family life cycle perspective

family of origin
family resilience perspective
family systems perspective
family timeline
feminist perspective
   on families
genogram
intersectionality feminist theory

lone-parent families
multilevel family
   practice model
nonnormative stressors
normative stressors
stress pileup
transition points
triangulation

ACTIVE LEARNING

1. *Theory and your family.* We have used different theoretical lenses to look at the family of Bobby Sharpe. If you were a social worker working with a family similar to the Sharpes, you would want to be aware of how your own family experiences influence your practice with families. You can use theory to help you do that as well. To begin this process, reflect on the following questions related to your family of origin and your childhood:

   • What value was placed on connectedness, and what value was placed on the differentiated self?

   • What were the external boundaries—who was in and who was out of the family? What were the commonly shared beliefs? What roles did family members play? What were the patterns of communication?

   • Were there any transition points that were particularly difficult for your family? What made those transitions difficult?

   • How traditional were the gender roles in your family? How was power distributed?

   • Can you recall any periods of stress pileup? If so, how did your family cope during those periods?

   • How did your family use belief systems, organizational patterns, and communication to be resilient in the face of adversity?

   After you have reflected on these questions, write a brief paper addressing the following points:

   • Summarize your reflections on each question.

   • How do you think your experiences in your family of origin might serve as a barrier or an aid in work with a family similar to the Sharpe family?

2. *Visualizing your family.* Sometimes we learn new things about families when we prepare visual representations of them. There are several tools available for doing this. You will use three of them here to visualize your own family.

   • Referring back to Exhibit 10.3, prepare a family ecomap of your current family situation.

   • Referring to Exhibit 10.2, prepare a multigenerational genogram of your family, going back to your maternal and paternal grandparents.

- Referring to Exhibit 10.4, prepare a family timeline, beginning at the point of your birth, or earlier if you think there were significant earlier events that need to be noted.

After you have prepared these materials, work in small groups in class to discuss how useful each tool was in helping you think about your family of origin. Were any new insights gained from using these visual tools? What is your overall reaction to using tools like these to understand your family?

WEB RESOURCES

Administration for Children and Families (ACF)
http://www.acf.hhs.gov/

ACF is a government agency that is part of the U.S. Department of Health and Human Services. Site contains fact sheets about children and families and information about ACF programs such as child support enforcement, Head Start, and Temporary Assistance for Needy Families (TANF).

The Clearinghouse on International Developments in Child, Youth and Family Policies
www.childpolicyintl.org

Site contains comparative information on child, youth, and family policies and programs in the industrialized nations of the world.

Council on Contemporary Families
www.contemporaryfamilies.org/

Official site of the Council on Contemporary Families, a non-profit organization that promotes an inclusive view of families, contains information and research on families, along with links to other Internet resources.

Families and Work Institute
www.familiesandwork.org/

Site contains information on work–life research, community mobilization forums, information on the Fatherhood Project, and frequently asked questions.

Forum on Child and Family Statistics
www.childstats.gov/

Official website of the Federal Interagency Forum on Child and Family Statistics, offers easy access to federal and state statistics and reports on children and families, including international comparisons.

National Council on Family Relations (NCFR)
www.ncfr.org/

The Public Policy section of this site contains NCFR Fact Sheets and Policy Briefs on a variety of family issues.

Small Groups

Elizabeth P. Cramer

OPENING QUESTIONS

- Small groups have become a common form of human service delivery. In today's age of managed care and increased human isolation, why would groups be an important form of social work practice?

- People find themselves a part of many different formal and informal small groups during their lifetimes. Why might it be helpful for a social worker to know about the groups to which a client belongs?

KEY IDEAS

As you read this chapter, take note of these central ideas:

1. Small groups are typically defined as collections of individuals who interact with each other, perceive themselves as belonging to a group, are interdependent, join together to accomplish a goal or fulfill a need through joint association, and are influenced by a set of rules and norms.

2. Types of social work groups include therapy, mutual aid, psychoeducational, self-help, and task groups. A group may be a combination of two or more types.

3. Small groups in social work vary in how they develop, how long they last, and how they determine membership.

4. In determining group composition, small groups must resolve issues of inclusion versus exclusion, heterogeneity versus homogeneity, and group cohesiveness.

5. To understand small group processes, social workers may draw on psychodynamic theory, symbolic interaction theory, status characteristics and expectation states theory, exchange theory, and self-categorization theory.

6. Both stage theories and process models have been used to understand how small groups develop.

7. Group dynamics are patterns of interaction, including factors such as leadership, roles, and communication networks.

8. Social workers often work in interdisciplinary teams with other professionals representing a variety of disciplines.

Case Study

Terry's Support Group

As she drove to a meeting of her Wednesday night support group, Terry popped a Melissa Etheridge CD into the player. A year ago, she would have barely recognized the singer's name. Now she listens to her music incessantly. But much more has changed in Terry's life these past several months. Last year at this time, she was married—to a man. Terry and Brad had an amiable 2-year marriage, but Terry had felt a sense of loneliness and discomfort throughout their marriage. She loved Brad, but could not commit to him deep in her heart.

She also felt an unhappiness beyond her marriage. Terry realized she had to discover what was contributing to her unhappiness. After some serious soul searching, she joined a support group run for women much like her. The group members have gradually learned much of Terry's history.

In sixth grade, Terry was inseparable from her best friend, Barb. Barb and Terry shared a similar family background—White, middle class, Protestant—and shared many of the preteen rites of passage together: starting menstruation, kissing boys for the first time, being picked on as the youngest children in the middle school, and wearing shirts that show your belly button. Barb loved Terry and Terry loved Barb in that very special way that best friends do.

One night when Terry was sleeping over at Barb's house, Barb suggested that they play the dating game. Terry had played the game before at a boy–girl party. The lights go out, and the boys and the girls pair up to plan a make-believe date. At Barb's house, when Terry protested because there were no boys to play the game with them, Barb suggested that they could switch off playing boys and girls. So Terry and Barb enacted the date themselves, including a long good-night kiss. That was the first and last time Barb and Terry played the dating game. They did not discuss this incident ever again.

Terry went through her preteen and adolescent years dating boys and imagining the kind of guy she might marry. In college, Terry had another sexual experience with a female. She had been at a party with some friends where heavy drinking occurred. The group of friends with whom she went to the party decided to spend the night at the home of the hostess instead of trying to drive home drunk. Bed space was sparse, so beds had to be shared. Terry and Patricia shared a twin-size bed in a private room. The two women crawled into bed and giggled about the fact that the two of them were sharing this tiny space. The giggling turned into tickling, and the tickling turned into kissing and touching. The next morning, Terry blamed this sexual experience on the alcohol.

After college, Terry worked as a loan officer in a bank. A few years into her job, at age 26, she met Brad. After several relationships with men, she was ready to leave the dating scene. Brad and Terry developed a close relationship quickly and were engaged within 9 months of meeting each other. They bought a house, combined their possessions, and began what they both thought would be the rest of their lives together. But that scenario didn't work out.

When Terry came to the Women's Coming-Out Support Group for the first time, she was petrified. Beverly, a woman on Terry's softball team, promised she would meet Terry in the parking lot and they'd go in together. Sure enough, Beverly was in the parking lot with a big smile and hug: "Hey, girl. You'll be all right." They walked to the front of the building, past the sign that read "Gay and Lesbian Community Center" (Terry was sure the sign must have been at least as big as a Ping-Pong table). Beverly rang the doorbell and gave Terry a reassuring look. An African American woman who looked to be in her fifties answered the door: "Hi, Beverly. Nice to meet you, Terry. I'm Doris. I'm so glad you could make it here tonight. Come on in."

What was so new that evening is now familiar. Terry has told the group that she looks forward to seeing the faces of those faithful members who return each week; she empathizes with the nervousness and shyness of the new members. Each of the group members' stories is unique. The group includes bisexual women and women questioning their sexual orientation, as Terry did when first attending the group. "Temperature reading"—a review of group members' excitements, concerns, and hopes and wishes—begins each group session. Sometimes, temperature reading is short and superficial; other times, it goes on for nearly the whole meeting, with much disclosure, intensity, and sometimes crying. The facilitators, both lesbians, plan activities for each session but are flexible enough to allow the members to control the flow of the session. They share a good deal about themselves and their own coming out processes (e.g., how they came to identify themselves as lesbian and to whom they've disclosed their sexual orientation and experiences).

(Continued)

(Continued)

One of the first people in the group to befriend Terry was Kathy, another woman who had been hetero-sexually married. Kathy approached Terry during social time, an informal gathering after the meeting to schmooze and have refreshments. Kathy shared that she, too, had questioned her sexual orientation during the time she was married. Kathy and Terry became friends outside the group; in fact, much of Terry's current friendship network has grown out of the group. She often sees group members at gay and lesbian functions that she has begun to attend, such as the gay/lesbian theater company and the monthly women's potlucks. How different her circle of friends has become compared to when she and Brad were together and they social-ized primarily with other White, childless, heterosexual couples.

Terry still feels like a "baby dyke" (a woman who has newly emerged in her lesbian identity) around her friends, most of whom have been "out" (living openly as lesbians/bisexuals) for much longer than she. She still has many questions about lesbian and gay culture, but she feels comfortable to ask them in the group. She has also found that she can help other women who are just beginning to come out by sharing her experiences. Sometimes she is embarrassed by the discussion in the group, however. For example, the facilitators keep an envelope marked "sex questions," where group members can anonymously submit questions about lesbian sex; the facilitators periodically read them to the group to open a discussion. The frankness of such discussions makes Terry blush sometimes, but she's glad she has a place to find answers about these things. Terry also did-n't realize some of the differences between the predominantly White lesbian community and the Black lesbian community, and has now learned from her friends about some of the issues faced by African American lesbians.

Terry is consistently amazed at the diversity within the group—women of different races, educational backgrounds, socioeconomic classes, disabilities, religions, and ages. Just last week, for example, seven women attended the group: three African Americans, two women who self-identify as bisexual, one who iden-tifies herself as disabled, one woman who is Jewish, and two women younger than 21.

Tonight, Terry tells the group, as she pulled into the parking lot and got out of the car, a woman pulled into the space next to her. Terry hadn't seen her before. The woman stepped out of the car and looked around nervously. Terry walked over to her: "Hi, have you been to the group before?" "No." "C'mon, I'll walk in with you." And now Terry is introducing the new woman to the rest of the group.

SMALL GROUPS IN SOCIAL WORK

Small groups play a significant role in our lives. Terry's support group is a type with special relevance to social work practice, but most people also become involved in other types of small groups: friendship groups, task groups at work, self-help groups, or sports teams, to name but a few.

In a mobile society, where family members may live in different parts of the country and community gathering places (such as a town hall) may be few, groups serve a useful function. They offer individuals an opportunity to meet others and work together to achieve mutual goals. Exhibit 11.1 shows how group members may benefit from belonging to a group. Groups may provide the social support, connection, and healing that various persons (such as neighbors) or institutions (such as houses of worship) did in the past (Specht & Courtney, 1994). Identifying with a group is one way that people can "try to find a sense of purpose or meaning" in life (p. 48). In the hustle and bustle of everyday lives, the warmth and sense of "realness" of a productive and healthy group is inviting. Robert Putnam (2000) suggests that in our rapidly changing globalized society, small groups are an important source of *social capital*, or con-nections among individuals based on reciprocity and trustworthiness.

Humanistic perspective

Small groups may be formally defined in a number of ways. A few scholarly definitions of small groups, along with examples from Terry's story, are displayed in Exhibit 11.2. Although these definitions differ, there is general agreement that small groups are more than a collection of individuals who may have similar traits or be in physical proximity. Persons who live on the same block may be in close proximity but have little social interaction and not perceive themselves as a group. Thus, we may define a **small group** as a collection of individuals who interact with each other, perceive themselves as belonging to a group, are interdependent, join together to accomplish a goal or fulfill a need, and are influenced by a set of rules and norms (D. W. Johnson & Johnson, 1994).

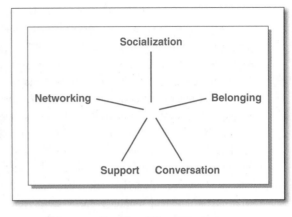

▲ **Exhibit 11.1**   Benefits of Small Groups

A significant element of social work practice today is **group work,** which serves people's needs by bringing them together in small groups. Group work emerged in the United States in the late 1800s and early 1900s. Early group work took place within the settlement houses, YMCA/YWCA, Jewish community centers, and the Boy Scouts and Girl Scouts. These groups focused primarily on recreation, social integration, immigration issues, character building, and social reform. We are now seeing a resurgence in recreation and social skill–building

Social behavioral perspective

Author(s)	Definition	Example
Shaw (1981)	Two or more individuals who through their interactions influence and are influenced by each other	At the party Terry attended while in college, a group of friends were drinking and chose to stay overnight at the home of the hostess rather than drive after drinking.
D. W. Johnson & Johnson (1994)	Two or more individuals who are each aware of membership in the group and of who else belongs to the group, who have a positive interdependence, and who develop and achieve mutual goals	The friends Terry has developed through her association with the coming-out group are aware of themselves as a group of friends, are interdependent, and achieve goals of socialization and companionship through attending gay and lesbian functions together.
Hare, Blumberg, Davies, & Kent (1994)	Two or more individuals who share values that help them maintain an overall pattern of activity, acquire or develop resources and skills to use in that activity, and conform to a set of norms that define roles in the activity, and who have enough cohesiveness and leadership to coordinate their resources and roles in order to accomplish their goals	The coming-out group at the Gay and Lesbian Community Center shares such values as exploration and acknowledgment of sexual orientation, an overall pattern of activity (weekly meetings), resources and skills (center space, two trained facilitators), norms or roles for the activity (structured group meetings, group guidelines), cohesiveness, and leadership (facilitators).

▲ **Exhibit 11.2**   Definitions of Small Groups

groups, reminiscent of early group work. Social skills groups with elementary-age children (LeCroy, 1992), hoops groups (basketball) with adolescent males (Pollio, 1995), physical activity and reminiscence and motivation groups for older adults (S. Hughes et al., 2005; Link, 1997) are three examples.

By the 1930s and 1940s, formal organizations were promoting group work. In 1935, the Group Work Section of the National Conference on Social Work emerged, and in 1937, the American Association for the Study of Group Work formed. The American Association of Group Workers, which started in 1946, later merged with other organizations to become the National Association of Social Workers (NASW).

During World War II, group work became popular in hospitals and other clinical settings in the United States, resulting in some tension between group workers and caseworkers. Following the war, the philosophy of group work shifted from a strengths focus to a more problem-focused orientation. Nevertheless, group workers continued to attempt to influence the social work profession as a whole. During the 1960s and 1970s, social work education centered on teaching group work, and some students even majored in "group work." But then group work content declined as social work education shifted its focus to individuals and families. Ironically, at the same time, joining groups became more common in the United States. The 1980s and 1990s saw the rise of mutual aid groups (Gitterman & Shulman, 1994), today a popular type of social work group.

In today's managed care era, groups are viewed as a financially prudent method of service delivery (S. Hurdle, 2001; Roller, 1997). In addition, empirical studies have shown the effectiveness of groups in addressing a number of social, health, and emotional problems, such as mental illness (Yalom, 1995) and cancer (Spiegel & Classen, 2000). One researcher (Garrett, 2004) found that a small sample of school social workers make extensive use of group work methods. Group work content is coming back into the social work curriculum, and social work students are being exposed to group work through their field placements. Furthermore, graduating students have informed me that potential employers ask if they have had course content on group work.

A number of scholars have established classifications for groups encountered in social work (see, e.g., Corey & Corey, 2006; Kottler & Englar-Carlson, 2010; Toseland & Rivas, 2009). This chapter focuses on five: therapy groups, mutual aid groups, psychoeducational groups, self-help groups, and task groups. Exhibit 11.3 compares these five types of groups on several major features—purpose, leadership, size of membership, duration—and gives examples of each. As you read about them, remember that groups may not fall exclusively into one category; rather, they may share elements of several group types. For example, a group for parents and friends of seriously mentally ill persons may include psychoeducational material about the nature of mental illness and its impact on family members, provide mutual aid to its members through discussion of taboo areas, and offer a therapeutic component in the examination of family patterns and dynamics.

Therapy Groups

Psychodynamic
perspective

One common type of group is known as the **therapy group,** or psychotherapy group. Group psychotherapy uses the group milieu to enable individuals to work out emotional and behavioral difficulties. The individuals in the group often reproduce their emotional and behavioral problems within the group setting, thus giving the leader and group members an opportunity to provide feedback about them (Husaini et al., 2004; K. E. Reid, 1997). An example of this type of group is a therapy group for adult incest survivors.

Therapy groups typically have fewer members and meet for a longer duration than self-help, psychoeducational, or mutual aid groups. Such a group may have six or fewer members, may be led by a person who considers himself or herself to be a therapist, may meet weekly for a year or more, and may involve intrapsychic

Type of Group	Main Purpose	Leadership	Typical Number of Members	Duration	Examples
Therapy	Uses group modality to assist individuals to resolve emotional and behavioral problems	Typically led by a trained clinician or psychotherapist	Typically small in size; sometimes six or fewer members.	Brief therapy groups usually meet for 6 weeks or less. Long-term psychotherapy groups can last years.	Groups for college students run by university counseling centers; groups for male adolescents who engage in sexual harm
Mutual aid	Uses mutual aid processes to create a helping environment within the group milieu	Typically led by a facilitator who may be a professional or a layperson trained to lead the group. The leader may or may not have experienced the issue on which the group is focused.	These groups may be small (less than 5 persons) or large (12 or more), especially if run in a drop-in format.	Drop-in mutual aid groups may be ongoing for a number of years with members coming in and out of the group. Time-limited mutual aid groups typically run for between 4 and 12 weeks.	Groups for cancer survivors; groups in schools for children whose parents are going through a divorce
Psychoeducational	Focuses on the provision of information about an experience or problem	Typically led by a trained professional who is knowledgeable about the subject	Limiting the group size is usually not as critical with these types of groups because of their purpose.	One-time meetings of psychoeducation groups may be offered on a regular schedule; they might be offered in a series of sessions (e.g., a 4-week educational series); or they might be offered on an as-needed basis.	Groups for couples preparing to adopt a child; groups to teach parents how to use adaptive equipment for children with disabilities
Self-help	Uses the commonality of the problem or issue to build social support among members	Typically led by a layperson who has experience with the problem (e.g., a person in recovery from alcohol and drug addition)	Typically, since self-help groups operate on a drop-in basis, the group size is not limited.	Most often, self-help groups are run on a drop-in basis; however, some may be offered in a time-limited format.	Twelve-step groups (e.g., AA, ACOA, NA)
Task	Created to accomplish a specific task or to advocate around a particular social issue or problem	These groups may be led by professionals or nonprofessionals; leaders may be appointed or elected.	Often limited in size to successfully accomplish the task. When advocating for change, membership may be larger.	Meet until the task has been accomplished or the desired social change has been accomplished	A committee to examine low-income housing needs that is instructed to submit a report of their findings to the city council

▲ Exhibit 11.3   Types of Groups

▲ **Photo 11.1**   Therapy group—Members in therapy groups share experiences and obstacles they have encountered. Through openness and self-disclosure, members feel supported and encouraged.

exploration of thoughts and emotions. Talk or verbal therapy groups are not the only type. Increasingly popular are art therapy groups, which have demonstrated the standard therapeutic factors of verbal therapy groups as well as some factors unique to art therapy (Shechtman & Perl-Dekel, 2000). In addition, therapy groups do not necessarily meet for long periods. **Brief treatment models,** which usually last 6 weeks or less, are becoming more and more popular in a managed care environment.

Mutual Aid Groups

In **mutual aid groups,** the members meet to help one another deal with common problems. The members of the group thus become as important to its success as the facilitator is (Gitterman & Shulman, 1994; Lesser et al., 2004). In Terry's story, we witness many benefits of mutual aid groups:

- *Sharing data:* coming-out stories, events in the lesbian community

- *Engaging in a dialectical process of discovery:* theories about sexual orientation, insight into when one first felt one was not heterosexual

- *Discussing taboo subjects:* the "sex questions" envelope

- *Realizing that one is not alone (all in the same boat):* others who are not heterosexual and have had similar feelings regarding coming-out and disclosure

- *Finding support:* a place to be oneself in a homophobic society

- *Making mutual demands:* gentle challenges to internalized homophobia and unhealthy coping mechanisms, such as alcohol use or thoughts of suicide, that lesbian and bisexual women may use as a way to live in two worlds

- *Problem solving:* disclosure decisions for individuals and the larger issue of self-disclosure of a stigmatized identity

- *Rehearsing new behaviors:* role-playing of disclosure scenarios or confrontations with people who make homophobic jokes

- *Finding strength in numbers:* pride march

In general, mutual aid groups are led by someone, either a professional or a trained individual, who identifies with the population that the group targets. For example, the two facilitators of the women's coming-out group self-identify as lesbians. In fact, some mutual aid groups form as an alternative to professionally led therapy groups. In this way, they may be similar in purpose to self-help groups. There is no requirement, however, that in order to be an effective leader, one must have "been there." The groups may be time-limited (for example, a 10-week group for siblings of children with disabilities) or ongoing (such as a weekly support group for incarcerated males).

Mutual aid groups also have the potential for activism. A group of people may meet initially to gain support and share concerns but may transform some of their healing energy into social change efforts. For instance, members of a mutual aid groups for battered women may attend a Take Back the Night march (to protest violence against women) as a group and then courageously approach the microphone to speak about their own experiences of victimization and empowerment.

Psychoeducational Groups

Psychoeducational groups, in which social workers and other professionals share their expertise with group members, are becoming more common in the United States. The topics include problems such as substance abuse and divorce as well as more general interests, such as child development or the aging process. Those who participate are primarily looking for information rather than treatment of emotional and behavioral problems. Thus, the format of group meetings may be a lecture by the group leader or a guest speaker with minimal group discussion. The group could be a one-time workshop or it could last several sessions.

> Social behavioral perspective

Although a psychoeducational group is not a therapy group, it can be therapeutic when members share feelings and concerns. An example would be a one-time group meeting for family and friends of persons in a drug rehabilitation center. The stated purpose may be to provide education about the recovery process to family members and friends, but during the session, group members may share feelings about their loved one's addiction and how it has affected their lives.

Self-Help Groups

In general, **self-help groups** are not professionally led, although a professional may serve in the role of consultant. An informal leader may emerge in a self-help group, or leadership may be rotated among the membership. Self-help groups are often used as a supplement to professional treatment. For example, someone who is receiving outpatient substance abuse treatment may be referred to Alcoholics Anonymous; someone in a family preservation program may be referred to Parents Anonymous. Self-help groups often have no limit on their life span and have rotating membership (people come and go from the group).

There are more than 800 self-help organizations in the United States, and it is estimated that 7% of U.S. adults participate in

▲ **Exhibit 11.2** Mothers support group—Here, mothers join together to share stories, struggles, and insights about the adjustment of becoming a parent.

some type of self-help group (Klaw & Humphreys, 2004; Kottler & Englar-Carlson, 2010). Self-help groups have several benefits. They are composed of people who voluntarily meet because of a common identity or life situation, thus offering members an opportunity to receive assistance from others who are also struggling with similar issues. At the same time, people are able to offer help to others, as well as receive help, which produces psychological rewards (Mok, 2004; Zastrow, 2009). In addition, self-help groups can run with few resources. For example, a religious institution might donate space for meetings, and there generally are no costs for the group facilitators.

Self-help groups offer their members some of the social functions mentioned in the beginning of this chapter—a chance to meet others and have meaningful interactions, a place to feel as though one belongs and to give support to others. In short, self-help groups offer a social support system. As discussed in Chapter 5, social support has been shown to help people prevent and overcome disease and to maintain good psychological health (Coker, Sanderson, Ellison, & Fadden, 2006). In addition, some believe that attending a self-help group is less stigmatizing than a "treatment" or "therapy" group, the latter being more often associated with those who are seriously ill or have major problems in living. Some people view self-help groups as a form of support by and for laypersons ("folks just like me"), and the idea of attending one can be much less intimidating than a therapy or mutual aid group. The absence of agency affiliation for many self-help groups is attractive to those who would rather think of themselves as getting support from people in similar situations than going to an agency for assistance. Yet others may find comfort in knowing that a particular self-help group has an affiliation with a national, state, or local organization (Wituk, Shepherd, Slavich, Warren, & Meissen, 2000). Self-help groups can demonstrate helping characteristics (e.g., universality, support, and communication of experiential knowledge) similar to those of mutual aid groups. In one study, however, self-help group members reported more satisfaction with the group and gave higher evaluations for most of the helping characteristics than mutual aid group members did (Schiff & Bargal, 2000).

Another benefit of self-help groups is their potential for activism. In a popular manual used in domestic violence programs (Duluth Domestic Abuse Intervention Project, n.d.), one of the steps in the group process is titled "Options for Actions." These options include personal, institutional, and cultural activities. A vigil in honor of battered women killed by their assailants is an example of such an action. One study found that parents of children with cancer who were members of self-help groups were significantly more involved than other parents of such children in working to improve the medical system in which their children were involved (Chesney & Chesler, 1993). Another researcher (Tesoriero, 2006) found that women's self-help groups in India become active in community action projects and sometimes move their activism beyond the local community.

Task Groups

Most of us have been involved in task groups, such as a committee at school or at work or a task force in the community. It appears that the use of task groups is increasing in the workplace (Kottler & Englar-Carlson, 2010). In social work practice, task groups are often short term and are formed to accomplish specific goals and objectives. Task groups are used frequently by social workers involved in planning, administration, and community organizing roles but are much less common in other social work roles. An example would be a needs assessment committee formed at an agency to determine the problems and concerns of the population the agency serves. Although members of other types of groups may take on tasks (e.g., researching a subject and presenting it to the group), the **task group** is created with the express purpose of completing some specific task.

Task groups are often formally led by professionals who are appointed or elected to chair the group. Leaders may be chosen because of their position in the agency or their expertise in the area. Task groups formed in the community to advocate for change may be led by community members or co-led by professionals and community (lay) members.

In task groups as well as other kinds of groups, members fulfill what are commonly referred to as "task and maintenance" roles. The task specialist focuses on the goals set by the group and the tasks needed to accomplish them.

These may include providing information to aid group discussion, giving directions for how to proceed with a task, or summarizing members' ideas. Maintenance roles refer to those that enhance the social and emotional bonding within the group. These include inquiring about how close members feel to each other, encouraging open and respectful discussion of conflicts, and inviting reluctant members to participate in group discussion (Zastrow, 2009).

Technology and Group Practice

Any of the above group types can and have utilized technology, either as the primary format for running the group or as a supplement to a group that meets face-to-face. For example, use of telephone technology in agency-led groups has been recommended for persons who have transportation challenges (such as in rural areas or locales without public transportation systems), persons with disabilities, people with financial limitations who cannot afford to travel to a location for a group, and those who lack time or child care (Mallon & Houtstra, 2007). Computer technology offers several potential support group outlets including chat rooms, news groups, videoconferencing, and discussion forums. Yet studies have shown that social workers express some discomfort with facilitation of groups that utilize telephone and computer technology (Galinsky, Schopler, & Abell, 1997). Based on their experience leading telephone-based groups for patients who are survivors of brain injury, spinal cord injury, and stroke, Mallon and Houtstra note that the skills needed to lead such groups do not differ from the skills required for face-to-face group facilitation. The skills need to be *altered* for telephone group work, however. For example, group leaders may need to inquire more about silences and the feelings that participants may be experiencing because of the inability to observe group members' nonverbal cues. According to the Association for the Advancement of Social Work With Groups' publication, *Standards for Social Work Practice With Groups* (2005), when utilizing technology for group work, "issues such as member interaction, decision making, group structure, mutual aid, and, particularly, confidentiality are of vital concern" (p. 26).

It is also important to remember that a considerable number of persons do not own a telephone or have a computer with private Internet access. According to the U.S. Census Bureau, about 62% of U.S. households have Internet access in their homes (cited in M. Martz, 2009). Those with a college education and Caucasians and Asians have the highest home Internet use. Those who are in the top three-fourths of earnings in the United States are also more likely to have Internet home connection, while persons living below the poverty level tend to use the Internet at public centers such as libraries (M. Martz, 2009). Computer and Internet use among persons with disabilities also significantly lags behind those without disabilities (Kaye, 2000). Thus, organizations who are considering Internet-based group intervention should assess whether their client population would have private access to the Internet as well as the technological skills to benefit from web-based groups.

Some people enjoy the anonymity of web-based groups. In some of these groups, the use of pseudonyms and withholding other identifying information is appealing for persons who desire support but don't want to feel too vulnerable. Social workers who refer clients to web-based groups may want to first discuss the potential negative consequences of using such groups. For example, because of the anonymity of the site, participants may engage in hostile or bullying behavior to an extent that they would not do in person. A good group moderator will intervene in such behavior. Also, *cyberstalking* is another danger for those who desire to participate in web-based groups (Hitchcock, 2006).

Critical Thinking Questions 11.1

There are more than 800 self-help organizations in the United States. What factors do you think are driving the interest in self-help groups? Why do you think self-help groups may be less intimidating to some people than therapy groups?

DIMENSIONS OF GROUP STRUCTURE

Terry's coming-out group serves a variety of functions. But that one group cannot provide for all of Terry's needs. She also belongs to a group of friends with whom she attends social functions, a group of coworkers, and a softball team. Each group plays a unique part in Terry's life. For example, the softball team provides an outlet for competition and team building, and the work group offers a context for achievement and accomplishment. But all these groups are obviously structured quite differently. They can be categorized along three dimensions:

1. *How they develop.* The types of groups encountered in social work have typically been organized for a purpose. Such **formed groups** have a defined purpose and come about through the efforts of outsiders, such as an agency (K. E. Reid, 1997). Examples of formed groups include not only therapy groups, mutual aid groups, psychoeducational groups, self-help groups, and task groups, but also such groups as college classes, PTAs, and choirs. **Natural groups,** in contrast, "develop in a spontaneous manner on the basis of friendship, location, or some naturally occurring event. Without external initiative, the members simply come together" (K. E. Reid, 1997). Peer groups, street gangs, and a group of patients who have befriended each other in a psychiatric hospital are examples of natural groups.

2. *How long they last.* A **time-limited group** is one with a set time for termination; an **ongoing group** has no defined endpoint. Both formed and natural groups may be time limited or ongoing, short or long term. A formed group, for example, may last for a 2-hour period (e.g., a focus group) or for months or years (e.g., Terry's coming-out group). A natural group may last a lifetime (a group of close friends from high school) or just through some event (tablemates at a workshop).

3. *How they determine membership.* Finally, both natural and formed groups may be open or closed or may fluctuate between open and closed. **Open groups** permit the addition of new members throughout the group's life. In **closed groups,** the minimum and maximum size of the group is determined in advance, before the group begins or as it is being formed, and others are prohibited from joining once that limit is reached. A group can start off open and then become closed. An example would be a group of people who have been attending a drop-in support group for women in abusive relationships who decide after a few months that they would like to close the group to do some more intensive work in group sessions. Alternatively, a closed group may open up, as when the number of members has decreased considerably and new members are needed to keep the group going.

These three dimensions of group structure interact in complex ways. The coming-out group that Terry attends, although it is a formed group, is open and ongoing. Attendance has ranged from 3 to 18 persons, and the group may continue indefinitely. An example of a closed natural group is an informal group of middle school girls who call themselves the "lunch bunch." The five girls eat lunch together every day and have let it be known among their peers that no others are welcome. An example of a formed, time-limited, closed group is a 12-week group for men and women who are going through a divorce. Interested persons must register prior to the group's beginning, and once the first session begins, no new members are permitted.

An example of an ongoing, open, formed group is a bereavement group that meets every Tuesday evening at the local hospital and allows anyone who would like support to join the group on any Tuesday. Another example is a group that spontaneously meets at the basketball courts on Sunday afternoons to play ball. Whoever shows up can get into a game, with no predetermined limit to the number of people allowed to play.

Particular structures and types of groups may lend themselves especially well to group work with certain populations. For example, mutual aid groups of a time-limited or ongoing nature are recommended when working with abused women (Duluth Domestic Abuse Intervention Project, n.d.); groups modeled along the stages of recovery are recommended when doing group work with people who are addicted to alcohol or other drugs (Martin, Giannandrea, Rogers, & Johnson, 1996). Funding and space limitations, lack of personnel, and the agency's philosophy of treatment (e.g., brief vs. long term) may also influence the structure and type of group that an agency provides.

GROUP COMPOSITION

Another important element of small groups is their composition—the types of people who are members. Three issues regarding group composition are discussed in this section: inclusiveness/exclusiveness, heterogeneity/homogeneity, and cohesiveness.

Inclusion Versus Exclusion

Terry's coming-out group is relatively inclusive. It is open to any woman who is lesbian, bisexual, or questioning her sexual identity. The members self-identify, and the facilitators do not have criteria for determining whether a person is lesbian, bisexual, or questioning. In contrast, the heterosexual couples with whom Terry formerly associated make up a relatively exclusive group. Very few new couples have joined the group over the years, and in fact Terry herself is excluded now that she is no longer part of a heterosexual couple.

Natural groups often have implicit or explicit rules about who gets to belong and who doesn't. Take the previous example of the lunch bunch: The girls determined who would belong. Formed groups have rules of membership, too. A sorority or fraternity establishes a process to select who will belong. A group for persons with serious mental illness includes those who either define themselves as such or are defined as such by powerful others. Space constraints and personnel issues may determine who gets to belong: The room may only hold eight people, or only one social worker may be hired to facilitate the group. Task groups may be composed of those with the most relevant experience to contribute, those who have been appointed by a person in authority, or those who show the greatest interest in the task. Effective task groups often include members with a variety of resources for the task at hand.

Heterogeneity Versus Homogeneity

The degree of heterogeneity/homogeneity of groups may vary along several dimensions such as age, race, sexual orientation, gender, level of education, coping style, religion, socioeconomic status, disabilities, and problem areas or strengths. Usually groups are homogeneous on one or a few of these dimensions and heterogeneous on the rest. For example, Terry's group is homogeneous regarding gender and sexual orientation but quite heterogeneous on other dimensions, including race, age, socioeconomic status, disabilities, educational status, occupation, age at first awareness of sexual orientation, and amount of disclosure of sexual orientation to others.

Often heterogeneity/homogeneity is a matter of perception (Chau, 1990; Dufrene & Coleman, 1992). For example, in several studies of racially mixed groups, European American group members had a different perception from African American members regarding the racial balance of the group (L. E. Davis, 1984). If the group was in proportion to the population of African Americans in the geographic area, then the European American members perceived the group as balanced. If the group had equal numbers of White and Black members, the Black members viewed the group as balanced. The White members, however, perceived the group as imbalanced because the number of African Americans exceeded the psychological threshold of tolerance for European American members.

Conflict perspective

Another interesting finding is that proportional representation acts as a significant influence on levels of participation and leadership for those in the numerical minority. In one study, Asian persons showed higher levels of participation and leadership skills in work groups that were racially balanced or all Asian compared to Asians in White-dominated groups (Li, Karakowsky, & Siegel, 1999).

Which is better for group work, heterogeneity or homogeneity? For "long-term intensive interactional group therapy," heterogeneous groups appear to be better (Yalom, 1995, p. 255). Homogeneous groups, on the other hand, are often better for "support or symptomatic relief over a brief period" and "for individuals with monosymptomatic complaints or for the noncompliant patient" (p. 255). Homogeneous groups tend to build commitment more quickly, offer more immediate support to members, and have better attendance and less conflict.

Homogeneous groups are generally not beneficial for long-term psychotherapeutic work that involves personality change, because they tend to remain at superficial levels and don't challenge individuals' behavioral patterns and dynamics as much as heterogeneous groups (Yalom, 1995). However, homogeneous groups based on such characteristics as race or sex may be an exception. In group therapy for Black women, homogeneous membership allows for more intensive exploration of common problems (Boyd-Franklin, 1987). In a study of 32 group counseling clients at a university counseling center, group members in homogeneous groups (by gender, race, or presenting problem) reported higher levels of commitment to and satisfaction with the group than the heterogeneous group members (Perron & Sedlacek, 2000).

Psychodynamic perspective

Even heterogeneous groups usually have a homogeneous factor: the purpose or common goal of the group. Differences among people may be overridden by the overall function of groups—a place for people to seek human connection and a sense of belonging (Wasserman & Danforth, 1988). I am reminded of a friend who spoke to me of her experiences attending a support group for family members who had lost their loved ones. As the only African American group member, she said she felt like a "fly in a milk carton," but her fellow group members were the only people she knew who truly understood her grief.

An interesting research finding is that the heterogeneity/homogeneity issue takes on less importance the briefer and more structured the group. Compositional issues are more significant in groups that are less structured and that focus on group interaction (Yalom, 1995). In Terry's group, the homogeneity of sexual orientation provides the safety and support to explore the heterogeneous aspects of the group.

In natural groups, heterogeneity or homogeneity may be affected by such variables as the location (some geographic areas are highly homogeneous), preferences of group members (people tend to form natural groups with those with whom they feel some connection), and social norms and values (acceptance or condemnation of mixed groups).

For task or work groups, heterogeneity has been shown to positively influence group productivity. Among the 42 student project groups examined in one study, racial/ethnic diversity was positively associated with group efficacy (Sargent & Sue-Chan, 2001). The lowest levels of group efficacy occurred in groups with low commitment and less racial/ethnic diversity; conversely, the highest efficacy was in the high-commitment/high-diversity groups.

Another study of work groups assessed diversity by race, age, sex, and functional background in terms of their contribution to quality of innovation (the usefulness of an idea or the impact it might have on a business) and quantity of innovation (the number of new ideas that the group produces) (Cady & Valentine, 1999). These four dimensions of diversity had no significant impact on quality of innovation. There were significant differences in *quantity* of innovation, however. Teams with greater gender diversity had a lower quantity of innovation; teams with greater racial diversity had a higher quantity of ideas. In other words, as the gender diversity of teams increases, the number of new ideas decreases, and conversely, when the racial diversity of teams increases, the number of new ideas increases. Another study found that increasing the number of dimensions of diversity in work group membership mitigates the negative effects of tensions between majority and minority group members based on a single trait such as gender or race (Valenti & Rockett, 2008).

Cohesiveness

One important variable related to group composition is **group cohesiveness**—group identity, commitment, and sense of belonging. Groups with a "greater sense of solidarity, or 'we-ness,' value the group more highly, and will defend it against internal and external threats" (Yalom, 1995, p. 48). Groups that are cohesive tend to have higher rates of attendance, participation, and mutual support. But cohesiveness does not mean the absence of conflict or dislike among group members. Even a cohesive group may sometimes experience bickering, frustration, or alienation. Cohesion is thought to be dynamic: It changes in extent and form throughout the life of a group. Thus, measuring the degree of group cohesiveness across different contexts can be a challenge (Carron & Brawley, 2000). It is important for group leaders to try to prevent heterogeneous groups from splitting into coalitions that are not committed to the interest of the whole group (T. Jones, 2005).

Some groups may develop rituals or habits to increase cohesiveness among members. For example, a gang member may receive a tattoo as an initiation rite, the group may name itself (the "lunch bunch"), a member who has been in the group for 6 months may receive a pin, or group members may be expected to call another member when he or she is having difficulty.

BASIC GROUP PROCESSES

To be effective, group workers need tools for understanding the group processes in which they participate. Group processes are those unique interactions between group members that result from being in a group together. How people behave in groups is of interest to us because we spend much of our time in groups, and groups have a strong influence on our behaviors.

Theories of Group Processes

The fields of social psychology and sociology have been in the forefront of empirical research on group processes. Five of the major theories of group processes are discussed in this section: psychodynamic theory, symbolic interaction theory, status characteristics and expectation states theory, exchange theory, and self-categorization theory. Each one helps us understand why and how certain members of a group develop and maintain more power than other members to influence the group's activities.

Psychodynamic Theory

You were introduced to the psychodynamic theoretical perspective in Chapter 2. When applied to small groups, psychodynamic theory "focuses on the relationship between the emotional unconscious processes and the rational processes of interpersonal interaction" (McLeod & Kettner-Polley, 2005, p. 63). It is assumed that understanding the emotional processes in the group is essential for accomplishing the group's task. The psychodynamic theoretical perspective is especially important to therapy groups where understanding emotional processes is the central task of the group, but some group leaders argue that it is an important perspective for increasing the effectiveness of any type of group. Small groups can be challenging because they satisfy our need to belong, and yet they also arouse our fears about social acceptance and social competence (Geller, 2005).

> Psychodynamic perspective

McLeod and Kettner-Polley (2005) identify three broad assumptions of psychodynamic theory for understanding small groups:

1. Emotional, unconscious processes are always present in every group.

2. Emotional, unconscious processes affect the quality of interpersonal communication and task accomplishment.

3. Group effectiveness depends on bringing emotional, unconscious processes to group members' conscious awareness.

Group leaders in a psychodynamic therapy group would look for opportunities to assist group members in identifying how their interactions within the group may mirror their patterns of interactions with others outside of group; in other words, the group experience becomes a microcosm of members' lives outside the group. For example, a female group member who tends to defer to the opinions of male group members and who is afraid to confront them may be demonstrating a general theme in her life of being intimidated by males because of childhood experiences of severe physical abuse by her father.

Symbolic Interaction Theory

In Chapter 4, you read about symbolic interaction theory and how it is used to understand the self. This theory is also used to understand what happens in small groups. According to symbolic interaction theory, humans are symbol-using creatures. We make meaning of the world by interacting with others through symbols—words, gestures, and objects. Some small group theorists find it helpful to think about the small group as a place where symbols are created, exchanged, and interpreted, and to think about individual and social change happening as meanings are made and changed through the use of symbols (Frey & Sunwolf, 2005). In fact, they think that a "group" is itself a symbol that is used to describe a relationship that people understand themselves to have with each other. Group members create a sense of being a "group" through their symbolic actions with each other, through their language and their behaviors over time. Groups may use such symbols as metaphors, stories, and rituals to communicate and build cohesion. In this way, they also build a culture with its own symbols and meanings. The symbols provide group identity and stimulate commitment to struggle with the tensions of group life.

> Constructionist perspective

The symbols used in a group, and the meaning made of those symbols, are influenced by the environments in which the group is embedded (Frey & Sunwolf, 2005). Group members are also members of other groups and bring symbolic meanings with them from these groups. This may lead to tension and conflict in the group as members struggle to develop shared meaning about who they are as a group, what their goals are, and how they will operate as a group.

An example of symbolic interaction within a group is a ritual developed by the chapter author and a co-facilitator for a support group for incarcerated battered women. At the beginning and end of each session, the group would light five candles and recite five affirmations related to the group's theme, loving and healing ourselves: "I am worthy of a good life," "I am worthy of positive friendship," "I am a loveable person," "I desire inner healing," and "I will recognize the good things about myself and others." The lighting of the candles symbolized bringing to awareness the inner strength and healing power of each woman in the group.

Status Characteristics and Expectation States Theory

Status characteristics and expectation states theory proposes that the influence and participation of group members during initial interactions are related to their status and to expectations others hold about their ability to help the group accomplish tasks (Fisek, Berger, & Moore, 2002; Oldmeadow, Platow, Foddy, & Anderson, 2003). **Status characteristics** are any characteristics that are evaluated in the broader society to be associated with competence; they may be either specific or diffuse. Let's look first at an example of a specific status characteristic. Joan and Bob are both members of a task force formed in a housing project community to increase healthy social interactions among the children and beautify the grounds. Joan, who is known to be artistic, makes a suggestion that the group involve children in painting murals on communal buildings and then hold a contest for the best mural. Bob, who is not known to be artistic, suggests that the group solicit volunteer contributions from local artists who would donate paintings and other artwork to display on the inside of buildings. It can be expected that group members will be more willing to go along with Joan's idea than with Bob's because of Joan's greater perceived expertise in artistic matters. Their **performance expectations**—predictions of how well an act will accomplish a group's task—are influenced by this specific status characteristic.

> Rational choice perspective

In Terry's coming-out group, Beverly carries some influence. She has attended for quite a long time and is one of the core members who come to the group consistently. As an influential member, she is expected to articulate and enforce the group's rules and to assist new members in acclimating to the group. Group members expect Beverly to share her insights about the coming-out process, and they perceive her as a knowledgeable person, especially when discussing issues faced by African American lesbians.

Now, let's look at an example of a diffuse status characteristic. In the coming-out group, Beverly is perceived as a knowledgeable person regarding coming out and the unique issues faced by African American lesbians. But in another setting, the color of Beverly's skin might negatively influence how she is perceived by other people. Stereotypes about African Americans may cause other people to question Beverly's interests, skills, or values. Such stereotypes are the basis of *diffuse status characteristics* whereby the power and prestige of group members are correlated with their status in the external world, regardless of their specific characteristics relative to the task at hand.

> Social constructionist perspective

For example, if people expect that someone using a wheelchair is incapable of playing basketball for a charity fundraiser, then they will act as if a person using a wheelchair is unable to play basketball. They may disqualify that person from playing, thereby demoralizing the individual with the disability and preventing the person from contributing to the success of the fund-raiser.

Gender is an influential diffuse status characteristic in our society, perhaps because it is so easily discerned. In mixed-gender groups, males have greater participation and influence than females (Balkwell, 1994; Garvin & Reed, 1983), and males or females with traditionally masculine personality traits are likely to exhibit more dominant behavior (Seibert & Gruenfeld, 1992). In same-sex groups, gender is not an initial status differential; instead, members develop expectations of each other based on other status characteristics, such as education, race, or experience. Regardless of gender, a person's perceived ability also affects performance expectations. For example, a female may be perceived as incapable of handling a complex mechanical problem in a work group, but she may be able to develop influence if she shows that she can accomplish the task successfully (Schneider & Cook, 1995).

One assumption of status characteristics and expectation states theory is that people rely on their stereotypes in the absence of proof that those characteristics are irrelevant (Balkwell, 1994). In our example of assumptions people may make about persons using wheelchairs, the burden of proof would be on the persons using wheelchairs to demonstrate that they could indeed play basketball, thus establishing the inapplicability of others' assumptions about the disability.

Exchange Theory

Sometimes in coming-out groups, those who have been out for the longest time have implicit power over those newly out, the baby dykes. A "let me show you the ropes and tell you what this is about" attitude can be used to gain

Rational choice
perspective

power and influence over another person and to create dependency: "You need me to help you understand what you are getting yourself into." But social power can also be used in a positive way in a coming-out group, as when those who have been in the lesbian community for a long time offer support and information to others with the intention of providing mutual aid. To understand power as a social commodity, we can look to exchange theory (Lovaglia, Mannix, Samuelson, Sell, & Wilson, 2005; Thibaut & Kelley, 1959), which assumes that human interactions can be understood in terms of rewards and costs.

According to exchange theory, social power is what determines who gets valued resources in groups and whether those resources are perceived as being distributed in a just manner. Conflicts within the group often revolve around power issues among members—those who want the power in the group, those who have power and don't want to give it up, and those who don't want others to have power over them.

Groups are particularly vulnerable to conflicts over power because social power arises within the context of the group itself rather than being an innate quality of an individual.

> Sometimes it [power] works within a relationship between two people, but often it works within the complex relationships among a set of three, four, or many more people. Different primary and secondary social networks, where variations occur in who interacts with whom, make up the social situations in which power emerges and produces effects in predictable ways. (Stolte, 1994, p. 173)

Power not only determines the distribution of group resources, but it also influences people's expectations of others' abilities, even when the power results from structural conditions (such as luck) and not from innate personal ability (Lovaglia, 1995). Emotion also has an impact on perceived power and influence, regardless of status. If a person has negative emotions toward a high-status person, the power of the high-status person will lessen (Lovaglia, 1995).

Power differences among group members can create status differences, but not necessarily. Group members may rate more highly the abilities and influences of high-power members, which may in turn influence expectations for high-power members, but negative feelings toward high-power members may mitigate their influence.

The exercise of social power often brings with it a concern about justice, fairness, and equality. Most of us would agree that power should not be exercised to the special benefit or detriment of some group members. However, justice is a relative rather than absolute term. Any two persons may have quite different ideas about what constitutes justice. For some, justice would be an equal distribution of resources; for others, justice would be an equitable (but not necessarily equal) distribution.

How persons evaluate the equity of a situation depends on such factors as cultural values, self-interest, the situation, the relationships between those affected, and personal characteristics (Hegtvedt, 1994). People tend to operate more from self-interest in impersonal conditions than when they have personal bonds with others. The status of the person for whom justice claims are being considered also affects the definition of justice, the perception of injustice,

Conflict perspective

and the resolution of injustices. In addition, what may be perceived as fair on an individual level may be perceived as unfair when viewed from a group perspective. For example, suppose a group member is in crisis and asks for extended time in the group. The other five group members agree to give the person an extra 10 minutes because of the crisis. This extension, however, requires each group member to give up 2 minutes of his or her floor time. Giving one individual an extra 10 minutes may not seem like much, but that one action has a cost for five other group members. And what if one group member decides that he or she has a pressing issue to discuss and does not want to give up the 2 minutes? How the group would resolve this dilemma relates to its spoken and unspoken guidelines for handling matters of justice within the group.

Self-Categorization Theory

This theory builds on social identity theory, which, as discussed in Chapter 5, is a stage theory of socialization that articulates the process by which we come to identify with some social groups and develop a sense of difference from other social groups. Self-categorization theory expands social identity theory by suggesting that in this process, we come to divide the world into in-groups (those to which we belong) and out-groups (those to which we do not belong). We begin to stereotype the attributes of in-groups and out-groups by comparing them to each other, with bias toward in-groups. When we encounter new group situations, we are more likely to be influenced by in-group members than by out-group members. We give more credence to those who are similar to us than to those who are different from us, particularly when situations are conflicted or unclear. Doing so is consistent with our categorization schemes, but it also helps us maintain distinctive and positive social identities (Abrams, Hogg, Hinkle, & Otten, 2005; Hogg, 2005; Oldmeadow et al., 2003). So, in this approach, we are influenced in group situations by members of our in-groups, whether or not they hold high status in society.

An example of the above is Katie, a member of Terry's support group, who was raised in an Evangelical Protestant Church. Katie struggled with her sexuality and what she was taught in church about homosexuality. She accompanied another group member to a Metropolitan Community Church one day and immediately "felt at home" there. She felt she had found a place where both her sexual orientation and faith could be affirmed—a place where she could belong.

Recently, researchers have studied the impact of both status characteristics and self-categorization on social influence in group settings, recording who agrees with whom and who defers to whom. They have found that group members are influenced by both status characteristics and social identity. More specifically, they found that group members are more highly influenced by high-status members who also belong to the in-group than by either a low-status in-group member or a high-status out-group member (Kalkhoff & Barnum, 2000).

Critical Thinking Questions 11.2

The psychodynamic perspective on groups proposes that emotional processes in the small group affect the effectiveness of the group. Some proponents of this perspective argue that dealing with the emotional processes in the group is important in any type of group, not just therapy groups. What do you think about this argument? How important are emotional processes to mutual aid groups, psychoeducational groups, self-help groups, and task groups? Can you think of an example where unconscious emotional processes interfered with task accomplishment in a task group of which you were a member?

Group Development

To understand the unique nature of groups and why they are effective in helping people, we need to examine the ways groups develop. Two common ways of viewing group development are by the stages the group passes through and by the processes that facilitate the work of a group. This section provides a brief overview of stage theories and models and then discusses an example of the analysis of processes that facilitate the work of groups.

Stage Theories and Models

A variety of scholars have attempted to delineate the life cycle of small groups. But researchers who focus on the stages of group development have reached no consensus as to how many stages there are, the order in which they appear, or the nature of those stages. Exhibit 11.4 displays seven of the models commonly cited in social

Life-Span Metaphor	Bales (1950)	Tuckman (1965)	Sarri & Galinsky (1967)	Hartford (1971)	J. Garland, Jones, & Kolodny (1973)	Northen (1988)	Levine (1991)
Conception			Origin	Pregroup planning		Planning and intake	
Birth	Orientation	Forming	Formation	Convening	Preaffiliation	Orientation	Parallel relations Authority crisis
Childhood			Intermediate I	Group formulation	Power and control Intimacy		Inclusion
Adolescence	Evaluation	Storming Norming	Revision Intermediate II	Integration, disintegration and conflict, reintegration or reorganization, synthesis	Differentiation	Exploring and testing	Intimacy crisis
Adulthood (Maturity)	Decision making	Performing	Maturation	Group functioning and group maintenance	Separation	Problem solving	Mutuality
Death			Termination	Pretermination Termination		Termination	Separation crisis Termination

▲ **Exhibit 11.4**   Stage Models of Group Development

SOURCE: From *Social Work Practice With Groups: A Clinical Perspective*, 2nd edition, by K. Reid, 1997. Reprinted with permission of Wadsworth, a division of Thomson Learning.

work literature to describe the development of groups. Note, however, that controlled experiments investigating group stages are rare. Most theories of group stages have been developed by observing patterns and changes in groups, usually after the group has disbanded. Because most of the stage theories have been based on studies of time-limited, closed groups, they may not even be applicable to open-ended or ongoing groups.

> Developmental perspective

Most stage theorists agree, however, on some basic principles: Groups don't necessarily move through each stage in order, groups may revert to an earlier stage, stages are not distinct entities but may be a blend or combination, the group's development is influenced by the leader and the members, and groups do not need to reach the most advanced developmental stage in order to be effective (K. E. Reid, 1997; Wheelan, 2005).

Process Models

If stage theories are inadequate for explaining how groups develop, what are we to use instead?

▲ **Photo 11.3**   Small group—This exercise class is an example of a small group that come together to accomplish a goal: fitness.

The chief alternative is process models, which identify what goes on in groups and how those processes affect group members and their interactions. The advantage of process analysis is that it focuses on the interactions among group members rather than creating norms for development.

A good example of a process model is the one developed by Irving Yalom, one of the best-known group psychotherapists. Yalom (1995) describes 11 factors that operate in therapeutic groups to shape their functioning. These factors are listed and defined in Exhibit 11.5.

Some of Yalom's therapeutic factors may operate to a degree in groups other than therapy groups. For example, universality and imparting of information are two of the mutual aid processes described earlier in this chapter. In addition, certain factors may be more significant at particular stages of group development than at others. One study of 12 time-limited outpatient psychotherapy groups found that the development of cohesion varied according to the stage (or phase) of psychotherapy (Budman, Soldz, Demby, Davis, & Merry, 1993). For example, in the earliest stage of the group, members sharing issues about their lives outside the group built cohesion; however, too much focus on the therapist during this stage tended to be counter-cohesive. In Terry's coming-out group, several therapeutic factors are evi-

> Psychodynamic perspective; social behavioral perspective; humanistic perspective

dent at different times. When group members feel they can trust each other, catharsis and interpersonal learning are likely. When new members attend the group, they often desire to experience an instillation of hope, universality, imparting of information, and development of socializing techniques.

Group Dynamics

The overall development of the group is overlaid with patterns of interactions that can be characterized as **group dynamics**—such issues as how leaders are appointed or emerge, which roles members take in groups, and how communication networks affect interactions in groups.

Therapeutic Factor	Definition
Instillation of hope	Confidence and optimism in the ability of the group and individual members to resolve issues and grow
Universality	Sense that others share similar problems and feelings and that one is not alone
Imparting of information	Leader's and group members' sharing of information and guidance around problems and concerns
Altruism	Benefits experienced when one realizes that one has helped another person
Corrective recapitulation of primary family group	(Re)experience of relationship patterns like those in one's family of origin while learning different approaches to relationships
Development of socializing techniques	Examination of patterns of interacting with others and acquisition of new social skills
Imitative behavior	Observation of how other group members handle their problems and feelings and recognition of how those methods apply to one's own situation
Interpersonal learning	Process of learning about oneself through interaction with others
Group cohesiveness	Sense of belonging that group members have and sense of acceptance and support they feel in the group
Catharsis	Sharing of deep and sometimes painful emotions with nonjudgmental acceptance from group members
Existential factors	Search for meaning and purpose in one's life

▲ **Exhibit 11.5**   Therapeutic Factors Involved in Group Development

SOURCE: Yalom (1995).

Formal and Informal Leadership

Formal leaders are appointed or elected to lead the group by virtue of such characteristics as their position in the organization or community and their interest or expertise in relation to the group's focus. Informal leaders may emerge in groups where no formal leader exists or in ones where formal leaders are established. In the latter case, a group member may feel more comfortable in a helper or leader role than as a client in the group, thereby mimicking the actions of the formal leader.

Both formal and informal group leaders have a binary focus: the individuals in the group and the group as a whole. **Task-oriented leaders** facilitate problem solving within the context of the group; **process-oriented leaders,** also known an social-emotional leaders, identify and manage group relationships (S. Myers & Anderson, 2008; K. E. Reid, 1997; Yalom, 1995). Any given leader usually fluctuates from one role to the other, although people tend to be either more task oriented or more process oriented.

In natural groups, leaders may be formal or informal. A friendly softball game at the diamond on a Saturday morning may evolve into a complex hierarchy of leaders and followers as various activities are negotiated—who is on what team, who bats first, how long the game will last, who will decide batting order, and so on—and such process issues as team morale and cohesiveness are promoted.

Leaders of formed groups also take on various roles, depending on the purpose and structure of the group. A facilitator for a group for children with ADHD is a formal leader who may provide structured activities, support, and guidance for the children. Similarly, the leader of a one-time debriefing group may provide support and information to rescue workers after a fire. Informal leaders of formed groups might include a person who evolves into a leadership role in a work group assigned to some project.

Systems perspective

Groups often have coleaders, or one appointed leader and one or more group members who serve as self- or group-appointed coleaders. The coming-out group has two facilitators, both of whom are self-appointed coleaders. Doris is a 52-year-old African American lesbian in a long-term relationship. She tends to be the more nurturing facilitator and has a degree in social work. Marie is a European American, 28, who came out during high school. She considers herself a lesbian/gay activist and works at a clinic for persons with HIV/AIDS. She is more task oriented and does much of the record keeping and information sharing in the group.

Researchers have made a wide range of discoveries about the types of people who tend to become group leaders:

- They are likely to have personality traits of dominance, friendliness, task orientation, persuasiveness, and intelligence.

- First-born persons are likely to become task-oriented leaders; later-borns will likely be relationship-oriented leaders (Hare, Blumberg, Davies, & Kent, 1994).

Gender, class, and race influence leadership (both who takes leadership and the perception of leaders by group members). Status differences based on gender influence the behaviors of both male and female group members, including their reactions to male and female group leaders (Garvin & Reed, 1983). Both males and females tend to respect male leadership more quickly and easily. Males in a female-led group tend to challenge the leader(s) and expect female leaders to be more nurturing than male leaders. Persons of color may distrust

Conflict perspective

White leaders "from the system" (L. E. Davis, 1995, p. 49), because such leaders may be perceived as not being sensitive or responsive to minorities' needs. In addition, the significant difference in life experiences of persons of color and Whites may create a wide gap between White (often middle-class) leaders and group members who are persons of color or poor. White leaders of groups that include minorities may want to prepare themselves for three questions: "1. Are we people of goodwill? 2. Do we have sufficient mastery/skills to help them? 3. Do we understand their social realities?" (L. E. Davis, 1995, p. 53). White group leaders should also remember that their behavior should be purposeful and they should demonstrate respect, examine their own attitudes and beliefs regarding clients who are different from them, use culturally and class-appropriate techniques, know the resources that exist in the larger society that may be of help to their group members, make every effort to "get off to a good start" (p. 55), and expect success.

- Communication content, more than gender, influences leadership emergence in task-oriented groups. One study found task-relevant communication to be the sole significant predictor of emerged leadership, with no significant gender differences in the production of task-relevant communication (Hawkins, 1995).

- In general, leaders who are elected by members tend to be more favorably perceived than leaders who are self-appointed or appointed by others.

- Informal leaders may emerge in groups where formal leaders are present. Sometimes an informal leader takes the role of "assistant therapist," the person who "asks leading questions of other members, analyzes behavior, and is always ready with an interpretation" (K. E. Reid, 1997, p. 246).

Formal and Informal Roles

In addition to formal and informal leadership roles within the group, group members fill a variety of other roles. Those roles serve a purpose for the group as a whole and simultaneously fulfill group members' personal needs (S. Myers & Anderson, 2008; K. E. Reid, 1997). Thus, a person's group role often mirrors roles in other arenas. For instance, the group clown is often a clown in other areas of life.

Keep in mind, however, that role is only one element of social interaction: "The other variables include the biological systems of the actors, their personalities, the structure and process of the small groups and organizations that they belong to, and the society, culture, and environment in which these are embedded" (Hare, 1994, pp. 443–444). In other words, role is only one part of the picture.

Roles of group members may have both positive and negative aspects. The peacemaker, for example, may serve the function of reducing conflict and anxiety within the group—but perhaps at the cost of suppressing efforts to work through or resolve conflict within the group. The clown or jester reduces anxiety and stress in the group by joking, but also enables the group to avoid a painful subject. The scapegoat may remind group members of parts of themselves that they deny or of which they are fearful. The rescuer, who jumps in to defend anyone who appears to be confronted in the group, may be uncomfortable with others' pain or with unfair attacks against the group scapegoat, but may also keep the group from sanctioning an unacceptable violation of group norms (S. Myers & Anderson, 2008; K. E. Reid, 1997).

From a therapeutic perspective, Yalom (1995) has categorized several types of "problem members," whom he refers to as "problem patients": the monopolist, the silent member, the boring member, the help-rejecting complainer, the psychotic member, the characterologically difficult member, and the borderline member. Yalom observes that he has yet to encounter an unproblematic member; each member has some problems in living. Furthermore, the behavior of the problem patient does not exist in a vacuum; "that patient always abides in a dynamic equilibrium with a group that permits or encourages such behavior" (p. 370). The behaviors of the problem members are attempts to cope with underlying feelings. The monopolist, for instance, talks incessantly to handle anxiety and to avoid talking about "real" feelings.

Systems perspective

Roles are not necessarily fixed and rigid. Rather, they develop through give-and-take within the group (S. Myers & Anderson, 2008; Salazar, 1996). Roles are also a social construction. They reflect group members' expectations and both produce and reproduce elements of the social structure.

Communication Networks

Groups function more effectively when the members are able to communicate easily and with competence. Social workers who lead groups can set the tone for the group by being clear, direct, and compassionate in their own communication. The free flow of ideas among members enhances productivity, particularly in task groups.

Communication networks are the links among members—who talks to whom, how information is transmitted, whether communication between members is direct or uses a go-between. *Sociograms* may be used to depict the physical arrangement of these communication channels. Typically, the formal leader occupies the central position in a communication network, like the hub at the center of spokes on a wheel (Shaw, 1981). However, an informal leader may take the role of information giver and controller.

Systems perspective

Group members' satisfaction with a group tends to be higher in "web" networks, where information passes freely among all group members, than in centralized "wheel" networks. (Exhibit 11.6 diagrams these patterns.) Centralized networks are the more efficient configuration for task groups addressing simple problems, however. Decentralized networks are more effective if the group is attempting to solve more complex problems (Shaw, 1981).

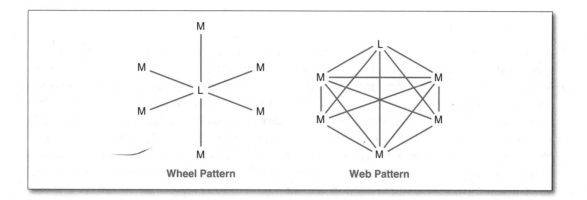

Wheel Pattern   **Web Pattern**

▲ **Exhibit 11.6** Common Communication Patterns in Groups

Communication patterns may also be affected by whether the group meets face-to-face or uses telephone or computer technology. Enhancing the leaders' and members' auditory skills for group participation may be important for telephone groups because of the absence of visual cues and in-person interaction. An active leader role in telephone and computer groups may be necessary to confront monopolizers and encourage those who are silent (Mallon & Houtstra, 2007).

INTERDISCIPLINARY TEAMS AND LEADERSHIP

In recent years, many organizations, including those where social workers work, have implemented organizational team structures to respond to rapidly changing conditions (Kogler Hill, 2007). Because it is anticipated that work teams will continue to be a part of organizational structure for the near future, it is important for social workers to understand what makes a team successful. Many scholars argue that team leadership is the primary ingredient of team success, and social workers will need to be prepared to function as team leaders.

Interdisciplinary Teams and Social Work

Social workers may be involved, on a regular or occasional basis, in a special type of group known as interdisciplinary teams. **Interdisciplinary teams** are composed of professionals representing a variety of disciplines, and they may include consumers or clients. Examples include Child Study and Early Intervention teams (Allen-Meares, 1995; Allen-Meares & Pugach, 1982; Kropf & Malone, 2004), medical teams in hospital units (Schofield & Amodeo, 1999), end-of-life and geriatric teams (Kornblatt, Cheng, & Chan, 2002; Reese & Sontag, 2001), and coordinated community response (CCR) teams to address domestic violence and sexual assault (Mederos & Perilla, 2003; Pence, 1999). Teams may be formed formally or informally, and may have representatives from within or outside of an agency. Andrews (1990) describes **interdisciplinary collaboration** as a process whereby "different professionals, possessing unique knowledge, skills, organizational perspectives, and personal attributes, engage in coordinated problem solving for a common purpose" (p. 175).

It is important that social workers have a good understanding of other professions and the roles of other members of interdisciplinary teams. Furthermore, learning to work well with team members regardless of differing perspectives and job responsibilities enables social workers to better achieve their desired outcomes (Ginsberg, 2001).

The Social Worker's Role on Interdisciplinary Teams

The social worker's role on an interdisciplinary team is often very crucial because the social worker may be the only professional who views clients from a person-in-environment and strengths perspective. Consequently, social workers sometimes find themselves needing to advocate for clients during a team meeting. Social workers may be assigned a specific function on interdisciplinary teams, such as conducting biopsychosocial assessments for geriatric teams. They may be requested by a team to meet with a client prior to a team meeting in which a client is expected to participate (Mellor & Lindeman, 1998). At times, social workers who work in a setting with an established professional hierarchy may experience marginalization within a team. In other words, the professionals who have more favorably perceived status characteristics may exert more influence in team decisions. There are situations, however, when team members may turn to the social worker on the team because he or she is perceived to have the most expertise about a given issue (C. S. Roberts, 1989). Social work training in group work can be a particular asset in facilitating team meetings (Andrews, 1990). Team members may also turn to social workers for their knowledge of community resources (broker function) (Mellor & Lindeman, 1998).

Conflict among interdisciplinary team members may be resolved in a number of ways, including attempting to sway others, backing down, or compromising. At times, team members may act more as representatives of their particular disciplines, influenced by their own theoretical principles, rather than as team members (Sands, Stafford, & McClelland, 1990). On the other hand, because of changing cultural values and norms in certain settings, such as hospice, social workers may find that the values of fellow team members are actually quite similar to their own (Reese & Sontag, 2001). Other potential barriers to effective interdisciplinary teams of which social workers should be aware include negative team norms, member inertia, unequal work distribution, power jockeying among team members, and lack of institutional resources to support the team's work (Reese & Sontag, 2001).

A review of studies of the efficacy of interdisciplinary teams in human services and health care found that while many of the studies' authors endorsed interdisciplinary teams, little evidence was presented to demonstrate their efficacy (Schofield & Amodeo, 1999). Schofield and Amodeo criticized the existing literature on interdisciplinary teams along several dimensions: inconsistency and lack of clarity in usage of terms (i.e., the use of the terms *interdisciplinary* and *multidisciplinary* without defining them), articles that described interdisciplinary teams or an aspect of them but did not delineate the process of such teams or conduct any empirical analysis of their effectiveness, articles that described the process of interdisciplinary teams but failed to use a research design, and empirical articles that demonstrated methodological and conceptual weaknesses. The authors did find, however, a few exemplary studies of interdisciplinary teams that were conceptually rigorous and methodologically sound. Social workers can play a critical role in advancing the state of the knowledge about interdisciplinary teams by attending to the weaknesses listed above.

Social work researchers can benefit by drawing on the work of researchers in other disciplines who have begun to engage in systematic study of what makes organizational teams successful. Based on interviews with members of highly effective teams, Larson and LaFasto (1989) identified several characteristics of successful teams:

- They have clear and motivating goals.

- They are structured in a way to facilitate goal accomplishment.

- They have the right number and mix of competent members.

- They have a collaborative and respectful climate.

- They have high standards of excellence.

- They have organizational support and adequate resources for goal accomplishment.

- They have effective leadership.

Social Workers and Leadership

Social workers may at times be elected or appointed to lead interdisciplinary teams. While there are many definitions of leadership, the definition by Northouse (2007) is "a process whereby an individual influences a group of individuals to achieve a common goal" (p. 3). Northouse's definition acknowledges that leadership is a process rather than a particular trait of an individual, it involves inspiring others, and it takes place within the context of groups who are working toward goal achievement. Social workers can bring their unique social work values, ethics, and training in interpersonal communication to bear on their leadership styles. While relational skills can be useful in leading interdisciplinary teams, a task orientation can also be beneficial for enacting the work of the team. Andrews (1990) notes that "leaders must be able to transcend disciplinary and organizational affiliation to plan, guide, and monitor the interactive process" (pp. 183–184). Social work leaders also need to know how to manage conflict and power dynamics in the team, attend to individuals' needs and strengths, and establish group norms (Andrews, 1990). In recent years, there has been a call for social workers to assume more leadership in interdisciplinary collaboration in several fields, including developmental disabilities (Kropf & Malone, 2004), legal services (Maidenberg & Golick, 2001), and failing to thrive in infants and children (Marino, Weinman, & Soudelier, 2001).

There is some evidence that social workers in leadership positions on interdisciplinary teams would benefit from an understanding of corporate management functions, namely planning, organizing, coordinating, encouraging, monitoring, and evaluating (Veeder & Dalgin, 2004). In one study, the presence of five management outcome variables, including coordinating an interdisciplinary team, predicted successful cases (Veeder & Dalgin, 2004). Social workers might also find it useful to use a self-analysis of leadership traits, such as the Leadership Trait Questionnaire, to measure their personal characteristics of leadership, or to examine their leadership style using an instrument such as a Leadership Style Questionnaire to assess task and relationship factors (Northouse, 2007).

While social workers may find themselves naturally gravitating to certain leadership styles, one approach to leadership has been termed *situational.* Proponents of this approach note that "different situations demand different kinds of leadership. From this perspective, to be an effective leader requires that an individual adapt his or her style to the demands of different situations" (Northouse, 2007, p. 91). Leaders using the situational approach would balance directive and supportive roles given the changing competence and commitment of members to carry out a task. There are times when the leader may need to assume a more directive style, whereas in other situations, the leader may find that a more supportive role would be appropriate. The effective leader "helps the team understand the problems . . . become cohesive and goal-focused . . . handle stressful circumstances . . . and coordinate team activities" (Kogler Hill, 2007, pp. 214–215). Leaders also can help the team develop shared expertise. There are instruments available for leaders to use to assess team members' perceptions of team effectiveness (for example, see LaFasto & Larson in Northouse, 2007, pp. 233–234). There are many other theories of leadership with which social workers can familiarize themselves (see Gini, 1997; Northouse, 2007; Woyach, 1993).

It is important to note that many of the functions noted above need not be carried out exclusively by the formal leader. Teams may have a cadre of experienced and competent members who take on and share leadership activities. In other situations, teams have no designated formal leader and the group works as a self-managed team. The important issue is that teams develop processes for monitoring progress toward goals and executing necessary actions (Kogler Hill, 2007).

Critical Thinking Questions 11.3

Think about a small group in which you have participated that was particularly effective. What factors do you think contributed to this effectiveness? Now, think of a small group in which you have participated that was particularly ineffective. What factors do you think contributed to this ineffectiveness?

IMPLICATIONS FOR SOCIAL WORK PRACTICE

The overview of formed and natural groups in this chapter suggests a number of principles for social work assessment, intervention, and evaluation:

- In the assessment process with individuals or families, identify any natural or formed groups to which the person or family belongs. Ecomaps or sociograms may be used to identify such groups.

- In the assessment process, determine whether the group modality or another intervention modality would be most appropriate for the client.

- In the assessment process with a potential group member, gather background information such as the motivation for joining the group, the expectations the person has of the leader and other group members, the strengths the person could offer the group, and previous experience with groups.

- Be aware of various groups in your community for referral and networking purposes.

- Develop and implement small groups when it is clear that a group would benefit the population you serve. Determine what type(s) of groups would be most appropriate for that population. Consider groups for prevention when appropriate.

- Collaborate with colleagues from other disciplines to co-facilitate groups in interdisciplinary settings.

- Seek to build alliances with natural and self-help groups that reinforce or supplement the services you are providing.

- In the groups that you facilitate, understand the stated and unstated purposes and functions of the group, and pay careful attention to issues of group structure, development, composition, and dynamics.

- Develop a plan for evaluating the effectiveness of a group prior to its formation, if possible. Use the information from ongoing evaluation to make needed changes in the group.

- Be aware of how managed care affects the use of groups as a practice modality.

KEY TERMS

brief treatment model	leadership	self-help group
closed group	mutual aid group	small group
communication networks	natural group	status characteristics
formed group	ongoing group	status characteristics and
group cohesiveness	open group	expectations states theory
group dynamics	performance expectations	task group
group work	process-oriented leader	task-oriented leader
interdisciplinary collaboration	psychoeducational group	therapy group
interdisciplinary team	self-categorization theory	time-limited group

ACTIVE LEARNING

1. Compare and contrast Terry's support group with a small group of which you are a member in terms of how they developed, how long they are lasting, how membership was determined, inclusiveness versus exclusiveness, heterogeneity versus homogeneity, cohesiveness, and leadership.

2. In a small group formed by your instructor, attempt to solve this problem: Draw a square. Divide it into four identical squares. Remove the bottom left-hand square. Now divide the resulting shape into four identical shapes. Work on the problem for 15 minutes. Observe the overall process in the group, the diversity of membership in the group, and the roles of each member while engaged in problem solving. Write up your observations.

3. In personal reflection, think about your behavior and your roles in important groups throughout your life to date, groups such as your family of origin, friendship groups, social groups, sports teams, work groups, therapy groups, and so on. What roles have you played in these different groups? Are there any patterns to the roles you have played across various types of groups? Do you notice any changes in your roles over time or in different types of groups? How do you understand both the patterns and the changes?

WEB RESOURCES

American Self-Help Group Clearinghouse, Self-Help Group Sourcebook
www.mentalhelp.net/selfhelp/

Provides a guide to locate self-help and support groups in the United States and other countries.

The Association for the Advancement of Social Work With Groups (AASWG)
www.aaswg.org/

Professional organization advocating in support of group work practice, education, research, and publication; includes links to newsletters, discussion lists, bibliographies, chapter information, syllabi, social work links, and other group work links. To order the association's bibliography on group work, write to Raymie H. Wayne, General Secretary, AASWG, Inc., 36 Rocklyn Drive, West Simsbury, CT 06092–2628.

Association for Specialists in Group Work (ASGW)
www.asgw.org/

Site maintained by a division of the American Counseling Association that promotes quality in group work training, practice, and research.

Google Groups
Groups.google.com

Site for creating or finding groups on the Internet, including support-related groups.

International Association for Group Psychotherapy and Group Processes
www.iagp.com/

Site contains information about the association, contact information for the board, membership information, and an electronic forum.

Formal Organizations

Elizabeth D. Hutchison

OPENING QUESTIONS

- How do the major theoretical perspectives on formal organizations help us to understand the functions they serve in contemporary society and their influence on human behavior?

- What are the contemporary trends in the formal organizations in which social workers work?

- How do social workers exercise leadership in formal organizations?

KEY IDEAS

As you read this chapter, take note of these central ideas:

1. Formal organizations—collectivities of people with a high degree of formality of structure, working together to meet a goal or goals—are important influences on human behavior. They help us in many ways, and they also cause stress and strain in our lives.

2. Perspectives on formal organizations can be classified into four broad categories: rational perspective, systems perspective, interpretive perspective, and critical perspective.

3. Theories in the rational perspective consider formal organizations to be purposefully designed machines that maximize efficiency and effectiveness.

4. The systems perspective sees the formal organization in constant interaction with multiple environments and composed of interrelated systems.

5. Both the interpretive and the critical perspectives emphasize human consciousness in creating organizations, but critical theories focus on patterns of domination and oppression in organizations, which interpretive theories largely ignore or negate.

6. Research in both public sector and business organizations indicates that formal organizations may be hazardous to the health of their members. Burnout—whose symptoms include emotional exhaustion, cynicism, and inefficacy—is the most identified hazard.

7. Social workers work in many diverse types of formal organizations.

Case Study

Changing Leadership at Beacon Center

Beacon Center (BC) has a short but proud history of providing innovative services to persons who are homeless in River Run, the mid-size midwestern city where it is located. It was established in 1980, thanks to one woman, Martha Green, and her relentless pursuit of a vision.

(Continued)

(Continued)

While serving as executive director of the YWCA, Martha became increasingly concerned about the growing homeless population in River Run. During the late 1960s and 1970s, she had worked in several positions in River Run's antipoverty agency, and she was well-known throughout the city for her uncompromising advocacy efforts for families living in poverty. Martha was also a skilled advocate and service planner, and she soon pulled together supporters for a new social service agency to address the special needs of homeless persons. A mix of private, public, federal, and local funds were secured, and BC opened with Martha Green as director, working with the assistance of one staff social worker. The agency grew steadily, and within a decade it had a staff of 15, as well as several subcontracted programs.

Martha valued client input into program development and made sure that client voices were heard at all levels: at city council meetings, in community discussions of program needs, in BC discussions of program needs and issues, in staff interviews, and at board meetings. She remained uncompromising in advocacy efforts, and she often angered city officials because she was unyielding in her demands for fair treatment of homeless persons. She advocated for their right to receive resources and services from other social service organizations as well as for their right to congregate in public places.

By the same token, Martha and the staff consistently reminded clients of their obligations as citizens and, gently but firmly, held them to those obligations. Clients were sometimes angered by this call for responsible behavior, but they appreciated the tireless advocacy of Martha and the staff. They also appreciated that they were kept fully informed about political issues that concerned them, as well as about actions taken by BC in relation to these issues.

Martha also had a vision regarding staff relationships. She was committed to working collaboratively, to trusting frontline workers to make their own decisions, and to securing the participation of all staff on important policy decisions. This commitment was aided by the fact that Martha and her staff came from similar backgrounds and had deep family roots in River Run. Rules were kept to a minimum, and staff relationships were very personal. For example, a staff member needing to keep a medical appointment would make informal arrangements with another staff member to exchange an hour of service, with no need to "go through channels" or invoke formal sick leave. Martha believed in hiring the best-trained and most experienced staff for frontline positions and, over the years, hired and retained a highly skilled, committed core staff. She had high expectations of her staff, particularly in terms of their commitment to the rights of homeless persons, but she was also a nurturing administrator who was concerned about the personal well-being and professional development of each staff member. She established a climate of mutual respect where people could risk disagreeing.

Martha spent some time every week working in each program area to ensure that she understood the agency's programs as they were experienced by clients and frontline staff. She kept staff fully informed about economic and political pressures faced by BC and about her actions in regard to these issues. She regularly sought their input on these issues, and decisions were usually made by consensus. On occasion, however, around really sensitive issues—such as the choice between forgoing a salary increase and closing a program—she asked staff to vote by secret ballot to neutralize any potential power dynamics.

Martha had a vision, as well, about how a board of directors can facilitate a successful client-centered program. She saw the board as part of the BC system, just as staff and clients were part of the system. She worked hard to ensure that members chosen for the board shared the BC commitment to the rights of homeless persons, and she developed warm, personal relationships with them. She kept the board fully informed about issues facing BC, and she was successful in securing their support and active involvement in advocacy and resource development activities.

Over the years, BC became known as an innovative, client-centered service center, as well as a hardheaded advocacy organization. Staff and board members took pride in being part of what they considered to be a very special endeavor—one that outstripped other social service organizations in its expertise, commitment, and compassion. Clients were not always satisfied with the services, but generally acknowledged among themselves that they were lucky to have the dedication of BC.

Reactions from the community were more mixed, however. The respect offered up was, in many circles, a grudging one. Many city officials as well as staff of other social service organizations complained about the self-righteous attitudes and uncompromising posture of Martha and the staff at BC. These detractors acknowledged that the tactics of BC staff were successful in countering discrimination against homeless persons, but suggested that BC succeeded at much cost of goodwill. Although Martha believed in keeping staff, clients, and board members informed about the economic and political pressures faced by BC, she saw it as her job to carry the major responsibility for responding to, and absorbing, those pressures, to protect staff energy for serving clients.

Martha retired 15 years ago and relocated with her husband to be closer to their children. An acting director was appointed at BC while a search for a permanent director was underway. The acting director had worked several years at BC and shared much of Martha's administrative and service philosophy. She was not as good, however, at juggling the multiple demands of the position. Staff and clients felt a loss of support, board members lost some of their enthusiasm and confidence, and antagonists in the community saw an opportunity to mute some of BC's advocacy efforts. Staff maintained a strong commitment to the rights of homeless persons, but they lost some of their optimism about making a difference.

After 8 months, Helen Blue, a former community college administrator, was hired as the new executive director. Like Martha Green, she was of European American heritage, but she had only lived in River Run for a few years. She was excited about this new professional challenge, but she had a vision for BC that was somewhat different from Martha's. She was concerned about the alienation that had resulted, in some circles, from BC's hard-hitting advocacy stance, and she favored a more conciliatory approach. For example, after meeting with city officials, she assigned staff social workers the task of convincing clients to stop congregating in the city park near BC and to stay out of the business district during business hours. After meeting with directors of other social service organizations, she directed staff to be less demanding in their advocacy for clients.

Helen was also concerned about the lack of rules and the looseness of attention to chain of command, and she began to institute new rules and procedures. Staff meetings and open community meetings with clients became presentations by Helen. Staff were no longer allowed to attend board meetings and were not informed about what happened at them. Frontline staff often found their decisions overturned by Helen. When the first staff resignation came, Helen hired the replacement with no input from staff, clients, or board members.

Helen stayed a few years at BC and then decided to return to community college administration. Since she left BC, two executive directors have come and gone. In the recession of 2009, funding streams became more restricted at a time of growing homelessness caused by home foreclosures and a weakened economy. Needs increased and resources declined. The board of directors has recently hired a consultant to assist them in beginning a strategic planning process.

A DEFINITION OF FORMAL ORGANIZATIONS

You were probably born in a hospital. There is a good chance that you began to attend a house of worship at an early age. You may have been enrolled in a child care or education center by the age of 4. You have, by now, spent close to two decades in school. Along the way, you may have joined organizations such as Girl Scouts, Boy Scouts, YMCA, YWCA, or other athletic clubs. You may also have participated in programs offered by civic and social service organizations as a member, recipient of services, or volunteer. You probably manage your finances with the assistance of a bank or credit union, and you meet your basic survival needs as well as fulfill your consumer wants through a variety of business organizations. Some of you are, or have been, members of sororities and fraternities, and some may be student members of the National Association of Social Workers (NASW). Most of you have been a paid employee of at least one formal organization, and many of you are currently enrolled in a field practicum in a social service organization like Beacon Center. When you die, a news organization may announce your death, a public organization will issue a death certificate, and your loved ones will probably seek the service of several other organizations to plan your funeral.

For those of us who live in contemporary complex societies, formal organizations are pervasive in our lives, a most important but usually taken-for-granted part of life. But what, exactly, are they? A **formal organization** is a collectivity of people with a high degree of formality of structure, working together to meet a goal or goals. This definition, like most found in the organization literature (see Greenwald, 2008; Shafritz & Ott, 2005), has three key components: a collectivity of people, a highly formal structure, and the common purpose of working together to meet a goal or goals.

This definition leaves a lot of room for variation. Formal organizations differ in size, structure, culture, and goals. They also perform a variety of functions in contemporary society and influence human behavior in many ways. Exhibit 12.1 is a list of what contemporary organizations do. You can see that formal organizations are intricately woven into the fabric of life in contemporary society, that formal organizations can be both functional and dysfunctional for society or for specific groups, and that some members of organizations benefit more than others from organizational goals and structure. You might want to think about how well the list of functions in Exhibit 12.1 describes Beacon Center, your school of social work, your field agency, and an organization where you have been an employee.

Formal organizations are human facilitators. Organizations help us get things done and meet our needs. Collective activities are often superior to individual efforts because of speed, accuracy, human connectedness, and other factors.

Formal organizations organize society. Every aspect of contemporary life is systematized and coordinated through formal organizations.

Formal organizations are political institutions. All organizations perform some type of political activity. In addition, all organizations are involved in the promotion of the ideology of the political system in which they operate.

Formal organizations are instruments of system maintenance and enhancement. Organizations engage in activities that maintain or enhance the economic, political, and social systems in which they operate.

Formal organizations are change agents. Although organizations often resist change, they also play a role in societal reform and change.

Formal organizations create culture and counterculture. Organizations produce and promote the general cultural values of the popular culture as well as specific organizational cultural values that run counter to the popular culture. In this way, organizations may play a proactive role in the societies in which they operate.

Formal organizations are tools of policy implementation. Organizations provide some stability and predictability as they implement policy over time.

Formal organizations are tools of development. Organizations produce advancements in science, technology, and other aspects of human functioning. Some of these "advancements" improve the human condition, some aggravate it, and many result in both benefits and costs.

Formal organizations are destructive forces. The processes that organizations use to accomplish organizational goals may create environmental degradation or work conditions that are hazardous to the well-being of organizational members. The goals of the organization may be to develop products for waging war or products detrimental to the health of citizens.

Formal organizations are instruments of repression and domination. Organizations may be, and often are, instruments of control, domination, class rule, and exploitation.

Formal organizations are alienators. In many organizations, hierarchical structures with their arrangements of power generate inequality and alienation.

Formal organizations are tension-management systems. Organizations develop processes for managing the tensions between individual goals and organizational goals, among competing organizational goals, or among competing individual goals. Processes are also developed to manage class tensions related to inequalities in organizational structure.

Formal organizations threaten individual rights. Individual rights are limited, to varying degrees, by organizational roles, rules, and norms.

Formal organizations form the administrative state of governance. Webs of corporate organizations and government organizations create a highly centralized and concentrated social structure.

Formal organizations are instruments of globalization. Organizations are tools to facilitate globalization of capital and cultures, consolidating money and power for wealthy nations.

Formal organizations are a forum for discourse. Their members have multiple perspectives about goals, processes, and structures. Organizations, therefore, become sites for more or less democratic disagreement and negotiation, the active construction of meaning and purpose, and problem resolution.

▲ **Exhibit 12.1**   The Functions of Formal Organizations

SOURCES: From "Introduction: The multifaceted nature of modern organizations." In A. Farazmand (Ed.), *Modern Organizations: Theory and Practice*, 2002. Copyright © 2002 by Ali Farazmand. Reproduced with permission of ABC-CLIO, LLC.

Think, too, about how much formal organizations influence our behavior. They meet our needs, help us fulfill goals, and nurture our development. They also make stressful demands, thwart our goals, inhibit our holistic development, and constrain our behavior.

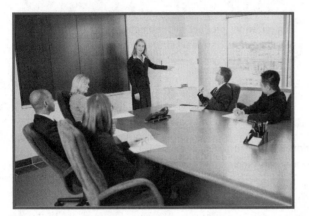

▲ **Photo 12.1** Formal organizations are defined as a collectivity of people with a high degree of formality, working together to meet a common goal.

The purpose for introducing theory and research about formal organizations in this chapter is twofold: (1) to help you understand the pervasive and multifaceted influence of formal organizations on human behavior—yours as well as your clients'—and (2) to assist you in understanding the organizations in which social workers practice.

PERSPECTIVES ON FORMAL ORGANIZATIONS

Almost three decades ago, the ways of thinking about organizational life in the United States had grown so numerous, and so fragmented, that one observer noted that the state of organization theory can be described as "more of a weed patch than a well-tended garden" (Pfeffer, 1982, p. 1). That is still an apt description of current U.S. theorizing about organizations (J. Walsh, Meyer, & Schoonhoven, 2006). Likewise, the research on organizations and the related prescriptions for organizational administration reflect great variety. Nevertheless, three generalizations can be made about the abundant multidisciplinary literature on formal organizations in the United States:

1. Early theories of organizations assumed that a rational organizational structure (bureaucracy) would ensure the effective and efficient accomplishment of organizational goals, which were assumed to be clear and specific.

Rational choice perspective

Contemporary theories challenge the rationality of formal organizations, but the image of the modern organization as a rational instrument (machine) of efficiency and predictability has had a lasting influence on theories of organizations (Farazmand, 2002; G. Morgan, 2006; Shafritz & Ott, 2005).

2. Early theories focused on what happens inside organizations and ignored all aspects of their external environments. In contrast, contemporary theories generally propose some sort of relationship between organization and environment (Garrow & Hasenfeld, 2010; G. Morgan, 2006; Northouse, 2007).

Systems perspective

Attention to the effects of the physical environment, both external and internal, on organizational life has been lacking, suggesting a possible new direction for organizational theory and research.

3. Most organizational theory has been biased toward the interests of owners and managers rather than those of workers (Farazmand, 2002; G. Morgan, 2006). In recent years, critical theorists have challenged this

Conflict perspective

one-sided view of organizations and raised questions about domination and oppression in organizational life (Farazmand, 2002; Garrow & Hasenfeld, 2010; G. Morgan, 2006).

Before going further, it is important to recognize that national culture has a great influence on the theories that are developed, and this is nowhere more true than in theorizing about formal organizations. Geert Hofstede (1996, 2001) argues that nationality has a large influence on organization theories, noting particularly that European organization theory shares some commonalities with that of the United States, but there are also some striking differences. Indeed, Hofstede suggests that there are philosophical differences in the way scholars in different European countries theorize about organizations. In his analysis, Hofstede asserts that organization theory is always constructed according to a worldview about where organizations come from, the foundation on which they are built. This worldview, he argues, is tied up in culture and varies from nation to nation. Here is what he suggests as the worldview undergirding organization theory in selected countries:

- Britain: systems

- China: the family

- Eastern Europe: efficiency

- France: power

- Germany: order

- Japan: Japan

- Netherlands: consensus

- Nordic countries: equality

- United States: the market

Recently, organization theorists have suggested the possibility of developing a more globally relevant theory of organizations (see Soulsby & Clark, 2007). They note that existing theories of organizations have been developed and studied in stable market-economic systems, usually in North America and Europe. They propose that study of the transformation of organizations in former socialist countries as they transitioned to market economies is a fruitful area for beginning to develop a more globally relevant theory (see Uhlenbruck, Meyer, & Hitt, 2003). However, at the moment, it appears that around the world, in Asia, Arab countries, Eastern Europe, and Russia, business schools are using translations of North American books on organization theory (Czarniawska, 2007). It is possible that the scholars in other countries will develop original theory as they try to adapt existing theory to fit their unique situations.

As noted above, Hofstede (1996) suggests that organization theory in the United States is strongly influenced by the high reverence for the market expressed in U.S. culture. You will probably note the market theme in some of the dominant organization theories in the United States. Often for social workers, particularly as we navigate human service organizations, this worldview is alienating and seems at odds with our ethic of care. Indeed, this is a major challenge to U.S. social workers, and perhaps increasingly to social workers in other countries in a globalized economy: how to provide caring services in organizations that operate within a societal context that reveres the market.

Please keep the important role of culture in mind as you read the discussion of theoretical perspectives in this chapter, which focuses primarily on organization theory developed in the United States. To date, there is little cross-pollination of organization theory across national lines. Several people have attempted to organize the weed patch of U.S. organizational theory into a garden—to bring some order to the diversity of viewpoints without denying the complexity and multifaceted nature of contemporary formal organizations (e.g., Garrow & Hasenfeld, 2010; Greenwald, 2008; G. Morgan, 2006). Here we use a classification system that includes four perspectives: rational perspective, systems perspective, interpretive perspective, and critical perspective. None of these perspectives, taken individually, accounts for all 16 functions of organizations listed in Exhibit 12.1, but taken together, they elaborate the multifaceted nature of organizations reflected in those functions. Each perspective encompasses both classical and contemporary theories, and each has relevance for social work practice.

As you read about these perspectives, you may want to keep in mind a recent suggestion (J. Walsh et al., 2006) that to be useful, contemporary research on organization theory needs to address three basic questions: (1) How can we understand current changing organizations (the theory question)? (2) How can we live *in* these organizations? (3) How can we more healthily live *with* these organizations? James Walsh and colleagues (2006) argue that existing theories of organizations fail to consider the powerful impact that contemporary organizations have on "human's social and material lives and on our planet's ecosystem" (p. 661) and that new theorizing is needed that takes these issues into account (see Marti, Etzion, & Leca, 2008, for a similar argument). This argument is consistent with social work's interest in social justice, and in the discussion below, I have tried to incorporate contemporary theories that are beginning to address these issues.

Critical Thinking Questions 12.1

Think of a formal organization of which you have been a part, for which you have positive feelings. What words come to mind when you think of this organization? Now, think of a formal organization of which you have been a part, for which you have negative feelings. What words come to mind when you think of this organization?

Rational Perspective

Rational choice
perspective

When Helen Blue became the executive director at Beacon Center, she was concerned about the lack of administrative formality, the lack of rules, and the ambiguous chain of command, among other things. She also wanted greater authority over planning and decision making. These concerns reflect the **rational perspective on organizations,** which views the formal organization as a "goal-directed, purposefully designed machine" (Garrow & Hasenfeld, 2010, p. 34). It assumes that organizations can be designed with structures and processes that maximize efficiency and effectiveness, concepts that are highly valued in this perspective. *Efficiency* means obtaining a high ratio of output to input, achieving the best outcome from the least investment of resources. *Effectiveness* means goal accomplishment. Exhibit 12.2 summarizes the central theories in this perspective.

Major theme: The organization is a goal-directed, purposefully designed machine (closed system).	
Theory	**Central Idea**
The ideal-type bureaucracy (Weber)	Formal rationality—rules, regulations, and structures—is essential to goal accomplishment.
Scientific management (Taylor)	The most effective organizations maximize internal efficiency, the "one best way."
Human relations theory	Human relationships are central to organizational efficiency and effectiveness.

▲ **Exhibit 12.2**   The Rational Perspective on Formal Organizations

The Ideal-Type Bureaucracy

In the modern era, formal organization is often equated with bureaucracy. Indeed, Max Weber (1947), the German sociologist who formulated a theory of bureaucracy at the beginning of the 20th century, saw bureaucracy and capitalism as inseparable. Weber proposed a **bureaucracy** as the most efficient form of organization for goal accomplishment. The characteristics of Weber's ideal-type bureaucracy are presented in Exhibit 12.3.

Weber (1947) was enthusiastic about the advantages of the ideal-type bureaucracy over other ways of organizing for goal accomplishment, but he did not see bureaucracies as problem free. He was concerned about the dehumanizing potential of bureaucracies—their potential to become an **iron cage of rationality**, trapping people and denying many aspects of their humanity. Researchers have noted that the excessive use of rules and procedures often limits the efficiency and effectiveness of bureaucratic organizations.

Despite the potential negative effects of bureaucracies, they continue to be the predominant form of organization in contemporary modern and postmodern societies, and the goal of maximization of efficiency is taken for granted. There is evidence, however, that some newer organizations are using less bureaucratic structures. This is true for human service organizations as well as organizations formed for other purposes (Hasenfeld, 2010b). Indeed, as Mary Katherine O'Connor and Ellen Netting (2009) suggest, most of the organizations that employ social workers have been influenced by the rational perspective but do not typically operate purely from this perspective. Moreover, as is the case with other types of organizations, their research has found that newer social service organizations are less likely than older ones to have traditional bureaucratic cultures. This means that a rational perspective will be less useful in understanding these newer organizations than it might be for understanding older social service organizations. How closely do the social work organizations you have worked in fit the ideal-type bureaucracy? How much emphasis is put on efficiency? Helen Blue and the two executive directors who followed her wanted to move Beacon Center closer to the ideal-type bureaucracy than it was under Martha Green's leadership.

Both Martha Green and Helen Blue might be interested in one researcher's findings that client satisfaction decreased as the level of bureaucracy increased in transitional housing programs for homeless families (Crook, 2001). In addition, conflict among residents increased as the level of organizational bureaucracy increased. The indirect impact of organizational bureaucracy on clients is called *trickle-down bureaucracy.*

Scientific Management

Another early 20th-century approach to formal organizations has had lasting influence. Frederick W. Taylor's (1911) **scientific management**, sometimes referred to as Taylorism, was directed toward maximizing internal

Ideal-Type Bureaucracy
Clear hierarchy and chain of command
Clear division of labor based on specialized skills
Formal rules of operation
Formal and task-oriented communications
Merit-based recruitment and advancement
Keeping of files and records for administrative action

▲ **Exhibit 12.3** Weber's Ideal-Type Bureaucracy

efficiency. The set of principles that Taylor developed to guide the design of organizations was widely adopted by both industry and government, first in the United States and then worldwide. These principles are listed in Exhibit 12.4.

In his provocative book *The McDonaldization of Society*, George Ritzer (2008a) proposes that McDonald's Corporation is a prototype organization, whose organizational style is coming to dominate much of the world. This new type of organization, which operates on the combined principles of bureaucratization and scientific management, has four key traits:

1. *Efficiency,* which is valued in a fast-paced society

2. *Calculability,* with an emphasis on saving time and money rather than on quality of product

3. *Predictability,* with the assurance that a Big Mac will be the same in San Francisco as in Washington, D.C., or Hong Kong

4. *Control,* with workers trained to do a limited number of things exactly as they are told to do them, and with maximum use of nonhuman technology

---

Scientific Management

Time and motion studies to find the "one best way" to perform each organizational task

Scientific selection and training of workers

Training focused on performing tasks in the standardized one best way

Close managerial monitoring of workers to ensure accurate implementation of task prescriptions and to provide appropriate rewards for compliance

Managerial authority over planning and decision making, with no challenge from workers

---

▲ **Exhibit 12.4**   Taylor's Scientific Management

▲ **Photo 12.2**   Formal organizations have important influences on human behavior—think about the impact McDonald's has had on human eating behaviors and our concept of "fast" food.

Ritzer gives many examples of the proliferation of the McDonald's model, including shopping malls; packaged tours; managed medical care; weight loss organizations; the "junk-food journalism" of *USA Today;* the use of machine-graded, multiple-choice examinations; reliance on GPAs, PSATs, SATs, and GREs for evaluating educational potential; franchised hotels; planned communities; and franchised child care centers.

Principles of scientific management are frequently followed in social service organizations. For example, some organizations undertake task and workload analyses to improve effectiveness and efficiency, and managers develop procedures, regulations, and decision trees to be implemented by direct service workers. The recent emphasis on *best practices* and *evidence-based practice* are derivative of scientific management thinking, but they do not typically conceive of "one best way." Have you encountered any of these in your field setting? Although Helen Blue initiated more procedures and regulations and believed in managerial authority over planning and decision making, she did not share scientific management's enthusiasm for "one best way" of delivering services.

Human Relations Theory

Human relations theory introduced a new twist on maximizing organizational efficiency and effectiveness. The theory grew out of a series of studies conducted by Elton Mayo (1933) and associates at the Hawthorne plant of the Western Electric Company in the 1920s and 1930s. Seeking to improve the rationality of the organization, the researchers were studying the effects of working conditions, such as intensity of lighting, on productivity. As expected, the researchers found that productivity increased as the lighting intensity increased. To their surprise, however, productivity continued to increase even when they began to dim the lights in an attempt to confirm their findings. The researchers concluded that technical rationality—the development of rational structures, procedures, and processes—is not sufficient to ensure maximum productivity. Social factors, they concluded, are as important as, if not more important than, technical factors in accomplishing organizational goals. They based this conclusion, which became the central proposition of a new theory, on their observation that productivity appeared to be related to worker morale and sense of social responsibility to the work group.

This interpretation of the research findings has been criticized on the basis of the **Hawthorne effect**—the tendency of experimental participants to perform in particular ways simply because they know they are being studied. In other words, critics have suggested that the participants in the study may have become more productive simply because they knew that their behavior was being studied.

Regardless of the validity of the initial findings, subsequent research led to the human relations theory of organizational management, which emphasized the heretofore unrecognized importance of human interaction in organizational efficiency and effectiveness. As the theory developed, it also proposed that democratic leadership is more effective than authoritarian management in securing worker cooperation.

The human relations approach has been a favorite theory in social service organizations because it calls attention to how staff attitudes about the work situation can influence how they relate to clients (see Garrow & Hasenfeld, 2010). The social workers at Beacon Center did indeed respond more cooperatively to Martha Green's democratic leadership than to Helen Blue's more authoritarian leadership. Furthermore, it appears that the staff cohesion did "trickle down" to improve consumer satisfaction as well.

It is important to note, however, that human relations theory is still in the rational tradition. Like scientific management, it focuses on maximizing efficiency and effectiveness, and it endorses the interests of owners and managers. Managers must become leaders capable of securing the cooperation of workers, but they are still in control of the organization. Although the consideration of human interaction opens the possibility of nonrational factors in organizational life, human relations theorists still assume that, with "leadership skills," human interactions can be as rationally managed as structures and procedures.

> Conflict perspective

After losing ground during the 1950s, human relations theory was reinvigorated in the 1960s by **organizational humanism** and a subfield called organizational development. These theories suggest that organizations can maximize efficiency and effectiveness while also promoting individual happiness and well-being. Douglas McGregor (1960), for example, a proponent of organizational humanism, identified two opposing sets of assumptions from which managers view workers (summarized in Exhibit 12.5). McGregor suggested that *Theory X* calls for directive management, but *Theory Y* calls for greater democratization of decision making in organizations. In your work experiences, have you encountered either of these theories about workers? If so, how did you react as a worker?

> Humanistic perspective

Assumptions of Theory X	Assumptions of Theory Y
Workers have an inherent dislike of work.	Workers see work as a natural activity.
Workers prefer to be told what to do.	Workers are self-directed when working on projects to which they are committed.
Workers respond to money as the primary motivator.	Workers seek responsibility when organizational goals are congruent with their needs. They have more creative contributions to make than organizations generally allow.

▲ **Exhibit 12.5**   Assumptions of Theory X and Theory Y

SOURCE: Based on McGregor (1960).

Although the rational perspective on organizations has been dominant in the design of organizations, including social service organizations, and has had some positive impact on productivity, it has been criticized on a number of grounds: It fails to consider external pressures on organizational decision makers. It overstates the rational capacity of organizational actors, assuming too much about their ability to understand all possible alternatives for action and the consequences of those actions. It fails to attend to the issue of power in organizational life. Garrow and Hasenfeld (2010) suggest that the rational perspective fails to take the moral basis of human service organizations into account.

Systems Perspective

Martha Green and Helen Blue had different styles of managing what happened inside Beacon Center, but they also had different styles of managing external pressures and resources. Martha focused on giving homeless persons a voice in efforts to secure political and economic resources for Beacon Center; Helen focused on conciliation with community and political leaders. In her own way, however, each was attentive to Beacon Center's relationship with its environment. In this respect, they negated the rational perspective's view of the organization as a closed system that can be controlled by careful attention to internal structure and processes. During the 1950s and 1960s, the rationalist view of organizations was challenged by the systems perspective, which seems to inform the efforts of both Martha Green and Helen Blue. All subsequent theorizing about organizations has been influenced by the systems perspective.

Systems perspective

The **systems perspective on organizations** builds on the fundamental principle that the organization is in constant interaction with its multiple environments—social, political, economic, cultural, technological—and must be able to adapt to environmental change. Some systems theorists suggest mutual influence between organizations and their environments; other theorists see the influence as unidirectional, with organizational structure and processes being determined by the environment. A second important principle of the systems perspective is that organizations are composed of interrelated subsystems that must be integrated in order to achieve the organization's goals and meet environmental demands. Finally, in contrast to the rational approach, the systems perspective holds that there are many different ways, rather than one best way, to reach the same ends. The idea that a system can attain its goals in a variety of ways is known as *equifinality*.

Several systems theories of organizations have been developed over time, but we look at only two here: the political economy model and the learning organization theory. These two theories are summarized in Exhibit 12.6.

Major theme: The organization is in constant interaction with multiple environments.	
Theory	**Central Idea**
Political economy model	The organization depends on the environment for political and economic resources.
Learning organization theory	The organization must be able to learn and change in a rapidly changing environment.

▲ **Exhibit 12.6** The Systems Perspective on Formal Organizations

Political Economy Model

The **political economy model** focuses on the dependence of organizations on their environments for necessary resources and on the impact of organization–environment interactions on the internal structure and processes of the organization (Wamsley & Zald, 1973). More specifically, it focuses on two types of resources necessary to organizations: political resources (legitimacy and power) and economic resources. The greater the dependence of the organization on the environment for either of these types of resources, the greater the influence the environment will have on the organization. Likewise, the greater control one unit of the organization has over resources, the more power that unit has over the organizational processes.

The political economy model is particularly potent for clarifying how social service organizations resolve such important issues as which clients to serve, which services to provide, how to organize service provision, and how to define staff and client roles (Garrow & Hasenfeld, 2010). Both Martha Green and Helen Blue were trying to read their political and economic environments as they made these kinds of decisions, but their different ways of thinking led them to attend to different aspects of the environment. The political economy model recognizes clients as resources and as potential players in the political arena. Social workers have an important role to play in facilitating their inclusion in the political process, a role that was part of Martha Green's vision for Beacon Center.

Learning Organization Theory

The **learning organization theory** was developed on the premise that rational planning is not sufficient for an organization to survive in a rapidly changing environment such as the one in which we live. Formal organizations must become complex systems that are capable of constant learning (Argyris, 1999; Argyris & Schön, 1978, 1996; Senge, 1990). The learning organization is one that can

- *Scan the environment, anticipate change, and detect "early warning" signs of trends and patterns.* In a social work context, this facility means understanding services from the points of view of clients as well as those of a variety of actors in the environment. It seems that Martha Green was more tuned in to the points of view of clients than Helen Blue was. On the other hand, Helen Blue seemed more sensitive to the points of view of some collaborating agencies.

- *Question, challenge, and change customary ways of operating.* Certainly, Helen Blue, like many new administrators, was questioning and challenging Martha Green's customary ways of operating. The important issue, however, was whether she was developing ways of operating that allowed and encouraged ongoing questioning, challenging, and changing. Ongoing growth requires dialogue, expression of conflicting points of view, and some risk taking.

Martha Green tried to develop a climate that allowed such dialogue, but the lack of staff diversity may have limited the nature of that dialogue.

- *Allow the appropriate strategic direction to emerge.* The learning organization needs vision, norms, values, and limits to guide organizational behavior (G. Morgan, 2006). But these should serve as guideposts, not straitjackets. Even these guideposts must be open for questioning. Ironically, both Martha Green's egalitarian vision and Helen Blue's vision of a more hierarchical organization had the potential to become straitjackets. Organizations need to be willing to look at both the benefits and the downside of their favored ways of operating—and to alter their strategic direction accordingly. Gareth Morgan emphasizes the importance of organizational limits, the "thou shalt nots" that guide organizational behavior. He suggests that Western organizations have put great emphasis on developing goals and objectives but have downplayed the limits needed to guide the actions taken to achieve those goals. There have been many reports of corporate misbehavior in the first decade of the 21st century, in both the private and public sectors, including social welfare organizations. Perhaps that is why we have been seeing an increasing call for "strong ethical leadership" in both sectors (Northouse, 2007). There is growing concern that organizations have established too few limits on behavior as they compete in a globalized and increasingly competitive and complex world.

- *Evolve designs that support continuous learning.* The challenge is to avoid anarchy on one hand and over-centralization on the other. The learning organization develops methods for shared decision making and avoids over-defining its members' actions. From this perspective, Beacon Center was more likely to be a learning organization under the leadership of Martha Green than under the leadership of Helen Blue.

Theories in the systems perspective have advanced organizational understanding by calling attention to the influence of the external environment on organizations. They provide useful concepts for considering how organizations survive in turbulent environments, and, indeed, Uhlenbruck et al. (2003) suggest that learning organization theory is an appropriate theoretical approach for understanding how organizations in former socialist countries successfully adapted to the transition to market economies. But the systems perspective has little to say about the moral purposes of social service organizations, or how organizations can be positive rather than negative forces in society. Recently, however, Stephen Gill (2010) has proposed learning organization theory as an appropriate model for nonprofit organizations. As we can see from the experience of Beacon Center, we live in a world that values the kind of order that Helen Blue wants to bring to Beacon Center, and there can be much environmental resistance to the development of learning organizations. But if nothing else, the idea of the learning organization serves as a bridge between the systems perspective and the interpretive perspective.

Interpretive Perspective

As I have been suggesting, when Helen Blue became executive director at Beacon Center, she wanted to introduce more "rational order" and have fewer internal voices speaking about the kind of place the center should be. It might be said that she found Martha Green's vision for Beacon Center to be too "interpretive." Theories of organizations within the **interpretive perspective on organizations** are quite diverse, but they all share one basic premise: Organizations are creations of human consciousness and reflect the worldviews of the creators; they are social constructions of reality.

> Social constructionist perspective

The interpretive perspective rejects both the rational and the systems perspectives. Contrary to the rational perspective, the interpretive perspective focuses on processes rather than goals, emphasizes flexibility rather than control and reason, and is interested in a diversity of approaches rather than one right way. From this perspective, organizations are seen as increasingly fragmented into multiple realities, and they should be studied through multiple voices rather than through the unitary voice of the manager. Contrary to the systems perspective, the interpretive perspective emphasizes human agency in creating organizations and challenges the constraining influence of external forces.

Different interpretive theorists focus on different themes in relation to the basic premises stated above. The three separate approaches summarized in Exhibit 12.7 will give you some sense of these differences.

Major theme: The organization is a social construction of reality	
Theory	**Central Idea**
Social action model (Silverman)	The organization is defined by individual actors.
Organizational culture model	Organizations are cultures with shared experiences and shared meanings.
Managing diversity model	Organizational systems and practices should maximize the potential advantages of diversity in organizational membership.

▲ **Exhibit 12.7**   The Interpretive Perspective on Formal Organizations

Social Action Model

One of the most influential contributions to the interpretive study of organizations is that of British sociologist David Silverman, presented in his 1971 book *The Theory of Organizations: A Sociological Framework*. Criticizing both rational and systems perspectives, Silverman proposed an approach that emphasizes the active role of individual organizational actors in creating the organization—an approach known as **Silverman's social action model.** He proposed a set of questions, presented in Exhibit 12.8, to ask when studying a specific organization.

In a more recent work, Silverman (1994) criticized the singular emphasis on organizational actors in his earlier model. He suggested that in reacting against deterministic theories of environmental constraints, he failed to acknowledge the influence of history and social structure. He further suggested that his portrayal of human behavior as free and undetermined failed to acknowledge the influence of cultural scripts and the tendency of humans to see their behavior as freer than it is. This self-critique is consistent with other criticisms of the limitations of the interpretive perspective (e.g., Reed, 1993; P. Thompson, 1993).

Who are the principal actors in the organization?

What goals are the actors trying to achieve?

How are the different actors involved in the organization?

What strategies do they use to achieve their goals?

What are the consequences of their actions for each other and for the development of interactional patterns in the organization?

▲ **Exhibit 12.8**   Silverman's Questions for Studying a Specific Organization (Social Action Model)

SOURCE: Silverman (1971).

Organizational Culture Model

In contrast to Silverman's de-emphasis on culture, Edgar Schein (1992) focuses on organizations as cultures whose members have shared experiences that produce shared meanings, or interpretations. Organizations, therefore, exist as much in the heads of their members as in policies, rules, and procedures. The **organizational culture model** views organizations as ongoing, interactive processes of reality construction, involving many organizational actors. Organizational culture is made up of language, slogans, symbols, rituals, stories, and ceremonies (G. Morgan, 2006), but also of mundane, routine, day-to-day activities. For example, under Martha Green's leadership, the slogan "client input" was an important feature of the Beacon Center culture, buttressed by the day-to-day practice of soliciting client opinions.

When we become new members of an organization, some aspects of its culture are immediately obvious. But other aspects are more difficult to decipher, causing us to feel uncomfortable and confused. For example, after one day in a field practicum agency, we may understand the cultural norms about casual versus professional dress and extended versus brief lunch hours, but it may take us several weeks to decipher whether we are in a cooperative or competitive culture. There may be a clear slogan about commitment to clients, but it may take some time to decipher how that commitment is implemented, or whether it is.

Organizational culture is always evolving, and it is not always unitary. In many organizations, like Beacon Center under the administration of Helen Blue, competing beliefs and value systems produce subcultures. Given the evolution of organizational culture and rapid societal changes, it is not unusual to find a split between the old guard and the new guard or to find cultural divisions based on organizational function. For example, members of prevention units in community mental health centers may speak a different language from clinicians in the same agency. The result may be cultural fragmentation or cultural warfare.

According to the organizational culture approach, organizations choose their environments and interact with them based on their interpretive schemes. It could be said that when Martha Green was executive director, Beacon Center saw itself as more humane than, and therefore superior to, other organizations serving homeless persons. Founders, staff, and board members had certain definitions of other agencies and of their client group that they used to influence referring agencies, funding sources, and clientele. They clearly saw themselves as proactive, capable of influencing their environments. This interpretive scheme could serve as a motivating factor, but it could also create barriers to their effective work with clients or other organizations. Indeed, other agencies often felt a certain resentment toward the arrogance and self-righteousness of Beacon Center under Martha Green's leadership. Under Helen Blue, on the other hand, clients and staff resented not being included in decisions.

Criticisms of the organizational culture approach are twofold (G. Morgan, 2006). One criticism is leveled at theorists who write about managing organizational culture. These theorists are sometimes criticized for being biased in favor of management and potentially exploitative of employees. They are also criticized for overstating managers' potential to control culture, negating the role of multiple actors in the creation of shared meaning. The second criticism of the organizational culture approach is that it fails to take account of the fact that some members have more power than others to influence the construction of culture.

Managing Diversity Model

In the 1990s, organizational theorists developed an approach to organizational management called the **managing diversity model.** Given the trend toward greater diversity in the labor force, several social scientists (e.g., T. Cox, 1993, 2001; Kossek, Lobel, & Brown, 2006; Mor Barak, 2005; Mor Barak & Travis, 2010) have suggested that contemporary organizations cannot be successful unless they can learn to manage diverse populations. Diversity is a permanent, not transitory, feature of contemporary life.

The purpose in managing diversity is to maximize the advantages of diversity while minimizing its disadvantages. Taylor Cox (1993), a leading proponent of the model, says "I view the goal of managing diversity as maximizing the ability of all employees to contribute to organizational goals and to achieve their full potential unhindered by group identities such as gender, race, nationality, age, and departmental affiliation" (p. 11). He argues that this goal requires that a new organizational culture must be institutionalized, a culture that welcomes diversity (T. Cox, 2001).

Mor Barak and Travis (2010) analyzed a decade of research about the linkages between organizational diversity and organizational performance. This research can be divided into the study of individual outcomes, workgroup outcomes, and organizational outcomes. The results were mixed in terms of individual outcomes, with some researchers finding that job satisfaction improves when workers find a higher proportion of people similar to them in values and ethnicity, and other researchers finding no such association. Likewise, mixed results were found in regard to diversity and workgroup outcomes. Some researchers found that the quality of ideas produced by workgroups increased as racial and ethnic diversity increased, other researchers found that racially diverse groups had more emotional conflict than racially homogeneous workgroups, and still other researchers found no relationship between extent of diversity of workgroup cohesion and performance. The results were also mixed regarding the relationship between diversity and organizational performance, but the majority of studies report positive relationships in both the corporate sector and the human service sector, meaning that organizational performance improves as diversity in the workforce increases.

Management of diversity is still a young idea and a long distance from the one right way of the rational perspective, which has dominated modern thinking about organizations. Pioneering organizations in the United States have begun to develop specific tools to assist organizations to become more effective at managing diversity. They emphasize a vision that values diversity, reflection of diversity in hiring and promotion policies, diversity training, language training, use of identity-based advisory groups, incorporating minority perspectives into organizational norms and culture, affirmative action programs, mentoring programs, and company-based social events (T. Cox, 2001). Mor Barak (2005) emphasizes the need to recognize different cultural expectations about interpersonal relationships in the workplace. Mor Barak and Travis (2010) note that social service organizations have historically served a diverse client population but have not historically hired a diverse workforce. Although the workforce in social service organizations has been gradually becoming more diverse, it lags behind the diversity of the clients served.

Critical Perspective

Although it may appear that Martha Green administered Beacon Center from an interpretative perspective, it is probably more accurate to describe her worldview as a **critical perspective on organizations.** She tried to minimize the power differences in her organization, and when she asked her staff to vote on sensitive issues, she invoked the secret ballot to neutralize any possible power dynamics. Critical theorists share the interpretive perspective's bias about the role of human consciousness in human behavior, but critical theory undertakes, as its central concern, a critique of existing power arrangements and a vision for change suggested by this critique. More specifically, critical theories see organizations as instruments of exploitation and domination, where conflicting interests are decided in favor of the most powerful members. This focus distinguishes the critical perspective from the interpretive perspective, which generally ignores or negates issues of power and the possibility that people in power positions can privilege their own versions of reality and marginalize other versions, thus controlling the organizational culture.

> Conflict perspective

The critical perspective has roots in Robert Michels' work in the early 20th century. Michels (1911/1959) wrote about the "iron law of oligarchy" (rule by the few), arguing that as bureaucracies grow, they always end up under the control of a very narrow, elite group. The elite make decisions with an eye toward preserving their own power, and other voices are suppressed (G. Morgan, 2006). Gareth Morgan draws on the work of a diverse group of theorists and researchers to identify several ways in which organizations serve as "instruments of domination":

- Formal organizations create and continually reproduce patterns of social inequality through organizational hierarchies.

- Employees are exposed to work conditions that are hazardous to their health and welfare—such as working with toxic materials or dangerous equipment—and to work expectations that interfere with personal health maintenance and family life.

- Employees experience mental health problems caused by job insecurity in a downsizing and globalizing economy.

Exhibit 12.9 summarizes the two contemporary critical approaches to formal organizations discussed here: organizations as multiple oppressions and nonhierarchical organizations.

Organizations as Multiple Oppressions

Have you ever felt oppressed—voiceless, powerless, abused, manipulated, unappreciated—in any of the organizations of which you have been a member? Do you think that whole groups of people have felt oppressed in any of those organizations? In the contemporary era, the critical perspective has taken a more focused look at who is oppressed in organizations and the ways in which they are oppressed. This approach was influenced by feminist critiques, during the 1970s and 1980s, of the failure of traditional organization theories to consider gender issues (J. Hearn & Parkin, 1993). Feminist critiques led to the recognition that other groups besides women had also been marginalized by formal organizations and by organization theory.

Jeff Hearn and Wendy Parkin (1993) recommend viewing **organizations as multiple oppressions**—social constructions that exclude and discriminate against some categories of people. According to these authors, oppression happens through a variety of processes, including "marginalization, domination and subordination, degradation, ignoring, harassment, invisibilizing, silencing, punishment, discipline and violence" (p. 153). These processes may also be directed at a variety of organizational actors, including "staff, members, employees, residents, patients and clients" (p. 153). Organizational domination can become compounded by multiple oppressions. Hearn and Parkin cite the example of a children's home where children were being sexually abused by male staff, and female staff were dissuaded, by intimidation, from reporting the situation. This idea that multiple oppressions are usually embedded in organizational life has also been addressed in a book by Sharon Kurtz (2002), who argues that addressing the situation of only one oppressed group will never get to the heart of the matrix of domination in organizations.

Major Theme: Organizations Are Instruments of Domination	
Theory	Central Idea
Organizations as multiple oppressions	Organizations exclude and discriminate against multiple groups.
Nonhierarchical organizations	Organizations run by consensus, with few rules and with informality, are least likely to oppress employees.

▲ **Exhibit 12.9**   The Critical Perspective on Formal Organizations

According to Hearn and Parkin (1993), frequently oppressed groups include women, younger and older people, persons with disabilities, those of lower economic class, persons of color, and sexual minorities. These groups may be excluded from organizations; admitted only in subordinate roles as clients, patients, or students; or admitted but discriminated against within the organization. If groups that are excluded or otherwise oppressed form their own organizations, dominant groups construct a hierarchy of organizations that maintains the oppression, as when a Black organization is viewed as inferior to similar White organizations.

Hearn and Parkin (1993) suggest that at the current time, the group most marginalized by formal organizations is people with disabilities. They are often physically excluded from organizations by inaccessible physical environments, and they are further marginalized by a "prevailing ideology . . . of medicine and medication, with people's disabilities being seen as sickness or illness and able-bodied people being seen as able and well, rather [than] the environment being disabling" (pp. 157–158).

Critical theory, with its focus on domination and oppression, reminds us that mainstream organizational theory is theory for the elite and not theory for the exploited. Therefore, our understanding of organizations is incomplete and biased. If you have felt somewhat alienated in reading about other theories in this chapter, you may be reacting to this bias. However, critical theory has been criticized for being ideological, giving priority to the voices of oppressed persons, just as Martha Green was criticized for giving too strong a voice to homeless persons. Critical theorists reply that their focus is no more ideological than is recognizing only the voices of the elite.

The critical perspective on organizations has special relevance to social workers. It helps us recognize the ways in which clients' struggles are related to oppressive structures and processes in the formal organizations with which they interact. It can help us to understand the ways in which social service organizations are gendered, with women constituting the majority of human service workers and men assuming key administrative roles. It also calls our attention to the power imbalance between clients and social workers and helps us think critically about how we use our power. We must be constantly vigilant about the multiple oppressions within the organizations where we work, as well as those with which we interact, as we try to promote social justice.

Nonhierarchical Organizations

Helen Blue preferred a more hierarchical organizational structure than the one developed at Beacon Center under Martha Green's leadership. A constant theme in critical theory is that hierarchical organizational structures lead to alienation and internal class conflict. Critical theorists directly challenge the rational perspective argument that hierarchy is needed to maximize efficiency; they point out that in fact hierarchy is often inefficient, but that it is maintained because it works well to protect the positions of those in power. For example, the staff at Beacon Center wasted much time and energy trying to find ways to thwart Helen Blue's decisions.

> Humanistic perspective

The idea of the **nonhierarchical organization** is not new. Human relations theorists have recommended "participatory management," which involves lower-level employees in at least some decision making, for several decades. Historical evidence indicates that since the 1840s, experiments with nonhierarchical organizations have accompanied every wave of antimodernist social movements in the United States (Rothschild-Whitt & Whitt, 1986). There have also been unsuccessful experiments with power sharing in French organizations (Hofstede, 1996). Beginning in the 1970s, feminist critiques of organizational theory helped to stimulate renewed interest in nonhierarchical organizations (Kravetz, 2004). Nevertheless, such organizations constitute only a small portion of the population of formal organizations, and research on nonhierarchical organizations constitutes a very small part of the massive body of research on organizations (Garrow & Hasenfeld, 2010; Iannello, 1992).

Exhibit 12.10 lists the traits of a model of nonhierarchical organization that Kathleen Iannello (1992) calls the consensual model. Studies of nonhierarchical organizations summarize some of the special challenges, both

Authority vested in the membership rather than in an elite at the top of a hierarchy

Decisions made only after issues have been widely discussed by the membership

Rules kept to a minimum

Personal, rather than formal, relationships among members

Leadership based on election, with rotation of leadership positions

No financial reward for leadership roles

No winners and losers in decision making—decisions made based on unchallenged "prevailing sentiment" (consensus)

▲ **Exhibit 12.10**   Traits of a Consensual Model of Formal Organizations

SOURCE: Iannello (1992).

internal and external, faced by consensual organizations (Ferree & Martin, 1995; Kravetz, 2004; Rothschild-Whitt & Whitt, 1986). Internal challenges include increased time needed for decision making, increased emotional intensity due to the more personal style of relationships, and difficulty incorporating diversity. External challenges are the constraints of social, economic, and political environments that value and reward hierarchy (Garrow & Hasenfeld, 2010).

On the basis of her study of two successful feminist organizations, Iannello (1992) proposed that the internal challenges of the nonhierarchical organization could be addressed by what she calls a "modified consensual organization" model. Critical decisions continue to be made by the broad membership, but routine decisions are made by smaller groups; members are recognized by ability and expertise, but not by rank and position; there are clear goals, developed through a consensual process. Similarly, reporting on the life course of five feminist organizations initiated in the 1970s, Diane Kravetz (2004) found that these organizations developed "modified hierarchies" as they grew and faced new external challenges. They gradually delegated authority to individuals and committees but retained some elements of consensus decision making.

The two most prominent contemporary examples of organizations based on consensus are feminist organizations and Japanese firms. Both types of organizations typically feature a strong shared ideology and culture, which should lead to relatively easy consensus. However, the available evidence suggests that feminist organizations in which membership crosses either ideological or cultural lines have not been successful in operating by consensus (Barnoff & Moffatt, 2007; Ferree & Martin, 1995; Iannello, 1992; Riger, 1994). Under Martha Green's administration, most decisions at Beacon Center were made by consensus, but Martha was sometimes criticized for building a staff with little ideological or cultural diversity.

One trend to watch is the one toward worker-owned corporations, both in the United States and Europe. Sometimes these corporations are not truly democratic, with strong worker input into decisions, but there is evidence that they are moving toward greater democratization (Alperovitz, 2005). The fact that the number of worker-owned companies in the United States increased from 1,600 in 1975 to 11,000 in 2003 seems to be a sign that the idea of shared leadership is gaining in popularity (Alperovitz, 2005).

Given the increasing diversity of the workforce in the United States, management of difference and conflict can be expected to become an increasing challenge in organizational life. This is as true for social work organizations as for others. To date, the literature on consensual organizations has failed to address the difficult challenges of diverse ideological and cultural perspectives among organizational members—issues that are the focus of the managing diversity model. This is an area in which social work should take the lead.

In Canada, one notable exception has occurred. Feminist critiques of social service organizations have led to growing interest in *anti-oppressive* social work practice at both the direct practice and organizational practice levels. The anti-oppression model seeks to develop social service organizations that are free from all types of domination and privilege (Barnoff & Moffatt, 2007). This is not an easy task, and researchers have identified some barriers to these efforts. First, they have found that when different groups of women encounter each other, they develop a *hierarchy of oppression,* in which women in different identity groups engage in ongoing competition about which group is most oppressed, with the different groups failing to look beyond their own experience to recognize the plight of other oppressed groups. Second, tension often develops between White women and women of color when White women try to control the agenda but lack awareness of how they are using White privilege to advance their own positions in the organization. Lisa Barnoff and Ken Moffatt conclude that anti-oppressive social work practice can be advanced only when privilege is a central concept in the discussion of oppression. Members of different identity groups need to recognize their own sources of privilege and give serious thought to how exercise of that privilege results in the subordination of others.

Critical Thinking Questions 12.2

Think back to your earlier ideas about the characteristics of an organization for which you have positive feelings. Which of the theoretical perspectives discussed above seem to best describe that organization? Can you use specific theoretical concepts to talk about that organization? Now, think of your ideas about the characteristics of an organization for which you have negative feelings? Which of the theoretical perspectives seems to best describe that organization? Can you use specific theoretical concepts to describe the organization?

BURNOUT: A NEGATIVE ORGANIZATIONAL OUTCOME

It was suggested at the beginning of this chapter that formal organizations meet our needs, assist us to fulfill goals, and nurture our development—but that they also make stressful demands, thwart our goals, inhibit our holistic development, and constrain our behavior. Robert T. Golembiewski (1994) used more colorful language to talk about the negative effects of organizations, suggesting that "organizational life bends people out of shape, and may even make them crazy" (p. 211). Indeed, some of the staff at Beacon Center were heard to say, after Helen Blue took over, that they must leave the center before they go crazy. This same lament has been heard from the current social workers who have struggled with the chaos of the brief stay of the last executive director.

In the past two decades, researchers have attempted to answer the question, is organizational membership hazardous to your health? The answer, to date, is that organizational membership is *often* hazardous to health, and burnout is the identified hazard. **Burnout** is a "prolonged response to chronic emotional and interpersonal stressors on the job, and is defined by the three dimensions of exhaustion, cynicism, and inefficacy" (Maslach, Schaufeli, & Leiter, 2001, p. 397). The study of burnout has appeal because it can give voice to individuals who are dominated or exploited in organizations, providing "organizational theory for the exploited," as recommended by Gareth Morgan (2006).

Burnout is most often studied using the Maslach Burnout Inventory (MBI) (Maslach & Jackson, 1981). The MBI, first developed for use with human service workers and later revised for use with teachers, analyzes three dimensions of burnout: (1) emotional exhaustion, or a feeling of being near the end of one's rope; (2) depersonalization, or a strong tendency to distance oneself from others, thinking of them as things or objects; and (3) reduced personal accomplishment, which refers to perceptions of doing well on a worthwhile project. In recent years, the MBI has been revised for use in occupations other than human services and education that are not as people oriented. The three dimensions of burnout have been conceptualized in the broader terms found in the previous definition of burnout: exhaustion, cynicism, and inefficacy (reduced personal accomplishment).

Golembiewski (1994) has built an eight-phase model of burnout based on these three domains, with depersonalization representing the least serious domain; reduced personal accomplishment a more serious domain; and emotional exhaustion the most serious domain, occurring in late-phase burnout. Golembiewski reports on extensive research with a large number of both public sector and business organizations, and found several indicators of well-being to be associated with the phases of burnout. With progression through the phases of burnout, research participants report increasingly less work satisfaction; lower self-esteem; greater physical symptoms; lower performance appraisals; and greater hostility, anxiety, and depression.

Golembiewski (1994) found that approximately 45% of 16,476 participants from 55 organizations were in the last three phases of burnout, with high levels of emotional exhaustion, as indicated by their scores on the MBI. Recent international research has noted high levels of burnout among physicians and other health care providers (Bell, Davison, & Sefcik, 2002; Clever, 2002; Jancin, 2002; McManus, Winder, & Gordon, 2002). The high level of hazard in so many settings suggests that social workers need to be attuned to symptoms of job-related burnout in their clients and in themselves.

Burnout has been found to be associated with absenteeism, turnover, lower productivity and effectiveness at work, decreased job satisfaction, and reduced commitment to the job or the organization. Burnout can be contagious, causing interpersonal conflict and disrupting work.

After 25 years of research on the subject, researchers found six dimensions of work life to be associated with burnout (Maslach et al., 2001):

1. *Workload.* Work overload makes too many demands and exhausts people's capacity to recover. Workload has been found to be directly related to the exhaustion dimension of burnout. Cross-national comparisons have found that workers in North America have higher levels of burnout than workers in Western Europe, particularly higher levels of exhaustion and cynicism (Maslach et al., 2001). As you may recall, we noted in Chapter 9 that workers in the United States work longer hours than those in Western Europe.

2. *Control.* People may have inadequate control over the resources needed to do their work, or they may be given responsibilities without the authority to do the work. These situations are associated with inefficacy (reduced personal accomplishment). The social workers at Beacon Center missed Martha Green's trust in them to make their own decisions, and they chafed at their diminishing control over their work and the direction of the organization after Helen Blue became the administrator.

3. *Reward.* Organizations may fail to provide appropriate rewards for the work that people do. There may be inadequate financial rewards, but social rewards, such as recognition and appreciation for contributions made, may also be missing. In addition, the work itself may not have intrinsic rewards because it does not feel important and useful. Lack of reward is associated with inefficacy. The social workers at Beacon Center once found that the social rewards more than made up for the poor pay, but they now miss the feeling that they are working in a special place and making a difference.

4. *Community.* In some organizations, people do not have a sense of positive connections to others. People may work in isolation from others, their interactions may be impersonal, or there may be chronic and unresolved conflict with others on the job. Social support from supervisors has been found to be particularly important. It is clear that a sense of community broke down when Martha Green left Beacon Center.

5. *Fairness.* There may be inequity of workload or pay, or work evaluations and promotions may be handled unfairly. Feelings of being treated unfairly are associated with exhaustion as well as with cynicism about the workplace.

6.   *Values.* Sometimes people face situations where the job requires them to compromise their ethical standards. Or they may find that there is a discrepancy between what the organization says it values and the day-to-day activities in the organization. Increasingly, human service organizations face a conflict between the competing values of high-quality service and cost containment. Little research has been done on the role of values in burnout. The original social workers at Beacon Center put high value on advocating for their homeless clients, and they were alienated by Helen Blue's request that they become more moderate in those efforts.

The research to date indicates that organizational factors play a bigger role in burnout than individual factors. And yet, greater attention has been given to individual-oriented approaches to preventing burnout than to changing aspects of organizations.

It has been suggested that social work is an occupation with above-average risk of burnout, but research does not seem to support this. One research team compared the burnout profiles for five occupational groups—teaching, social services, medicine, mental health, and law enforcement—in the United States and Holland (Schaufeli & Enzmann, 1998). They found that the comparisons differed by nation. In the United States, the levels of cynicism were higher for social service workers and mental health workers than for the other occupational groups, but they were about average in Holland. Other than that, the levels of burnout were about average for social service workers in both countries. We know that our work as social workers has many satisfactions as well as many stressors, but further research is needed to discover which way the balance tilts and why.

Mary Guy and colleagues (Guy, Newman, Mastracci, & Maynard-Moody, 2010) have examined the relationship between emotional labor and burnout. They define **emotional labor** as "the engagement, suppression, or evocation of the worker's emotions necessary to get the job done" (p. 292). They argue that emotional labor is the key feature of the therapeutic relationship between social worker and client. Their research indicates that emotional labor can lead to burnout, but it can also lead to job satisfaction. When it leads to burnout, the worker feels emotional exhaustion, stress, cynicism, and lack of effectiveness. When emotional labor leads to job satisfaction, the worker feels energetic, involved, and a sense of accomplishment. Guy et al. found that social workers are more likely to experience burnout if they have to fake their emotional expressions in the course of their work and if they lack confidence in their ability to perform emotional work.

One recent small-scale research project attempted to discover the balance of job satisfaction and burnout among one sample of social workers. David Conrad and Yvonne Kellar-Guenther (2006) investigated burnout among child protection workers in Colorado. They sought to understand the relationship between *compassion fatigue* (reduced capacity for empathy caused by an overexposure to suffering), burnout (emotional exhaustion, depersonalization, and inefficacy), and *compassion satisfaction* (fulfillment from helping others and from positive collegial relationships). They found that about 50% of their sample suffered from compassion fatigue, only 7.7% suffered from burnout, and 75% had high levels of compassion satisfaction. Furthermore, they found that the respondents with higher compassion satisfaction had lower levels of burnout and compassion fatigue than respondents with lower levels of compassion satisfaction. This is consistent with the findings of Guy et al. that emotional labor can lead to job satisfaction as well as burnout, and may help to explain earlier findings that social workers are not much more prone to burnout than people in other occupations. These findings suggest that the concept of compassion satisfaction is worthy of further attention by social work researchers.

SOCIAL WORK AND FORMAL ORGANIZATIONS

You have probably learned already that social work is a diverse profession; we use diverse methods to address a diversity of social problems—and we work in diverse types of organizations. We work in hospitals, outpatient health and mental health clinics, in-home programs, nursing homes and other residential programs, crisis shelters, prisons and jails, government social service agencies, private family and children's agencies, schools, the workplace, community centers, social movement organizations, research centers, planning organizations, social entrepreneurial organizations, and in private practice, among other places.

We can think about the differences among the organizations in which social workers are found in several ways. One is to divide them into host organizations, social work–oriented organizations, and human service organizations (Popple & Leighninger, 2005). In *host organizations*—such as schools, the workplace, correctional facilities, the military, and hospitals—social service is not the primary purpose of the organization. Social workers in these settings work with other disciplines to meet organizational goals, and they often serve as mediators between clients and the organization. In contrast, *social work–oriented organizations* have social service delivery as their purpose and are staffed primarily by social workers. Family and children's agencies and government social service programs are examples of social work–oriented organizations. Social workers also work in *human service organizations,* whose staff come from a variety of disciplines but work in a coordinated fashion to provide an array of services. Community mental health centers and drug treatment programs are examples of human service organizations.

Another way to think about formal organizations in which social workers work has traditionally been to divide them into public and private organizations. *Public social service organizations* are those funded and administered by local, state, or federal government; *private social service organizations* are privately funded and administered. This distinction made some sense in earlier eras, but it is not very useful in the contemporary era. Today, many public agencies contract programs out to private organizations, and many private organizations, like Beacon Center, receive public as well as private funding. The Social Security Act of 1935 ushered in an era of government dominance in both the funding and administering of social service programs, but for the past two decades, we have seen increasing **privatization** of social services, shifting the administration of programs back to private organizations (Karger & Stoesz, 2006; L. Lynn, 2002). This trend is based on a belief that privatization will lead to more efficient and effective service delivery. It has been estimated that more than half of public social service dollars are contracted to private organizations (O'Connor & Netting, 2009).

Among private service organizations, the distinction between *nonprofit* and *for-profit* organizations is increasingly important, but also increasingly blurred. Social workers have a long history with nonprofit organizations, also called

▲ **Photo 12.3** The 100,000-square-foot Children and Family Services Center in Charlotte, North Carolina, an innovative marriage of public and private sector organizations.

voluntary agencies and *nongovernmental organizations* (NGOs), but their extensive involvement in for-profit organizations is more recent and has been increasing steadily since the 1970s (Karger & Stoesz, 2006; L. Lynn, 2002). Since the passage of the Personal Responsibility and Work Opportunity Reconciliation Act (PRWORA) of 1996, a number of high-profile for-profit corporations, like Lockheed Martin, have entered the welfare-to-work market (Karger & Stoesz, 2006). Large for-profit organizations have had the resources to move quickly into new markets and have become serious competitors for nonprofit organizations in vying for government contracts. Some nonprofit organizations are responding by developing partnerships with for-profit organizations; others are changing to for-profit status. Indeed, many nonprofits use some profit-making programs, such as thrift stores, to shore up their income base. There is general agreement that for-profit organizations will continue to have a large presence in the social service landscape in the future. This is the case even though the current research evidence indicates that they have not met their promise to cut costs (Karger & Stoesz, 2006).

The entry of for-profit organizations into the social service arena poses questions that have been raised by many observers: Will for-profit organizations, in search of profitable business opportunities, voluntarily serve the common good? Will they engage in advocacy and community-building activities that are the hallmark of the social work profession and the history of nonprofit organizations? Will they deny service as a cost-cutting measure, particularly service to clients with the most entrenched problems? Historically, social service agencies funded advocacy and community-building activities out of surplus from other programs. Social workers will need to be vigilant to see that these important social work functions do not disappear. There is also some fear that very large for-profit organizations will have undue influence on social welfare policy in a way that protects their own interests (Karger & Stoesz, 2006).

Organizations in which social workers work have not been immune to the economic trends discussed in Chapter 9. Downsizing and the resulting "do more with less" climate have increased work-related stressors, and increasing economic inequality is producing stubborn social problems that must be addressed with shrinking resources. Social workers, like other workers, are increasingly involved in "contingent" labor situations—that is, in part-time, temporary, and contractual arrangements. There is increasing evidence that social service organizations are favoring clients who can pay, or who qualify for payment by a third party, and they are failing to serve people who are poor or have the most challenging problems (L. Lynn, 2002; W. Ryan, 1999). The "information revolution" has raised new issues about protection of client confidentiality. Unfortunately, social welfare organizations, particularly in the nonprofit sector, have not been immune to the fraud and scandal that have embroiled many large corporations in the past decade. Given these challenges, a solid grounding in organizational theory can be an important tool in the social work survival kit.

Social service organizations, like other organizations, are trying to survive in turbulent, complex times. They must continuously adjust their services in response to changing societal trends, such as growing diversity in population and lifestyles and growing inequality. In recent times, they have had to adapt to a political environment that shifted from thinking of social service organizations in terms of social care to an emphasis on the market and personal responsibility (Hasenfeld, 2010b). It is unclear whether recent failures in the market will undermine popular reverence for the market model.

Two types of human service organizations are becoming more prominent in the social service landscape: hybrid organizations and social entrepreneurial organizations. **Hybrid organization** is the name given to organizations that combine political advocacy and service provision in their core identity (Minkoff, 2010). This type of social service organization has a history in organizations developed by women, Blacks, and other ethnic groups in the 1960s. These organizations make a strong commitment to service to typically underserved populations, but they also engage in advocacy work that is often focused on changing the perspectives of political figures and the general public on specific social problems. For example, homeless service organizations like Beacon Center have attempted to change public perception of homelessness, pushing for a framework that focuses on homelessness as the failure of housing policy rather than a consequence of personal failings. Advocacy work by nonprofit organizations has been steadily increasing in the past few decades (M. Meyer, 2010).

A **social entrepreneurial organization** is one that is formed by a social entrepreneur who recognizes a social problem and uses ideas from business entrepreneurs to organize, create, and manage a new venture to bring about social change related to that problem. The most famous social entrepreneurial organization is the Grameen Bank developed by Muhammad Yunus, a Bangladeshi economist who was the winner of the 2006 Nobel Peace Prize. The idea of using social entrepreneurship to solve social problems is spreading around the world (O'Connor & Netting, 2009).

Yeheskel Hasenfeld (2010a) has asked the question, "What is different about human service organizations?" In answering it, he identifies six attributes that set human service organizations apart from other organizations:

1. They engage in moral work, making judgments about what constitutes good behavior and a good society.

2. They get their legitimacy from the broader institutional society.

3. They must negotiate different interest groups that have different goals for the organization.

4. Client–staff relationships are the primary vehicle of service provision.

5. Emotional labor is their primary resource and must be harnessed through recruitment, training, and supervision.

6. They are gendered organizations where women are the majority of the frontline workers, matching the societal ideology that emotional work is women's work.

If this is an accurate representation of the attributes of human service organizations, we can ask another question: Is one kind of leadership better than another for the human service organization? That is exactly the question that the staff and board of directors of Beacon Center are asking as they begin to search for a new executive director.

SOCIAL WORK LEADERSHIP IN FORMAL ORGANIZATIONS

With the pervasive influence of formal organizations in complex societies, attention has turned to a fascination with organization leadership. Books are being written, academic programs in leadership studies are being developed, and professional associations (including the Council on Social Work Education) are developing "leadership initiatives." This intense focus on leadership seems to be driven by a frustration with the performance and impact of formal organizations as well as by a hope that we can engineer and manage them better—in such a way to minimize their adverse effects and magnify their positive ones (Northouse, 2007). This concern applies to the formal organizations where social work is practiced, as well as to other formal organizations that affect our lives and those of our clients.

In Chapter 11, we presented Northouse's (2007) definition of leadership: *a process whereby an individual influences a group of individuals to achieve a common goal* (p. 3). Northouse made a distinction between *assigned leadership* and *emergent leadership*. Assigned leaders occupy organizational positions that carry with them *formal authority* to influence others toward a common goal. They might be in a position called director, department head, administrator, supervisor, committee chair, or team leader. An emergent leader, on the other hand, is someone whose influence is recognized by others regardless of position; the emergent leader has *personal authority* rather than *formal authority*.

As social workers carry out their work in formal organizations, they may act sometimes as assigned leaders and sometimes as emergent leaders. I agree with O'Connor and Netting's (2009) premise that every social worker carries leadership responsibility in the organizations where he or she works; such responsibility goes with being a social worker. They define leadership as "an attitude about responsibilities in an organization based on professional skills and a set of values that compel an individual to act" (p. 29).

There are a number of theories of leadership (see, e.g., Northouse, 2007), and different perspectives on organizations call for different approaches to leadership. Certainly, you can imagine how the approach to thinking about leadership from a scientific management perspective is different from the approaches of an interpretive or critical perspective.

In addition, it seems obvious that the nature of the organization itself will render some ways of leading more effective than others. Social work leaders pay attention to all of this. In spite of the complexity, some core leadership competencies can be identified. They include the following: problem-identification, problem-solving, and solution-generating skills; ability to critically analyze our own beliefs and attitudes; ability to critically analyze the beliefs and attitudes of others; ability to forgo early judgments; ability to conceptualize and articulate a vision and a plan; and good written, verbal, and nonverbal communication skills. In the contemporary, globalized, multicultural world, social work leaders must be able to live with change and flux, live with ambiguity, and recognize multiple perspectives on situations. We must know how to maneuver bureaucracies and complex systems, manage diversity, and recognize and struggle against the multiple oppressions that we encounter in our own and other organizations. Every social worker is responsible to build this set of capabilities.

Social work scholars have also been interested in assigned leadership and the skills needed to direct social service agencies and social work educational programs. Michael Rank and William Hutchison (2000) undertook telephone interviews with a random sample of 75 executive directors and presidents of social service agencies and 75 deans and directors of social work education programs, with the goal of learning their views on social work leadership. The top three leadership skills identified by this sample were as follows: (1) building community; (2) communicating orally and in writing; and (3) performing comprehensive analysis of social, political, and cultural events. A decade later, one can conjecture that these leaders would identify skills in the use of computer-based technologies as an important part of the skill set for social work leaders.

Globalization is leading to a need to develop and maintain effective organizations that cross national borders. Increasingly, social workers work in and provide leadership to transnational service and advocacy organizations. Hofstede, Deusen, Mueller, and Charles (2002) suggest that transnational organizations are often unsuccessful because of cultural differences in attitudes about goals and appropriate traits of leaders. What is needed in such organizations are leaders who can become competent in cross-cultural awareness and communication. To that end, Robert House and colleagues (2004) have engaged in ongoing study of the attitudes about leadership in 62 societies. They have found that societies vary in their attitudes about leadership on a number of identified dimensions: uncertainty avoidance, power sharing, collective spirit and action, gender egalitarianism, assertiveness, future orientation, performance orientation, and humane orientation. For U.S. social workers working in transnational organizations, it is important to know that in this research the Anglo cluster of societies—which includes the United States, Australia, Ireland, United Kingdom, White South Africa, and New Zealand—puts much more value on performance orientation and much less value on collectivism than respondents in other societies.

CULTURALLY SENSITIVE CARE SYSTEMS

Issues of diversity, and managing diversity, are important for all formal organizations, but they take on special urgency in social service organizations. Social workers have a commitment to provide competent service to diverse populations. (We take a broad view of diversity, including, but not limited to, gender, race, ethnicity, social class, religion, disability, age, and sexual orientation.) In recent years, a growing body of literature has recommended ways of providing culturally competent practice (e.g., Devore & Schlesinger, 1999; Green, 1999; Lum, 2007; Rothman, 2008). When I lived in Washington, D.C., in an area where one school might serve a student body representing well over 100 national heritages, I came to think in terms of providing *culturally sensitive practice,* rather than culturally competent practice. As Ruth G. Dean (2001) so aptly stated, to work effectively across cultural lines typically requires that we begin with a recognition that we are not competent in the culture of another, and from this position of "informed not knowing" (Laird, 1998), we establish a goal to understand.

Although there is much an individual social worker can do to provide more culturally sensitive practice, individual efforts will not go far unless the vision of cultural sensitivity is encoded into the fabric of social service organizations. Some effective guidelines for developing a culturally sensitive system of care can be gleaned from a number of sources (see Beckett & Dungee-Anderson, 1998; Green, 1999; Lum, 2007; Mor Barak, 2000; Rothman, 2008). As you read these traits, keep in mind that some social service organizations serve a multicultural population, while others target a specific cultural group.

- The organization is located where it is accessible to the targeted population, and it is decorated in a manner appealing to the population. Particular attention is paid to the accessibility of the physical environment for people with a variety of disabilities.

- A name is chosen for the organization that is acceptable to the targeted population. For example, for some ethnic groups, "mental health services" carries a social stigma, and these words should be avoided when naming the organization. A name like Beacon Center carries no such stigma.

- Diversity is reflected in the board of directors, administrators, and professional and nonprofessional staff, in accordance with the targeted population. The organization is engaged in an ongoing audit of the diversity represented at all levels, from clients to the board of directors.

- The organization conducts or supports ongoing training and communication about diversity issues and multicultural communication. A collection of resource materials on culturally diverse groups is available to staff.

- Ongoing efforts are made to create a climate where people can recover from multicultural miscommunications. This is especially important where there is a multicultural staff and multicultural client population.

- The ability to work cross-culturally is included in job descriptions and in the hiring process.

- Ongoing efforts are made to involve minority staff members in information networks and decision-making processes.

- Staff are actively engaged in learning about the community, its norms, values, and formal as well as informal resources, as well as the ways in which it is changing. They use what they learn in ongoing program planning. They pay particular attention to the cultural understanding of and preferences for caregiving and care receiving.

- Staff engage in active outreach, attending local functions, giving talks at community organizations, and so forth, particularly when the targeted population is not inclined to use formal social services. Outreach activities will help build credibility.

- The staff maintains working relationships with other organizations that serve the same population, such as ethnic agencies, agencies for sexual minority clients, or disability service centers.

Critical Thinking Questions 12.3

What does it mean to be a leader? What makes a "bad leader"? A "good leader"? How might ideas about good and bad leaders be influenced by culture? Why do you think there has been so much fascination with the issue of organizational leadership in recent years?

IMPLICATIONS FOR SOCIAL WORK PRACTICE

Several principles for social work action are recommended by this discussion of formal organizations:

- Be alert to the influence of formal organizations on the client's behavior. Be particularly alert to the ways in which the social service organization where you work, as well as other social service organizations to which you frequently refer clients, influences the client's behavior.

- Develop an understanding of the organizational goals of the social service organization where you work and how the tasks that you perform are related to these goals.

- Develop an understanding of the shared meanings in the social service organization where you work and of the processes by which those meanings are developed and maintained.

- Develop an understanding of the forces of inertia and other constraints on rational decision making in the social service organization where you work.

- Develop an understanding of the social, political, economic, cultural, and technological environments of the social service organization where you work.

- Develop an understanding of the sources of legitimacy, power, and economic resources for the social service organization where you work and an understanding of how they influence internal decisions.

- Collaborate with colleagues at the social service organization where you work to understand and enhance the creative use of diversity.

- Collaborate with colleagues at the social service organization where you work to facilitate the inclusion of clients in the political process, internally as well as externally.

- Collaborate with colleagues at the social service organization where you work to develop an understanding of multiple oppressions within the organization.

- Be attuned to the symptoms of job-related burnout in yourself, your colleagues, and your clients.

- Collaborate with colleagues to create a culturally sensitive care system.

KEY TERMS

bureaucracy
burnout
critical perspective
    on organizations
emotional labor
formal organizations
Hawthorne effect
human relations theory
hybrid organization

interpretive perspective on
    organizations
iron cage of rationality
learning organization theory
managing diversity model
nonhierarchical organization
organizational culture model
organizational humanism
organizations as multiple oppressions

political economy model
privatization
rational perspective on
    organizations
scientific management
Silverman's social action model
social entrepreneurial organization
systems perspective on
    organizations

ACTIVE LEARNING

1. In the case study at the beginning of the chapter, you read about the transition in leadership at Beacon Center. You have also read about four theoretical perspectives on formal organizations. Imagine that you, and not Helen Blue, succeeded Martha Green as executive director at Beacon Center. Write a brief paper covering the following points: What vision would you have for Beacon Center? What would you want to keep the same as it had been, and what would you want to change? Use theory to back up your position.

2. Examine aspects of diversity in your workplace, your field practicum agency, or another organization you are familiar with. What can you observe or discover about diversity in the organization on the following variables: gender, age, social class, religion, ethnicity, race, and disability? Compare the diversity found among the management to that among the line workers and clientele. Write a brief paper describing what you found and addressing the following points: How does diversity (or the lack of it) appear to affect organizational effectiveness? What changes would you suggest for the organization in terms of diversity? (Questions are based on Strom-Gottfried & Morrissey, 1999.)

WEB RESOURCES

Alliance for Nonprofit Management
www.allianceonline.org

Site contains information on board development, financial management, strategic planning, fund-raising, and risk management, as well as a newsletter and FAQs.

ARNOVA
www.arnova.org

Site presented by the Association for Research on Nonprofit Organizations and Voluntary Action, contains member directory, conference information, publications, partners, and links.

Center on Nonprofits & Philanthropy
www.urban.org/nonprofits/index.cfm

Site maintained by the Center on Nonprofits & Philanthropy at the Urban Institute contains fact sheets, state profiles, resources, and databases.

Communities

Elizabeth D. Hutchison and Soon Min Lee

OPENING QUESTIONS

- What impact has globalization had on communities and on sense of community?

- What are the implications of the different theoretical approaches to community for community social work practice?

KEY IDEAS

As you read this chapter, take note of these central ideas:

1. Global communication technologies are having a profound impact on the nature of communities.

2. Community consists of people bound either by geography or webs of communication, sharing common ties, and interacting with one another.

3. Sense of community is based on belonging, being important to each other, and having mutual commitment.

4. Both relational communities, based on voluntary association, and territorial communities, based on geography, are relevant to social work.

5. Five approaches to community have relevance for contemporary social work: the contrasting types approach, spatial arrangements approach, social systems approach, social capital approach, and conflict approach.

6. Long-standing disagreements about social work's relationship to communities center on four points of tension: community as context for practice versus target of practice, agency orientation versus social action, conflict model versus collaborative model, and expert versus partner in the social change process.

Case Study

Filipina Domestic Workers Creating Transnational Communities

Filipina domestic workers scattered around the globe read the multinational magazines *Tinig Filipino* and *Diwaliwan*, and many contribute articles to *Tinig Filipino* describing the realities of their lives as overseas domestic workers. Sometimes their children back in the Philippines write articles about the pain of separation from their mothers or about the heroic sacrifices their mothers make to provide much-needed economic resources to their families back home. Filipino women (Filipinas) work as domestic workers in more than 130 countries, working in elderly care, child care, and housecleaning in private homes. They are among the ranks of service workers of globalization.

Globalization has created both a pull and push for Filipinas to become global domestic workers. It has created a heightened demand (pull) for low-wage service workers in major global cities of affluent nations to maintain the lifestyles of professional and managerial workers. It has also produced large geographical economic inequalities, and many poor countries, like the Philippines, are depending on the export of labor to help with debt repayment. Over 6 million Filipinos work overseas as contract workers, and the money and goods these workers send home to families, known as remittances, are an important source of revenue at home. In 1999, the Philippines ranked second among countries receiving the largest remittances from overseas workers (McMichael, 2008). The large outflow of labor also helps to decrease very high unemployment and underemployment rates. In the Philippines, about 70% of families live in poverty. There is quite a push for exporting Filipino labor.

Since the early 1990s, women have made up over half of Filipino contract workers. Filipino men work as seamen, carpenters, masons, and mechanics, many in the Middle East. Two-thirds of the migrant Filipinas are domestic workers, and they work in cities around the world. Many of them have a college education, but they earn more as domestic workers in affluent nations than they would as professional workers in the Philippines. They migrate for economic gain, but also, in many instances, to escape domestic violence or other domestic struggles. Most migrate alone. The Philippine government has applauded the legion of female migrant workers as "modern-day heroes." The remittances they send home allow families to buy houses, computers, and college educations for siblings, children, and other relatives.

The two most popular destinations for Filipina domestic workers are Rome and Los Angeles, both destinations that are difficult to access. In Italy, Filipina domestic workers are restricted to the status of guest worker, but they are allowed to stay for as long as 7 years, longer than in many other countries. A majority of Filipina domestic workers in Rome entered the country clandestinely, and often faced much danger and trauma on the journey. In contrast, most Filipina domestic workers in Los Angeles entered the country with valid legal documents. Migrants to both cities used their social networks to learn about the opportunities and the process for migrating.

The community life of the Filipina domestic workers in Rome and Los Angeles is alike in a number of ways; most importantly, both groups see themselves as simultaneously members of more than one community. They see themselves as part of a global community of Filipina domestic workers across geographic territories. They see themselves as part of their Philippine communities and only temporarily part of their receiving communities, referring to their sending communities as "home." While they are doing domestic work for class-privileged women in their receiving communities, they purchase the domestic services of even lower-paid women left behind in the Philippines to help care for their own families. They leave children, who are often very young, at home to be cared for by the extended family that benefits from the remittances that they send. They keep contact with their families in the Philippines by mail and by telephone. Both in Rome and in Los Angeles, they face anti-immigrant sentiment in their receiving communities.

There are great differences, however, in the local cultures of community life among Filipina domestic workers in Rome and Los Angeles. These differences seem to reflect the larger social and political contexts of the migration experience. Let's look first at the community of domestic workers in Rome. There, Filipina migrants are restricted to domestic work, and they live segregated lives in a society that is not welcoming. Consequently, they have built a community of much solidarity that congregates in multiple private and public gathering places.

(Continued)

(Continued)

The domestic workers are residentially dispersed throughout the city, and gathering places are likewise geographically dispersed. Specific gathering places are associated with specific regions of the Philippines.

On their days off, the workers tend to congregate in private gathering places in church centers and apartments. Several churches, mostly Catholic, have opened day-off shelters or church centers where the workers can spend time watching television or listening to music, visiting, and purchasing Filipino food. These centers are often developed out of the joint efforts of local churches in the Philippines and in Rome. The Filipino Chaplaincy, a coalition of 28 Roman Catholic churches, is the strongest advocate for Filipino workers in Rome. It publishes a directory of religious, government, and civic organizations relevant to the Filipino workers. The Santa Prudenziana parish, besides offering regular spiritual activities, also provides a variety of social services, including job placement referrals, free medical care, legal assistance, and Italian language classes. The migrant workers can also participate in choirs, dance groups, and a theater group.

Apartments are another site of private gathering for the Filipinas in Rome. Domestic workers who can navigate the barriers to rent their own apartments sometimes rent out rooms or beds to other migrant workers. They also rent access to their apartments to live-in workers on their days off. Apartments are furnished with televisions and equipment for watching Filipino movies, and at night, renters congregate in the kitchen, eating and relaxing, playing card games and mahjong.

There are also particular train stations and bus stops that are known as public gathering places for Filipinos in Rome. However, the city authorities have discouraged congregating in such public places. After much harassment at one bus stop, the Filipino migrants moved to a spot under an overpass, near the Tiber River. They subsequently turned the spot into a shopping bazaar that includes food shops, restaurants, hair salons, and tailoring shops.

These gathering spots allow for network building, sharing information, and providing a variety of assistance to new migrants. The domestic workers often discuss their problems at work and share information about housing. There is an ethic of mutual assistance and solidarity, although occasionally, some migrants take advantage of others in activities such as money lending.

The community of Filipina domestic workers in Los Angeles is not nearly as cohesive as the one in Rome. In contrast to Rome, the Los Angeles Filipino population is class stratified. There has been a long stream of migration from the Philippines to the United States, going back a century, and many earlier streams involved professional workers, particularly in the medical professions. Although many of the Filipina domestic workers have connections to more economically privileged Filipinos in Los Angeles, often securing work through these connections, they perceive the class distinctions as impeding cohesion and do not feel supported by the middle-class Filipino community. This is so even though they often spend their days off with relatives or friends in middle-class homes, or even live alongside middle-class neighbors. The domestic workers perceive the Filipino enclaves as middle-class spaces.

A subcommunity of Filipina domestic workers does seem to form from time to time, however. Live-in workers often congregate in the parks and playgrounds of the wealthy communities where they work. Those who work as part-time rather than live-in workers often meet on the buses traveling to and from work. Like their counterparts in Rome, they talk about work situations, but these gatherings are neither as large nor as regular as they are in Rome. The domestic workers also often participate in parties in the homes of middle-class Filipinos, but these associations do not seem to lead to the type of solidarity that occurs among the workers in Rome (Parrenas, 2001).

A DEFINITION OF COMMUNITY

Rhacel Salazar Parrenas (2001) chronicled the lives of Filipina domestic workers between June 1995 and August 1996, a period before the wide use of the Internet and cell phones. We can wonder how these technologies might have changed the connections of these women to their multiple communities. Although the circumstances of their lives are different in some important ways, the Filipinas in Rome and Los Angeles both appear to see themselves as members of multiple communities. But exactly what is community? Actually, this question has not been an easy one for social scientists. In fact, George Hillery's 1955 review of the sociological literature found 94 distinct definitions of *community*. Twenty years later, Seymour Sarason (1974) struggled to define the related concept of *sense of community*. Sarason concluded that even though sense of community is hard to define, "you know when you have it and when you don't" (p. 157).

How should we interpret the fuzziness of the concepts of community and sense of community? Some suggest that any concept with so many meanings is unscientific, and its potential utility is therefore highly suspect. On the other hand, Larry Lyon (1987) suggests that the multiplicity of definitions of community is evidence that the concept is meaningful to scholars with diverse interests and perspectives. We would certainly agree that a concept such as community should not be discarded simply because it has been hard to define. Over the past two decades, sociologists have in fact worked to develop greater agreement about the meaning of community, and community psychologists have been equally diligent about developing greater clarity for sense of community. Both lines of inquiry are relevant to social work.

Sociological attempts to reach agreement on the definition of community have centered on the report that approximately three-fourths of the 94 definitions found in the sociological literature included the same three elements: geographic area, social interaction, and common ties (Hillery, 1955, p. 118). The Filipina domestic workers' understanding of community seems very similar, but they would, most likely, suggest that community can be built across geographical distance. Historically, community did have a geographic meaning in sociology. More recently, however, two different sociological meanings of community have developed: community as a geographic or territorial concept and community as an interactional or relational concept. In this chapter, we discuss both meanings of community because both appear to have relevance for human behavior in the contemporary era. Recently, researchers are finding more similarities than differences in these two types of community (Obst & White, 2004; Obst, Zinkiewicz, & Smith, 2002a, 2002b). We use the following definition to cover both territorial and relational communities: **Community** is people who are bound either by geography or by webs of communication, sharing common ties, and interacting with one another.

Does it appear to you that the Filipina domestic workers in Rome have a sense of community with other domestic workers in the city? What about the Filipina domestic workers in Los Angeles? In 1974, Seymour Sarason proclaimed the enhancement of "psychological sense of community" as the mission of community psychology. He saw the basic characteristics of **sense of community** as

> the perception of similarity with others, an acknowledged interdependence with others, a willingness to maintain this interdependence by giving to or doing for others what one expects from them, the feeling that one is part of a larger dependable and stable structure. (p. 157)

These characteristics of sense of community are very similar to the "common ties" element of the definition of community. The elements of community and sense of community are presented in Exhibit 13.1. We look more closely at the concept of sense of community in a later section.

Community (from community sociology literature)
Linked by geography or webs of communication
Common ties
Interaction
Sense of Community (from community psychology literature)
Similarity with others
Interdependence
Mutual exchanges to fulfill needs
Sense of belonging

▲ **Exhibit 13.1** Essential Elements of Community and Sense of Community

SOURCES: Based on Hillery (1955); Sarason (1974); Wellman (1999).

TERRITORIAL COMMUNITY AND RELATIONAL COMMUNITY

Some would argue that community in the contemporary era is based on voluntary interaction (**relational community**), not on geography or territory (**territorial community**). For the Filipina domestic workers, community seems to be both relational and territorial. They are a part of a growing trend of transnational families who are also creating *transnational communities*. They maintain a sense of community connection to their sending communities in the Philippines as well as to other Filipina domestic workers in their territorial communities. In addition, they imagine themselves as a part of a global community of Filipina domestic workers, especially when they read magazines such as *Tinig Filipino*. Their sense of belonging to this global community is based on common ties but does not include much interaction. They do, however, draw support from feeling a part of this community. What about for you? Are your strongest supports based on territorial or relational community?

In premodern times, human groups depended, by necessity, on the territorial community to meet their human needs. But each development in communication and transportation technology has loosened that dependency somewhat. Electronic communication now connects people over distant spaces, with a high degree of both immediacy and intimacy. The development of the World Wide Web in the early 1990s allowed rapid growth in the use of e-mail; beginning in the mid-1990s, hundreds of millions of people around the world began to use e-mail to communicate with other individuals and to develop e-mail discussion groups. Toward the end of 2004, Web 2.0 technologies, a second generation of the World Wide Web that allows people to collaborate and share information online, came to prominence. Web 2.0 includes blogs, wikis, podcasting, multimedia sharing sites, and social networking sites (SNSs). By 2008, a major research study of the use of digital technologies by adults in 17 industrialized nations found an average use of these technologies for one-third of leisure time (Harrison & Thomas, 2009). The SNS Facebook reportedly has more than 175 million users worldwide. Other SNSs have sprung up in specific countries—for example, Cyworld (Korea), Hyves (Holland), LunarStorm (Sweden), Mixi (Japan), Orkut (Brazil), QQ (China), and Skyrock (France). SNSs have been defined as web-based services that allow individuals to "construct a public or semi-public profile within a bounded system, articulate a list of other users with whom they share a connection, and view and traverse their list of connections and those made by others within the system" (Boyd & Ellison, 2007, ¶ 5). This definition is consistent with the aspects of the above-stated definition of community: linked by webs of communication, common ties, and interaction.

Since the last edition of this book (2008), first author Lib Hutchison has continued to enjoy e-mail conversations with former students, former colleagues at three universities, contributing authors in four countries and nine states plus the District of Columbia, her editor in Los Angeles, members of a national committee spread across the United States and Canada, and numerous friends and relatives. She is struck by how much larger her e-mail network has grown since she worked on the first edition of this book in the late 1990s. In the past year, she has also developed a community of friends on the SNS Facebook and enjoys keeping up with a growing community of friends scattered around the world. She is recognizing that many members of her Facebook community now prefer Facebook communication to e-mail, and also make regular use of text messaging and Twittering (or tweeting). No doubt, new technological innovations will continue to provide new ways of building community. Lib is also recognizing that members of her Facebook community are struggling with issues of privacy, and have had to deal with unsettling situations in which their Facebook communications, especially those that were political in nature, were responded to in different ways in different sectors of their Facebook communities. When the second author (Soon Min) was studying in the United States, she kept in touch with her family and friends in Korea by using Cyworld, one of the most popular Korean

▲ **Photos 13.1a and 13.1b**   Communities are linked together by geography and webs of communication, common ties, and interaction. Here, contrast two different types of neighborhoods, a suburban neighborhood in the United States and the village of Cantondougou in the Ivory Coast.

online social networking sites, similar to MySpace or Facebook. Users of Cyworld first create a cyber home or "minihompy" and a "minime," which is an avatar that represents them. Then, users add friends or family members to the network so that they can visit with them. Most of Soon Min's friends and family in Korea were registered as Cyworld members, and it was easy for her to connect with them. She could also store and edit photos and share her life in the United States with her community back home.

In Cyworld, members use a virtual currency called the "dotori," Korean for "acorn." Members buy dotori with credit cards and use it to purchase decorations or songs for their minihompies or to buy special clothes for their avatars. Soon Min sometimes buys songs with dotori to play on her minihompy. A friend sent her several dotori as a birthday gift on her last birthday. Dotori and what it "buys" are important symbols in Cyworld.

In terms of privacy, Cyworld has a function to control access to a user's photos or journals. Users can decide what information they do or do not want to be viewed or searched by visitors. Also, users of the Cyworld register with Korean Social Security numbers and real names, which can prevent anonymous postings and help assure responsibility and trust between Cyworld members. This is an important way that Cyworld allows virtual communities to control their membership.

While studying in the United States, Soon Min regularly updated the stories on her minihompy with pictures and music while checking how others were doing. She visited Cyworld many times daily and sometimes spent hours checking her minihompy, visiting her friends, and exchanging messages and pictures. She used Cyworld for enhancing existing relationships rather than for meeting new people, focusing on relationships with relatives, neighborhood friends, and high school and college friends. Given her busy life and the great geographical distance across several time zones, it would have been hard for her to stay in touch with her Korean community without Cyworld.

After she went back to Korea, Cyworld still helped Soon Min to keep in touch with her old friends in Korea as well as in the United States. Her old high school friend found out that Soon Min was back home and contacted her through her minihompy. They finally met in person after all these years. However, they did not feel any distance, since they had been communicating with each other through Cyworld. Soon Min still uses Cyworld for connecting to Korean American friends in the United States. The other day, Soon Min visited her Korean American friend's minihompy and found out that she was visiting Korea. Soon Min was able to talk to her by calling the phone number her friend posted on her minihompy.

Soon Min is now using Facebook to connect with her American friends. She uploads her recent pictures and personal news on her Facebook page. She believes that she will be able to catch up with her American friends easily when she visits the United States again. Cyworld and Facebook are examples of virtual communities that overcome geographical distances. They are a type of communication tool that helps Soon Min and many others maintain relational community with those at a distance.

For a number of years, researchers have been finding that local ties make up a decreasing portion of our social connections, and they have interpreted that finding to mean that territorial community is no longer important in our lives (A. Hunter & Riger, 1986; Wellman, 1982; Wellman & Wortley, 1990). A more careful look at this research suggests, however, that even highly mobile people continue to have a lot of contacts in their territorial communities. One study in Toronto (Wellman, 1996) found that if we study *ties,* the number of people with whom we have connections, it is true that the majority of ties for most of us are nonterritorial. However, when we study *contacts,* our actual interactions, two-thirds of all contacts are local, in the neighborhood or work setting. This may well be the case for the Filipina domestic workers who often complain about how isolating their domestic work is.

When technology opens the possibilities for relational communities, it does not necessarily spell the death of territorial community, but there have been conflicting findings about this. One research team found that Internet-wired suburbanites were more likely than their nonwired neighbors to engage in "active neighboring," actually using the Internet to support neighboring (Hampton & Wellman, 2003). A widely publicized 2006 study by McPherson et al. found the opposite. This study found that since 1985, people in the United States have become more socially isolated, the size of their discussion networks has declined, and the diversity of their networks has decreased. More specifically, the researchers found that people had fewer close ties in their neighborhoods and from voluntary associations (clubs, neighborhood associations, etc.). They suggested that use of the Internet and mobile phones pulls people away from neighborhood and other locally based social settings. To address the inconsistencies in prior research, the most comprehensive study of social isolation and new technology in the United States to date was reported by researchers with the Pew Internet & American Life Project (Hampton, Sessions, Her, & Rainie, 2009). These researchers undertook a study to compare the social networks of people who use particular technologies with those of demographically similar people who do not use these technologies. Here are their major findings about the trends in social networks since 1985:

- There has been a small-to-modest drop in the number of people reporting that they have no one to talk to about important matters; 6% of adults report they have no one with whom they can discuss such matters.

- The average size of people's core discussion networks has declined, with a drop of about one confidant.

- The diversity of people's core discussion network has markedly declined.

However, the research indicates that use of technology is not the driving force behind these changes. Here are their findings about the relationship between new technology and social networks:

- People who own a cell phone and use the Internet for sharing photos and messages have larger core discussion networks than those who do not use this technology.

- People who use these technologies have more nonkin in their networks than people who do not.

- People who use the Internet to share photos are more likely to have discussion partners that cross political lines.

- People who use Internet social networking sites have social networks that are about 20% more diverse.

- In-person contact remains the most frequent way to have contact in the geographical community.

- The mobile phone has replaced the landline as the most frequently used medium for communication.

- Text messaging tied with the landline as the third most popular way to communicate.

- Those who use SNSs are 25% less likely to use neighbors for companionship, but use of other technologies is associated with higher levels of neighborhood involvement.

- Internet users are less likely to depend on neighbors to provide concrete services.

Wendy Griswold (2008) proposes that people can have ties to both relational and territorial communities at the same time, and this does seem to be the case for the Filipina domestic workers in both Rome and Los Angeles. They maintain relationships with their sending communities while also building community in local gathering places in their receiving communities. Griswold recognizes the possibility that the new technologies will simply allow us to develop and maintain a larger network of increasingly superficial relationships. But she also points out the possibility that the new capacity to be immediately and intimately connected across space could help us to develop more shared meanings and become more tolerant of our differences. We can imagine that e-mail and Internet SNSs are now helping the Filipina mothers maintain more intimate contact with their children back in the Philippines. You might want to pause and think about how this technology is changing the lives of such transnational families.

As social workers concerned about social justice, however, we must understand the multiple implications of inequality of access to the new technologies. These technologies open opportunities for relational community and the multitude of resources provided by such communities. Skills in using the new technologies are also increasingly rewarded in the labor market. Unless access to these technologies is equalized, however, territorial community will remain central to the lives of some groups—most notably, young children and their caregivers; older adults; poor families; and many persons with disabilities, who have their own special technological needs. On the other hand, the new technologies may make it easier for some people with disabilities to gain access to relational community, even while inaccessible physical environments continue to block their access to territorial community. One of my former students who is African American has told me that she likes the Internet because it is color blind, and she can have encounters of various kinds without feeling that race gets in the way.

Although both territorial and relational communities are relevant to social work, social work's commitment to social justice has led to continued concern for territorial communities. That same commitment also requires social workers to work toward equalization of access to both territorial and relational community.

Critical Thinking Questions 13.1

Review the cited research above about the impact of the new technologies on territorial and relational community. Which technologies have you used in the past week to keep in touch with people you know? Which type of technology do you use the most these days to build and maintain relationships? Do you use different types of technology to keep in touch with different people or for different types of situations? How important is territorial community to you? What methods do you use to stay in touch with your territorial community?

SOCIAL WORKERS AND COMMUNITIES: OUR HISTORY

From the earliest history of social work in the United States, social workers have been interested in the health of communities and in the influence of community on individual behavior (Fisher, 2005; Hardcastle, Wenocur, & Powers, 2004). Social work grew from two different approaches to social problems, one of which—the settlement house movement—was community focused. (The other was the social casework approach, which was focused on individual and family adjustment.) Social workers in the settlement houses provided a wide range of services to help individual poor families cope with the challenges of poverty, including day nurseries, employment bureaus, a place to take a shower, English classes for immigrants, health clinics, pasteurized milk, information on workers' compensation, legal assistance, and emergency financial assistance. Their interests went beyond helping individual families, however; they were also interested in identifying and addressing community conditions that jeopardized the health and well-being of neighborhood families. They campaigned for social reforms such as tenement protection, improved sanitation, and labor reform. In addition, the settlement house social workers were interested in building a sense of mutual support in the poor neighborhoods where they were located. They developed dance, drama, and arts classes; sports and hobby clubs; summer camps; cultural events; and libraries. During this same period, African American social work pioneers developed settlement houses and engaged in active community work to "improve the collective social functioning of their racially segregated communities" (Carlton-LaNey, 1999, p. 312).

Social work's interest in community has ebbed and flowed since then, with more interest shown in some periods than in others. Stanley Wenocur and Steven Soifer (1997) suggest that there have been three peak periods of intense social work interest in community in the United States: the Progressive Era at the turn of the 20th century, the Depression years of the 1930s, and the Civil Rights Era of the 1960s. Contemporary critiques of social work accuse the profession of replacing its original focus on community with a preoccupation with personality problems of individuals (Specht & Courtney, 1994). The social work literature, however, reflects a recent expansion in community practice in the United States and around the world (e.g., Ewalt, Freeman, & Poole, 1998; Fisher & Karger, 1997; Hardcastle et al., 2004; Weil, 2005a). It is hard to say what mix of societal trends has produced this expanded interest in community practice, but some have credited the far-reaching impact of economic and cultural globalization, growing social inequality, massive movement of refugees, the devolution of policy decisions about social welfare programs to the state and local levels in the United States, and social work's renewed commitment to the goal of social justice (see, e.g., Daley & Marsiglia, 2000; Weil, 2005b).

THEORETICAL APPROACHES TO COMMUNITY

Social workers traditionally have turned to *community sociology* for theory and research on community. During the 1950s and 1960s, however, community theory and research were scant—almost nonexistent—in the United States and Europe (Lyon, 1987; Puddifoot, 1995). Although this decline in academic interest in community sociology probably had multiple causes, sociologists suggest that it was related in large part to the rising prominence of the concept of mass society (Lyon, 1987; Woolever, 1992). **Mass society** is standardized and homogenized—a society that has no ethnic, class, regional, or local variations in human behavior. Standardized public education, mass media, and residential mobility are cited as the primary mechanisms by which societies become standardized and homogenized. If we assume that mass society has no local or group-based variations in norms, values, and behavior, then community, which is local and group based, loses its relevance to the study of human behavior.

Just as the rising prominence of the concept of mass society contributed to the eclipse of community theory and research, recognition of the limits of mass society as a way of understanding human behavior contributed to the revitalization of community sociology. Beginning in the late 1960s, it became apparent that even though some standardization and homogenization had occurred, mass society had not eradicated ethnic, class, regional, and local variations in human behavior. In the 1980s, a more balanced view of community developed within sociology, a view that recognizes the contributions that both community and mass society make to human behavior (Cuba & Hummon, 1993; W. Flanagan, 1993; Keane, 1991; Lyon, 1987; Woolever, 1992). In this view, some standardization is present, but local variations still occur. Certainly, we note that there are similarities in the experiences of the Rome and Los Angeles Filipinas, but there are also many differences.

More recently, scholars in a variety of disciplines have been interested in how globalization interacts with local cultural norms in the development, maintenance, and deterioration of community (Francescato & Tomai, 2001). They have been particularly interested in social inequalities as well as conflicts between communities of competing interests in a globalized, postmodern world. These scholars identify strong and hotly contested group-based variations in norms, values, and behavior.

At the same time that the concept of community was regaining prominence in sociology, it also emerged as an important concept in psychology. In the midst of concern about the ineffectiveness of existing psychotherapeutic methods, the concept of community was discovered—or rediscovered—by the community mental health movement. The field of community psychology developed and became Division 27 of the American Psychological Association in the United States (Heller, 1989). During the 1980s, community psychology was also established as a division in some European countries, and in 1995, the European Network of Community Psychologists was formed (Francescato & Tomai, 2001). Like social workers, community psychologists have turned to the sociological literature for community theory, but they have also developed their own theory of psychological sense of community.

In a 1979 paper presented to the Community Section of the American Sociological Association, Roland Warren (1988) suggested that theorizing about community, like sociological theory in general, includes multiple perspectives. He recommended that multiple theoretical approaches be used to understand communities because each approach explains particular aspects of community. Three decades later, it still seems wise for social workers to follow Warren's advice and use multiple theoretical approaches for understanding multidimensional community. That approach is, of course, consistent with the multidimensional approach of this book.

Five perspectives on community seem particularly relevant for social work: the contrasting types approach, spatial arrangements approach, social systems approach, social capital approach, and conflict approach. The second of these, the spatial arrangements approach, applies only to territorial communities, but the other four can be applied equally well to both relational and territorial communities. In combination, these five approaches to community should enable you to scan more widely for factors contributing to the problems of living among vulnerable populations, to recognize community resources, and to think more creatively about possible interventions. Using approaches that are not only varied but even discordant should assist you in thinking critically about human behavior and prepare you for the often ambiguous practice situations that you will encounter.

Contrasting Types Approach

The Filipina domestic workers in Rome and Los Angeles are concerned about commitment, identification, and relationships within their communities. The Los Angeles Filipinas seem especially concerned about the nature of their relationship to the wider Filipino community in their area. This concern is at the heart of the oldest theory of community, Ferdinand Tonnies' (1887/1963) concepts of *gemeinschaft* and *gesellschaft* (translated from the German as community and society). Actually, Tonnies was trying to describe contrasting types of societies, rural preindustrial societies (gemeinschaft) versus urban industrial societies (gesellschaft), but his ideas continue to be used by community sociologists today to understand differences between communities, both spatial and online (Ballantine & Roberts, 2009; Memmi, 2006). In **gemeinschaft** communities, relationships are personal and traditional; in **gesellschaft** communities, relationships are impersonal and contractual. The defining characteristics of gemeinschaft and gesellschaft communities are listed in Exhibit 13.2.

Tonnies (1887/1963) saw gemeinschaft and gesellschaft as ideal types that will never exist in reality. However, they constitute a hypothetical dichotomy against which the real world can be compared. Although Tonnies' work is more than a century old, the gemeinschaft/gesellschaft dichotomy has proven to be a powerful analytical construct, and it continues to be used and validated in community research. It is also reflected in later typological theories. For example, Charles Cooley (1902/1964) proposed that the social world can be defined in terms of *primary groups* (intimate, face-to-face groups to which we form attachments) and *secondary groups* (less intimate, more impersonal groups). Mark Granovetter (1973) made a distinction between strong ties and weak ties. *Strong ties* entail frequent contact between members, emotional intensity in interactions, and cohesion. *Weak ties* are impersonal and superficial, connecting acquaintances rather than friends. Some theorists have envisioned more of a continuum than a dichotomy, such as Robert Redfield's (1947) folk/urban continuum and Howard Becker's sacred/secular (1957) continuum.

Tonnies (1887/1963) shared the view of other early European sociologists, such as Max Weber and Émile Durkheim, that modernization was leading us away from gemeinschaft and toward gesellschaft. Capitalism, urbanization, and industrialization have all been proposed as causes of the movement toward gesellschaft. Many typology theorists lament the "loss of community" that occurs in the process. But some theorists suggest that electronic technology is moving us into a third type of community—sometimes referred to as a *postgesellschaft*, or postmodern, community—characterized by diversity and unpredictability (Griswold, 2008; Lyon, 1987; G. Smith, 1996). This view has become more prominent with increasing globalization, and it is well illustrated by the Filipina

Gemeinschaft	Gesellschaft
Strong identification with community	Little identification with community
Authority based on tradition	Authority based on laws and rationality
Relationships based on emotionalism	Relationships based on goal attainment and emotional neutrality
Others seen as whole persons	Others seen as role enactors

▲ **Exhibit 13.2**   Gemeinschaft and Gesellschaft Communities

SOURCE: Based on Lyon (1987).

domestic workers and their families back in the Philippines. Back home in their rural, newly industrializing sending communities, children, relatives, and friends talk about the loss of emotional intimacy in their relationships with the migrant workers. Although the Filipina domestic workers feel the pain of separation from family and friends back home, they talk about relationships based on goal attainment—meeting the goal of improving the financial situation of their families. Likewise, Soon Min lives with much diversity in the nature of her relationships with her Korean and U.S. communities.

Howard Becker (1957) sees the evolution of community in a different light. He suggests that modern society does not always move toward the secular but instead moves back and forth a great deal on the sacred/secular continuum. To Becker, the sacred is best characterized by reluctance to change (traditional authority in Tonnies' gemeinschaft), and the secular is best characterized by readiness to change (emotional neutrality in Tonnies' gesellschaft).

Tonnies and other theorists who have studied communities as contrasting types have focused their attention on territorial communities. Indeed, empirical research supports the idea that territorial communities vary along the gemeinschaft/gesellschaft continuum (Cuba & Hummon, 1993; A. Hunter & Riger, 1986; Keane, 1991; Woolever, 1992). More recently, however, Barry Wellman (1999) and research associates have attempted to understand contrasting types of relational communities that are based on networks of interaction rather than territory. In his early work, Wellman (1979) identified three contrasting types of communities:

1. *Community lost:* Communities that have lost a sense of connectedness, social support, and traditional customs for behavior

2. *Community saved:* Communities that have retained a strong sense of connectedness, social support, and customs for behavior

3. *Community liberated:* Communities that are loosely knit, with unclear boundaries and a great deal of heterogeneity

Wellman (1999) suggested that as societies change, community is not necessarily lost but becomes transformed, and new forms of community develop. Daniel Memmi (2006) argues that online communities are just another form of community and another example of the long-term evolution of looser social relationships. There are differences of opinion about whether community is lost or merely transformed in the exportation of labor around the world.

Wellman and associates have continued to study the idea of contrasting types of relational communities for over 20 years, seeking to understand multiple dimensions of communities. Their more recent work (e.g., Wellman & Potter, 1999) suggests that it is more important to think in terms of *elements* of communities rather than *types* of communities. Using factor analytic statistical methods, they have identified four important elements of community—contact, range, intimacy, and immediate kinship/friendship—which are described in Exhibit 13.3. These elements are configured in different ways in different communities, and in the same community at different times.

Social workers might benefit by recognizing both the gemeinschaft and gesellschaft qualities of the communities they serve as well as the histories of those communities. Approaches like Wellman and Potter's multiple elements of communities could be helpful in this regard.

Spatial Arrangements Approach

If we think about the Filipina community in Rome in terms of spatial arrangements, we note the dispersed gathering places where they congregate. We think about how their gathering places are segregated from the public space of the dominant society. We also think about the crowded apartments that sometimes hold as many as four residents in a small room. If we think about the Filipinas in Los Angeles, we think about domestic workers isolated in houses in

Contact	Level of interaction; how accessible community members are for contact and how much contact they actually have
Range	Size and heterogeneity of community membership
Intimacy	Sense of relationships being special; desire for companionship among members; interest in being together in multiple social contexts over a long period of time; sense of mutuality in relationships, with needs known and supported
Immediate kinship/friendship	Proportion of community membership composed of immediate kin (parents, adult children, siblings) versus friends

▲ **Exhibit 13.3** Four Elements of Communities

SOURCE: Based on Wellman and Potter (1999).

▲ **Photo 13.2** Teenagers can often be characterized as a community held together via social bonds; they share a common spirit, trust, art, and emotional connection. In this case, they also share a common territory.

wealthy neighborhoods and visiting middle-class Filipino neighborhoods where they feel like outsiders on their days off. We also think about their lack of transportation to get beyond their live-in and day-off neighborhoods.

Beginning with Robert Park's (1936) human ecology theory, a diverse group of sociological theorists have focused on community as spatial arrangements. Their interests have included city placement; population growth; land use patterns; the process of suburbanization; the development of "edge" cities (newly developed business districts of large scale located on the edge of major cities); and the relationships among central cities, suburbs, and edge cities. They are also interested in variations in human behavior related to the type of spatial community, such as rural area, small town, suburb, or central city, and more recently, in how human health and well-being are related to physical features of the community (Sternberg, 2009).

Social constructionist perspective

Symbolic interactionists have studied how symbolic images of communities—the way people think about their communities—are related to spatial arrangements (G. Wilson & Baldassare, 1996). A survey of a random sample of Denver employees found that a large majority thought of themselves as either a "city person" or a "suburbanite" (Feldman, 1990). Participants largely agreed about the spatial attributes that distinguish cities from suburbs. On the whole, both city people and suburbanites reported a preference for the type of spatial community in which they resided.

One research team set out to discover the meanings that residents of seven distressed neighborhoods in one midwestern city make of the physical aspects of their neighborhoods (Nowell, Berkowitz, Deacon, & Foster-Fishman, 2006). They used a *photovoice* methodology, putting cameras in the hands of participants and asking them to use the cameras to tell a story about their community. They found that physical aspects of the neighborhood carry many meanings for the residents. Positive physical landmarks, such as parks and monuments, communicate a message of pride and identity, but physical conditions such as dilapidated houses, graffiti, and overflowing garbage convey negative meaning that invites frustration and shame. The researchers concluded that community physical conditions are important because they carry symbolic meanings for the residents. We are reminded that the Los Angeles Filipina domestic workers interpret the middle-class neighborhoods where they visit on their days off as "middle-class spaces."

The multidisciplinary theory on human behavior and the physical environment, discussed in Chapter 7, has also been extended to the study of community as spatial arrangements. Social scientists have focused on elements of environmental design that encourage social interaction as well as those that encourage a sense of control and the motivation to look out for the neighborhood. They have identified such elements as large spaces broken into smaller spaces, personalized spaces, and spaces for both privacy and congregation. One research team that studied the spatial arrangements in a suburban region found that people who had a sense of adequate privacy from neighbors' houses also reported a greater sense of community (G. Wilson & Baldassare, 1996). Another researcher found that opportunities to visit nearby shared space and having views of nature from home are correlated with increased neighborhood satisfaction (Kearney, 2006). Still another researcher found that neighborhood physical environments that provide opportunity for physical activity are particularly valued by children and recommends that social work assessment with children should include aspects of the child–neighborhood relationship (Nicotera, 2005). Recently, the new urbanist designers have been interested in aspects of community design that encourage physical activity for people of all ages; they are thinking of the health benefits that physical activity provides (see discussion in Chapter 7).

Systems perspective

Early settlement house social workers at Hull House in Chicago developed community maps for assessing the spatial arrangements of social and economic injustices in local neighborhoods (Wong & Hillier, 2001). Social work planners and administrators have recently returned to the idea of geographical mapping, making use of advancements in **geographic information system (GIS)** computer technology, which can map the spatial distribution of a variety of social data. Social workers have used GIS to map (1) the distribution of child care facilities in a geographic region (Queralt & Witte, 1998a, 1998b); (2) prior residences of persons admitted to homeless shelters (Culhane, Lee, & Wachter, 1997); (3) the geographical distribution of rates of child physical abuse, neglect, and sexual abuse (Ernst, 2000); and (4) the geographical areas of greatest unmet service needs (Wong & Hillier, 2001). GIS is also being used to map public health risk factors and to examine the match of physicians to community needs (see Cervigni, Suzuki, Ishii, & Hata, 2008); to target neighborhoods for community-building initiatives (Huber, Egeren, Pierce, & Foster-Fishman, 2009); to understand the match of welfare recipients, child care providers, and potential employers (M. Chen, Harris, Folkoff, Drudge, & Jackson, 1999); and to study race disparities in the national distribution of hazardous waste treatment, storage, and disposal facilities (Mohai & Saha, 2007). Huber et al. (2009) emphasize that community resources as well as community risk factors can be identified through the use of GIS.

GIS holds much promise for future social work planning, administration, and research (see Lohmann & McNutt, 2005). Amy Hillier (2007), a leading proponent of the use of GIS by social workers, emphasizes the important role that GIS can play in identifying where social work clients live in relation to both resources and hazards. She also argues that GIS has the potential to empower community groups, particularly disenfranchised groups, but that it is rarely used this way by social workers. If you have access to GIS technology, you might want to do some mapping of your territorial community: its ethnic makeup, socioeconomic class, crime rate, libraries, parks, hospitals, social services, and so on. If you do not have access to GIS, you can accomplish the same task with a good map blowup and multicolored pushpins.

Thinking about territorial communities as spatial arrangements can help social workers decide which territorial communities to target, for which problems, and with which methods. An interdisciplinary literature has recently focused on the compounding and interrelated nature of problems in deteriorating, impoverished neighborhoods in central cities. Philanthropic funders have responded with comprehensive community initiatives (CCIs) to fund mul-

> Systems perspective

tifaceted community-building programs that address the economic and physical conditions, as well as social and cultural issues, of these impoverished communities (Huber et al., 2009; Nowell et al., 2006). Typical elements of CCIs are economic and commercial development, education, health care, employment, housing, leadership development, physical revitalization, neighborhood security, recreation, social services, and support networks. Although CCIs have been thought of as a development strategy for impoverished urban neighborhoods, Lori Messinger (2004) argues that the model is also relevant for work in rural communities. She suggests, however, that in rural communities, it is particularly important to pay attention to both current and historical points of tension and conflict. Another recent development is that many communities are using neighborhood youth for neighborhood cleanup and revitalization (Ross & Coleman, 2000; Twiss & Cooper, 2000).

Social Systems Approach

A third way to think about communities is as social systems with cultures and patterns of interactions. We have looked at some of the ways that the cultures and patterns of interactions of the Filipina community in Rome are simi-

> Systems perspective

lar to and different from those in Los Angeles. A closer look at these communities as social systems might help us understand both the differences and similarities. The social systems perspective focuses on social interaction rather than on the physical, spatial aspects of community. Social interaction in a community can be understood in two different ways: as culture and as structure (Griswold, 2008). Exhibit 13.4 shows the differences between these two aspects of community.

For thinking about community in terms of its culture, symbolic interaction theory is promising because of its emphasis on the development of meaning through interaction. *Ethnography* is also particularly useful for studying community culture. The goal of ethnographic research is to understand the underlying rules and patterns of everyday

Community Culture
Pattern of meanings
Enduring patterns of communication
Symbols that guide thinking, feelings, and behaviors
Community Structure
Pattern of interactions
Institutions
Economic factors
Political factors

▲ **Exhibit 13.4** Aspects of Community Culture and Community Structure

SOURCE: Based on Griswold (2008).

life, in a particular location or among a particular group, from the native point of view rather than the researcher's point of view. One example of this is work by Italian community psychologists Donata Francescato and Manuela Tomai (2001). Their method of building a profile of a territorial community of interest combines demographic data with ethnographic methods that include "environmental walks, drawings, movie scripts, narratives, and telling jokes" (p. 376). For the movie script, they ask different target groups in the community to develop a plot for a movie script about the future they imagine for the neighborhood; sometimes these different groups perform parts of their "movies" for each other. Francescato and Tomai have used the movie script method to build understanding between Blacks, Afrikaners, and Indians in a college town in South Africa; old farmers and young students in an Austrian town; and immigrants and locals in several neighborhoods in Italy.

> Social constructionist perspective

Community can also be studied in terms of its structure. Roland Warren (1963, 1978, 1987) made significant contributions to the understanding of patterns of interactions in communities. Warren pointed out that members of communities have two distinctive types of interactions. The first are those that create **horizontal linkage,** or interactions with other members of the community. The second are interactions that create **vertical linkage,** or interaction with individuals and systems outside the community. Warren suggested that healthy communities must have both types of interactions. Communities with strong horizontal linkage provide a sense of identity for community members, but without good vertical linkage they cannot provide all the necessary resources for the well-being of community members. Communities with strong vertical linkage but weak horizontal linkage may leave community members searching and yearning for a sense of community.

More recently, a similar distinction has been made by scholars who write about community as social capital (to be discussed later; see Putnam, 2000). They differentiate between bonding social capital and bridging social capital. **Bonding social capital** is inward looking and tends to mobilize solidarity and in-group loyalty, and it leads to exclusive identities and homogenous communities. It may also lead to strong out-group hostilities. This type of social capital is often found in minority ethnic enclaves that provide psychological, social, and economic support to members. **Bridging social capital** is outward looking and diverse, and it links community members to assets and information across community boundaries. Robert Putnam (2000) describes the difference between the two types of social capital this way: "Bonding social capital constitutes a kind of sociological superglue, whereas bridging social capital provides a sociological WD-40" (p. 23). One research team (N. Ellison, Steinfield, & Lampe, 2007) found that the SNS Facebook is particularly useful for bridging social capital, but much less useful for bonding social capital. Tomai et al. (2010) found that both bridging and bonding social capital were increased for youth who joined an online community of high school students outside Rome, Italy; however, increased intensity of use was associated with increased bridging social capital but not with increased bonding social capital.

Researchers have found support for the advantages and disadvantages of horizontal and vertical linkage discussed above. But consider also the experiences of the Filipina domestic workers in Rome and Los Angeles. We see much evidence that the workers in Rome have built strong horizontal linkages, but their opportunities to build vertical linkages are hampered by anti-immigrant sentiment. Unfortunately, the Filipina domestic workers in Los Angeles seem to be limited in both horizontal and vertical linkages, although middle-class Filipinos appear to be a source of bridging social capital for them.

For almost three decades, network theorists and researchers have been using network analysis to study community structure. They suggest that communities, like small groups and organizations, should be thought of as networks of social interaction (Wellman, 1999, 2001, 2005). They have tended to define community as **personal community,** which is composed of ties with friends, relatives, neighbors, workmates, and so on. Community is personal because the makeup of community membership varies from person to person. Another name for personal community is **network,** which has been defined as "the set of social relations or social ties among a set of actors" (Emirbayer & Goodwin, 1994). Network theorists suggest that the new communication technologies, particularly the Internet, have played a large role in transforming community from solidary community, which seeks the participation of all members in an integrated fashion, to what Barry Wellman has called community as networked individualism, where individuals operate in large, personalized, complex networks (Boase, Horrigan, Wellman, & Rainie, 2006). Some network theorists value this transformation (see, e.g., Boase et al., 2006). Others argue that communication technologies, and particularly the Internet, can and should be used to develop solidary community, which is friendlier, richer, and more socially binding than networked individualism, which they argue is a North American idea (see, e.g., Day & Schuler, 2004). It seems that both sides are correct. Certainly, we know that the Internet has been used to develop support groups as one form of solidary community. It is interesting to note that the Los Angeles Filipina domestic workers seem to be closer to a network individualism model, while the Rome Filipinas seem to have built solidary community.

In the mid-1990s, when Parrenas (2001) did her study of Filipina domestic workers, the Internet was a tool that was accessible only to the technically elite, but a decade later, it was a part of everyday life for a large majority of people. That represents an unusually rapid diffusion of innovation, which has been accompanied by debates about whether it is helping to build or destroy community. In 2004–2005, the PEW Internet & American Life Project undertook a research project to study this question (Boase et al., 2006). Using a random digit sample of telephone numbers in the United States, the researchers studied two types of connection people have in their social networks: *core ties,* or our closest relationships, and *significant ties,* or relationships that are only somewhat closely connected. They found surprisingly large networks among the respondents, a median of 15 core ties and 16 significant ties. There was no difference in the number of core ties between Internet users and nonusers, but Internet users were found to have larger numbers of significant ties.

In-person encounters continued to be the most common form of interaction, followed by landline phone, cell phone, e-mail, and instant messaging (IM). E-mail was not found to be replacing other forms of contact, either with core ties or significant ties. In fact, higher levels of e-mail communication were associated with higher levels of other forms of contact, and with both local and distant ties. This latter finding led the researchers to conclude that e-mail is a tool of *glocalization,* a term that has been invented to emphasize the bringing together of the global and the local. Finally, as found in earlier research, the amount of support offered to network members increases as the *range* of the network— size and heterogeneity—increases. In interpreting these results, it is important to note that 74% of respondents are cell phone users, 63% are e-mail users, and 27% (mostly teens) are instant messaging (IM) users (Boase et al., 2006). This raises important concerns about the digital divide discussed in Chapter 9.

Network analysis has been used to study social ties in both territorial and relational communities. In doing so, researchers have found that for many people, community is based more on relationships than territory. One research team (B. Lee & Campbell, 1999) did find, however, that barriers of segregation and discrimination make neighborhood relationships more important for Blacks than for Whites. They found that Blacks have more intimate and long-standing ties with neighbors than Whites do in similar neighborhoods, and they engage in more frequent contact with neighbors. Similarly, it would seem that the network of relationships built in Filipina gathering places in Rome is highly important to the Filipinas, who face much segregation and anti-immigrant discrimination.

Social Capital Approach

When the Filipinas in Rome talk about solidarity in their migrant community, they are talking about the quality of the connections that community members make with each other and the commitment they feel to one another. They are thinking about community as a social bond that unifies people. Similarly, when the Filipinas in Los Angeles talk about the lack of camaraderie in the Los Angeles Filipino community, they are talking about a lack of a social bond in the community.

In the midst of globalization, it is not unusual to hear both the general public and social scientists lamenting the weakening of community bonds and talking longingly about searching for community, strengthening community, or building a sense of community. These concerns have been consistently voiced in public opinion polls for some time in the United States, and they were the subject of Robert Putnam's (2000) best-selling book *Bowling Alone: The Collapse and Revival of American Community*. To be sure, concerns about the waxing and waning of community are not new, but the nature of those concerns has shifted over time. In the past decade, community psychologists and community sociologists have turned to the concept of social capital to conceptualize this social bond aspect of community. This approach has been reinforced by the World Bank (2009), which has endorsed such an approach for international development work.

In simplest terms, social capital is community cohesion, which is thought to be based in dense social networks, high levels of civic engagement, a sense of solidarity and equality among members, and norms of reciprocity and trustworthiness (see Kay, 2006; Putnam, 1993). The World Bank (2009) identifies five components of their social capital implementation framework: groups and networks, trust and solidarity, collective action and cooperation, social cohesion and inclusion, and information and communication. In *Bowling Alone*, Putnam (2000) argues that for the first two-thirds of the 20th century, social capital was expanding in the United States, but that tide reversed in the final decades of the century. He calls for reconnection and revitalization of networks, civic engagement, solidarity and equality, and reciprocity and trustworthiness.

Putnam (2000) presents large amounts of empirical evidence to build a powerful argument for the loss of community in the United States. Here is some of that evidence: a 25% decline in voting and large declines in other forms of political participation in recent decades, a steep decline in face-to-face involvement in civic associations, a 25% to 50% decline in involvement in religious activities, less stable work settings and less involvement in unions, and less time socializing with friends and neighbors. He also provides evidence that we are relying increasingly on formal systems, such as the legal system, to regulate reciprocity and trustworthiness. On the other hand, he reports an increase in volunteering during this same time period. Putnam also draws on a variety of data to consider what is driving the above trends and identifies four contributing factors: pressures of time and money (about 10% of the decline); suburbanization, commuting, and sprawl (about 10% of the decline); electronic communication (about 25% of the decline); and generation change (perhaps 50% of the decline). Factors that he did not find to be associated with the decline in social capital are changing family structure and larger government. Finally, Putnam argues, with supportive data, that social capital has an important impact on human well-being in several domains, including economic, educational, and physical and mental health (see also Campbell & Jovchelovitch, 2000).

While respecting his empirical analysis, the network researchers are critical of Putnam's conceptual analysis. They argue that community has been changing rather than declining and that, while people in the United States may not be participating in group-based community activities to the same extent as in the past, their networks remain large and strong (Boase et al., 2006). They see no inherent disadvantage to the more fragmented nature of contemporary social networks, while Putnam (2000) suggests that it takes dense integrated networks that exist over time to build cohesion and trust. The work of Robert Sampson and colleagues (see Sampson, 2003; Sampson, Morenoff, & Earls, 1999) seems to support and expand this concern of Putnam's. They have proposed a theory of collective efficacy, which is "the capacity of community residents to achieve social control over the environment and to engage in collective action for the common good" (Sampson, 2003, p. S56). Collective efficacy involves a working trust, a shared belief in the neighborhood's ability for action, and a shared willingness to intervene to gain social control. Research to date indicates that as collective efficacy in a neighborhood decreases, a host of individual and social ills increase (Odgers et al., 2009; Sampson, 2003). It is important to note, however, that Sampson and colleagues (1999) have found that the spatial dynamics and quality of the physical environment of the neighborhood have an impact on collective efficacy. The Filipinos in Rome showed a great deal of collective efficacy when they developed their shopping bazaar by the Tiber River after the city authorities challenged their right to congregate in public spaces.

This idea of a social bond among community members is what Seymour Sarason (1974) had in mind when he declared the enhancement of *psychological sense of community* (PSOC) as the mission of community psychology. We looked earlier at Sarason's definition of sense of community (see Exhibit 13.1). Community psychologists

David McMillan and David Chavis (McMillan, 1996; McMillan & Chavis, 1986) turned to the literature on group cohesiveness to understand how to enhance the social bonds of community. They presented a theory of PSOC that identified four essential elements:

1. *Membership* is a sense of belonging, of being part of a collective, something bigger than oneself. Reading *Tinig Filipino* provides the Filipina domestic workers with this sense of belonging to something bigger than themselves. Membership is based on boundaries, emotional safety, personal investment, and a common symbol system. Boundaries clarify who is in and who is out, and they protect against threat. Personal investment in a community is enhanced when we feel that we have worked for membership. Common symbols facilitate integration of the community, in part by intentionally creating social distance between members and nonmembers. However, communities built on exclusion, rather than inclusion, contribute to the fragmentation of social life (Fisher & Karger, 1997; Hardcastle et al., 2004).

2. *Influence* is bidirectional. On the one hand, members are more attracted to a community where they have some sense of control and influence. On the other hand, to be cohesive, a community has to be able to exert influence over members. In this way, behavioral conformity comes from the need to belong, and conformity promotes cohesiveness. The Filipinas in Rome have established a clear set of expectations that members engage in mutual assistance; this expectation promotes a sense of belonging, and conformity to it promotes cohesiveness.

Rational choice perspective

3. *Integration and fulfillment of needs* refers to individual reinforcement or reward for membership. The community must be rewarding to its members, but McMillan and Chavis (1986) conclude that "a strong community is able to fit people together so that people meet others' needs while they meet their own" (p. 13). Both in Rome and in Los Angeles, the Filipina domestic workers share information about jobs and job-related problems. In Rome, solidarity compels the women to support each other's day-off business ventures, such as working as vendors. There is a mutual understanding that "I will buy your wares if you buy mine." However, on occasion, some workers take advantage of others and violate the norm of integration and mutual meeting of needs.

Social behavioral perspective

4. *Shared emotional connection* is based on a shared history and identification with the community. It is enhanced when members are provided with "positive ways to interact, important events to share and ways to resolve them positively, opportunities to honor members, opportunities to invest in the community, and opportunities to experience a spiritual bond among members" (McMillan & Chavis, 1986, p. 14). The Filipinas in Rome and Los Angeles have found positive ways to interact with each other, and they feel camaraderie in their shared migrant experience. When they read the stories in *Tinig Filipino*, they also feel a shared emotional connection to Filipina domestic workers around the world.

Humanistic perspective

On the basis of this definition of PSOC, McMillan and Chavis (1986) developed a 12-item Sense of Community Index (SCI) that has been used extensively for research on sense of community in such diverse settings as religious communities (Miers & Fisher, 2002), the workplace (Pretty & McCarthy, 1991), student communities (Pretty, 1990; Obst & White, 2007), Internet communities (Obst et al., 2002a), immigrant communities (Sonn, 2002), political groups (Sonn & Fisher, 1996), and residential and geographic communities (Brodsky & Marx, 2001; Brodsky, O'Campo, & Aronson, 1999). Recently, researchers have suggested some need to make minor revisions to the SCI (Obst & White, 2004). One research team cautioned that the SCI was developed and validated in Western societies and may not be a good fit for the meaning of community for non-Western people (Mak, Cheung, & Law, 2009). Another research team

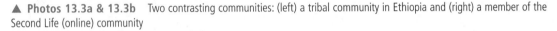

▲ **Photos 13.3a & 13.3b**   Two contrasting communities: (left) a tribal community in Ethiopia and (right) a member of the Second Life (online) community

developed separate measures for each of the four components of POSC and tested their psychometric properties in the first known study of POSC in a community of gay men (Proescholdbell, Roosa, & Nemeroff, 2006). They found that membership could not be distinguished from integration and need fulfillment.

An Australian research team (Obst et al., 2002a, 2002b) has used McMillan and Chavis's theory of PSOC to compare PSOC in territorial and relational communities. More specifically, the researchers asked 359 science fiction aficionados attending a World Science Fiction Convention to complete questionnaires rating PSOC both for their fandom community and for their territorial community. Research participants reported significantly higher levels of PSOC in their fandom communities than in their territorial communities. They also found that although the ratings on all dimensions of McMillan and Chavis's four theorized dimensions of PSOC were higher in the fandom communities than in the geographical communities, the dimensions received essentially the same rank ordering in both communities. The researchers also suggest that a fifth dimension, *conscious identification* with the community, should be added to McMillan and Chavis's theory of PSOC. They found this cognitive identification to be an important component of PSOC. Other researchers have found that social bonding and intimacy take time to mature in computer-mediated communication (Harrison & Thomas, 2009).

In recent years, the social work literature has paid much attention to the issue of community building. This literature often focuses broadly on community revitalization, in terms of the economic and physical, as well as the social relationship dimensions of communities (e.g., E. Beck & Eichler, 2000; Halperin, 2001; Hendricks & Rudich, 2000; Zachary, 2000). The literature on youth leadership development is particularly noteworthy for its attention to building a sense of community among youth in neighborhoods (Finn & Checkoway, 1998; Tilton, 2009; Twiss & Cooper, 2000). Recent social work literature on community youth development has returned to its settlement house roots, recommending the use of arts, humanities, and sports to build a sense of community, as well as to empower youth and help them build skills (Delgado, 2000; Tilton, 2009). Building social capital has been a particularly popular public health strategy in the United Kingdom and Australia (Baum, 1999; Campbell & Jovchelovitch, 2000).

Social capital theorists acknowledge that social capital can be used for antisocial as well as prosocial purposes. Think of the elements of social capital and sense of community and you will have to agree that they apply equally well to the Ku Klux Klan (KKK) and a neighborhood committee formed to welcome the influx of new immigrants. The literature on networks often suggests that birds of a feather flock together. It is quite possible, as the KKK example demonstrates, that groups can be socially cohesive and yet quite exclusionary, distrustful, and hostile (even violently so) to outsiders. That has led Putnam (2000) and others (Baum, 1999; Potocky-Tripodi, 2004) to accede the dark side of social capital.

Putnam notes that in the same time period that social capital was declining in the United States, social tolerance was growing. On another dark note, Australian public health educator Fran Baum (1999) states a fear that has also been presented by European community psychologists (see Riera, 2005):

> Social capital may come to be seen as a shorthand way of putting responsibility on communities that do not have the economic, educational or other resources to generate social capital. Networks, trust and cooperation are not substitutes for housing, jobs, incomes and education even though they might play a role in helping people gain access to them. (p. 176)

We would suggest that the dark side of social capital calls for a conflict approach to understanding community.

Conflict Approach

Conflict perspective

The Filipina domestic workers in Rome and Los Angeles have confronted anti-immigrant sentiment. They often feel exploited by their privileged employers. They feel shut out of all sectors of the labor market except for low-status domestic work. In Los Angeles, they have felt marginalized by and alienated from middle-class Filipinos. Back in the Philippines, many were abused or abandoned by their husbands. They blame the Philippines government for providing so little security to its residents, but they seldom blame the inequities of economic globalization for their limited options. Conflict theory's emphasis on dissension, power, and exploitation adds another dimension to our understanding of their story.

Writing about how European approaches to community psychology differ from U.S. community psychology, Francescato and Tomai (2001) suggest that European theorizing is much more in the conflict tradition than U.S. theorizing. They propose that, particularly in continental Europe (Germany, Italy, Spain, and Portugal), the work of community psychologists shows that they "do not believe in the myth of the self-made man" (p. 372) that undergirds much of the work in the United States. They further suggest that the longer historical view in Europe leads to more critical emphases in European theory on social and economic inequalities, the historical interpretations that have been presented by power elites to legitimize existing social hierarchies, and the historical collective struggles by which groups of people have become empowered. Indeed, they report that European textbooks on community psychology typically devote chapters to historical social struggles that have led to greater empowerment for specific groups. Francescato and Tomai argue that Putnam's findings of declining social capital in the United States can be explained by U.S. fascination with neoliberal economics and individual success, which has led to increasing inequality. They insist that social capital cannot exist at the community level without state policy that supports it. In their view, community practice should involve strategies that focus on unequal power distribution and stimulate community participants to challenge community narratives that legitimize the status quo.

Writing from the United Kingdom, Isabelle Fremeaux (2005) criticizes the social capital approach on several fronts. She argues that it typically romanticizes community and fails to recognize the internal coercion and divisions that often are at play in communities. Failure to recognize the power politics operating in communities does damage to the least powerful members. And, much like Francescato and Tomai, she criticizes Putnam and other social capital theorists for neglecting to analyze the impact of the macro political and economic contexts on local networks. The story of the Filipinas in Rome and Los Angeles is an excellent example of the influence of macro political and economic contexts on social networks among migrant domestic workers.

Other European social scientists argue that community is "as much about struggle as it is about unity" (Brent, 1997, p. 83). Community workers are often faced with heterogeneous settings with diverse opinions, attitudes, and emotional attachments (Dixon, Dogan, & Sanderson, 2005). Carles Riera (2005), community development specialist from Spain, argues that managing the conflicts in such diversity should be the focus of community theorists and practitioners. Riera notes that European society, like U.S. society, is becoming more and more multicultural, caused by migrations from non-European countries as well as by the loosening of the borders of the European Union. Migrating groups often have strong internal cohesion, but the receiving communities are often fragmented. The task for community workers is to work for both inclusion and equality of opportunities in a framework of coexistence.

Riera (2005) describes a model of practice developed in Barcelona, Spain, called the Intercultural Mediation Programme. The program is three-pronged: It strives (1) to facilitate the resolution of intercultural community conflicts that occur in public spaces, (2) to facilitate the resolution of intercultural conflict situations among neighbors living in the same buildings, and (3) to provide information and advice to service professionals struggling with intercultural conflicts. The program is carried out by community mediator teams who use both linguistic and sociocultural interpreters. Perhaps such mediation could have helped when the Filipinos in Rome were being harassed to stop congregating in public spaces, and it might also be helpful to bridge divisions in the Los Angeles Filipino community.

Conflict theory is not new to U.S. social workers and social scientists, but its popularity has waxed and waned over time. Like European theorists, Robert Fisher and Eric Shragge (2000) argue that the worldwide spread of neoliberal faith in the free market (see discussion in Chapter 9) has "dulled the political edge" (p. 1) of community social workers. They argue for renewed commitment to a form of community social work that is willing to build opposition and use a range of confrontational tactics to challenge privilege and oppression. Given economic globalization, Fisher and Shragge recommend that effective community organizing in the current era will need to be tied to a global social movement (social movements are the topic of Chapter 14). To work effectively with community conflict, social workers must be able to analyze the structure of community power and influence (Martinez-Brawley, 2000). They must understand who controls which types of resources and how power brokers are related to one another. That means understanding the power held internally in the community as well as the power that resides external to the community. This type of analysis allows social workers to understand both the possibilities and limits of community empowerment. Emilia Martinez-Brawley suggests that social workers working in small communities should keep in mind that memories are usually long in such places, and conflictual relationships established on one issue may have an impact on future issues. Historical understanding is important.

Contemporary life also calls for the type of mediation programs recommended by Riera (2005). In many areas of life, from race relations to family relations, the mediator role is becoming more prominent for social workers. We will have to become more comfortable with conflict if we are to take leadership roles in healing these social fractures. In recent years, some rural communities have faced sudden influxes of refugees from a particular trouble spot in the world. Some of these communities have responded in exclusionary and punitive ways, while others have responded in inclusive and collaborative ways. It is more than likely that communities in the United States and other affluent countries will continue to face such influxes, and social workers should be able to assist communities in managing such change. One suggestion recently forwarded is that restorative justice programs similar to the ones used in criminal justice could be used to heal friction and conflict within neighborhoods (Verity & King, 2007). Restorative justice gatherings would allow storytelling and dialogue about social fractures and allow communities to move toward a more just future. This suggestion is consistent with Riera's Intercultural Mediation Programme.

Critical Thinking Questions 13.2

If we put a camera in your hands, what story would you tell about your territorial community? What images would you capture, and what meaning would you make of those images? Would social cohesion or social conflict be more prominent in the photographic story?

SOCIAL WORKERS AND COMMUNITIES: CONTEMPORARY ISSUES

As suggested in Chapter 9, modernization, capitalism, industrialization, urbanization, and globalization have great costs for society as well as benefits. The profession of social work was developed as one force to minimize the costs—a communal force to correct for extremes of individualism. In its efforts to promote the general social welfare, social work has always been involved with communities in some way. But, as suggested earlier, there is expanding interest in community among social workers around the world. The expanded interest in the United States has been nurtured by the Association for Community Organization & Social Administration (ACOSA), which was formed in 1987, and by the journal started by ACOSA, *Journal of Community Practice*. The 2005 publication of *The Handbook of Community Practice* (Weil, 2005a) was a major advance in knowledge building for community social work practice.

The nature of social work's relationships with communities has changed over time, however, and there are long-standing disagreements about appropriate roles for social workers in communities. Depending on the preferred community model or perspective, social workers can play a number of different roles in the community, such as guide, facilitator, expert, therapist, organizer, administrator, activist, broker, or educator. Here, we summarize the issues involved in four of these points of disagreement.

Community as Context for Practice Versus Target of Practice

Social workers who view community as a context for practice focus on working with individuals and families, although they recognize the ways in which communities provide opportunities and barriers for client behaviors and agency responses. They are most likely to enact the therapist role, but may also engage in individual or family education. In contrast, social workers who view community as a target of practice focus on enhancing the health of the community. They are most likely to enact the organizer, activist, broker, and educator roles.

There seems to be a growing consensus that social work needs to recognize community as both context and target of practice (Hardcastle et al., 2004; M. Lynn, 2006; Mulroy, Nelson, & Gour, 2005). During the 1990s, there was a reemergence of the idea of comprehensive multifocused community interventions (Mulroy et al., 2005). Recent initiatives to revitalize impoverished neighborhoods have combined resource development and individual asset building with efforts to strengthen sense of community (Padilla & Sherraden, 2005). Community agencies are working to help individual families and at the same time to help in building strong and caring communities. For example, they are combining family therapy and parent education with community building to help children succeed at school (Feikema, Segalavich, & Jeffries, 1997). A similar continuum of practice has been developed for community building with and care of older adults (Mulroy et al., 2005). The Wellbriety Movement in Native American communities in the United States is focusing on recovery from alcohol and other addictions at both the individual and community level (Coyhis & Simonelli, 2005). They use the metaphor of a "healing forest" to suggest that youth can't get well in an unhealthy community.

Even with a combined, or comprehensive, community practice model, questions still arise about when to intervene with individuals and families and when to focus on larger collectivities and groups. Many projects focus almost exclusively on capacity building at the community level. For example, around the world, communities are engaging in community capacity-building projects as a strategy to prevent family violence in distressed neighborhoods (see Chan, Lam, & Cheng, 2009). They attempt to develop a sense of community, stimulate a sense of mutual responsibility, activate a process of communal problem solving, and improve access to resources. In a similar vein, the asset-building movement focuses on creating asset-rich communities for children and youth. These projects seek to engage adults in building supportive relationships with neighborhood children and youth, mobilize youth to become active participants in community life, and stimulate resource development and collaborative problem solving (see Mannes, Roehlkepartain, & Benson, 2005). On the other hand, the majority of social work interventions continue to occur at the individual and family level, with far too little attention to the context of individual and family lives.

In a much-cited work, Harry Specht and Mark Courtney (1994) called for putting the "social" back in social work with a "community-based system of social care" and elimination of the psychotherapeutic role. We would not recommend that the psychotherapeutic role be eliminated from social work's repertoire, but social workers may have come to rely too heavily on this role. They may be using it for problems for which it is neither efficient nor effective. An integrated community practice should avoid an overreliance on one-to-one and family sessions, opting, where appropriate, for collective and group formats. Two promising models for this are family group conferencing and peacemaking circles used in child protection and youth services (see Boyes-Watson, 2005; Connolly, 2006).

Agency Orientation Versus Social Action

Community social work practice has roots in a **social action model** of community organization, which was developed by leaders of the settlement house movement. This model of community practice is political in nature, emphasizing social reform and challenge of structural inequalities. But by the 1930s, this social action model had been replaced by an **agency-based model,** which promoted social agencies and the services they provided (Fisher & Karger, 1997). This model of community practice is nonpolitical and puts little or no emphasis on social change. It is based on the assumption that the best way to strengthen communities is to provide social services. Proponents of the agency-based model of community organizing often focus on coordination of services across agencies (see Altshuler, 2005; Chahine, van Straaten, & Williams, 2005; Steves, & Blevens, 2005).

Saul Alinsky (1971), founder of one of the best-known community organizing training centers, was critical of the agency-based model of community social work. He did not think that social justice was ensured by providing social services. A contemporary African social worker, Tlamelo Mmatli (2008), makes a similar argument. Mmatli argues that the main problems facing people in Africa are "unemployment, poverty, inequality, illiteracy, homelessness, child streetism, ill-health, HIV/AIDS, abuse of human right and civil liberties, civil conflicts and official corruption" (p. 297). He further argues that these problems require political advocacy, not social services.

We suggest that agency-based provision of social services, and interagency coordination of services, often do contribute to the well-being of communities. We need social workers who will advocate for the retention of threatened services as well as the development of new services, but we also need good program evaluation to guide those advocacy efforts. We also agree with DeFilippis, Fisher, and Shragge (2009) that although community-based nonprofit organizations are growing in number and influence, too many focus narrowly on service delivery and have lost sight of social and economic justice. DeFilippis et al. argue that it is possible to engage in both service provision and social action and provide examples of community organizations that are doing this. An integrated approach to community social work practice enhances community-based services, builds a sense of community, and advocates for social reform.

Conflict Model of Practice Versus Collaborative Model

Over the years, social work has taken different positions on the question of whether social workers should lean toward conflict or collaboration, ebbing and flowing in its "tradition of nagging the conscience of America" (Fisher & Karger, 1997, p. 188). In liberal times, social work has been more willing to embrace conflict approaches; in conservative times, more collaborative approaches have been preferred (Fisher, 2005). In the early 1900s, social work reformers used social surveys

Conflict perspective

to expose exploitive industries and disseminated the results widely in newspapers and magazines (Fisher & Karger, 1997). In the current era of transnational corporations and high transnational mobility, these methods might be revisited by contemporary social workers. Today, however, as suggested above, the trend is away from challenging the establishment and toward creating partnerships between community groups, government agencies, and corporations (DeFilippis et al., 2009; Fisher, 2005).

In his historical review of community practice, Robert Fisher (2005) argues that the global context of contemporary community practice is dominated by a conservative, corporate-oriented ethos. In this climate, the market dominates, issues are seen as private and not public, and people are becoming more isolated from each other. In such a climate, social action approaches both inside and outside social work have been viewed as inappropriate. Social workers depend on political and financial support from governmental and private philanthropies, which have, for the most part, a heavy investment in the status quo (Mmatli, 2008).

The contemporary tension between conflict and collaborative models of practice is exemplified by two articles that appeared in the *Journal of Community Practice* during 2000. Robert Fisher, a social work educator from the United States, and Eric Shragge, a social work educator from Canada, contrast social action and community-building approaches to practice (Fisher & Shragge, 2000). *Social action* works for social change by organizing people to put pressure on governments or private organizations. It challenges social inequalities. Community development is based on an assumption of shared interests, rather than conflicting interests. It seeks to bring together diverse community interests for the betterment of the community as a whole, with attention to community building and an improved sense of community. Fisher and Shragge acknowledge that many community practitioners interweave social action and community development. They suggest, however, that the community development approach to community practice has become dominant. They lament this turn of events, arguing that we are in an era of growing inequality that requires more, not less, social action.

An article by Elizabeth Beck and Michael Eichler (2000) argues the other side of the coin. They propose consensus organizing, based in feminist theory, as a practice model for community building. *Consensus organizing* has four basic assumptions:

1. Power does not have to be redistributed; it can be grown.

2. Human behavior is motivated by mutual self-interest, not just individual self-interest.

3. People are basically good, and power holders will make decisions that improve community well-being when given the opportunity.

4. The wealthy and the poor, the powerful and the powerless can be knit together rather than become adversaries.

Like Fisher and Shragge (2000), Beck and Eichler (2000) suggest that both social action and community development are needed, but they argue for an emphasis on community work that strengthens relationships. They claim that social action calls for a redistribution of power, but consensus organizing does not assert that redistribution of power is necessary to end oppression. Indeed, Beck and Eichler argue that conflict tactics often don't reach the goal of redistribution of power anyway.

Contemporary social trends call for a contemporary style of community practice that draws on both conflict and collaborative models. Community social workers need skills for exposing and challenging social injustice as well as for resolving conflict and building coalitions. The choice of tactics will depend on the specific person–environment configurations encountered. Michael Reisch (2005) astutely observes that in conservative times, social workers can use opportunities to work in collaborative, community-based projects to help create a radical vision of justice and fairness.

Some person–environment configurations call for community social workers to elevate community conflict for the purpose of challenging exploitation and oppression. Throughout this book, we emphasize the need for social workers to take a critical perspective that recognizes power and oppression as important factors in the negotiation of social life. A critical perspective also calls for social workers to challenge existing patterns of domination and oppression. With the trend toward devolution of government responsibilities to the local level, the local territorial community becomes increasingly important to these efforts. Social work research can identify and expose local patterns of exploitation. Community social workers can use consciousness-raising tactics to help oppressed groups understand their situations. They can use a variety of advocacy skills to make appeals for the rights and needs of oppressed groups. Many contemporary social critics "see grassroots community organizations as potentially the most effective progressive balance to the elite domination" (Fisher & Karger, 1997, p. 130).

Other person-environment configurations call for community social workers to resolve community conflicts. Robert Fisher and Howard Karger (1997) remind us that "public life is about difference, and about learning to create a society by interacting with others who have different opinions and experiences" (p. 26). This notion seems to be left out of the community psychology literature on PSOC. Social work's professional organizations have taken a position that values diversity. But they should go beyond that position and value the conflict that accompanies diversity. Communities often need help in negotiating their differences. Social workers can help to develop a civil discourse on controversial issues, a discourse that includes the voices of people who have previously been marginalized and excluded. Community social workers can use a variety of conflict resolution skills to help different community groups understand and respect each other's experiences and to engage in respectful and effective problem-solving activities.

There is considerable agreement among social work scholars that social workers should focus on helping to develop broad issues that can unite diverse groups in social reform efforts; two examples of such issues are health care and financial security in a global economy (Fisher & Karger, 1997; Hardcastle et al., 2004). Recently, actions of the antiglobalization movement have suggested that a spark of resistance is alive for the issue of financial security in a global economy. But these efforts are less likely to succeed if they do not build greater solidarity between poor and middle-class people, something that is very much lacking even among immigrant groups like the Filipinos in Los Angeles. Another problem requiring coalition building is the viability of impoverished central-city neighborhoods for which regional solutions will be necessary. Coalitions across cultural groups are also increasingly desirable. For example, domestic workers from different ethnic backgrounds might benefit from working collaboratively rather than competitively. The social work literature is beginning to grapple with the complexities of coalition building (Dunlop & Angell, 2001; Mizrahi & Rosenthal, 2001; Roberts-DeGennaro & Mizrahi, 2005).

Expert Versus Partner in the Social Change Process

The traditional social planning model of community social work is based on the premise that the complexities of modern social problems require expert planners schooled in a rational planning model. In this model, the community power structure is the author of social change efforts. This is often referred to as a top-down approach to social change.

Community-building models of community social work take a different view: Community practice should support and enhance the ability of community members to identify their own community's needs, assets, and solutions to problems (Daley & Marsiglia, 2000; Foster-Fishman et al., 2006; Weil, 2005c). These approaches are commonly called participatory community planning. Social workers work in partnership with community members and groups, and remain open to learning from the community (Weil, 2005c). This approach is often referred to as a bottom-up approach to social change.

Many local community development corporations (CDCs) are experimenting with ways of building partnerships with community members for community revitalization. When one community intervention team encountered difficulties in getting community residents to focus on possibilities rather than problems, they borrowed the miracle question from solution focused therapy:

> Imagine you've gone to sleep and while you're sleeping, you have a dream. And in your dream, Westlane becomes exactly the way you'd like to see it. . . . Keeping your eyes closed: What do you see that lets you know the goal has been accomplished, that your dream has become a reality. (Hollingsworth, Allen-Meares, Shanks, & Gant, 2009, p. 334)

Laura Ross and Mardia Coleman (2000) provide one model for community partnerships, a model they call Urban Community Action Planning (UCAP). They have adapted this approach from Participatory Rural Appraisal (PRA), a grassroots approach used in rural areas of Africa, Latin America, and Asia. The PRA model is based on three assumptions:

1. *Local knowledge.* Community members have knowledge about local problems, but they need help to organize it.

2. *Local resources.* Community members have resources, but these resources need to be mobilized.

3. *Outside help.* Outside resources are available, but they need to be matched to community-identified priorities.

Efforts at community building often rely heavily on indigenous leaders, or leaders who are indigenous to the targeted community, to facilitate meaningful community participation. These efforts do not always run smoothly. Community practitioners have had little guidance on how to identify indigenous leaders and how to prepare them to lead. Recent literature has begun to address this important issue, noting both aids and barriers to effective indigenous leadership (Zachary, 2000). Seeing that many potential indigenous leaders have had limited opportunities to play such roles, some community organizers have suggested a need for preparation or training for the role of indigenous leader.

A traditional social planning model is appropriate for problems requiring specialized technical knowledge. Community members are the experts, however, about community needs and assets. They also have the capacity to be active partners in identifying solutions to community problems. The Generations of Hope intergenerational communities project, which forms intentional communities where older adults serve as resources to foster and adoptive families, is an example of a community intervention that makes a distinction between tasks for which the professional is the expert and tasks for which community members are the expert (Eheart, Hopping, Power, Mitchell, & Racine, 2009). For example, staff are seen as the experts about who should live in the community, how to secure and manage financial resources and relationships with the external environment, and providing counseling and therapeutic support. But members of the community are considered to be the experts on the needs of families, and older adults in the community are the primary resources for children and families.

Critical Thinking Questions 13.3

What intercultural conflicts have you seen in or around your local territorial community or in your online community? What social justice issues are involved in those conflicts? What approaches to community practice do you think could be useful in helping to manage these conflicts?

IMPLICATIONS FOR SOCIAL WORK PRACTICE

The preceding discussion of community has many implications for social work practice:

- Be informed about the communities you serve; learn about their readiness to change, their spatial arrangements (for territorial communities), their cultures, their patterns of internal and external relationships, their social capital, and their conflicts.

- Avoid overreliance on individual and family sessions; make use of small- and large-group formats where appropriate.

- When working with individuals and families, assess their opportunities to be supported by and to make contributions to the community, and assess the limits imposed by their territorial and relational communities.

- Recognize the central role of territorial community in the lives of many young persons and their caregivers, older adults, and poor families.

- If you are a social work planner or administrator, become familiar with computer-based geographical information systems for mapping social data.

- Where appropriate, strengthen interaction within the community (horizontal linkages) to build a sense of community and maximize the use of internal resources. Strengthen intercommunity interactions (vertical linkages) to ensure there are adequate resources to meet the community's needs.

- Where appropriate, advocate for the retention of threatened social services, the coordination of existing services, and the development of new services.

- Where appropriate, collaborate with others to challenge exploitation and oppression in communities. Use consciousness-raising tactics to help oppressed groups understand their situations.

- Where appropriate, assist communities to negotiate differences and resolve conflicts.

- Where appropriate, assist in the development of coalitions to improve the resource base for community problem solving.

- Involve community members in identification of community strengths and community problems, in goal setting, and in intervention activities.

- When working with impoverished communities, work with other individuals and organizations, both inside and outside these communities, to develop comprehensive, multidimensional, integrated strategies.

KEY TERMS

agency-based model	gesellschaft	social action model
bonding social capital	horizontal linkage	social capital
bridging social capital	mass society	social planning model
collective efficacy	network	solidary community
community	networked individualism	territorial community
community development	personal community	vertical linkage
gemeinschaft	relational community	
geographic information system (GIS)	sense of community	

ACTIVE LEARNING

1. You have read about two communities with geographical properties, one based in Rome and one based in Los Angeles. Now think about your own geographic community. Compare and contrast it with the communities of Filipina domestic workers in Rome and in Los Angeles according to the following characteristics:

   - Sense of community
   - Physical environment
   - Horizontal and vertical linkages

2. One research team has found that the majority of our ties to other people are nonterritorial, but two-thirds of our actual interactions are local, in the neighborhood or work setting. To test this idea, for one day keep a record of all contacts you have with other people and the time spent in such contacts—face-to-face contacts as well as telephone and electronic contacts. What percentage of your contacts occur in your neighborhood, at work, or at school?

3. Visit a neighborhood house or center, a YMCA or YWCA, or another community action organization in your town or city. Interview the director or another staff member about the mission of the organization, asking them to address the following questions:

   - Is the focus on working with individuals and families or on enhancing the health of the community?
   - Is the focus of the work political in nature, emphasizing social reform and challenge of structure inequalities, or is it on providing and coordinating services?
   - Are the methods used confrontational in nature ("challenging the establishment") or collaborative in nature ("creating partnerships")?
   - How involved are community members in planning and carrying out the change activities of the organization?

WEB RESOURCES

The Annie E. Casey Foundation
www.aecf.org

Site maintained by the Annie E. Casey Foundation, a grant-making organization that works to build better futures for disadvantaged children and their families, contains a description of initiatives, and projects and publications.

Association for Community Organization & Social Administration (ACOSA)
www.acosa.org

Site includes recent paper presentations, hot topics, important news about community organizing, and links to other Internet sites.

National Community Action Foundation (NCAF)
www.ncaf.org

Site maintained by NCAF, an advocacy group for community action agencies, contains news, events, and current issues.

National People's Action (NPA)
www.npa-us.org

Site maintained by NPA, an advocacy organization that helps neighborhood people take on corporate America and political institutions, contains conference information, issues, and links to other advocacy groups.

Social Psychology Network: Community Psychology
www.socialpsychology.org/

An online guide to community psychology maintained by Scott Plous at Wesleyan University, contains links to sites covering a wide range of community psychology issues.

United Neighborhood Houses of New York Inc.
www.unhny.org

Site maintained by United Neighborhood Houses of New York Inc., a federation of 36 settlement houses in New York City, includes information about the settlement house movement, current activities of settlement houses in the United States, and job vacancies.

CHAPTER

14

Social Movements

Elizabeth D. Hutchison

OPENING QUESTIONS

- How might the literature on social movements help social work with its social reform mission?

- What are the major theoretical perspectives on social movements?

KEY IDEAS

As you read this chapter, take note of these central ideas:

1. Social movements are formed when people feel that one or more social institutions are unjust and need to be changed.

2. The profession of social work has its origins in the confluence of two social movements: the charity organization society movement and the settlement house movement.

3. Three theoretical perspectives on social movements have emerged in the past two decades: the political opportunities perspective, the mobilizing structures perspective, and the cultural framing perspective. None of these perspectives taken individually is sufficient for understanding social movements, but taken together, they provide a multidimensional understanding. Dissatisfaction with these three perspectives is leading to emerging theories of social movements.

4. Social movements are neither completely successful nor completely unsuccessful.

5. Recently, there has been a rise in transnational social movement organizations (TSMOs).

6. Contemporary social work, like historical social work, must manage a tension between professional services and social reform.

Case Study

Fighting for a Living Wage

Greg Halpern was in his senior year at Harvard University in 1998 when Aaron Bartley, his labor activist roommate and childhood friend, "dragged" him to a meeting of the Harvard Living Wage Campaign (Terkel, 2003). Greg remembers that he was in the lunch line a few days later when a friend made a joke about how bad the food was. Greg laughed, and then he looked up and exchanged glances with one of the young women working behind the lunch counter. He saw her anger and hurt. He was deeply embarrassed and realized that most Harvard students had never been taught about the people who clean the bathrooms, serve the food, or clean the classrooms. Greg became active in the living wage campaign at Harvard, attending weekly rallies and sending letters to the university president, calling for the custodians, security guards, and food service workers at Harvard to be paid a living wage. In March 1999, the campaign presented the university president with the "Worst Employer in Boston" award while he was addressing a group of high school students. At graduation, some students chartered an airplane to pull a sign behind it that read, "Harvard needs a living wage" (Tanner, 2002).

That same spring, in his final year at Harvard, Greg Halpern did an independent study in which he interviewed and photographed university workers. He decided to blow the interviews up on 10-foot pages and stick them up in the public space provided for students, so that other students could know the stories of the low-wage workers. Greg had never been an activist, but he was dismayed at what he was hearing from workers, and he remained active in the Harvard Living Wage Campaign after he graduated. The campaign had been holding rallies at Harvard for 3 years, but nothing was happening. During the spring of 2001, just 2 years after Greg graduated from Harvard, there was growing interest among the members of the Harvard Living Wage Campaign to engage in a sit-in. As they discussed this option, Greg remembered the custodian he had interviewed 2 years earlier. Bill Brook, who cleaned the room in which they were meeting, was 65 years old, worked two full-time jobs, and slept 4 hours per night (Terkel, 2003).

Greg became one of the leaders of the Harvard Living Wage Campaign sit-in strike that occupied Massachusetts Hall, the president's building, for 21 days, demanding that the university raise the wages for 1,400 employees who were making less than a living wage. Throughout the strike, the students, who had never participated in such an event before, kept in touch with the media by cell phones and e-mail (sent and received on their laptops).

There were 50 students inside Massachusetts Hall and a growing group of students on the outside. Three hundred professors or more took out a full-page ad in the *Boston Globe* in support of the students. The dining hall workers and food workers began to deliver pizzas to the students on the inside, and many workers took the risk to wear buttons on the job that said "We Support the Living Wage Campaign." Every local labor union in Cambridge, Massachusetts, endorsed the students, and national labor leaders came to speak. The AFL-CIO union sent one of its top lawyers to negotiate with the university administration. Several high-profile religious leaders made appearances to support the students. On the 15th day of the sit-in, the Cambridge mayor and city council, along with other sympathizers, marched from City Hall to Harvard Yard in support of the students. During the second week of the sit-in, between 30 and 40 Harvard Divinity School students held a vigil, chanting, "Where's your horror? Where's your rage? Div School wants a living wage." On the last night of the sit-in, there was a rally of about 3,000 people outside Massachusetts Hall (Gourevitch, 2001; Tanner, 2002; Terkel, 2003).

In the end, the Harvard administration agreed to negotiate higher wages with the unions. Higher wages were paid, but the students were not fully satisfied with the results of their campaign. Two of the student activists later coproduced an advocacy film based on the sit-in, *Occupation: The Harvard University Living Wage Sit-in,* narrated by Ben Affleck (Raza & Velez, 2002).

The sit-in at Harvard was neither the beginning nor the end of the gathering living wage movement in the United States. The sit-in built on the momentum that had started in Baltimore, Maryland, in 1994, and it fueled new actions on other university campuses. It was one piece of a story of a rapidly growing social movement.

In 1994, religious groups in Baltimore were seeing an increase in use of soup kitchens and food pantries by the working poor (Quigley, 2001; Tanner, 2002). They were angry that working people could not afford to feed their families. A coalition of 50 religious groups joined forces with the American Federation of State, County, and Municipal Employees (AFSCME) and low-wage service workers to create a local campaign, which they called Baltimoreans United in Leadership Development (BUILD). BUILD worked to develop a law that would require businesses that had contracts with the city to pay their workers a "living wage," a pay rate that would lift a family of four over the federal poverty level. At the time, the federal minimum wage was $4.25 an hour, a wage that could not lift a family out of poverty. Both the religious groups and AFSCME provided people and funds to educate the public about the problem of low wages and to lobby for signing of the living wage bill. The living wage law was enacted in July 1996, requiring city contractors with municipal contracts over $5,000 to pay a minimum wage of $6.16 an hour in 1996, with increments to reach $7.70 an hour in 1999. The law is estimated to have affected 1,500 to 2,000 workers.

(Continued)

(Continued)

The BUILD coalition had no intention of sparking a national social movement, but their success helped to trigger a nationwide alliance of religious and labor groups that has come to be known as the living wage movement. Local grassroots coalitions of activists have used a variety of tactics, including lobbying, postcard campaigns, rallies, door-knocking, leafleting, workshops, and sit-ins to achieve their goals in over 120 localities by 2004, just 10 years after BUILD began work in Baltimore. The policy solutions have varied from locality to locality, with some bolder than others, but all have established a wage above the federal minimum wage for some group of workers. Some of the local living wage ordinances, like the one in Baltimore, cover only municipal workers. Others have been more expansive in their approach, like the Chicago ordinance passed on July 26, 2006, which requires "big box" stores—those making over $1 billion per year—to pay a wage of $10 plus $3 in benefits per hour, beginning in 2010. The living wage movement has also helped to enact legislation at the state rather than local level. By the end of 2006, a total of 22 states plus the District of Columbia had enacted minimum wage laws that set the minimum wage higher than the federal requirement (Vanden Heuvel & Graham-Felsen, 2006).

Each local coalition is different. In Alexandria, Virginia, the living wage campaign started with the Tenants' and Workers' Support Committee, which had formed in 1986 to fight evictions of residents in low-rent housing. They were eventually joined by seven religious congregations and 17 unions. In Los Angeles, the living wage campaign was orchestrated by the Los Angeles Alliance for a New Economy (LAANE), which was created by a coalition of the Hotel Employees and Restaurant Employees Union, Hispanic neighborhood groups, a tenant group, Communities for a Better Environment, and religious organizations (Bernstein, 2002).

These campaigns benefited from much assistance from the Living Wage Resource Center established by the Association of Community Organizations for Reform Now (ACORN). ACORN developed a 225-page guide to assist local activists in organizing a successful living wage campaign, written by labor economist David Reynolds. ACORN, an organization that once had neighborhood chapters in over 90 cities, organized national training conferences and also regularly dispatched staff to consult to local coalitions.

The living wage movement has drawn on stories of the impact of living wage ordinances on the lives of low-wage workers to ignite public support for new campaigns. Here are some of the stories told:

- A retail worker at the Los Angeles airport was able to drop one of her part-time jobs to enroll in a class to build career skills;

- A parking lot attendant in Alexandria, Virginia, was able to quit one of his three jobs to spend more time with his family;

- A security guard in Tucson, Arizona, could finally take care of some small car repairs and start a savings account.

In 2006, a documentary called *Waging a Living* (Weisberg, 2006), which chronicles the daily struggles of four low-wage workers, premiered on public television and became available for sale and rental.

Along the way, the living wage movement has benefited from the support of a number of organizations. The Economic Policy Institute developed a guide to living wage initiatives and their economic impacts on its website. The National Low Income Housing Coalition compiled a report that calculated the amount of money a household needs to afford a rental unit in specific localities. The Brennan Center for Justice, located at the New York University School of Law, provided assistance to design and implement living wage campaigns, including economic impact analysis, legislative drafting, and legal analysis and defense. Responsible Wealth, a national network of businesspeople, investors, and affluent citizens, developed a living wage covenant for businesses who are interested in economic fairness. The Political Economy Research Institute (PERI), at the University of Massachusetts at Amherst, collected a number of research reports on the effects of living wage laws.

One of the more promising developments in the living wage social movement is the entry of university and high school students into the movement. The Living Wage Action Coalition (LWAC), made up of university students and recent graduates who have participated in living wage campaigns around the country, was created in the summer of 2005. LWAC has been touring around colleges and universities in the United States, running workshops about strategies for successful living wage campaigns for low-wage workers on campus. In May 2005, Brookline, Massachusetts, passed Article 19 to amend the town's living wage bylaws to be more inclusive. Article 19 was researched and proposed by the Students Action for Justice and Education group at Brookline High School (Living Wage Resource Center, 2006).

The living wage movement started in the United States, but by 2001, it had crossed national lines to London, England, where it has spread to hospitals, finance companies, universities, art galleries, and hotels. The movement there has also secured agreements that all new jobs at the Olympic site for the 2012 Summer Olympics will be living wage jobs (Willis, 2010). In October 2009, activists in 11 European countries participated in events to demand that retailers pay a living wage to all garment workers in their supply chains; the events included leafleting, public debates, visiting corporate headquarters, and hosting film screenings. These events were organized by a coalition of activists involved in a "clean clothes campaign" (fighting for the rights of workers in the global garment industry) (Clean Clothes Campaign, 2009).

A DEFINITION OF SOCIAL MOVEMENTS

What happens when a group of people, like the many people involved in living wage campaigns, think that certain arrangements are unjust and need to be changed? Sometimes they work together to try to bring about the desired changes—not just for themselves but for a large group of people. These joint efforts are social movements—ongoing, large-scale, collective efforts to bring about (or resist) social change.

We can think of social movements as either offensive or defensive (L. Ray, 1993). Offensive social movements seek to "try out new ways of cooperating and living together" (Habermas, 1981/1987, p. 394). The living wage and Amnesty International movements are examples of offensive social movements. Defensive social movements, on the other hand, seek to defend traditional values and social arrangements. Christian and Islamic fundamentalist and property rights movements are examples of defensive social movements. Both types of social movements are common today in the United States and across the world.

Mario Diani (della Porta & Diani, 2006) identifies the following properties that distinguish social movements from other social collectivities. They

- Are involved in conflictual relations with clearly identified opponents;

- Are linked by dense informal networks;

- Share a distinct collective identity. (p. 20)

It is protest that distinguishes social movements from other types of social networks, but a single episode of protest is not a social movement unless it is connected to a longer-lasting network of public action (della Porta & Diani, 2006; Tarrow, 2006).

SOCIAL MOVEMENTS AND THE HISTORY OF SOCIAL WORK

Like many of the world's religions, some nation-states, labor unions, the YMCA/YWCA, and the Boy Scouts and Girl Scouts, the profession of social work is generally considered to have its origin in social movements (G. Marx & McAdam, 1994). More specifically, the social work profession developed out of the confluence of two social movements: the charity organization society movement and the settlement house movement (Popple & Leighninger, 2007). You have probably studied these social movements in some of your other courses, so they will not be discussed in great detail here. But as social workers, we should recognize how intertwined the history of social work is with social movements.

Both the charity organization society movement and the settlement house movement emerged out of concern during the late 1800s about the ill effects of industrialization, including urban overcrowding and economic instability among low-paid workers. Both social movements developed in England and spread to the United States. But from the beginning, their orientations were very different.

The **charity organization society (COS) movement** developed because private charity organizations became overtaxed by the needs of poor people. Middle- and upper-class individuals were fearful that a coalition of unemployed people and low-paid workers would revolt and threaten the stability of established political and economic institutions. Leaders of the COS movement saw poverty as based in individual pathology and immorality, and set the goal of coordinating charity giving to ensure that no duplication occurred. Volunteer "friendly visitors" were assigned to poor families to help them correct character flaws and develop strong moral fiber. Leaders of the COS movement believed in private, rather than public, charity. The provision of efficient and effective service was the primary agenda of the COS.

The **settlement house movement** was stimulated by the same social circumstances but was based on very different values and goals. Whereas COS leaders focused on individual pathology, leaders of the settlement house movement focused on environmental hazards. They developed settlement houses in urban neighborhoods where "settlers" lived together as "good neighbors" to poor families and were actively involved in research, service, and reform (Popple & Leighninger, 2007). The settlers supported labor activities, lobbied for safe and sanitary housing, provided space for local political groups, offered day care, and provided a variety of cultural and educational programs. They published the results of their research widely and used it to push for governmental reform. **Social reform**—the creation of more just social institutions—was the primary agenda of the settlement house movement.

Over time, workers from the two social movements began to interact at annual meetings of the National Conference of Charities and Corrections, and social work as an occupation took shape. With efforts to professionalize the occupation of social work and, later, to win acceptance for the public social welfare institution, the social reform agenda of the settlement house movement lost ground. Direct service became the focus—specifically, individual and family casework in health and welfare agencies and social work with groups in the settlement houses and YMCAs/YWCAs. This transition away from reform toward a service model is not an uncommon trajectory of social movements. However, almost a century later, social work continues to experience a tension between service and social reform.

Although social work emerged from social movements, it is now a profession, not a social movement. Some social workers work for social movement organizations, however, and the social work profession struggles with its relationship to a variety of social movements. For example, Chapter 13 discussed the tensions in community social work around issues of social action. With the profession's emphasis on social justice, we should understand how social movements emerge and become successful. That is why this chapter on social movements is included in this book and why the professional literature is beginning to make use of social movement theory and to call for greater social work involvement with social movements (see, e.g., Fisher & Shragge, 2000; MacNair, Fowler, & Harris, 2000; Reisch, 2008).

PERSPECTIVES ON SOCIAL MOVEMENTS

Early social science literature on social movements was based on a relatively unified perspective, commonly called **strain theory**. According to this theory, social movements develop in response to some form of strain in society, when people's efforts to cope with stress become collective efforts. Different versions of strain theory focus on

Conflict perspective

different types of social strains, such as strain due to rapid social change, social inequality, social isolation and lack of community, or conflicts in cultural beliefs (M. Hall, 1995; G. Marx & McAdam, 1994). Discussion in earlier chapters has built a case that each of these types of strain exists in the United States today.

Recent social science theory and research have been critical of social strain theory, however. Critics argue that strain is always present to some degree in all societies, but social movements do not always appear in response, and their intensity does not vary systematically with the level of strain (della Porta & Diani, 2006; Goodwin & Jasper, 2004; McAdam, McCarthy, & Zald, 1996). These critics suggest that social strain is a necessary but not sufficient condition to predict the development of a social movement. Any social movement theory must start, they insist, with the condi-

tion of social strain, but other theories are needed to understand why a particular social movement develops when it does, what form that movement takes, and how successful the movement is in accomplishing its goals. Without the sense of outrage felt by the religious leaders in Baltimore in 1994, BUILD would not have developed, at least not its social reform mission, and without a sense of outrage in many localities, the living wage movement could not have capitalized on the Baltimore momentum. But the situation of low-wage workers had not changed suddenly, so why did the social reform movement develop when it did?

Instead of focusing on social strains, some social psychologists have looked for psychological factors or attitudes that might explain which individuals are likely to get involved in social movements. A variety of psychological characteristics have been

▲ **Photo 14.1** Social work experiences a tension between service (helping those in need) and reform (changing organizational structures and systems). Here, workers fight for a living wage.

investigated, including authoritarian personality, emotional conflicts with parents, alienation, aggression, and relative deprivation. Empirical investigations have found very little support for a relationship between such psychological characteristics and social movement participation, however. Indeed, research indicates that social movement activists tend to be people who are rich in relational resources and well-integrated into their communities. Research also indicates that a great many people who never join social movements have similar attitudes about movement goals to those of active movement participants (della Porta & Diani, 2006).

Psychodynamic perspective

Recently, however, some social movement scholars have suggested that it is time to take a look at what motivates people to participate in social movement activities (Flacks, 2004; D. Gould, 2004). We will examine some of those ideas later, under the discussion of emerging perspectives.

Theory and research about social movements have flourished in the past four decades. Throughout the 1970s, social movement scholars in the United States and Europe worked independently of each other and developed different theories and different research emphases (McAdam et al., 1996). In the past 20 years, however, U.S. and

European social movement scholars have begun to work together and to engage in comparative analysis of social movements across place and time. Originally, these collaborative efforts focused only on social movements in the United States and Western Europe. Since the momentous political events in Eastern Europe in the late 1980s, however, Eastern European social movements have received extensive and intensive investigation. Social movement scholarship has begun to extend comparative analysis beyond the United States and Europe to nonindustrialized countries as well as to social movements that cross national lines (J. Smith, Chatfield, & Pagnucco, 1997; Tarrow, 2006).

Three perspectives on social movements have emerged out of this lively interest. I will be referring to these as the political opportunities perspective, the mobilizing structures perspective, and the cultural framing perspective. There is growing agreement among social movement scholars that none of these perspectives taken alone provides adequate tools for understanding social movements (della Porta & Diani, 2006; Goodwin & Jasper, 2004; McAdam et al., 1996; Tarrow, 1994, 1998, 2006). Each perspective adds important dimensions to our understanding, however, and taken together they provide a relatively comprehensive theory of social movements. Social movement scholars recommend research that synthesizes concepts across the three perspectives. The recent social movement literature offers one of the best examples of contemporary attempts to integrate and synthesize multiple theoretical perspectives to give a more complete picture of social phenomena.

Political Opportunities Perspective

Many advocates have been concerned about the deteriorating economic situation of low-wage workers in the United States for some time. After Republicans regained control of Congress in 1994, advocates saw little hope for major increases in the federal minimum wage. The federal minimum wage was increased slightly, from $4.25 an hour to $5.15 an hour in 1996, with a Democratic president and a Republican Congress. However, under the circumstances, advocates of a living wage decided it was more feasible to engage in campaigns at the local rather than the federal level to ensure a living wage for all workers. A shift occurred at the federal level when the Democrats regained control of Congress in November 2006. After being stalled at $5.15 for 10 years, Congress voted in a three-step increase in the minimum wage on May 24, 2007, and Republican President George W. Bush signed the new wage bill into law. The law called for an increase of the federal minimum wage to $5.85 in the summer of 2007, to $6.55 in the summer of 2008, and to $7.25 in the summer of 2009 (Labor Law Center, 2009). These observations are in line with the **political opportunities (PO) perspective,** whose main ideas are summarized in Exhibit 14.1.

Social movements emerge when political opportunities are open.

Political systems differ from each other, and change over time, in their openness to social movements.

A given political system is not equally open or closed to all challengers.

Success of one social movement can open the political system to challenges from other social movements.

A given political system's openness to social movements is influenced by international events.

Opportunities for social movements open at times of instability in political alignments.

Social movements often rely on elite allies.

▲ **Exhibit 14.1**   Key Ideas of the Political Opportunities Perspective

The PO perspective begins with the assumption that social institutions—particularly political and economic institutions—benefit the more powerful members of society, often called elites, and disadvantage many. The elites typically have routine access to institutionalized political channels, whereas disadvantaged groups are

denied access. Power disparities make it very difficult for some groups to successfully challenge existing institutions, but the PO perspective suggests that institutions are not consistently invulnerable to challenge by groups with little power. Social movements can at times take advantage of institutional arrangements that are vulnerable to challenge. The BUILD coalition was convinced that it was morally unjust for workers to receive wages that kept them below the federal poverty line, but they astounded even themselves by setting in motion a process that would spark a national social movement. Theories of social movements often underestimate the ability of challengers to mount and sustain social movements (Morris, 2000).

The political system itself may influence whether a social movement will emerge at a given time, as well as the form the movement will take. Social movement scholars have identified several influential dimensions of political systems and analyzed the ways in which changes in one or more of these dimensions make the political system either receptive or vulnerable to challenges (della Porta & Diani, 2006; Tarrow, 2006). Here, we examine four of those dimensions: openness of the political system, stability of political alignments, availability of elite allies, and international relations.

Openness of the Political System

It might seem reasonable to think that activists will undertake collective action when political systems are open and avoid such action when political systems are closed. The relationship of system openness or closure to social movement activity is not that simple, however. They have instead a curvilinear relationship: Neither full access nor its total absence encourages the greatest degree of collective action. Some resistance stimulates movement solidarity, but too much resistance makes collective action too costly for social movement participants (D. Meyer, 2004). The nature of the political structure will also affect the types of social movement activities that emerge in a given society. Researchers have found that France, with its highly centralized government and hostility to professional social movement organizations, is more prone to strikes, demonstrations, and collective violence than other European countries that are more fragmented and democratic in their governmental structures (Koopmans, 2004).

More generally, but in a similar vein, democratic states facilitate social movements and authoritarian states repress them (della Porta & Diani, 2006). However, because democratic states invite participation, even criticism, many challenging issues that might spark social movements are "processed" out of existence through electoral processes. It is hard to mount a social movement if it seems that the political system is easily influenced without serious collective action. On the other hand, the repression found in authoritarian states may serve to radicalize social movement leaders (della Porta, 1996). Furthermore, as was evident in Eastern Europe in the late 1980s, authoritarian states are not always effective in repressing challenges. The political leadership's efforts to appease the population by offering small liberties had a snowball effect. Relaxation of social control in a previously repressive political system often has the unintended consequence of fueling the fire of long-held grievances (G. Marx & McAdam, 1994).

Social movement researchers are interested in how police handle protest events. They have identified two contrasting styles of policing: the escalated-force model and the negotiated control model. The escalated-force model puts little value on the right to protest, has low tolerance for many forms of protest, favors little communication between the police and demonstrators, and makes use of coercive and even illegal methods to control protests. The negotiated control model honors the right to demonstrate peacefully, tolerates even disruptive forms of protest, puts high priority on communication between police and demonstrators, and avoids coercive control as much as possible. Social movement scholars suggest that in Western societies, including the United States, the escalated-force model lost favor and the negotiated control model became prominent after the intense protest wave of the 1960s (della Porta & Diani,

2006). They also argue, however, that preference for the negotiated control model has proven fragile in the face of the new challenge of transnational protest movements. In the United States, political activists have been spied upon and disrupted in the name of the war on terror since September 11, 2001. In February 2003, in the weeks leading up to the beginning of the Iraq War, New York City authorities refused march permits to United for Peace and Justice, a coalition of more than 800 antiwar and social justice groups. Later that same year, the Philadelphia police commissioner classified the Free Trade Area of America (FTAA) as outsiders who were coming to terrorize the city; this was done to allow the city to receive $8.5 million in war-on-terror money (A. Bornstein, 2009).

A given political system is not equally open or closed to all challengers at a given time; some social movements are favored over others. Even in a democracy, universal franchise does not mean equal access to the political system; wealth buys access not easily available to poor people's movements (A. Bornstein, 2009; della Porta & Diani, 2006; Piven & Cloward, 1977). Indeed, the rapid success and growth of the living wage movement has been a surprise to many who support it ideologically, because it has been hard to sustain poor people's movements in the past.

The success of one social movement can open the political system to challenges by other social movements. For example, successful legislative action by the Black civil rights movement during the 1960s opened the way for other civil rights movements, particularly the women's movement, which benefited from Title VII of the Civil Rights Act of 1964, which included prohibiting employment discrimination on the basis of sex (McAdam, 1996a). But the successful movement may also open the way for opponent movements, called **countermovements,** as well as for allied movements. The women's movement has been countered by a variety of antifeminist movements, including the antiabortionist movement and a set of interrelated movements that focus on traditional gender roles for family life. Indeed, the living wage movement has engendered opposition coalitions that have launched intensive lobbying campaigns to convince state legislators in several states to bar cities from establishing their own minimum wages (B. Murray, 2001; Quigley, 2001).

Stability of Political Alignments

PO theorists agree that the routine transfer of political power from one group of incumbents to another group, as when a different political party takes control of the U.S. presidency or Congress, opens opportunities for the development or reactivation of social movements (Tarrow, 2006). At such times, some social movements lose favor and others gain opportunity. In both the 1930s and 1960s, changes in political party strength appear to have been related to increased social movement activity among poor people. Some observers note that social movements on the Left mobilized during the Kennedy and Johnson administrations, and social movements on the Right mobilized during the Reagan and George H. W. Bush administrations and again when the Republicans took over Congress in 1994 (McAdam et al., 1996); social movements on the Right also appear to have gained momentum when George W. Bush became president in 2000. That did not mean, however, that local grassroots movements for a living wage could not be mounted.

Disruption of political alliances also occurs at times other than political elections, for both partisan and nonpartisan reasons, and such disruptions produce conflicts and divisions among elites. When elites are divided, social movements can sometimes encourage some factions to take a stand for disenfranchised groups and support the goals of the movement. The Harvard Living Wage Campaign garnered the support of the mayor and city council in Cambridge, Massachusetts. Disruptions in political alliances also occur when different branches of the government—such as the executive branch and the legislative branch—are at odds with each other. Such conflict was the case in the early days of the living wage campaign, but may have had little effect on the campaign because it was being fought at the local level. New coalitions may be formed, and the uncertainty that ensues may encourage groups to make new or renewed attempts to challenge institutional arrangements, hoping to find new elite allies. The new local coalitions formed during the living wage campaigns have often breathed new life into local progressive advocates (B. Murray, 2001).

The events in Eastern Europe in the late 1980s represent another type of political opportunity—one that has received little attention by social movement scholars—the opportunity that opens when a political regime loses legitimacy with those it governs. A political regime that has lost both legitimacy and effectiveness "is skating on very thin ice" (Oberschall, 1996, p. 98). As reported in Chapter 9, many political analysts suggest that the current era is marked by a reduced capacity of nations to govern and increasing cynicism on the part of citizens about the ability of governments to govern. Some social movement scholars suggest that this sort of instability is contributing to the global spread of social movement activity (Oberschall, 1996; J. Smith et al., 1997; Tarrow, 1998).

Availability of Elite Allies

Participants in social movements often lack both power and resources for influencing the political process. But they may be assisted by influential allies who play a variety of supportive roles. These elite allies may provide financial support, or they may provide name and face recognition that attracts media attention to the goals and activities of the movement. Research indicates a strong correlation between the presence of elite allies and social movement success (della Porta & Diani, 2006). The Harvard students, who mostly came from elite families themselves, were able to attract a number of elite allies, including Congressman Edward M. Kennedy, former Labor Secretary Robert Reich, Chairman of the NAACP Julian Bond, high-profile religious leaders, and actors Ben Affleck and Matt Damon.

Social movement participants often have ambivalent relationships with their elite allies, however. On the one hand, powerful allies provide needed resources; on the other hand, they may limit or distort the goals of the movement (della Porta & Diani, 2006; Kriesi, 1996). The early relationship between participants in the disability movement and actor Christopher Reeve is a good example of the tension that can develop between movement participants and their elite allies. When Reeve was paralyzed following an equestrian accident in 1995, the media quickly assigned him the role of star speaker for the disability community. Many in the disability movement were offended. Reeve's personal agenda was to find a cure for spinal cord injuries, but the movement's emphasis was on personal assistance for people with disabilities—on living with disability, not curing it. People in the disability movement were concerned that the emphasis on cure would undermine their efforts to win public acceptance of their disabilities and to make their environments more accessible.

International Relations

Since the 18th century, social movements have diffused rapidly across national boundaries, and the fate of national social movements has been influenced by international events. In the 19th century, the antislavery movement spread from England to France, the Netherlands, and the Americas (Tarrow, 2006). The mid–20th-century Black civil rights movement in the United States was influenced by international attention to the gap between our national image as champion of human rights and the racial discrimination that permeated our social institutions (McAdam, 1996a). The fight for the right of women to vote was first won in New Zealand in the 1880s; the United States followed almost 40 years later, in 1920. It took some time, but gradually the movement for women's suffrage spread around the world (Sernau, 2006).

The recent revolution in communication technology, coupled with the globalization of market systems, is quickening the diffusion of collective action, as evidenced by peace and global social justice movements (della Porta & Diani, 2006; Tarrow, 2006). The protest against corporate globalization that took place at the 1999 meeting of the World Trade Organization (WTO) in Seattle was only one action in several years of work by an international coalition of more than 1,200 labor, religious, consumer, environmental, farm, academic, and human rights groups from over 90 nations (D. Newman, 2006). On February 15, 2003, an estimated 16 million people around the world marched in protest of the impending U.S.-led war in Iraq, including 2.5 million in Italy, 1.75 million in London, 1.3 million in Barcelona, 1 million

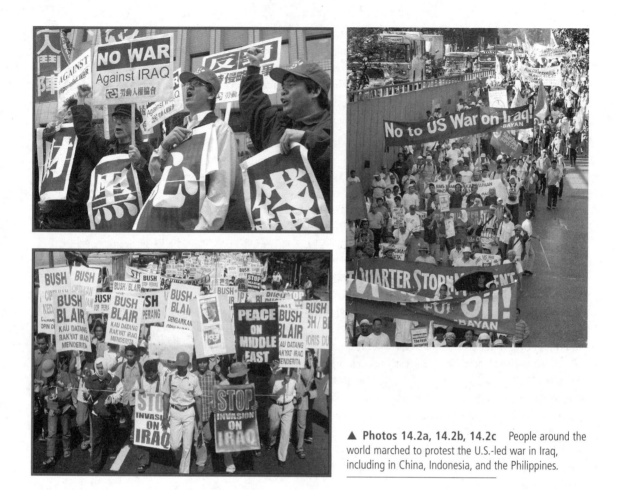

▲ **Photos 14.2a, 14.2b, 14.2c**   People around the world marched to protest the U.S.-led war in Iraq, including in China, Indonesia, and the Philippines.

in Madrid, 500,000 in Berlin, 500,000 in New York City, and 250,000 in Paris. This is probably the largest international protest in history (Tarrow, 2006).

Tarrow (2006) suggests that the international spread of social movements was aided by two growing trends. First, there was a growing attitude, after the end of the Cold War, that it is acceptable for nations to interfere with the affairs of other nations. Second, the end of classical colonialism—a policy by which one nation maintains control over a foreign nation and makes use of its resources—left a large number of weak states in its wake. With these two trends working together, opportunities were opened for minorities who were dispossessed in one nation to appeal for support from allies in another nation. It is also important to note that global social movements have been aided by human rights legislation from multi-state governments like the United Nations (A. Bornstein, 2009).

Mobilizing Structures Perspective

Rational choice perspective

Most analysts would agree that much of the success of the living wage movement can be attributed to strong existing networks of local progressive advocates. The movement also benefited from strong advocacy organizations like ACORN that developed and provided resources to grassroots organizers. These views are consistent with the

mobilizing structures (MS) perspective, which starts from this basic premise: Given their disadvantaged position in the political system, social movement leaders must seek out and mobilize the resources they need—people, money, information, ideas, and skills—in order to reduce the costs and increase the benefits of movement activities (G. Davis, McAdam, Scott, & Zald, 2005; della Porta & Diani, 2006; Morris, 2004). In the MS perspective, social movements have no influence without effective organization of various kinds of **mobilizing structures**—existing informal networks and formal organizations through which people mobilize and engage in collective action. Mobilizing structures are the collective building blocks of social movements. The main ideas of the MS perspective are summarized in Exhibit 14.2.

Informal and Formal Structures

MS scholars agree that social movements typically do not start from scratch but build on existing structures. They disagree, however, on the relative importance of informal versus formal structures. The MS perspective has two theoretical building blocks, one that emphasizes formal mobilizing structures and the other that emphasizes informal mobilizing structures:

Resource mobilization theory focuses on the organization and coordination of movement activities through formal organizations called **social movement organizations (SMOs)** (G. Davis et al., 2005). Theorists in this tradition are particularly interested in **professional social movement organizations** staffed by leaders and activists who make a professional career out of reform causes (della Porta & Diani, 2006; Morris, 2004). The professional staff engages in fund-raising and attempts to speak for the constituency represented by the movement. There are advantages to professional SMOs, because social movements are more likely to meet their goals when they have a well-structured organization to engage in continuous fund-raising and lobbying. There are also problems, however. Professional SMOs must respond to the wishes of the benefactors who may be comfortable with low-level claims only. Theda Skocpol (2003) argues that professionalization can lead to movement defeat by taming protest. Della Porta and Diani (2006) remind us that although social movements need organizations, organizations are not social movements. They insist that one thing that distinguishes social movements is that they are linked by dense informal networks.

Global social movements are being supported by growing numbers of **transnational social movement organizations (TSMOS),** or social movement organizations that operate in more than one nation-state. The number of TSMOs grew each decade of the 20th century, with particularly rapid growth in the last three decades of the century. There were fewer than 200 TSMOs in the 1970s, but nearly 1,000 by the year 2000 (A. Bornstein, 2009; G. Davis et al., 2005). Some examples of TSMOs are Green Peace and Amnesty International.

The **network model** focuses on everyday ties between people, in grassroots settings, as the basic structures for the communication and social solidarity necessary for mobilization (della Porta & Diani, 2006; Tindall, 2004). The focus

---

Social movements must be able to mobilize various kinds of formal and informal networks.

Resource mobilization theory focuses on the coordination of movement activities through social movement organizations (SMOs).

The network model focuses on mobilization of the movement through informal networks.

Mobilizing structures have a strong influence on the life course of social movements.

To survive, social movements must be able to attract new members and sustain the involvement of current members.

▲ **Exhibit 14.2** Key Ideas of the Mobilizing Structures Perspective

is thus on naturally existing networks based in family, work, religious, educational, and neighborhood relationships, or such networks as those that can be found at alternative cafes and bookshops and social and cultural centers. Naturally existing social networks facilitate recruitment to movement activities and support continued participation. These natural networks are hard to repress and control because, in a democratic society, people have the right to congregate in their private homes and other informal settings.

Some social movement scholars argue that the shift in the organization of work to home-based work, smaller factories, and offshore industrial production is limiting the development of work-based networks of activism. On the other hand, the increased presence of women in higher education and places of employment is facilitating new ties between women. Not only do people get involved in social movements because of previous connections, but they also make new connections through their movement activities, connections that may generate continued loyalty. Proponents of the network model emphasize that individual, not just organizational, participation is essential for social movements, and they argue that social movements have participants, not members, and must find ways to keep participants involved. Although the benefits of informal networks are often noted in the social movement literature, some researchers are beginning to explore cases where networks do not lead to participation (della Porta & Diani, 2006, Tindall, 2004).

Although resource mobilization theory and the network model disagree about the relative merits of formal and informal structures, they do agree that the costs of mobilizing social movements are minimized by drawing on preexisting structures and networks (G. Davis et al., 2005; Tindall, 2004). The living wage campaign in Baltimore got its start in an existing coalition of religious leaders, and the growing living wage movement was able to generate support from existing social movement organizations and university students. This is very common in the life of social movements. Black churches and Black colleges played an important role in the U.S. civil rights movement (McAdam, 1982; Morris, 1981, 1984). The student movements of the 1960s benefited from friendship networks among activists of the civil rights movement (Oberschall, 1992). The radical wing of the women's movement emerged out of informal friendship networks of women who had been active in the civil rights and New Left movements of the 1960s (S. Evans, 1980). Antiabortion and other New Right movements have benefited from strong ties and commitments found in Catholic and conservative Protestant churches (Oberschall, 1992; L. Ray, 1993). The global justice movement depends on a broad coalition of organizations with a strong background in activism, including trade unions and other worker organizations, ethnic organizations, farmers, religious organizations, consumer groups, environmental groups, women's groups, and youth groups (della Porta & Diani, 2006; Tarrow, 2006).

Several social movement scholars have noted the particularly "religious roots and character of many American movements" (McAdam et al., 1996, p. 18; R. Wood, 2002). They suggest that this link is not surprising, given the higher rates of church affiliation and attendance in the United States than in other comparable Western democracies.

The Life Course of Social Movements

Developmental perspective

Social movements are by definition fluid in nature. The MS perspective asserts that mobilizing structures have a strong influence on the life course of a social movement, making time an important dimension. Although most social movements fade relatively soon, some last for decades. Movements typically have brief periods of intense activity and long latent periods when not much is happening. One pattern for the movements that persist is as follows: At the outset, the movement is ill defined, and the various mobilizing structures are weakly organized (Kriesi, 1996; G. Marx & McAdam, 1994). Once the movement has been in existence for a while, it is likely to become larger, less spontaneous, and better organized. The mature social movement is typically led by the SMOs that were developed in the course of mobilization. The living wage movement seems to be in this position currently, with several organizations, including some transnational ones, playing a major role, but it was not always so.

Social movement scholars disagree about whether the increasing role of formal organizations as time passes is a good thing or a bad thing. Many suggest that movements cannot survive without becoming more organized and taking on many of the characteristics of the institutions they challenge (Tarrow, 2006). On the other hand, this tendency of social movements to become more organized and less spontaneous has often doomed them—particularly poor people's movements—to failure (Skocpol, 2003). Organizations that become more formal commonly abandon the oppositional tactics that brought early success and fail to seize the window of opportunity created by the unrest those tactics generated. But that is not always the case. Sometimes SMOS become more radical over time, and most current large-scale social movements are strengthened by the support of a number of different types of organizations (della Porta & Diani, 2006). One of the most important problems facing social movement organizers is to create mobilizing structures that are sufficiently strong to stand up to opponents but also flexible enough to respond to changing circumstances (Tarrow, 2006). The living wage movement appears to have managed that tension in its first decade, but it is still a work in progress.

Jo Freeman (1995) asserts that there is "no such thing as a permanent social movement" (p. 403). She suggests that every movement, at some point, changes into something else, often into many other things, through three basic processes:

1. *Institutionalization.* Some movements become part of existing institutions or develop durable SMOs with stable income, staff, and routine operations. The profession of social work is an example of a social movement that became institutionalized.

2. *Encapsulation.* Some social movements, or at least some parts of them, lose their sense of mission and begin to direct their activities inward, to serve members, rather than outward, to promote or resist change. That has been the trajectory of some labor unions (Clemens, 1996). Social work's history also includes periods of encapsulation, when social workers became more concerned about "professional advancement and autonomy, status, and financial security" (Reamer, 1992, p. 12) than about social justice and the public welfare. This appears to be the current state of the social work profession.

3. *Factionalization.* Still other movements fall apart, often disintegrating into contentious, competing factions. This was the trajectory of the U.S. student protest movements after the violence at the 1968 Democratic Party convention in Chicago (della Porta & Diani, 2006; Tarrow, 1994).

It is too early to tell what the long-term trajectory of the living wage movement will be.

Computer-Mediated Social Movement Communication

Increasingly, social movements are being mounted and maintained by the use of computer technology. Both progressive and conservative social movements have benefited from the use of e-mail Listservs, Internet blogs, and organizational websites to communicate with potential members. These methods are used to provide information, solicit funds, recommend political action, and organize activities. They provide easy entry into activism. One recent example is MomsRising (2006), which uses a primarily web-based model of organizing to pull together a coalition of existing organizations and new recruits. MomsRising is dedicated to these core issues: maternity/paternity leave; open, flexible work; safe television and after-school programs; health care for all children; quality child care; and fair wages. Cell phones and text messaging are also increasingly used to help groups mobilize.

Communication scholars suggest that the Internet is a rich resource for social movements because it can be used to bypass mainstream media, which often ignores or distorts movement activity. They have identified several ways that communication can be facilitated by the Internet, including providing information, coordinating action and mobilization, making linkages, promoting interaction and dialogue, serving as an outlet for creative expression, and promoting fund-raising. However, one researcher found that U.S.-based SMOs are not using the Internet to its full potential (Stein, 2009). On the other hand, della Porta and Mosca (2009) reviewed the websites of 261 organizations involved in the global justice movement worldwide and found that they are making use of a number of democratic concepts, including information sharing, identity building, transparency/accountability, mobilization, and intervening in the digital divide.

The widespread use of computer-mediated communication (CMC) in social movement mobilization is raising new questions for social movement scholars. Are dense, face-to-face networks still necessary to mobilize social movements? How essential is shared direct experience and face-to-face interaction to keep activists involved? To date, the answers to these questions appear mixed. It is true that the Internet can connect diverse communities that would never be connected otherwise. In addition, there are clear instances of solidarity and mutual trust developed by people who only know each other on the Internet (della Porta & Diani, 2006). Transnational computer-based networks contribute to efficient coordination of international campaigns, as demonstrated by the February 15, 2003, worldwide demonstrations against the impending Iraq War. On the other hand, participants on Listservs often hide their personal identity, participate only occasionally and typically only with one other person, and do not have a strong sense of loyalty to the network as a whole (Tilly, 2004). It appears that the best results come from a combination of local grassroots organizing and CMC (Bennett, 2004; Van Aelst & Walgrave, 2004).

Cultural Framing Perspective

> Social constructionist perspective

The **cultural framing (CF) perspective** asserts that a social movement can succeed only when participants develop shared understandings and definitions of the situation. These shared meanings develop through a transactional process of consciousness raising, which social movement scholars call cultural framing. **Cultural framing** involves "conscious strategic efforts by groups of people to fashion shared understandings of the world and of themselves that legitimate and motivate collective action" (McAdam et al., 1996, p. 6). Exhibit 14.3 summarizes the central ideas of the CF perspective.

Social movement leaders and participants engage in a delicate balancing act as they construct cultural frames. To legitimate collective action, cultural frames must impel people to feel aggrieved or outraged about some situation they consider unjust. But to motivate people to engage in collective action, cultural frames must be optimistic about the possibilities for improving the situation. Consider the chant developed by the divinity students at Harvard: "Where's your horror? Where's your rage? Div School wants a living wage." The chant dramatized the severity of the situation and the

---

Social movements must be able to develop shared understandings that legitimate and motivate collective action.

Social movements actively participate in the naming of grievances and injustices.

Social movement leaders must construct a perception that change is possible.

Social movements must articulate goals.

Social movements must identify and create tactical choices for accomplishing goals.

Contests over cultural frames are common in social movements.

Social movements must be able to create cultural frames to appeal to diverse audiences.

▲ **Exhibit 14.3** Key Ideas of the Cultural Framing Perspective

fairness of their cause, but it also expressed hope for a solution. Simultaneously, social movements want to draw heavily on existing cultural symbols so that the movement frame will resonate with people's cultural understandings while they add new frames to the cultural stock, thus sponsoring new ways of thinking about social conditions. The challenge of this balancing act is "how to put forward a set of unsettling demands for unconventional people in ways that will not make enemies out of potential allies" (Tarrow, 1994, p. 10). The BUILD coalition was wise in choosing to call their cause a "living wage" rather than a "minimum wage." The notion that workers should draw a wage that allows them to "live" is morally persuasive, and even those who oppose the living wage movement have suggested that it is hard to take a public stance that you are opposed to such an idea (Malanga, 2003).

▲ **Photo 14.3** Social movements can be categorized as offensive (trying out new ways of living and cooperating) or defensive (defending traditional values). The U. S. civil rights movement was an example of an offensive social movement.

Cultural frames are "metaphors, symbols, and cognitive cues that cast issues in a particular light and suggest possible ways to respond to these issues" (G. Davis et al., 2005, pp. 48–49). Exhibit 14.4 presents some cultural frames provided by social movements in the United States during the past few decades. You may not be familiar with all of these cultural frames, and you might want to check with your classmates to see if, collectively, you can identify the social movement with which each of the frames is associated. How well do you think these cultural frames serve both to legitimate and to motivate collective action? How well do they draw on existing symbols while promoting new ways of thinking?

A complication in the process of constructing frames is that frames attractive to one audience are likely to be rejected by other audiences. Social movement groups "must master the art of simultaneously playing to a variety of

Pro-life	**MAKE LOVE, NOT WAR**	**Deaf Now**	CIVIL RIGHTS	*12 Steps*
The Color Lavender		**I May Be Disabled But I'm Not Dead Yet**		Pro Choice
	The Peace Sign	Stonewall	*We Shall Overcome*	
A woman's body is her own		Family Values	*Take Back the Night*	
Welfare Rights	Unborn Child	*Our Homes, Not Nursing Homes*		GAY RIGHTS
	Every Child a Wanted Child	Reverence for Life	Piss on Pity	
I Have a Dream	**Hell No, We Won't Go**		*Our Daughters and Our Sons*	
black power	*Do Not Speak For Me, Listen To Me*		**Disability Rights**	

▲ **Exhibit 14.4** Selected Cultural Frames Presented by Social Movements in the United States

publics, threatening opponents, and pressuring the state, all the while appearing nonthreatening and sympathetic to the media and other publics" (McAdam, 1996b, p. 344). Activists desire media attention because that is the most effective way to reach wide audiences, but they also know that they cannot control the way the movement will be framed by the media. The media are attracted to dramatic, even violent, aspects of a movement, but these aspects are likely to be rejected by other audiences (Stein, 2009). They are often more interested in scandal than in providing substantive information on movement issues (della Porta & Diani, 2006). ACORN, an SMO that was very helpful to the living wage campaign in the United States, became the subject of a highly publicized scandal in September 2009 regarding a few local staff caught in unethical behavior on hidden camera (Farrell, 2009). This scandal led to loss of federal funding and private donations, and by March 2010, ACORN announced that it was closing its offices after 40 years of successful advocacy efforts (Urbina, 2010). Indeed, it was their success in fighting for the rights of poor people that led to a backlash from conservative forces that wanted to destroy them. That is a possibility with which successful social movements must always contend. It remains to be seen how ACORN's demise will affect the living wage movement.

Movement activists are particularly concerned about the impact of the media on their **conscience constituency**—people attracted to the movement because it appears just and worthy, not because they will benefit personally. The students at Harvard gave serious thought to whether a sit-in demonstration would cause them to lose some support for their cause. They also were aware that they could face repercussions, such as being expelled from the university.

Social movement framing is never a matter of easy consensus building, and intense **framing contests** may arise among a variety of actors, particularly in the later stages. Representatives of the political system and participants in countermovements influence framing through their own actions and public statements, and internal conflicts may become more pronounced. Leaders and followers often have different frames for the movement (G. Marx & McAdam, 1994), and there are often splits between moderate and radical participants. It is not at all unusual for movements to put forth multiple frames, with different groups sponsoring different frames. For example, Bill Hughes (2009) suggests that disability activism in the UK is splitting into two branches, the disabled people's movement (DPM) and the "biological citizens." The DPM takes the position that disability is a social phenomenon created by discrimination and oppression, and suggests that impairment is irrelevant to disability. The "biological citizens" organize politically around specific diagnostic labels and embrace medical and scientific knowledge associated with their "condition," with the goal of enhancing their ability to exercise citizenship. When a movement captures media attention, there is often an intense struggle over who speaks for the movement and which cultural frame is put forward.

Qualitative analysis of social movement framing has been a popular topic in the social movement literature in the past few years. This literature indicates that cultural framing provides language, ideology, and symbols for understanding that a problem exists, for recognizing windows of opportunity, for establishing goals, and for identifying pathways for action (Polletta, 2004).

Frames for Understanding That a Problem Exists

Social movements are actively involved in the "naming" of grievances and injustices. They do so in part by drawing on existing cultural symbols, but they also underscore, accentuate, and enlarge current understanding of the seriousness of a situation. In essence, they call attention to contradictions between cultural ideals and cultural realities. For example, the living wage movement calls attention to the discrepancy between working and receiving a wage that does not allow a person to rise out of poverty. Calling attention to this discrepancy is important in the United States, where the public tends to believe that people are poor because they don't work. The international antiglobalization movement has used "globalization" as a catchword to symbolize the misery and exploitation caused by the dominance of market forces in contemporary life. Many of the ill effects of global markets, such as growing inequality, were present before antiglobalization activists were able to turn "globalization" into a negative symbol that could mobilize people to action. When 50,000 demonstrators protested against the WTO meeting in Seattle on November 30, 1999, they used a number of slogans to frame globalization as a problem (della Porta & Diani, 2006, p. 163):

- The world is not for sale.
- No globalization without representation.
- We are citizens, not only consumers.
- WTO = Capitalism without conscience.

In the United States, movement frames are often articulated in terms of rights—civil rights, disability rights, GLBT rights, animal rights,

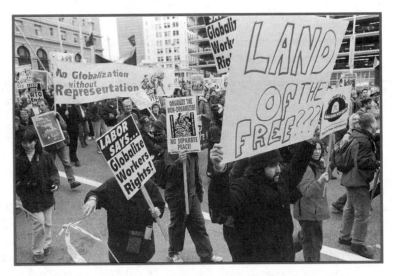

▲ **Photo 14.4**   The international antiglobalization movement has used "globalization" as a catchword to symbolize the misery and exploitation caused by the dominance of market forces in contemporary life. On November 30, 1999, an estimated 50,000 demonstrators protested against the WTO meeting in Seattle.

children's rights. In Europe, where there is less emphasis on individual liberty, rights frames are far less common in social movements (Hastings, 1998; Tarrow, 1998).

In the past decade, fundamentalist religious movements have sprung up in many countries, including the United States. These movements have used morality frames, focusing on good and evil rather than justice versus injustice. Compared to Europe, the United States has historically produced a high number of such movements (G. Marx & McAdam, 1994). Prohibition, abolition, anticommunism, and antiabortionism have all had religious roots. A contemporary religious frame that crosses national boundaries as well as liberal and conservative ideologies is "reverence for life," expressed in such disparate movements as the environmental, health, antiabortion, animal rights, antiwar, and anti–capital punishment movements.

Frames for Recognizing a Window of Opportunity

The perception of opportunity to change a troublesome situation is also culturally framed, to some extent (della Porta & Diani, 2006; Gamson & Meyer, 1996; Polletta, 2004). On occasion, it is easy to develop a shared frame that opportunity exists or does not exist, but most situations are more ambiguous. Social movement leaders must successfully construct a perception that change is possible, because an opportunity does not exist unless it is recognized. They typically attempt to overcome concerns about the dangers and futility of activism by focusing on the risks of inaction, communicating a sense of urgency, and emphasizing the openness of the moment. They are intent on keeping hope alive.

Calibrating this type of frame is a difficult task. On the one hand, overstating an opportunity can be hazardous (Piven & Cloward, 1977). Without "fortifying myths," which allow participants to see defeats as mere setbacks, unrealistically high expectations can degenerate into pessimism about possibilities for change (K. Voss, 1996). On the other hand, "movement activists systematically overestimate the degree of political opportunity, and if they did not, they would not be doing their job wisely" (Gamson & Meyer, 1996, p. 285). Unrealistic perceptions about what is possible can actually make change *more* possible. The Harvard students were not happy with the size of the worker raise that came out of their sit-in, but their expectations led them to bold action, which brought some improvements in the lives of workers and has been an inspiration for students at other universities around the country.

Frames for Establishing Goals

Once it has been established that both problem and opportunity exist, the question of social movement goals arises. Is change to be narrow or sweeping, reformist or revolutionary? Will the emphasis be on providing opportunities for individual self-expression or on changing the social order? At least three different goals have been adopted by different segments of the antiglobalization movement: rejection, opt out, and reform. The rejectionists reject capitalism as an ethical economic form. The "opt out" segment of the movement focuses on experiments in local sustainable economic development, which they hope will allow them to avoid participation in the global economic system dominated by large, transnational companies. The reformists see economic globalization as a potentially good thing, but favor measures to reduce the power of transnational businesses (della Porta & Diani, 2006). U.S. social movements have generally set goals that are more reformist than revolutionary (G. Marx & McAdam, 1994). Parents, Families and Friends of Lesbians and Gays (PFLAG) is a fairly typical example of a contemporary U.S. social movement that has struck a balance between goals of individual change and changes in the social order. Exhibit 14.5 demonstrates how PFLAG strikes this balance in its statement of goals.

Typically, goals are poorly articulated in the early stages of a movement but are clarified through ongoing negotiations about the desired changes. Manuals for social activism suggest that modest and winnable objectives in the early stages of a movement help to reinforce the possibility of change (Gamson & Meyer, 1996). Indeed, the early goals for the living wage movement were quite modest. The wage increase secured by BUILD only covered 1,500 to 2,000 workers. By 2001, it was estimated that the combined efforts of all local living wage campaigns had brought the number to only about 100,000 workers. Some progressives were critical of a movement that was yielding so little, but other analysts argued that it was the modest and winnable nature of the early campaigns that neutralized opposition and built a momentum of success (B. Murray, 2001). Certainly, it is true that the movement has become more ambitious in its goals over time, moving from improving the wages of a small number of municipal contract workers to large-scale, citywide ordinances like the one in Chicago, as well as to statewide minimum wage laws. Likewise, the European activists' demands that all garment workers in retail supply chains be paid a living wage would have far-reaching results across national lines (Clean Clothes Campaign, 2009).

Social workers Ray MacNair, Leigh Fowler, and John Harris (2000) suggest that progressive, or offensive, social movements have a three-pronged goal: (1) They must confront oppression, (2) they must attend to the damaged identities of oppressed persons, and (3) they must "renovate" the cultural roles of both oppressor groups and oppressed groups. The living wage movement has paid a lot of attention to the first two of these goals. It has named the oppression, and it has actively engaged low-wage earners in the struggle. It is not clear how much work is being done on the third goal, but the European activists for the garment workers may well be thinking in those terms.

Three "identity movements"—the Black civil rights movement, the women's movement, and the lesbian-gay-bisexual-transgender movement—demonstrate the process of goal setting. Each of these movements has a long history

---

To cope with an adverse society, PFLAG PROVIDES SUPPORT.

To enlighten a sometimes frightened and ill-informed public, PFLAG EDUCATES AND INFORMS.

To combat discrimination and secure equal rights, PFLAG ADVOCATES JUSTICE.

▲ **Exhibit 14.5**   Goals Statement of Parents, Families and Friends of Lesbians and Gays (PFLAG)

SOURCE: PFLAG (1995).

of emerging, waning, and reemerging in the United States, changing its framing of the movement's goals along the way. For these three social movements, the framing of goals followed an evolutionary path through six different frames:

1. *Assimilation:* Persuade the mainstream to recognize the capabilities of the oppressed group while also working to uplift the oppressed group.

2. *Normative antidiscrimination:* Place the onus for change completely on oppressor groups and oppressive institutions. Take a confrontational approach of legal challenges and political lobbying. Recognize the positive attributes of the oppressed group.

3. *Militant direct action:* Reject the legitimacy of normal decision-making processes, and attempt to disrupt them. Develop a "culture of rebellion" to energize disruptive actions (MacNair et al., 2000, p. 75).

4. *Separatism:* Avoid oppression by avoiding oppressor groups.

5. *Introspective self-help:* Focus on building a healthy identity.

6. *Pluralistic integration:* Appreciate themselves and promote connections to other cultures.

Frames for Identifying Pathways for Action

Some of the most important framing efforts of a social movement involve tactical choices for accomplishing goals. Social movement scholars generally agree that each society has a repertoire of forms of collective action that are familiar to social movement participants as well as the elites they challenge (Tarrow, 2006). New forms are introduced from time to time, and they spread quickly if they are successful. In the United States, for example, marches on Washington have come to be standard fare in collective action, and activist groups exchange information on the logistics of organizing such a march on the nation's capital. On the other hand, the sit-down strike is no longer as common as it once was, although university students in the living wage movement have brought it back in the form of sit-in strikes in recent years (Gourevitch, 2001; McAdam, 1996b). Contemporary social movements draw power from the large selection of forms of collective action currently in the cultural stock, and many movements have wisely used multiple forms of action (della Porta & Diani, 2006; Tarrow, 2006). The living wage movement has made use of lobbying, postcard campaigns, door-knocking campaigns, leafleting, rallies, sit-ins, workshops, newspaper ads, and advocacy videos.

The repertoire of collective action is handed down, but there is some improvisation by individual movements. For example, public marches are a standard part of the repertoire, but there have been innovations to the march in recent years, such as closing rallies and the incorporation of theatrical forms. Participants in the global justice movement are using some long-standing action forms such as petitions, reports and press releases, sit-ins, marches, lobbying, blockades, and boycotts. They are also using recent action innovations as well as developing new action forms. Their repertoire includes concerts, vigils, theatrical masks, puppets, electronic advocacy, documentaries, and "buycotts" (active campaign to buy the products) of fair trade products. Computer technology is being used in two new forms of disruptive action. *Net striking* is an action form in which a large number of people connect to the same website at a prearranged time. This jams the site and makes it impossible for other users to reach it. *Mailbombing* is an action form in which large numbers of e-mails are sent to a web address or a server until it overloads (della Porta & Diani, 2006).

Just as social movement goals fall on a continuum from reform to revolution, forms of collective action can be arranged along a continuum from conventional to violent, as shown in Exhibit 14.6. Nonviolent forms of collective action are the core of contemporary U.S. movements. Nonviolent disruption of routine activities is today considered

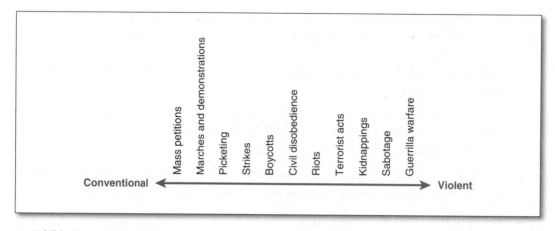

▲ **Exhibit 14.6**   Forms of Collective Action

the most powerful form of activism in the United States and in other Western democracies with relatively stable governments (della Porta & Diani, 2006). The power of nonviolent disruption is that it creates uncertainty and some fear of violence, yet provides authorities in democratic societies with no valid argument for repression. Violent collective action, on the other hand, destroys public support for the movement. Martin Luther King was ingenious in recognizing that the best path for the U.S. civil rights movement was "successfully courting violence while restraining violence in his followers" (McAdam, 1996b, p. 349). Consequently, it was the police who lost public favor for their brutality, not the demonstrators.

Some action forms, such as marches, petitions, and Net strikes, are used to demonstrate numerical strength. Other action forms, such as conferences, concerts, documentaries, and buycotts of fair products, are used to bear witness to the substantive issues. Still other action forms are designed to do damage to the parties reputed to be to blame for an unfair situation. Small-scale violence does this, as do boycotts. Not only do these latter action forms run the risk of escalating repression and alienating sympathizers, but boycotts also run the risk of harming workers (della Porta & Diani, 2006).

In an interesting development, a new organizing tactic has been used in peace and justice campaigns. The proponents of this tactic call it "creative play." They argue that "changing entrenched systems of oppression requires shifts in emotional as well as intellectual attitudes" (Shephard, 2005, p. 52). Furthermore, "culture-poems, songs, paintings, murals, chants, sermons, quilts, stories, rhythms, weavings, pots, and dances can make such emotional and visceral breakthroughs possible" (Si Kahn, cited in Shephard, 2005, p. 52). One global movement, Reclaim the Streets (RTS), uses street parties as its organizing tool. During the 2004 presidential election, Billionaires for Bush used humor to lampoon the role of money in U.S. politics. They appeared at both pro-Bush and anti-Bush rallies in tuxedos and top hats, and fake jewels and gowns, often carrying signs that read "Because Inequality Is Not Growing Fast Enough." Paul Bartlett, a member of the Billionaires group, suggests that "Performance with humor can disarm fear. When we laugh, we can listen, we can learn. . . . When people participate in a play, opportunities for new perspectives and transformation emerge" (cited in Shepherd, 2005, p. 55).

Social movement scholars agree that for the past 200 years, social movement actions have become less violent (Tarrow, 2006). They also suggest, however, that beginning in the 1990s, violent social movements began to flourish again around the world. This trend was exemplified by White supremacist armed militias in the United States and militant Islamic fundamentalist movements in the Middle East, Central Asia, and Africa. Out of these two movements have come (respectively) the bombing of a state building in Oklahoma City and the somber events of September 11, 2001. It is unclear whether the increased violence of social movements will be a long-term trend, and if so, whether existing theories of social movements will be relevant to the new forms of movement actions.

Emerging Perspectives

Some social movement scholars have suggested that the three dominant perspectives discussed above—political opportunities, mobilizing structures, and cultural framing—fail to attend to some important dimensions of social movements. Two emerging perspectives are discussed here.

First, Deborah Gould (2004) argues that social movement researchers should take another look at the role of emotions in motivating people to participate in social movement activities. She contends that the social movement literature has fallen short by attending to rationality but not emotions of movement participants. She applauds the rejection of earlier attempts to understand social movement actors in terms of psychopathologies, but suggests that social movements are passionate political processes and emotions must be considered. She proposes that social movement researchers should study the role that emotions such as anger, indignation, hope, and pride play in motivating social movement involvement. She recounts her own qualitative research with lesbians and gays who participate in the AIDS activism group ACT UP, noting the important role that grief and anger about AIDS and the slow response to it played in moving participants to action. In another analysis, Karen Stanbridge and J. Scott Kenney (2009) suggest that victims' rights advocates must manage the grief, fear, and anger related to the victim experience in their public protest action.

When reconsidering the living wage campaign, it seems that Deborah Gould has a point. Certainly, it appears that Greg Halpern was touched emotionally as well as intellectually by the stories he heard from workers at Harvard. The divinity students who participated in the vigil chanted, "Where's your horror? Where's your rage?" Perhaps they were thinking that such strong emotions move people to action. We know that the religious leaders who started the action in Baltimore were angry at the plight of the working poor. This raises an important question for social movement leaders: Should they appeal to both emotional and intellectual understandings of injustice? If so, what are the best methods to do this? These are the questions that Gould recommends social movement researchers investigate.

Second, Richard Flacks (2004) suggests that the literature on resource mobilization has failed to consider the fundamental differences in the way that different members participate in social movements. He asserts that there may be very different explanations for the participation of leaders, organizers, and mass participants. He thinks we should be more interested in why some people come to see societal change as a major priority in their lives while others don't, and he suggests that social movement scholars should study the biographies of activists to learn more about that. Studs Terkel was an activist, not a social movement scholar, but he was interested in exactly the same question that Flacks raises. For his book *Hope Dies Last* (2003), he interviewed 55 activists about what motivated them to activism. As the title of the book indicates, he found hope to be a major motivator.

From another perspective, Robert Putnam (2000) notes that many people are participating at a very superficial level in contemporary social movements, responding to direct mail campaigns with a one-time contribution but making no greater commitment to the cause. Putnam argues that this type of involvement in social movements fails to build the social capital that is built in grassroots coalitions like those driving the living wage movement. There are, indeed, different ways to participate in social movements, and social movement leaders need to understand the different motivations involved.

Critical Thinking Questions 14.1

Think of a social justice issue that you have some passion about. How would you talk about this issue in terms of social justice? How global is the issue? How open is the political system (in the United States or internationally) to social action about the issue? What existing networks might be available to organize reform efforts regarding this issue? Think of two or three cultural frames that would motivate people to engage in collective action on this issue?

SOCIAL MOVEMENT OUTCOMES

Because social movements are processes, not structures, they are not easy to research. The case study has been the predominant method used, with recent emphasis on comparative case studies. Unfortunately, one researcher may declare a particular movement a failure, while another researcher will see it as having succeeded (Goodwin & Jasper, 2004). Often the impact of a movement cannot be determined until well past its heyday. Different analyses may be based, in part, on different guidelines for success, but the researchers may also be evaluating the movement from different time perspectives. This is a reminder, again, of the importance of the time dimension in changing person-environment configurations.

Like other human endeavors, social movements are neither completely successful nor completely unsuccessful. In general, however, the most successful social movements have outcomes that are far less radical than their proponents would like and far more radical than their opponents would like. Social movements rarely produce the major redistribution of power that activists desire and movement goals specify. The women's movement has not achieved its goal of equality and nondiscrimination for women. The conservative Christian movement has not reached its goal of restoring traditional family and gender roles. And yet, social movements do have an effect on society. Thus, their success should perhaps be measured not by their survival, but by the institutional changes they influence. For example, should any credit be given to the living wage movement for the 2007, 2008, and 2009 federal minimum wage increases in the United States? This is a hard question to answer.

Sidney Tarrow (1998) suggests that the power of social movements is cumulative and can be appreciated only from a long-term historical perspective. Many of the gains of social movements get reversed, but "they often leave behind incremental expansions in participation, changes in popular culture, and residual movement networks" (p. 202). Research on social movements documents a range of direct and indirect effects. Contemporary social movements have accomplished an impressive list of specific federal legislation, including the Civil Rights Act of 1964; Title IX, the federal law that prohibits gender-based discrimination in athletics and educational programs at institutions that receive federal funds; and the Americans with Disabilities Act of 1990. Considered by some scholars to be the most successful social movement in the United States since World War II, the Black civil rights movement has served as a model for organizing, opened opportunities, and provided hope for other aggrieved groups. Because of social movements, the political system has become more open and responsive to previously ignored groups, and voicing grievances has become an expected part of life in a democratic country. New decision-making bodies, such as ad hoc committees and new governmental ministries, have been created in many nations (della Porta & Diani, 2006). Many SMOs have become a stable part of the social environment, and activist-oriented networks outlast the movements that spawned them. Research indicates that although individual activists are often temporarily disillusioned at the end of a social movement, in the long term, they are empowered and politicized by their participation (Tarrow, 1998).

Although the success of a given social movement depends on its unique configuration of political opportunities, mobilizing efforts, and cultural frames, social movement researchers agree on the factors that influence success or failure. Some of these factors are outside the control of the movement, but some of them can be successfully manipulated by movement leaders. The most obvious factor is the ability to attract a large number of participants. The most successful movements tap into existing networks and associations that have a shared culture, a strong sense of solidarity, and a common identity. These groups are the most likely to be willing to make sacrifices and remain committed over time, and to have the shared symbols to frame the movement. Religious movements, for example, benefit from long-lasting and widely cherished religious symbols. Other forces, however, can serve as serious threats to the success of a social movement. Internal conflicts and factionalism weaken the chances for success, as does a strong opponent. Initial successes may stimulate strong countermovements, or a backlash may develop in reaction to the radical flank of a movement.

SOCIAL MOVEMENT TRENDS

Social movement scholars generally agree that social movements will continue to be a part of the social landscape in the foreseeable future (della Porta & Diani, 2006; McMichael, 2008). In fact, some have predicted that we are entering an era of "movement societies," in which challenge and disruption of institutional arrangements will become a routine part of life (Tarrow, 2006). Della Porta and Diani (2006) predict that the antiglobalization movement will become a new political force in the world. They also see a trend toward the return of working class movements and "mobilization by the dispossessed" (p. viii). They suggest that this may be happening because the size of social groups that lack full citizenship is growing around the world.

Tarrow (2006) suggests that the extraordinary international protests of the late 1990s and beginning years of the 21st century represent something new on the planet. Indeed, as suggested earlier, there has been a rapid expansion of TSMOs (McMichael, 2008; J. Smith, 2002; Soyez, 2000). To date, the TSMOs have developed primarily in the areas of human rights, women's rights, environmental protection, antiglobalization, and peace (McMichael, 2008). Greenpeace, Amnesty International, Service for Peace and Justice (SERPAJ), and Friends of the Earth are examples of TSMOs. One benefit of TSMOs is that they can include people who speak out about an issue in one country while people are silenced in other countries. TSMOs rarely use violent, or even seriously disruptive, methods. Many observers suggest that given the globalization of the economy, any successful labor challenge to growing inequality will have to be international in scope, and there is evidence that this is, indeed, happening. That is one aim of the antiglobalization movement, which is made up of a collection of labor activists as well as environmentalists and feminists (McMichael, 2008; Weil & Gamble, 2005).

Two examples of this global labor movement are the International Confederation of Free Trade Unions (ICFTU) and the Transnationals Information Exchange (TIE). The ICFTU, set up in 1949, has over 200 organizations in 145 countries and a membership of 155 million. It has regional offices in Asia, Africa, and the Americas and close links to the European Trade Union Confederation. The ICFTU priorities include eradication of forced and child labor, equal rights for working women, and protecting the environment (ICFTU, n.d.). TIE is an international grassroots network of workers and union activists established in 1978 (McMichael, 2008; TIE Internationales, 2009). Its primary aim is to promote international consciousness of work conditions and to encourage cooperation among workers. TIE is a good example of the form taken by many emerging global movements. It has a flexible, decentralized structure with offices in the Netherlands, Brazil, Sri Lanka, Russia, Germany, and the United States, and grassroots activities going on worldwide. For example, TIE–Asia has organized campaigns to support garment workers in Bangladesh and Cambodia, and it has supported a seminar on the plight of women workers in Asian political conflict areas.

Another strong trend that began in the 1990s was a shift from single-issue organizing to multi-issue organizing by TSMOs (Tarrow, 2006). Traditionally, social movements and the SMOs that supported them focused tightly on a single issue, such as poverty or gender equality. The majority of TSMOs still focus on single issues, but the number of multi-issue TSMOs doubled in the 1990s, growing twice as fast as the overall TSMO population (G. Davis et al., 2005). Increasingly, for example, TSMOs are bridging labor issues with such other issues as the environment, gender equality, peace, and global justice (della Porta & Diani, 2006).

SOCIAL MOVEMENTS AND CONTEMPORARY SOCIAL WORK

Early in this chapter, I suggested that the professionalization of social work was accomplished by sacrificing the social reform fervor of its settlement house tradition. Some social movement scholars have found that it is difficult, if not impossible, to be both a profession and a reform movement (J. Freeman, 1995). Other social work scholars see a dual focus on professional service and social reform as achievable and even natural. The history of social work is a history of tension between the goal of professional service and the goal of social reform. This tension has been quite obvious in recent years. On the one hand, social workers and their professional organizations have devoted a lot of resources to obtaining licensure for clinical social workers and to securing private and public reimbursement for clinical social work services. On the other hand, social work's leading professional organizations have in recent times revised documents, including the NASW Code of Ethics and CSWE's Curriculum Policy Statement, to add forceful language about the social justice goals of the profession.

Philip Popple (1992) suggests that each generation of social workers must struggle anew with the tension between a conservative mandate from society for efficient service that manages problems of dependency and a liberal or radical mandate from the profession to promote social justice. He also suggests that social workers experience this tension differently in different political eras. In conservative political times, there is great disparity between the societal mandate for social workers to act as social control agents and the profession's social reform tradition. In such times, the social reform goal is not prominent. In liberal political times, however, there is less tension between the two goals, and social work's social reform goal is more visible. Popple's analysis is consistent with a tenet of the PO perspective on social movements: Shifts in political alignments open or close opportunities for social movement activity. Even though the social work profession's emphasis on social reform at any given time is influenced by political opportunities, the valuing of social justice is a permanent feature of social work in the United States (Popple, 1992). Thus, all social workers should be familiar with developments in social movement theory and research.

Some social workers practice in **social movement service organizations (SMSOs),** also known as *social movement agencies, alternative social agencies,* and *hybrid organizations,* which pursue social change while delivering services (M. Meyer, 2010). These organizations make a fundamental commitment both to social service provision and to advocacy efforts. They often attempt to provide revolutionary services that are oriented toward empowerment and cognitive liberation. Their advocacy efforts are often focused on reframing public understanding of social problems and their solutions. For example, SMSOs serving homeless persons have attempted to reframe homelessness as being a consequence of failed housing policies, rather than a consequence of individual failings. Likewise, rape crisis centers have focused on gaining public affirmation that rape is not the victim's fault (Hasenfeld, 2010a).

Megan Meyer (2010) identifies five characteristics of SMSOs:

1. They are driven by controversial values that they see as socially beneficial.

2. They closely integrate service provision and advocacy roles.

3. They develop a close sense of community among their clients.

4. They often mobilize their members to advocate for change.

5. They typically develop a hybrid structure that incorporates elements of both collective and bureaucratic forms of operation.

Some examples of SMSOs are feminist health and rape crisis centers, peace and conflict resolution organizations, and national women's and racial minority organizations. Unfortunately, there is very little research on SMSOs to date, and our knowledge of them and their impact is limited.

Recent critics of existing social movement theory have suggested that SMOs can be divided into a reform or moderate tradition and a radical tradition (K. Fitzgerald & Rodgers, 2000). Radical social movement organizations tend to be organized nonhierarchically and operate with little structure. Their goal is usually radical change in social institutions, rather than social reform. Exhibit 14.7 contrasts the characteristics of moderate and radical SMOs. As you can see, existing social movement theories are a better fit with moderate SMOs than with radical SMOs (K. Fitzgerald & Rodgers, 2000).

	Moderate SMOs	Radical SMOs
Internal structure	Hierarchical leadership; formal bureaucratic organization; development of large membership base for resource generation	Nonhierarchical leadership; participatory democratic organization; egalitarian; "membership" based on involvement; indigenous leadership
Ideology	Reform agenda, emphasis on being a contender in the existing political system; national focus	Radical agenda; emphasis on structural change; flexible ideology; radical networks; global consciousness
Tactics	Nonviolent legal action	Nonviolent direct action; mass actions; innovative tactics
Communication	Mainstream media and communication channels	Either ignored or misrepresented by mainstream media; reliance on alternative forms of communication (music, street theater, pamphlets, newsletters, digital technology, cell phones, text messaging)
Assessment of success	Measured in terms of reform of existing political/economic system; longevity	Measured in terms of contribution to larger radical agenda; subject to intense opposition and government surveillance; may be purposefully short lived

▲ **Exhibit 14.7**   Characteristics of Moderate and Radical SMOs

SOURCE: Based on Fitzgerald and Rodgers (2000), Table 1.

This model helps us understand the dimensions of contemporary SMOs but does not capture their changing trajectories over time. After studying six feminist SMOs, Cheryl Hyde (2000) suggests that many social movement agencies fall somewhere between the moderate SMO and radical SMO. The six agencies that she studied had begun as grassroots organizations with traits consistent with the description of radical SMOs. They changed in varying ways over the years, however, falling on a continuum from moderate to radical at the point that she studied them.

We are living in a time of growing inequality, hot spots of ethnic hatred, and activism based on social identity. It is easy to get overwhelmed and feel powerless about the situations we confront. Social movement theory is an important ingredient in our social work survival kit. It helps us see, as the title of Sidney Tarrow's (1998) book suggests, that there is "power in movement." It provides a conceptual base to reinvigorate our social reform mission. We may take inspiration from some contemporary examples of courage and conviction that led to social change (Sernau, 2006):

- Rosa Parks, a tired seamstress on a public bus, helped launch the U.S. civil rights movement.

- C. P. Ellis, a former Ku Klux Klan leader, started action that changed the racial climate of an entire community.

- Craig Kielburger, a 12-year-old Canadian boy, began an international movement, Free the Children, to end child labor after reading a story about child workers in Pakistan.

- In 1999, college students around the United States began a boycott of Reebok sports shoes, prompting improved conditions in that company's Indonesian factories.

These are just a few of the empowering stories we can recall in our most discouraged moments, to give us hope.

Critical Thinking Questions 14.2

Do you see the goals of professional service and social reform as incompatible or as dual goals that can be fruitfully integrated? How prominent do you think the social reform goal is in the social work profession at the current time? What factors do you think are influencing the current emphasis (or lack of emphasis) on social reform by the profession? How important are social movements in the search for social justice?

IMPLICATIONS FOR SOCIAL WORK PRACTICE

This discussion of social movements recommends several principles for social work activism:

- Become skillful in assessing political opportunities for social reform efforts.

- Become skillful in recognizing and mobilizing formal and informal networks for social reform activities.

- In conservative political eras, be vigilant about the temptation to encapsulate and lose sight of social work's social reform mission.

- Become skillful at attracting new recruits to social reform activities and sustaining the morale and commitment of current participants.

- Become skillful in managing internal movement conflicts and avoiding factionalism.

- Become skillful in developing cultural frames that legitimate and motivate collective action.

- Assist social workers in direct practice to assess the benefits and costs to clients of involvement in social movement activities.

- Assist social workers in the traditional social welfare institution to recognize the important role that reform social movements play in identifying new or previously unrecognized social injustices and social service needs.

KEY TERMS

charity organization society (COS) movement
conscience constituency
countermovement
cultural framing
cultural framing (CF) perspective
defensive social movement
elites
framing contests

mobilizing structures
mobilizing structures (MS) perspective
network model
offensive social movement
political opportunities (PO) perspective
professional social movement organizations
resource mobilization theory

settlement house movement
social movements
social movement organizations (SMOs)
social movement service organizations (SMSOs)
social reform
strain theory
transnational social movement organizations (TSMOs)

ACTIVE LEARNING

1. You read about some of the early history of the living wage movement in the case study at the beginning of this chapter. The living wage movement is just over a decade old. What, if anything, had you heard about this movement before reading the case story in the chapter? At this point, how do you evaluate its outcomes? How do you explain its successes? What challenges might lie ahead?

2. In this chapter, I suggested that successful social movements often open the way for countermovements. I also suggested that social movements may be either offensive or defensive. In considering these ideas, it is helpful to look at two social movements that hold competing views on issues related to women. Go to the websites of the National Organization for Women (NOW) at www.now.org and the National Right to Life Committee (NRLC) at www.nrlc.org. Study carefully the positions that each of these social movement organizations takes on the issue of abortion. What language and symbols does each organization use for framing the issue?

WEB RESOURCES

Amnesty International
www.amnesty.org

Site contains recommendations for protection and promotion of human rights and a timeline for accomplishing them, good news, FAQs, and links to other human rights activist groups.

Critical Social Work
www.criticalsocialwork.com

Site organized at the University of Windsor in Ontario, Canada, is an international, interdisciplinary e-journal whose goal is to promote dialogue about methods for achieving social justice.

Free the Children
www.freethechildren.com

Site maintained by the social movement organization developed by Craig Kielburger when he was 12 years old, contains information about accomplishments, campaigns, planned activities and projects, conferences, and speakers' bureau.

Greatergood.com
http://greatergood.com

Site maintained as part of a family of cause-related websites operated by Charity USA LLC, contains merchandise from over 100 leading online merchants; up to 15% of each purchase goes to a charitable organization of the purchaser's selection.

National Organizers Alliance (NOA)
www.noacentral.org

Site maintained by NOA, a nonprofit organization with the mission to advance progressive organizing for social, economic, environmental, and racial justice, contains information about national gatherings, a job bank, a newsletter, a calendar of events, and links to other activist organizations.

New Organizing Institute (NOI)
www.neworganizing.com

Site maintained by NOI, a grassroots program that trains young political organizers for progressive campaigns, contains information about training programs, internships, and jobs as well as a blog.

References

Abma, J., & Martinez, G. (2006). Childlessness among older women in the United States: Trends and profiles. *Journal of Marriage and Family, 68,* 1045–1056.

Abrams, D., Hogg, M., Hinkle, S., & Otten, S. (2005). The social identity perspective on small groups. In M. Poole & A. Hollingshead (Eds.), *Theories of small groups: Interdisciplinary perspectives* (pp. 99–137). Thousand Oaks, CA: Sage.

Abu-Lughod, L. (1999). The interpretation of culture(s) after television. In S. B. Ortner (Ed.), *The fate of culture: Geertz and beyond* (pp. 110–135). Berkeley: University of California Press.

Adams, B., & Trost, J. (2005). *Handbook of world families.* Thousand Oaks, CA: Sage.

Adelman, E. (2006). Mind–body intelligence. *Holistic Nursing Practice, 20*(3), 147–151.

Adler, J. (1995). *Arching backwards: The mystical initiation of a contemporary woman.* Rochester, VT: Inner Traditions.

Adler, N. (2001). A consideration of multiple pathways from socioeconomic status to health. In J. Auerbach & B. Krimgold (Eds.), *Income, socioeconomic status, and health: Exploring the relationships* (pp. 56–66). Washington, DC: Academy for Health Services Research & Health Policy.

Adler, N. (2006, October). *Health disparities: Monitoring, mechanism, and meaning.* Paper presented at the NIH Conference on Understanding and Reducing Health Disparities: Contributions from the Behavioral and Social Sciences, Bethesda, MD.

Aguilar, M. A. (2001). Catholicism. In M. Van Hook, B. Hugen, & M. Aguilar (Eds.), *Spirituality within religious traditions in social work practice* (pp.120–145). Pacific Grove, CA: Brooks/Cole.

Ainsworth, M. S., Blehar, M. C., & Waters, E. (1978). *Patterns of attachment: A psychological study of the strange situation.* Oxford, UK: Erlbaum.

Ajzen, I., & Fishbein, M. (1977). Attitude–behavior relations: A theoretical analysis and review of empirical research. *Psychological Bulletin, 84,* 888–918.

Akande, A. (1997). Determinants of personal space among South African students. *Journal of Psychology, 131,* 569–571.

Al-Ansari, E. (2002). Effects of gender and education on the moral reasoning of Kuwait university students. *Social Behavior & Personality, 30*(1), 75–82.

Alan Guttmacher Institute. (2002a). *Sexuality education.* Retrieved October 24, 2006, from http://www.guttmacher.org.

Alan Guttmacher Institute. (2002b). *Teenagers' sexual and reproductive health: Developed countries.* Retrieved October 24, 2006, from http://www.guttmacher.org.

Alan Guttmacher Institute. (2006). *Facts on American teens' sexual and reproductive health.* Retrieved October 24, 2006, from http://www.guttmacher.org.

Albrecht, G. H. (2002). *Hitting home: Feminist ethics, women's work, and the betrayal of "family values."* London: Continuum.

Albrecht, G. L., Seelman, K. D., & Bury, M. (Eds.). (2001). *Handbook of disability studies.* Thousand Oaks, CA: Sage.

Aldashev, G., & Verdier, T. (2009). When NGOs go global: Competition on international markets for development donations. *Journal of International Economics, 79*(2), 198–210.

Aldwin, C. M. (2007). *Stress, coping, and development: An integrative perspective* (2nd ed.). New York: Guilford Press.

Aldwin, C. M., & Yancura, L. A. (2004). Coping and health: A comparison of the stress and trauma literatures. In P. Schnurr & B. Green (Eds.), *Trauma and health: Physical health consequences of exposure to extreme stress* (pp. 99–125). Washington, DC: American Psychological Association.

Alinsky, S. (1971). *Rules for radicals.* New York: Vintage.

Allan, K. (2007). *The social lens: An invitation to social and sociological theory.* Thousand Oaks, CA: Sage.

Allen, K., Lloyd, S., & Few, A. (2009). Reclaiming feminist theory, method, and praxis for family studies. In S. Lloyd, A. Few, & K. Allen (Eds.), *Handbook of feminist family studies* (pp. 3–17). Thousand Oaks, CA: Sage.

Allen-Meares, P. (1995). *Social work with children and adolescents.* White Plains, NY: Longman.

Allen-Meares, P., & Pugach, M. (1982). Facilitating interdisciplinary collaboration on behalf of handicapped children and youth. *Teaching Education and Special Education, 5,* 30–36.

Almaas, A. H. (1995). *Luminous night's journey.* Berkeley, CA: Diamond Books.

Almaas, A. H. (1996). *The point of existence.* Berkeley, CA: Diamond Books.

Alperovitz, G. (2005). *America beyond capitalism: Reclaiming our wealth, our liberty, and our democracy.* Hoboken, NJ: Wiley.

Altman, I. (1975). *The environment and social behavior: Privacy, personal space, territory, and crowding.* Monterey, CA: Brooks/Cole.

Altman, I. (1993). Dialectics, physical environments, and personal relationships. *Communication Monographs, 60,* 26–34.

Altshuler, S. (2005). Drug-endangered children need a collaborative community response. *Child Welfare, 84*(2), 171–190.

Amato, P., & Irving, S. (2006). Historical trends in divorce and dissolution in the United States. In M. Fine & J. Harvey (Eds.), *Handbook of divorce and relationship dissolution* (pp. 41–57). Mahwah, NJ: Erlbaum.

American Anthropological Association. (2007). *Race: Are we so different?* Retrieved November 1, 2009, from http://www.understandingrace.org/home.html.

American Diabetes Association. (n.d.). *Direct and indirect costs of diabetes in the United States.* Retrieved October 18, 2006, from http://www.diabetes.org/linkforlife?WTLPromo=all aboutdia betes_linkforlife.

American Heart Association. (2005). *Heart disease and stroke statistics—2005 update.* Retrieved May 18, 2010, from http://www.americanheart.org/download/heart/ 110539098119hDSStats2005Update.

American Heart Association. (2006). *AHA statistical update. Heart disease and stroke statistics—2006 Update* [Electronic version]. *Circulation, 113,* 85–151. Retrieved August 4, 2006, from http:// circ.ahajournals.org/cgi/ content/short/113/6/e85.

American Heart Association. (2009). *Cardiovascular disease statistics.* Retrieved December 4, 2009, from http://www.american heart.org/presenter.jhtml?identifier=4478.

American Heart Association. (2010). *Cardiovascular disease statistics.* Retrieved April 19, 2010, from http://www.american heart.org/presenter.jhtml?identifier=4478.

American Psychiatric Association. (2000). *Diagnostic and statistical manual of mental disorders* (4th ed., Text Rev.). Washington, DC: Author.

American Religious Identification Survey. (2001). Retrieved July 25, 2006, from http://www.gc.cuny.edu/ faculty/research_studies/ aris.pdf

Amole, D. (2005). Coping strategies for living in student residential facilities in Nigeria. *Environment & Behavior, 37*(2), 201–219.

Anandarajah, G., & Hight, E. (2001). Spirituality and medical practice: Using the HOPE questions as a practical tool for spiritual assessment. *American Family Physician, 63*(1), 81–99.

Anderson, C. M. (2005). Single-parent families: Strengths, vulnerabilities, and interventions. In B. Carter & M. McGoldrick (Eds.), *The expanded family life cycle: Individual, family, and social perspectives* (3rd ed., pp. 399–416). Boston: Allyn & Bacon.

Anderson, H. (2009). A spirituality for family living. In F. Walsh (Ed.), *Spiritual resources in family therapy* (2nd ed.) (pp. 194–211). New York: Guilford Press.

Anderson, R. (2002). Deaths: Leading causes for 2000. *National Vital Statistics Report, 50*(16), 1–86. Retrieved August 4, 2006, from http://www.cdc.gov/nchs/data/nvsr/ nvsr50/nvsr50_16.pdf.

Anderson, R., & Carter, I. (1974). *Human behavior in the social environment: A social systems approach.* Chicago: Aldine.

Andrews, A. B. (1990). Interdisciplinary and interorganizational collaboration. In L. Ginsberg, S. Khinduka, J. A. Hall, F. Ross-Sheriff, & A. Hartman (Eds.), *Encyclopedia of social work* (18th ed., 1990 supplement, pp. 175–188). Silver Spring, MD: NASW Press.

Angell, G. B., Dennis, B. G., & Dumain, L. E. (1998). Spirituality, resilience, and narrative: Coping with parental death. *Families in Society, 79*(6), 615–630.

Angers, M. E. (2008). Psychoanalysis, politics, and "the repressed feminine": Toward a psychoanalytically informed sociology of knowledge. *Issues in Psychoanalytic Psychology, 30*(2), 137–155.

Appelrouth, S., & Edles, L. (2007). *Sociological theory in the contemporary era.* Thousand Oaks, CA: Pine Forge.

Applegate, J., & Shapiro, J. (2005). *Neurobiology for clinical social work.* New York: Norton.

Argyris, C. (1999). *On organizational learning.* Cambridge, MA: Blackwell.

Argyris, C., & Schön, D. (1978). *Organizational learning: A theory of action perspective.* Reading, MA: Addison-Wesley.

Argyris, C., & Schön, D. (1996). *Organizational learning II: Theory, method, and practice.* Reading, MA: Addison-Wesley.

Aronowitz, S. (2003). Global capital and its opponents. In S. Aronowitz & H. Gautney (Eds.), *Implicating empire: Globalization & resistance in the 21st century world order* (pp. 179–195). New York: Basic Books.

Ashford, J., LeCroy, C., & Lortie, K. (2010). *Human behavior in the social environment* (4th ed.). Belmont, CA: Cengage.

Ashkanani, H. R. (2009). The relationship between religiosity and subjective well-being: A case of Kuwaiti car accident victims. *Traumatology, 15*(1), 23–28.

Assagioli, R. (1965). *Psychosynthesis: A manual of principles and techniques.* New York: Viking.

Assagioli, R. (1973). *The act of will.* New York: Penguin.

Assagioli, R. (1989). Self-realization and psychological disturbances. In S. Grof & C. Grof (Eds.), *Spiritual emergency: When personal transformation becomes a crisis* (pp. 27–48). Los Angeles: Jeremy P. Tarcher.

Association for the Advancement of Social Work With Groups. (2005). *Standards for social work practice with groups* (2nd ed.). Alexandria, VA: Author.

Auerbach, J., & Krimgold, B. (2001). Improving health: It doesn't take a revolution. In J. Auerbach & B. Krimgold (Eds.), *Income, socioeconomic status, and health: Exploring the relationships* (pp. 1–11). Washington, DC: Academy for Health Services Research & Health Policy.

Australian Government: Department of Family and Community Services, Office for Women. (2006). *What the Australian government is doing for women.* Retrieved April 10, 2010, from http://www.fahcsia.gov.au/sa/women/pubs/govtint/budgetpubs/govt_for_women/Documents/booklet.pdf

Averill, J. R. (1997). The emotions: An integrative approach. In R. Hogan, J. A. Johnson, & S. R. Briggs (Eds.), *Handbook of personality psychology* (pp. 513–541). San Diego, CA: Academic Press.

Bagdikian, B. (2004). *The new media monopoly* (5th ed.). Boston: Beacon Press.

Baker, M., Das, D., Venugopal, K., & Howden-Chapman, P. (2008). Tuberculosis associated with household crowding in a developed country. *Journal of Epidemiology and Community Health, 62*(8), 715–721.

Bal, S., Crombez, G., & Oost, P. V. (2003). The role of social support in well-being and coping with self-reported stressful events in adolescents. *Child Abuse & Neglect, 27*(12), 1377–1395.

Bales, R. (1950). *Interaction process analysis: A method for the study of small groups.* Cambridge, MA: Addison-Wesley.

Balkwell, J. W. (1994). Status. In M. Foschi & E. J. Lawler (Eds.), *Group processes: Sociological analyses* (pp. 119–148). Chicago: Nelson-Hall.

Ballantine, J., & Roberts, K. (2009). *Our social world: Introduction to sociology* (2nd ed.). Thousand Oaks, CA: Pine Forge.

Balsam, K., Beauchaine, T., Rothblum, E., & Solomon, S. (2008). Three-year follow-up of same-sex couples who had civil unions in Vermont, same-sex couples not in civil unions, and heterosexual married couples. *Developmental Psychology, 44*(1), 102–116.

Bandura, A. (1977a). Self-efficacy: Toward a unifying theory of behavioral change. *Psychological Review, 84,* 191–215.

Bandura, A. (1977b). *Social learning theory.* Englewood Cliffs, NJ: Prentice Hall.

Bandura, A. (1986). *Social foundations of thought and action: A social cognitive theory.* Englewood Cliffs, NJ: Prentice Hall.

Bandura, A. (2001). Social cognitive theory: An agentic perspective. *Annual Review of Psychology, 52,* 1–26.

Bandura, A. (2002). Social cognitive theory in cultural context. *Applied Psychology: An International Review, 51*(2), 269–290.

Banerjee, M. M., & Canda, E. R. (2009). Spirituality as a strength of African-American women affected by welfare reform. *Social Thought, 28*(3), 239–262.

Barber, B., & Demo, D. (2006). The kids are alright (at least, most of them): Links between divorce and dissolution and child well-being. In M. Fine & J. Harvey (Eds.), *Handbook of divorce and relationship dissolution* (pp. 289–311). Mahwah, NJ: Erlbaum.

Barker, R. G. (1968). *Ecological psychology: Concepts and methods for studying the environment of human behavior.* Palo Alto, CA: Stanford University Press.

Barker, R. G., & Gump, P. (1964). *Big school, small school: High school size and student behavior.* Palo Alto, CA: Stanford University Press.

Barnard, M., & McKeganey, N. (2004). The impact of parental drug use on children: What is the problem and what can be done to help? *Addiction, 99,* 552–559.

Barnekow, K., & Kraemer, G. (2005). The psychobiological theory of attachment. A viable frame of reference for early intervention providers. *Physical & Occupational Therapy in Pediatrics, 25*(1 & 2), 3–15.

Barnes, P. M., Bloom, B., & Nahin, R. (2008, December 10). Complementary and alternative medicine use among adults and children: United States, 2007. *CDC National Health Statistics Report #12.* Retrieved April 17, 2010, from http://nccam.nih.gov/news/2008/ nhsr12.pdf.

Barnett, S., & Scotch, R. (2002). *Disability protests.* Washington, DC: Gallaudet University Press.

Barnoff, L., & Moffatt, K. (2007). Contradictory tensions in anti-oppression practice in feminist social services. *Affilia, 22*(1), 56–70.

Barret, R., & Barzan, R. (1996). Spiritual experiences of gay men and lesbians. *Counseling and Values, 41,* 4–15.

Barrett, C. E., Noble, P., Hanson, E., Pine, D. S., Winslow, J. T., & Nelson, E. E. (2009). Early adverse rearing experiences alter sleep–wake patterns and plasma cortisol levels in juvenile rhesus monkeys. *Psychoneuroendocrinology, 34*(7), 1029–1040.

Barrett, M. J. (1999). Healing from trauma: The quest for spirituality. In F. Walsh (Ed.), *Spiritual resources in family therapy* (pp. 192–208). New York: Guilford Press.

Bartholomae, S., & Fox, J. (2010). Economic stress and families. In S. Price, C. Price, & P. McKenry (Eds.), *Families &*

change: Coping with stressful events and transitions (4th ed., pp. 185–209). Thousand Oaks, CA: Sage.

Bartholomew, R. E. (2000). *Exotic deviance: Medicalizing cultural idioms—From strangeness to illness.* Boulder: University Press of Colorado.

Baskin, C. (2006). Aboriginal world views as challenges and possibilities in social work education. *Critical Social Work, 7*(2).

Baum, F. (1999). The role of social capital in health promotion. Australian perspectives. *Health Promotion Journal of Australia, 9*(3), 171–178.

Bauman, L., Silver, E., & Stein, R. (2006). Cumulative social disadvantage and child health. *Pediatrics, 117*(4), 1321–1328.

Bauman, Z. (1998). *Globalization: The human consequences.* New York: Columbia University Press.

Baxter, L., & Braithwaite, D. (2006). Introduction: Metatheory and theory in family communication research. In D. Braithwaite & L. Baxter (Eds.), *Engaging theories in family communication: Multiple perspectives* (pp. 1–15). Thousand Oaks, CA: Sage.

Beauchemin, K., & Hays, P. (1996). Sunny hospital rooms expedite recovery from severe and refractory depressions. *Journal of Affective Disorders, 40*(1–2), 49–51.

Beauchemin, K., & Hays, P. (1998). Dying in the dark: Sunshine, gender, and outcomes in myocardial infarction. *Journal of the Royal Society of Medicine, 91,* 352–354.

Bechtel, R. (2000). Assumptions, methods, and research problems of ecological psychology. In S. Wapner, J. Demick, T. Yamamoto, & H. Minami (Eds.), *Theoretical perspectives in environment-behavior research: Underlying assumptions, research problems, and methodologies* (pp. 61–66). New York: Kluwer Academic.

Beck, A. T. (1976). *Cognitive therapy and the emotional disorders.* New York: International Universities Press.

Beck, E., & Eichler, M. (2000). Consensus organizing: A practice model for community building. *Journal of Community Practice, 8*(1), 87–102.

Beck, J. S. (1995). *Cognitive therapy: Basics and beyond.* New York: Guilford Press.

Beck, U. (1992). *Risk society: Towards a new modernity.* Thousand Oaks, CA: Sage.

Beck, U. (1999). *World risk society.* Cambridge, UK: Polity.

Becker, D. (2004). Post-traumatic stress disorder. In P. J. Caplan & L. Cosgrove (Eds.), *Bias in psychiatric diagnosis* (pp. 207–212). Lanham, MD: Jason Aronson.

Becker, D. (2005). *The myth of empowerment: Women and the therapeutic culture in America.* New York: New York University Press.

Becker, G. (1981). *A treatise on the family.* Cambridge, MA: Harvard University Press.

Becker, G. (2002). Dying away from home: Quandaries of migration for elders in two ethnic groups. *Journals of Gerontology, Series B, 57*(2), S79–S95.

Becker, H. (1957). Current sacred–secular theory and its development. In H. Becker & A. Boskoff (Eds.), *Modern sociological theory in continuity and change* (pp. 137–185). New York: Dryden.

Becker, M. (1974). The health belief model and sick role behavior. *Health Education Monographs, 2,* 409–419.

Becker, M., & Joseph, J. (1988). AIDS and behavioral change to avoid risk: A review. *American Journal of Public Health, 78,* 384–410.

Beckett, J., & Dungee-Anderson, D. (1998). Multicultural communication in human services organizations. In A. Daly (Ed.), *Workplace diversity: Issues and perspectives* (pp. 191–214). Washington, DC: NASW Press.

Becvar, D., & Becvar, R. (1996). *Family therapy: A systemic integration* (3rd ed.). Boston: Allyn & Bacon.

Beitel, M., Genova, M., Schuman-Olivier Z., Arnold R., Avants, S. K., & Margolin A. (2007). Reflections by inner-city drug users on a Buddhist-based spirituality-focused therapy: A qualitative study. *American Journal of Orthopsychiatry, 77*(1), 1–9.

Belanger, K., Copeland, S., & Cheung, M. (2009). The role of faith in adoption: Achieving positive adoption outcomes for African American children. *Child Welfare, 87*(2), 99–123.

Belcher, J. R., Fandetti, D., & Cole, D. (2004). Is Christian religious conservatism compatible with the liberal social welfare state? *Social Work, 49*(2), 269–276.

Bell, L. (1997). Theoretical foundations for social justice education. In M. Adams, L. Bell, & P. Griffin (Eds.), *Teaching for diversity and social justice* (pp. 1–15). New York: Routledge.

Bell, L. (2009). Mindful psychotherapy. *Journal of Spirituality in Mental Health, 11*(1–2), 126–144.

Bell, R., Davison, M., & Sefcik, D. (2002). A first survey: Measuring burnout in emergency medicine physician assistants. *Journal of the American Academy of Physician Assistants, 15*(3), 40–48.

Bell, Y. R., Bouie, C. L., & Baldwin, J. (1998). Afrocentric cultural consciousness and African American male–female relationships. In J. D. Hamlet (Ed.), *Afrocentric visions: Studies in culture and communication* (pp. 47–71). Thousand Oaks, CA: Sage.

Benedetti, F., Colombo, C., Barbini, B., Campori, E., & Smeraldi, E. (2001). Morning sunlight reduces length of hospitalization in bipolar depression. *Journal of Affective Disorders, 62*(3), 221–223.

Benedict, R. (1946). *The chrysanthemum and the sword.* Boston: Houghton Mifflin.

Benedict, R. (1989). *Patterns of culture.* Boston: Houghton Mifflin. (Original work published 1934)

Bennett, W. L. (2004). Communicating global activism: Strength and vulnerabilities of networked politics. In W. van de Donk,

B. Loader, P. Nixon, & D. Rucht (Eds.), *Cyberprotest: New media, citizens and social movements* (pp. 109–126). London: Routledge.

Bennion, J. (2009, June 23). Drowning in electronics: Where the law stands on e-waste. *Frontline World.* Retrieved October 17, 2009, from http://www.pbs.org/frontlineworld/stories/ghana804/resources/ewaste.html.

Benokraitis, N. V. (2004). *Marriages and families: Changes, choices, and constraints* (5th ed.). Upper Saddle River, NJ: Prentice Hall.

Bentley, K. J., & Walsh, J. (2006). *The social worker and psychotropic medication: Toward effective collaboration with mental health clients, families, and providers* (3rd ed.). Pacific Grove, CA: Brooks/Cole.

Berck, J. (1992). *No place to be: Voices of homeless children.* Boston: Houghton Mifflin.

Berg, P., Appelbaum, E., Bailey, T., & Kalleberg, A. (2004). Contesting time: International comparisons of employee control of working time. *Industrial and Labor Relations Review, 57*(3), 331–349.

Berger, P. L. (1969). *The sacred canopy: Elements of a sociological theory of religion.* Garden City, NY: Doubleday.

Berger, P. L., & Luckmann, T. (1966). *The social construction of reality.* Garden City, NY: Doubleday.

Berke, E., Koepsell, T., Moudon, A., Hoskins, R., & Larson, E. (2007). Association of the built environment with physical activity and obesity in older persons. *American Journal of Public Health, 97*(3), 486–492.

Bernstein, J. (2002, May/June). Making a living: How the living wage movement has prevailed. *Shelterforce Online #123.* Retrieved December 4, 2006, from http://www.nhi.org/online/issues/123/makingaliving.html.

Berry, M. E. (2009). *The sacred universe: Earth, spirituality, and religion in the 21st century.* New York: Columbia University Press.

Besser, G. M., & Thorner, M. O. (1994). *Clinical endocrinology* (2nd ed.). London: Times Mirror International.

Best, J. (1989). Extending the constructionist perspective: A conclusion and introduction. In J. Best (Ed.), *Images of issues: Typifying contemporary social problems* (pp. 243–252). New York: Aldine de Gruyter.

Besthorn, F. H. (2001). Transpersonal psychology and deep ecology: Exploring linkages and applications for social work. In E. R. Canda & E. D. Smith (Eds.), *Transpersonal perspectives on spirituality in social work* (pp. 23–44). Binghamton, NY: Haworth Press.

Besthorn, F. H., & Canda, E. R. (2002). Revisioning environment: Deep ecology for education and teaching in social work. *Journal of Teaching in Social Work, 22*(1/2), 79–101.

Bidart, C., & Lavenu, D. (2005). Evolutions of personal networks and life events. *Social Networks, 27*(4), 359–376.

Biorck, G. (1977). The essence of the clinician's art. *Acta Medica Scandinavica, 201*(3), 145–147.

Bjorklund, B., & Bee, H. (2008). *The journey of adulthood* (6th ed.). Upper Saddle River, NJ: Pearson.

Black, H. K. (1999). Life as gift: Spiritual narratives of elderly African American women living in poverty. *Journal of Aging Studies, 13*(4), 441–455.

Blau, P. (1964). *Exchange and power in social life.* New York: Wiley.

Bloch, D. P., & Richmond, L. J. (Eds.). (1998). *Finding the work you love, loving the work you have.* Palo Alto, CA: Davies-Black.

Bloom, M. (1984). *Configurations of human behavior: Life span development in social environments.* New York: Macmillan.

Blumberg, R., & Devlin, A. (2006). Design issues in hospitals: The adolescent client. *Environment and Behavior, 38*(3), 293–317.

Blumer, H. (1998). *Symbolic interactionism: Perspective and method.* Berkeley: University of California Press.

Boas, F. (1948). *Race, language and culture.* New York: Free Press. (Original work published 1940)

Boase, J., Horrigan, J., Wellman, B., & Rainie, L. (2006). *The strength of Internet ties: The Internet and email aid users in maintaining their social networks and provide pathways to help when people face big decisions.* Washington, DC: Pew Internet & American Life Project. Retrieved November 27, 2006, from http://www.pewinternet.org.

Boddie, S. C., & Cnaan, R. A. (Eds.). (2006). *Faith-based social services: Measures, assessments, and effectiveness.* Binghamton, NY: Haworth Press.

Bohannan, P. (1995). *How culture works.* New York: Free Press.

Bolen, J. S. (1984). *Goddesses in every woman: A new psychology of women.* San Francisco: Harper & Row.

Bolland, K., & Atherton, C. (1999). Chaos theory: An alternative approach to social work practice and research. *Families in Society, 80*(4), 367–373.

Bonnie, R., & Wallace, R. (Eds.). (2003). *Elder mistreatment: Abuse, neglect, and exploitation in an aging America.* Washington, DC: National Academies Press.

Borden, W. (2009). *Contemporary psychodynamic theory and practice.* Chicago: Lyceum.

Bornstein, A. (2009). N30 + 10: Global civil society, a decade after the Battle of Seattle. *Dialectical Anthropology, 33*, 97–108.

Bornstein, M., & Bradley, R. (Eds.). (2003). *Socioeconomic status, parenting, and child development.* Mahwah, NJ: Erlbaum.

Borysenko, J. (1996). *A woman's book of life: The biology, psychology, and spirituality of the life cycle.* New York: Riverhead Books.

Boss, P. (2006). *Loss, trauma, and resilience: Therapeutic work with ambiguous loss.* New York: Norton.

Boubekri, M., Hull, R., & Boyer, L. (1991). Impact of window size and sunlight penetration on office workers' mood and satisfaction. *Environment and Behavior, 23,* 474–493.

Bourdieu, P. (1977). *Outline of a theory of practice.* New York: Cambridge University Press.

Bowen, M. (1978). *Family therapy in clinical practice.* New York: Aronson.

Bowman, P. J. (2006). Role strain and adaptation issues in the strength-based model: Diversity, multilevel, and life-span considerations. *Counseling Psychologist, 34*(1), 118–133.

Boyatzis, R., & McKee, A. (2005). *Resonant leadership: Renewing yourself and connecting with others through mindfulness, hope, and compassion.* Boston: Harvard Business School Press.

Boyd, D., & Ellison, N. (2007). Social networks: Definition, history, and scholarship. *Journal of Computer-Mediated Communication, 13*(1). Retrieved November 13, 2009, from http://jcmc.indiana.edu/vol13/issue1/boyd.ellison.html.

Boyd-Franklin, N. (1987). Group therapy for Black women: A therapeutic support model. *American Journal of Orthpsychiatry, 57,* 394-401.

Boyes-Watson, C. (2005). Seeds of change: Using peacemaking circles to build a village for every child. *Child Welfare, 82*(2), 191–208.

Bradley, R., & Corwyn, R. (2002). Socioeconomic status and child development. *Annual Review of Psychology, 53,* 371–399.

Bradshaw, Y., Healey, J., & Smith, R. (2001). *Sociology for a new century.* Thousand Oaks, CA: Pine Forge.

Brain Injury Association of America. (2001). *Brain Injury Awareness Month 2001: Awareness kit.* Retrieved January 21, 2002, from www.biausa.org.

Braithwaite, D., & Baxter, L. (2006). *Engaging theories in family communication: Multiple perspectives.* Thousand Oaks, CA: Sage.

Brandon, D. (1976). *Zen in the art of helping.* New York: Delta/Seymour Lawrence.

Brantley, J., Doucette, D., & Lindell, A. (2008). Mindfulness, meditation, and health. In A. L. Strozier & J. E. Carpenter (Eds.), *Introduction to alternative and complementary therapies* (pp. 9–29). New York: Haworth Press.

Braude, A. (1997). Women's history is American religious history. In T. A. Tweed (Ed.), *Retelling U.S. religious history* (pp. 87–107). Berkeley: University of California Press.

Brave Heart, M. Y. H. (2001). Clinical interventions with American Indians. In R. Fong & S. Furuto (Eds.), *Cultural competent social work practice: Practice skills, interventions, and evaluation* (pp. 285–298). New York: Longman.

Braver, S., Shapiro, J., & Goodman, M. (2006). Consequences of divorce for parents. In M. Fine & J. Harvey (Eds.), *Handbook of divorce and relationship dissolution* (pp. 313–337). Mahwah, NJ: Erlbaum.

Brawley, E. (2006). *Design innovations for aging and Alzheimer's.* Hoboken, NJ: Wiley.

Bredy, T., Weaver, I., Champagne, F. C., & Meaney, M. J. (2001). Stress, maternal care, and neural development in the rat. In C. A. Shaw & J. C. McEachern (Eds.), *Toward a theory of neural plasticity* (pp. 288–300). Philadelphia: Psychology Press/Taylor & Francis.

Breitman, B. E. (1995). Social and spiritual reconstruction of self within a feminist Jewish community. *Woman and Therapy: A Feminist Quarterly, 16*(2/3), 73–82.

Brent, J. (1997). Community without unity. In P. Hoggett (Ed.), *Contested communities: Experiences, struggles, policies* (pp. 68–83). Bristol, UK: Policy Press.

Brodsky, A., & Marx, C. (2001). Layers of identity: Multiple psychological senses of community within a community setting. *Journal of Community Psychology, 29*(2), 161–178.

Brodsky, A., O'Campo, P., & Aronson, R. (1999). PSOC in community context: Multilevel correlates of a measure of psychological sense of community in low-income, urban neighborhoods. *Journal of Community Psychology, 27,* 659–679.

Bronfenbrenner, U. (1989). Ecological systems theory. *Annals of Child Development, 6,* 187–249.

Bronfenbrenner, U. (1999). Environments in developmental perspective: Theoretical and operational models. In S. Friedman & T. Wachs (Eds.), *Measuring environment across the life span* (pp. 3–28). Washington, DC: American Psychological Association.

Brown, G. (2009). NICU noise and the preterm infant. *Neonatal Network, 28*(3), 165–173.

Brown, G., Lawrence, T., & Robinson, S. (2005). Territoriality in organizations. *Academy of Management Review, 30*(3), 577–594.

Brown, K. A., Jemmott, F. F., Mitchell, H. J., & Walton, M. L. (1998). The Well: A neighborhood-based health promotion model for Black women. *Health and Social Work, 23*(2), 146–152.

Brown, L., Shepherd, M., Wituk, S. & Meissen, G. (2007). How settings change people: Applying behavior setting theory to consumer-run organizations. *Journal of Community Psychology, 35*(3), 399–416.

Bucko, R. A., & Iron Cloud, S. (2008). Lakota health and healing. *Southern Medical Journal, 101*(6), 596–598.

Budman, S. H., Soldz, S., Demby, A., Davis, M., & Merry, J. (1993). What is cohesiveness? An empirical examination. *Small Group Research, 24,* 199–216.

Bullis, R. K. (1996). *Spirituality in social work practice.* Washington, DC: Taylor & Francis.

Burke, M. T., Chauvin, J. C., & Miranti, J. G. (2005). *Religious and spiritual issues in counseling: Applications across diverse populations.* New York: Brunner/ Routledge.

Burrell, G., & Morgan, G. (1979). *Sociological paradigms and organizational analysis.* London: Heinemann.

Burston, D., & Frie, R. (2006). *Psychotherapy as a human science.* Pittsburgh, PA: Duquesne University Press.

Burt, M., & Katz, B. (1987). Dimensions of recovery from rape: Focus on growth outcomes. *Journal of Interpersonal Violence, 2,* 57–82.

Burtless, G. (2001). *Has widening inequality promoted or retarded U.S. growth?* Retrieved April 20, 2010, from http://www.brookings .edu/articles/2003/0901useconomics_burtless.aspx.

Burton, L. (1981). *A critical analysis and review of the research on Outward Bound and related programs.* Unpublished doctoral dissertation, Rutgers University, New Brunswick, NJ.

Bush, K., Bohon, S., & Kim, H. (2010). Adaptation among immigrant families: Resources and barriers. In S. Price, C. Price, & P. McKenry (Eds.), *Families & change: Coping with stressful events and transitions* (4th ed., pp. 285–310). Thousand Oaks, CA: Sage.

Bussolari, C., & Goodell, J. (2009). Chaos theory as a model of life transitions counseling: Nonlinear dynamics and life's changes. *Journal of Counseling & Development, 87,* 98–107.

Buzzell, L. (Ed.). (2009). *Ecotherapy: Healing with nature in mind.* San Francisco: Sierra Club Books.

Byoung-Suk, K., Ulrich, R., Walker, V., & Tassinary, L. (2008). Anger and stress: The role of landscape posters in an office setting. *Environment & Behavior, 40*(3), 355–381.

Cacioppo, J. T., Amaral, D. G., Blancard, J. J., Cameron, J. L., Carter, C. S., Crews, D., et al. (2007). Social neuroscience: Progress and promise. *Perspectives on Psychological Science, 2,* 99–123.

Cacioppo, J. T., Bernston, G. G., Sheridan, J. F., & McClintock, M. K. (2000). Multilevel integrative analysis of human behavior: Social neuroscience and the complementary nature of social and biological approaches. *Psychological Bulletin, 126*(6), 829–843.

Cady, S. H., & Valentine, J. (1999). Team innovation and perceptions of consideration: What difference does diversity make? *Small Group Research, 30*(6), 730–750.

Cairns, D. B. (2005). The journey to resiliency: An integrative framework for treatment for victims and survivors of family violence. *Social Work & Christianity, 32*(4), 305–320.

Calasanti, T. (1996). Incorporating diversity: Meaning, levels of research, and implications for theory. *The Gerontologist, 36*(2), 147–156.

Cameron, J. (1992). *The artist's way: A spiritual path to higher creativity.* New York: Putnam.

Campbell, C., & Jovchelovitch, S. (2000). Health, community and development: Towards a social psychology of participation. *Journal of Community & Applied Social Psychology, 10,* 255–270.

Campbell, D. (1997). *The Mozart effect: Tapping the power of music to heal the body, strengthen the mind, and unlock the creative spirit.* New York: Harper Trade.

Canda, E. R. (1983). General implications of shamanism for clinical social work. *International Social Work, 26*(4), 14–22.

Canda, E. R. (1988). Conceptualizing spirituality for social work: Insights from diverse perspectives. *Social Thought, 14*(1), 30–46.

Canda, E. R. (1997). Spirituality. *Encyclopedia of social work: 1997 supplement* (19th ed.). Washington, DC: NASW Press.

Canda, E. R. (2001). Buddhism. In M. V. Hook, B. Hugen, & M. Aguilar (Eds.), *Spirituality within religious traditions in social work practice* (pp. 53–72). Pacific Grove, CA: Brooks/Cole.

Canda, E. R. (2005). The future of spirituality in social work: The farther reaches of human nature. *Advances in Social Work, 6*(1), 97–108.

Canda, E. R., & Furman, L. D. (1999). *Spiritual diversity in social work practice: The heart of helping.* New York: Free Press.

Canda, E. R., & Furman, L.D. (2010). *Spiritual diversity in social work practice: The heart of helping* (2nd ed.). New York: Oxford University Press.

Canda, E. R., Nakashima, M., & Furman, L. D. (2004). Ethical considerations about spirituality in social work: Insights from a national qualitative study. *Families in Society: The Journal of Contemporary Social Services, 85*(1), 27–35.

Canda, E. R., & Phaobtong, T. (1992). Buddhism as a support system for Southeast Asian refugees. *Social Work, 37,* 61–67.

Canda, E. R., Shin, S., & Canda, H. (1993). Traditional philosophies of human services in Korea and contemporary social work implications. *Social Development Issues, 15*(3), 84–104.

Canda, E. R., & Yellow Bird, M. J. (1996). Cross-tradition borrowing of spiritual practices in social work settings. *Society for Spirituality and Social Work Newsletter, 3*(1), 1–7.

Cannon, W. B. (1924). *Bodily changes in pain, hunger, fear, and rage.* New York: Appleton.

Caplan, G. (1990). Loss, stress, and mental health. *Community Mental Health Journal, 26,* 27–48.

Caplan, G., & Caplan, R. B. (2000). The future of primary prevention. *Journal of Primary Prevention, 21*(2),131–136.

Carey, J. (Ed.). (1990). *Brain facts: A primer on the brain and nervous system.* Washington, DC: Society for Neuroscience.

Carley, G. (2005). An influence of spiritual narrative in community work. *Canadian Social Work, 7*(1), 81–94.

Carlton-LaNey, I. (1999). African American social work pioneers' response to need. *Social Work, 44*(4), 311–321.

Carnes, R., & Craig, S. (1998). *Sacred circles: A guide to creating your own women's spirituality group.* San Francisco: HarperSan Francisco.

Carolan, M. T., Bagherinia, G., Juhari, R., Himelright, J., & Mouton-Sanders, M. (2000). Contemporary Muslim families: Research and practice. *Contemporary Family Therapy, 22*(1), 67–79.

Carpenter, M. B. (1991). *Core text of neuroanatomy* (4th ed.). Baltimore: Williams & Wilkins.

Carroll, M. (1998). Social work's conceptualization of spirituality. *Social Thought, 18*(2), 1–14.

Carron, A. V., & Brawley, L. R. (2000). Cohesion: Conceptual and measurement issues. *Small Group Research, 31*(1), 89–106.

Carter, B., & McGoldrick, M. (2005a). Coaching at various stages of the life cycle. In B. Carter & M. McGoldrick (Eds.), *The expanded family life cycle: Individual, family, and social perspectives* (3rd ed., pp. 436–454). New York: Pearson.

Carter, B., & McGoldrick, M. (2005b). *The expanded family life cycle: Individual, family, and social perspectives* (3rd ed.). New York: Pearson.

Carter, R. (2009). *The human brain book.* London: DK.

Castex, G. M. (1994). Providing services to Hispanic/Latino populations: Profiles in diversity. *Social Work, 39*(3), 288–296.

Catalano, S. (2007). *Intimate partner violence in the United States. Bureau of Justice Statistics.* Retrieved, December 15, 2009, from http://www.ojp.usdoj.gov/bjs/intimate/ipv.htm.

Cattich, J., & Knudson-Martin, C. (2009). Spirituality and relationship: A holistic analysis of how couples cope with diabetes. *Journal of Marital & Family Therapy, 35*(1), 111–124.

Center for Health Design. (2006). *Transforming healthcare buildings into healing environments.* Retrieved August 31, 2006, from http://www.healthdesign.org.

Centers for Disease Control and Prevention. (2005a). *HIV/AIDS among African Americans.* Retrieved May 18, 2010, from http://www.cdc.gov/hiv/topics/aa/resources/factsheets.aa.htm.

Centers for Disease Control and Prevention. (2005b). *Preventing heart disease and stroke.* Retrieved October 20, 2006, from http://www.cdc.gov/nccdphp/publishers/factsheets/Prevention/cvh.htm.

Centers for Disease Control and Prevention. (2006a). *Facts about traumatic brain injury.* Retrieved October 24, 2009, from http://www.biausa.org/aboutbi.htm.

Centers for Disease Control and Prevention. (2006b). State-specific prevalence of obesity among adults: United States. *Morbidity and Mortality Weekly Report, 55*(36), 985–988.

Centers for Disease Control and Prevention. (2007). *Youth Risk Behavior Surveillance System (YRBSS). 2007 national, state, and local data.* Retrieved January 1, 2010, from http://www.cdc.gov/HealthyYouth/yrbs/index.htm.

Centers for Disease Control and Prevention. (2009a). *Basic Statistics. HIV/AIDS surveillance report: Cases of HIV infection in the United States and Dependent Areas, 2007.* Retrieved December 4, 2009, from http://www.cdc.gov/hiv/topics/surveillance/basic.htm#hivaidscases.

Centers for Disease Control and Prevention. (2009b). *Life expectancy.* Retrieved February 23, 2010, from http://www.cdc.gov/nchs/fastats/lifexpect.htm.

Centers for Disease Control and Prevention. (2009c). *Preventing teen pregnancy: An update in 2009.* Retrieved January 17, 2010, from http://www.cdc.gov/reproductivehealth/adolescentreprohealth/AboutTP.htm.

Centers for Disease Control and Prevention. (2009d). *Trends in reportable sexually transmitted diseases in the United States, 2007.* Retrieved May 18, 2010, from http://www.cdc.gov/std/stats07/trends.htm.

Cervigni, F., Suzuki, Y., Ishii, T., & Hata, A. (2008). Spatial accessibility to pediatric services. *Journal of Community Health, 33,* 444–448.

Chachamovich, J., Chachamovich, E., Fleck, M., Cordova, F., Knauth, D., & Passos, E. (2009). Congruence of quality of life among infertile men and women: Findings from a couple-based study. *Human Reproduction, 24*(9), 2151–2157.

Chahine, Z., van Straaten, J., & Williams, I. (2005). The New York City neighborhood–based services strategy. *Child Welfare, 84*(2), 141–152.

Challenger, Gray, & Christmas, Inc. (2006). *May 2006 Challenger employment report.* Retrieved November 12, 2006, from http://chicagobusiness.com/cgi-bin/article.pl?portal_id=131@page_id=2000.

Chan, Y., Lam, G., & Cheng, H. (2009). Community capacity building as a strategy of family violence prevention in a problem-stricken community: A theoretical formulation. *Journal of Family Violence, 24,* 559–568.

Charon, J. (1998). *Symbolic interactionism: An introduction, an interpretation, and integration* (6th ed.). Englewood Cliffs, NJ: Prentice Hall.

Chau, K. (1990). Social work with groups in multicultural contexts. *Group Work, 7*(3), 8–21.

Chen, J., Rehkopf, D., Waterman, P., Subramanian, S., Coull, B., Cohen, B., et al. (2006). Mapping and measuring social disparities in premature mortality: The impact of census tract poverty within and across Boston. *Journal of Urban Health, 83*(6), 1063–1084.

Chen, M., Harris, D., Folkoff, M., Drudge, R., & Jackson, C. (1999). Developing a collaborative GIS in social services. *Geo Info Systems, 9,* 44–47.

Chesney, B. K., & Chesler, M. A. (1993). Activism through self-help group membership: Reported life changes of parents of children with cancer. *Small Group Research, 24,* 258–273.

Chibucos, T., & Leite, R. (2005). *Readings in family theory.* Thousand Oaks, CA: Sage.

Child Trends Data Bank. (2010). *Education attainment (youth).* Retrieved February 22, 2010, from http://www.childtrends databank.org/?q=node/182.

Childress, H. (2004). Teenagers, territory and the appropriation of space. *Childhood: A Global Journal of Child Research, 11,* 195–205.

China Education and Research Network. (2000). *Basic education in China (IV).* Retrieved November 6, 2006, from http://www.edu.cn/20010101/21778.shtml.

Choi, G., & Tirrito, T. (1999). The Korean church as a social service provider for older adults. *Arete, 23*(2), 69–83.

Christ, C. P. (1995). *Odyssey with the goddess: A spiritual quest in Crete.* New York: Continuum.

Chung, D. K. (2001). Confucianism. In M. V. Hook, B. Hugen, & M. Aguilar (Eds.), *Spirituality within religious traditions in social work practice* (pp. 73–97). Pacific Grove, CA: Brooks/Cole.

Chung, G., Tucker, M., & Takeuchi, D. (2008). Wives' relative income production and household male dominance: Examining violence among Asian American enduring couples. *Family Relations, 57,* 227–238.

Chung, I. W. (2006). A cultural perspective on emotions and behavior: An empathic pathway to examine intergenerational conflicts in Chinese immigrant families. *Families in Society, 87*(3), 367–376.

Cingolani, J. (1984). Social conflict perspective on work with involuntary clients. *Social Work, 29,* 442–446.

Clammer, J. (2009). Sociology and beyond: Towards a deep sociology. *Asian Journal of Social Science, 37*(3), 332–346.

Clark, C. C. (2002). *Health promotion in communities: Holistic and wellness approaches.* New York: Springer.

Clark, J. L. (2007). Listening for meaning: A research-based model for attending to spirituality culture, and worldview in social work practice. *Critical Social Work, 7*(1). Retrieved February 26, 2010, from http://www.uwindsor.ca/criticalsocialwork/2006-volume-7-no-1.

Clayton, S., & Opotow, S. (2003). *Identity and the natural environment: The psychological significance of nature.* Cambridge: MIT Press.

Clean Clothes Campaign. (2009, October 5). *Asia wage demand put to Euro retailers.* Retrieved October 23, 2009, from http://www.cleanclothes.org/media-inquiries/press-releases/asia-wage-demand-put-to-euro-retailers.

Clearinghouse on International Developments in Child, Youth and Family Policies at Columbia University. (2004). *Maternity and parental leaves, 1999–2002.* Retrieved April 25, 2010, from http://www.childpolicyintl.org.

Clemens, E. (1996). Organizational form as frame: Collective identity and political strategy in the American labor movement, 1880–1920. In D. McAdam, J. McCarthy, & M. Zald (Eds.), *Comparative perspectives on social movements* (pp. 205–226). New York: Cambridge University Press.

Cleveland Clinic. (2005–2009). *Your pulse and your target heart rate.* Retrieved December 20, 2009, from http://www.cchs .net/health/health-info/docs/0900/0984.asp?index=5508.

Clever, L. (2002). Who is sicker: Patients or residents? *Annals of Internal Medicine, 136*(5), 391–393.

Coates, J. (2003). *Ecology and social work: Toward a new paradigm.* Halifax, NS: Fernwood.

Coates, J. (2007). From ecology to spirituality and social justice. In J. Coates, J. R. Graham, B. Swartzentruber, & B. Ouelette (Eds.), *Spirituality and social work: Selected Canadian readings* (pp. 213–227). Toronto, Ont.: Canadian Scholars' Press.

Cohen, S., Gottlieb, B. H., & Underwood, L. G. (2001). Social relationships and health: Challenges for measurement and intervention. *Advances in Mind–Body Medicine, 17*(2), 129–141.

Cohn, T. (1997). Art as a healing force: Creativity, healing, and spirituality. *Artweek, 28,* 15–17.

Coker, A., Sanderson, M., Ellison, G., & Fadden, M. (2006). Stress, coping, social support, and prostate cancer risk among older African American and Caucasian men. *Ethnicity & Disease, 16*(4), 978–987.

Cole, S. (1992). *Making science: Between nature and society.* Cambridge, MA: Harvard University Press.

Coleman, J. (1990). *Foundations of social theory.* Cambridge, MA: Belknap Press.

Coleman, M., Ganong, I., & Warzinik, K. (2007). *Family life in the 20th century America.* Westport, CT: Greenwood.

Coles, R. (1990). *The spiritual life of children.* Boston: Houghton Mifflin.

Collins, G. (2009). *When everything changed: The amazing journey of American women from 1960 to the present.* New York: Little, Brown.

Collins, P. H. (1990). *Black feminist thought: Knowledge, consciousness, and empowerment.* Boston: Unwin Hyman.

Collins, P. H. (2000). It's all in the family: Intersections of gender, race, and nation. In U. Narayan & S. Harding (Eds.), *Decentering the center: Philosophy for a multicultural post-colonial, and feminist world* (pp. 156–176). Bloomington: Indiana University Press.

Collins, R. (1981). On the micro-foundations of macro-sociology. *American Journal of Sociology, 86,* 984–1014.

Collins, R. (1988). *Theoretical sociology.* San Diego, CA: Harcourt Brace Jovanovich.

Collins, R. (1990). Conflict theory and the advance of macro-historical sociology. In G. Ritzer (Ed.), *Frontiers of social theory: The new syntheses* (pp. 68–87). New York: Columbia University Press.

Collins, R. (1994). *Four sociological traditions.* New York: Oxford University Press.

Colonial Williamsburg. (n.d.). *The Native-American family.* Retrieved December 3, 2009, from http://www.history.org/almanack/life/family/first.cfm.

Conger, R., & Conger, K. (2008). Understanding the processes through which economic hardship influences families and children. In D. R Crane & T. Heaton (Eds.), *Handbook of families & poverty* (pp. 64–81). Thousand Oaks, CA: Sage.

Conger, R., & Elder, G. (1994). *Linking economic hardship to marital quality and instability. Families in troubled times: Adapting to change in rural America.* New York: Aldine De Gruyter.

Conger, R., Wallace, L., Sun, Y., Simons, R., McLoyed, V., & Brody, G. (2002). Economic pressure in African American families: A replication and extension of the family stress model. *Developmental Psychology, 38,* 179–193.

Connolly, M. (2006). Fifteen years of Family Group Conferencing: Coordinators talk about their experiences in Aotearoa New Zealand. *British Journal of Social Work, 36*(4), 523–540.

Conrad, D., & Kellar-Guenther, Y. (2006). Compassion fatigue, burnout, and compassion satisfaction among Colorado child protection workers. *Child Abuse & Neglect, 30,* 1071–1080.

Conrad, P. (2007). *The medicalization of society: On the transformation of human conditions into treatable disorders.* Baltimore, MD: Johns Hopkins University Press.

Cook, K. (Ed.). (1987). *Social exchange theory.* Newbury Park, CA: Sage.

Cook, K., O'Brien, J., & Kollock, P. (1990). Exchange theory: A blueprint for structure and process. In G. Ritzer (Ed.), *Frontiers of social theory: The new syntheses* (pp. 158–181). New York: Columbia University Press.

Cooley, C. (1964). *Human nature and the social order.* New York: Scribner's. (Original work published 1902)

Coombs, D., & Capper, S. (1996). Public health and mortality: Public health in the 1980s. In D. Peck & J. Hollingsworth (Eds.), *Demographic and structural change: The effects of the 1980s on American society* (pp. 101–126). Westport, CT: Greenwood.

Corbett, J. M. (1997). *Religion in America* (3rd ed.). Upper Saddle River, NJ: Prentice Hall.

Corcoran, J., & Walsh, J. (2006). *Clinical assessment and diagnosis in social work practice.* New York: Oxford University Press.

Corey, M. S., & Corey, G. (2006). *Groups: Process and practice* (7th ed.). Belmont, CA: Thomson Brooks/Cole.

Cornwall, M. (1989). Faith development of men and women over the life span. In S. Bahr & E. Peterson (Eds.), *Aging and the family* (pp. 115–139). Lexington, MA: Lexington Books/DC Heath.

Cortright, B. (1997). *Psychotherapy and spirit: Theory and practice in transpersonal psychotherapy.* Albany: SUNY Press.

Coser, L. (1956). *The functions of conflict.* New York: Free Press.

Coser, L. (1975). Presidential address: Two methods in search of a substance. *American Sociological Review, 40,* 691–700.

Costas, O. E. (1991). Hispanic theology in North America. In L. M. Getz & R. O. Costa (Eds.), *Strategies for solidarity: Liberation theologies in tension* (pp. 63–74). Minneapolis, MN: Fortress Press.

Council for a Parliament of the World's Religions. (2010). *About us: Our mission.* Retrieved February 20, 2010, from http://www.parliamentofreligions.org/index.cfm?n=1.

Council on Social Work Education. (2008). *Educational policy and accreditation standards.* Alexandria, VA: Author.

Cousins, L. (1994). *Community High: The complexity of race and class in a Black urban high school.* Unpublished doctoral dissertation, University of Michigan, Ann Arbor.

Cousins, L. (2008). Black students' identity and acting White and Black. In J. U. Ogbu (Ed.), *Minority status, oppositional culture and schooling* (pp. 167–189). New York: Routledge.

Cousins, L., & Mabrey, T. (1998). Re-gendering social work practice and education: The case for African American girls. *Journal of Human Behavior in the Social Environment, 1*(2/3), 91–104.

Cousins, L., & Mabrey, T. (2007). Revisiting the regendering of social work practice with African American girls. In L. A. See (Ed.), *Human behavior in the social environment from an African American perspective* (2nd ed., pp. 235-252). New York: Haworth.

Cowley, A. S. (1993). Transpersonal social work: A theory for the 1990s. *Social Work, 38,* 527–534.

Cowley, A. S. (1996). Transpersonal social work. In F. J. Turner (Ed.), *Social work treatment: Interlocking theoretical approaches* (4th ed., pp. 663–698). New York: Free Press.

Cowley, A. S. (1999). Transpersonal theory and social work practice with couples and families. *Journal of Family Social Work, 3*(20), 5–21.

Cowley, A. S., & Derezotes, D. (1994). Transpersonal psychology and social work education. *Journal of Social Work Education, 30,* 32–39.

Cox, G. R. (2000). Children, spirituality, and loss. *Illness, Crisis & Loss, 8*(1), 60–70.

Cox, K. (2000). Parenting the second time around for parents in recovery: Parenting class using the twelve-step recovery model. *Sources, 10,* 11–14.

Cox, T., Jr. (1993). *Cultural diversity in organizations: Theory, research, and practice.* San Francisco: Berrett-Koehler.

Cox, T., Jr. (2001). *Creating a multicultural organization: A strategy for capturing the power of diversity.* San Francisco: Jossey-Bass.

Coyhis, D., & Simonelli, R. (2005). Rebuilding Native American communities. *Child Welfare, 84*(2), 323–336.

Coyle, J., Nochajski, T., Maguin, E., Safyer, A., DeWit, D., & Macdonald, S. (2009). An exploratory study of the nature of family resilience in families affected by parental alcohol abuse. *Journal of Family Issues, 30*(12), 1606–1623.

Crabtree, S. A., Husain, F., & Spalek, B. (2008). *Islam and social work: Debating values, transforming practice.* Bristol, UK: Policy Press.

Cressey, T., & Lallemant, M. (2007). Pharmacogenetics of antiretroviral drugs for the treatment of HIV-infected patients: An update. *Infection, Genetics and Evolution, 7*(2), 333–342.

Crocetti, E., Rubini, M., & Meeus, W. (2008). Capturing the dynamics of identity formation in various ethnic groups: Development and validation of a three-dimensional model. *Journal of Adolescence, 31*(2), 207–222.

Crompton, R. (2006). *Employment and the family: The reconfiguration of work and family life in contemporary societies.* Cambridge, UK: Cambridge University Press.

Crook, W. (2001). Trickle-down bureaucracy: Does the organization affect client responses to programs? *Administration in Social Work, 26*(1), 37–59.

Cross, W., Parham, T., & Black, E. (1991). The stages of Black identity development: Nigrescence models. In R. Jones, *Black psychology* (3rd ed., pp. 319–338). Berkeley, CA: Cobb & Henry.

Croteau, D., & Hoynes, W. (2006). *The business of media: Corporate media and the public interest* (2nd ed.). Thousand Oaks, CA: Pine Forge.

Cuba, L., & Hummon, D. (1993). A place to call home: Identification with dwelling, community, and region. *Sociological Quarterly, 34*(1), 111–131.

Culhane, D., Lee, C., & Wachter, S. (1997). Where the homeless come from: A study of the prior address distribution of families admitted to public shelters in New York City and Philadelphia. In D. Culhane & S. Hornburg (Eds.), *Understanding homelessness: New policy and research perspectives* (pp. 225–263). Washington, DC: Fannie Mae Foundation.

Cumes, D. (1998). Nature as medicine: The healing power of the wilderness. *Alternative Therapies, 4,* 79–86.

Curtis, S. (2004). *Health and inequality: Geographical perspectives.* London: Sage.

Czarniawska, B. (2007). Has organization theory a tomorrow? *Organization Studies, 28,* 27–29.

Dainton, M., & Zelley, E. (2006). Social exchange theories: Interdependence and equity. In D. Braithwaite & L. Baxter (Eds.), *Engaging theories in family communication: Multiple perspectives* (pp. 243–259). Thousand Oaks, CA: Sage.

Daley, J., & Marsiglia, F. (2000). Community participation: Old wine in new bottles? *Journal of Community Practice, 8*(1), 61–86.

D'Andrade, R. G. (1995). Cultural meaning systems. In R. Shweder & R. LeVine (Eds.), *Culture theory: Essays on mind, self, and emotion* (pp. 88–122). New York: Cambridge University Press. (Original work published 1984)

Danto, E. (2008). Same words: Different meanings: Notes toward a typology of postmodern social work education. *Social Work Education, 27*(7), 710–722.

Das, A., & Harries, B. (1996). Validating Fowler's theory of faith development with college students. *Psychological Reports, 78,* 675–679.

David, T., & Weinstein, C. (1987). The built environment and children's development. In C. Weinstein & T. David (Eds.), *Spaces for children: The built environment and child development* (pp. 3–18). New York: Plenum.

Davidoff, A., & Kenney, G. (2005). *Uninsured Americans with chronic health conditions: Key findings from the National Health Interview Survey.* Retrieved April 25, 2010, from http://www.urban.org/UploadedPDF/ 411161_uninsured_americans.pdf.

Davidson, R. J., Kabat-Zinn, J., Schumacher, J., Rosenkranz, M., Muller, D., Santorelli, S. F., et al. (2003). Alterations in brain and immune function produced by mindfulness meditation. *Psychosomatic Medicine, 65*(4), 564–570.

Davies, S. (2006). *Challenging gender norms: Five genders among the Bugis in Indonesia.* Belmont, CA: Wadsworth.

Davis, G., McAdam, D., Scott, W. R., & Zald, M. (2005). *Social movements and organization theory.* New York: Cambridge University Press.

Davis, L. E. (1984). Essential components of group work with Black Americans. *Social Work With Groups, 7*(3), 97–109.

Davis, L. E. (1995). The crisis of diversity. In M. D. Feit, J. H. Famey, J. S. Wodarski, & A. R. Mann (Eds.), *Capturing the power of diversity* (pp. 47–57). New York: Haworth.

Davis, M. (2000). *Magical urbanism: Latinos reinvent the U.S. city.* New York: Verso.

Davis, S., Greenstein, T., & Marks, J. (2007). Effects of union type on division of household labor: Do cohabiting men really perform more housework? *Journal of Family Issues, 28*(9), 1246–1272.

Day, P., & Schuler, D. (2004). *Community practice in the network society: Local action/global interaction.* New York: Routledge.

Dean, R. G. (2001). The myth of cross-cultural competence. *Families in Society, 82*(6), 623–630.

Deater-Deckard, K. (2004). *Parenting stress.* New Haven, CT: Yale University Press.

DeFilippis, J., Fisher, R., & Shragge, E. (2009). What's left in the community? Oppositional politics in contemporary practice. *Community Development Journal, 44*(1), 38–52.

Delgado, M. (1988). Groups in Puerto Rican spiritism: Implications for clinicians. In C. Jacobs & D. D. Bowles (Eds.), *Ethnicity and race: Critical concepts in social work* (pp. 34–37). Silver Spring, MD: NASW Press.

Delgado, M. (2000). *New arenas for community social work practice with urban youth: Use of arts, humanities, and sports.* New York: Columbia University Press.

Delgado, M., & Humm-Delgado, D. (1982). Natural support systems: Sources of strength in Hispanic communities. *Social Work, 27,* 83–89.

della Porta, D. (1996). Social movements and the state: Thoughts on the policing of protest. In D. McAdam, J. McCarthy, & M. Zald (Eds.), *Comparative perspectives on social movements* (pp. 62–92). New York: Cambridge University Press.

della Porta, D., & Diani, M. (2006). *Social movements: An introduction* (2nd ed.). Malden, MA: Blackwell.

della Porta, D., & Mosca, L. (2009). Searching the net: Democratic styles of global justice movements' websites. *Information, Communication & Society, 12*(6), 771–792.

Deloria, V., Jr. (1994). *God is red: A native view of religion.* Golden, CO: Fulcrum Publishing.

Demo, D., & Fine, M. (2010). *Beyond the average divorce.* Thousand Oaks, CA: Sage.

DeNavas-Walt, C., Proctor, B., & Hill Lee, C. (2006). *Income, poverty, and health insurance coverage in the United States: 2005.* Washington, DC: U.S. Census Bureau.

DeNavas-Walt, C., Proctor, B., & Smith, J. (2009). *Income, poverty, and health insurance coverage in the United States: 2008.* Washington, DC: U.S. Census Bureau.

Denzin, N. K. (2001). *Interpretive interactionism.* Thousand Oaks, CA: Sage.

DePoy, E., & Gilson, S. F. (2004). *Rethinking disability: Principles for professional and social change.* Belmont, CA: Wadsworth.

DePoy, E., & Gilson, S. F. (2007). *The human experience: Description, explanation, and judgment.* New York: Rowman & Littlefield.

DePoy, E., & Gilson, S. (2008). Healing the disjuncture: Social work disability practice. In K. Sowers & C. Dulmus (Series Eds.) & B. White (Vol. Ed.), *Comprehensive handbook of social work and social welfare: The profession of social work* (Vol. 1, pp. 267–282). Hoboken, NJ: Wiley.

DePoy, E., & Gilson, S. F. (2010). *Studying disability: Multiple theories and responses.* Thousand Oaks, CA: Sage.

DePree, M. (1997). *Leading without power.* San Francisco: Jossey-Bass.

Derezotes, D. S. (2001). Transpersonal social work with couples: A compatibility-intimacy model. In E. R. Canda & E. D. Smith (Eds.), *Transpersonal perspectives on spirituality in social work* (pp. 163–174).Binghamton, NY: Haworth Press.

Derezotes, D. S. (2006). *Spiritually oriented social work practice.* Boston: Pearson Education.

Devereux. E. (2008). *Understanding the media* (2nd ed.). Thousand Oaks, CA: Sage.

Devine-Wright, P. (2009). Rethinking NIMYism: The role of place attachment and place identity in explaining place-protective action. *Journal of Community & Applied Social Psychology, 19*(6), 426–441.

Devlin, A. (1992). Psychiatric ward renovation: Staff perception and patient behavior. *Environment and Behavior, 24,* 66–84.

Devore, W., & Schlesinger, E. (1999). *Ethnic-sensitive social work practice* (5th ed.). Boston: Allyn & Bacon.

Diamond, J. (1999). *Guns, germs, and steel: The fates of human societies.* New York: Norton.

Dixon, J., Dogan, R., & Sanderson, A. (2005). Community and communitarianism: A philosophical investigation. *Community Development Journal, 40*(1), 4–16.

Dosser, D. A., Smith, A. L., Markowski, E. W., & Cain, H. I. (2001). Including families' spiritual beliefs and their faith communities in systems of care. *Journal of Family Social Work, 5*(3), 63–78.

Downes, D. M., & Rock, P. (2003). *Understanding deviance: A guide to the sociology of crime and rule-breaking.* New York: Oxford University Press.

Drescher, K. D, Burgoyne, M., Casas, E., Lovato, L., Curran, E., Pivar, I., et al. (2009). Issues of grief, loss, honor, and remembrance: Spirituality and work with military personnel and their families. In S. M. Freeman, B. A. Moore, & A. Freeman (Eds.), *Living and surviving in harm's way: A psychological treatment handbook for pre- and post-deployment of military personnel* (pp. 437–466). New York: Routledge.

Drosdzol, A., & Skrzypulec, V. (2008). Quality of life and sexual function of Polish infertile couples. *European Journal of Contraceptive and Reproductive Health Care, 13,* 271–281.

Duba, J. D., & Watts, R. E. (2009). Therapy with religious couples. *Journal of Clinical Psychology, 65*(2), 210–223.

Dufrene, P. M., & Coleman, V. S. (1992). Counseling Native Americans: Guidelines for group process. *Journal of Specialists in Group Work, 17*(4), 229–234.

Duluth Domestic Abuse Intervention Project. (n.d.). *In our best interest.* (Support group manual available from the Duluth Domestic Abuse Intervention Project, 206 W. Fourth Street, Duluth, MN 55806.)

Dunlop, J., & Angell, G. B. (2001). Inside-outside: Boundary-spanning challenges in building rural health coalitions. *Professional Development, 4*(1), 40–48.

Duran, E., & Duran, B. (1995). *Native American postcolonial psychology.* Albany: State University of New York Press.

Duvall-Early, K., & Benedict, J. (1992). The relationship between privacy and different components of job satisfaction. *Environment and Behavior, 24,* 670–679.

Dybicz, P. (2004). An inquiry into practice wisdom. *Families in Society, 85*(2), 197–203.

Eagle, M., & Wolitzky, D. L. (2009). Adult psychotherapy from the perspectives of attachment theory and psychoanalysis. In J. H. Obegi & E. Berant (Eds.), *Attachment theory and research in clinical work with adults* (pp. 351–378). New York: Guilford Press.

Earle, A. M. (1987). *An outline of neuroanatomy.* Omaha: University of Nebraska Medical Center.

Edin, K., Kefalas, M., & Reed, J. (2004). A peak inside the black box: What marriage means for poor unmarried parents. *Journal of Marriage and the Family, 66,* 1007–1014.

Edin, K., & Reed, J. (2005). Why don't they just get married? Barriers to marriage among the disadvantaged. *The Future of Children, 15*(5), 117–137.

Education Trust. (2006a). *Missing the mark: An Education Trust analysis of teacher-equity plans.* Retrieved April 28, 2010, from http://www.edtrust.org/print/525.

Education Trust. (2006b, September 1). *Yes we can: Telling truths and dispelling myths about race and education in America.* Retrieved April 28, 2010, from http://www.edtrust.org/print/159.

Eheart, B., Hopping, D., Power, M., Mitchell, E., & Racine, D. (2009). Generations of Hope Communities: An intergenerational neighborhood model of support and service. *Children and Youth Services Review, 31,* 47–52.

Eitzen, D. S., & Zinn, B. C. (Eds.). (2006). *Globalization: The transformation of social worlds.* Belmont, CA: Wadsworth.

Ekeh, P. (1974). *Social exchange theory: The two traditions.* Cambridge, MA: Harvard University Press.

Elder, G. H., Jr. (1974). *Children of the Great Depression: Social change in life experience.* Chicago: University of Chicago Press.

Elder, G. H., Jr. (1998). The life course as developmental theory. *Child Development, 69*(1), 1–12.

Elder, G. H., Jr., & Giele, J. (Eds.). (2009). *The craft of life course research.* New York: Guilford Press.

Ellis, A. (1989). Is rational emotive therapy (RET) "rationalist or constructivist"? In W. Dryden (Ed.), *The essential Albert Ellis* (pp. 199–233). New York: Springer.

Ellison, C. G., & Levin, J. S. (1998). The religion–health connection: Evidence, theory, and future directions. *Health, Education, and Behavior, 25*(6), 700–720.

Ellison, J. W., & Plaskow, J. (Eds.). (2007). *Heterosexism in contemporary world religion: Problem and prospect.* Cleveland, OH: Pilgrim Press.

Ellison, N., Steinfield, C., & Lampe, C. (2007). The benefits of Facebook "friends": Social capital and college students' use of online social network sites. *Journal of Computer-Mediated Communication, 12,* 1143–1168.

Ellsworth, P. C. (1991). Some implications of cognitive appraisal theories of emotion. In K. T. Strongman (Ed.), *International review of studies on emotion* (pp. 143-161). New York: Wiley.

El-Messidi, A., Al-Fozan, H., Lin Tan, S., Farag, R., & Tulandi, T. (2004). Effects of repeated treatment failure on the quality of life of couples with infertility. *Journal of Obstetrics and Gynaecology Canada, 26,* 333–336.

Elwan, A. (1999). *Poverty and disability: A survey of the literature.* Retrieved April 28, 2010, from http://asksource.ids.ac.uk/cf/display/bibliodisplay.cfm?ID=26550&topic=dis&Search=QL%5FDISPOV05&display=full.

Emerson, R. (1972a). Exchange theory: Part I. A psychological basis for social exchange. In J. Berger, M. Zelditch Jr., & B. Anderson (Eds.), *Sociological theories in progress* (Vol. 2, pp. 38–57). Boston: Houghton Mifflin.

Emerson, R. (1972b). Exchange theory: Part II. Exchange relations and networks. In J. Berger, M. Zelditch Jr., & B. Anderson (Eds.), *Sociological theories in progress* (Vol. 2, pp. 58–87). Boston: Houghton Mifflin.

Emery, R. (1999). *Marriage, divorce, and children's adjustment* (2nd ed.). Thousand Oaks, CA: Sage.

Emirbayer, M., & Goodwin, J. (1994). Network analysis, culture, and the problem of agency. *American Journal of Sociology, 99,* 1411–1454.

Engel, G. (1977). The need for a new medical model: A challenge for biomedicine. *Science, 196,* 129–136.

Engels, F. (1970). *The origins of the family, private property and the state.* New York: International. (Original work published 1884)

Engels, F. (1892). *The condition of the working class in England in 1844* (F. K. Wischnewtzky, Trans.). London: Sonnenschein.

Engle, J., & Theokas, C. (2010). *Top gainers: Some public four-year colleges and universities make big improvements in minority graduation rates.* Retrieved February 21, 2010, from http://www.edtrust.org/dc/publication/college-results-online-brief-top-gainers.

Epel, E., Wilhelm, F., Wolkowitz, O., Cawthorn, R., Adler, N., Dolbier, C., et al. (2006). Cell aging in relation to stress arousal and cardiovascular disease risk factors. *Psychoneuroendocrinology, 31*(3), 277–287.

Equal Rights Center. (2009). *Civil rights lawsuit filed against the city of Manassas, VA and its school system for discriminating against Hispanic residents.* Retrieved April 28, 2010, from http://www.equalrightscenter.org/releases/CivilRightsLawsuitFiledAgainsttheCityofManassasVAanditsSchoolSystemforDiscriminiatingAg.php.

Erera, P. (2002). *Family diversity: Continuity and change in the contemporary family.* Thousand Oaks, CA: Sage.

Erikson, E. (1963). *Childhood and society* (2nd ed.). New York: Norton.

Erikson, E. (1968). *Identity: Youth and crisis.* New York: Norton.

Erikson, K. (1976). *Everything in its path: Destruction of community in the Buffalo Creek flood.* New York: Simon & Schuster.

Ernst, J. (2000). Mapping child maltreatment: Looking at neighborhoods in a suburban county. *Child Welfare, 79,* 555–572.

Evans, C. J., Boustead, R. S., & Owens, C. (2008). Expressions of spirituality in parents with at-risk children. *Families in Society: The Journal of Contemporary Social Services, 89*(2), 245–252.

Evans, G. (2006). Child development and the physical environment. *Annual Review of Psychology, 57,* 423–451.

Evans, G., Lepore, S., & Allen, K. (2000). Cross-cultural differences in tolerance for crowding: Fact or fiction? *Journal of Personality and Social Psychology, 79*(2), 204–210.

Evans, G., & Saegert, S. (2000). Residential crowding in the context of inner city poverty. In S. Wapner, J. Demick, T. Yamamoto, & H. Minami (Eds.), *Theoretical perspectives in environment–behavior research: Underlying assumptions, research problems, and methodologies* (pp. 247–267). New York: Kluwer Academic.

Evans, S. (1980). *Personal politics.* New York: Vintage.

Ewalt, P., Freeman, E., & Poole, D. (Eds.). (1998). *Community building: Renewal, well-being, and shared responsibility.* Washington, DC: NASW Press.

Ewert, A., & Heywood, J. (1991). Group development in the natural environment: Expectations, outcomes, and techniques. *Environment and Behavior, 23,* 529–615.

Ewing, R., Schmid, T., Killingsworth, R., Zlot, A., & Raudenbush, S. (2003). Relationship between urban sprawl and physical activity, obesity, and morbidity. *American Journal of Health Promotion, 18*(1), 47–57.

Faber, A., Willerton, E., Clymer, S., MacDermid, S., & Weiss, H. (2008). Ambiguous absence, ambiguous presence: A qualitative study of military reserve families in wartime. *Journal of Family Psychology, 22*(2), 222–230.

Fadiman, A. (1998). *The spirit catches you and you fall down: A Hmong child, her American doctors, and the collision of two cultures.* New York: Farrar, Straus and Giroux.

Faiola, A. (2006, July 28). The face of poverty ages in rapidly graying Japan. *The Washington Post,* p. A01.

Falicov, C. J. (2003). Immigrant family processes. In F. Walsh (Ed.), *Normal family processes: Growing diversity and complexity* (3rd ed., pp. 280–300). New York: Guilford Press.

Farazmand, A. (2002). Introduction: The multifaceted nature of modern organizations. In A. Farazmand (Ed.), *Modern organizations: Theory and practice* (2nd ed., pp. xv–xxix). Westport, CT: Praeger.

Farmer, R. (2009). *Neuroscience and social work practice: The missing link.* Thousand Oaks, CA: Sage.

Farrell, M. (2009, September 19). ACORN scandal: How much federal funding does it get? *The Christian Science Monitor.* Retrieved April 28, 2010, from http://www.csmonitor.com/USA/2009/0919/p02s13-usgn.html.

Farrelly-Hansen, M. (2009). *Spirituality and art therapy: Living the connection.* London: Jessica Kingsley Publishers.

Faull, K., & Hills, M. (2006). The role of the spiritual dimensions of the self as the prime determinant of health. *Disability and Rehabilitation, 28*(11), 729–740.

Fauri, D. P. (1988). Applying historical themes of the profession in the foundation curriculum. *Journal of Teaching in Social Work, 2,* 17–31.

Faver, C. A., & Trachte, B. L. (2005). Religion and spirituality at the border: A survey of Mexican-American social work students. *Social Thought, 24*(4), 3–18.

Feikema, R., Segalavich, J., & Jeffries, S. (1997). From child development to community building: One agency's journey. *Families in Society, 78,* 185–195.

Feldman, R. (1990). Settlement-identity: Psychological bonds with home places in a mobile society. *Environment and Behavior, 22*(2), 183–229.

Felty, K., & Poloma, M. (1991). From sex differences to gender role beliefs: Exploring effects on six dimensions of religiosity. *Sex Roles, 23,* 181–193.

Ferguson, K. M., Wu, Q., Dryness, G., & Spruijt-Metz, D. (2007). Perceptions of faith and outcomes in faith-based programs for homeless youth: A grounded theory approach. *Journal of Social Service Research, 33*(4), 25–43.

Ferraro, K., & Shippee, T. (2009). Aging and cumulative inequality: How does inequality get under the skin? *The Gerontologist, 49*(3), 333–343.

Ferree, M. M., & Martin, P. Y. (1995). *Feminist organizations: Harvest of the new women's movement.* Philadelphia: Temple University Press.

Figley, C. R. (2002). Compassion fatigue: Psychotherapist's chronic lack of self care. *Journal of Clinical Psychology, 58*(11), 1433–1441.

Fine, M., Ganong, L., & Demo, D. (2010). Divorce: A risk and resilience perspective. In S. Price, C. Price, & P. McKenry (Eds.), *Families & change: Coping with stressful events and transitions* (4th ed., pp. 211–233). Thousand Oaks, CA: Sage.

Finger, W., & Arnold, E. M. (2002). Mind–body interventions: Applications for social work practice. *Social Work in Health Care, 35*(4), 57–78.

Finkelhor, D., Ormrod, R., Turner, H., & Hamby, S. (2005). The victimization of children and youth: A comprehensive national survey. *Child Maltreatment, 10,* 5–25.

Finn, J., & Checkoway, B. (1998). Young people as competent community builders: A challenge to social work. *Social Work, 43*(4), 335–345.

Firebaugh, G., & Goesling, B. (2004). Accounting for the recent decline in global income inequality. *American Journal of Sociology, 110*(2), 283–312.

Fischer, D. (1989). *Albion's seed: Four British folkways in American.* New York: Oxford University Press.

Fischer, J., Lyness, K., & Engler, R. (2010). Families coping with alcohol and substance abuse. In S. Price, C. Price, & P. McKenry (Eds.), *Families & change: Coping with stressful events and transitions* (4th ed., pp. 141–162). Thousand Oaks, CA: Sage.

Fisek, M. H., Berger, J., & Moore, J. (2002). Evaluations, enactment, and expectations. *Social Psychology Quarterly, 65*(4), 329–345.

Fisher, R. (2005). History, context, and emerging issues for community practice. In M. Weil (Ed.), *The handbook of community practice* (pp. 34–58). Thousand Oaks, CA: Sage.

Fisher, R., & Karger, H. (1997). *Social work and community in a private world.* New York: Longman.

Fisher, R., & Shragge, E. (2000). Challenging community organizing: Facing the 21st century. *Journal of Community Practice, 8*(3), 1–19.

Fitzgerald, J. (1997). Reclaiming the whole: Self, spirit, and society. *Disability and Rehabilitation, 19*(10), 407–413.

Fitzgerald, K., & Rodgers, D. (2000). Radical social movement organizations: A theoretical model. *Sociological Quarterly, 41*(4), 573–592.

Flacks, R. (2004). Knowledge for what? Thoughts on the state of social movement studies. In J. Goodwin & J. Jasper (Eds.), *Rethinking social movements: Structure, meaning, and emotion* (pp. 135–153). Lanham, MD: Rowman & Littlefield.

Flake, E., Davis, B., Johnson, P., & Middleton, L. (2009). The psychosocial effects of deployment on military children. *Journal of Developmental & Behavioral Pediatrics, 30*(4), 271–278.

Flanagan, L. M. (2008a). Object relations theory. In J. Berzoff, L. M. Flanagan, & L. Melano (Eds.), *Inside out and outside in: Psychodynamic clinical theory and psychopathology in contemporary multicultural contexts* (2nd ed., pp. 121–169). Lanham, MD: Jason Aronson.

Flanagan, L. M. (2008b). The theory of self psychology. In J. Berzoff, L. M. Flanagan, & P. Hertz (Eds.), *Inside out and outside in: Psychodynamic clinical theory and psychopathology in contemporary multicultural contexts* (2nd ed., pp. 161–188). Lanham, MD: Jason Aronson.

Flanagan, W. (1993). *Contemporary urban sociology.* New York: Cambridge University Press.

Floyd, K., & Morman, M. (Eds.). (2006). *Widening the family circle: New research on family communication.* Thousand Oaks, CA: Sage.

Flores-Gonzalez, N. (1999). Puerto Rican high achievers: An example of ethnic and academic identity compatibility. *Anthropology & Education Quarterly, 30*(3), 343–362.

Fong, R., & Furuto, S. B. C. L. (Eds.). (2001). *Culturally competent practice: Skills, interventions, and evaluations.* Boston: Allyn & Bacon.

Fontana, A. (1984). Introduction: Existential sociology and the self. In J. Kotarba & A. Fontana (Eds.), *The existential self in society* (pp. 3–17). Chicago: University of Chicago Press.

Ford, D., & Lerner, R. (1992). *Developmental systems theory: An integrative approach.* Newbury Park, CA: Sage.

Fordham, S. (1993). Those loud Black girls: (Black) women, silence, and gender "passing" in the academy. *Anthropology and Education Quarterly, 2*(1), 3–32.

Fordham, S. (1996). *Blacked out: Dilemmas of race, identity, and success at Capital High.* Chicago: University of Chicago Press.

Fordham, S., & Ogbu, J. (1986). Black students' school success: Coping with the "Burden of 'Acting White.'" *Urban Review, 18*(3), 176–206.

Foster-Fishman, P., Fitzgerald, K., Brandell, C., Nowell, B., Chavis, D., & Van Egeren, L. (2006). Mobilizing residents for action: The role of small wins and strategic supports. *Journal of Community Psychology, 38*(3/4), 143–152.

Foucault, M. (1969). *The archaeology of knowledge and the discourse on language.* New York: Harper Colophon.

Fowler, J. F. (1981). *Stages of faith: The psychology of human development and the quest for meaning.* San Francisco: Harper.

Fowler, J. F. (1995). *Stages of faith: The psychology of human development and the quest for meaning.* New York: HarperCollins.

Fowler, J. F. (1996). *Faithful change: The personal and public challenges of postmodern life.* Nashville, TN: Abingdon Press.

Fox, C., & Miller, H. (1995). *Postmodern public administration: Toward discourse.* Thousand Oaks, CA: Sage.

Fox, M. (1994). *The reinvention of work: A new vision of livelihood for our time.* San Francisco: HarperSanFrancisco.

Frame, M. W. (2003). *Integrating religion and spirituality into counseling: A comprehensive approach.* Pacific Grove, CA: Brooks/Cole Thompson Learning.

Francescato, D., & Tomai, M. (2001). Community psychology: Should there be a European perspective? *Journal of Community & Applied Social Psychology, 11,* 371–380.

Frank, A. (1967). *Capitalism and development in Latin America.* New York: Monthly Review Press.

Frank, L., Andresen, M., & Schmid, T. (2004). Obesity relationships with community design, physical activity, and time spent in cars. *American Journal of Preventive Medicine, 27*(2), 87–96.

Frankl, V. E. (1988). *The will to meaning: Foundations and applications of logotherapy.* New York: Meridian.

Franklin, C. (1995). Expanding the vision of the social constructionist debates: Creating relevance for practitioners. *Families in Society, 76,* 395–407.

Franklin, R. M. (1994). The safest place on earth: The culture of Black congregations. In J. P. Wind & J. W. Lewis (Eds.), *American congregations* (Vol. 2, pp. 257–260). Chicago: University of Chicago Press.

Fraser, C., McIntyre, A., & Manby, M. (2009). Exploring the impact of parental drug/alcohol problems on children and parents in a Midlands county in 2005/06. *British Journal of Social Work, 39*, 846–866.

Fraser, M. (Ed.). (2004). *Risk and resilience in childhood: An ecological perspective* (2nd ed.). Washington, DC: NASW Press.

Freedberg, S. (2007). Re-examining empathy: A relational-feminist point of view. *Social Work, 52*(3), 251–259.

Freedom House. (2010). *Freedom of the press.* Retrieved February 23, 2010, from http://www.freedomhouse.org/template.cfm?page=16.

Freeman, D. R. (2006). Spirituality in violence and substance abusing African American men: An untapped resource in healing. *Social Thought, 25*(1), 3–22.

Freeman, E., & Couchonnal, G. (2006). Narrative and culturally based approaches in practice with families. *Families in Society: The Journal of Contemporary Social Services, 87*(2), 198–208.

Freeman, J. (1995). From seed to harvest: Transformations of feminist organizations and scholarship. In M. Ferree & P. Martin (Eds.), *Feminist organizations: Harvest of the new women's movement* (pp. 397–408). Philadelphia: Temple University Press.

Fremeaux, I. (2005). New labour's appropriation of the concept of community: A critique. *Community Development Journal, 40*(3), 265–274.

French, L. A., & White, W. L. (2004). Alcohol and other drug addictions among Native Americans: The movement toward tribal-centric treatment programs. *Alcoholism Treatment Quarterly, 22*(1), 81–91.

Freud, S. (1928). *The future of an illusion.* London: Hogarth Press and Institute of Psychoanalysis.

Freud, S. (1953). Three essays on the theory of sexuality. In J. Strachey (Ed. & Trans.), *The standard edition of the complete psychological works of Sigmund Freud* (Vol. 7, pp. 135–245). London: Hogarth Press. (Original work published 1905)

Freud, S. (1978). *The interpretation of dreams* (A. A. Brill, Trans.). New York: Modern Library. (Original work published 1899)

Frey, L., & Sunwolf. (2005). The symbolic-interpretive perspective of group life. In M. Poole & A. Hollingshead (Eds.), *Theories of small groups: Interdisciplinary perspectives* (pp. 185–239). Thousand Oaks, CA: Sage.

Friedman, B., Kahn, P., Hagman, J., Severson, R., & Gill, B. (2006). The watcher and the watched: Social judgments about privacy in a public place. *Human–Computer Interaction, 21*(2), 235–272.

Frith, U., & Frith, C. (2010). The social brain: Allowing humans to boldly go where no other species has been. *Philosophical Transactions of the Royal Society B: Biological Science, 365*(1537), 165–176.

Fromm, E. (1941). *Escape from freedom.* New York: Avon.

Fromm, E., & Maccoby, M. (1970). *Social character in a Mexican village.* Englewood Cliffs, NJ: Prentice Hall.

Frumkin, H. (2001). Beyond toxicity: Human health and the natural environment. *American Journal of Preventive Medicine, 20*(3), 234–240.

Frumkin, H. (2003). Healthy places: Exploring the evidence. *American Journal of Public Health, 93*(9), 1451–1456.

Frumkin, P. (2002). Service contracting with nonprofit and for-profit providers. In J. D. Donahue & J. S. Nye Jr. (Eds.), *Market-based governance* (pp. 66–87). Washington, DC: Brookings Institution Press.

Fukuyama, M. A., & Sevig, T. D. (1999). *Integrating spirituality into multicultural counseling.* Thousand Oaks, CA: Sage.

Furman, L. E., & Chandy, J. M. (1994). Religion and spirituality: A long-neglected cultural component of rural social work practice. *Human Services in the Rural Environment, 17*(3/4), 21–26.

Furushima, R. Y. (1983). Faith development in a cross-cultural perspective. *Religious Education, 80*, 414–420.

Galambos, C. (2001). Community healing rituals for survivors of rape. *Smith College Studies in Social Work, 71*(3), 441–457.

Gale, J. (2009). Meditation and relational connectedness: Practices for couples and families. In F. Walsh (Ed.), *Spiritual resources in family therapy* (2nd ed., pp. 247–266). New York: Guilford Press.

Galinsky, E., Aumann, K., & Bond, J. (2009). *Times are changing: Gender and generation at work and at home.* Washington, DC: Families and Work Institute. Retrieved December 3, 2009, from http://www.familiesandwork.org.

Galinsky, M. J., Schopler, J. H., & Abell, M. D. (1997). Connecting group members through telephone and computer groups. *Health & Social Work, 22*, 181–188.

Gallagher, M. (1996). *The abolition of marriage: How we destroy lasting love.* Washington, DC: Regnery.

Gallagher, W. (1993). *The power of place: How our surroundings shape our thoughts, emotions, and actions.* New York: Poseidon.

Gallup. (2008). *Religion.* Retrieved February, 26, 2010, from http://www.gallup.com/ poll/1690/religion.aspx.

Gallup, G., & Jones, T. (2000). *The next American spirituality: Finding God in the twenty-first century.* Colorado Springs, CO: Cook Communication Ministries.

Gallup, G., & Lindsay, D. M. (1999). *Surveying the religious landscape: Trends in U.S. beliefs.* Harrisburg, PA: Morehouse.

Galotti, K. M. (1989). Gender differences in self-reported moral reasoning: A review and new evidence. *Journal of Youth and Adolescence, 18*, 475–488.

Galvin, K. (2006). Joined by hearts and words: Adoptive family relationships. In K. Floyd & M. Morman (Eds.), *Widening the family circle: New research on family communication* (pp. 137–152). Thousand Oaks, CA: Sage.

Galvin, K., Bylund, C., & Brommel, B. (2003). *Family communication: Cohesion and change* (6th ed.). New York: Allyn & Bacon.

Galvin, K., Dickson, F., & Marrow, S. (2006). Systems theory: Patterns and wholes in family communication. In D. Braithwaite & L. Baxter (Eds.), *Engaging theories in family communication: Multiple perspectives* (pp. 309–324). Thousand Oaks, CA: Sage.

Gambrill, E. (2006). *Critical thinking in clinical practice: Improving the quality of judgments and decisions* (2nd ed.). Hoboken, NJ: Wiley.

Gamson, W., & Meyer, D. (1996). Framing political opportunity. In D. McAdam, J. McCarthy, & M. Zald (Eds.), *Comparative perspectives on social movements* (pp. 273–290). New York: Cambridge University Press.

Garbarino, J., & Bedard, C. (1997). Spiritual challenges to children facing violent trauma. *Childhood: A Global Journal of Child Research, 3*(4), 467–478.

Garden, F., & Jalaludin, B. (2009). Impact of urban sprawl on overweight, obesity, and physical activity in Sydney, Australia. *Journal of Urban Health, 86*(1), 19–30.

Gardiner, H. W., & Kosmitzki, C. (2008). *Lives across cultures: Cross-cultural human development* (4th ed.). Boston: Pearson.

Gardner, H. (1999). *Intelligence reframed: Multiple intelligences for the 21st century.* New York: Basic Books.

Gardner, H. (2006). *Multiple intelligences: New horizons.* New York: Basic Books.

Garland, D. R., Myers D. M., & Wolfer, T. A. (2008). Social work with religious volunteers: Activating and sustaining community involvement. *Social Work, 53*(3), 255–265.

Garland, E., & Howard, O. (2009). Neuroplasticity, psychosocial genomics, and the biopsychosocial paradigm in the 21st century. *Health & Social work, 34*(3), 191–199.

Garland, J., Jones, H., & Kolodny, R. (1973). A model for stages of development in social work groups. In S. Bernstein (Ed.), *Explorations in groupwork* (pp. 17–71). Boston: Milford.

Garrett, K. (2004). Use of groups in school social work: Group work and group processes. *Social Work with Groups, 27*(2/3), 75–92.

Garrow, E., & Hasenfeld, Y. (2010). Theoretical approaches to human service organizations. In Y. Hasenfeld (Ed.), *Human services as complex organizations* (2nd ed., pp. 33–57). Thousand Oaks, CA: Sage.

Garvin, C. D., & Reed, B. G. (1983). Gender issues in social group work: An overview. *Social Work With Groups, 6*(3/4), 5–18.

Gates, G., & Ost, J. (2004). *The gay and lesbian atlas.* Washington, DC: The Urban Institute.

Geertz, C. (1973). *The interpretation of cultures.* New York: Basic Books.

Geertz, C. (1983). Common sense as a cultural system. In C. Geertz, *Local knowledge: Further essays in interpretive anthropology* (pp. 73–93). New York: Basic Books.

Gelberg, L., & Linn, L. S. (1988). Social and physical health of homeless adults previously treated for mental health problems. *Hospital and Community Psychiatry, 39,* 510–516.

Geller, M. (2005). The psychoanalytic perspective. In S. Wheelan (Ed.), *The handbook of group research and practice* (pp. 87–105). Thousand Oaks, CA: Sage.

Gelles, R. (2010). Violence, abuse, and neglect in families and intimate relationships. In S. Price, C. Price, & P. McKenry (Eds.), *Families & change: Coping with stressful events and transitions* (4th ed., pp. 119–139). Thousand Oaks, CA: Sage.

George, L. (1993). Sociological perspectives on life transitions. *Annual Review of Sociology, 19,* 353–373.

Gergen, K. (1985). The social constructionist movement in modern psychology. *American Psychologist, 40,* 266–275.

Gerhardt, S. (2004). *Why love matters: How affection shapes a baby's brain.* Philadelphia: Routledge/Taylor & Francis.

Germain, C. (1973). An ecological perspective in casework practice. *Social Casework, 54,* 323–330.

Germain, C. (1978). Space: An ecological variable in social work practice. *Social Casework, 59,* 515–522.

Germain, C. (1981). The physical environment and social work practice. In A. N. Maluccio (Ed.), *Promoting competence in clients* (pp. 103–124). New York: Free Press.

Germain, C. (1994). Human behavior and the social environment. In R. Reamer (Ed.), *The foundations of social work knowledge* (pp. 88–121). New York: Columbia University Press.

Germain, C., & Gitterman, A. (1980). *The life model of social work practice.* New York: Columbia University Press.

Gevirtz, C. (2006). Managing postpolio syndrome pain. *Nursing, 36*(12), 17.

Gibbs, N. (2009, October 14). What women want now. *Time.* Retrieved December 3, 2009, from http://www.time.com/time/specials/packages/article/0,28804,1930277_1930145,00.html.

Gibson, M. (1988). *Accommodation without assimilation: Sikh immigrants in an American high school.* Ithaca, NY: Cornell University Press.

Gibson-Davis, C., Edin, K., & McLanahan, S. (2005). High hopes but even higher expectations: The retreat from marriage among low-income couples. *Journal of Marriage and Family, 65*(5), 1301–1312.

Giddens, A. (1979). *Central problems in social theory: Action, structure, and contradiction in social analysis.* Berkeley: University of California Press.

Giddens, A. (2000). *Runaway world: How globalization is reshaping our lives.* New York: Routledge.

Gifford, R. (2007). *Environmental psychology: Principles and practice* (4th ed.). Colville, WA: Optimal Books.

Gill, S. (2010). *Developing a learning culture in nonprofit organizations.* Thousand Oaks, CA: Sage.

Gilligan, C. (1982). *In a different voice.* Cambridge, MA: Harvard University Press.

Gilligan, C. (1988). Remapping the moral domain: New images of self in relationship. In C. Gilligan, J. V. Ward, & J. M. Taylor (Eds.), *Mapping the moral domain* (pp. 3–20). Cambridge, MA: Harvard University Press.

Gillis, J. (1996). *A world of their own making: Myth, ritual, and the quest for family values.* New York: Basic Books.

Gilson, S. F. (1996). *The disability movement and federal legislation.* Unpublished manuscript.

Gilson, S. F., & DePoy, E. (2000). Multiculturalism and disability: A critical perspective. *Disability & Society, 15*(2), 207–218.

Gilson, S. F., & DePoy, E. (2002). Theoretical approaches to disability content in social work education. *Journal of Social Work Education, 37,* 153–165.

Gini, A. (1997). Moral leadership: An overview. In W. E. Rosenbach & R. L. Taylor (Eds.), *Contemporary issues in leadership* (4th ed., pp. 5–16). Boulder, CO: Westview Press.

Ginsberg, L. H. (2001). *Careers in social work* (2nd ed.). Boston: Allyn & Bacon.

Gitterman, A. (2009). The life model. In A. R. Roberts (Ed.), *Social workers' desk reference* (2nd ed., pp. 231–235).

Gitterman, A., & Shulman, L. (1994). *Mutual aid groups, vulnerable populations, and the life cycle* (2nd ed.). New York: Columbia University Press.

Glynn M., & Rhodes P. (2005, June). *Estimated HIV prevalence in the United States at the end of 2003.* Paper presented at the National HIV Prevention Conference, Atlanta. Retrieved August 4, 2006, from http://www.cdc.gov/hiv/topics/surveillance/basic.htm.

Godsall, R., Jurkovic, G., Emshoff, J., Anderson, L., & Stanwyck, D. (2004). Why some kids do well in bad situations: Relation of parental alcohol misuse and parentification to children's self-concept. *Substance Use & Misuse, 39*(5), 789–809.

Goffman, E. (1959). *Presentation of self in everyday life.* Garden City, NY: Archer.

Goggin, G. (Ed.). (2008). *Mobile phone cultures.* New York: Routledge.

Goldberg, A. (2010). Lesbian- and gay-parent families: Development and functioning. In S. Price, C. Price, & P. McKenry (Eds.), *Families & change: Coping with stressful events and transitions* (pp. 263–284). Thousand Oaks, CA: Sage.

Goldman, J. (1996). *Healing sounds: The power of harmonics.* Rockport, MA: Element Books.

Goldstein, A. (2006, August 7). Welfare changes a burden to states: Work rules also threaten study, health programs. *The Washington Post,* p. A01.

Goldstein, C. (n.d.). *Spiritual activism: Co-creating the world we seek.* Retrieved February 26, 2010, from http://www.feminist.com/activism/spiritualactivism1.html.

Goldstein, D. (1996). Ego psychology theory. In F. Turner (Ed.), *Social work treatment* (4th ed., pp. 191–217). New York: Free Press.

Goldstein, E. (1995). *Ego psychology and social work practice* (2nd ed.). New York: Free Press.

Goldstein, E. (2001). *Object relations theory and self psychology in social work practice.* New York: Free Press.

Goldstein, E. (2008). Ego psychology theory. In B. A. Thyer, K. M. Sowers, & C. N. D. Dulmus (Eds.), *Comprehensive handbook of social work and social welfare, Vol. 2: Human behavior in the social environment* (pp. 135–162). Hoboken, NJ: Wiley.

Goleman, D. (2005). *Emotional intelligence* (10th anniv. ed.). New York: Bantam.

Golembiewski, R. T. (1994). Is organizational membership bad for your health? Phases of burnout as covariants of mental and physical well-being. In A. Farazmand (Ed.), *Modern organizations: Administrative theory in contemporary society* (pp. 211–227). Westport, CT: Praeger.

Golsworthy, R., & Coyle, A. (1999). Spiritual beliefs and the search for meaning among older adults following partner loss. *Mortality, 4*(1), 21–40.

Goodenough, W. (1996). Culture. In D. Levison & M. Ember (Eds.), *Encyclopedia of cultural anthropology* (Vol. 1, pp. 291–298). New York: Holt.

Goodson-Lawes, J. (1994). Ethnicity and poverty as research variables: Family studies with Mexican and Vietnamese newcomers. In E. Sherman & W. Reid (Eds.), *Qualitative research in social work* (pp. 22–31). New York: Columbia University Press.

Goodwin, J., & Jasper, J. (Eds.). (2004). *Rethinking social movements: Structure, meaning, and emotion.* Lanham, MD: Rowman & Littlefield.

Gordon, M. (1964). *Assimilation in American life: The role of race, religion, and national origins.* New York: Oxford University Press.

Gordon, W., Zafonte, R., Cicerone, K., Cantor, J., Brown, M., Lombard, L., et al. (2006). Traumatic brain injury rehabilitation: State of the science. *American Journal of Physical Medicine & Rehabilitation, 85*(4), 343–382.

Gould, D. (2004). Passionate political processes: Bring emotions back into the study of social movements. In J. Goodwin & J. Jasper (Eds.), *Rethinking social movements: Structure, meaning, and emotion* (pp. 155–175). Lanham, MD: Rowman & Littlefield.

Gould, S. (1981). *The mismeasure of man.* New York: Norton.

Gourevitch, A. (2001, May 30). Awakening the giant: How the living wage movement can revive progressive politics. *American Prospect Online.* Retrieved May 5, 2010, from http://www .prospect.org/cs/articles? article=awakening_the_giant.

Granovetter, M. (1973). The strength of weak ties. *American Journal of Sociology, 78,* 1360–1380.

Graven, S., Bowen, W., Brooten, D., Eaton, A., Graven., M., Hack, M., et al. (1992). The high-risk environment, Part I: The role of the neonatal intensive care unit and the outcome of high-risk infants. *Journal of Perinatology, 12,* 64–172.

Greeff, A. P., & Fillis, A. J. (2009). Resiliency in poor single-parent families. *Families in Society: The Journal of Contemporary Social Services, 90*(3), 279–285.

Green, J. (1999). *Cultural awareness in the human services: A multiethnic approach* (3rd ed.). Boston: Allyn & Bacon.

Greenberg, L. S. (2008). The clinical application of emotion in psychotherapy. In M. Lewis, J. M. Havilland-Jones, & L. F. Barrett (Eds.), *Handbook of emotions* (3rd ed., pp. 88–101). New York: Guilford Press.

Greene, R. R., & Cohen, H. L. (2005). Social work with older adults and their families: Changing practice paradigms. *Families in Society, 86*(3), 367–373.

Greenwald, H. (2008). *Organizations: Management without control.* Thousand Oaks, CA: Sage.

Griswold, W. (2008). *Cultures and societies in a changing world* (3rd ed.). Thousand Oaks, CA: Pine Forge.

Grof, S. (1988). *The adventure of self-discovery.* New York: SUNY Press.

Grof, S. (2003). Physical manifestations of emotional disorders: Observations from the study of non-ordinary states of consciousness. In K. Taylor (Ed.), *Exploring holotropic breathwork: Selected articles from a decade of The Inner Door.* Santa Cruz, CA: Hanford Mead Publishers.

Grof, S., & Bennett, H. Z. (1992). *The holotropic mind: The three levels of human consciousness and how they shape our lives.* New York: HarperCollins.

Grossman, P., Niemann, I., Schmidt, S., & Walach, H. (2004). Mindfulness-based stress reduction and health benefits: A meta-analysis. *Journal of Psychosomatic Research, 57*(1), 35–43.

Gudmunson, C., Beutler, I., Israelsen, C., McCoy, J., & Hill, E. (2007). Linking financial strain to marital instability: Examining the roles of emotional distress and marital interaction. *Journal of Family and Economic Issues, 28*(3), 357–376.

A guide to African Americans and religion. (2007). Retrieved May 20, 2010, from http://www.religionlink.com/tip_070108.php.

Gump, P. (1987). School and classroom environments. In D. Stokols & I. Altman (Eds.), *Handbook of environmental psychology* (pp. 691–732). New York: Wiley.

Gump, L., Baker, R., & Roll, S. (2000). Cultural and gender differences in moral judgment: A study of Mexican Americans and Anglo-Americans. *Hispanic Journal of Behavioral Sciences, 22*(1), 78–93.

Gunnar, M. R., Broderson, L., Nachimas, M., Buss, K., & Rigatuso, J. (1996). Stress reactivity and attachment security. *Developmental Psychobiology, 29*(3), 191–204.

Gutheil, I. (1991). The physical environment and quality of life in residential facilities for frail elders. *Adult Residential Care Journal, 5,* 131–145.

Gutheil, I. (1992). Considering the physical environment: An essential component of good practice. *Social Work, 37,* 391–396.

Gutierrez, L. (1990). Working with women of color: An empowerment perspective. *Social Work, 35*(2), 149–153.

Gutierrez, L. (1994). Beyond coping: An empowerment perspective on stressful life events. *Journal of Sociology and Social Welfare, 21*(3), 201–219.

Gutman, L., McLoyd, V., & Tokoyawa, T. (2005). Financial strain, neighborhood stress, parenting behaviors, and adolescent adjustment in urban African American families. *Journal of Research on Adolescence, 15*(4), 425–449.

Guy, M., Newman, M., Mastracci, S., & Maynard-Moody, S. (2010). Emotional labor in the human service organization. In Y. Hasenfeld (Ed.), *Human services as complex organizations* (2nd ed., pp. 291–309). Thousand Oaks, CA: Sage.

Haan, N. (1991). Moral development and action from a social constructivist perspective. In W. Kurtines & J. Gewirtz (Eds.), *Handbook of moral behavior and development: Theory* (Vol. 1, pp. 251–273). Hillsdale, NJ: Erlbaum.

Habash, A. (2008). *Counting on graduation: An agenda for state leadership.* Retrieved May 5, 2010, from http://www.nass gap.org/library/docs/counting_on_graduation_Habash_10 08.pdf.

Habash Rowan, A., Hall, D., & Haycock, K. (2010). *Gauging the gaps: A deeper look at student achievement.* Retrieved February 21, 2010, from http://www.edtrust.org/sites/edtrust.org/files/ publications/files/NAEP%20Gap_0.pdf.

Habermas, J. (1984). *The theory of communicative action, Vol. 1: Reason and the rationalization of society.* Boston: Beacon Press.

Habermas, J. (1987). *The theory of communicative action, Vol. 2: Lifeworld and system: A critique of functionalist reason* (T. McCarthy, Trans.). Boston: Beacon Press. (Original work published 1981)

Haddad, Y. Y. (1997). Make room for the Muslims? In W. H. Conser Jr., & S. B. Twiss (Eds.), *Religious diversity and American religious history: Studies in traditions and cultures* (pp. 218–261). Athens: University of Georgia Press.

Hagan, J. (1994). *Crime and disrepute.* Thousand Oaks, CA: Pine Forge.

Hagerman, I., Rasmanis, G., Blomkvist, V., Ulrich, R., Eriksen, C. A., & Theorell, T. (2005). Influence of intensive coronary care acoustics on the quality of care and physiological state of patients. *International Journal of Cardiology, 98*(2), 267–270.

Haig-Brown, C. (1988). *Resistance and renewal: Surviving the Indian residential school.* Vancouver, BC, Canada: Tillacum Library.

Hall, D. (2005, June). Getting honest about grad rates: How states play the numbers and students lose. *The Education Trust.* Retrieved May 5, 2010, from http://www.ccsso.org/content/pdfs/GettingHonestAboutGradRates.pdf.

Hall, E. (1966). *The hidden dimension.* New York: Doubleday.

Hall, M. (1995). *Poor people's social movement organizations: The goal is to win.* Westport, CT: Praeger.

Halperin, D. (2001). The play's the thing: How social group work and theatre transformed a group into a community. *Social Work With Groups, 24*(2), 27–46.

Hames, A. M., & Godwin, M. C. (2008). The "out of control" balloon: Using spirituality as a coping resource. In C. F. Sori, & L. L. Hecker (Eds.), *The therapist's notebook: More homework, handouts, and activities for use in psychotherapy* (pp. 171–176). New York: Routledge/Taylor & Francis.

Hamilton, B., Martin, J., & Ventura, S. (2009, March 18). Births: Preliminary data for 2007. *National Vital Statistics Reports, 57*(12). Hyattsville, MD: National Center for Health Statistics.

Hampton, K., Sessions, L., Her, E. J., & Rainie, L. (2009, November 4). *Social isolation and new technology.* Washington, DC: Pew Internet & American Life Project. Retrieved May 5, 2010, from http://www.pewinternet.org/Reports/2009/18—Social-Isolation-and-New-Technology.aspx?r=1.

Hampton, K., & Wellman, B. (2003). Neighboring in Netville: How the Internet supports community and social capital in a wired suburb. *City & Community, 2*(4), 277–311.

Handel, G., Cahill, S. E., & Elkin, F. (2007). *Children and society: The sociology of children and childhood socialization.* Los Angeles: Roxbury.

Hannerz, U. (1992). *Cultural complexity: Studies in the social organization of meaning.* New York: Columbia University Press.

Hansen, L. S. (1997). *Integrative life planning: Critical tasks for career development and changing life patterns.* San Francisco: Jossey-Bass.

Hardcastle, D., Wenocur, S., & Powers, P. (2004). *Community practice: Theories and skills for social workers* (2nd ed.). New York: Oxford University Press.

Hare, A. P. (1994). Types of roles in small groups: A bit of history and a current perspective. *Small Group Research, 25,* 433–448.

Hare, A. P., Blumberg, H. H., Davies, M. F., & Kent, M. V. (1994). *Small group research: A handbook.* Norwood, NJ: Ablex.

Hareven, T. K. (2000). *Families, history, and social change: Life-course and cross-cultural perspectives.* Boulder, CO: Westview Press.

Harrison, R., & Thomas, M. (2009). Identity in online communities: Social networking sites and language learning. *International Journal of Emerging Technologies & Society, 7*(2), 109–124.

Hart, J. (1970). The development of client-centered therapy. In J. T. Hart & T. M. Tomlinson (Eds.), *New directions in client-centered therapy* (pp. 3–22). Boston: Houghton Mifflin.

Hartford, M. (1971). *Groups in social work.* New York: Columbia University Press.

Hartig, T., Evans, G., Jamner, L., Davis, D., & Gärling, T. (2003). Tracking restoration in natural and urban field settings. *Journal of Environmental Psychology, 23*(2), 109–123.

Hartig, T., Mang, M., & Evans, G. (1991). Restorative effects of natural environment experiences. *Environment and Behavior, 23,* 3–26.

Hartig, T., & Staats, H. (2006). The need for psychological restoration as a determinant of environmental preferences. *Journal of Environmental Psychology, 26*(3), 215–226.

Hartman, A. (1970). To think about the unthinkable. *Social Casework, 51,* 467–474.

Hartman, A. (1995). Diagrammatic assessment of family relationships. *Families in Society, 76,* 111–122.

Hartman, A., & Laird, J. (1983). *Family-centered social work practice.* New York: Free Press.

Hasenfeld, Y. (2010a). The attributes of human service organizations. In Y. Hasenfeld (Ed.), *Human services as complex organizations* (2nd ed., pp. 9–32). Thousand Oaks, CA: Sage.

Hasenfeld, Y. (2010b). Introduction. In Y. Hasenfeld (Ed.), *Human services as complex organizations* (2nd ed., pp. 1–5). Thousand Oaks, CA: Sage.

Hastings, M. (1998). Theoretical perspectives on social movements. *New Zealand Sociology, 13*(2), 208–238.

Hauser, M., Cushman, F., Young, L., Mikhail, J., & Jin, R. K. (2007). A dissociation between moral judgments and justifications. *Mind & Language, 22*(1), 1–21.

Hawkins, K. W. (1995). Effects of gender and communication content on leadership emergence in small task-oriented groups. *Small Group Research, 26,* 234–249.

Hay, D., & Nye, R. (2006). *The spirit of the child* (Rev. ed.). London: Jessica Kingsley.

Hay, D., Nye, R., & Murphy, R. (1996). Thinking about childhood spirituality: Review of research and current directions. In L. J. Francis, W. K. Kay, & W. S. Campbell (Eds.), *Research in religious education* (pp. 47–71). Macon, GA: Smyth & Helwys.

Haycock, K. (2006, August 1). *Promise abandoned: How policy choices and institutional practices restrict college opportunities.* Retrieved May 5, 2010, from http://www.edtrust.org/dc/publication/promise-abandoned-how-policy-choices-and-institutional-practices-restrict-college-opp.

Healey, J. F. (1995). *Race, ethnicity, gender, and class: The sociology of group conflict and change.* Thousand Oaks, CA: Pine Forge.

Healey, J. F. (2010). Race, ethnicity, gender, and class: The sociology of group conflict and change (5th ed.). Thousand Oaks, CA: Pine Forge.

Hearn, G. (1958). *Theory building in social work.* Toronto, Ont., Canada: University of Toronto Press.

Hearn, G. (1969). *The general systems approach: Contributions toward an holistic conception of social work.* New York: Council on Social Work Education.

Hearn, J., & Parkin, W. (1993). Organizations, multiple oppressions and postmodernism. In J. Hassard & M. Parker (Eds.), *Postmodernism and organizations* (pp. 148–162). Newbury Park, CA: Sage.

Hedberg, P., Brulin C., & Alex, L. (2009). Experiences of purpose in life when becoming and being a very old woman. *Journal of Women & Aging, 21*(2), 125–137.

Hegtvedt, K. A. (1994). Justice. In M. Foshci & E. J. Lawler (Eds.), *Group processes: Sociological analyses* (pp. 177–204). Chicago: Nelson-Hall.

Heller, K. (1989). The return to community. *American Journal of Community Psychology, 17*(1), 1–14.

Henderson, L. (2000). The knowledge and use of alternative therapeutic techniques by social work practitioners: A descriptive study. *Social Work in Health Care, 30*(3), 55–71.

Hendricks, C., & Rudich, G. (2000). A community building perspective in social work education. *Journal of Community Practice, 8*(3), 21–36.

Hepworth, D., Rooney, R., Rooney, G. D., Strom-Gottfried, K., & Larsen, J. (2010). *Direct social work practice: Theory and skills* (8th ed.). Belmont, CA: Brooks/Cole.

Herman, D. (Ed.). (2003). *Narrative theory and the cognitive sciences.* Chicago: Center for the Study of Language and Information.

Herzog, T., Herbert, E., Kaplan, R., & Crooks, C. (2000). Cultural and developmental comparisons of landscape perceptions and preferences. *Environment and Behavior, 32*(3), 323–346.

Hetherington, E., & Kelly, J. (2002). *For better or worse.* New York: Norton.

Heuveline, P., & Timberlake, J. (2004). The role of cohabitation in family formation: The United States in comparative perspective. *Journal of Marriage and Family, 66,* 1214–1230.

Hickson, J., & Phelps, A. (1998). Women's spirituality: A proposed practice model. In D. S. Becvar (Ed.), *The family,* spirituality, and social work (pp. 43–57). Binghamton, NY: Haworth Press.

Hidalgo, M., & Hernandez, B. (2001). Place attachment: Conceptual and empirical questions. *Journal of Environmental Psychology, 21,* 273–281.

Hilger, N. (2003, May). *Market liberalization, labor unions and real wages in Mexico, 1984–1998.* Honors thesis in economics, Stanford University, Palo Alto, California. Retrieved November 9, 2006, from http://economics.stanford.edu/files/Theses/Theses_2004/Hilger.pdf.

Hill, R. (1949). *Families under stress.* Westport, CT: Greenwood.

Hill, R. (1958). Generic features of families under stress. *Social Casework, 49,* 139–150.

Hillery, G. (1955). Definitions of community: Areas of agreement. *Rural Sociology, 20,* 111–123.

Hillier, A. (2007). Why social work needs mapping. *Journal of Social Work Education, 43*(2), 205–221.

Hillier, B. (2004). Can streets be safe? *Urban Design International, 9,* 31–45.

Himmelstein, D., Thorne, D., Warren, E., & Woolhandler, S. (2009). Medical bankruptcy in the United States, 2007: Results of a national study. *American Journal of Medicine, 122*(8), 741–746.

Hines, P. M., Preto, N. G., McGoldrick, M., Almeida, R., & Weltman, S. (2005). Culture and the family life cycle. In B. Carter & M. McGoldrick (Eds.), *The expanded family life cycle: Individual, family, and social perspectives* (3rd ed., pp. 69–87). Boston: Allyn & Bacon.

Hing, B. (2004). *Defining America through immigration policy.* Philadelphia: Temple University Press.

Hitchcock, J. (2006). *Net crimes and misdemeanors: Outmaneuvering web spammers, stalkers, and con artists.* Medford, NJ: CyberAge Books.

Ho, M., Rasheed, J., & Rasheed, M. (2004). *Family therapy with ethnic minorities* (2nd ed.). Thousand Oaks, CA: Sage.

Hobfoll, S. E. (1996). Social support: Will you be there when I need you? In N. Vanzetti & S. Duck (Eds.), *A lifetime of relationships* (pp. 46–74). Belmont, CA: Thomson Brooks/Cole.

Hobsbawm, E. (1983). Introduction: Inventing tradition. In E. Hobsbawm & T. Ranger (Eds.), *The invention of tradition* (pp. 1–14). New York: Cambridge University Press.

Hodge, D. R. (2002). Does social work oppress evangelical Christians? A new class analysis of society and social work. *Social Work, 47,* 401–414.

Hodge, D. R. (2003). Differences in worldviews between social workers and people of faith. *Families in Society: The Journal of Contemporary Social Services, 84,* 285–295.

Hodge, D. R. (2004). Working with Hindu clients in a spiritually sensitive manner. *Social Work, 49*(1), 27–38.

Hodge, D. R. (2005a). Developing a spiritual assessment toolbox: A discussion of the strengths and limitation of five different assessment methods. *Health & Social Work, 30*(4), 314–323.

Hodge, D. R. (2005b). Social work and the House of Islam: Orienting practitioners to the beliefs and values of Muslims in the United States. *Social Work, 50*(2), 162–173.

Hodge, D. R., Cardenas, P., & Montoya, H. (2001). Substance use: Spirituality and religious participation as protective factors among rural youths. *Social Work Research, 25*(3), 153–161.

Hofstede, G. (1996). An American in Paris: The influence of nationality on organization theories. *Organization Studies, 17*(13), 525–537.

Hofstede, G. (1998). A case for comparing apples with oranges: International differences in values. *International Journal of Comparative Sociology, 39*, 16–31.

Hofstede, G. (2001). *Culture's consequences: Comparing values, behaviors, institutions and organizations across nations* (2nd ed.). Thousand Oaks, CA: Sage.

Hofstede, G., Deusen, C., Mueller, C., & Charles, T. (2002). What goals do business leaders pursue? A study in fifteen countries. *Journal of International Business Studies, 33*(4), 785–803.

Hogg, M. (2005). The social identity perspective. In S. Wheelan (Ed.), *The handbook of group research and practice* (pp. 133–157). Thousand Oaks, CA: Sage.

Holder, D. W., Durant, R. H., Harris, T. L., Daniel, J., Obeidallah, D., & Goodman, E. (2000). The association between adolescent spirituality and voluntary sexual activity. *Journal of Adolescent Health, 26*(4), 295–302.

Hollinghurst, S., Kessler, D., Peters, T., & Gunnell, D. (2005). Opportunity cost of antidepressant prescribing in England: Analysis of routine data. *British Medical Journal, 330*(7948), 999–1000.

Hollingsworth, L., Allen-Meares, P., Shanks, T., & Gant, L. (2009). Using the miracle question in community engagement and planning. *Families in Society, 90*(3), 332–335.

Holm, J., & Bowker, J. (Eds.). (1994). *Women in religion.* New York: Pinter.

Holman, A., & Silver, R. (1998). Getting "stuck" in the past: Temporal orientation and coping with trauma. *Journal of Personality and Social Psychology, 74*(5), 1146–1163.

Holtzworth-Munroe, A., & Stuart, G. (1994). Typologies of male batterers: Three subtypes and the differences among them. *Psychological Bulletin, 116*(3), 476–497.

Homans, G. (1958). Social behavior as exchange. *American Journal of Sociology, 63*, 597–606.

Hood, L. (2003). *Immigrant students, urban high schools: The challenge continues.* New York: Carnegie Corporation of New York. Retrieved May 17, 2010, from http://carnegie.org/fileadmin/Media/Publications/PDF/immigrantstudents.pdf.

Horney, K. (1939). *New ways in psychoanalysis.* New York: Norton.

Horney, K. (1967). *Feminine psychology.* New York: Norton.

Hornik, R. (1991). Alternative models of behavior change. In J. Wasserheit, S. Aral, K. Holmes, & P. Hitchcock (Eds.), *Research issues in human behavior and sexually transmitted diseases in the AIDS era* (pp. 201–218). Washington, DC: American Society for Microbiology.

Hornsey, M. J. (2008). Social identity theory and self-categorization theory: A historical review. *Social and Personality Psychology Compass, 2*(1), 204–222.

House, R., Hanges, P., Javidan, M., Dorfman, P., Gupta, V., and Associates (Eds.). (2004). *Culture, leadership, and organizations: The GLOBE study of 62 societies.* Thousand Oaks, CA: Sage.

Houston, J. B., Pfefferbaum, B., Sherman, M., Meison, A., Jeon-Slaughter, H., Brand, M., et al. (2009). Children of deployed National Guard troops: Perceptions of parental deployment to Operation Iraqi Freedom. *Psychiatric Annals, 39*(8), 805–811.

Hsu, S. H., Grow, J., Marlatt, A., Galanter, M., & Kaskutas, L. A. (Eds). (2008). *Research on Alcoholics Anonymous and spirituality in addiction recovery.* New York: Springer Science.

Huber, M. S., Egeren, L., Pierce, S., & Foster-Fishman, P. (2009). GIS applications for community-based research and action: Mapping change in a community-building initiative. *Journal of Prevention & Intervention in the Community, 27*, 5–20.

Hudson, C. (2000). At the edge of chaos: A new paradigm for social work? *Journal of Social Work Education, 36*(2), 215–230.

Hughes, B. (2009). Disability activisms: Social model stalwarts and biological citizens. *Disability & Society, 24*(6), 677–688.

Hughes, S., Williams, B., Molina, L., Bayles, C., Bryant, L., Harris, J., et al. (2005). Characteristics of physical activity programs for older adults: Results of a multisite survey. *Gerontologist, 45*(5), 667–675.

Human Rights Campaign. (2009). *Statewide marriage prohibitions.* Retrieved May 11, 2010, from http://www.hrc.org/documents/marriage_prohibitions.pdf.

Human Rights Campaign. (2010). *Marriage equality & other relationship recognition laws.* Retrieved May 12, 2010, from http://www.hrc.org/statelaws.

Hunler, O. S., & Gencoz, T. (2005). The effect of religiousness on marital satisfaction: Testing the mediator role of marital problem solving between religiousness and marital satisfaction relationship. *Contemporary Family Therapy, 27*(1), 123–136.

Hunter, A., & Riger, S. (1986). The meaning of community in community mental health. *Journal of Community Psychology, 14*, 55–71.

Hunter, J. D. (1994). *Before the shooting begins: Searching for democracy in America's culture wars.* New York: Free Press.

Huntington, S. (1996). *The clash of civilizations and the remaking of world order.* New York: Simon & Schuster.

Hurdle, D. E. (2002). Hawaiian traditional healing: Culturally based interventions for social work practice. *Social Work, 47*(2), 183–192.

Hurdle, S. (2001). "Less is best"—A group-based treatment program for persons with personality disorders. *Social Work With Groups, 23*(4), 71–80.

Hurst, J. (2007). Disability and spirituality in social work practice. *Journal of Social Work in Disability & Rehabilitation, 6*(1/2), 179–194.

Husaini, B., Cummings, S., Kilbourne, B., Roback, H., Sherkat, D., Levine, R., et al. (2004). Group therapy for depressed elderly women. *International Journal of Group Psychotherapy, 54*(3), 295–319.

Hutchison, E. (1987). Use of authority in direct social work practice with mandated clients. *Social Service Review, 61*(4), 581–598.

Hutchison, E. (2007). Community violence. In E. Hutchison, H. Matto, M. Harrigan, L. Charlesworth, & P. Viggiani (Eds.), *Challenges of living: A multidimensional model for social workers* (pp. 71–104). Thousand Oaks, CA: Sage.

Hutchison, E., & Charlesworth, L. (2000). Securing the welfare of children: Policies past, present, and future. *Families in Society, 81*(6), 576–586.

Hutchison, E., Charlesworth, L., Matto, H., Harrigan, M., & Viggiani, P. (2007). Elements of knowing and doing in social work. In E. Hutchison, H. Matto, M. Harrigan, L. Charlesworth, & P. Viggiani, *Challenges of living: A multidimensional working model for social workers* (pp. 13–33). Thousand Oaks, CA: Sage.

Hutchison, E., Matto, H., Harrigan, M., Charlesworth, L., & Viggiani, P. (2007). *Challenges of living: A multidimensional working model for social workers.* Thousand Oaks, CA: Sage.

Huynh-Nhu, L., Ceballo, R., Chao, R., Hill, N., Murry, V., & Pinderhughes, E. E. (2008). Excavating culture: Disentangling ethnic differences from contextual influences in parenting. *Applied Developmental Science, 12*(4), 163–175.

Hyde, C. (2000). The hybrid nonprofit: An examination of feminist social movement organizations. *Journal of Community Practice, 8*(4), 45–67.

Iannello, K. (1992). *Decisions without hierarchy: Feminist interventions in organization theory and practice.* New York: Routledge.

Ignatow, G. (2006). Cultural models of nature and society: Reconsidering environmental attitudes and concern. *Environment and Behavior, 38*(4), 441–461.

Imre, R. (1984). The nature of knowledge in social work. *Social Work, 29,* 41–45.

Ingram, R. E., & Luxton, D. D. (2005). Vulnerability-stress models. In B. L. Hankin & J. R. Z. Abela (Eds.), *Development of psychopathology: A vulnerability-stress perspective* (pp. 32–46). Thousand Oaks, CA: Sage.

Ingstad, B., & Whyte, S. (Eds.). (1995). *Disability and culture.* Berkeley: University of California Press.

International Confederation of Free Trade Unions. (n.d.). *ICFTU: What it is, what it does.* Retrieved May 17, 2010, from http://www.icftu.org/displaydocument.asp?DocType=Overview&Index=990916422&Language=EN.

International Telecommunications Union. (2008). *Global ICT developments.* Retrieved May 17, 2010, from http://www.itu.int/ITU-D/ict/statistics/ict/ index.html.

Internet World Stats. (2010). *Internet usage statistics: The Internet big picture.* Retrieved February 23, 2010, from http://www.internetworldstats.com/stats.htm.

Jackson, J. (2006, October). *Capstone presentation.* Paper presented at the NIH Conference on Understanding and Reducing Health Disparities: Contributions from the Behavioral and Social Sciences, Bethesda, MD.

Jackson, M. A. (2002). Christian womanist spirituality: Implications for social work practice. *Social Thought, 21*(1), 63–76.

Jackson, R. L. (Ed.). (2004). *African American communication & identities: Essential readings.* Thousand Oaks, CA: Sage.

James, R. K., & Gilliland, B. E. (2001). *Crisis intervention strategies* (4th ed.). Pacific Grove, CA: Brooks/Cole.

James, W. (1890). *Principles of psychology.* New York: Holt.

Jancin, B. (2002). Work–family conflict fuels physician burnout. *OB GYN News, 37*(1), 22.

Jandt, F. (2010). *An introduction to intercultural communication: Identities in a global community* (6th ed.). Thousand Oaks, CA: Sage.

Jenkins, R. (Ed.). (1998). *Questions of competence: Culture, classification and intellectual disability.* New York: Cambridge University Press.

Jenkins, W. (2008). *Ecologies of grace: Environmental ethics and Christian theology.* Oxford, UK: Oxford University Press.

Johnson, D. W., & Johnson, F. P. (1994). *Joining together: Group theory and skills* (5th ed.). Boston: Allyn & Bacon.

Johnson, G. R., Jang, S. J., Larsen, D. B., & De Li, S. (2001). Does adolescent religious commitment matter? A re-examination of the effects of religiosity on delinquency. *Journal on Research in Crime and Delinquency, 38*(1), 22–43.

Johnson, H. C. (2001). Neuroscience in social work practice and education. *Journal of Social Work Practice in the Addictions, 1*(3), 81–102.

Johnson, K., Whitbeck, L., & Hoyt, D. (2005). Predictors of social network composition among homeless and runaway adolescents. *Journal of Adolescence, 28*(2), 231–248.

Johnson, M. (Ed.). (1992). *People with disabilities explain it all for you.* Louisville, KY: Advocado Press.

Johnson, M. (1995). Patriarchal terrorism and common couple violence: Two forms of violence against women. *Journal of Marriage and the Family, 57*(2), 283–294.

Johnson, S. K. (1997). Does spirituality have a place in rural social work? *Social Work and Christianity, 24*(1), 58–66.

Johnson, T., & Colucci, P. (2005). Lesbians, gay men, and the family life cycle. In B. Carter & M. McGoldrick (Eds.), *The expanded family life cycle: Individual, family, and social perspectives* (3rd ed., pp. 346–361). Boston: Allyn & Bacon.

Johnstone, B., Yoon, D. P., Rupright, J., & Reid-Arndt, S. (2009). Relationships among spiritual beliefs, religious practices, congregational support and health for individuals with traumatic brain injury. *Brain Injury, 23*(5), 411–419.

Joint United Nations Programme on HIV/AIDS. (2009). *Eight-year trend shows new HIV infections down by 17%—Most progress seen in sub-Saharan Africa.* Retrieved December 4, 2009, from http://www.unaids .org/en/KnowledgeCentre/Resources/FeatureStories/archive/2009/20091124_pr_EpiUpdate.asp.

Jones, S., & Fernyhough, C. (2007). A new look at the neural diathesis-stress model of schizophrenia: The primacy of social-evaluative and uncontrollable situations. *Schizophrenia Bulletin, 33*(5), 1171–1177.

Jones, T. (2005). Mediating intragroup and intergroup conflict. In S. Wheelan (Ed.), *The handbook of group research and practice* (pp. 463–483). Thousand Oaks, CA: Sage.

Jordan, M. (2009). Back to nature. *Therapy Today, 20*(3), 26–28.

Joseph, M. V. (1988). Religion and social work practice. *Social Casework, 69,* 443–452.

Joye, Y. (2007). Architectural lessons from environmental psychology: The case of biophilic architecture. *Review of General Psychology, 11*(4), 305–328.

Jung, C. (1933). *Modern man in search of a soul.* New York: Harcourt, Brace & World.

Jung, C. (1969). *The archetypes and the collective unconscious* (R. F. C. Hull, Trans.). Princeton, NJ: Princeton University Press. (Original work published 1959)

Kagan, J. (2007). *What is emotion? History, measures, and meanings.* New Haven, CT: Yale University Press.

Kahana, B. (1992). Late-life adaptation in the aftermath of extreme stress. In M. Wykel, E. Kahana, & J. Kowal (Eds.), *Stress and health among the elderly* (pp. 5–34). New York: Springer.

Kahn, J., & Pearlin, L. (2006). Financial strain over the life course and health among older adults. *Journal of Health & Social Behavior, 47*(1), 17–31.

Kahn, M., & Scher, S. (2002). Infusing content on the physical environment into the BSW curriculum. *Journal of Baccalaureate Social Work, 7*(2), 1–14.

Kahn, P. (1999). *The human relationship with nature: Development and culture.* Cambridge: MIT Press.

Kahneman, D., & Tversky, A. (1982). The psychology of preferences. *Scientific American, 246,* 160–173.

Kahneman, D., & Tversky, A. (1984). Choices, values, and frames. *American Psychologist, 39,* 341–350.

Kaitz, M., Bar-Haim, Y., Lehrer, M., & Grossman, E. (2004). Adult attachment style and interpersonal distance. *Attachment & Human Development, 6*(3), 285–304.

Kalkhoff, W., & Barnum, C. (2000). The effects of status-organizing and social identity processes on patterns of social influence. *Social Psychology Quarterly, 63,* 95–115.

Kamp Dush, C., & Amato, P. (2005). Consequences of relationship status and quality for subjective well-being. *Journal of Social and Personal Relationship, 22*(5), 607–627.

Kapit, W., Macey, R. I., & Meisami, E. (2000). *The physiology coloring book* (2nd ed.) Cambridge, MA: HarperCollins.

Kaplan, R. (1983). The role of nature in the urban context. In I. Altman & J. F. Wohlwill (Eds.), *Behavior and the natural environment* (pp. 127–161). New York: Plenum.

Kaplan, R., & Kaplan, S. (1989). *The experience of nature: A psychological perspective.* New York: Cambridge University Press.

Kaplan, S. (1995). The restorative benefits of nature: Toward an integrative framework. *Journal of Environmental Psychology, 15,* 169–182.

Karenga, M. (1995). Making the past meaningful: Kwanzaa and the concept of Sankofa. *Reflections: Narratives of Professional Helping, 1*(4), 36–46.

Karger, H., & Stoesz, D. (2006). *American social welfare policy: A pluralist approach* (5th ed.). Boston: Pearson.

Karls, J. M. & O'Keefe, M. (2008). *Person-in-environment system manual* (2nd ed.). Washington, DC: NASW Press.

Kasee, C. R. (1995). Identity, recovery, and religious imperialism: Native American women and the new age. *Women and Therapy: A Feminist Quarterly, 16*(2/3), 83–93.

Katyal, N. (2002). Architecture as crime control. *Yale Law Journal, 111*(5), 1039–1139.

Kawachi, I., & Kennedy, B. (2001). How income inequality affects health: Evidence from research in the United States. In J. Auerbach & B. Krimgold (Eds.), *Income, socioeconomic status, and health: Exploring the relationships* (pp. 16–28). Washington, DC: National Policy Association, Academy for Health Services Research and Health Policy.

Kay, A. (2006). Social capital, the social economy and community development. *Community Development Journal, 41*(2), 160–173.

Kaya, N., & Burgess, B. (2007). Territoriality: Seat preferences in different types of classroom arrangements. *Environment & Behavior, 39*(6), 859–876.

Kaya, N., & Weber, M. (2003). Territorial behavior in residence halls: A cross-cultural study. *Environment and Behavior, 35*(3), 400–414.

Kaye, H. S. (2000). *Computer and Internet use among people with disabilities.* Washington, DC: National Institute on Disability and Rehabilitation Research.

Keane, C. (1991). Socioenvironmental determinants of community formation. *Environment and Behavior, 23*(1), 27–46.

Kearney, A. (2006). Residential development patterns and neighborhood satisfaction: Impacts of density and nearby nature. *Environment and Behavior, 38*(1), 112–139.

Keefe, T. (1996). Meditation and social work treatment. In F. J. Turner (Ed.), *Social work treatment: Interlocking theoretical approaches* (4th ed., pp. 434–460). New York: Free Press.

Kellert, S., & Wilson, E. (Eds.). (1993). *The biophilia hypothesis.* Washington, DC: Island Press.

Kelley, H., & Thibaut, J. (1978). *Interpersonal relations: A theory of interdependence.* New York: Wiley.

Kempes, M. M., Gulickx, M. M. C., van Daalen, H. J. C., Sterck, E. H. M., & Louwerse, A. L. (2008). Social competence is reduced in socially deprived rhesus monkeys. *Journal of Comparative Psychology, 122*(1) 62–67.

Kendler, K. S., Gardner, C., & Prescott. C. (1997). Religion, psychopathology and substance use and misuse: A multimeasure, genetic-epidemiology study. *American Journal of Psychiatry, 154*(3), 322–329.

Kendler, K. S., Liu, X. Q., Gardner, C. O., McCullough, M. E., Larson, D., & Prescott, C. A. (2003). Dimensions of religiosity and their relationship to lifetime psychiatric and substance use disorders. *The American Journal of Psychiatry, 160*(3), 496–503.

Kennedy, S., Kiecolt-Glaser, J. K., & Glaser, R. (1988). Immunological consequences of acute and chronic stressors: Mediating role of interpersonal relationships. *British Journal of Medical Psychology, 61,* 77–85.

Kent, S. (1991). Partitioning space: Cross-cultural factors influencing domestic spatial segmentation. *Environment and Behavior, 23,* 438–473.

Keutzer, C. (1982). Physics and consciousness. *Journal of Humanistic Psychology, 22,* 74–90.

Kher, U. (2008). Outsourcing your heart. In S. Sernau (Ed.), *Contemporary readings in globalization* (pp. 143–145). Thousand Oaks, CA: Pine Forge.

Kidd, S. M. (1996). *The dance of the dissident daughter: A woman's journey from Christian tradition to the sacred feminine.* New York: HarperCollins.

Kilbury, R., Bordieri, J., & Wong, H. (1996). Impact of physical disability and gender on personal space. *Journal of Rehabilitation, 62*(2), 59–61.

Kim, J., Siegel, S., & Patenall, V. (1999). Drug-onset cues as signals: Intraadministration associations and tolerance. *Journal of Experimental Psychology: Animal Behavior Processes, 25*(4), 491–504.

Kimura, H., Nagao, F., Tanaka, Y., Sakai, S., Ohnishi, S., & Okumura, K. (2005). Beneficial effects of the Nishino breathing method on immune activity and stress level. *Journal of Alternative and Complementary Medicine, 11*(2), 285–291.

Kinkade, K. (1973). *A Walden Two experiment: The first five years of Twin Oaks Community.* New York: Morrow.

Kinnunen, U., & Feldt, T. (2004). Economic stress and marital adjustment among couples: Analyses at the dyadic level. *European Journal of Social Psychology, 34*(5), 519–532.

Kirk, S., & Reid, W. (2002). *Science and social work: A critical appraisal.* New York: Columbia University Press.

Kissman, K., & Maurer, L. (2002). East meets West: Therapeutic aspects of spirituality in health, mental health and addiction recovery. *International Social Work, 45*(1), 35–43.

Kivel, P. (1991). Men, spirituality, and violence. *Creation Spirituality, 7*(4), 12–14, 50.

Klapper, B. (2006, September 25). Swiss voters toughen asylum, immigration laws. *The Washington Post,* p. A16.

Klaw, E., & Humphreys, K. (2004). The role of peer-led mutual help groups in promoting health and well-being. *Handbook of group counseling and psychotherapy* (pp. 630–640). Thousand Oaks, CA: Sage.

Kline, G., Stanley, S., Markman, H., Olmos-Gallo, P. A., Peters, M., Whitton, S., et al. (2004). Timing is everything: Pre-engagement cohabitation and increased risk for poor marital outcomes. *Journal of Family Psychology, 18*(2), 311–318.

Knudsen, E. I. (2004). Sensitive periods in the development of the brain and behavior. *Journal of Cognitive Neuroscience, 16*(8), 1412–1425.

Kobayashi, M., & Miura, K. (2000). Natural disaster and restoration housings. In S. Wapner, J. Demick, T. Yamamoto, & H. Minami (Eds.), *Theoretical perspectives in environment-behavior research: Underlying assumptions, research problems, and methodologies* (pp. 39–49). New York: Kluwer Academic.

Koenig, H. G. (1999). *The healing power of faith: Science explores medicine's last great frontier.* New York: Simon & Schuster.

Koenig, H. G. (2001a). Religion and medicine IV: Religion, physical health, and clinical implications. *International Journal of Psychiatry in Medicine, 31*(3), 321–336.

Koenig, H. G. (2001b). Religion and mental health II: Religion, mental health, and related behaviors. *International Journal of Psychiatry in Medicine, 31*(10), 97–109.

Koenig, H. G. (2005). *Faith and mental health: Religious sources for healing.* Philadelphia: Templeton Foundation Press.

Koenig, H. G., Larson, D. B., & Larson, S. S. (2001). Religion and coping with serious medical illness. *Annals of Pharmacotherapy, 35*(3), 352–359.

Koenig, H. G., McCullough, M. E., & Larson, D. B. (2000). *Handbook of religion and health.* New York: Oxford University Press.

Kogler Hill, S. (2007). Team leadership. In P. Northouse (Ed.), *Leadership: Theory and practice* (4th ed., pp. 207–236). Thousand Oaks, CA: Sage.

Kohlberg, L. (1969). *Stages in the development of moral thought and action.* New York: Holt, Rinehart and Winston.

Kohli, M., & Albertini, M. (2009). Childlessness and intergenerational transfers: What is at stake? *Ageing & Society, 29,* 1171–1183.

Kondrat, M. E. (1999). Who is the "self" in self-aware: Professional self-awareness from a critical theory perspective. *Social Service Review, 73*(4), 451–477.

Koopmans, R. (2004). Political. Opportunity. Structure: Some splitting to balance the lumping. In J. Goodwin & J. Jasper (Eds.), *Rethinking social movements: Structure, meaning, and emotion* (pp. 61–73). Lanham, MD: Rowman & Littlefield.

Kornblatt, S., Cheng, S., & Chan, S. (2002). Best practice: The On Lok model of geriatric interdisciplinary team care. *Journal of Gerontological Social Work, 4*(1/2), 15–22.

Kosmin, B. A, Mayer, E., & Keysar, A. (2001). *American Religious Identification Survey 2001.* Retrieved April 10, 2010, from http://www.gc.cuny.edu/faculty/research_briefs/aris.pdf.

Kossek, E., Lobel, S., & Brown, J. (2006). Human resource strategies to manage workforce diversity: Examining "the business case." In A. Konrad & J. Pringle (Eds.), *Handbook of workplace diversity* (Vol. 1, pp. 53–74). Thousand Oaks, CA: Sage.

Kottak, C. P. (1994). *Anthropology: The exploration of human diversity.* New York: McGraw-Hill.

Kottak, C. P. (1996). *Mirror for humanity: A concise introduction to cultural anthropology.* New York: McGraw-Hill.

Kottak, C. P. (2008). *Anthropology: The exploration of human diversity* (12th ed.). Boston: McGraw-Hill.

Kottak, C. P., & Kozaitis, K. (2008). *On being different: Diversity and multiculturalism in the North American mainstream.* Boston: McGraw-Hill.

Kottler, J., & Englar-Carlson, M. (2010). *Learning group leadership: An experiential approach.* Thousand Oaks, CA: Sage.

Kozol, J. (2000). *Ordinary resurrections: Children in the years of hope.* New York: Harper Perennial.

Kozol, J. (2005). *The shame of the nation: The restoration of apartheid schooling in America.* New York: Crown.

Kraemer, G. (1992). A psychobiological theory of attachment. *Behavioral and Brain Sciences, 15*(3), 493–511.

Kravetz, D. (2004). *Tales from the trenches: Politics and practice in feminist service organizations.* Lanham, MD: University Press of America.

Kriesi, H. (1996). The organizational structure of new social movements in a political context. In D. McAdam, J. McCarthy, & M. Zald (Eds.), *Comparative perspectives on social movements* (pp. 152–184). New York: Cambridge University Press.

Krill, D. (1986). Existential social work. In F. Turner (Ed.), *Social work treatment: Interlocking theoretical approaches* (pp. 181–217). New York: Free Press.

Krill, D. F. (1996). Existential social work. In F. J. Turner (Ed.), *Social work treatment* (4th ed., pp. 250–281). New York: Free Press.

Kroeber, A., & Kluckhohn, C. (1963). *Culture: A critical review of concepts and definitions.* New York: Vintage.

Kroeber, A., & Kluckhohn, C. (1978). *Culture: A critical review of concepts and definitions.* Cambridge, MA: Peabody Museum. (Original work published 1952)

Kroll, B. (2004). Living with an elephant: Growing up with parental substance misuse. *Child and Family Social Work, 9,* 129–140.

Kropf, N., & Malone, D. M. (2004). Interdisciplinary practice in developmental disabilities. *Journal of Social Work in Disability & Rehabilitation, 3*(1), 21–36.

Kruel, M. (1995). Women's spirituality and healing in Germany. *Women and Therapy: A Feminist Quarterly, 16*(2/3), 135–147.

Kunkel, A., Hummert, M. L., & Dennis, M. R. (2006). Social learning theory: Modeling and communication in the family context. In D. Braithwaite & L. A. Baxter (Eds.), *Engaging theories in family communication: Multiple perspectives* (pp. 250–275). Thousand Oaks, CA: Sage.

Kuo, F., Bacaicoa, M., & Sullivan, W. (1998). Transforming innercity landscapes: Trees, sense of safety, and preference. *Environment and Behavior, 30,* 28–59.

Kuo, F., & Faber Taylor, A. (2004). A potential treatment for attention deficit/hyperactivity disorder: Evidence from a national study. *American Journal of Public Health, 94*(9), 1580–1586.

Kupritz, V. (2003). Accommodating privacy to facilitate new ways of working. *Journal of Architectural and Planning Research, 20*(2), 122–135.

Kurdek, L. (2004). Are gay and lesbian cohabiting couples really different from heterosexual married couples? *Journal of Marriage and Family, 60,* 553–568.

Kurdek, L. (2006). Differences between partners from heterosexual, gay, and lesbian cohabiting couples. *Journal of Marriage and Family, 68,* 509–528.

Kurtz, L. (2007). *Gods in the global village: The world's religions in sociological perspective* (2nd ed.). Thousand Oaks, CA: Pine Forge.

Kurtz, S. (2002). *Workplace justice: Organizing multi-identity movements.* Minneapolis: University of Minnesota Press.

Kvarfordt, C., & Sheridan, M. J. (2007). The role of religion and spirituality in working with children and adolescents: Results of a national survey. *Social Thought, 26*(3), 1–23.

Kyle, G., Graefe, A., Manning, R., & Bacon, J. (2004). Effect of activity involvement and place attachment on recreationists' perceptions of setting density. *Journal of Leisure Research, 36*(2), 209–231.

Labor Law Center. (2009). *Federal minimum wage increase for 2007, 2008, & 2009.* Retrieved October 6 26, 2009, from http://www.laborlawcenter.com/t-federal-minimum-wage.aspx.

LaDue, R. A. (1994). Coyote returns: Twenty sweats does not an Indian expert make. *Women & Therapy, 15*(1), 93–111.

Laing, R. D. (1967). *The politics of experience.* New York: Ballantine.

Laing, R. D. (1969). *The politics of the family.* New York: Pantheon.

Laird, J. (1994). Changing women's narratives: Taking back the discourse. In L. Davis (Ed.), *Building on women's strengths: A social work agenda for the twenty-first century* (pp. 179–210). New York: Haworth.

Lajoie, D. H., & Shapiro, S. I. (1992). Definitions of transpersonal psychology: The first twenty-three years. *Journal of Transpersonal Psychology, 4,* 79–98.

Lakoff, G. (2004). *Don't think of an elephant! Know your values and frame the debate: The essential guide for progressives.* White River Junction, VT: Chelsea Green.

Lakoff, G. (2006). *Whose freedom? The battle over America's most important ideas.* New York: Farrar, Straus & Giroux.

Lane, C. (2007). *Shyness: How normal behavior became a sickness.* New Haven, CT: Yale University Press.

Langer, E., Fiske, S., Taylor, S., & Chanowitz, B. (1976). Stigma, staring, and discomfort: A novel-stimulus hypothesis. *Journal of Experimental Social Psychology, 12,* 451–463.

Lantz, J., & Walsh, J. (2007). *Short-term existential intervention in clinical practice.* Chicago: Lyceum.

Larson, C., & LaFasto, F. (1989). *Teamwork: What must go right/what can go wrong.* Newbury Park, CA: Sage.

Lau, J. T., Wang, Q., Cheng, Y. Kim, J., Yang, X., & Tsui, H. (2008). Infertility-related perceptions and responses and their associations with quality of life among rural Chinese infertile couples. *Journal of Sexual and Marital Therapy, 34,* 248–267.

Lau, J. Y. F., Eley, T. C., & Stevenson, J. (2006). Examining the state–trait anxiety relationship: A behavioural genetic approach. *Journal of Abnormal Child Psychology, 34*(1), 19–27.

Lauer, R. (1981). *Temporal man: The meaning and uses of social time.* New York: Praeger.

Lawrence, C., & Andrews, K. (2004). The influence of perceived prison crowding on male inmates' perception of aggressive events. *Aggressive Behavior, 30*(4), 273–283.

Lazarus, R. S. (1999). *Stress and emotion: A new synthesis.* New York: Springer.

Lazarus, R. S. (2001). Relational meaning and discrete emotions. In K. R. Scherer, A. Schorr, & T. Johnstone (Eds.), *Appraisal processes in emotion: Theory, methods, research* (pp. 37–67). New York: Oxford University Press.

Lazarus, R. S. (2007). Stress and emotion: A new synthesis. In A. Monat, R. S. Lazarus, & G. Reevy (Eds.), *The Praeger handbook on stress and coping* (Vol. 1, pp. 33–51). Westport, CT: Praeger/Greenwood.

LeCroy, C. W. (1992). *Case studies in social work practice.* Belmont, CA: Wadsworth.

LeDoux, J. E., & Phelps, E. A. (2008). Emotional networks in the brain. In M. Lewis, J. M. Havilland-Jones, & L. F. Barrett (Eds.), *Handbook of emotions* (3rd ed., pp. 159–179). New York: Guilford Press.

Lee, B., & Campbell, K. (1999). Neighbor networks of Black and White Americans. In B. Wellman (Ed.), *Networks in the global village* (pp. 119–146). Boulder, CO: Westview Press.

Lee, J. (2001). *The empowerment approach to social work practice: Building the beloved community.* New York: Columbia University Press.

Lee, J. (2006). *Tracking achievement gaps and assessing the impact of NCLB on the gaps: An in-depth look into national and state reading and math outcome trends.* Cambridge, MA: The Civil Rights Project at Harvard University. Retrieved May 17, 2010, from http://www.publiceducation .org/nclb_main/Reports CRP.asp.

Lee, M. (2008). A small act of creativity: Fostering creativity in clinical social work practice. *Families in Society, 89*(1), 19–31.

Lee, M. Y., Ng, S., Leung, P. P. Y., & Chan, C. L. W. (2009). *Integrative body–mind–spirit social work: An empirically based approach to assessment and treatment.* New York: Oxford University Press.

Leeder, E. (2004). *The family in global perspective: A gendered journey.* Thousand Oaks, CA: Sage.

Leiby, J. (1985). Moral foundations of social welfare and social work: A historical view. *Social Work, 30,* 323–330.

Lengermann, P., & Niebrugge-Brantley, G. (2007). Contemporary feminist theories. In G. Ritzer (Ed.), *Contemporary sociological theory and its classical roots* (2nd ed., pp. 185–214). Boston: McGraw-Hill.

Lenski, G. (1966). *Power and privilege.* New York: McGraw-Hill.

Leonard, K., & Eiden, R. (2007). Marital and family processes in the context of alcohol use and alcohol disorders. *Annual Review of Clinical Psychology, 3,* 285–310.

LePoire, B. (2006). *Family communication: Nurturing and control in a changing world.* Thousand Oaks, CA: Sage.

Lesser, J., O'Neill, M., Burke, K., Scanlon, P., Hollis, K., & Miller, R. (2004). Women supporting women: A mutual aid group fosters new connections among women in midlife. *Social Work With Groups, 27*(1), 75–88.

Levi, M., Cook, K., O'Brien, J., & Faye, H. (1990). The limits of rationality. In K. Cook & M. Levi (Eds.), *The limits of rationality* (pp. 1–16). Chicago: University of Chicago Press.

Levin, J. D. (1992). *Theories of the self.* Washington, DC: Hemisphere.

Levine, B. (1991). *Group psychotherapy.* Prospect Heights, IL: Waveland Press.

Levine, R. (2006). A geography of time. In D. Newman & J. O'Brien (Eds.), *Sociology: Exploring the architecture of everyday life: Readings* (6th ed., pp. 73–83). Thousand Oaks, CA: Pine Forge.

Levine, S. (1999). Children's cognition as the foundation of spirituality. *International Journal of Children's Spirituality, 4*(2), 121–140.

Levinson, D. (1996). *The seasons of a woman's life.* New York: Knopf.

Lewandowski, C. A., & Canda, E. R. (1995). A typological model for the assessment of religious groups. *Social Thought, 18*(1), 17–38.

Lewis, C. (1979). Healing in the urban environment: A person/plant viewpoint. *Journal of American Planning Association, 45,* 330–338.

Lewis, C. (1996). *Green nature/human nature: The meaning of plants in our lives.* Urbana: University of Illinois Press.

Li, J., Karakowsky, L., & Siegel, J. (1999). The effects of proportional representation on intragroup behavior in mixed-race decision-making groups. *Small Group Research, 30*(3), 259–279.

Lichter, D., & Qian, Z. (2008). Serial cohabitation and the marital life course. *Journal of Marriage and Family, 70,* 861–878.

Lightfoot, C., Lalonde, C., & Chandler, M. (Eds.). (2004). *Changing conceptions of psychological life.* Mahwah, NJ: Erlbaum.

Limb, G. E., & Hodge, D. R. (2008). Developing spiritual competency with Native Americans: Promoting wellness through balance and harmony. *Families in Society: The Journal of Contemporary Social Services, 89*(4), 615–622.

Lincoln, Y., & Guba, E. (1985). *Naturalistic inquiry.* Beverly Hills, CA: Sage.

Lindsey, D. (2004). *The welfare of children* (2nd ed.). New York: Oxford.

Lindsey, E. W., Kurtz, P. D., Jarvis, S., Williams, N. R., & Nackerud, L. (2000). How runaway and homeless youth navigate troubled waters: Personal strengths and resources. *Clinical and Adolescent Social Work Journal, 17*(2), 115–140.

Link, A. L. (1997). *Group work with elders: 50 therapeutic exercises for reminiscence, validation, and remotivation.* Sarasota, FL: Professional Resource Press.

Linver, M., Brooks-Gunn, J., & Kohen, D. (2002). Family processes as pathways from income to young children's development. *Developmental Psychology, 38,* 719–734.

Lippa, R. A. (2005). *Gender, nature, and nurture* (2nd ed.). Mahwah, NJ: Erlbaum.

Living Wage Resource Center. (2006). *The living wage resource center: Introduction.* Retrieved May 17, 2010, from http://highboldtage.wordpress.com/2008/03/12/acorns-living-wage-resource-center/.

Lloyd, S., Few, A., & Allen, K. (2009). Preface. In S. Lloyd, A. Few, & K. Allen (Eds.), *Handbook of feminist family studies.* Thousand Oaks, CA: Sage.

Logan, G. (2000). Information-processing theories. In A. E. Kazdi (Ed.), *Encyclopedia of psychology* (Vol. 4, pp. 294–297). Washington, DC: American Psychological Association.

Logan, S. L. (1997). Meditation as a tool that links the personal and the professional. *Reflections: Narratives of Professional Helping, 3*(1), 38–44.

Logan, S. L. (Ed.). (2001). *The Black family: Strengths, self-help, and positive change* (2nd ed.). Boulder, CO: Westview Press.

Lohmann, R., & McNutt, J. (2005). Practice in the electronic community. In M. Weil (Ed.), *The handbook of community practice* (pp. 636–646). Thousand Oaks, CA: Sage.

Lopez, R. (2004). Urban sprawl and risk for being overweight or obese. *Research and Practice, 94*(9), 1574–1579.

Lopez, R., & Hynes, P. (2006). Obesity, physical activity, and the urban environment: Public health research needs. *Environmental Health: A Global Access Science Source, 5,* 25. Retrieved October 15, 2009, from http://www.ehjournal.net/content/5/1/25.

Lovaglia, M. J. (1995). Power and status: Exchange, attribution, and expectation states. *Small Group Research, 26,* 400–426.

Lovaglia, M., Mannix, E., Samuelson, C., Sell, J., & Wilson, R. (2005). Conflict, power, and status in groups. In M. Poole & A. Hollingshead (Eds.), *Theories of small groups: Interdisciplinary perspectives* (pp. 63–97). Thousand Oaks, CA: Sage.

Low, S., & Altman, I. (1992). Place attachment: A conceptual inquiry. In I. Altman & S. Low (Eds.), *Place attachment* (pp. 1–12). New York: Plenum.

Lowe, J. (1997). A social-health model: A paradigm for social work in health care. In M. Reisch & E. Gambrill (Eds.), *Social work in the 21st century* (pp. 209–218). Thousand Oaks, CA: Pine Forge.

Lowenberg, F. M. (1988). *Religion and social work practice in contemporary American society.* New York: Columbia University Press.

Lownsdale, S. (1997). Faith development across the lifespan: Fowler's integrative work. *Journal of Psychology and Theology, 25,* 49–63.

Lubin, H., & Johnson, D. R. (1998). Healing ceremonies. *Family Networker, 22*(5), 38–39, 64–67.

Luhmann, N. (1987). Modern systems theory and the theory of society. In V. Meja, D. Misgeld, & N. Stehr (Eds.), *Modern German sociology* (pp. 173–186). New York: Columbia University Press.

Lum, D. (2007). *Culturally competent practice: A framework for understanding diverse groups and justice issues* (3rd ed.). Belmont, CA: Thomson.

Lupien, S. J., King, S., Meaney, M. J., & McEwen, B. S. (2000). Child's stress hormone levels correlate with mother's socioeconomic status and depressive state. *Biological Psychiatry, 48*(10), 976–980.

Lutz, A., Dunne, J. D., & Davidson, R. J. (2007). Meditation and the neuroscience of consciousness. In P. Zelazo, M. Moscovitch, & E. Thompson (Eds.), *The Cambridge handbook of consciousness* (pp. 499–552). Cambridge, UK: Cambridge University Press.

Lynn, L. (2002). Social services and the state: The public appropriation of private charity. *Social Service Review, 76*(1), 58–83.

Lynn, M. (2006). Discourses of community: Challenges for social work. *International Journal of Social Welfare, 15,* 110–120.

Lyon, L. (1987). *The community in urban society.* Philadelphia: Temple University Press.

Lyotard, J. (1984). *The postmodern condition.* Minneapolis: University of Minnesota Press.

MacArthur Network on Mind–Body Interactions. (2001). *Vital connections: Science of mind–body interactions: A report on the interdisciplinary conference held at NIH, March 26–28, 2001.* Chicago: Author.

MacDonald, C., & Mikes-Liu, K. (2009). Is there a place for biopsychosocial formulation in a systemic practice? *Australian & New Zealand Journal of Family Therapy, 30*(4), 269–283.

MacDonald, D. (2000). Spirituality: Description, measurement, and relation to the five factor model of personality. *Journal of Personality, 68,* 157–197.

MacKinley, E. (Ed.). (2006). *Aging, spirituality and palliative care.* Binghamton, MA: Haworth Press.

MacNair, R., Fowler, L., & Harris, J. (2000). The diversity functions of organizations that confront oppression: The evolution of three social movements. *Journal of Community Practice, 7*(2), 71–88.

Mader, S. M. (2003). *Biology* (8th ed). New York: McGraw-Hill.

Madigan, S., Moran, G., & Pederson, D. R. (2006). Unresolved states of mind, disorganized attachment relationships, and disrupted interactions of adolescent mothers and their infants. *Developmental Psychology, 42*(2), 293–304.

Magai, C. (2001). Emotions over the life span. In J. E. Birren & K. W. Schale (Eds.), *Handbook of the psychology of aging* (5th ed., pp. 399–426). San Diego, CA: Academic Press.

Mahoney, M. (1991). *Human change processes: The scientific foundations of psychotherapy.* New York: Basic Books.

Maidenberg, M. P., & Golick, T. (2001). Developing or enhancing interdisciplinary programs: A model for teaching collaboration. *Professional Development: The International Journal of Continuing Social Work, 4*(2), 15–24.

Major branches of religions ranked by number of adherents. (2005). Retrieved May 20, 2007, from http://www.adherents.com/ adh _branches.html

Major religions of the world ranked by numbers of adherents. (2005). Retrieved July 10, 2006, from http://www.adherents .com/Religions_By_Adherents.html.

Mak, W., Cheung, R., & Law, L. (2009). Sense of community in Hong Kong: Relations with community-level characteristics and residents' well-being. *American Journal of Community Psychology, 44,* 80–92.

Malanga, S. (2003). How the "living wage" sneaks socialism into cities. *City Journal, Winter,* 1–8 [Electronic version]. Retrieved May 17, 2010, from http://www.city-journal.org/ html/13_1_how_the_living_wage.html.

Maller, C., Townsend, M., Pryor, A., Brown, P., & St. Leger, L. (2005). Healthy nature healthy people: "Contact with nature" as an upstream health promotion intervention for populations. *Health Promotion International, 21*(1), 45–54.

Mallon, B., & Houtstra, T. (2007). Telephone technology in social work group treatment. *Health & Social Work, 32,* 139–141.

Malti, T., Gasser, L., & Buchmann, M. (2009). Aggressive and prosocial children's emotion attributions and moral reasoning. *Aggressive Behavior, 35*(1), 90–102.

Mann, M. (1986). *The sources of social power* (Vol. 1). New York: Cambridge University Press.

Mannes, M., Roehlkepartain, & Benson, P. (2005). Unleashing the power of community to strengthen the well-being of children, youth, and families: An asset-building approach. *Child Welfare, 84*(2), 233–250.

Manning, M., Cornelius, L., & Okundaye, J. (2004). Empowering African Americans through social work practice: Integrating an Afrocentric perspective, ego psychology, and spirituality. *Families in Society: The Journal of Contemporary Social Services, 85*(2), 229–235.

Manzo, L., & Perkins, S. (2006). Finding common ground: The importance of place attachment to community participation and planning. *Journal of Planning Literature, 20*(4), 335–350.

Mapp, S. (2008). *Human rights and social justice in a global perspective: An introduction to international social work.* New York: Oxford University Press.

March, J., & Simon, H. (1958). *Organizations.* New York: Wiley.

Marecek, J., Kimmel, E. B., Crawford, M., & Hare-Mustin, R. T. (2003). Psychology of women and gender. In D. K. Freedheim (Ed.), *Handbook of psychology: History of psychology* (Vol. 1, pp. 249–268). Hoboken, NJ: Wiley.

Margolin, A., Beitel, M., Schuman-Olivier, Z., & Avants, S. K. (2006). A controlled study of a spirituality-focused intervention for increasing motivation for HIV prevention among drug users. *AIDS Education and Prevention, 18*(4), 311–322.

Marino, R, Weinman, M. L., & Soudelier, K. (2001). Social work intervention and failure to thrive in infants and children. *Health and Social Work, 26*(2), 90–97.

Markovitzky, G., & Mosek, A. (2005). The role of symbolic resources in coping with immigration. *Journal of Ethnic & Cultural Diversity in Social Work, 14*(1/2), 145–158.

Markovsky, B. (2005). Network exchange theory. In G. Ritzer (Ed.), *Encyclopedia of social theory* (pp. 530–534). Thousand Oaks, CA: Sage.

Markowitz, M. (1997). HIV infection, An oncologic model of pathogenesis and treatment. *Oncologist, 2*(3), 187.

Markus, H., & Kitayama, S. (2003). Models of agency: Sociocultural diversity in the construction of action. In G. Berman & J. Berman (Eds.), *Cross-cultural differences in perspectives on the self* (pp. 2–57). Lincoln: University of Nebraska Press.

Markus, H., & Kitayama, S. (2009). Culture and the self: Implications for cognition, emotion, and motivation. In P. Smith & D. Best (Eds.), *Cross-cultural psychology.* (Vol. 1, pp. 265–320). Thousand Oaks, CA: Sage.

Marti, I., Etzion, D., & Leca, B. (2008). Theoretical approaches for studying corporations, democracy, and the public good. *Journal of Management Inquiry, 17,* 148–151.

Martin, E. P., & Martin, J. M. (2002). *Spirituality and the Black helping tradition in social work.* Washington, DC: NASW Press.

Martin, J., & Sherman, M. (2010). The impact of military duty and military life on individuals and families. In S. Price, C. Price, & P. McKenry (Eds.), *Families & Change: Coping with stressful events and transitions* (4th ed., pp. 381–397). Thousand Oaks, CA: Sage.

Martin, J. G. (1993). Why women need a feminist spirituality. *Women's Studies Quarterly, 1,* 106–120.

Martin, M., Giannandrea, P., Rogers, B., & Johnson, J. (1996). Beginning steps to recovery: A challenge to the "Come Back When You're Ready" approach. *Alcoholism Treatment Quarterly, 14*(2), 45–57.

Martin, P. Y., & O'Connor, G. G. (1989). *The social environment: Open systems applications.* New York: Longman.

Martinez-Brawley, E. (2000). *Close to home: Human services and the small community.* Washington, DC: NASW Press.

Marty, M. (1980). Social service: Godly and godless. *Social Service Review, 54,* 463–481.

Martz, E. (2004). Do reactions of adaptation to disability influence the fluctuation of future time orientation among individuals with spinal cord injuries? *Rehabilitation Counseling Bulletin, 47*(2), 86–95.

Martz, M. (2009, June 18). Internet access widespread in Va. *Richmond Times-Dispatch,* p. B5.

Marx, G., & McAdam, D. (1994). *Collective behavior and social movements: Process and structure.* Englewood Cliffs, NJ: Prentice Hall.

Marx, K. (1967). *Capital: A critique of political economy* (S. Moore & E. Aveling, Trans; Vol. 1). New York: International. (Original work published 1887)

Maslach, C., & Jackson, S. (1981). *Maslach Burnout Inventory: Research edition.* Palo Alto, CA: Consulting Psychologists Press.

Maslach, C., Schaufeli, W., & Leiter, M. (2001). Job burnout. *Annual Review of Psychology, 52,* 397–422.

Maslow, A. (1954). *Motivation and personality.* New York: Harper.

Maslow, A. (1962). *Toward a psychology of being.* New York: Van Nostrand.

Maslow, A. (1971). *Farther reaches of human nature.* New York: Viking.

Mason, M., Skolnick, A., & Sugarman, S. (Eds.). (2003). *All our families: New policies for a new century: A report of the Berkeley family forum.* New York : Oxford University Press.

Mathambo, V., & Gibbs, A. (2009). Extended family childcare arrangements in a context of AIDS: Collapse or adaptation? *AIDS Care, 21,* 22–27.

Matheson, L. (1996). Valuing spirituality among Native American populations. *Counseling and Values, 41,* 51–58.

Matsumoto, D. (2007). Culture, context, and behavior. *Journal of Personality, 75*(6), *1285–1320.*

Mattaini, M. (1997). *Clinical practice with individuals.* Washington, DC: NASW Press.

Matthews, D. A., McCullough, M. E., Larson, D. B., Koenig, H. G., Swyers, J. P., & Milano, M. G. (1998). Religious commitment and health status: A review of the research and implications for family medicine. *Archives of Family Medicine, 7*(2), 118–124.

Matto, H., Berry-Edwards, J., Hutchison, E. D., Bryant, S. A., & Waldbillig, A. (2006). An exploratory study on multiple intelligences and social work education. *Journal of Social Work Education, 42*(2), 405–416.

Maturana, H. (1988). Reality: The search for objectivity or the question for a compelling argument. *Irish Journal of Psychology, 9,* 25–82.

Maxwell, L. (2003). Home and school density effects on elementary school children: The role of spatial density. *Environment and Behavior, 35*(4), 566–578.

Mayo, E. (1933). *The human problems of an industrial civilization.* New York: Macmillan.

Mayo, K. R. (2009). *Creativity, spirituality, and mental health: Exploring connections.* Surrey, UK: Ashgate.

McAdam, D. (1982). *Political process and the development of Black insurgency, 1930–1970.* Chicago: University of Chicago Press.

McAdam, D. (1996a). Conceptual origins, current problems, future directions. In D. McAdam, J. McCarthy, & M. Zald (Eds.), *Comparative perspectives on social movements* (pp. 23–40). New York: Cambridge University Press.

McAdam, D. (1996b). The framing function of movement tactics: Strategic dramaturgy in the American civil rights movement. In D. McAdam, J. McCarthy, & M. Zald (Eds.), *Comparative perspectives on social movements* (pp. 338–355). New York: Cambridge University Press.

McAdam, D., McCarthy, J., & Zald, M. (1996). Introduction: Opportunities, mobilizing structures, and framing processes: Toward a synthetic, comparative perspective on social movements. In D. McAdam, J. McCarthy, & M. Zald (Eds.), *Comparative perspectives on social movements* (pp. 1–20). New York: Cambridge University Press.

McAvoy, M. (1999). *The profession of ignorance: With constant reference to Socrates.* Lanham, NY: University Press of America.

McBee, L., Westreich, L., & Likourezos, A. (2004). A psychoeducational relaxation group for pain and stress management in the nursing home. *Journal of Social Work in Long-Term Care, 3*(1), 15–28.

McCarroll, J., Ursano, R., Fan, Z., & Newby, J. (2004). Patterns of mutual and nonmutual spouse abuse in the U.S. Army (1998–2002). *Violence and Victims, 19*(4), 453–468.

McCarthy, J., & Zald, M. (1977). Resource mobilization in social movements: A partial theory. *American Journal of Sociology, 82,* 1212–1239.

McCleod, P., & Kettner-Polley, R. (2005). Psychodynamic perspectives on small groups. In M. Poole & A. Hollingshead (Eds.), *Theories of small groups: Interdisciplinary perspectives* (pp. 63–97). Thousand Oaks, CA: Sage.

McCreary, L., & Dancy, B. (2004). Dimensions of family functioning: Perspectives on low-income African American single-parent families. *Journal of Marriage and Family, 66,* 690–701.

McCubbin, H. I., & Figley, C. R. (1983). *Stress and the family, Vol. 1: Coping with normative transitions.* New York: Brunner/Mazel.

McCubbin, H. I., & Patterson, J. M. (1983). The family stress process: The double ABCX model of adjustment and adaptation. In H. I. McCubbin, M. B. Sussman, & J. M. Patterson (Eds.), *Social stress and the family: Advances and developments in family stress theory and research* (pp. 7–37). New York: Haworth.

McDermott, M. L. (1997). Voting cues in low-information elections: Candidate gender as a social information variable in contemporary United States elections. *American Journal of Political Science, 41*(1), 270–283.

McFague, S. (2001). *Life abundant: Rethinking theology and economy for a planet in peril.* Minneapolis, MN: Fortress Press.

McGregor, D. (1960). *The human side of enterprise.* New York: McGraw-Hill.

McHale, S., Updegraff, K., Ji-Yeon, K., & Cansler, E. (2009). Cultural orientations, daily activities, and adjustment in Mexican American youth. *Journal of Youth and Adolescence, 38*(5), 627–641.

McIntosh, P. (2007). White privilege: Unpacking the invisible knapsack. In P. Rothenberg (Ed.), *Race, class, and gender in the United States* (6th ed., pp. 163–168). New York: Worth.

McKee-Ryan, F., Song, Z., Wanberg, C., & Kinicki, A. (2005). Psychological and physical well–being during unemployment: A meta-analytic study. *Journal of Applied Psychology, 90*(1), 53–76.

McKnight, P., Snyder, C., & Lopez, S. (2007). Western perspectives on positive psychology. In C. Snyder & S. Lopez, *Positive psychology: The scientific and practical explorations of human strengths* (pp. 23–35). Thousand Oaks, CA: Sage.

McManus, I., Winder, B., & Gordon, D. (2002). The causal links between stress and burnout in a longitudinal study of UK doctors. *Lancet, 359*(9323), 2089–2090.

McMichael, P. (2004). *Development and social change: A global perspective* (3rd ed.). Thousand Oaks, CA: Pine Forge.

McMichael, P. (2008). *Development and social change: A global perspective* (4th ed.). Thousand Oaks, CA: Pine Forge.

McMillan, D. (1996). Sense of community. *Journal of Community Psychology, 24,* 315–325.

McMillan, D., & Chavis, D. (1986). Sense of community: A definition and theory. *Journal of Community Psychology, 14,* 6–23.

McNeill, J. J. (1995). *Freedom, glorious freedom: The spiritual journey to the fullness of life for gays, lesbians, and everybody else.* Boston: Beacon Press.

McPherson, M., Smith-Lovin, L., & Brashears, M. (2006). Social isolation in America: Changes in core discussion networks over two decades. *American Sociological Review, 71*(3), 353–375.

McWhorter, J. (2000). *Losing the race: Self-sabotage in Black America.* New York: Free Press.

Mead, G. H. (1934). *Mind, self, and society.* Chicago: University of Chicago Press.

Mead, G. H. (1959). *The philosophy of the present.* LaSalle, IL: Open Court.

Mead, M. (1961). *Coming of age in Samoa.* New York: Morrow Quill. (Original work published 1928)

Mead, M. (1968). *Growing up in New Guinea: A comparative study of primitive education.* New York: Dell. (Original work published 1930)

Mead, M. (1950). *Sex and temperament in three primitive societies.* New York: New American Library. (Original work published 1935)

Mederos, R., & Perilla, J. (2003). *Community connections: Men, gender, and violence.* Retrieved May 17, 2010, from http://www.melissainstitute.org/documents/eighth/men_gender_violence.pdf.

Meinert, R. G., Pardeck, J. T., & Murphy, J. W. (Eds.). (1998). *Postmodernism, religion, and the future of social work.* Binghamton, NY: Haworth Press.

Meisenhelder, J. B., & Marcum, J. P. (2009). Terrorism, post-traumatic stress, coping strategies, and spiritual outcomes. *Journal of Religion and Health, 48*(1), 46–57.

Melchior, A., & Telle, K. (2001). Global income distribution 1965–98: Convergence and marginalization. *Forum for Development Studies, 1,* 75–98.

Mellor, M. J., & Lindeman, D. (1998). The role of the social worker in interdisciplinary geriatric teams. *Journal of Gerontological Social Work, 30*(3/4), 3–7.

Melton, J. G. (1993). *Encyclopedia of American religion.* Detroit, MI: Gale Research.

Memmi, D. (2006). The nature of virtual communities. *AI & Society: Journal of Knowledge, Culture and Communication, 20,* 288–300.

Menezes, P., Scazufca, M., Rodrigues, L., & Mann, A. (2000). Household crowding and compliance with outpatient treatment in patients with non-affective functional psychoses. *Social Psychiatry and Psychiatric Epidemiology, 35*(3), 116–120.

Messinger, L. (2004). Comprehensive community initiatives: A rural perspective. *Social Work, 49*(4), 529–624.

Meyer, C. (1976). *Social work practice* (2nd ed.). New York: Free Press.

Meyer, C. (Ed.). (1983). *Clinical social work in an eco-systems perspective.* New York: Columbia University Press.

Meyer, C. (1993). *Assessment in social work practice.* New York: Columbia University Press.

Meyer, D. (2004). Tending the vineyard: Cultivating political process research. In J. Goodwin & J. Jasper (Eds.), *Rethinking social movements: Structure, meaning, and emotion* (pp. 47–59). Lanham, MD: Rowman & Littlefield.

Meyer, M. (2010). Social movement service organizations: The challenges and consequences of combining service provision and political advocacy. In Y. Hasenfeld (Ed.), *Human services as complex organizations* (2nd ed., pp. 533–550). Thousand Oaks, CA: Sage.

Mezzich, A., Tarter, R., Kirisci, L., Feske, U., Day, B., & Gao, Z. (2007). Reciprocal influence of parent discipline and child's behavior on risk for substance disorder: A nine-year prospective study. *American Journal of Drug and Alcohol Abuse, 33*(6), 851–867.

Michels, R. (1959). *Political parties: A sociological study of the oligarchical tendencies of modern democracy* (Eden & Cedar Paul, Trans.). New York: Dover. (Original work published 1911)

Miers, R., & Fisher, A. (2002). Being church and community: Psychological sense of community in a local parish. In A. T. Fisher, C. C. Sonn, & B. J. Bishop (Eds.), *Psychological sense of community: Research applications and implications* (pp. 123–140). New York: Plenum.

Mijares, S. G., & Khalsa, G. S. (2005). *The psychospiritual clinician's handbook: Alternative methods for understanding and treating mental disorders.* New York: Haworth Reference Press.

Mikulas, W. L. (2002). *The integrative helper: Convergence of Eastern and Western traditions.* Pacific Grove, CA: Brooks/Cole Thompson Learning.

Mikulincer, M. (1994). *Human learned helplessness: A coping perspective.* New York: Plenum.

Miles, M. (1995). Disability in an Eastern religious context: Historical perspectives. *Disability and Society, 10,* 49–69.

Millennium Ecosystem Assessment. (2005). *Ecosystems and human well-being: Synthesis.* Washington, DC: Island Press.

Miller, L., Davies, M., & Greenwald, S. (2000). Religiosity and substance use and abuse among adolescents in the National Comorbidity Survey. *Journal of the American Academy of Child and Adolescent Psychiatry, 19*(9), 1190–1197.

Minami, H., & Tanaka, K. (1995). Social and environmental psychology: Transaction between physical space and group-dynamic processes. *Environment and Behavior, 27,* 43–55.

Minami, H., & Yamamoto, T. (2000). Cultural assumptions underlying concept-formation and theory building in environment-behavior research. In S. Wapner, J. Demick, T. Yamamoto, & H. Minami (Eds.), *Theoretical perspectives in environment-behavior research: Underlying assumptions, research problems, and methodologies* (pp. 237–246). New York: Kluwer Academic.

Mind. (2007). *Ecotherapy: The green agenda for mental health.* Retrieved October 9, 2009, from http:www.mind.org.uk/mindweek.

Minkoff, D. (2010). The emergence of hybrid organizational forms: Combining identity-based provision and political action. In Y. Hasenfeld (Ed.), *Human services as complex organizations* (2nd ed., pp. 117–138). Thousand Oaks, CA: Sage.

Miringoff, M. (2003). *2003 Index of Social Health: Monitoring the social well-being of the nation.* Unpublished paper. Tarrytown, NY: Fordham Institute for Innovation in Social Policy.

Miringoff, M. L., & Miringoff, M. (1999). *The social health of the nation: How America is really doing.* New York: Oxford University Press.

Miringoff, M. L., Miringoff, M., & Opdycke, S. (1996). The growing gap between standard economic indicators and the nation's social health. *Challenge,* 17–22.

Miringoff, M. L., & Opdycke, S. (2008). *America's social health: Putting social issues back on the public agenda.* Armonk, NY: M.E. Sharpe.

Mischey, E. J. (1981). Faith, identity, and personality in late adolescence. *Character Potential: A Record of Research, 9*(4), 175–185.

Mishel, L., Bernstein, J., & Allegretto, S. (2006). *The state of working America 2006/2007.* Washington, DC: Economic Policy Institute.

Mishel, L., Bernstein, J., & Shierholz, H. (2009). *The state of working America 2008/2009.* Washington, DC: Economic Policy Institute

Mistry, R., Lowe, D., Renner, A., & Chien, N. (2008). Expanding the Family Economic Stress Model: Insights from a mixed-methods approach. *Journal of Marriage and Family, 70*(1), 196–209.

Mistry, R., Vandewater, E., Huston, A., & McLoyd, V. (2002). Economic well-being and children's social adjustment: The role of family process in an ethnically diverse low-income sample. *Child Development, 73,* 935–951.

Mizrahi, T., & Rosenthal, B. (2001). Complexities of coalition building: Leaders' successes, strategies, struggles, and solutions. *Social Work, 46*(1), 63–78.

Mmatli, T. (2008). Political activism as a social work strategy in Africa. *International Social Work, 51*(3), 297–310.

Mohai, P., & Saha, R. (2007). Racial inequality in the distribution of hazardous waste: A national-level reassessment. *Social Problems, 54*(3), 343–370.

Mok, V. (2004). Self-help group participation and empowerment in Hong Kong. *Sociology and Social Welfare, 31*(3), 153–168.

MomsRising. (2006). *About MomsRising.* Retrieved April 21, 2007, from http://www.momsrising.org/aboutmomsrising.

Monette, D., Sullivan, T., & DeJong, C. (2008). *Applied social research: A tool for the human services* (7th ed.). Belmont, CA: Brooks/Cole.

Monte, C., & Sollod, R. (2003). *Beneath the mask: An introduction to theories of personality* (7th ed.). Hoboken, NJ: Wiley.

Moore, E. (1981). A prison environment's effect on health care service demands. *Journal of Environmental Systems, 11,* 17–34.

Mor Barak, M. (2000). The inclusive workplace: An ecosystem approach to diversity management. *Social Work, 45*(4), 339–352.

Mor Barak, M. (2005). *Managing diversity: Toward a globally inclusive workplace.* Thousand Oaks, CA: Sage.

Mor Barak, M., & Travis, D. (2010). Diversity and organizational performance. In Y. Hasenfeld (Ed.), *Human services as complex organizations* (2nd ed., pp. 341–378). Thousand Oaks, CA: Sage.

Moren-Cross, J. L., & Lin, N. (2006). Social networks and health. In R. H. Binstock & L. K. George (Eds.), *Handbook of aging and the social sciences* (6th ed., pp. 111–126). Amsterdam: Elsevier.

Morgan, G. (2006). *Images of organizations* (Updated ed.). Thousand Oaks, CA: Sage.

Morgan, J. P. (2002). Dying and grieving are journeys of the spirit. In R. B. Gilbert (Ed.), *Health care and spirituality: Listening, assessing, caring* (pp. 53–64). Amityville, NY: Baywood.

Morreale, D. (Ed.). (1998). *The complete guide to Buddhist America.* Boston: Shambhala.

Morris, A. (1981). The Black southern sit-in movement: An analysis of internal organization. *American Sociological Review, 46,* 744–767.

Morris, A. (1984). *The origins of the civil rights movement: Black communities organizing for change.* New York: Free Press.

Morris, A. (2000). Reflections on social movement theory: Criticisms and proposals. *Contemporary Sociology, 29*(3), 445–454.

Morris, A. (2004). Reflections on social movement theory: Criticisms and proposals. In J. Goodwin & J. Jasper (Eds.), *Rethinking social movements* (pp. 233–246). Lanham, MD: Rowman & Littlefield.

Moss, T. (2004, November). *Adolescent pregnancy and childbearing in the United States.* Retrieved August 4, 2006, from http://www.advocatesforyouth.org/PUBLICATIONS/factsheet/fsprechd.htm.

The Moynihan report revisited: Lessons and reflections after four decades. (2009, January). *The Annals of the American Academy of Political and Social Science, 621*(1).

Mueller, P. C., Plevak, D. J., & Rummans, T. A. (2001). Religious involvement, spirituality, and medicine: Implications for clinical practice. *Mayo Clinical Proceedings, 76*(12), 1225–1235.

Mullings, L. (2005). Interrogating racism: Toward an antiracist anthropology. *Annual Review of Anthropology, 34,* 667–693.

Mulroy, E., Nelson, K., & Gour, D. (2005). Community building and family-centered service collaboratives. In M. Weil (Ed.), *The handbook of community practice* (pp. 460–474). Thousand Oaks, CA: Sage.

Murray, B. (2001). Living wage comes of age: An increasingly sophisticated movement has put opponents on the defense. *The Nation, 273*(4), 24.

Murray, C., & Herrnstein, R. (1994). *The bell curve: Intelligence and class structure in American life.* New York: Free Press.

Myers, B. K. (1997). *Young children and spirituality.* New York: Routledge.

Myers, S., & Anderson, C. (2008). *The fundamentals of small group communication.* Thousand Oaks, CA: Sage.

Naidoo, R., & Adamowicz, W. (2006). Modeling opportunity costs of conservation in transitional landscapes. *Conservation Biology, 20*(2), 490–500.

Natale, S. M., & Neher, J. C. (1997). Inspiriting the workplace: Developing a values-based management system. In D. P. Bloch & L. J. Richmond (Eds.), *Connections between spirit and work in career development: New approaches and practical perspectives* (pp. 237–255). Palo Alto, CA: Davies-Black.

Nathanson, I. G. (1995). Divorce and women's spirituality. *Journal of Divorce and Remarriage, 22,* 179–188.

National Alliance to End Homelessness. (2005, May 16). *Alliance online news.* Retrieved August 31, 2006, from http://www.endhomelessness.org.

National Alliance to End Homelessness. (2009). Geography of Homelessness, Part 1: Defining the spectrum. Retrieved

October 16, 2009, from http://www.endhomelessness.org/content/article/detail/2437.

National Association of Social Workers. (1999). *Code of ethics.* Washington, DC: Author.

National Association of Social Workers. (2002). *NASW priorities on faith-based human services initiatives.* Retrieved February 26, 2010, from http://www.socialworkers.org/advocacy/positions/faith.asp.

National Association of Social Workers. (n.d.). *Social work speaks abstracts: Environmental policy.* Retrieved August 30, 2006, from http:www.socialworkers.org/resources/ abstracts/abstracts/environmental.asp.

National Center for Complementary and Alternative Medicine. (n.d.). *What is CAM?* Retrieved February 26, 2010, from http:// nccam.nih.gov/health/whatiscam/overview.htm.

National Coalition for the Homeless. (2009a). *How many people experience homelessness?* Retrieved May 17, 2010, from http://www.nationalhomeless.org/factsheets/How_Many.html.

National Coalition for the Homeless. (2009b). *Who is homeless?* Retrieved October 16, 2009, from http://www.nationalhomeless.org/factsheets/who.html.

National Conference of State Legislatures. (2009). *State laws regarding marriages between first cousins.* Retrieved December 9, 2009, from http://www.ncsl.org/default.aspx?tabid=4266.

National Institute of Diabetes and Digestive and Kidney Diseases (NIDDK) NIH. National Diabetes Information Clearing House (NDIC). (2008, June). National Diabetes statistics, 2007. Retrieved December 4, 2009, from http://diabetes.niddk.nih.gov/ dm/pubs/statistics/index.htm#allages.

National Institute of Neurological Disorders and Stroke. (2006). *Post-polio syndrome fact sheet* (NIH Publication No. 06–4030) [Electronic version]. Bethesda, MD: Author. Retrieved October 20, 2006, from http://www.ninds.nih.gov/disorders/post_polio/detail_post_polio.htm.

National Marriage Project. (2006). *The state of our unions 2006: The social health of marriage in America.* Piscataway, NJ: Rutgers, The State University of New Jersey: Author.

National Network of Libraries of Medicine. (2008). *Health literacy.* Retrieved January 1, 2010, from http://nnlm.gov/outreach/consumer/hlthlit.html.

The National Religious Partnership for the Environment. (n.d.). *What is the partnership?* Retrieved May 17, 2010, from http://www.nrpe.org/whatisthepartnership/index.html.

Navarro, V., Muntaner, C., Borrell, C., Benach, J., Quiroga, A., Rodriguez-Manz, M., et al. (2006). Politics and health outcomes. *Lancet, 368*(9540), 1033–1037.

Nelson, C. A. (1999). How important are the first three years of life? *Applied Developmental Science, 3*(4), 235–238.

Nelson, C. A. (2000). The neurobiological basis of early intervention. In J. P. Shonkoff & S. J. Meisels (Eds.), *Handbook of early childhood intervention* (2nd ed., pp. 204–227). New York: Cambridge University Press.

Nelson-Becker, H. B. (2006). Voices of resilience: Older adults in hospice care. *Journal of Social Work in End-of-Life & Palliative Care, 2*(3), 87–106.

Nesdale, D. (2004). Social identity processes and children's ethnic prejudice. In M. Bennett & M. Sani (Eds.), *The development of the social self* (pp. 219–245). New York: Psychology Press.

Netting, F. E., O'Connor, M. K., & Singletary, J. (2007). Finding homes for their dreams: Strategies founders and program initiators use to position and sustain faith-based programs. *Families in Society: The Journal of Contemporary Social Services, 88*(1), 19–29.

Neufeld, P., & Knipemann, K. (2001). Gateway to wellness: An occupational therapy collaboration with the National Multiple Sclerosis Society. *Occupational Therapy in Health Care, 12*(3/4), 67–84.

Newell, P. (1997). A cross-cultural examination of favorite places. *Environment and Behavior, 29,* 495–514.

Newman, D. (2006). *Sociology: Exploring the architecture of everyday life* (6th ed.). Thousand Oaks, CA: Pine Forge.

Newman, D. (2008). *Sociology: Exploring the architecture of everyday life* (7th ed.). Thousand Oaks, CA: Sage.

Newman, O. (1972). *Defensible space.* New York: Macmillan.

Newman, O. (1980). *Community of interest.* Garden City, NY: Anchor/Doubleday.

Newman, O., & Franck, K. (1980). *Influencing crime and stability in urban housing development.* Washington, DC: National Institute of Justice, U.S. Department of Justice.

News Corporation. (2006). *News Corporation: Creating and distributing top-quality news, sports and entertainment around the world.* Retrieved October 13, 2006, from http://www.newscorp.com/operations.

News Corporation. (2010). *News Corporation: Operations.* Retrieved February 23, 2010, from http://www.newscorp.com/operations.

New York City Commission on Human Rights. (2003, Summer). *Discrimination against Muslims, Arabs, and South Asians in New York City since 9/11.* Retrieved February 26, 2010, from http://www.nyc.gov/ html/cchr/pdf/sur_report.pdf.

Nichols, M., & Schwartz, R. (2006). *Family therapy: Concepts and methods* (7th ed.). Boston: Allyn & Bacon.

Nicotera, N. (2005). The child's view of neighborhood: Assessing a neglected element in direct social work practice. *Journal of Human Behavior in the Social Environment, 11*(3/4), 105–133.

Niemann, S. (2005). Persons with disabilities. In M. T. Burke, J. C. Chauvin, & J. G. Miranti (Eds.), *Religious and spiritual issues in counseling: Applications across diverse populations* (pp. 105–133). New York: Brunner-Routledge.

Nobles, W. W. (1980). African philosophy: Foundations for Black psychology. In R. L. Jones (Ed.), *Black psychology* (2nd ed., pp. 23–36). New York: Harper & Row.

Noddings, N. (2002). *Starting at home: Caring and social policy.* Berkeley: University of California Press.

Noddings, N. (2005). *Educating citizens for global awareness.* New York: Teacher's College Press.

Nomaguchi, K., & Milkie, M. (2005). Costs and rewards of children: The effects of becoming a parent on adults' lives. In T. Chibucos & R. Leite, with D. Weis (Eds.), *Readings in family theory* (pp. 140–164). Thousand Oaks, CA: Sage.

Northcut, T. (2000). Constructing a place for religion and spirituality in psychodynamic practice. *Clinical Social Work Journal, 28*(2), 155–169.

Northen, H. (1988). *Social work with groups* (3rd ed.). New York: Columbia University Press.

Northouse, P. (2007). *Leadership: Theory and practice* (4th ed.). Thousand Oaks, CA: Sage.

Northridge, M., & Sclar, E. (2003). A joint urban planning and public health framework: Contributions to health impact assessment. *American Journal of Public Health, 93*, 118–121.

Nowell, B., Berkowitz, S., Deacon, Z., & Foster-Fishman, P. (2006). Revealing the cues within community places: Stories of identity, history, and possibility. *American Journal of Community Psychology, 37*(1/2), 29–46.

Nyamathi, A., Leake, B., Keenan, C., & Gelberg, L. (2000). Type of social support among homeless women: Its impact on psychosocial resources, health and health resources, and the use of health services. *Nursing Research, 49*(6), 318–326.

Nye, I. (Ed.). (1982). *Family relationships: Rewards and costs.* Beverly Hills, CA: Sage.

Nye, R., & Hay, D. (1996). Identifying children's spirituality: How do you start without a starting point? *British Journal of Religious Education, 18*(3), 144–154.

Oates, S. (2008). *Introduction to media and politics.* London: Sage.

Oberschall, A. (1992). *Social movements: Ideologies, interests, and identities.* New Brunswick, NJ: Transaction.

Oberschall, A. (1996). Opportunities and framing in the Eastern European revolts of 1989. In D. McAdam, J. McCarthy, & M. Zald (Eds.), *Comparative perspectives on social movements: Political opportunities, mobilizing structures, and cultural framings* (pp. 93–121). New York: Cambridge University Press.

O'Brien, P. (1992). Social work and spirituality: Clarifying the concept for practice. *Spirituality and Social Work Journal, 3*(1), 2–5.

O'Brien, P. (2001). Claiming our soul: An empowerment group for African-American women in prison. *Journal of Progressive Human Services, 12*(1), 35–51.

Obst, P., & Tham, N. (2009). Helping the soul: The relationship between connectivity and well-being within a church community. *Journal of Community Psychology, 37*(3), 342–361.

Obst, P., & White, K. (2004). Revisiting the Sense of Community Index: A confirmatory factor analysis. *Journal of Community Psychology, 32*(6), 691–705.

Obst, P., & White, K. (2007). Choosing to belong: The influence of choice on social identification and psychological sense of community. *Journal of Community Psychology, 35*(1), 77–90.

Obst, P., Zinkiewicz, L., & Smith, S. (2002a). Sense of community in science fiction fandom, Part 1. Understanding sense of community in an international community of interest. *Journal of Community Psychology, 30*(1), 87–103.

Obst, P., Zinkiewicz, L., & Smith, S. (2002b). Sense of community in science fiction fandom, Part 2. Comparing neighborhood and interest group sense of community. *Journal of Community Psychology, 30*(1), 105–117.

Ochshorn, J., & Cole, E. (Eds.). (1995). *Women's spirituality, women's lives.* Binghamton, NY: Haworth Press.

O'Connor, M., & Netting, E. (2009). *Organization practice: A guide to understanding human service organizations* (2nd ed.). Hoboken, NJ: Wiley.

Odgers, C. Moffitt, T., Tach, L., Sampson, R., Taylor, A., Matthews, C., et al. (2009). The protective effects of neighborhood collective efficacy on British children growing up in deprivation: A developmental analysis. *Developmental Psychology, 45*(4), 942–957.

OECD Family Database. (2008). *Cohabitation rate and prevalence of other forms of partnership.* Retrieved December 8, 2009, from http://www.oecd.org/els/social/family/database.

Office of Faith-Based and Neighborhood Partnerships. (2009). *The work of the office: Office of Faith-Based and Neighborhood Partnerships.* Retrieved May 17, 2010, from http://www.white house.gov/blog/2009/11/12/work-office-white-house-office-faith-based-and-neighborhood-partnerships

Ogbu, J. (2003). *Black American students in an affluent suburb: A study of academic disengagement.* Mahwah, NJ: Erlbaum.

Oldmeadow, J., Platow, M., Foddy, M., & Anderson, D. (2003). Self-categorization, status, and social influence. *Social Psychology Quarterly, 66*(2), 138–152.

Orbuch, T., & Brown, E. (2006). Divorce in the context of being African American. In M. Fine & J. Harvey (Eds.), *Handbook of divorce and relationship dissolution* (pp. 481–498). Mahwah, NJ: Erlbaum.

O'Reilly, B. (2007). *Culture warrior.* New York: Broadway Books.

Organisation for Economic Co-operation and Development. (2006a). *OECD health data 2006: Statistics and indicators for 30 countries.* Retrieved November 3, 2006, from http://www.ecosante.org/OCDEENG68.html.

Organisation for Economic Co-operation and Development. (2006b). Social Expenditure Database. Retrieved May 17, 2010, from http://www.oecd.org/document/9/0,3343,en_2649_34637_38141385_1_1_1_1,00.html.

Ortner, S. B. (1973). On key symbols. *American Anthropologist, 75,* 1338–1346.

Ortner, S. B. (1984). Theory in anthropology since the sixties. *Comparative Studies in History and Society, 26*(1), 126–166.

Ortner, S. B. (1989). *High religion: A cultural and political history of Sherpa Buddhism.* Princeton, NJ: Princeton University Press.

Ortner, S. B. (1996). *Making gender: The politics and erotics of culture.* Boston: Beacon Press.

Ortner, S. B. (Ed.). (1999). *The fate of culture: Geertz and beyond.* Berkeley: University of California Press.

Ortner, S. B. (2006). *Anthropology and social theory: Culture, power, and the acting subject.* Durham, NC: Duke University Press.

Ozdemir, A. (2008). Shopping malls: Measuring interpersonal distance under changing conditions and cultures. *Field Methods, 20*(3), 226–248.

Ozorak, E. W. (1996). The power, but not the glory: How women empower themselves through religion. *Journal for the Scientific Study of Religion, 35*(1), 17–29.

Padilla, Y., & Sherraden, M. (2005). Communities and social policy issues: Persistent poverty, economic inclusion, and asset building. In M. Weil (Ed.), *The handbook of community practice* (pp. 103–116). Thousand Oaks, CA: Sage.

Pals, D. L. (1996). *Seven theories of religion.* New York: Oxford University Press.

Pan, P. (2002, December 28). Three Chinese workers: Jail, betrayal and fear; Government stifles labor movement. *The Washington Post,* p. A01.

Panksepp, J. (2008). The affective brain and core consciousness: How does neural activity generate emotional feelings? In M. Lewis, J. M. Havilland-Jones, & L. F. Barrett (Eds.), *Handbook of emotions* (3rd ed., pp. 47–67). New York: Guilford Press.

Paradies, Y. (2006). A systematic review of empirical research on self-reported racism and health. *International Journal of Epidemiology, 35*(4), 888–901.

Parappully, J., Rosenbaum, R., van den Daele, L., & Nzewi, E. (2002). Thriving after trauma: The experience of parents of murdered children. *Journal of Humanistic Psychology, 42*(1), 33–70.

Pardini, D. A., Plante, T. G., Sherman, A., & Stump, J. E. (2000). Religious faith and spirituality in substance abuse recovery: Determining the mental health benefits. *Journal of Substance Abuse Treatment, 19,* 347–354.

Parents, Families and Friends of Lesbians and Gays (PFLAG). (1995). *Our daughters and sons: Questions and answers for parents of gay, lesbian and bisexual people.* Washington, DC: Author.

Pargament, K. I. (1997). *The psychology of religious coping: Theory, research, practice.* New York: Guilford Press.

Pargament, K. I. (2007). *Spiritually integrated psychotherapy: Understanding and addressing the sacred.* New York: Guilford Press.

Pargament, K. I. (2008). The sacred character of community life. *American Journal of Community Psychology, 41*(1–2), 22–34.

Pargament, K. I., Koenig, H. G., & Perez, L. M. (2000). The many methods of religious coping: Development and initial validation of the RCOPE. *Journal of Clinical Psychology, 56,* 519–543.

Paris, P. J. (1995). *The spirituality of African peoples: The search for a common moral discourse.* Minneapolis, MN: Fortress Press.

Parish, S. L., Magana S., & Cassiman, S. A. (2008). It's just that much harder: Multi-layered hardship experiences of low-income mothers with disabilities. *AFFILIA: Journal of Women and Social Work, 23*(1) 51–65.

Park, C., Edmondson, D., Hale-Smith, A., & Blank, T. (2009). Religiousness/spirituality and health behaviors in younger adult cancer survivors: Does faith promote a healthier lifestyle? *Journal of Behavioral Medicine, 32*(6), 582–591.

Park, R. (1936). Human ecology. *American Journal of Sociology, 17,* 1–15.

Parkinson, B., Fischer, A. H., & Manstead, A. S. R. (2005). *Emotion in social relations: Cultural, group, and interpersonal processes.* New York: Psychology Press.

Parrenas, R. (2001). *Servants of globalization: Women, migration, and domestic work.* Palo Alto, CA: Stanford University Press.

Parrillo, V. (2009). *Diversity in America* (3rd ed.). Thousand Oaks, CA: Pine Forge.

Parsons, R., Tassinary, L, Ulrich, R., Hebl, M., & Grossman-Alexander, M. (1998). The view from the road: Implications for stress recovery and immunization. *Journal of Environmental Psychology, 18,* 113–140.

Pasley, K., & Lee, M. (2010). Stress and coping within the context of stepfamily life. In S. Price, C. Price, & P. McKenry (Eds.), *Families & change: Coping with stressful events and transitions* (4th ed., pp. 235–261). Thousand Oaks, CA: Sage.

Patterson, T., Shaw, W., Semple, S., Cherner, M., McCutchan, J., Atkinson, K., et al. (1996). Relationship of psychosocial factors to HIV disease progression. *Annals of Behavioral Medicine, 18,* 30–39.

Paulino, A. (1995). Spiritism, santeria, brujeria, and voodooism: A comparative view of indigenous healing systems. *Journal of Teaching in Social Work, 12*(1/2), 105–124.

Paulino, A. (1998). Dominican immigrant elders: Social service needs, utilization patterns, and challenges. *Journal of Gerontological Social Work, 30*(1/2), 61–74.

Payne, R. (2000). *Relaxation techniques: A practical handbook for the health care professional* (2nd ed.). Edinburgh, NY: Churchill Livingstone.

Pearson, J. (1996). *Discovering the self through drama and movement: The Sesame Approach.* London: Jessica Kingsley.

Pedrotti, J., Snyder, C., & Lopez, S. (2007). Eastern perspectives on positive psychology. In C. Snyder & S. Lopez (Eds.), *Positive psychology: The scientific and practice explorations of human strengths* (pp. 37–50). Thousand Oaks, CA: Sage.

Pence, E. (1999). An introduction: Developing a coordinated community response. In E. Pence & M. Shepard (Eds.), *Coordinating community responses: Lessons from Duluth and beyond* (pp. 3–23). Newbury Park, CA: Sage.

Peplau, L., & Fingerhut, A. (2007). The close relationships of lesbians and gay men. *Annual Review of Psychology, 58,* 373–408.

Perron, K. M., & Sedlacek, W. E. (2000). A comparison of group cohesiveness and client satisfaction in homogeneous and heterogeneous groups. *Journal for Specialists in Group Work, 25*(3), 243–251.

Perry, A. V., & Rolland, J. S. (2009). The therapeutic benefits of a justice-seeking spirituality: Empowerment, healing, and hope. In F. Walsh (Ed.), *Spiritual resources in family therapy* (2nd ed., pp. 379–396). New York: Guilford Press.

Perry, B. G. F. (1998). The relationship between faith and well-being. *Journal of Religion and Health, 37*(2), 125–136.

Pert, C. (1997). *Molecules of emotion: Why you feel the way you feel.* New York: Scribner.

Peterson, B., Newton, C., & Rosen, K. (2003). Examining congruence between partners' perceived infertility-related stress and its relationship to marital adjustment and depression in infertile couples. *Family process, 42,* 59–70.

Pew Forum on Religion & Public Life. (2008). *U.S. religious landscape survey: Religious affiliation—diverse and dynamic.* Washington, DC: Author.

Pew Forum on Religion & Public Life. (n.d.). *Religion and public life.* Retrieved February 26, 2010, from http://www.pewtrusts .org/ our_work_category.aspx?id=318.

Pew Research Center. (2009, November 16). *Faith-based programs still popular, less visible.* Retrieved February 23, 2010, from http://people-press.org/report/563/faith-based-programs.

Pfeffer, J. (1982). *Organizations and organization theory.* Boston: Pitman.

Pharr, S. (1988). *Homophobia: A weapon of sexism.* Inverness, CA: Chardon Press.

Phillips, J., & Sweeny, M. (2005). Premarital cohabitation and marital disruption among White, Black, and Mexican American women. *Journal of Marriage and Family, 67,* 296–314.

Pincus, A., & Minahan, A. (1973). *Social work practice: Model and method.* Itasca, IL: Peacock.

Pinto, R. (2006). Using social network interventions to improve mentally ill client's well-being. *Clinical Social Work Journal, 34*(1), 83–100.

Pirog, M., & Ziol-Guest, M. (2006). Child support enforcement: Programs and policies, impacts and questions. *Journal of Policy Analysis and Management, 25,* 943–990.

Piven, F., & Cloward, R. (1977). *Poor people's movements: Why they succeed, how they fail.* New York: Pantheon.

Plasse, B. R. (2001). A stress reduction and self-care group for homeless and addicted women: Meditation, relaxation and cognitive methods. *Social Work With Groups, 24*(3/4), 117–133.

Plutchik, R. (2005). The nature of emotions. In P. W. Sherman & J. Alcock (Eds.), *Exploring animal behavior: Readings from American Scientist* (4th ed., pp. 85–91). Sunderland, MA: Sinauer Associates.

Polletta, F. (2004). Culture is not just in your head. In J. Goodwin & J. Jasper (Eds.), *Rethinking social movements* (pp. 97–110). Lanham, MD: Rowman & Littlefield.

Pollio, D. E. (1995). Hoops group: Group work with young "street" men. *Social Work With Groups, 18*(2/3), 107–116.

Pons, F., Laroche, M., & Mourali, M. (2006). Consumer reactions to crowded retail settings: Cross-cultural differences between North America and Middle East. *Psychology & Marketing, 23*(7), 555–572.

Popenoe, D. (1996). *Life without father: Compelling new evidence that fatherhood and marriage are indispensable for the good of children and society.* New York: Martin Kessler Books.

Popple, P. (1992). Social work: Social function and moral purpose. In P. Reid & P. Popple (Eds.), *The moral purposes of social work: The character and intentions of a profession* (pp. 141–154). Chicago: Nelson-Hall.

Popple, P., & Leighninger, L. (2001). *The policy-based profession: An introduction to social welfare policy analysis for social workers* (2nd ed.). Boston: Allyn & Bacon.

Popple, P., & Leighninger, L. (2005). *Social work, social welfare, and American society* (6th ed.). Boston: Allyn & Bacon.

Popple, P., & Leighninger, L. (2007). *The policy-based profession: An introduction to social welfare policy analysis for social workers* (4th ed.). Boston: Allyn & Bacon.

Potocky-Tripodi, M. (2004). The role of social capital in immigrant and refugee economic adaptation. *Journal of Social Service Research, 31*(1), 59–91.

Praglin, L. (2004). Spirituality, religion, and social work: An effort towards interdisciplinary conversation. *Social Thought, 23,* 67–84.

Pretty, G. (1990). Relating psychological sense of community to social climate characteristics. *Journal of Community Psychology, 18,* 60–65.

Pretty, G., & McCarthy, M. (1991). Exploring psychological sense of community among men and women of the corporation. *Journal of Community Psychology, 19,* 351–361.

Prewitt, K. (2000, October). Census 2000: *A new picture of America.* Plenary Session at George Warren Brown School of Social Work 75th Anniversary Celebration. St. Louis, MO.

Price, S., Price, C., & McKenry, P. (2010). *Families & change: Coping with stressful events and transitions* (4th ed.). Thousand Oaks, CA: Sage.

Prichard, D. (2004). Critical incident stress and secondary trauma: An analysis of group process. *Groupwork, 14*(3), 44–62.

Procidano, M. E., & Smith, W. W. (1997). Assessing perceived social support: The importance of context. In G. R. Pierce, B. Lakey, & B. R Sarason (Eds.), *Sourcebook of social support and personality* (pp. 93–106). New York: Plenum Press.

Proescholdbell, R., Roosa, M., & Nemeroff, C. (2006). Component measures of psychological sense of community among gay men. *Journal of Community Psychology, 34*(1), 9–24.

Puchalski, C., & Romer, A. L. (2000). Taking a spiritual history allows clinicians to understand patients more fully. *Journal of Palliative Medicine, 3*(1), 129–137.

Puddifoot, J. (1995). Dimensions of community identity. *Journal of Community & Applied Social Psychology, 5,* 357–370.

Putnam, R. (1993). *Making democracy work.* Princeton, NJ: Princeton University Press.

Putnam, R. (2000). *Bowling alone: The collapse and revival of American community.* New York: Simon & Schuster.

Pyroos, J., & Nishita, C. (2003). The cost and financing of home modifications in the United States. *Journal of Disability Studies, 14*(2), 68–73.

Queralt, M., & Witte, A. (1998a). Influences on neighborhood supply of child care in Massachusetts. *Social Service Review, 72*(1), 17–46.

Queralt, M., & Witte, A. (1998b). A map for you? Geographic information systems in the social services. *Social Work, 43*(5), 455–469.

Quigley, B. (2001). The living wage movement. *Blueprint for Social Justice, LIV*(9), 1–7.

Ragland, D., Krause, N., Greiner, B., & Fisher, J. (1998). Studies of health outcomes in transit operators: Policy implications of the current scientific database. *Journal of Occupational Health Psychology, 3*(2), 172–187.

Rai, S. (2006, February 10). Labor rigidity in India stirs investors' doubts. *The International Herald Tribune,* p. 14.

Raines, J. (1997). Co-constructing the spiritual tree. *Society for Social Work and Social Work Newsletter, 4*(1), 3, 8.

Rainie, L. (2010, January 5). *Internet, broadband, and cell phone statistics.* Retrieved February 23, 2010, from http://www.pewinternet.org/~/media/Files/Reports/2010/PIP_December09_update.pdf.

Ramirez, R. (1985). Hispanic spirituality. *Social Thought, 11*(3), 6–13.

Ramos, B., Siegel, S., & Bueno, J. (2002). Occasion setting and drug tolerance. *Integrative Physiological & Behavioral Science, 37*(3), 165–177.

Rampell, C. (2009, February 5). As layoffs surge, women may pass men in job force. *New York Times.* Retrieved December 3, 2009, from http://www.nytimes.com/2009/02/06/business/06women.html.

Rank, M., & Hutchison, W. (2000). An analysis of leadership within the social work profession. *Journal of Social Work Education, 36*(3), 487–502.

Rapoport, A. (1990). *Meaning of the built environment.* Tucson: University of Arizona Press.

Rappaport, H., Enrich, K., & Wilson, A. (1985). Relation between ego identity and temporal perspective. *Journal of Personality and Social Psychology, 48*(6), 1609–1620.

Rathus, S., Nevid, J., & Fichner-Rathus, L. (1998). *Essentials of human sexuality.* Boston: Allyn & Bacon.

Raustiala, K. (2005). The evolution of territoriality. *International Studies Review, 7,* 515–519.

Ray, L. (1993). *Rethinking critical theory: Emancipation in the age of global social movements.* Newbury Park, CA: Sage.

Ray, O. (2004). How the mind hurts and heals the body. *American Psychologist, 59*(1), 29–40.

Ray, R., Gornick, J., & Schmitt, J. (2009). *Parental leave policies in 21 countries: Assessing generosity and gender equality.* Washington, DC: Center for Economic and Policy Research. Retrieved May 17, 2010, from http://www.cepr.net/index.php/publications/reports/plp/.

Raza, M., & Velez, P. (Directors). (2002). *Occupation: The Harvard University living wage sit-in* [Motion picture]. Waterville, ME: EnMasse Films.

Reamer, F. (1992). Social work and the public good: Calling or career? In P. Reid & P. Popple (Eds.), *The moral purposes of social work: The character and intentions of a profession* (pp. 11–33). Chicago: Nelson-Hall.

Rector, R., & Hederman, R. (1999). *Income inequality: How census data misrepresent income distribution.* Retrieved May 17, 2010, from http://www.heritage.org/ Research/Reports/1999/09/Income-Inequality.

Rector, R., Johnson, K., & Fagan, P. (2008). Increasing marriage would dramatically reduce child poverty. In D. R. Crane & T. Heaton (Eds.), *Handbook of families & poverty* (pp. 457–470). Thousand Oaks, CA: Sage.

Redfield, R. (1947). The folk society. *American Journal of Sociology, 52,* 293–308.

Redman, D. (2008). Stressful life experiences and the roles of spirituality among people with a history of substance abuse and incarceration. *Social Thought, 27*(1–2), 47–67.

Reed, M. (1993). Organizations and modernity: Continuity and discontinuity in organization theory. In J. Hassard & M. Parker (Eds.), *Postmodernism and organizations* (pp. 163–182). Newbury Park, CA: Sage.

Reese, D. J., & Kaplan, M. S. (2000). Spirituality, social support, and worry about health: Relationships in a sample of HIV+ women. *Social Thought, 19*(4), 37–52.

Reese, D. J., & Sontag, M. A. (2001). Successful interprofessional collaboration on the hospice team. *Health and Social Work, 26*(3), 167–175.

Reeves, T. C. (1998). *The empty church: Does organized religion matter anymore?* New York: Simon & Schuster.

Regoeczi, W. (2008). Crowding in context: An examination of the differential responses of men and women to high-density living environments. *Journal of Health and Social Behavior, 49*(3), 254–268.

Reichert, E. (2006). *Understanding human rights: An exercise book.* Thousand Oaks, CA: Sage.

Reid, K. E. (1997). *Social work practice with groups: A clinical perspective* (2nd ed.). Pacific Grove, CA: Wadsworth/Thomson Learning.

Reid, T. R. (2004). *The United States of Europe: The new superpower and the end of American supremacy.* New York: Penguin.

Reid, W., & Smith, A. (1989). *Research in social work* (2nd ed.). New York: Columbia University Press.

Reilly, P. (1995). The religious wounding of women. *Creation Spirituality, 11*(1), 41–45.

Reinhardt, U., Hussey, P., & Anderson, G. (2002). Cross-national comparisons of health systems using OECD data, 1999. *Health Affairs, 21*(3), 169–181.

Reinhardt, U., Hussey, P., & Anderson, G. (2004). U.S. health care spending in an international context. *Health Affairs, 23*(3), 10–25.

Reisch, M. (1997). The political context of social work. In M. Reisch & E. Gambrill (Eds.), *Social work in the 21st century* (pp. 80–92). Thousand Oaks, CA: Pine Forge.

Reisch, M. (2005). Radical community organizing. In M. Weil (Ed.), *The handbook of community practice* (pp. 287–304). Thousand Oaks, CA: Sage.

Reisch, M. (2008). Social movements. In T. Mizrahi & L. Davis (Eds.), *Encyclopedia of social work* (20th ed., Vol. 4, pp. 52–56). New York: NASW Press and Oxford University Press.

Reporters Without Borders. (2010). *World Press Freedom Index 2009.* Retrieved May 17, 2010, from http://en.rsf.org/IMG/pdf/ classement_en.pdf.

Resnick, H., & Jaffee, B. (1982). The physical environment and social welfare. *Social Casework, 63,* 354–362.

Ressler, L. E., & Hodge, D. R. (2003). Silenced voices: Social work and the oppression of conservative narratives. *Social Thought, 22,* 125–142.

Reuther, R. (1983). *Sexism and God-talk: Toward a feminist theology.* Boston: Beacon Press.

Reynald, D., & Elffers, H. (2009). The future of Newman's defensible space theory: Linking defensible space and the routine activities of place. *European Journal of Criminology, 6*(1), 25–46.

Richards, M. (2005). Spirituality and social work in long-term care. *Journal of Gerontological Social Work, 45*(1/2), 173–183.

Richman, J. M., Rosenfeld, L. B., & Hardy, C. J. (1993). The social support survey: A validation study of a clinical measure of the social support process. *Research on Social Work Practice, 3,* 288–311.

Richmond, M. (1901). Charitable cooperation. In *Proceedings of the National Conference of Charities and Corrections* (pp. 298–313). Boston: George H. Elles.

Richmond, M. (1917). *Social diagnosis.* New York: Russell Sage Foundation.

Riera, C. (2005). Social policy and community development in multicultural contexts. *Community Development Journal, 40*(4), 433–438.

Riger, S. (1994). Challenges of success: Stages of growth in feminist organizations. *Feminist Studies, 20*(2), 275–300.

Ritzer, G. (2008a). *The McDonaldization of Society* (5th ed.). Thousand Oaks, CA: Pine Forge.

Ritzer, G. (2008b). *Sociological theory* (7th ed.). Boston: McGraw-Hill.

Ritzer, G., & Goodman, D. (2004). *Modern sociological theory* (6th ed.). Boston: McGraw-Hill.

Robbins, S., Chatterjee, P., & Canda, E. (2006a). *Contemporary human behavior theory: A critical perspective for social work* (2nd ed.). Boston: Pearson.

Robbins, S., Chatterjee, P., & Canda, E. (2006b). Theories of assimilation, acculturation, bicultural socialization, and ethnic minority identity. In *Contemporary human behavior theory: A critical perspective for social work* (2nd ed., pp. 126–161). Boston: Allyn & Bacon.

Roberson, W. W. (2004). *Life and livelihood: A handbook for spirituality at work.* Harrison, PA: Morehouse Publishing.

Roberts, C. S. (1989). Conflicting professional values in social work and medicine. *Health and Social Work, 14*(3), 211–218.

Roberts, K. A. (2004). *Religion in sociological perspective* (4th ed.). Belmont, CA: Wadsworth.

Roberts-DeGennaro, M., & Mizrahi, T. (2005). Coalitions as social change agents. In M. Weil (Ed.), *The handbook of community practice* (pp. 305–318). Thousand Oaks, CA: Sage.

Robertson, R. (1992). *Globalization.* London: Sage.

Robinson, T. L. (2000). Making the hurt go away: Psychological and spiritual healing for African American women survivors of childhood incest. *Journal of Multicultural Counseling and Development, 28*(3), 160–176.

Roehlkepartain, E. C., King, P. E., Wagener, L., & Benson, P. L. (2006). *Spiritual development in childhood and adolescence.* Thousand Oaks, CA: Sage.

Roff, S. (2004). Nongovernmental organizations: The strengths perspective at work. *International Social Work, 47*(2), 202–212.

Rogers, C. (1951). *Client-centered therapy.* Boston: Houghton Mifflin.

Rogge, M. (1993). Social work, disenfranchised communities, and the natural environment: Field education opportunities. *Journal of Social Work Education, 29,* 111–120.

Roller, B. (1997). *The promise of group therapy: How to build a vigorous training and organizational base for group therapy in managed behavioral health care.* San Francisco: Jossey-Bass.

Ronen, T., & Freeman, A. (Eds.). (2007). *Cognitive behavior therapy in clinical social work practice.* New York: Springer.

Roof, W. C. (1993). *A generation of seekers: The spiritual journeys of the baby boom generation.* San Francisco: HarperCollins.

Roof, W. C. (1999). *Spiritual marketplace: Baby boomers and the remaking of American religion.* Princeton, NJ: Princeton University Press.

Rosaldo, R. (1993). *Culture and truth: The remaking of social analysis.* Boston: Beacon Press.

Rose, S. (1992). *Case management and social work practice.* White Plains, NY: Longman.

Rose, S. (1994). Defining empowerment: A value-based approach. In S. P. Robbins (Ed.), *Melding the personal and the political: Advocacy and empowerment in clinical and community practice. Proceedings of the Eighth Annual Social Work Futures Conference, May 13–14, 1993* (pp. 17–24). Houston, TX: University of Houston Graduate School of Social Work.

Rosen, R. (2004). *Time and temporality in the ancient world.* Philadelphia: University of Pennsylvania Museum of Archaeology and Anthropology.

Rosenzweig, M. R., Breedlove, S. M., & Watson, N. W. (2004). *Biological psychology: An introduction to behavioral and cognitive neuroscience* (4th ed.). Sunderland, MA: Sinauer Associates.

Rosenzweig, M. R., & Leiman, A. L. (1989). *Physiological psychology* (2nd ed.). Lexington, MA: Heath.

Ross, L., & Coleman, M. (2000). Urban community action planning inspires teenagers to transform their community and their identity. *Journal of Community Practice, 7*(2), 29–45.

Rostow, W. (1990). *The stages of economic growth: A non-communist manifesto.* Cambridge, UK: Cambridge University Press.

Rothenberg, P. (2006). Preface. In P. Rothenberg (Ed.), *Beyond borders: Thinking critically about global issues* (pp. xv–xvii). New York: W. H. Freeman.

Rothenberg, P. (2007). *Race, class, and gender in the United States* (7th ed.). New York: Worth.

Rothman, J. (2008). *Cultural competence in process and practice: Building bridges.* Boston: Pearson.

Rothschild-Whitt, J., & Whitt, J. (1986). *The cooperative workplace.* Cambridge, UK: Cambridge University Press.

Roulstone, A. (2004). Employment barriers and inclusive futures? In *Disabling barriers—Enabling environments* (2nd ed., pp. 195–200). Thousand Oaks, CA: Sage.

Rubin, A., & Babbie, E. (1993). *Research methods for social work* (2nd ed.). New York: Columbia University Press.

Rudacille, D. (2005). *The riddle of gender: Science, activism, and transgender rights.* New York: Pantheon.

Ruger, J., & Kim, H. (2006). Global health inequalities: An international comparison. *Journal of Epidemiology and Community Health, 60,* 928–936.

Russel, R. (1998). Spirituality and religion in graduate social work education. *Social Thought, 18*(2), 15–29.

Ryan, M., David, B., & Reynolds, K. (2004). Who cares? The effect of gender and context on the self and moral reasoning. *Psychology of Women Quarterly, 28*(3), 246–255.

Ryan, P. L. (1998). Spirituality among adult survivors of childhood violence: A literature review. *Journal of Transpersonal Psychology, 30*(1), 39–51.

Ryan, W. (1999). The new landscape for nonprofits. *Harvard Business Review, 77*(1), 127–136.

Sabatelli, R. (1984). The Marital Comparison Level Index: A measure for assessing outcomes relative to expectations. *Journal of Marriage and the Family, 46,* 651–662.

Sadock, B., & Sadock, V. (2007). *Kaplan & Sadock's synopsis of psychiatry: Behavioral sciences/clinical psychiatry* (10th ed.). Baltimore: Wolters Kluwer.

Saez, E. (2009). *Striking it richer: The evolution of top incomes in the United States (Update with 2007 estimates).* Retrieved February 20, 2010, from http://elsa.berkeley.edu/~saez.

Safyer, A. W., & Spies-Karotkin, G. (1988). The biology of AIDS. *Health and Social Work, 13,* 251–258.

Sahlins, M. (1981). *Historical metaphors and mythical realities: Structure in the early history of the Sandwich Islands kingdom.* Ann Arbor: University of Michigan Press.

Saint Louis Healthy Family Coalition. (2009). *Stepfamilies in the United States: A fact sheet.* Retrieved December 11, 2009, from http://www.stl-healthymarriage.org/stepfamilies-in-the-united-states-a-fact-sheet.

Salamon, L., Anheier, H., List, R., Toepler, S., & Sokolowski, W. (1999). *Global civil society: Dimensions of the nonprofit sector.* Baltimore: The Johns Hopkins Comparative Center for Civil Society Studies.

Salazar, A. J. (1996). An analysis of the development and evolution of roles in the small group. *Small Group Research, 27,* 475–503.

Saleebey, D. (1994). Culture, theory, and narrative: The intersection of meanings in practice. *Social Work, 39,* 351–359.

Saleebey, D. (2001). *Human behavior and social environments: A biopsychosocial approach* (3rd ed.). New York: Columbia University Press.

Saleebey, D. (2006). *The strengths perspective in social work practice.* Boston: Pearson/Allyn & Bacon.

Sampson, R. (2003). The neighborhood context of well-being. *Perspectives in Biology and Medicine, 46*(3), S53–S65.

Sampson, R., Morenoff, J., & Earls, F. (1999). Beyond social capital: Spatial dynamics of collective efficacy for children. *Science, 277,* 918–924.

Sanders, S. (2005). Is the glass half empty or half full? Reflections on strain and gain in caregivers of individuals with Alzheimer's disease. *Social Work in Health Care, 40*(3), 57–73.

Sands, R. G., Stafford, J., & McClelland, M. (1990). "I beg to differ": Conflict in the interdisciplinary team. *Social Work in Health Care, 14*(3), 55–72.

Saperstein, A. (1996). The prediction of unpredictability: Applications of the new paradigm of chaos in dynamical systems to the old problem of the stability of a system of hostile nations. In L. D. Kiel & E. Elliott (Eds.), *Chaos theory in the social sciences: Foundations and applications* (pp. 139–163). Ann Arbor: University of Michigan Press.

Sapolsky, R. (2005). Sick of poverty. *Scientific American, 293*(6), 92–99.

Sarafino, E. P. (2008). *Health psychology: Biopsychosocial implications* (6th ed.). Belmont, CA: Wiley.

Sarason, S. (1974). *The psychological sense of community: Prospects for a community psychology.* San Francisco: Jossey-Bass.

Sargent, L. D., & Sue-Chan, C. (2001). Does diversity affect group efficacy? The intervening role of cohesion and task independence. *Small Group Research, 32*(4), 426–450.

Sarri, R., & Galinsky, M. (1967). A conceptual framework for group development. In R. Vinter (Ed.), *Readings in group work practice* (pp. 72–94). Ann Arbor, MI: Campus Publishers.

Satir, V. (1983). *Conjoint family therapy* (3rd ed.). Palo Alto, CA: Science and Behavior Books.

Savin-Williams, R. (2008). Then and now: Recruitment, definition, diversity, and positive attributes of same-sex populations. *Developmental Psychology, 44,* 135–138.

Sayer, L. (2006). Economic aspects of divorce and relationship dissolution. In M. Fine & J. Harvey (Eds.), *Handbook of divorce and relationship dissolution* (pp. 385–406). Mahwah, NJ: Erlbaum.

Scales, T. L., Wolfer, T. A., Sherwood, D. A., Garland, D. R., Hugen, B., & Pittman, S. W. (2002). *Spirituality and religion in social work practice: Decision cases with teaching notes.* Alexandria, VA: Council on Social Work Education.

Scanzoni, J., & Szinovacz, M. (1980). *Family decision-making: A developmental sex role model.* Beverly Hills, CA: Sage.

Schackman, B. R., Gebo, K. A., Walensky, R. P., Losina, E. L., Muccio, T., Sax, P. E., et al. (2006). The lifetime cost of current Human Immunodeficiency Virus care in the United States. *Medical Care, 44*(11), 990–997.

Schacter, S., & Singer, J. E. (1962). Cognitive, social, and physiological determinants of emotional states. *Psychological Review, 69,* 379–399.

Schaufeli, W., & Enzmann, D. (1998). *The burnout companion to study and practice: A critical analysis.* London: Taylor & Francis.

Schein, E. (1992). *Organizational culture and leadership* (2nd ed.). San Francisco: Jossey-Bass.

Schiff, M., & Bargal, O. (2000). Helping characteristics of self-help and support groups: Their contribution to participants' subjective well-being. *Small Group Research, 31*(3), 275–304.

Schmid, H. (2004). The role of nonprofit human service organizations in providing social services: A prefatory essay. *Administration in Social Work, 28*(3/4), 1–21.

Schneider, J., & Cook, K. (1995). Status inconsistency and gender: Combining revisited. *Small Group Research, 26,* 372–399.

Schofer, E., & Hironaka, A. (2005). The effects of world society on environmental protection outcomes. *Social Forces, 84*(1), 25–47.

Schofield, R. F., & Amodeo, M. (1999). Interdisciplinary teams in health care and human service settings: Are they effective? *Health and Social Work, 24*(3), 210.

Schore, A. N. (2001). The effects of a secure attachment relationship on right brain development, affect regulation, and infant mental health. *Infant Mental Health Journal, 22,* 7–66.

Schore, A. N. (2002). Dysregulation of the right brain: A fundamental mechanism of traumatic attachment and the psychopathogenesis of post-traumatic stress disorder. *Australian and New Zealand Journal of Psychiatry, 36,* 9–30.

Schriver, J. (2004). *Human behavior and the social environment: Shifting paradigms in essential knowledge for social work practice* (4th ed.). Boston: Pearson.

Schuster, M. A., Stein, B. P., Jaycox, L. H., Collins, R. L., Marshall, G. N., Zhou, A. J., et al. (2001). A national survey of stress reactions after the September 11, 2001, terrorist attacks. *New England Journal of Medicine, 345*(20), 1507–1512.

Schutt, R. (2009). *Investigating the social world: The process and practice of research* (6th ed.). Thousand Oaks, CA: Sage.

Schutz, A. (1967). *The phenomenology of the social world* (G. Walsh & F. Lehnert, Trans.). Evanston, IL: Northwestern University Press. (Original work published 1932)

Schwalbe, M. (2006). Afterword: The costs of American privilege. In P. Rothenberg (Ed.), *Beyond borders: Thinking critically about global issues* (pp. 603–605). New York: Worth.

Schweitzer, J., Woo Kim, J., & Mackin, J. (1999). The impact of the built environment on crime and fear of crime in urban neighborhoods. *Journal of Urban Technology, 6*, 59–73.

Scott, A. H., Butin, D. N., Tewfik, D., Burkhardt, A., Mandel, D., & Nelson, L. (2001). Occupational therapy as a means to wellness with the elderly. *Physical and Occupational Therapy in Geriatrics, 18*(4), 3–22.

Scott, M. (2005). A powerful theory and a paradox: Ecological psychologists after Barker. *Environment and Behavior, 37*(3), 295–329.

Scott, W. R. (2008). *Institutions and organizations: Ideas and interests* (3rd ed.). Thousand Oaks, CA: Sage.

Seabury, B. (1971). Arrangement of physical space in social work settings. *Social Work, 16*, 43–49.

Sebba, R. (1991). The landscapes of childhood: The reflection of childhood's environment in adult memories and in children's attitudes. *Environment and Behavior, 23*, 395–422.

Seccombe, K., & Warner, R. (2004). *Marriages and families: Relationships in social context.* New York: Thomson Learning.

Segerstrom, S. S., & Miller, G. E. (2004). Psychological stress and the human immune system: A meta-analytic study of 30 years of inquiry. *Psychological Bulletin, 130*(4), 601–630.

Seibert, S., & Gruenfeld, L. (1992). Masculinity, femininity, and behavior in groups. *Small Group Research, 23*, 95–112.

Seligman, M. (1991). *Learned optimism.* New York: Knopf.

Seligman, M. (1992). *Helplessness: On depression, development, and death.* New York: Freeman.

Seligman, M. (1998). *Learned optimism: How to change your mind and your life* (2nd ed.). New York: Pocket Books.

Seligman, M. (2002). *Authentic happiness: Using the new positive psychology to realize your potential for lasting fulfillment.* New York: Free Press.

Selye, H. (1991). History and present status of the stress concept. In A. Monat & R. S. Lazarus (Eds.), *Stress and coping: An anthology* (3rd ed., pp. 21–35). New York: Columbia University Press.

Sen, A., Partelow, L., & Miller, D. (2005). *Comparative indicators of education in the United States and other G8 countries: 2004* (NCES 2005–021). U.S. Department of Education, National Center for Education Statistics. Washington, DC: U.S. Government Printing Office.

Senge, P. (1990). *The fifth discipline.* New York: Doubleday.

Sennett, R. (2006). *The culture of the new capitalism.* New Haven, CT: Yale University Press.

Sernau, S. (2006). *Worlds apart: Social inequalities in a global economy* (2nd ed.). Thousand Oaks, CA: Pine Forge.

Shafritz, J., & Ott, J. (2005). *Classics of organization theory* (6th ed.). Belmont, CA: Thomson Wadsworth.

Sharma, S., Mittal, S., & Aggarwal, P. (2009). Management of infertility in low resource countries. *BJOG: An International Journal of Obstetrics & Gynaecology, 116*, 71–76.

Shaw, M. E. (1981). *Group dynamics: The psychology of small group behavior* (3rd ed.). New York: McGraw-Hill.

Shechtman, Z., & Perl-Dekel, O. (2000). A comparison of therapeutic factors in two group treatment modalities: Verbal and art therapy. *Journal for Specialists in Group Work, 25*(3), 288–304.

Sheets, V., & Manzer, C. (1991). Affect, cognition, and urban vegetation: Some effects of adding trees along city streets. *Environment and Behavior, 23*, 285–304.

Shek, D. (2003). Economic stress, psychological well-being and problem behavior in Chinese adolescents with economic disadvantage. *Journal of Youth and Adolescence, 32*(4), 259–266.

Shephard, B. (2005). Play, creativity, and the new community organizing. *Journal of Progressive Human Services, 16*(2), 47–69.

Sheridan, M. J. (1995). Honoring angels in my path: Spiritually sensitive group work with persons who are incarcerated. *Reflections: Narratives of Professional Helping, 1*(4), 5–16.

Sheridan, M. J. (2002). Spiritual and religious issues in practice. In A. R. Roberts & G. J. Greene (Eds.), *Social workers' desk reference* (pp. 567–571). New York: Oxford University Press.

Sheridan, M. J. (2004). Predictors of use of spiritually-derived interventions in social work practice: A survey of practitioners. *Journal of Spirituality and Religion in Social Work: Social Thought, 23*(4), 5–25.

Sheridan, M. J. (2009). Ethical issues in the use of spiritually-based interventions in social work practice: What are we doing and why? *Social Thought, 28*(1/2), 99–126.

Sheridan, M. J., & Amato-von Hemert, K. (1999). The role of religion and spirituality in social work education and practice: A survey of student views and experiences. *Journal of Social Work Education, 35*(1), 125–141.

Sheridan, M. J., & Bullis, R. K. (1991). Practitioners' views on religion and spirituality: A qualitative study. *Spirituality and Social Work Journal, 2*(2), 2–10.

Sheridan, M. J., Bullis, R. K., Adcock, C. R., Berlin, S. D., & Miller, P. C. (1992). Practitioners' personal and professional attitudes and behaviors toward religion and spirituality: Issues for social work education and practice. *Journal of Social Work Education, 28*(2), 190–203.

Sheridan, M. J., Wilmer, C., & Atcheson, L. (1994). Inclusion of content on religion and spirituality in the social work curriculum: A study of faculty views. *Journal of Social Work Education, 30*, 363–376.

Shilts, R. (1987). *And the band played on.* New York: St. Martin's Press.

Shmotkin, D. (1991). The role of time orientation in life satisfaction across the life span. *Journal of Gerontology, 46*(5), 243–250.

Shore, R., & Shore, B. (2009). *Increasing the percentage of children living in two-parent families.* Baltimore: The Annie E. Casey Foundation. Retrieved December 9, 2009, from http://www.kidscount.org.

Shorey, H. S., & Snyder, C. R. (2006). The role of adult attachment styles in psychopathology and psychotherapy outcomes. *Review of General Psychology, 10*(1), 1–20.

Shu, L., & Li, Y. (2007). How far is enough? A measure of information privacy in terms of interpersonal distance. *Environment & Behavior, 39*(3), 317–331.

Shweder, R. (1995). Anthropology's Romantic rebellion against the Enlightenment, or there's more to thinking than reason and evidence. In R. Shweder & R. LeVine (Eds.), *Culture theory: Essays on mind, self, and emotion* (pp. 27–66). New York: Cambridge University Press. (Original work published 1984)

Shweder, R., & LeVine, R. (Eds.). (1995). *Culture theory: Essays on mind, self, and emotion.* New York: Cambridge University Press. (Original work published 1984)

Sideridis, G. D. (2006). Coping is not an "either" "or": The interaction of coping strategies in regulating affect, arousal and performance. *Stress and Health: Journal of the International Society for the Investigation of Stress, 22*(5), 315–327.

Siegel, S. (1991). Feedforward processes in drug tolerance and dependence. In R. Lister & H. Weingartner (Eds.), *Perspectives on cognitive neuroscience* (pp. 405–416). New York: Oxford University Press.

Siegel, S. (2001). Pavlovian conditioning and drug overdose: When tolerance fails. *Addiction Research & Theory, 9*(5), 503–513.

Siegel, S. (2005). Drug tolerance, drug addiction, and drug anticipation. *Current Directions in Psychological Science, 14*(6), 296–300.

Siegel, S., & Allan, L. (1998). Learning and homeostasis: Drug addiction and the McCollough effect. *Psychological Bulletin, 124*(2), 230–239.

Siegel, S., Hinson, R., Krank, M., & McCully, J. (1982). Heroin "overdose" death: Contribution of drug-associated environmental cues. *Science, 216,* 436–437.

Silverman, D. (1971). *The theory of organizations: A sociological framework.* New York: Basic Books.

Silverman, D. (1994). On throwing away ladders: Re-writing the theory of organizations. In J. Hassard & M. Parker (Eds.), *Towards a new theory of organizations* (pp. 1–23). New York: Routledge.

Singh, G., & Hiatt, R. (2006). Trends and disparities in socioeconomic and behavioural characteristics, life expectancy, and cause-specific mortality of native-born and foreign-born populations in the United States, 1979–2003. *International Journal of Epidemiology, 35*(4), 903–919.

Singh, R. (2001). Hinduism. In M. V. Hook, B. Hugen, & M. Aguilar (Eds.), *Spirituality within religious traditions in social work practice* (pp. 34–52). Pacific Grove, CA: Brooks/Cole.

Singh-Manoux, A., Marmot, M., & Adler, N. (2005). Does subjective social status predict health and change in health status better than objective status? *Psychosomatic Medicine, 67*(6), 855–861.

Sinha, S., & Mukherjee, N. (1996). The effect of perceived cooperation on personal space requirements. *Journal of Social Psychology, 136,* 655–657.

Sinha, S., & Nayyar, P. (2000). Crowding effects of density and personal space requirements among older people: The impact of self-control and social support. *Journal of Social Psychology, 140*(6), 721–726.

Sinha, S., Nayyar, P., & Mukherjee, N. (1995). Perception of crowding among children and adolescents. *Journal of Social Psychology, 135,* 263–268.

Siporin, M. (1975). *Introduction to social work practice.* New York: Macmillan.

Siporin, M. (1986). Contribution of religious values to social work and the law. *Social Thought, 12*(4), 35–50.

Siragusa, N. (2001). *The language of gender* [Electronic version]. New York: Gay Lesbian Straight Education Network. Retrieved December 29, 2006, from http://www.glsen.org/cgi-bin/iowa/all/libarary/record/811.html.

Skinner, B. F. (1948). *Walden Two.* New York: Macmillan.

Skocpol, T. (1979). *States and social revolutions.* New York: Cambridge University Press.

Skocpol, T. (2003). *Diminished democracy: From membership to management in American civil life.* New York: Cambridge University Press.

Skolnick, A. (1997, May/June). Family values: The sequel. *American Prospect, 32,* 86–94.

Skye, W. (2002). E.L.D.E.R.S. gathering for Native American youth: Continuing Native American traditions and curbing substance abuse in Native American youth. *Journal of Sociology and Social Welfare, 24*(1), 117–135.

Smith, C., & Denton, M. L. (2005). *Soul searching: The religious and spiritual lives of American teenagers.* New York: Oxford University Press.

Smith, E. D. (1995). Addressing the psychospiritual distress of death as reality: A transpersonal approach. *Social Work, 40,* 402–413.

Smith, E. D., & Gray, C. (1995). Integrating and transcending divorce: A transpersonal model. *Social Thought, 18*(1), 57–74.

Smith, G. (1996). Ties, nets and an elastic bund: Community in the postmodern city. *Community Development Journal, 31*(3), 250–259.

Smith, J. (2002). Bridging global divides: Strategic framing and solidarity in transnational social movement organizations. *International Sociology, 17*(4), 505–528.

Smith, J., Chatfield, C., & Pagnucco, R. (1997). *Transnational social movements and global politics: Solidarity beyond the state.* Syracuse, NY: Syracuse University Press.

Smith, N. R. (2006). *Workplace spirituality: A complete guide for business leaders.* Lynn, MA: Axial Age Publishing.

Smith, S. (2010). The political economy of contracting and competition. In Y. Hasenfeld (Ed.), *Human services as complex organizations* (2nd ed., pp. 139–160). Thousand Oaks, CA: Sage.

Snipp, C. M. (1998). The first Americans: American Indians. In M. L. Andersen & P. H. Collins (Eds.), *Race, class, and gender: An anthology* (pp. 357–364). Belmont, CA: Wadsworth.

Snyder, C., & Lopez, S. (2007). *Positive psychology: The scientific and practical explorations of human strengths.* Thousand Oaks, CA: Sage.

Snyder, S., & Mitchell, D. (2001). Re-engaging the body: Disability studies and the resistance to embodiment. *Public Culture, 13*(3), 367–389.

Solantaus, T., Leinonen, J., & Punamaki, R. (2004). Children's mental health in times of economic recession: Replication and extension of the Family Economic Stress Model in Finland. *Developmental Psychology, 40*(3), 412–429.

Sollod, R., Wilson, J., & Monte, C. (2009). *Beneath the mask: An introduction to theories of personality* (8th ed.). Hoboken, NJ: Wiley.

Solomon, B. (1976). *Black empowerment: Social work in oppressed communities.* New York: Columbia University Press.

Solomon, B. (1987). Empowerment: Social work in oppressed communities. *Journal of Social Work Practice, 2*(4), 79–91.

Sommer, R. (1969). *Personal space: The behavioral basis of design.* Englewood Cliffs, NJ: Prentice Hall.

Sommer, R. (2002). Personal space in a digital age. In R. Bechtel & A. Churchman (Eds.), *Handbook of environmental psychology* (pp. 647–660). New York: Wiley.

Sonn, C. (2002). Immigrant adaptation: Understanding the process through the sense of community. In A. T. Fisher, C. S. Sonn, & B. J. Bishop (Eds.), *Psychological sense of community: Research, applications, and implications* (pp. 205–222). New York: Plenum.

Sonn, C., & Fisher, A. (1996). Psychological sense of community in a politically constructed group. *Journal of Community Psychology, 24,* 417–430.

Soulsby, A., & Clark, E. (2007). Organization theory and the post-socialist transformation: Contributions to organizational knowledge. *Human Relations, 60*(10), 1419–1442.

Soyez, D. (2000). Anchored locally—linked globally. Transnational social movement organizations in a (seemingly) borderless world. *Earth and Environmental Science, 52*(1), 7–16.

Specht, H., & Courtney, M. E. (1994). *Unfaithful angels: How social work has abandoned its mission.* New York: Free Press.

Spiegel, D., & Classen, C. (2000). *Group therapy for cancer patients: A research-based handbook of psychosocial care.* New York: Basic Books.

Sprecher, S. (2005). Equity and social exchange in dating couples: Associations with satisfaction, commitment, and stability. In T. Chibucos & R. Leite, with D. Weis (Eds.), *Readings in family theory* (pp. 165–182). Thousand Oaks, CA: Sage.

Sprent, J., & Surth, C. (2001). Generation and maintenance of memory T cells. *Current Opinion in Immunology, 13*(2), 248–254.

Staats, H., Kieviet, A., & Hartig, T. (2003). Where to recover from attentional fatigue: An expectancy-value analysis of environmental preference. *Journal of Environmental Psychology, 23*(2), 147–157.

Stanbridge, K., & Kenney, J. S. (2009). Emotions and the campaign for victims' rights in Canada. *Canadian Journal of Criminology & Criminal Justice, 51*(4), 473–509.

Stanley, S., Markman, H., & Whitton, S. (2002). Communication, conflict, and commitment: Insights on the foundations for relationship success from a national survey. *Family Process, 41,* 659–675.

Stansfeld, S., Head, J., Bartley, M., & Fonagy, P. (2008). Social position, early deprivation and the development of attachment. *Social Psychiatry and Psychiatric Epidemiology, 43*(7), 516–526.

Staral, J. M. (2000). Building on mutual goals: The intersection of community practice and church-based organizing. *Journal of Community, 7*(3), 85–95.

Starhawk. (1979). *The spiral dance: A rebirth of the ancient religion of the great Goddess.* San Francisco: Harper & Row.

Stark, M. (2003). Restoring attention in pregnancy: The natural environment. *Clinical Nursing Research, 12*(3), 246–265.

Stein, L. (2009). Social movement web use in theory and practice: A content analysis of US movement websites. *New Media & Society, 11*(5), 749–771.

Stephens, K., & Clark, D. (1987). A pilot study on the effect of visible stigma on personal space. *Journal of Applied Rehabilitation Counseling, 18,* 52–54.

Sternberg, E. (2009). *Healing spaces: The science of place and well-being.* Cambridge, MA: Belknap Press.

Steves, L., & Blevins, T. (2005). From tragedy to triumph: A segue to community building for children and families. *Child Welfare, 84*(2), 311–322.

Stewart, C., Koeske, G., & Pringle, J. L. (2007). Religiosity as a predictor of successful post-treatment abstinence for

African-American clients. *Journal of Social Work Practice in the Addictions, 7*(4), 75–92.

Stewart, J. (2001). Radical constructivism in biology and cognitive science. *Foundations of Science, 6*(1–3), 99–124.

Stirling, K., & Aldrich, T. (2008). Child support: Who bears the burden? *Family Relations, 57,* 376–389.

Stocking, G. W., Jr. (1968). *Race, culture, and evolution: Essays on the history of anthropology.* New York: Free Press.

Stokols, D., & Montero, M. (2002). Toward an environmental psychology of the Internet. In R. Bechtel & A. Churchman (Eds.), *Handbook of environmental psychology* (pp. 661–675). New York: Wiley.

Stolte, J. F. (1994). Power. In M. Foshci & E. J. Lawler (Eds.), *Group processes: Sociological analyses* (pp. 149–176). Chicago: Nelson-Hall.

Stone, D. (2002). *Policy paradox: The art of political decision making* (Rev. ed.). New York: Norton.

Street, K., Harrington, J., Chiang, W., Cairns, P., & Ellis, M. (2004). How great is the risk of abuse in infants born to drug-using mothers? *Child Care, Health and Development, 30*(4), 325–330.

Streeter, C., & Gillespie, D. (1992). Social network analysis. *Journal of Social Service Research, 16,* 201–221.

Streifel, C., & Servaty-Seib, H. L. (2009). Recovering from alcohol and other drug dependency: Loss and spirituality in a 12-step context. *Alcoholism Treatment Quarterly, 27*(2), 184–198.

Strom-Gottfried, K., & Morrissey, M. (1999). The organizational diversity audit. In K. Strom-Gottfried (Ed.), *Social work practice: Cases, activities, and exercises* (pp. 168–172). Thousand Oaks, CA: Pine Forge.

Stuart, R. (1989). Social learning theory: A vanishing or expanding presence? *Psychology: A Journal of Human Behavior, 26,* 35–50.

Stuening, K. (2002). *New family values: Liberty, equality, diversity.* Lanham, MD: Rowman & Littlefield.

Sullivan, W., Kuo, F., & DePooter, S. (2004). The fruit of urban nature: Vital neighborhood spaces. *Environment and Behavior, 36*(5), 678–700.

Sunderman, G. (2006). *The unraveling of No Child Left Behind: How negotiated changes transform the law.* Cambridge, MA: The Civil Rights Project at Harvard University.

Suomi, S. J. (2005). Mother–infant attachment, peer relationships, and the development of social networks in rhesus monkeys. *Human Development,* 48(1–2), 67–79.

Swain, J., French, S., Barnes, C., & Thomas, C. (2004). *Disabling barriers—Enabling environments* (2nd ed.). Thousand Oaks, CA: Sage.

Swatos, W. H. (2005). Globalization theory and religious fundamentalism. In P. Kivisto (Ed.), *Illuminating social life:*

Classical and contemporary theory revisited (3rd ed., pp. 319–339). Thousand Oaks, CA: Pine Forge.

Swenson, C. H., Fuller, S., & Clements, R. (1993). Stage of religious faith and reactions to terminal cancer. *Journal of Psychology and Theology, 21,* 238–245.

Swidler, A. (1986). Culture in action: Symbols and strategies. *American Sociological Review, 51,* 273–286.

Swift, D. C. (1998). *Religion and the American experience.* Armonk, NY: M.E. Sharpe.

Swinton, J. (1997). Restoring the image: Spirituality, faith, and cognitive disability. *Journal of Religion and Health, 36*(1), 21–27.

Takano, T., Nakamura, K., & Watanabe, M. (2002). Urban residential environments and senior citizens' longevity in megacity areas: The importance of walkable green spaces. *Journal of Epidemiology and Community Health, 56*(12), 913–918.

Tan, P. P. (2006). Spirituality and religious beliefs among South-East Asians. *Reflections: Narratives of Professional Helping, 12*(3), 44–47.

Tangenberg, K. M. (2008). Saddleback Church and the P.E.A.C.E. plan: Implications for social work. *Social Work & Christianity, 35*(4), 391–412.

Tangenberg, K. M., & Kemp, S. (2002). Embodied practice: Claiming the body's experience, agency, and knowledge for social work. *Social Work, 47*(1), 9–18.

Tanielian, T., & Jaycox, L. (Eds.). (2008). *Invisible wounds of war: Psychological and cognitive injuries, their consequences, and services to assist recovery.* Santa Monica, CA: RAND Corporation.

Tanner, J. (2002). Do laws requiring higher wages cause unemployment? *CQ Researcher, 12*(33), 769–786.

Tarrow, S. (1994). *Power in movement: Social movements, collective action, and politics.* New York: Cambridge University Press.

Tarrow, S. (1998). *Power in movement: Social movements and contentious politics* (2nd ed.). New York: Cambridge University Press.

Tarrow, S. (2006). *The new transnational activism.* New York: Cambridge University Press.

Taylor, A., Kuo, F., Sullivan, W. (2002). Views of nature and self-discipline: Evidence from inner city children. *Journal of Environmental Psychology, 22*(1–2), 49–63.

Taylor, A., Wiley, A., Kuo, F., & Sullivan, W. (1998). Growing up in the inner city: Green spaces as places to grow. *Environment and Behavior, 30,* 3–27.

Taylor, F. W. (1911). *Principles of scientific management.* New York: Harper & Row.

Taylor, R. (1988). *Human territorial functioning: An empirical, evolutionary perspective on individual and small group territorial cognitions, behaviors, and consequences.* Cambridge, UK: Cambridge University Press.

Taylor, R. J., Ellison, C. G., Chatters, L. M., Levin, J. S., & Lincoln, D. L. (2000). Mental health services in faith communities: The role of clergy in Black churches. *Social Work, 45*(1), 73–87.

Taylor, S. E., Lewis, B., Gruenewald, T., Gurung, R., Updegraff, J., & Klein, L. (2002). Sex differences in biobehavioral responses to threat. *Psychological Review, 109*(4), 751–753.

Taylor, S. E., & Stanton, A. L. (2007) Coping resources, coping processes, and mental health. *Annual Review of Clinical Psychology, 3*, 377–401.

Teachman, J. (2003). Premarital sex, premarital cohabitation, and the risk of subsequent marital dissolution among women. *Journal of Marriage and Family, 65*(2), 444–455.

Teeple, G. (2000). *Globalization and the decline of social reform: Into the twenty-first century.* Aurora, Ont., Canada: Garamond Press.

Tennessen, C., & Cimprich, B. (1995). Views to nature: Effects on attention. *Journal of Environmental Psychology, 15*, 77–85.

Terkel, S. (2003). *Hope dies last: Keeping the faith in difficult times.* New York: The New Press.

Tesoriero, F. (2006). Strengthening communities through women's self-help groups in South India. *Community Development Journal, 41*(3), 321–333.

Thibaut, J. W., & Kelley, H. H. (1959). *The social psychology of groups.* New York: Wiley.

Thomas, M. L. (2009). Faith collaboration: A qualitative analysis of faith-based social service programs in organizational relationships. *Administration in Social Work, 33*(1), 40–60.

Thomas, W. I., & Thomas, D. S. (1928). *The child in America: Behavior problems and programs.* New York: Knopf.

Thompson, P. (1993). Postmodernism: Fatal distraction. In J. Hassard & M. Parker (Eds.), *Postmodernism and organizations* (pp. 183–203). Newbury Park, CA: Sage.

Thomson, R. G. (Ed.). (1996). *Freakery: Cultural spectacles of the extraordinary body.* New York: New York University Press.

Thyer, B. A. (2005). The misfortunes of behavioral social work: Misprized, misread, and misconstrued. In S. A. Kirk (Ed.), *Mental disorders in the social environment: Critical perspectives* (pp. 330–343). New York: Columbia University Press.

Thyer, B., & Wodarski, J. (2007). *Social work in mental health: An evidence-based approach.* Hoboken, NJ: Wiley.

TIE Internationales. (2009). *A global workers network.* Retrieved May 18, 2010, from http:www.tie-germany.org/who_we_are/index.html.

Tilly, C. (2004). *Social movements, 1768–2004.* Boulder, CO: Paradigm.

Tilton, J. (2009). Youth uprising: Gritty youth leadership development and communal transformation. In L. Nybell, J. Shook, & J. Finn (Eds.), *Childhood, youth, & social work in transformation: Implications for policy & practice* (pp. 385–400). New York: Columbia University Press.

Timberlake, E. M., & Cook, K. O. (1984). Social work and the Vietnamese refugee. *Social Work, 29*(2), 108–114.

Tindall, D. (2004). Social movement participation over time: An ego-network approach to micro-mobilization. *Sociological Focus, 37*, 163–184.

Titone, A. M. (1991). Spirituality and psychotherapy in social work practice. *Spirituality and Social Work Communicator, 2*(1), 7–9.

Tjaden, P., & Thoennes, N. (2000). *Full report of the prevalence, incidence, and consequence of violence against women: Findings from the National Violence Against Women Survey.* Research Report. Washington, DC: National Institute of Justice and Centers for Disease Control and Prevention. Retrieved May 17, 2010, from http://www.ncjrs.gov/ pdffiles1/nij/183781.pdf.

Tolliver, D. E. (2001). African-American female caregivers of family members living with HIV/AIDS. *Families in Society, 82*(2), 145–156.

Tomai, M., Veronica, R., Mebane, M., D'Acunti, A., Benedetti, M., & Francescato, D. (2010). Virtual communities in schools as tools to promote social capital with high school students. *Computers & Education, 54*, 265–274.

Tonnies, F. (1963). *Community and society* (C. P. Loomis, Ed.). New York: Harper & Row. (Original work published 1887)

Torrez, E. (1984). *The folk-healer: The Mexican-American tradition of curanderismo.* Kingsville, TX: Nieves Press.

Toseland, R. W., & Rivas, R. F. (2009). *An introduction to group work practice* (6th ed.). New York: Pearson.

Tracy, E., & Johnson, P. (2007). Personal social networks of women with co-occurring substance use and mental disorders. *Journal of Social Work Practice in Addictions, 7*(1/2), 69–70.

Tracy, E., & Martin, T. (2007). Children's roles in the social networks of women in substance abuse treatment. *Journal of Substance Abuse Treatment, 32*, 81–88.

Trees, A. (2006). Attachment theory: The reciprocal relationship between family communication and attachment patterns. In D. Braithwaite & L. Baxter (Eds.), *Engaging theories in family communication: Multiple perspectives* (pp. 165–180). Thousand Oaks, CA: Sage.

Tripses, J., & Scroggs, L. (2009). Spirituality and respect: Study of a model school–church–community collaboration. *School Community Journal, 19*(1), 77–97.

Troiden, R. (1989). The formation of homosexual identities. *Journal of Homosexuality, 17*, 43–73.

Tuckman, B. (1965). Developmental sequence in small groups. *Psychological Bulletin, 63*, 384–399.

Turner, R. P., Lukoff, D., Barnhouse, R. T., & Lu, F. G. (1995). Religious or spiritual problem: A culturally sensitive diagnostic category in the DSM–IV. *Journal of Nervous and Mental Disease, 183*, 435–444.

Tweed, T. T. (1997). Asian religions in the United States. In W. H. Conser, Jr., & S. B. Twiss (Eds.), *Religious diversity and American religious history: Studies in traditions and cultures* (pp. 189–217). Athens: University of Georgia Press.

Twiss, P., & Cooper, P. (2000). Youths revitalizing Main Street: A case study. *Social Work in Education, 22*(3), 162–176.

Uchino, B. N. (2009). Understanding the links between social support and physical health: A life-span perspective with emphasis on the separability of perceived and received support. *Perspectives on Psychological Science, 4*(3), 236–255.

Uchino, B. N., Holt-Lunstad, J., Smith, T. W., & Bloor, L. (2004). Heterogeneity in social networks: A comparison of different models linking relationships to psychological outcomes. *Journal of Social & Clinical Psychology, 23*(2), 123–139.

Uhlenbruck, K., Meyer, K., & Hitt, M. (2003). Organizational transformation in transition economies: Resource based and organizational learning perspectives. *Journal of Management Studies, 40,* 257–282.

Ulrich, R. (1984). View through a window may influence recovery from surgery. *Science, 224,* 420–421.

Ulrich, R. (1993). Biophilia, biophobia, and natural landscapes. In S. Kellert & E. Wilson (Eds.), *The biophilia hypothesis* (pp. 73–137). Washington, DC: Island Press.

Ulrich, R. (2006). Evidence-based health-care architecture. *Lancet, 368,* 538–539.

Ulrich, R., & Zimring, C. (2005). *The role of the physical environment in the hospital of the 21st century: A once-in-a-lifetime opportunity.* Retrieved October 10, 2009, from http://www.health design.org/research/ reports/physical_environ.php.

UNAIDS. (2005). Global summary of the HIV and AIDS epidemic in 2004. Retrieved April 24, 2005, from http://www.unaids .org/ en/resources/epidemiology.

UNESCO. (2010). *Education for All global monitoring report 2010: Summary.* Paris: Author.

Ungar, M. (2002). A deeper, more social ecological social work practice. *Social Service Review, 76*(3), 480–497.

UNICEF. (2000). *Child poverty in rich nations.* Florence, Italy: United Nations Children's Fund.

UNICEF. (2005). *Child poverty in rich countries 2005: Report card no. 6.* Florence, Italy: UNICEF Innocenti Research Centre.

UNICEF. (2007). *Child poverty in perspective: An overview of child well-being in rich countries.* Florence, Italy: United Nations Children's Fund.

UNICEF. (2009). *The state of the world's children: Special edition statistical tables.* New York: Author.

UNICEF. (n.d.). *Information by country and programme.* Retrieved January 13, 2010, from http://www.unicef.org/infobycountry/ index.html.

United Nations. (1948). *The universal declaration of human rights.* Retrieved January 14, 2010, from http://www.un.org/ Overview/rights.html.

United Nations Development Program. (2005). *Human development report 2005: International cooperation at the crossroads: Aid, trade and security in an unequal world.* New York: Oxford University Press.

University of Cincinnati. (2001–2010). *About COM. Polio.* University of Cincinnati, College of Medicine. Retrieved January 1, 2010, from http://www.med.uc.edu/about/history/htmlversion/polio.cfm.

Urban Institute. (2006). *Welfare reform: Ten years later.* Retrieved May 17, 2010, from http://www.urban.org/toolkit/issues/ welfarereform.cfm.

Urbina, I. (2010, March 23). Acorn to shut all offices by April 1. *New York Times,* p. A17.

U.S. Census Bureau. (2002a). *Census brief. Coming to America: A profile of the nation's foreign born (2000 update).* Washington, DC: Author

U.S. Census Bureau. (2002b). *Current population survey.* Washington, DC: Author.

U.S. Census Bureau. (2004). *The foreign born population 2004.* Washington, DC: Author.

U.S. Census Bureau. (2005). *People: Disability.* Retrieved June 11, 2005, from http://factfinder.census.gov.

U.S. Census Bureau. (2007). *Table 3. Marital history for people 15 years and over. Survey of income and program participation (SIPP), 2004 panel, wave 2 topic module.* Retrieved December 16, 2009, from http:// www.census.gov/population/socdemo/marital_ hist/2004/Table3.2004.xls.

U.S. Census Bureau (2009a). *America's families and living arrangements: 2007.* Retrieved December 9, 2009, from http:://www.census.gov/.

U.S. Census Bureau. (2009b). *Definition: Household and family.* Retrieved November 30, 2009, from http://www.census .gov/

U.S. Census Bureau. (2009c). *Population estimates program: National characteristics.* Retrieved July 23, 2009, from http://www .census.gov/popest/national/asrh/NC-EST2008-srh.html.

U.S. Census Bureau. (2009d). *U.S. POPClock projection.* Retrieved July 23, 2009, from http://www.census.gov/population/ www/popclockus.html.

U.S. Commission on Human Rights. (1998). Indian tribes: A continuing quest for survival. In P. S. Rothenberg (Ed.), *Race, class and gender in the United States: An integrated study* (4th ed., pp. 378–382). New York: St. Martin's Press.

U.S. Conference of Mayors. (2007). *A hunger and homelessness survey, 2007.* Retrieved October 16, 2009, from http://usmayors .org/uscm/home.asp.

U.S. Department of Health and Human Services. (2000). *Tracking healthy people 2010.* Washington, DC: U.S. Government Printing Office.

U.S. Department of Health and Human Services. (2008). *Child maltreatment 2006.* Washington, D.C.: Government Printing Office.

U.S. Department of Housing and Urban Development. (2009). *Federal definition of homeless.* Retrieved October 16, 2009, from http://www.hud.gov/homeless/definition.cfm.

U.S. Department of Labor, Bureau of Labor Statistics. (2008). *Employment and earnings, 2008 annual averages and the monthly labor review.* Retrieved December 3, 2009, from http://www.dol.gov/wb/stats/main.htm.

U.S. Department of Labor, Bureau of Labor Statistics. (2010). *Economic news release: Employment situation summary.* Retrieved February 20, 2010, from http://www.bls.gov/news.release/empsit.nr0.htm.

Vaillant, G. (2002). *Aging well.* Boston: Little, Brown.

Valenti, M., & Rockett, T. (2008). The effects of demographic differences on forming intragroup relationships. *Small Group Research, 39*(2), 179–2002.

Van Aelst, P., & Walgrave, S. (2004). New media, new movements? The role of the Internet in shaping the "ant-globalization" movement. In W. van de Donk, B. Loader, P. Nixon, & D. Rucht (Eds.), *Cyberprotest: New media, citizens and social movements* (pp. 87–108). London: Routledge.

VanDeMark, N., Russelol, L, O'Keefe, M., Finkelstein, N., Noether, C., & Gambell, J. (2005). Children of mothers with histories of substance abuse, mental illness, and trauma. *Journal of Community Psychology, 33,* 445–459.

Vanden Heuvel, K., & Graham-Felsen, S. (2006). Chicago's living wage. *The Nation, 283*(9), 8–9.

Van Hook, M., Hugen, B., & Aguilar, M. (Eds.). (2001). *Spirituality within religious traditions in social work practice.* Pacific Grove, CA: Brooks/Cole.

Varela, F. (1989). Reflections on the circulation of concepts between the biology of cognition and systemic family therapy. *Family Process, 28,* 15–24.

Veeder, N. W., & Dalgin, R. E. (2004). Social work as management: A retrospective study of 245 hospital care management practice outcomes. *Journal of Social Service Research, 31*(1), 33–58.

Verity, F., & King, S. (2007). Responding to intercommunal conflict—What can restorative justice offer? *Community Development Journal, 43*(4), 470–482.

Vetere, A. (2005). Structural family therapy. In T. Chibucos & R. Leite (Eds.), *Readings in family theory* (pp. 293–302). Thousand Oaks, CA: Sage.

Viacom. (2008–2009). *Our brands.* Retrieved May 19, 2010, from http://www.viacom.com_ourbrands/Pages/default.aspx.

Vickrey, B. G., Strickland, T. L., Fitten, L. J., Admas, G. R., Ortiz, F., & Hays, R. D. (2007). Ethnic variations in dementia caregiving experiences: Insights from focus groups. *Journal of Human Behavior in the Social Environment, 15*(2/3), 233–249.

Virilio, P. (2000). *The information bomb.* London: Verso.

Vlahov, D., Galea, S., & Freudenberg, N. (2005). The urban health "advantage." *Journal of Urban Health, 82*(1), 1–4.

Vohra-Gupta, S., Russell, A., & Lo, E. (2007). Meditation: The adoption of Eastern thought to Western social practices. *Social Thought, 26*(2), 49–61.

Vosler, N. R. (1996). *New approaches to family practice: Confronting economic stress.* Thousand Oaks, CA: Sage.

Voss, K. (1996). The collapse of a social movement: The interplay of mobilizing structures, framing, and political opportunities in the Knights of Labor. In D. McAdams, J. McCarthy, & M. Zald (Eds.), *Comparative perspectives on social movements* (pp. 227–258). New York: Cambridge University Press.

Voss, R. W., Douville, V., Little Soldier, A., & Twiss, G. (1999). Tribal and shamanic-based social work practice: A Lakota perspective. *Social Work, 44*(3), 228–241.

Vranic, A. (2003). Personal space in physically abused children. *Environment and Behavior, 35*(4), 550–565.

Vryan, K. D., Adler, P. A., & Adler, P. (2003). Identity. In L. T. Reynolds & N. J. Herman-Kinney, *Handbook of symbolic interactionism* (pp. 367–390). Walnut Creek, CA: AltaMira Press

Waanders, C., Mendez, J., & Downer, J. (2007). Parent characteristics, economic stress and neighborhood context as predictors of parent involvement in preschool children's education. *Journal of School Psychology, 45*(6), 619–636.

Wachs, T. (1992). *The nature of nurture.* Newbury Park, CA: Sage.

Wadsworth, M., & Santiago, C. (2008). Risk and resiliency processes in ethnically diverse families in poverty. *Journal of Family Psychology, 22*(3), 399–410.

Wagner, R. (1981). *The invention of culture.* Chicago: University of Chicago Press.

Wainwright, J., Russell, S., & Patterson, C. (2004). Psychosocial adjustment, school outcomes, and romantic relationships of adolescents with same-sex parents. *Child Development, 75,* 1886–1898.

Walch, J., Day, R., & Kang, J. (2005). The effect of sunlight on post-operative analgesic medication use: A prospective study of patients undergoing spinal surgery. *Psychosomatic Medicine, 67,* 156–163.

Waldron-Hennessey, R., & Sabatelli, R. (1997). The Parental Comparison Level Index: A measure of assessing parental rewards and costs relative to expectations. *Journal of Marriage and the Family, 59,* 823–833.

Wallerstein, I. (1974). *The modern world system: Capitalist agriculture and the origins of the European world economy in the 16th century.* New York: Academic Press.

Wallerstein, I. (1979). *The capitalist world economy.* London: Cambridge University Press.

Wallerstein, I. (1980). *The modern world-system: Mercantilism and the consolidation of the European world economy, 1600–1750.* New York: Academic Press.

Wallerstein, I. (1989). *The modern world-system: The second great expansion of the capitalist world-economy, 1730–1840's.* San Diego: Academic Press.

Wallerstein, J., & Blakeslee, S. (1990). *Second chances.* New York: Ticknor & Fields.

Walker, D. F., Reid, H. W., O'Neill, T., & Brown, L. (2009). Changes in personal religion/spirituality during and after childhood abuse: A review and synthesis. *Psychological Trauma: Theory, Research, Practice, and Policy, 1*(2), 130–145.

Walsh, F. (2003a). Changing families in a changing world: Reconstructing family normality. In F. Walsh (Ed.), *Normal family processes: Growing diversity and complexity* (3rd ed., pp. 3–26). New York: Guilford Press.

Walsh, F. (2003b). Family resilience: Strengths forged through adversity. In F. Walsh (Ed.), *Normal family processes: Growing diversity and complexity* (3rd ed., pp. 399–423). New York: Guilford Press.

Walsh, F. (2006). *Strengthening family resilience* (2nd ed.). New York: Guilford Press.

Walsh, F. (2009a). Integrating spirituality in family therapy: Wellsprings for health, healing, and resilience. In F. Walsh (Ed.), *Spiritual resources in family therapy* (2nd ed., pp. 31–61). New York: Guilford Press.

Walsh, F. (2009b). Spiritual resources in family adaptation to death and loss. In F. Walsh (Ed.), *Spiritual resources in family therapy* (2nd ed., pp. 81–102). New York: Guilford Press.

Walsh, J. (2000). *Clinical case management with persons having mental illness: A relationship-based perspective.* Pacific Gove: Brooks/Cole.

Walsh, J. (2010). *Theories for direct social work practice* (2nd ed.). Belmont, CA: Wadsworth.

Walsh, J., Meyer, A., & Schoonhoven, C. (2006). A future for organization theory: Living in and living with changing organizations. *Organization Science, 17*(5), 657–671.

Walsh, J., & Zacharias-Walsh, A. (2008). Working longer, living less: Understanding Marx through the workplace today. In P. Kivisto (Ed.), *Illuminating social life* (4th ed., pp. 5–40). Thousand Oaks, CA: Sage.

Wamsley, G., & Zald, M. (1973). *The political economy of public organizations.* Lexington, MA: Heath.

Wanyeki, I., Olson, S., Brassard, P., Menzies, D., Ross, N., Behr, M., et al. (2006). Dwellings, crowding, and tuberculosis in Montreal. *Social Science & Medicine, 63*(2), 501–511.

Wapner, S. (1995). Toward integration: Environmental psychology in relation to other subfields of psychology. *Environment and Behavior, 27,* 9–32.

Warner, S. R. (1993). Work in progress: Toward a new paradigm for the sociological study of religion in the United States. *American Journal of Sociology, 98,* 1044–1093.

Warren, K., Franklin, C., & Streeter, C. (1998). New directions in systems theory: Chaos and complexity. *Social Work, 43*(4), 357–372.

Warren, R. (1963). *The community in America.* Chicago: Rand McNally.

Warren, R. (1978). *The community in America* (2nd ed.) Chicago: Rand McNally.

Warren, R. (1987). *The community in America* (3rd ed.). Chicago: Rand McNally.

Warren, R. (1988). Observations on the state of community theory. In R. Warren & L. Lyon, *New perspectives on the American community* (5th ed., pp. 84–86). Chicago: Dorsey.

Warwick, L. L. (1995). Feminist Wicca: Paths to empowerment. *Women and Therapy: A Feminist Quarterly, 16*(2/3), 121–133.

Wasserman, H., & Danforth, H. E. (1988). *The human bond: Support groups and mutual aid.* New York: Springer.

Watters, E. (2010). *Crazy like us: The globalization of the American psyche.* New York: Free Press.

Watts, F., Dutton, K., & Gulliford, L. (2006). Human spiritual qualities: Integrating psychology and religion. *Mental Health, Religion & Culture, 9*(3), 277–289.

Weaver, H. (1999). Indigenous people and the social work profession: Defining culturally competent services. *Social Work, 44*(3), 217–225.

Weaver, H. (2007). Cultural competence with First Nations peoples. In D. Lum (Ed.), *Culturally competent practice: A framework for understanding diverse groups and justice issues* (3rd ed., pp. 254–275). Belmont, CA: Thomson.

Webb, J., & Weber, M. (2003). Influence of sensory abilities on the interpersonal distance of the elderly. *Environment and Behavior, 35*(5), 695–711.

Webb, S. J., Monk, C. S., & Nelson, C. A. (2001). Mechanisms of postnatal neurobiological development: Implications for human development. *Developmental Neuropsychology, 19*(2), 147–171.

Weber, M. (1947). *The theory of economic and social organization.* New York: Free Press.

Weber, M. (1958). *The Protestant ethic and the spirit of capitalism* (T. Parsons, Trans.). New York: Scribner's. (Original work published 1904–1905)

WebUrbanDesign. (2009). *New urbanism & urban design.* Retrieved October 15, 2009, from http://www.weburbandesign.com.

Weil, M. (Ed.). (2005a). *The handbook of community practice.* Thousand Oaks, CA: Sage.

Weil, M. (2005b). Introduction: Contexts and challenges for 21st-century communities. In M. Weil (Ed.), *The handbook of community practice* (pp. 3–33). Thousand Oaks, CA: Sage.

Weil, M. (2005c). Social planning with communities: Theory and practice. In M. Weil (Ed.), *The handbook of community practice* (pp. 215–243). Thousand Oaks, CA: Sage.

Weil, M., & Gamble, D. (2005). Evolution, models, and the changing context of community practice. In M. Weil (Ed.), *The handbook of community practice* (pp. 117–149). Thousand Oaks, CA: Sage.

Weiner, B. (2008). Reflections on the history of attribution theory and research: People, personalities, publications, problems. *Social Psychology, 39*(3), 151–156.

Weisberg, R. (Producer/Director). (2006). *Waging a living* [Motion picture]. New York: Public Policy Productions.

Weisman, G. (1981). Modeling environment–behavior systems: A brief note. *Journal of Man–Environment Relations, 1*(2), 32–41.

Weitz, R. (2009). *The sociology of health, illness, and health care: A critical approach* (5th ed.). Beverly, MA: Wadsworth.

Wellman, B. (1979). The community question. *American Journal of Sociology, 84,* 1201–1231.

Wellman, B. (1982). Studying personal communities. In P. Marsden & N. Lin (Eds.), *Social structure and network analysis* (pp. 61–80). Beverly Hills, CA: Sage.

Wellman, B. (1996). Are personal communities local? A Dumptarian reconsideration. *Social Networks, 18,* 347–354.

Wellman, B. (1999). The network community: An introduction. In B. Wellman (Ed.), *Networks in the global village* (pp. 1–47). Boulder, CO: Westview Press.

Wellman, B. (2001). *The persistence and transformation of community: From neighborhood groups to social networks*: Report to the Law Commission of Canada. Retrieved November 13, 2009, from http://www.chass.utoronto.ca/~wellman/publications/index.html

Wellman, B. (2005). Community: From neighborhood to network. *Communications of the ACM, 48*(10), 53–55.

Wellman, B., & Potter, S. (1999). The elements of personal communities. In B. Wellman (Ed.), *Networks in the global village* (pp. 49–81). Boulder, CO: Westview Press.

Wellman, B., & Wortley, S. (1990). Different strokes from different folks: Community ties and social support. *American Journal of Sociology, 96,* 558–588.

Welwood, J. (2000). *Toward a psychology of awakening: Buddhism, psychotherapy, and the path of personal and spiritual transformation.* Boston: Shambhala.

Wenger, G. C. (2009). Childlessness at the end of life: Evidence from rural Wales. *Ageing and Society, 29*(8), 1243–1259.

Wenocur, S., & Soifer, S. (1997). Prospects for community organization. In M. Reisch & E. Gambrill (Eds.), *Social work in the 21st century* (pp. 198–209). Thousand Oaks, CA: Pine Forge.

Werner, C., & Altman, I. (2000). Humans and nature: Insights from a transactional view. In S. Wapner, J. Demick, T. Yamamoto, & H. Minami (Eds.), *Theoretical perspectives in environment-behavior research: Underlying assumptions, research problems, and methodologies* (pp. 21–37). New York: Kluwer Academic.

Werner, C., Altman, I., & Oxley, D. (1985). Temporal aspects of homes: A transactional perspective. In I. Altman & C. Werner (Eds.), *Home environments* (pp. 1–32). New York: Plenum.

Werner, C., Brown, B., & Altman, I. (2002). Transactionally oriented research: Examples and strategies. In R. Bechtel & A. Churchman, *Handbook of environmental psychology* (pp. 203–221). Hoboken, NJ: Wiley.

Werner, E., & Smith, R. (2001). *Journeys from childhood to midlife.* Ithaca, NY: Cornell University Press.

West, M. (1986). *Landscape views and stress responses in the prison environment.* Unpublished master's thesis, University of Washington, Seattle.

Westrin, A., & Lam, R. (2007). Seasonal affective disorder: A clinical update. *Annals of Clinical Psychiatry, 19*(4), 239–246.

Wethington, E., Moen, P., Glasgow, N., & Pillemer, K, (2000). Multiple roles, social integration, and health. In K. Pillemer, P. Moen, & N. Glasgow (Eds.), *Social integration in the second half of life* (pp. 48–71). Baltimore: Johns Hopkins University Press.

Wettenhall, R. (1999). Privatization in Australia: How much and what impacts? *Asian Review of Public Administration, 10*(1–2), 144–158.

Wheelan, S. (2005). The developmental perspective. In S. Wheelan (Ed.), *The handbook of group research and practice* (pp. 119–132). Thousand Oaks, CA: Sage.

Wheeler, H. (Ed.). (1973). *Beyond the punitive society.* San Francisco: Freeman.

White, J., & Klein, D. (2002). *Family theories* (2nd ed.). Thousand Oaks, CA: Sage.

White, J., & Klein, D. (2008a). The conflict framework. In *Family theories* (3rd ed., pp. 179–204). Thousand Oaks, CA: Sage.

White, J., & Klein, D. (2008b). The feminist framework and post-structuralism. In J. White & D. Klein, *Family theories* (3rd ed., pp. 205–240). Thousand Oaks, CA: Sage.

White, J., & Klein, D. (2008c). The social exchange and rational choice framework. In *Family theories* (3rd ed., pp. 65–92). Thousand Oaks, CA: Sage.

White, J., & Klein, D. (2008d). The systems framework. In *Family theories* (3rd ed., pp. 151–177). Thousand Oaks, CA: Sage.

White, P. (Ed.). (2005). *Biopsychosocial medicine: An integrated approach to understanding illness.* Oxford, UK: Oxford University Press.

Whitehead, B. (1997). *The divorce culture.* New York: Knopf.

Whitehouse.gov. (2010). *Health care.* Retrieved May 8, 2010, from http://www.whitehouse.gov/issues/health-care.

Whiting, B., & Whiting, J. (1975). *Children of six cultures: Studies of childrearing.* Cambridge, MA: Harvard University Press.

Wicker, A. (1979). *An introduction to ecological psychology.* Monterey, CA: Brooks/Cole.

Wicker, A. (1987). Behavior settings reconsidered: Temporal stages, resources, internal dynamics, context. In D. Stokols & I. Altman (Eds.), *Handbook of environmental psychology* (Vol. 1, pp. 613–654). New York: Wiley.

Wilber, K. (1977). *Spectrum of consciousness.* Adyar, India: Quest Books.

Wilber, K. (1995). *Sex, ecology, spirituality: The spirit of evolution.* Boston: Shambhala.

Wilber, K. (1996). *A brief history of everything.* Boston: Shambhala.

Wilber, K. (1997a). *The eye of spirit: An integral vision for a world gone slightly mad.* Boston: Shambhala.

Wilber, K. (1997b). An integral theory of consciousness. *Journal of Consciousness Studies, 4*(1), 71–93.

Wilber, K. (2000a). *Integral psychology: Consciousness, spirit, psychology, therapy.* Boston: Shambhala.

Wilber, K. (2000b). *Sex, ecology, spirituality: The spirit of evolution* (2nd ed.). Boston: Shambhala.

Wilber, K. (2001). *A theory of everything: An integral vision for business, politics, science, and spirituality.* Boston: Shambhala.

Wilber, K. (2006). *Integral spirituality.* Boston: Integral Books.

Wilkin, A. C. (2009). Masculinity dilemmas: Sexuality and intimacy talk among Christians and Goths. *Signs, 34*(2), 343–368.

Wilkinson, R. (2001). Why is inequality bad for health? In J. Auerbach & B. Krimgold (Eds.), *Income, socioeconomic status, and health: Exploring the relationships* (pp. 29–43). Washington, DC: National Policy Association, Academy for Health Services Research and Health Policy.

Willer, D. (1987). *Theory and the experimental investigation of social structures.* New York: Gordon and Breach.

Williams, A., & Nussbaum, J. (2001). *Intergenerational communication across the life span.* Mahwah, NJ: Erlbaum.

Williams, C. (2006). The epistemology of cultural competence. *Families in Society: The Journal of Contemporary Social Services, 87*(2), 209–220.

Williams, M., Teasdale, J. D., Segal, Z., & Kabat-Zinn, J. (2007). *The mindful way through depression: Freeing yourself from unhappiness.* New York: Guilford Press.

Williams, R. (1977). *Marxism and literature.* Oxford, UK: Oxford University Press.

Williams, R. (1983). *Key words: A vocabulary of culture and society* (Rev. ed.). New York: Oxford University Press.

Williamson, J. S., & Wyandt, C. M. (2001). New perspectives on alternative medicines. *Drug Topics, 145*(1), 57–66.

Willis, J. (2010). *Researching London's Living Wage Campaign.* Retrieved October 23, 2009, from http://www.geog/qmul.ac.uk/livingwage/.

Wills, T. A., Yaeger, A. M., & Sandy, J. M. (2003). Buffering effect of religiosity for adolescent substance abuse. *Psychology of Addictive Behaviors, 17*(1), 24–31.

Wilson, E. (1984). *Biophilia.* Cambridge, MA: Harvard University Press.

Wilson, E. (2007). Biophilia and the conservation ethic. In D. Penn & I. Mysterud (Eds.), *Evolutionary perspectives on environmental problems* (pp. 249–257). New Brunswick, NJ: Transaction Publishers.

Wilson, G., & Baldassare, M. (1996). Overall "sense of community" in a suburban region: The effects of localism, privacy, and urbanization. *Environment and Behavior, 28*(1), 27–43.

Wilson, J. Q. (1995). *On character.* Washington, DC: AIE Press.

Winant, H. (2004). *The new politics of race: Globalism, difference, justice.* Minneapolis: University of Minnesota Press.

Winnicott, D. W. (1975). *Collected papers: From paediatrics to psycho-analysis.* New York: Basic Books.

Winston, C. A. (2006). African American grandmothers parenting AIDS orphans: Grieving and coping. *Qualitative Social Work, 5*(1), 33–43.

Wirth, J. (2009). The function of social work. *Journal of Social Work, 9*(4), 405–419.

Wisniewski, C. (2008). Applying complementary and alternative medicine practices in a social work context: A focus on mindfulness meditation. *Praxis, 8*, 13–22.

Witkin, S., & Gottschalk, S. (1988). Alternative criteria for theory evaluation. *Social Service Review, 62*, 211–224.

Wittine, B. (1987, September/October). Beyond ego. *Yoga Journal*, pp. 51–57.

Wituk, S., Shepherd, M. D., Slavich, S., Warren, M. L., & Meissen, G. (2000). A topography of self-help groups: An empirical analysis. *Social Work, 45*(2), 157–165.

Wong, Y., & Hillier, A. (2001). Evaluating a community-based homelessness prevention program: A geographic information system approach. *Administration in Social Work, 25*(4), 21–45.

Wood, J. (2006). Critical feminist theories: A provocative perspective on families. In D. Braithwaite & L. Baxter (Eds.),

Engaging theories in family communication: Multiple perspectives (pp. 197–212). Thousand Oaks, CA: Sage.

Wood, R. (2002). *Faith in action: Religion, race, and democratic organizing in America.* Chicago: University of Chicago Press.

Woods, T., Antoni, M., Ironson, G., & Kling, D. (1999). Religiosity is associated with affective and immune status in symptomatic HIV-infected gay men. *Journal of Psychosomatic Research, 46*(2), 165–176.

Woolever, C. (1992). A contextual approach to neighbourhood attachment. *Urban Studies, 29*(1), 99–116.

World Bank. (2009). Social capital implementation framework. Retrieved November 16, 2009, from http://www.worldbank.org/.

World Health Organization. (2006a). *Countries.* Retrieved November 3, 2006, from http://www.who.int/countries/.

World Health Organization. (2006b). *Global access to HIV therapy tripled in past two years, but significant challenges remain.* Retrieved June 24, 2006, from http://www.who.int/hiv/mediacentre/news57/en/index.html.

World Health Organization. (2006c). *Global polio eradication initiative strategic plan 2004–2008. Polio Case Count.* Retrieved May 17, 2010, from http://www.comminit.com/en/node/267428/292.

World Health Organization. (2006d). *The world health report 2006.* Retrieved November 3, 2006, from http://www.who.int/whr/2006/.

World Health Organization. (2008a). Poliomyelitis. *Fact Sheet No. 114.* Retrieved January 1, 2010, from http:// www.who.int/mediacentre/factsheets/fs114/en/index.html.

World Health Organization. (2008b). *Primary health care: Now more than ever.* Geneva, Switzerland: Author. Retrieved February 22, 2010, from http://www.who.int/whr/ 2008/whr08_en.pdf.

Woyach, R. B. (1993). *Preparing for leadership: A young adult's guide to leadership skills in a global age.* Westport, CT: Greenwood Press.

Wright, V. H. (2005). *The soul tells a story: Engaging spirituality with creativity in the writing life.* Downers Grove, IL: InterVarsity Press.

Wronka, J. (2008). *Human rights and social justice: Social action and service for the helping and health professions.* Thousand Oaks, CA: Sage.

Wuthnow, R. (2001). *Creative spirituality: The way of the artist.* Berkeley: University of California Press.

Wuthnow, R. (2003). Studying religion, making it sociological. In M. Dillon (Ed.). *Handbook of the sociology of religion* (pp. 17–30). Cambridge, UK: Cambridge University Press.

Yalom, I. D. (1995). *The theory and practice of group psychotherapy* (4th ed.). New York: Basic Books.

Yang, B., & Brown, J. (1992). A cross-cultural comparison of preferences for landscape styles and landscape elements. *Environment and Behavior, 24,* 471–507.

Yellow Bird, M. J. (1995). Spirituality in First Nations story telling: A Sahnish-Hidatsa approach to narrative. *Reflections: Narratives of Professional Helping, 1*(4), 65–72.

Yoon, D. P., & Lee, E. K. O. (2004). Religiousness/spirituality and subjective well-being among rural elderly whites, African Americans, and Native Americans. *Journal of Human Behavior in the Social Environment, 10*(1), 191–211.

Zachary, E. (2000). Grassroots leadership training: A case study of an effort to integrate theory and method. *Journal of Community Practice, 7*(1), 71–93.

Zastrow, C.H. (2009). *Social work with groups: A comprehensive workbook* (7th ed). Belmont, CA: Brooks/Cole.

Zautra, A. (2003). *Emotions, stress, and health.* New York: Oxford University Press.

Zeisel, J. (2006). *Inquiry by design: Environment/behavior/neuroscience in architecture, interiors, landscape, and planning* (Rev. ed.). New York: Norton.

Zimbardo, P. (2007). *The Lucifer effect.* New York: Random House.

Zimmerman, S. (2001). *Family policy: Constructed solutions to family problems.* Thousand Oaks, CA: Sage.

Zimmet, P., Alberti, K., & Shaw, J. (2001). Global and societal implications of the diabetes epidemic. *Nature, 414,* 782–787.

Zinnbauer, B., Pargament, K., Cole, B., Rye, M., Butter, E., & Belavich, T. (1997). Religion and spirituality: Unfuzzying the fuzzy. *Journal for the Scientific Study of Religion, 36,* 549–564.

Zuniga, M. (1988). Chicano self-concept: A proactive stance. In C. Jacobs & D. Bowles (Eds.), *Ethnicity and race: Critical concepts in social work* (pp. 71–83). Silver Spring, MD: NASW Press.

Zunkel, G. (2002). Relational coping processes: Couples' response to a diagnosis of early stage breast cancer. *Journal of Psychosocial Oncology, 20*(4), 39–55.

Glossary

ABC-X model of family stress and coping A way of viewing families that focuses on stressor events and crises, family resources, family definitions and beliefs, and outcomes of stress pileup

Accommodation (cognitive) The process of altering a schema when a new situation cannot be incorporated within an existing schema

Accommodation (cultural) Process of partial or selective cultural change in which members of nondominant groups follow the norms, rules, and standards of the dominant culture only in specific circumstances and contexts

Acculturation A process of changing one's culture by incorporating elements of another culture; a mutual sharing of culture

Acquired immunodeficiency syndrome (AIDS) Disease caused by human immunodeficiency virus (HIV); involves breakdown of the immune system

Adaptation A change in functioning or coping style that results in a better adjustment of a person to his or her environment

Affect The physiological manifestation of a feeling

Afrocentric relational theory Assumes a collective identity for people rather than valuing individuality; places great value on the spiritual or nonmaterial aspects of life

Agency The capacity to intentionally make things happen

Agency-based model A model of community social work practice that focuses on promoting social agencies and the services they provide

Antibodies Protein molecules that attach to the surface of specific antigens in an effort to destroy them

Antigens Foreign substances such as bacteria, fungi, protozoa, and viruses that cause the immune system to react

Assimilation (cognitive) In cognitive theory, the incorporation of new experiences into an existing schema

Assimilation (cultural) The process of change whereby individuals of one society or ethnic group are culturally incorporated or absorbed into another by adopting the patterns and norms of the host culture

Assistive devices Devices that allow a person with a disability to communicate, see, hear, or maneuver. Examples include wheelchairs, motorized scooters, hearing aids, and telephone communications devices (TTD/TTY)

Assumption Something taken to be true without testing or proof

Atria (atrium) The two upper, thin-walled chambers of the heart

Attribution theory A theory of emotional behavior that asserts that the experience of emotion is based on conscious evaluations people make about their physiological sensations in particular social settings

Autoimmune diseases Diseases that occur when the immune system wrongly attacks systems that it should be protecting

Axon A conduction fiber that conducts impulses away from the body of a nerve cell

Behavior settings Settings where particular kinds of activities are performed. For example, a school classroom is a behavior setting where learning/teaching activities are performed.

Behavior settings theories Theories that propose that consistent, uniform patterns of behavior occur in particular places, or behavior settings

Bicultural socialization Process whereby members of nonmajority groups master both the dominant culture and their own culture

Bifurcate Divide into two branches, as in labor force bifurcation into a core of stable, well-paid labor and a periphery of casual, low-wage labor

Biological determinism Defining and differentiating social behavior on the basis of biological and genetic endowment

Biophilia A genetically based need of humans to affiliate with nature

Biopsychosocial approach An approach that considers human behavior to be the result of interactions of integrated biological, psychological, and social systems

Blood pressure Measure of the pressure of the blood against the wall of a blood vessel

Bonding social capital Community relationships that are inward looking and tend to mobilize solidarity and in-group loyalty; they lead to exclusive identities and homogenous communities

Boundary An imaginary line of demarcation that defines which human and nonhuman elements are included in a given system and which elements are outside the system

Boundary-regulating mechanisms Mechanisms, such as personal space and territoriality, that we use to gain greater control over our physical environments

Brain injury (BI) Damage to the brain arising from head trauma (falls, automobile accidents), infections (encephalitis), insufficient oxygen (stroke), or poisoning

Bridging social capital Community relationships that are outward looking and diverse and that link community members to assets and information across community boundaries

Brief treatment model A type of practice modality characterized by a brief time period for intervention (usually 6 weeks or less) and practice techniques that are solution focused

Built environment The portion of the physical environment attributable solely to human effort

Bureaucracy A form of organization, considered by Max Weber to be the most efficient form for goal accomplishment, based on formal rationality

Burnout A process in which a previously committed worker disengages from his or her work in response to stress and strain experienced in the job

Cardiovascular system Biological system made up of the heart and the blood circulatory system

Chaos theory A theory that emphasizes systems processes that produce change, even sudden, rapid change

Charity organization society (COS) movement A social movement, brought to the United States from England in the late 1800s, that emphasized the delivery of services through private charity organizations

Classical conditioning theory A theory in the social behavioral perspective that sees behavior as the result of the association of a conditioned stimulus with an unconditioned stimulus

Closed group A natural or formed group that is open to certain persons and closed to others based on such characteristics as age, gender, geographic location, or type of problem/issue; a natural or formed group that opens its membership for a certain time period and then closes the group when the ideal number of members has been reached or the time period has elapsed

Cognition Conscious thinking processes; mental activities of which the individual is fully aware. These processes include taking in information from the environment, synthesizing that information, and formulating plans of action based on that synthesis

Cognitive mediation The influence of thinking between the occurrence of a stimulus and one's response to the stimulus

Cognitive operations Use of abstract thoughts and ideas that are not tied to sensory and motor information

Cognitive social learning theory A theory in the social behavioral perspective that sees behavior as learned by imitation and through cognitive processes

Cohabiting When a couple lives together without marriage

Collective efficacy The ability of community residents to engage in collective action to gain control of the neighborhood

Colonialism The practice of dominant and powerful nations going beyond their boundaries; using military force to occupy and claim less dominant and powerful nations; imposing their culture, laws, and language upon the occupied nation through the use of settlers

Common sense Shared ways of perceiving reality and shared conclusions drawn from lived experience; an organized body of culture-bound beliefs that members of a community or society believe to be second nature, plain, obvious, and self-evident

Communication networks The organization and pattern of communication among group members

Community People bound either by geography or by webs of communication, sharing common ties, and interacting with one another

Community development A collaborative model of community social work that seeks to bring together diverse interests for the betterment of the community as a whole, with attention to community building and improved sense of community

Concept A word or phrase that serves as an abstract description, or mental image, of some phenomenon

Conflict perspective An approach to human behavior that draws attention to conflict, dominance, and oppression in social life

Conscience constituency People who are attracted to a social movement because it appears just and worthy, not because they will benefit personally

Conservative thesis A philosophy that inequality is the natural, divine order and no efforts should be made to alter it

Control theories Theories that focus on the issue of how much control we have over our physical environment and the attempts we make to gain control

Conventional morality In Kohlberg's theory of moral development, a stage in which moral decisions are based on adherence to social rules

Coping A person's efforts to master the demands of stress, including the thoughts, feelings, and actions that constitute those efforts

Countermovement A social movement that arises to oppose a successful social movement

Crisis A major upset in psychological equilibrium as a result of some hazardous event, experienced as a threat or loss, with which the person cannot cope

Critical consciousness The ongoing process of reflection and knowledge seeking about mechanisms and outcomes of social, political, and economic oppression; requires taking personal and collective action toward fairness and social justice.

Critical perspective on organizations A perspective that sees formal organizations as instruments of domination

Critical theorists Theorists who argue that as capitalism underwent change, people were more likely to be controlled by culture and their consumer role than by their work position

Critical thinking Engaging in a thoughtful and reflective judgment about alternative views and contradictory information; involves thinking about your own thinking and the influences on that thinking, as well as a willingness to change your mind

Crowding Unpleasant experience of feeling spatially cramped

Cultural conflict Conflict over the meaning of cultural symbols

Cultural framing A conscious effort by a group of people to develop shared understandings of the world and themselves

Cultural framing (CF) perspective An approach to social movements that asserts that they can be successful only when participants develop shared understandings and definitions of some situation that impels the participants to feel aggrieved or outraged, motivating them to action

Cultural hegemony The all-encompassing dominance of particular structures in society. Not limited to political control, but includes a way of seeing the world that includes cultural and political dominance

Cultural innovation A process of adapting, modifying, and changing culture through interaction over time

Cultural relativism The position that behavior in a particular culture should not be judged by the standards of another culture

Culture Shared cognitive and emotional frames and lenses that serve as the bases for an evolving map for living. It is constructed from the entire spectrum of human actions and the material circumstances of people in societies as they attempt to create order, meaning, and value

Culture of poverty A term coined by Oscar Lewis to describe the unique culture and ways of those who are impoverished; it has been used over time to look at impoverished people as having cultural deficits

Customs Beliefs, values, and behaviors, such as marriage practices, child-rearing practices, dietary preferences, and attire, that are handed down through generations and become a part of a people's traditions

Daily hassles Common occurrences that are taxing; used to measure stress

Deductive reasoning A method of reasoning that lays out general, abstract propositions that can be used to generate specific hypotheses to test in unique situations

Defense mechanisms Unconscious, automatic responses that enable a person to minimize perceived threats or keep them out of awareness entirely

Defensible space Newman's theory that certain physical design features can reduce crime and fear of crime in neighborhoods by enhancing residents' motivation to defend their territory

Defensive social movement A social movement with the goal of defending traditional values and social arrangements

Density Ratio of persons per unit area of a space

Determinism A belief that persons are passive products of their circumstances, external forces, or internal urges

Developmental perspective An approach that focuses on how human behavior changes and stays the same across stages of the life cycle

Devolution Delegation of authority and responsibility to a lower level of government, e.g., passing federal responsibilities down to state and local governments

Diabetes mellitus A disease of the endocrine system resulting from insulin deficiency or resistance to insulin's effects

Differential emotions theory A theory that asserts that emotions originate in our neurophysiology and that our personalities are organized around affective biases

Differentiation of self In family systems theory, the process of learning to differentiate between thoughts and feeling and to follow one's own beliefs rather than making decisions based on reactivity to the cues of others or the need to win approval

Dimension A feature that can be focused on separately, but that cannot be understood without considering its embeddedness with other features

Diversity Patterns of group differences

Downsizing Corporate layoff of workers for the purpose of greater efficiency

Ecocentric Perspective that the ecosphere and everything on earth has its own intrinsic worth, and should be valued and cared for, including earth (Gaia) itself; recognition that humans are only one part of the interconnected web of life

Ecomaps Visual representations of the relations between social network members. Members of the network are represented by points, and lines are drawn between pairs of points to demonstrate a relationship between them; also called a sociogram

Economic institution The social institution with primary responsibility for regulating the production, distribution, and consumption of goods and services

Ecotherapy Exposure to nature and the outdoors as a component of psychotherapy

Educational institution The social institution responsible for passing along formal knowledge from one generation to the next

Efficacy expectation In cognitive social learning theory, the expectation that one can personally accomplish a goal

Ego A mental structure of personality that is responsible for negotiating between internal needs of the individual and the outside world

Ego psychology A theory of human behavior and clinical practice that views activities of the ego as the primary determinants of behavior

Elites The most powerful members of a society

Emotion A feeling state characterized by one's appraisal of a stimulus, changes in bodily sensations, and expressive gestures

Emotional intelligence A person's ability to process information about emotions accurately and effectively, and consequently to regulate emotions in an optimal manner

Emotional labor A from of emotion regulation wherein workers are expected to engage, suppress, or evoke emotions as part of their job

Emotion-focused coping Coping efforts in which a person attempts to change either the way a stressful situation is attended to (by vigilance or avoidance) or the meaning of what is happening. Most effective when situations are not readily controllable by action

Empirical research A careful, purposeful, and systematic observation of events with the intent to note and record them in terms of their attributes, to look for patterns in those events, and to make one's methods and observations public

Empowerment theories Theories that focus on processes by which individuals and collectivities can recognize patterns of inequality and injustice and take action to increase their own power

Endocrine system A body system that is involved in growth, metabolism, development, learning, and memory. Made up of glands that secrete hormones into the blood system

Ethnic identity Feelings, beliefs, and behaviors associated with membership in an ethnic group that are based on common relations such as kinship, language, religion, geographic location, and historical experience

Ethnocentrism Considering one's own culture as superior, and judging culturally different practices (beliefs, values, behavior) by the standards and norms of one's own culture

Ethos The moral and aesthetic tone, character, and quality of a people's life; their underlying feelings toward themselves and the world

Evidence-based design Architectural design that reflects findings on physiological and health-outcome measures on the health benefits of specific design features

Faith As defined in Fowler's theory of faith development, a generic feature of the human search for meaning that provides a centering orientation from which to live one's life. May or may not be based in religious expression

Faith stages Distinct levels of faith development, each with particular characteristics, emerging strengths, and potential dangers. Fowler identifies seven faith stages in his theory of faith development.

Family A social group of two or more persons, characterized by ongoing interdependence with long-term commitments that stem from blood, law, or affection

Family and kinship institution The social institution primarily responsible for the regulation of procreation, for the initial socialization of new members of society, and for mutual support

Family economic stress model A model of family stress that suggests that economic hardship leads to economic pressure, which leads to parent distress, which leads to disrupted family relationships, which leads to child and adolescent adjustment problems

Family investment model Theoretical model that proposes that families with greater economic resources can afford to make large investments in the development of their children

Family life cycle perspective An approach that looks at how families change over time and proposes normative changes and tasks at different stages

Family of origin The family into which we were born and in which we were raised, when the two are the same

Family resilience perspective An approach to family that seeks to identify and strengthen family processes that allow families to bear up under and rebound from distressing life experiences

Family systems perspective A way of understanding families that focuses on the family as a social system, with patterns of interaction and relationships, and on changes in these patterns over time

Family timeline A visual representation of important dates and events in a family's life over time

Feedback control mechanism The mechanism by which the body controls the secretion of hormones and therefore their actions on target tissues

Feedback mechanism A process by which information about past behaviors in a system are fed back into the system in a circular manner

Feminist perspective on families A perspective that proposes that families should not be studied as whole systems, with the lens on the family level, but rather as patterns of dominance, subjugation, and oppression, particularly as those patterns are tied to gender

Feminist theories Theories that focus on male domination of the major social institutions and present a vision of a just world based on gender equity

First Force therapies Therapies based on dynamic theories of human behavior, with the prime concern being about repression and solving instinctual conflicts by developing insights

Formal organization A collectivity of people, with a high degree of formality of structure, working together to meet a goal or goals

Formed group A group that is formed for a specific purpose, such as a group for substance abusers, a therapy group for women with eating disorders, or a self-help group for gamblers

Four quadrants From Wilber's integral theory, the four most important dimensions of existence; the upper-left quadrant represents the interior of individuals, or the subjective aspects of consciousness or awareness; the upper-right quadrant represents the exterior of individuals, including the objective biological and behavioral aspects; the lower-left quadrant represents the interior of collectives, or the values, meanings, worldviews, and ethics that are shared by groups of individuals; the lower-right quadrant represents the exterior, material dimensions of collectives, including social systems and the environment

Fourth Force therapies Therapies that specifically target the spiritual dimension, focusing on helping the person let go of ego attachments and transcend the self through various spiritually based practices

Framing contests Competition among different factions of a social movement to control the definition of the problem, goals, and strategies for the movement

Fulcrum In Wilber's full-spectrum model of consciousness, a specific turning point in development, where the person must go through a three-step process of fusion/differentiation/integration in order to move from one level of consciousness to another

Gemeinschaft A community in which relationships are personal and traditional

General adaptation syndrome The physical process of coping with a stressor through the stages of alarm (awareness of the threat), resistance (efforts to restore homeostasis), and exhaustion (the termination of coping efforts because of the body's inability to sustain the state of disequilibrium)

Genogram A visual representation of the multigenerational family system, using squares, circles, and relationship lines

Geographic information system (GIS) Computer-based system for mapping the spatial distribution of a variety of social data

Gesellschaft A community in which relationships are impersonal and contractual

Gini index An index that measures the extent to which the distribution of income within a country deviates from a perfectly equal distribution; scores range from 0 (perfect equality) to 100 (perfect inequality)

Globalization The process by which the world's people are becoming more interconnected economically, politically, environmentally, and culturally

Government and political institution The social institution responsible for how decisions are made and enforced for the society as a whole

Group cohesiveness A sense of solidarity or "we-ness" felt by group members toward the group

Group dynamics The patterns of interaction that emerge in groups, including group leadership, roles, and communication networks

Group work A recognized social work method that involves teaching and practicing social work with groups

Hawthorne effect Tendency of participants in an experimental study to perform in particular ways simply because they know they are being studied

Health care institution The social institution with primary responsibility for promoting the general health of a society

Heterogeneity Individual-level variations, differences among individuals

Hierarchy of needs Abraham Maslow's humanistic theory that suggests that higher needs cannot emerge until lower needs have been satisfied; the hierarchy runs from physiological needs at the bottom, to safety needs, belongingness and love needs, and esteem needs, with self-actualization needs at the top

High blood pressure (hypertension) Blood pressure greater than 140/90; the leading cause of strokes and a major risk factor for heart attacks and kidney failure

Homeostasis Equilibrium; a positive, steady state of biological, psychological, or social functioning

Horizontal linkage Interaction within a community

Human immunodeficiency virus (HIV) The virus that causes acquired immunodeficiency syndrome (AIDS)

Humanistic perspective An approach that sees human behavior as based on freedom of action of the individual and focuses on the human search for meaning

Human relations theory A theory that focuses on the role of human relationships in organizational efficiency and effectiveness

Hybrid organization An organization that combines political advocacy and service provision in its core identity

Hypotheses Tentative statements to be explored and tested

Ideology (cultural) The dominant ideas within a culture about the way things are and should work, derived from a group's social, economic, and political interests

Ideology (personal) A particular body of ideas or outlook; a person's specific worldview

Immune system Organs and cells that interact and work together to defend the body against disease

Information processing theory A sensory theory of cognition that sees information as flowing from the external world through the senses to the nervous system, where it is coded

Interdisciplinary collaboration A process whereby different professionals coordinate problem solving for a common purpose

Interdisciplinary team A special type of task group composed of professionals representing a variety of disciplines; it may also include consumers or clients

Interpretist perspective Ways of understanding human behavior that share the assumption that reality is based on people's definition of it

Interpretive perspective on organizations A perspective that sees formal organizations as social constructions of reality

Intersectionality feminist theory A feminist theory that suggests that no single category is sufficient to understand social oppression, and that categories such as gender, race, and class intersect to produce different experiences for women of various races and classes.

Iron cage of rationality Max Weber's term for the dehumanizing potential of bureaucracies

Leadership A process of influencing a group to achieve a common goal

Learned helplessness In cognitive social learning theory, a situation in which a person's prior experience with environmental forces has led to low self-efficacy and efficacy expectation

Learning organization theory A theory of formal organizations that developed on the premise that rational planning is not sufficient for an organization to survive in a rapidly changing environment such as the one in which we live, that formal organizations must become complex systems that are capable of constant learning

Levels of consciousness From Wilber's integral theory, overall stages of awareness and being; moving from the prepersonal to the personal and transpersonal phases, each with multiple levels of development

Life course perspective An approach to human behavior that recognizes the influence of age, but also acknowledges the influences of historical time and culture

Life events Incidents or events that are brief in scope but are influential on human behavior

Linear time Time based on past, present, and future

Lines of consciousness From Wilber's integral theory, the approximately two dozen relatively independent developmental lines or streams that can evolve at different rates, with different dynamics, and on different time schedules; examples include cognitive, moral, interpersonal, self-identity, and socioemotional capacity

Lone-parent families Families composed of one parent and at least one child residing in the same household, headed by either a divorced or unmarried parent

Lymphocytes White blood cells

Managing diversity model An approach to formal organizations that focuses on the need to maximize the potential advantages, and minimize the potential disadvantages, of diversity in organizational membership

Mass media institution In a democratic society, the social institution responsible for managing the flow of information, images, and ideas

Mass society A society that is standardized and homogenized, with no ethnic, class, regional, or local variations in human behavior

Mobilizing structures Existing informal networks and formal organizations that serve as the collective building blocks for social movements

Mobilizing structures (MS) perspective An approach to social movements that suggests that they develop out of existing networks and formal organizations

Mood A feeling disposition that, in contrast to an emotion, is more chronic, less intense, and less tied to a specific situation

Multidetermined behavior A view that human behavior is developed as a result of many causes

Multidimensional Having several identifiable dimensions

Multilevel family practice model A way of viewing a family that focuses on stress from and resources provided (or not provided) by patterns and institutions within larger social systems, including the neighborhood, the local community, the state, the nation, and the global socioeconomic system

Multiple intelligences The eight distinct biopsychosocial potentials, as identified by Howard Gardner, with which people process information that can be activated in cultural settings to solve problems or create products that are of value in the culture

Musculoskeletal system Muscles that are attached to bone and cross a joint. Their contraction and relaxation are the basis for voluntary movements

Mutual aid group A formed group of persons who utilize the support, encouragement, and feedback from other persons in the group to work on certain problems they have in common

Narrative theory A theory that proposes that all of us are engaged in an ongoing process of constructing a life story

Natural environment The portion of the environment influenced primarily by geological and nonhuman biological forces

Natural group A group that occurs naturally, without external initiative, such as a group of peers or coworkers

Neocolonialism The practice of dominant and powerful nations going beyond their boundaries, utilizing international financial institutions such as the World Bank and the International Monetary Fund to exert influence over impoverished nations and to impose their culture, laws, and language upon the occupied nation through the use of financial incentives (loans) and disincentives

Neoliberal philosophy A philosophy that governments should keep their hands off the economic institution

Nervous system The biological system responsible for processing and integrating incoming sensory information; it influences and directs reactions to that information

Network A set of relationships and ties among a set of actors

Network model A social movement theory in the mobilizing structures perspective that focuses on the role of grassroots settings in the development and maintenance of social movements

Networked individualism A way of thinking about community in which individuals operate in large, personalized, complex networks

Neural plasticity The capacity of the nervous system to be modified by experience

Neuron Nerve cell that is the basic working unit of the nervous system. Composed of a cell body, dendrites (receptive extensions), and an axon

Neurotransmitters Messenger molecules that transfer chemical and electrical messages from one neuron to another

New federalism The downward movement of policy responsibilities from federal to state and local governments

Nonhierarchical organization An organization run by consensus, with few rules, characterized by informality

Nonnormative stressors Unexpected stressful events that can quickly drain a family's resources

Nonspecific immunity Immunity that includes physical barriers to infection, inflammation, and phagocytosis. Does not include antibodies or cell-mediated immunity

Normative stressors The stressors that families face as a result of typical family life cycle transitions

Objective reality The belief that phenomena exist and have influence, whether or not we are aware of them

Object relations theory A psychodynamic theory that considers that our ability to form lasting attachments is based on early experiences of separation from and connection with our primary caregivers

Offensive social movement A social movement with the goal of changing traditional social arrangements

Ongoing group A natural or formed group that is set up without a particular time limit and that meets until the group is disbanded

Open group A natural or formed group that includes any person who would like to become a member; a natural or formed group that accepts persons who meet the group's criteria after the group has begun and throughout its existence

Operant conditioning theory A theory in the social behavioral perspective that sees behavior as the result of reinforcement

Organizational culture model An approach to formal organizations that sees them as cultures with shared experiences and shared meanings

Organizational humanism An approach to formal organizations that assumes that organizations can maximize efficiency and effectiveness while also promoting individual happiness and well-being

Organizations as multiple oppressions A theory of organizations that views them as social constructions that exclude and discriminate against some categories of people

Othering Labeling people who fall outside of one's own group as abnormal, inferior, or marginal

Performance expectations The expectations group members have of other group members in terms of how they will act or behave in the group or how well they will perform a task

Personal community Networks of social interaction composed of friends, relatives, neighbors, workmates, and so on

Personal network Those from the social network who provide a person with his or her most essential support resources

Personal space The physical distance we choose to maintain in interpersonal relationships

Person-in-environment (PIE) classification system A classification system developed for the purpose of social work assessment. Assessment is based on four factors: social functioning problems, environmental problems, mental health problems, and physical health problems

Phenomenal self An individual's subjectively felt and interpreted experience of "who I am"

Place attachment A process in which individuals and groups form bonds with places

Place identity A process in which the meaning of a place merges with one's self-identity

Pluralistic theory of social conflict A theory that suggests that there is more than one social conflict going on at all times, that individuals often hold cross-cutting and overlapping memberships in status groups, and that these cross-cutting memberships prevent the development of solidarity among oppressed groups

Political economy model A model of formal organizations that focuses on the organization's dependence on its environments for political and economic resources and, more specifically, on the influence of political and economic factors on the internal workings of the organization

Political opportunities (PO) perspective An approach to social movements that suggests that they develop when windows of political opportunity are open

Positive psychology An approach to psychology that focuses on people's strengths and virtues and promotes optimal functioning of individuals and communities

Positivist perspective The perspective on which modern science is based. Assumes objective reality: that findings of one study should be applicable to other groups, that complex phenomena can be studied by reducing them to some component part, and that scientific methods are value-free

Postconventional morality In Kohlberg's theory of moral development, a stage in which moral decisions are based on moral principles that transcend those of one's own society

Postmodernism A term used to describe contemporary culture as a postindustrial culture in which people are connected across time and place through global electronic communications; emphasis is on the existence of different worldviews and concepts of reality

Post-poliomyelitis syndrome (PPS) Progressive atrophy of muscles in those who once had polio

Postpositivism A philosophical position that recognizes the complexity of reality and the limitations of human observers; proposes that scientists can never develop more than a partial understanding of human behavior

Posttraumatic stress disorder (PTSD) A set of symptoms experienced by some trauma survivors that include reliving the traumatic event, avoidance of stimuli related to the event, and hyperarousal

Practice orientation A way of thinking about culture that recognizes the relationships and mutual influences among structures of society and culture, the impact of history, and the nature and impact of human action

Preconscious Mental activity that is outside of awareness but can be brought into awareness with prompting

Preconventional morality In Kohlberg's theory of moral development, a stage in which moral decisions are made on the basis of avoiding punishment and receiving rewards

Primary emotions Emotions that developed as specific reactions and signals with survival value for the human species. They serve to mobilize an individual, focus attention, and signal one's state of mind to others; examples include anger, fear, sadness, joy, and anticipation

Primary territory A territory that evokes feelings of ownership, that we control on a relatively permanent basis, and that is vital to our daily lives

Privatization Shifting the administration of programs from government to nongovernment organizations

Privilege Unearned advantage enjoyed by members of some social categories

Problem-focused coping Coping efforts in which the person attempts to change a stress situation by acting on the environment. Most effective when situations are controllable by action

Process-oriented leader A leader who identifies and manages group relationships

Professional social movement organizations Organizations that are staffed by leaders and activists who make a career out of reform causes

Programs In behavior settings theories, the consistent, prescribed patterns of behavior that are developed and maintained in particular behavior settings

Proposition An assertion about a concept or about the relationship between concepts

Psychoanalytic theory A theory of human behavior and clinical intervention that assumes the primacy of internal drives and unconscious mental activity in determining human behavior

Psychodynamic perspective An approach that focuses on how internal processes motivate human behavior

Psychoeducational group A formed group that is focused on providing information and support concerning a particular problem area or issue; such groups usually meet over only a short period of time

Psychology The study of the mind and mental processes

Public territory A territory open to anyone, to which we generally make no attempt to control access

Qualitative methods of research Research methods that use flexible methods of data collection, seek holistic understanding, present findings in words rather than numbers, and attempt to account for the influence of the research setting and process on the findings

Quantitative methods of research Research methods, based on the tenets of modern science, that use quantifiable measures of concepts, standardize the collection of data, attend only to preselected variables, and use statistical methods to look for patterns and associations

Race A system of social identity based on biological markers such as skin color that influence economic, social, and political relations

Racism Discriminatory thoughts, beliefs, and actions based on the assignment of an individual or group to a racial classification

Radical antithesis Philosophy that equality is the natural, divine order, and that inequality is based on abuse of privilege and should be minimized

Rational choice perspective An approach that sees human behavior as based in self-interest and rational choices about effective goal accomplishment

Rational perspective on organizations A perspective that sees formal organizations as goal-directed, purposefully designed machines that maximize efficiency and effectiveness

Relational community A community based on voluntary association rather than geography

Relational coping Coping that takes into account actions that maximize the survival of others as well as oneself

Relational theory A theory that proposes that the basic human tendency is relationships with others, and that our personalities are formed through ongoing interactions with others

Religion A systematic set of beliefs, practices, and traditions experienced within a particular social institution over time

Religious institution The social institution with primary responsibility for answering questions about the meaning and purpose of life

Resource mobilization theory A social movement theory in the mobilizing structures perspective that focuses on the role of formal organizations in the development and maintenance of social movements

Role A set of usual behaviors of persons occupying a particular social position

Role strain Problems experienced in the performance of specific roles. Used by sociologists to measure stress

Schema (plural: schemata) An internalized representation of the world, including systematic patterns of thought, action, and problem solving

Science A set of logical, systematic, documented methods for answering questions about the world

Scientific management A set of principles developed by Frederick Taylor to maximize the internal efficiency of formal organizations; it is focused on finding the "one best way" to perform every organizational task

Second Force therapies Therapies based on behavioral theories; they focus on learned habits and seek to remove symptoms through various processes of direct learning

Secondary emotions Emotions that are socially acquired. They evolved as humans developed more sophisticated means of learning, controlling, and managing emotions to promote flexible cohesion in social groups. Examples include envy, jealousy, anxiety, guilt, shame, relief, hope, depression, pride, love, gratitude, and compassion

Secondary territory A territory less important to us than primary territories, control of which does not seem essential

Self An essence of who we are that is more or less enduring

Self-categorization theory A theory of small groups that proposes that in the process of social identity development, we come to divide the world into in-groups (those to which we belong) and out-groups (those to which we do not belong) and to be biased toward in-groups

Self-efficacy A sense of personal competence

Self-help group A formed group, which may or may not be professionally led, composed of persons who share a common life situation

Self psychology A theory, based in psychoanalytic theory, that conceives of the self as experienced cohesion through action and reflection

Self-system In Wilber's full-spectrum model of consciousness, the active self or person who moves through the stages of consciousness and mediates between the basic and transitional structures of development

Sense of community A feeling of belonging and mutual commitment

Settlement house movement A social movement, brought to the United States from England in the late 1800s, that turned attention to the environmental hazards of industrialization and focused on research, service, and social reform

Silverman's social action model A model of formal organizations that focuses on the active role of individual actors in creating the organization

Small group A small collection of individuals who interact with each other, perceive themselves as belonging to a group, are interdependent, join together to accomplish a goal, fulfill a need through joint association, or are influenced by a set of rules and norms

Social action model (community organization) A model of community social work practice that emphasizes social reform and the challenge of structural inequalities

Social behavioral perspective An approach that sees human behavior as learned when individuals interact with their environments

Social capital Connections among individuals based on reciprocity and trustworthiness

Social class A particular position in a societal structure of inequality

Social constructionist perspective An approach that focuses on how people learn, through their interactions with each other, to classify the world and their place in it

Social entrepreneurial organization An organization formed by a social entrepreneur who recognizes a social problem and uses ideas from business entrepreneurs to organize, create, and manage a new venture to bring about social change related to that problem.

Social exchange theory A theory in the rational choice perspective that sees human behavior as based on the desire to maximize benefits and minimize costs in social interactions

Social identity theory A stage theory of socialization that articulates the process by which we come to identify with some social groups and develop a sense of difference from other social groups

Social institutions Patterned ways of organizing social relations in a particular sector of social life

Social movement organizations (SMOs) Formal organizations through which social movement activities are coordinated

Social movements Large-scale collective actions to make change, or resist change, in specific social institutions

Social movement service organizations (SMSOs) A type of social agency that has the explicit goal of social change and accomplishes this goal through the delivery of services

Social network The people with whom a person routinely interacts; the patterns of interaction that result from exchanging resources with others

Social network theory A developing theory in the rational choice perspective that focuses on the pattern of ties that link persons and collectivities

Social planning model A model of community social work based on the premise that the complexities of modern social problems require expert planners schooled in a rational planning model; also referred to as a top-down approach

Social reform Efforts to create more just social institutions

Social structure A set of interrelated social institutions developed by humans to impose constraints on human interaction for the purpose of the survival and well-being of the collectivity

Social support The interpersonal interactions and relationships that provide people with assistance or feelings of attachment to others they perceive as caring

Social welfare institution The social institution in modern industrial societies that promotes interdependence and provides assistance for issues of dependency

Socioeconomic status (SES) Social, economic, and political relations that are developed around education, economic, and occupational status; social class

Sociofugal spaces Physical designs that discourage social interaction

Sociopetal spaces Physical designs that encourage social interaction

Solidary community A type of community that seeks the participation of all members in an integrated fashion

Specific immunity Immunity that involves cells (lymphocytes) that not only respond to an infection, but also develop a memory of that infection and allow the body to defend against it rapidly during subsequent exposure

Spiritual bypassing Use of spiritual beliefs or practices to avoid dealing in any significant depth with unresolved issues and related emotional and behavioral problems; includes attempts to prematurely transcend the ego.

Spirituality A search for purpose, meaning, and connection between oneself, other people, the universe, and the ultimate reality, which can be experienced within either a religious or a nonreligious framework

Staffing In behavior settings theories, the participants in a particular behavior setting

State A personality characteristic that changes over time, depending on the social or stress context

States of consciousness From Wilber's integral theory, an understanding of experience that includes both ordinary (waking, sleeping, and dreaming) and non-ordinary experiences (peak experiences, religious experiences, altered state, and meditative or contemplative states)

Status A specific social position

Status characteristics In status characteristics and expectation states theory, any characteristics that are evaluated in the broader society to be associated with competence

Status characteristics and expectation states theory A theory of basic group process that assumes that the influence and participation of group members during initial interactions are related to their status and to expectations others hold about their ability to help the group accomplish tasks

Stimulation theories Theories that focus on the physical environment as a source of sensory information that is necessary for human well-being

Strain theory An approach to social movements that sees them as developing in response to some form of societal strain

Stress Any biological, psychological, or social event in which environmental demands or internal demands, or both, tax or exceed the adaptive resources of the individual

Stress/diathesis models Perspectives on mental and emotional disorders in which a disorder is considered to be the result of interactions of environmental stresses and the person's genetic or biochemical predisposition to the disorder

Stress pileup When a series of crises over time depletes a family's resources and exposes the family to increasing risk of very negative outcomes

Subjective reality The belief that reality is created by personal perception and does not exist outside that perception; the same as the interpretist perspective

Symbol Something verbal (language, words) or nonverbal (such as a flag) that comes to stand for something else; a way of expressing meaning

Symbolic interactionism A theory that stresses that we develop a sense of meaning in the world through interaction with our physical and social environments and interpretation of symbols

Synapse In the nervous system, the gap between an axon and a dendrite; the site at which chemical and electrical communication occurs

Systems perspective An approach that sees human behavior as the outcome of reciprocal interactions of persons operating within organized and integrated social systems

Systems perspective on organizations A perspective that focuses on formal organizations in constant interaction with multiple environments

Task group A group formed for the purpose of accomplishing a specific goal or objective

Task-oriented leader A leader who facilitates problem solving within the context of the group

Territorial community A community based on geography

Territoriality A pattern of behavior of a group or individual that involves marking or personalizing a territory to signify ownership and engaging in behaviors to protect it from invasion

Testes Male gonads, primarily responsible for producing sperm (mature germ cells that fertilize the female egg) and secreting male hormones called androgens

Theory A logically interrelated set of concepts and propositions, organized into a deductive system, that explain relationships among aspects of our world

Therapeutic medicine An approach to medicine that focuses on diagnosing and treating disease

Therapy group A formed group that uses an intensive group format to promote growth in its members and to assist its members in resolving emotional and behavioral problems

Third Force therapies Therapies rooted in experiential/humanistic/existential theories that focus on helping a person deal with existential despair, and that seek the actualization of the person's potential through techniques grounded in immediate experiencing

Time-limited group A natural or formed group whose members or leader establish a certain length of time that they will meet as a group

Time orientation The extent to which individuals and collectivities are invested in three temporal zones: past, present, and future time

Tradition A process of handing down from one generation to another particular cultural beliefs and practices. In particular, a process of ratifying particular beliefs and practices by connecting them to selected social, economic, and political practices

Trait A stable personality characteristic

Transactionalism An approach to understanding human behavior that starts from an assumption of person–environment unity rather than from an assumption of the person and environment as separate entities

Transition points Time when families face a transition in family life stage or in family composition

Transnational corporation (TNC) A very large company that carries on production and distribution activities in many nations

Transnational social movement organizations (TSMOs) Social movement organizations that operate in more than one nation-state

Transpersonal approach An approach to human behavior that includes levels of consciousness or spiritual development that move beyond rational-individuated-personal personhood to a sense of self that transcends the mind/body ego—a self-identity also referred to as transegoic

Traumatic stress Stress associated with events that involve actual or threatened severe injury or death of oneself or significant others

Triangulation A process that occurs when two family members (a family subsystem) inappropriately involve another family member to reduce the anxiety in the dyadic relationship

Ultimate environment Conceptualizations of the highest level of reality, understood differently by persons at various levels of spiritual development or consciousness

Unconscious Mental activities of which one is not aware but that influence behavior

Uterus Also called the womb, serves as the pear-shaped home for the fetus for the 9 months between implantation and birth

Ventricles The two lower, thick-walled chambers of the heart

Vertical linkage Interaction with systems external to the community

Voluntarism The belief that persons are free and active agents in the creation of their behaviors

Worldcentric Identification beyond the "me" (egocentric), or the "us" (ethnocentric), to identification and concern for "all of us" (worldcentric), or the entire global human family; a moral stance that is characteristic of higher levels of spiritual development.

Worldview A cognitive picture of the way things—nature, self, society—actually are

Index

ABC-X model of family stress/coping, 328
  double ABC-X model and, 328
  family timeline and, 329, 330 (exhibit)
  nonnormative stressors and, 329
  normative stressors and, 329
  potential outcomes and, 328
  stress pileup concept and, 328–329
  stressors-resources balance and, 329
  See also Family dimension; Family economic
      stress model
Ability, 19, 21
Abma, J., 334, 335
Accessibility, 211–213, 214 (exhibit), 232–233,
  233–234 (exhibit)
Accommodation, 109, 147, 232, 261
  See also Cultural accommodation
Accreditation standards, xv–xvii, 6–7
Acculturation, 15, 16, 261, 346
  See also Cultural change; Cultural
      dimension
Acetylcholine (ACh), 82, 94
ACORN (Association of Community
  Organizations for Reform Now),
  456, 462
Acquired brain injury (ABI), 80
Acquired immunodeficiency syndrome (AIDS),
  87, 89, 90, 198, 333, 467
ACT UP, 467
Activism, 363, 364, 458, 459, 462, 463
  collective action strategies, 465–466,
      466 (exhibit)
  creative play tactic, 466
  nonviolent disruption, 465–466
  redistribution of power and, 468
  violent collective action, 466
  See also Advocacy work; Social movement
      dimension
Adaptation, 145
  accumulation of loss and, 53
  bicultural socialization, 16
  cultural maintenance and, 257–262,
      257 (exhibit)
  defense mechanisms and, 147
  ego psychology theory and, 54
  gender and, 16

primary emotions and, 124
refugee resettlement and, 15, 16
See also ABC-X model of family
    stress/coping; Coping; General
    adaptation syndrome; Stress
Addams, J., 18, 193, 247
Addictions, 77
  See also Alcohol abuse; Substance abuse
Adequate yearly progress (AYP), 293
Adolescents:
  family violence and, 347
  physical environment and, 235
  substance abuse by, 350
  See also Child development
Adoption, 332, 333, 339
Adulthood:
  adult literacy rate, 291
  ongoing cognitive development
      and, 110
  personality development in, 54, 55
  weakened immune system and, 89
  See also Divorce; Domestic violence; Elder
      population
Advertising industry, 43
Advocacy centers, 79
Advocacy therapy, 130
Advocacy work, 409, 411, 439, 441, 462
  See also Activism; Social movement
      dimension; Social service
      organizations
Affect, 108
Affective biases, 118
African Americans, 194–195, 232, 246
  acting White, cultural capital and, 263
  adaptation to poverty and, 255
  Black behavior and, 263
  culture of poverty and, 254–255
  domestic servants and, 321–322
  Eurocentric customs/traditions and, 259
  extended kinship system and, 333
  graduation rates and, 293
  health insurance and, 295
  Latinos, conflict with, 260
  poverty among, 281
  race, meanings/uses of, 262–263

redlining and, 255
unequal education opportunities and, 292
upward mobility and, 255
urban youth culture and, 256
Afrocentric perspective, 56
  moral development, collective humanistic
      experience of, 114
  See also African Americans; Afrocentric
      relational theory
Afrocentric relational theory, 139
Age, 21, 199
  aging societies, 18, 298–299, 308
  time perceptions and, 17
  See also Elder population
Agency, 61, 256–257
  collective agency, 61, 63, 311
  female gender roles and, 265
  history and, 256
  information processing theory and, 111
  personal agency, 61
  proxy agency, 61, 63
  social class, structural determinism and,
      310–311
  social reform and, 63
  social structure and, 256
Agency-based model of community
  practice, 439
Aggression, 54
Agoraphobia, 125
AIDS. *See* Acquired immunodeficiency
  syndrome (AIDS)
Alcohol abuse:
  adult children of alcoholics, 350
  classical conditioning and, 61
  homelessness and, 232
  marital satisfaction/violence
      and, 350
  Wellbriety Movement and, 438
Alcoholics Anonymous (AA), 363
Alienation, 43, 45, 65, 139, 298, 466
Alinsky, S., 439
Allen-Meares, P., 442
Almaas, A. H., 192
Altman, I., 216, 218
Altman, L., 17

therapeutic medicine, 297
See also Health care institution;
    Health/illness
Meditation, 202
Melting pot metaphor, 18
Memmi, D., 427
Memory, 110
Mental health:
    community mental health movement, 425
    complementary and alternative medicine,
        201–202
    coping, psychiatric perspective on, 156
    disease model of abnormality and,
        156, 157 (exhibit)
    early childhood experiences and, 140–141
    infertility, emotional impact of, 335
    mental illness, homelessness and, 232
    mental illness, stress/diathesis
        models of, 145
    mindfulness practices and, 16
    natural light and, 223
    outdoor activities and, 221 (exhibit), 222
    positive psychology and, 65
    psychotropic medications and, 83
    seasonal affective disorder and, 223
    spirituality/religiosity and, 13, 176–177,
        200–201
    See also Health/illness
Merton, R., 39
Mesosystems, 13
Messinger, L., 430
Metacognition, 24
Metaphors, 262
Meyer, A., 392
Meyer, D., 463
Meyer, K., 398
Meyer, M., 470
Michels, R., 401
Microsystems, 13
Migrant workers, 288–289, 427
Migrations, 285, 307, 346
    See also Immigration
Mikulas, W. L., 192
Military families, 339–340
    active-duty families, 340, 341
    case study, 315–317
    children, psychosocial functioning of, 341
    emotional strain/role overload and, 340
    military spouses, single-parenting and, 340
    military-based support of, 341
    reservists and, 340, 341
    return from deployment, readjustment
        stresses and, 340–341, 346
    war zones, stress in, 340
    See also Family dimension; Military personnel
Military personnel, 288, 328
    See also Military families
Military power, 285
Militia movements, 466
Millennium Ecosystem Assessment, 223–224
Miller, H., 389
MIMBRA assessment tool, 204
Minami, H., 217

Mind:
    ego psychology theory and, 54
    mind-body interactions, 78–79
    states of, 54
    structural model of, 54
    topographical theory of, 54
    See also Brain function; Cognition;
        Consciousness; Information
        processing theory
Mind-body interactions, 78–79, 202
Mindfulness practices, 16
Minority groups:
    bonding social capital, 431
    cardiovascular disease and, 90–91
    environmental hazards and, 224
    hostile environments, coping strategies
        for, 56
    minority/local knowledge, credibility of, 52
    neighborhood toxic waste facilities and, 228
    psychodynamic bias and, 55, 56
    subjective social status and, 102
    See also Cultural change; Multidimensional
        concept of culture; Oppression; Power;
        Social constructionist perspective;
        Socioeconomic status (SES)
Miringoff, M., 279, 280
Miringoff, M. L., 279, 280
Mmatli, T., 439
Mobilizing structures (MS) perspective,
    456–457, 457 (exhibit)
    computer-mediated social movement
        communication and, 459–460
    costs of mobilizing, 458
    encapsulation of social movements and, 459
    factionalization of social movements
        and, 459
    informal/formal structures and, 457–458
    institutionalization of social movements
        and, 459
    life course of social movements and,
        458–459
    network model and, 457–458
    New Right/New Left movements and, 458
    professionalization and, 457
    resource mobilization theory and, 457
    social movement organizations and, 457, 458
    transnational social movement
        organizations and, 457
    work-based networks of activism and, 458
    See also Social movement dimension
Modeling, 111
Models, 26
Modern culture, 250, 250 (exhibit)
Modernism, 303
Modernization, 20, 65
    entrenched poverty and, 310
    gemeinschaft/gesellschaft dichotomy
        and, 426
    religious conflict and, 174–175
MomsRising, 459
Monette, D., 29
Monogamy, 307, 319
Monte, C., 62

Mood, 108, 115, 125, 224
Mor Barak, M., 401
Moral development:
    postconventional morality, 113
    poverty and, 252
    preconventional morality, 113
    religious practice and, 175
    social constructionist theory of, 114
    stages of, approaches to, 113–114,
        113–114 (exhibits)
    universal morality and, 51
    See also Moral reasoning theories
Moral reasoning theories, 112–113
    abstract thought and, 114
    cross-cultural moral reasoning, 114
    emotions, control of, 114
    ethic of care and, 113
    gender differences and, 113–114, 138
    justice-oriented approach and, 113
    morality and, 112
    self-other interdependence and, 114
    stages of moral development and, 113–114,
        113–114 (exhibits)
    See also Moral development; Psychological
        person dimension
Morality frames, 463
Morenoff, J., 433
Morgan, G., 402, 405
Mother blaming, 55
Multiculturalism:
    religious conflict and, 175
    See also Ethnic identity; Multidimensional
        concept of culture; Race
Multidetermined behavior, 10
Multidimensional approach, 7
    acculturation process and, 15, 16
    biological person dimension and,
        10–11 (exhibit), 12, 13
    case coordination model and,
        13, 14 (exhibit)
    case study for, 4–9
    clock time dimension and, 10 (exhibit),
        12 (exhibit), 16, 17
    community dimension and, 8, 10 (exhibit),
        12 (exhibit)
    cultural dimension and, 7, 10–11 (exhibits)
    dimension, definition of, 10
    dyadic relationships and, 10–11 (exhibits),
        13, 15
    ecological theory and, 9
    environmental dimensions and, 7–9,
        10–12 (exhibits), 13, 15
    event time dimension and, 10 (exhibit),
        12 (exhibit), 16–17
    family dimension and,
        8, 10–11 (exhibits), 15
    human behavior, multidimensional
        understanding of, xxi
    linear time dimension and, 10 (exhibit),
        12 (exhibit), 16, 17
    multidetermined behavior and, 10
    organizational dimension and,
        8, 10 (exhibit), 12 (exhibit)

About the Author

Elizabeth D. Hutchison, MSW, PhD, received her MSW from the George Warren Brown School of Social Work at Washington University in St. Louis and her PhD from the University at Albany, State University of New York. She was on the faculty in the Social Work Department at Elms College from 1980–1987, and was chair of the department from 1982–1987. She was on the faculty in the School of Social Work at Virginia Commonwealth University from 1987–2009, where she taught courses in human behavior and the social environment, social work and social justice, and child and family policy; she also served as field practicum liaison. She has been a social worker in health, mental health, aging, and child and family welfare settings. She is committed to providing social workers with comprehensive, current, and useful frameworks for thinking about human behavior. Her other research interests focus on child and family welfare. She currently lives in Rancho Mirage, California.

About the Contributors

Leanne Wood Charlesworth, LMSW, PhD, is assistant professor in the Department of Social Work at Nazareth College of Rochester. She has practiced within child welfare systems, and her areas of service and research interest include poverty and child and family well-being. She has taught human behavior and research at the undergraduate and graduate levels.

Linwood Cousins, MSW, MA, PhD, is professor and director of the School of Social Work at Western Michigan University. He is a social worker and an anthropologist who has practiced in child welfare and family services. His research, teaching, and practice interests include the sociocultural manifestations of race, ethnicity, and social class as well as other aspects of human diversity in the community life and schooling of African Americans and other ethnic and economic minorities.

Elizabeth P. Cramer, MSW, PhD, LCSW, ACSW, is professor in the School of Social Work at Virginia Commonwealth University. Her primary scholarship and service areas are domestic violence, lesbian and gay male issues, and group work. She is editor of the book *Addressing Homophobia and Heterosexism on College Campuses* (2002). She teaches in the areas of foundation practice, social justice, oppressed groups, and lesbian and bisexual women.

Stephen French Gilson, MSW, PhD, is professor and coordinator of interdisciplinary disability studies at the Center for Community Inclusion and Disability Studies; professor at the School of Social Work at the University of Maine; and Senior Research Fellow at Ono Academic College Research Institute for Health and Medical Professions, Kiryat Ono, Israel. After he completed his undergraduate degree in art, he shifted his career to social justice, pursuing a masters in social work. Realizing that knowledge of human biology and physiology was foundational to his work, he completed a PhD in medical sciences. Synthesizing the diversity and richness of this scholarly background, Dr. Gilson engages in research in disability theory, disability as diversity, design and access, social justice, health and disability policy, and the atypical body. He serves on the board of directors of the Disability Rights Center of Maine and is chair of the Disability Section of the American Public Health Association. He teaches courses in disability as diversity, policy, and human behavior from a legitimacy perspective. Along with his wife, Liz DePoy, Stephen is the owner of an adapted rescue farm in Maine. Living his passion of full access, the barn and farm area have been adapted not only to better assure human access and animal caretaking, but also to respond to the needs of the disabled and medically involved animals that live on the farm. Two other major influences on Dr. Gilson's writing, research, and work include his passion for and involvement in adaptive alpine skiing and dressage.

Beverly Koerin, MSW, PhD, is associate professor emerita in the School of Social Work at Virginia Commonwealth University. She practiced in public social services at the local and state levels. For over 10 years, she has been involved in research and service related to family caregiving. She cofacilitates a caregiver support group for the Richmond Alzheimer's Association, volunteers with Jewish Family Services in aging-related programs, and teaches ESL with Catholic Charities' Refugee and Immigration Services Program. She taught policy, macro practice, and diversity courses, and served as BSW Program Director, MSW Program Director, and Associate Dean.

Soon Min Lee, MSW, LSW, PhD, is assistant professor in the School of Social Work at Sejong Cyber University, Seoul, Korea. Her major areas of interest include Asian immigrant families, culturally diverse families, family therapy, career choices among Asian Americans, and culturally sensitive social work intervention.

Michael J. Sheridan, MSW, PhD, is currently a research associate professor at the National Catholic School of Social Service (NCSSS) of The Catholic University of America. Her practice experience includes work in mental health, health, corrections, and youth and family services. Her major areas of interest are spirituality and social work and issues related to diversity, oppression, and social and economic justice. She teaches courses on diversity and social justice, spirituality and social work, transpersonal theory, human behavior, international social development, and conflict resolution and peacebuilding at the BSW, MSW, and doctoral levels. She is also the Director of Research for NCSSS's Center for Spirituality and Social Work.

Joseph Walsh, MSW, PhD, LCSW, is professor in the School of Social Work at Virginia Commonwealth University. He was educated at Ohio State University and has worked for 30 years in community mental health settings. His major areas of interest are clinical social work, serious mental illness, and psychopharmacology. He teaches courses in social work practice, human behavior and the social environment, and research while maintaining a small clinical practice.

Maria E. Zuniga, MSW, PhD, is professor emeritus from the School of Social Work at San Diego State University. She taught there for 16 years; she also taught for 11 years at Sacramento State University. Her areas of focus were direct practice; gerontological practice; and practice with multicultural populations, in particular, practice with Latinos. She taught human behavior courses. She was also a member of the board of directors of the Council on Social Work Education (CSWE) and helped to develop a CSWE-sponsored conference on cultural competence held at the University of Michigan in 1999. She is a consultant on cultural competence for local, state, and national agencies and publishing houses.